CONTEMPORARY RUSSIAN PROSE

Edited by
Carl & Ellendea Proffer

ARDIS

ACKNOWLEDGEMENTS

Thanks to Priscilla Meyer for permission to use the translation of "Life in Windy Weather," from the forthcoming volume, Andrei Bitov, *Selected Short Stories*. Our continuing thanks to Lev Kopelev and Raisa Orlova, without whom twelve years of following Russian literature would not have been the same.

The following works have previously been copyrighted: V. Aksenov, "The Steel Bird" © 1979 by Ardis; V. Shukshin, "Snowball Berry Red" 1979 by Ardis; Sasha Sokolov, *A School for Fools* © 1976 by Ardis; Yury Trifonov, "The Exchange" © 1973 by Ardis.

Contemporary Russian Prose (introduction and all new materials)

Library of Congress Cataloging in Publication Data

An Anthology of contemporary Russian prose.

Contents: The steel bird / Vasily Aksyonov — Snowball berry red / Vasily Shukshin — A school for fools / Sasha Sokolov — [etc.]
1.   Russian   fiction—20th   century—Translations   into   English.
2. English fiction—Translations from Russian.
I. Proffer, Carl R.
PG3276.A58   891.73'44'08   81-14903
ISBN 0-88233-596-0   AACR2
ISBN 0-88233-597-9 (pbk.)

Photographs of the Authors: Rasputin [xxiv], Sokolov [xxviii],
Aksenov [2], Shukshin [56], Trifonov [254], Bitov [304],
Iskander [334].

INTRODUCTION: RUSSIAN FICTION INTO THE EIGHTIES

   The most important general development in Russian literature during the last fifteen years has been convergence—between
Russian writing done or published outside the USSR and that
written and published at home. The massive "Third Wave" of
Russian emigration which has occurred since 1971 has played a
major role in transporting much of the most important Russian
writing across the Soviet border. Some 250,000 people have
emigrated, and among them are many of the most interesting
Russian writers of our time. Russian-language literary journals
and publishing houses in the United States, France, Germany,
and Israel now publish about two hundred titles annually. These
books include not only much of the finest in contemporary
Russian prose and poetry, but also reprints of the Russian classics of this century, many of whom are unpublished, or selective-
ly published, in the USSR. Thus the only complete works of
Mandelstam, Pasternak, Akhmatova, Bulgakov, and many others
are the products of non-Soviet publishing houses. Although it is
still illegal to bring Russian-language books into the USSR, thousands of the books published in the West are smuggled into the
Soviet Union, where there is a thriving black market for them.
   Emigre Russian publishing has existed since the middle of the
last century—Alexander Herzen founded one of the early presses
in London himself. After the 1917 revolutions there was a brief
period when writers could work on either side of the border, if
they were careful. Between the 1920s and 1960s, however, a very

strict line was drawn between emigre Russian literature and "real" Soviet Russian literature. This line still exists, but during the last decade or so many holes have been punched in it. This is important, because in the past whole Soviet generations grew up ignorant of the greatest Russian prose writer of the century, Vladimir Nabokov, and some of their best poets, including both Marina Tsvetaeva and Vladislav Khodasevich (both were emigres). In the past decade, however, there has been a steady flow of manuscripts and microfilms out of the USSR and a reverse flow of books back into the country.

This anthology illustrates the situation. Everything in it was written in the USSR by writers born and educated in the Soviet period. Everything in it is set in the USSR. However, only the stories by Bitov, Shukshin, Trifonov, and Rasputin were actually published in the USSR. The Aksenov story was published in Russian, but in the United States, twelve years after it was written; at the time of publication Aksenov still lived in Moscow, but since then he has emigrated. Iskander still lives and publishes in the USSR, but "Belshazzar's Feasts" has been published only abroad. Sokolov emigrated in the year that *A School for Fools* was published in the United States. The enervating struggles that are behind this dry recitation of residencies and places of publication will be invisible to the American reading the selections. The intrinsic similarities among the writers are far more important than the extrinsic differences. They will all look Russian to you—and that is as it should be, because basically they are all part of the same Russian literature of the Soviet period. They share a common heritage, language and general subject matter, i.e., life in the USSR. They read and write for one another and their Soviet audience, both the one in the USSR and that composed of the quarter of a million new emigres.

Twenty years ago it would have been impossible to say such things, and it would have been impossible to select works representing so many styles and methods. Ten years ago one might have been able to select realistic works and fantastic ones, but still the choices would have been limited, and there were few works of the high quality that now exists. The last decade has been very productive. If we include only writers born after the Revolution, it is clear that the best Soviet Russian writing—both in poetry and in prose—dates from the 1970s.

The seven authors presented here all have reputations as being among the leading writers, at least with some segment of the reading and critical public. All of the novellas (if that is the word) in this anthology have been seen as important enough for serious critics to write about them, and nearly all of them have been translated into one or more other languages. Our goal was to offer substantial works by a few recognized writers, not to represent all of the worthwhile names by using a multitude of short pieces. Many things we would like to include cannot be used 'for a variety of purely practical reasons, but a second anthology of recent writing is already in the planning stage.

We have included here both "country prose" (one of the dominant types of fiction in the USSR) and urban prose (Trifonov and Aksenov are quintessential Moscow writers). There is realism and there is fantasy, even surrealism. There is straightforward psychological realism (Trifonov), instrospective realism (Bitov), retrospective realism (Rasputin), and even epic realism (Iskander) with a touch of the literature of the nationalities. And there is Sokolov, who doesn't fit any of the conventional categories. All in all it shows a diverse and healthy literature.

In the sections which follow, each devoted to an individual writer, we have tried to provide basic biographical information and some description not only of the works included in this anthology, but also other important works by the same author. The bibliography which follows these sections gives both general works about contemporary Russian writing and enough works in English by and about individual writers so that the reader can follow up on his favorites.

Carl R. Proffer
Ellendea Proffer

September 3, 1981
Ann Arbor

VASILY AKSENOV

Aksenov's career, from superstar of the sixties to non-person three years before 1984, is an extreme example of what has happened to honest Russian writing since 1960. He was born August 20, 1932; his parents were both Party members, and both were arrested in 1937. His mother, Evgenia Ginzburg, is famous as the author of her memoirs, *Into the Whirlwind*. When Aksenov was a young boy he joined his mother in exile in Magadan; he attended school there, later returning from the Far East to Leningrad where he eventually graduated from medical school. He practiced medicine only four years, until the publication of his novel *Colleagues* in 1960. The novel and such stories as "A Ticket to the Stars" (1961) and "Halfway to the Moon" (1962) made him probably the most popular writer of his country, and established him as the spokesman of a new generation, the post-Stalin intelligentsia, liberals who helped deepen the Thaw. But rapid fluctuations in the political temperature were reflected in his career.

Two months after his novella "Oranges from Morocco" (1963) appeared, Aksenov and others were called to the Kremlin where Khrushchev delivered a terrifying attack on them. Aksenov's works were published after this, but rather erratically and in censored form. His efforts to expand the stylistic, structural, and thematic limits of Soviet writing presented a continual challenge to editorial and political conservatives. *It's Time, My Friend, It's Time* (1964) and the inventive "Overstocked Tare of Barrels" (1968, "a tale with exaggerations and dreams") were his other main works of the sixties.

In 1975 Aksenov travelled to the United States and gave lectures, while working on his major novel *The Burn,* a work which could not pass Soviet censorship. It was only with great difficulty that he managed to get *In Search of a Genre* (1978) into print. His last publication in the USSR was his translation of E. L. Doctorow's *Ragtime.* It was a sensation for the Russians; and in spite of the editor's red ink, Aksenov managed to preserve some frank sexual descriptions. This brought down the wrath of the Party; the editor was summoned to the Central Committee with the original in one hand and Aksenov's version in the other. Separate book publication (it had appeared only in a journal) was forbidden.

But it was Aksenov's role in putting together the *Metropol* anthology (1979) of prose and poetry by twenty-three Soviet writers that was the last straw for the authorities. After *Metropol* was rejected by the Union of Writers, and then published in the West, Aksenov resigned from the Union over their harassment of the less well-known contributors to the anthology. The fact that several of the contributors were Soviet best-sellers, and their demand that the collection be published precisely as compiled, without any censorship or editng, were the greatest offenses from the point of view of literary superintendents. Aksenov was made the scapegoat, and he was given to feel that he would be healthier outside the USSR. He was given an exit visa, and then deprived of his Soviet citizenship (announced in January 1981), an honor conferred on other internationally known Russian writers such as Solzhenitsyn, Vladimir Voinovich, Vladimir Maximov, and Lev Kopelev. Aksenov now lives in the United States.

From the start of his career Aksenov consciously identified himself with his generation. The Khrushchev era, the time between Hungary and the invasion of Czechoslovakia, provided this generation with a breathing period, which they took to be a permanent state of affairs. They had hopes and illusions, ones of great force and charm: the truth could be told; a new Russia was rising from the devastation of the Stalinist past; the new generation, unlike the old, would never allow a return to the horrors of the past. Despite a number of unpleasant warning signs—trials, Khrushchev's fall, etc.—this generation of the intelligentsia was completely unprepared for the invasion of Czechoslovakia in 1968. After the Prague summer of brutality came the Prague winter, a time of re-evaluation of beliefs, a time of disillusionment and despair. This is the gestation period of *The Burn* (1980), which is dated "late sixties, early seventies"; this is the period which colors the fantastical *Crimea Island* (1981)—both of these novels, the major works of Aksenov's career, were published only after he left the Soviet Union. In a sense they are a two-part argument on the subject of the sins and expiations of the Russian intelligentsia, the intelligentsia which created the monster and was then devoured by it.

The first Aksenov work to appear in Russian only outside his homeland was "The Steel Bird" (written 1965, published

1977). Aksenov's semi-public reading of the entire tale at the Union of Writers' building in 1965 was a memorable occasion; the standing-room-only crowd and unusual length of the work read both set records for such literary try-outs. The fantastic and "modernistic" elements (such as the use of jazz imitations) irritated some listeners, but they mistakenly thought it would soon be allowed to appear in *Novy mir (New World,* the leading literary magazine). But in form and theme it scared the literary bureaucrats. Written before Czechoslovakia, but after the fall of Khrushchev, the story foreshadows thematically *The Burn.* A man who is not really a man, but a steel bird, gradually intimidates the inhabitants of a Moscow apartment house, becomes a tyrant, but is finally driven out. Significantly, the steel bird does not die; it simply flies away, perhaps to return one day. Instrumental in getting rid of this evil Stalinist henchman type are the four Samopalov brothers, who share an interest in the same things the heroes of *The Burn* do: one is a writer, one an artist, one a motorcyclist, one a musician.

"The Steel Bird" is a warning story: Stalin may have died, but there are other men of steel ready to take his place, if an ignorant, fearful populace permits it. The steel bird himself is clear in his intentions, often expressed through jazz: "There will be no past," he sings, "there will be no future, and I have already devoured the present." The path from the relatively hopeful fantasy of "The Steel Bird" to the self-destructive irony of *The Burn* can be traced through most of Aksenov's works, with the coloration gradually darkening. In *The Burn* "the steel bird" as a metaphor is transformed into a sculpture of a dinosaur done by one of the heroes. The sculpture's title is "Submissiveness" ("Smirenie"), and the dinosaur has the face of a Ryazan peasant. This dinosaur seems submissive and good-hearted, but it will destroy everything in its path nonetheless. The dinosaur is the ultimate destination of all art and science, no matter how humanistic its creators. In this change of central metaphor we may see the change in the author's attitude: in "The Steel Bird" the ordinary people are not really implicated in the doings of the tyrant, they are merely victims whose only crime is consenting to do nothing. In *The Burn* the dinosaur *is* the people, at least as they exist now, and its acts are the embodiment of the will of the people.

YURY TRIFONOV

Trifonov's early career gave no indication that he would become a controversial writer. Born in Moscow August 28, 1925 into a family with firm Party connections, he began publishing in 1947 and received a Stalin Prize for his novel *Students* in 1951. He wrote a number of well-received works: a novel, *The Quenching of Thirst* (1963), about the construction of a canal in Turkmenia; four books of short stories; a documentary work, *Reflection of the Fire* (1965); and the scenario for a movie *(The Hockey Players*, 1965). All of this established him as one of the leading Soviet writers. His only foreign taste was for the safe realist Hemingway; he seemed orthodox in almost every way. However, a qualitative change in his writing and his career took place when he published "The Exchange" (1969), quickly followed by "Taking Stock" (1970) and "The Long Goodbye" (1971), all in the influential journal *Novy mir*. Widely reviewed in the Soviet press, these novellas were seen by some critics as an attack on the intelligentsia as a whole—by one of their own. Other Soviet critics complained that the author was too objective, too alienated from the characters, that he was showing only the ugly side of contemporary life. Maybe this was realism, but it was not, by ordinary definitions, Socialist Realism. Indeed, from the educated outsider's point of view, it is "bourgeois realism"; and if one wants to know what Soviet urban life is and has been like, no Soviet writer provides a better picture than Trifonov. His prose is a solid machine, moving methodically through the moral and material crises of the intelligentsia and the middle class.

Following the historical novel *Impatience* (1973), about the People's Will revolutionary party, Trifonov published a fourth "Moscow novella"—"Another Life" (1975). Again we are in a world where people live with wives and husbands whom they no longer love, in-laws cause daily misery, children leave the nest, and death or sickness haunt the characters, who have often failed to find the peace they seek in life. Even more controversial was the novel *The House on the Embankment* (1976), a kind of variation of Trifonov's own first novel. The "house" in the title is a Moscow building where many Party leaders and government officials lived (including Trifonov's family), and the themes of betrayal and careerism are prominent. While Trifonov was an honest writer who was controversial in the Soviet Union because of his boldness and candor, he had to leave much beneath the surface. One senses a submerged anger in Trifonov, and it is doubtful that *The House on the Embankment* would contain so much that is purely implicit if he had written it "for abroad." Thus non-Soviet readers will miss much that Trifonov's home readers immediately understand—because of their shared experiences with Stalin and the history of the Party leaders in that "house." To some extent the same things are true of Trifonov's last published work, the novel *The Old Man* (1978). The struggle between usurpers of power and good, honest men is a central issue, as is the falsification of Soviet history. The archives of Trifonov's family (his father, killed in the purges, had been a revolutionary comrade of Stalin) and friends often figure in his historical novels. Unfortunately his career is now at an end; Trifonov died on March 31 this year, of complications following a routine operation. According to some reports a new novel entitled *Time and Place* was left in manuscript.

Like Balzac, Trifonov was interested in the specifics of existence: his characters are so firmly embedded in their social milieu that it is hard to imagine them alone, as individuals, without their relatives, friends and co-workers. What they have for breakfast, where they go on vacations, what they do with their money—all of these things go into the characterization of a Trifonov family. In the novellas the world of the middleclass professional is subjected to the somber, unblinking gaze of the moralist. For all his ethnographic description—many readers have been convinced that he knew *their* families—Trifonov's real interest lay not in excoriating the vices of his class, but rather in examining the precise moment when a man takes a wrong turn in his life, the moment of moral betrayal. This is the real subject of Trifonov's later work.

"The Exchange," for example, is firmly grounded in Moscow life, and it is no wonder that it was made into a very popular long-running play at Moscow's Taganka Theater. Its plot is based on the eternal housing shortage in Russia. What is not obvious to a non-Russian reader is miserably familiar to Russian readers: due to the chronic shortage of "living space," especially in Moscow, many people try to exchange different single rooms for one apartment where an entire family can live together. Otherwise one must wait for years to get into a decent apartment, or spend large sums to buy into a cooperative apartment house as it is being built.

The moral conflict in "The Exchange" seems simple at first glance: Dmitriev's aggressive wife Lena sees a chance to get a larger apartment by inviting her mother-in-law, whom she dislikes, to move in with them, exchanging both her old room and theirs for a real apartment. Lena's real motive, of course, is that she knows that her mother-in-law is dying, and will thus leave them with an extra room in the apartment they could not get otherwise—Soviet law allotting space on the basis of how many members there are in a family. From all of this, Dmitirev's wife would appear to be the villain. She is indeed unlikable, but in Trifonov's world nothing is quite so clear-cut. The reader of the story should pay close attention to the value systems and interrelations of all the characters; motivation is extremely complex.

The novellas Trifonov wrote in the 1970s are joined by a sober style, deliberately prosaic in its imagery. His heroes do not reach for poetic metaphors when they are happy or sad; they use concepts and objects from their everyday life, their ordinariness is emphasized. Which is the point about these people—they are not better or worse than others, they are ordinary, but they have serious problems, enjoy moments of euphoria when they feel that life has promise; in a word they are *human,* a category that comes up several times in his stories when it is affirmed that whether a man is an intellectual or not is not important—but whether he has humanity is.

Trifonov's Moscow stories give us the texture of everyday life, with the interlocking worlds of family, career, and conscience; but he provides no solutions, makes no conclusions that can be used. He is content to state the problem clearly, and show us that there are no heroes, no real villains. This is the gray blur of adult moral compromise, not the black-and-white photograph of childhood conceptions of honor. But Trifonov's characters long for the consoling sharpness and clarity of those early beliefs.

ANDREI BITOV

That emigre Russian writing does influence Soviet Russian writing can be seen clearly in the prose of Bitov; he has obviously read the Russian novels of Vladimir Nabokov, particularly *The Gift,* and he has put them to original use. To point this out is not at all to diminish Bitov's talent; he is one of the few Russian writers of importance whose style can be recognized even out of context, and he is one of the few whose fictional inventions have profited from the discoveries of such different classics as Dostoevsky and Proust, although until quite recently Proust was banned in the USSR.

Andrei Georgievich Bitov (b. Leningrad, May 27, 1937) seems to have specialized in writing books which were not immediately recognizable as books. Thus the story included in this collection, a piece which is generally regarded as his best short prose, is actually part of a longer cycle of stories entitled *Apothecary Island* (a locale in Leningrad), which focus on various moments and stages in the life of a strongly autobiographical hero, Alexei Monakhov ("monakh"="monk"). Bitov's novel *Pushkin House* has not been published in the USSR, but bits and pieces of it, in the guise of short stories and critical essays, were published there over a period of years and written about in some detail by Soviet critics, most of whom did not suspect that they were actually writing about a longer and unpublishable work.

Bitov is not a prolific writer, but aside from fiction he has published books of reportage and travel notes, such as *Lessons of Armenia* (1967-68) and *The Wheel* (1969-70). While by no stretch of the imagination a political person or dissident, he was one of the five editors of the ill-fated *Metropol* anthology presented to the Union of Writers in 1979. Virtually from the time Bitov's career began—his first book was *The Big Balloon* (1963)—he has been identified as a psychological writer, a subtle analyst of the most fugitive kinds of emotions and "thought about thought," as Soviet critic Lev Anninsky put it. Conservative defenders of Socialist Realism deplore excessive concentration on one's own developing thoughts, biographical minutiae, and other such "subjective" and socially useless notions. Party critics take too seriously Goethe's theory that if a person thinks about himself too much, he discovers he is sick. Thus "Dostoevskyism" is a pejorative term in the USSR, and somehow Tolstoi, for all his death-ridden, anti-scientific, anti-women, proto-religious work, is considered the Sun-God of Russian letters and the model to follow, in however debased the form. But Bitov's affinities with Dostoevsky are clear.

His early works, like the "Young Prose" of the early sixties in general, tended to concentrate on the lives of children and young people; as Bitov got older, his main heroes got older along with him. The relationships among the generations—particularly grandfather-father-son—are central concerns in many works, including "Life in Windy Weather" and *Pushkin House*. Deming Brown writes about the story:

It can be read as an account of the normal anxieties of a young, adult, urban, male professional. Likewise it can be viewed as a more special treatment of the psychology of creativity, of problems of aesthetics (several are brought up, directly or indirectly), and of the artist's inevitable loneliness. Throughout the story are arresting speculations on the relationship between subjective and objective knowledge, imagination and reality, and time—which sporadically either ceases to exist for the narrator or seems to rush with blinding speed.[1]

Another of the most knowledgeable critics of contemporary Russian prose, Priscilla Meyer, summarizes:

In "Life in Windy Weather" Alexei finally creates an acceptable version of himself through fiction, and can decide that sufficient meaning resides in the natural world around him, the pleasures of daily family life, and in his work. As a writer, Monakhov can reconcile fantasy and subjective reality, which he has associated with childhood, with the "reality" of adulthood. Bitov suggests that fiction is a means of renovating one's perception, analogous to seeing life through the eyes of a child.[2]

Bitov is now in the prime of his career, and as befits a writer of the first rank, his prose style is unique. The serpentine syntax, the complex series of subordinations, the startling but graceful use of abstractions and metaphors present a formidable challenge to the translator. This is especially true of *Pushkin House*. It is the major work of his life, and the one which Bitov could not get printed in the USSR. That it was first published in Russian in the United States is all the more ironic since the title refers to

Russia herself, to Pushkin's "home," as well as to the Leningrad literary archives which bear his name. The novel circulated in samizdat for some years, so it already has the status of a classic in the Soviet literary world, and when published here in 1978 it was met with universal acclaim among Russians abroad.

If Hemingway was Trifonov's early master, Bitov's masters are Dostoevsky and Nabokov. Among other things, they share St. Petersburg (Leningard). Like Nabokov's *The Gift, Pushkin House* is a "museum of Russian literature." It is the story of a 20th-century, Soviet, superfluous man, a "hero of his time" (the post-Stalin generation), who is playing his own version of "fathers and sons," a version in which the fatal purge year 1937 plays a decisive role. The classic Russian novels of the last century echo on almost every page, and one can say that an important theme in *Pushkin House* is the Russian novel and its development. Bitov's deeply introspective attention to motivation puts him with Dostoevsky as a psychological novelist; and Dostoevsky's characters, in modern dress, and character relationships are everywhere. But Dostoevsky's journalese, supernumeraries, and messy structures are utterly foreign to Bitov. Instead we find a neatly planned modern novel with structural symmetries, character parallels, the use of literary allusion, fatidic numbers, intentional ambiguities, and undermining of the fictional reality by variant versions of important events. As a melding of traditional and modern elements, *Pushkin House* is a true *tour de force*. It is as much Bitov's modern form and style that made the novel unpublishable at home as it was the themes—which include the sins of the fathers during Stalin's rule, the relative virtues of aristocracy and meritocracy, and alcohol as a Russian institution. But even if Bitov writes nothing else, his permanent place in Russian literature has been established by *Pushkin House* and "Life in Windy Weather," a story marked by all of the virtues of the novel.

FAZIL ISKANDER

Reading fiction is widely held to be an enjoyable experience, a fact which many Western Slavists, Russian writers and critics tend to lose sight of. When getting down to the grim business of discussing Russian literature they drag out the heavy artillery of Purpose and Truth. But one of the simplest and most unusual things to be reported about Iskander is that he is enjoyable to read.

Born Fazil Abdulovich Iskander (March 6, 1929) in Sukhum, he is of mixed Persian and Abkhazian descent, Abkhazia being a small so-called autonomous Soviet republic in the Caucasus, nestled along the eastern shore of the Black Sea. He has always divided his life between Abkhazia and Russia proper (Moscow). He graduated from the Gorky Literary Institute in Moscow in 1954, and began his career as a poet *(Mountain Paths,* 1957; *Green Rain,* 1960; *The Sea's Youth,* 1964). His early prose, like that of Bitov, Aksenov, and Sokolov, tends to deal with young people. Most of Iskander's stories are set in Abkhazia, and most of them have a first-person narrator (or something very close to one), a narrator who is apparently very autobiographical. One has to be careful on the latter count, because Iskander enjoys nothing more than making people believe some rather fantastic stories he has invented.

Iskander has created an entire fictional universe in and of Abkhazia; it has its regular settings and names (sometimes just slightly changed from real ones), its constant tribes (some invented) and characters; it has an entire *lore,* a mythology and history (which is which is hard to decide). He has been faithfully chronicling this world for twenty years. The story-teller often seems to treat the reader almost as a fellow countryman, someone who has sat through epic evenings of story-telling and is therefore familiar with at least the most colorful events and famous heroes.

For the most part Iskander's world is a fairly benign one, at least on the surface. He tells tales of cranks and eccentrics whose vices one can often forgive or ignore, and most events have some kind of happy ending. But Iskander also has dark stories of blood vengeance and historical injustice; and, like most satirists, at heart he is also a moralist.

Iskander's best-known work before *Sandro* was *The Goatibex Constellation* (1966). The author said (although this may be an intentional mystification) that it began when he read a newspaper account about a man who crossed a goat with a male ibex to produce the first "goatibex." The novel tells how this singular copulation led to an orgy of socialist competition and self-congratulation aimed at reforming the animal husbandry front, with the newspaper of the young narrator playing a major role in this fantastic project. The agricultural "reforms" of Khrushchev's day and the looney genetics of Lysenko are obvious targets of the satire, but one doesn't need any special historical knowledge to enjoy Iskander's portrayal of human fables and foibles. Here, as in most of his prose, Iskander's narration is relaxed and leisurely, completely open to entertaining digressions, presented in lucid prose which is misleadingly simple.

The story presented in this anthology is one of the twenty-one currently existing chapters of the major work of Iskander's life, a novel entitled *Sandro from Chegem*. (Its original title, *Zhitie Sandro chegemskogo, The Life of Sandro Chegemsky*, makes its relation to the tradition of Russian saints' lives clearer.) In a series of semi-independent tales, Iskander tells the 80-year story of Uncle Sandro from the 1880s to the 1960s—and Sandro's story is also the story of the Abkhazian people, with all their customs, superstitions, passions, and sufferings. In Iskander's case regionalism is not a barrier to understanding, because there is an epic, universal quality to his writing. He is a comic writer, and certainly much of the value of *Sandro* as entertainment is due to the humor. But again like many comic writers, Iskander is basically serious—even melancholic, reminiscent of Gogol. The section on Stalin presented here shows both Iskander's dark and light sides. The unflattering picture of a republic under Soviet domination is so violently at variance with the idealized, paternalistic Muscovite view that *Sandro,* the great work of Iskander's life (and no doubt of his people), quickly ran afoul of the censors. Roughly ten percent of the novel was published in Moscow as if it were the whole work (1973), and another chapter was published in 1981. But only abroad has the whole work seen the light of day: in 1978 a then complete edition was published in Russian here, and in 1981 a supplementary volume containing five new chapters was also issued by Ardis. In all what has been written so far makes the epic nearly as long as *War and Peace.*

Iskander's is an especially depressing case. He is a writer of the first rank, and he obviously has very little interest in politics as such. His role as an editor of the 1979 *Metropol* anthology, and his publication of some works abroad (including the allegorical animal novella *Rabbits and Boa Constrictors),* shows only the frustration of an independent mind, of a writer who wants to see his best work in print. *Sandro* was obviously a book from the heart and soul; its satire is more Horatian than Juvenalian, and only the unreasoning practices of Soviet literary superintendents kept a Soviet publishing house from having the honor of bringing out a book which would truly make the West look on with envy. Now translations are under way into English, French, German, Italian, and Swedish, and the pride of Abkhazia will soon be known all over the world.

VASILY SHUKSHIN

For Russians, Shukshin (b. July 25, 1929; d. October 2, 1974) was more than a writer—he was a phenomenon. His premature death (heart attack) at the height of his fame was mourned by millions of fans; pilgrims with fresh flowers still appear at his grave every day. The people loved him, and the officials loved him—an extraordinary confluence of opinion. Shukshin's two novels and 130-odd stories represent only one side of his talent. The part responsible for his celebrity status was his film work: a half dozen scripts, direction of six movies, and major roles in a dozen films.

"Snowball Berry Red" (1973) is unusual in that the story was written as a prelude or "treatment" for a film, a film which Shukshin actually did make in 1974 (he directed and starred in it). The reader can see Shukshin's cinematic intentions in the sequence and ratios of narration, scene and half-scene. The role of Egor was tailor-made for Shukshin the actor. Egor is the Soviet version of the John Garfield good-looking trying-to-reform tough whose past determines his tragic end; Shukshin's magnetic looks and personality helped him to create one of the most effective Soviet tear-jerkers ever made. Thus, while he could be represented in this anthology by more tightly constructed stories, "Snowball Berry Red" is obviously the only work which could represent Shukshin as a whole and convey some idea of what a Soviet best-seller is like.

Shukshin was born in Siberia, but after a stretch in the Soviet Navy, he moved to Moscow where he studied in the Institute of of Cinematography (1954-60) under the well-known director Mikhail Romm. He joined the Party in 1955. His first roles and story publications date from his student days. Shukshin's first col-lection, *Country Folk* (1963), was followed by prolific production of publishable works. Awards for his films ranged from the Venice Film Festival's Golden Lion to official Soviet medals, including a Lenin Prize for "Snowball Berry Red."

It would appear that, even more than Valentin Rasputin, Shukshin was a country boy who moved to the city and then found out that he never really felt at home anywhere, and that it isn't clear if you can't go home again because you have changed, or home has changed, or both. His chronicles of deracinated coun-try folk in search of they don't know what obviously have some autobiographical basis. His characters are often loners, indepen-dent, even anarchistic types who do not fit the most conservative rules for Soviet "positive heroes" (though in fact ever since the beginnings of country prose the noble eccentric from the back-woods has been an allowable, if not a stock, figure—as in Kazakov, Nagibin, etc.). But obviously hard-drinking romantics represent only one part of Shukshin's cast of characters, which is as varied as the country and country-to-city life which he usually describes.

Shukshin has what is usually called a "good ear" for speech. His dialogue strikes Russian readers as authentic and unhack-neyed, and his fast-moving scenes have the sort of virtues one would expect from someone with a cinematic mind. The heavy-handedness of Shukshin's nature descriptions may also be partly a result of movie training; he uses obvious symbolism and human emotions are underscored so heavily that one almost expects a musical sound-track next. Turgenev has a lot to answer for.

Interesting plots and surprise endings also help explain Shuk-shin's readability. He loves sudden and unexpected clashes, ironic and paradoxical endings. Russians say that no one likes scandals as much as Russians, and Shukshin has them in all forms—an outraged brother takes revenge but does so on the sister's wrong lover, minor points of honor lead people to disasters, and so on. Given the drabness of life described in most Soviet literature, Shukshin's lively conflicts are extremely exciting to his readers. Shukshin gives them heroes and situations easy to sympathize with. Above all, his naive (but not phoney) sentimentality accounts for his popularity among such different kinds of readers as Brezhnev and Solzhenitsyn. If Bitov represents the cerebral cortex of Soviet writing, Shukshin represents the heart and soul, the good old Russian soul that people have been writing about for two hundred years now. Free spirits emoting without control, laughing with drink and weeping with strangers, bold seekers after spontaneity and freedom—these are his typical heroes. Almost all of the Western critics who have written about Shukshin speak of his characters' quest for liberty (in Russian "volia"), unrestrained emotional (as opposed to political) freedom. The paradox of this is that Shukshin never felt strongly called to deal with the larger question of liberty which obviously faces everyone who lives in the USSR, and while he had his brushes with the censorship and made fun of official Soviet artistic conventions (in stories such as "The Craftsman" and "Point of View"), it was always acceptable fun, and he never pushed far beyond what authorities would tolerate from a Party member. Thus among Shukshin's weaknesses is the tendency to deal with little, or local, problems; the focus is narrow, and we may see a striking close-up, but essentially characterization is superficial.

One of the greatest difficulties a Soviet writer faces is how to be interesting and truthful while keeping the readers' mental eyes off the unmentionable backdrop against which all his characters work—totalitarian society cut off from the larger world by the Russian Great Wall. It is a measure of Shukshin's raw talent that when he is at his best he is able to create characters of such vitality that the reader focuses totally on them and honestly forgets to look at that backdrop. This makes him one of the best and truest practitioners of Socialist Realism.

VALENTIN RASPUTIN

The country writer who has received most attention in the last five years is Valentin Grigorievich Rasputin (b. March 15, 1937, in the Irkutsk region—and no relation to the more famous Rasputin). He is a Siberian, and his view and knowledge of the world are naturally rather different from what they would be if he had been born and reared in the literary capitals. Rasputin graduated from Irkutsk University in 1959, having majored in literature and history. He started publishing short stories in 1961, rather romantic versions of powerful characters living in the taiga.

His first book (1967) was published in Krasnoyarsk (incidentally the place of publication of Sasha Sokolov's only Soviet book, a student anthology from that same period). In Rasputin's compassionate tale "Money for Maria" (1967) a farm store manager faced with an unexplained one-thousand-ruble shortage in inventory is forced by authorities to find the amount in five days or go to jail, even though everyone knows she could not possibly have stolen anything herself. The outcome in left agonizingly up in the air. The short novel *Live and Remember* (1974) is unique in Soviet letters because the hero is a Red Army deserter (the extenuating circumstances are so exculpatory that only narrow-minded officials pursue the man), and the heroine, his wife, is faithful to him, not the law. Another strong and positive female figure in Rasputin's cast of characters, even though pregnant she leads the police away, eventually committing suicide to throw them off her husband's track.

Farewell to Matyora (1976) deals with the flooding of an island community as part of a hydroelectric project. But there are human mysteries which the engineers of progress cannot fathom; the ancient cemetery, the ancestors of the villagers, and a huge larch which the confident loggers are unable to fell with blade or fire, suggest forces and values of a kind not appreciated by modern society. *Farewell to Matyora* is easily the best thing Rasputin has written, and the main reason for including him in an anthology along with the other leading Russian writers. He has achieved a high level of honesty in describing life in his native regions; this and the fact that his prose style is rich—avoiding both the homogenized Party lingo and the extremes of dialect—make him a hope for the future, perhaps the only hope for literature published wholly in the USSR now that Trifonov has died. Because he is now being touted by the establishment as a success story, it will be interesting to see what happens to him. So far he has refused to do the hack work and jingoistic essays, the kinds of things that are usually demanded of an officially successful career (messages to the people on Soviet holidays, etc.). Given Rasputin's realism and honesty, it will be extremely difficult for him to remain detached, Moreover, as he approaches his mid-forties, traditionally the peak years for a prose writer), he may discover he has written something so truthful and so good that it will be unpublishable in his homeland. His attraction to tragedy, the irrational, and traditional humane values would seem to drive him in this direction. His interest for the non-Soviet reader is somewhat questionable; both of his novels were published here by Macmillan without creating stir beyond a meagre handful of tepid reviews.

"Downstream" represents an earlier stage in Rasputin's career, but many of the same themes which are found in *Farewell to Matyora* appear here too. Island communities are flooded, sometimes by design, sometimes by nature; and the young writer-narrator, returning to his family after five years away, contemplates the changing face of things with intelligence and sensitivity much greater than that of the other people around, those who remained in the villages and on the farms. He finds rapturous beauty in part of this remote life, but he also understands that he is no longer part of it. In spite of the intelligentsia narrator, the story is a fair sample of country prose; and the leisurely movement of the vast river downstream, both into the past and into the future, is an appropriate end to an anthology which has begun with the fantastic frenetic urban world of the capital.

SASHA SOKOLOV

Although we have put him at the end of this introduction, Sasha Sokolov represents a new beginning, and *A School for Fools* is the central selection of this anthology. Sokolov (b. 1943) is of a different generation than all the other writers in this volume, and the independent course which he has followed is one of the things which sets him apart from writers for whom social concerns are primary motivators. *A School for Fools* (1976) is one of the greatest first books ever written in Russian. Vladimir Nabokov, who was not known for easy praise, especially of totally unknown writers, said resoundingly: *"A School for Fools* is an enchanting, tragic, and touching book." In addition to English, it has been translated into German, French, Dutch, and Italian.

The author's life story is as extraordinary as his books. He was born in Ottawa during World War II; his father, who was spying on the Allies from the Soviet Embassy, and who later became a general in Soviet military intelligence (GRU), left with Sasha and his mother on a submarine. Sokolov grew up mostly in and around Moscow, attended the journalism department of Krasnoyarsk University, and was associated with an unofficial literary group called SMOG (which means "I could" and is a playful acronym for the Society of Youngest Geniuses). In style and structure his writing was totally unacceptable to Soviet editors. Indeed, Sokolov is a good example of the principle that subject matter is not the only thing censorable in the USSR—*how* one writes is almost as important as what one writes. After great difficulties and adventures, Sokolov emigrated in 1976. He was able to claim Canadian citizenship, and has divided his time between Canada and the United States since then.

A School for Fools describes life in the country, centering on a "special" school for retarded, and often psychotic, children. The novel's nameless hero, and one of the main narrators, is a former pupil in the special school. His father is a chief prosecutor, responsible among other things for the schizophrenia of his only son. The student's only hero is the eloquent geographer Norvegov, an idealist and dreamer who hates the way the school and the society are run. His speeches, along with the young man's hallucinatory reminiscences, are among the best parts of the novel, whose characters include the narrator's imagined mistress, some whimsical railroad workers, and some semimythic people whose existence remains in doubt. Sokolov is very Russian in his moral concerns, particularly in showing with imaginative force the past causes and future consequences of a given act. But in his sense of measure, his quiet wit, and his delicacy of touch he is rather un-Russian.

The modernistic devices Sokolov uses are an obvious feature of the novel, but they are not in themselves particularly important. The imaginative chronology and the few modest stream-of-

consciousness passages may have been calculated partly to annoy traditionalist Russian readers, but the devices arise naturally out of the characterization. The complexities of Sokolov's prose are amply rewarded by the fantastic lyricism, charm, and humor of almost every scene. Behind the most fanciful of digressions there is always a sense that the author is firmly in control, and the second reading makes one more aware of the careful plans and balanced architecture. Sokolov's prose is made of velvet-covered chains—lyrical, poetical, and mellifluous, but also somehow concise and inevitable, as if the final text had been distilled and refined from a much longer book. The diction is rich, playful, and completely original. The deft parodies of many Soviet literary conventions are not altogether visible to the reader of a translation; they reveal the author's furious contempt for the hackneyed words and themes of most Soviet writing, both official and dissident. On the political level, one has to look much harder for an axe to grind, because except in the very broadest sense, Sokolov is indifferent to literature of social comment.

He is equally as independent and innovative in his only other published novel, *Between the Dog and the Wolf* (1980). Sections of prose and poetry alternate. Potentially sensational subject matter—incest, patricide—is heavily veiled. The action takes place "between the dog and the wolf," i.e., the twilight zone when the shepherd cannot tell the difference between the two. The difference between the past and future is blurred, along with the distinction between the living and the dead—and all of this is born ultimately out of a quotation from Pushkin's *Eugene Onegin.* The book is above all a hymn to the Russian language; and without Dahl's dictionary and some experience living on the upper Volga, the non-native reader will have a hard time with the novel in Russian (and it is not translatable). Sokolov shows the dull, plodding writers of so much ordinary "country prose" what true imagination can do with their language and settings. At the same time his world is a fictive one which has little in common with Socialist Realism or the real Russian countryside. "You are an incredible dreamer," says one of the characters in *A School for Fools,* and the same is clearly true of Sasha Sokolov.

1. Deming Brown, *Soviet Russian Literature since Stalin* (Cambridge: Cambridge University Press, 1978), p. 197.

2. Priscilla Meyer, quoted from her introduction to Andrei Bitov, *Selected Short Stories,* scheduled to be published by Ardis in 1982.

BIBLIOGRAPHY

INDIVIDUAL AUTHORS

AKSENOV, V. P. A Starry Ticket. Putnam, 1962.
— — —. The Steel Bird & Other Stories. Ann Arbor: Ardis, 1979.
— — —. It's Time, My Friend, It's Time. London: Macmillan, 1969.
— — —. Colleagues. Moscow: FLPH, n.d.

about Aksenov:
> Johnson, John J. "Introduction: The Life and Works of Aksenov," in Aksenov, The Steel Bird & Other Stories, ix-xxvii.
> Meyer, Priscilla, "Aksenov and Soviet Literature of the 1960s," Russian Literature Triquarterly, No. 6 (1973), pp. 447-63.
> Meyer, Priscilla, "A Bibliography of Works by and about Vasily Pavlovich Aksenov," in Fred Moody (ed.), Ten Bibliographies of 20th-Century Russian Literature (Ann Arbor: Ardis, 1977), pp. 119-26.

BITOV, Andrei. Selected Short Stories. Ann Arbor: Ardis, 1982.

about Bitov:
> Schmid, Wolf (comp.), "Materialen zu einer Bitov-Bibliographie," Wiener Slawistischer almanach. Band 4 (1979), pp. 480-92.

ISKANDER, F. Forbidden Fruit and Other Stories. Moscow: Progress, 1972.
— — —. The Thirteenth Labour of Hercules. Moscow: Progress, 1978.
— — —. The Goatibex Constellation. Ann Arbor: Ardis, 1975.
— — —. "A Very Sexy Little Giant" and "Vengeance" in the anthology Metropol (New York: Norton, 1982).

about Iskander:
> Burlingame, Helen P. "The Prose of Fazil Iskander," Russian Literature Triquarterly, No. 14 (Winter 1976), pp. 123-65.

RASPUTIN, V. Live & Remember. New York: Macmillan, 1978.
— — —. Farewell to Matyora. New York: Macmillan, 1980.
— — —. "Money for Maria," Soviet Literature, No. 1 (1969).
— — —. "The French Lesson," Soviet Literature, No. 1 (1975).

about Rasputin:
> Hosking, G. Beyond Socialist Realism (see below), pp. 70-81.

SHUKSHIN, V. I Want to Live. Moscow: Progress, 1973.
— — —. Snowball Berry Red & Other Stories. Ann Arbor: Ardis, 1979.

about Shukshin:
> The most detailed biographical, critical, and bibliographical information about him is in the book Snowball Berry Red & Other Stories.

SOKOLOV, Sasha. A School for Fools. Ann Arbor: Ardis, 1977.

about Sokolov:
> Johnson, D. Barton, "A Structural Analysis of Sasha Sokolov's *School for Fools: A Paradigmatic Novel*," in Fiction and Drama in Eastern and Southeastern Europe, eds. H. Birnbaum and T. Eeekman (Columbus, 1980), pp. 207-37.
> Karriker, Alexandra H. "Double Vision: Sasha Sokolov's *School for Fools*," World Literature Today, Vol. 53, No. 4 (Autumn 1979), pp. 610-14.
> Moody, Fred. "Madness and the Pattern of Freedom in Sasha Sokolov's *A School for Fools*," Russian Literature Triquarterly, No. 16 (1979), pp. 7-32.

TRIFONOV, Yury. The Long Goodbye: Three Novellas. Ann Arbor: Ardis, 1978.
− − −. The Impatient Ones. Moscow: Progress, 1978.
− − −. The Students. Moscow: FLPH, 1953.
− − −. The House on the Embankment. New York: Simon & Schuster, 1982.

about Trifonov:
> Kustanovich, Constantin. Review of *The Old Man,* in Ulbandus Review, Vol. 1, No. 2 (Spring 1978), pp. 169-72.
> Proffer, Ellendea. "Introduction," in Trifonov, The Long Goodbye.

HISTORIES AND CRITICISM

Brown, Deming. SOVIET RUSSIAN LITERATURE SINCE STALIN. Cambridge University Press, 1978.

Brown, E. J. RUSSIAN LITERATURE SINCE THE REVOLUTION. London, 1969.

−−− (ed.). MAJOR SOVIET WRITERS. Essays in Criticism. Oxford Univ. Press, 1973.

Brumberg, A. (ed.), IN QUEST OF JUSTICE PROTEST & DISSENT IN THE SOVIET UNION TODAY. New York: Praeger, 1970.

Gladilin, Anatoly. THE MAKING AND UNMAKING OF A SOVIET WRITER. Ann Arbor: Ardis, 1979.

Hayward, Max & E. Crowley (eds.), SOVIET LITERATURE IN THE SIXTIES. New York: Praeger, 1964.

Hingley, Ronald. RUSSIAN WRITERS AND SOVIET SOCIETY 1917-1978. New York: Random House, 1979.

Hosking, Geoffrey. BEYOND SOCIALIST REALISM. Soviet Fiction Since Ivan Denisovich. London: Granada Publishing, 1980.

Mathewson, Rufus. THE POSITIVE HERO IN RUSSIAN LITERATURE. 2nd ed. Stanford University Press, 1975.

Mihajlov, Mihajlo. RUSSIAN THEMES. New York: Farrar, Straus, 1968.

Proffer, Carl R. "Writing in the Shadow of the Monolith: A Guide to the New Russian Writers," NEW YORK REVIEW OF BOOKS. February 19, 1976.

Rothberg, Abraham. THE HEIRS OF STALIN: DISSIDENCE AND THE SOVIET REGIME 1953-1970. Ithaca: Cornell University Press, 1972.

Slonim, Marc. SOVIET RUSSIAN LITERATURE. Writers & Problems, 1917-77. Oxford University Press, 1977.

Solzhenitsyn, A. THE OAK AND THE CALF. New York: Harper & Row, 1980.

Svirski, G. A HISTORY OF POST-WAR SOVIET WRITING. Ann Arbor: Ardis, 1981.

Blake, Patricia & May Hayward (eds.), DISSONANT VOICES IN SOVIET LITERA-TURE. New York: Pantheon, 1962.

Bochkarev, Yuri (ed.), SOVIET RUSSIAN STORIES OF THE 1960s & 1970s. Moscow: Progress, 1977.

Field, Andrew (ed.), PAGES FROM TARUSA. Boston: Little, Brown, 1964.

Glagoleva, F. (ed.), BY THE LIGHT OF DAY. STORIES BY SOVIET WRITERS. Moscow: Progress, 1968.

Ivanov, Y. (ed.), A TREASURY OF RUSSIAN & SOVIET SHORT STORIES. New York: Fawcett, 1971.

Kazakova, R. (selector), THE TENDER MUSE (SOVIET POETESSES). Moscow: Progress, 1976.

Kunitz, Joshua (ed.), RUSSIAN LITERATURE SINCE THE REVOLUTION. New York, Boni and Gaer, 1948.

MacAndrew, A. R. (ed.), FOUR SOVIET MASTERPIECES. New York: Bantam, 1965 [Vladimov, Voinovich, Aksenov, Kazakov].

Massie, Suzanne (ed.), THE LIVING MIRROR. Five Young Poets from Leningrad. Garden City: Doubleday, 1972.

Milner-Gulland, Robin & Martin Dewhirst (eds.), RUSSIAN WRITING TODAY. Penguin Books, 1977.

Niyazi, Shovkat (comp.), VOICES OF FRIENDS. Soviet Poets. Moscow: Progress, 1973.

Pomorska, Krystyna (ed.), FIFTY YEARS OF RUSSIAN PROSE FROM PASTERNAK TO SOLZHENITSYN. Cambridge: MIT Press, 1971. 2 volumes.

Proffer, Carl and Ellendea Proffer (eds.), THE ARDIS ANTHOLOGY OF RECENT RUSSIAN LITERATURE. Ann Arbor: Ardis, 1975.

Proffer, Carl (ed.), AN ANTHOLOGY OF CONTEMPORARY RUSSIAN PROSE. Ann Arbor: Ardis, 1981.

Reeve, F. D. (ed.), CONTEMPORARY RUSSIAN DRAMA. New York: Pegasus, 1967.

Scammel, Michael (ed.), RUSSIA'S OTHER WRITERS. London: Longman, 1970.

Whitney, T. P. (ed.), THE NEW WRITING IN RUSSIA. Ann Arbor: University of Michigan Press, 1964.

Yarmolinsky, Avrahm (ed.), SOVIET SHORT STORIES. Garden City: Anchor, 1960.

PERIODICALS

KONTINENT. Anthologies made up from the best-known emigre periodical are regularly published by Doubleday. To date 3 volumes have appeared, containing both fiction and non-fiction.

RUSSIAN LITERATURE TRIQUARTERLY. 1971- . Every issue of this journal contains translations of Russian poetry, fiction, and criticism, primarily 20th-century works.

SOVIET LITERATURE. Published in Moscow by Progress Publishers, the official Soviet propaganda publisher, the twelve annual issues of this magazine are the best place to see the conservative Party presentation of Soviet literature and politics.

CONTEMPORARY
RUSSIAN
PROSE

Vasily Aksenov

THE STEEL BIRD
A Tale with Digressions and a Solo for Cornet.

Enter the Hero, and an Attempt at a Portrait

It would appear that the hero of my tale appeared in Moscow in the spring of 1948, at any rate that is when he was first observed on Fonarnii[1] Lane. It is possible that he had inhabited the capital even earlier, no one denies it, maybe even a number of years, there are plenty of blank spots on the city map, after all.

A sharp smell of mold, of filthy damp underwear, a mouse-like smell struck the folk crowded round the beer vendor opposite No. 14 Fonarnii as the hero walked past. Their nostrils were invaded by decay and foul weather, disintegration and putrefaction, by the twilight of civilization. Even seasoned veterans who had marched from the Volga to the Spree were stunned, so out of keeping was this smell, this sign of preposterous destructive forces with the Moscow spring evening, with the voices of Vadim Siniavskii and Claudia Shulzhenko, with the peaceful lowing of captive BMWs and Opel-Admirals, with the abolition of ration cards, with reminiscences of retreats and advances, with the beer, the rusty, but astonishingly tasty sardelle,[2] with the wife of Deputy Minister Z., whose charming hands had fluttered the first-floor curtains literally one minute earlier.

The smell conjured up something that not even the most desperate times had produced, that a normal person would never dream of, not even hell, something far worse.

The stunned episodic characters stared mutely at my hero's frail back, and at this moment he stopped. Even ex-paratrooper Fuchinian, a man of snap and precise decisions, was taken aback by the sight of our hero, his pale, somewhat hairy hands, with their two string bags and the scraps of yellow newspaper poking out of the holes in these string bags. The string bags dripped something dark onto the asphalt. Even so, Fuchinian resolved to rouse the crowd with a joke, to terminate the oppressive situation, to get his cronies in formation for the rebuff.

"Now here's a little rat," he said. "If I were a cat I'd gobble him up, and that would be the end of him."

His cronies were about to roar laughing, were just about to line up, but just then my hero turned to them and choked off their laughter with the inexpressible sadness of his eye-sockets, deep and dark as railway tunnels in scorching Mesopotamia.

"Could you please tell me, Comrades," he said in an ordinary sort of voice which still gave each of the beer-drinkers the shudders, "how to get to 14 Fonarnii Lane."

The episodic characters were silent, even Fuchinian said nothing.

"Would you be so good as to indicate No. 14 Fonarnii," said the hero.

"Something is dripping from your bags," pronounced Fuchinian in a hollow jerky voice.

"No wonder," the hero smiled meekly. "This one is meat," he raised his right arm, "and this one is fish," raising his left arm. "Omnea mea mecum porto," he smiled again and there was a gleam of light in the Mesopotamian tunnels.

"No. 14 is across the street," someone said. "That entrance there. Who do you want there?"

"Thanks," said our hero and crossed the street, leaving two dark trails behind him.

"I've seen him somewhere before," said one.

"I've met him too," said another.

"His snout is familiar," said a third.

"Enough!" cried Fuchinian. "You know me, I'm Fuchinian! Whoever wants a beer had better drink, anybody who doesn't, needn't. Everyone knows me here."

And notwithstanding the terribly edgy atmosphere they all began drinking beer.

The Doctor's Recollections and a More Detailed Portrait

The history of his first illness and my part in it is a mystery to me to this day. Firstly, I don't understand how I, an experienced clinician and generally acknowledged diagnostician, was unable to make a diagnosis, or even a working assumption, on the nature of the illness. I have never seen anything like it—there was nothing to kick off from, not the slightest starting point for the development of a medical thought, nothing to catch on to at all.

Before me lay the naked body of a comparatively young man; the subcutaneous fatty layer was a little wanting, but in general near average; the cutaneous coverings were pale, dirty and unhappy (I remember going cold with horror when I made mental use of this highly unmedical term, but later things got much worse), breathing was even, there was no wheezing, all I could detect was the alveola's fussy whisper and the soft twitter of the hemoglobin absorbing oxygen; the heartbeat was distinct and rhythmic, but it became quite clear to me while I was listening that this was a suffering heart (we doctors laugh at a lyrical term like "suffering," for anyone with the slightest education knows that spiritual sufferings develop in the cortex of the large hemispheres, but in the given instance it was a spiritually suffering heart, and again I was overcome with fear). The stomach was soft and smooth to the touch, but the sigmoidal intestine showed signs of a strange playfulness (this threw me completely); the peripheral blood vessels were examined on the extremities under a layer of skin, and suddenly on the right thigh I read the blood formula, just as if it were typed on a form from our hospital: L-6500, ROE - 5mm/hour, NV-98 (the formula was normal)—that is, an objective examination yielded no sign of physical suffering, and only in his eyes, in their deep sockets, in the ancient cave city, raged pneumonia, military tuberculosis, syphilis, cancer, tropical fever all rolled into one.

In the first place there was all that, and in the second place I have no idea why I didn't send him to a clinic but instead leaped outside into the night and ran all over the place rousing my colleagues in my hunt for penicillin, which was very scarce in those days.

When I got back, I bent over him with the syringe containing the precious penicillin, and one of the countless women surrounding his bed babbled behind me:

"Doctor, it won't hurt him very much, will it?"

My own hands were trembling with pity for this creature, and the paltry injection I was planning to give him seemed almost like a laporotomy, but nevertheless I remembered my medical calling and ordered:

"Turn over onto your stomach."

He instantly rolled onto his stomach, I couldn't even work out which muscles were exerted to make this movement possible.

"Pull down your pants," I said.

He pulled down his pants, baring buttocks of a very unpleasant appearance, resembling the edge of a forest where stumps had been grubbed out prior to a forest fire coming through.

"Poor thing!" gasped the women from behind.

When the needle entered the upper outside square of the right buttock my patient began to tremble, at first gently gently, then his whole body began vibrating violently, something popped and gurgled inside him, something whistled, sweat stains spread across the pillow, but this lasted no more than a minute, then all abated and he was calm.

"What is this?" I thought, slowly pushing forward the plunger of the syringe. "What secret chains have suddenly forged me to this horrible behind, this transcendental being?"

When the procedure was over the patient immediately turned over onto his back, and his eyes lit up bright yellow, like the headlights of approaching trains. He smiled meekly, even humbly.

"When will we be having another jab, Doctor?" he asked me.

"Whenever you want, my friend, any time of day or night, the first beckoning of your hand, the first call, no matter where I am," I replied in all seriousness.

"Thank you, Doctor," he thanked me simply, but I immediately felt warm inside.

"Thank you, dear Doctor, you have saved him," whispered the women, closing the circle. We all fell silent in order to remember forever the majesty of this moment.

Nevertheless I couldn't resist measuring some of his body proportions with a tape measure. For years I kept this data secret, but recently it was codified by the committee for Coordination of Scientific Research.

Chapter One

Nikolaev, Nikolai Nikolaevich, manager of the houses[3] on Fonarnii Lane, was busy sorting out a dispute which had flared up between the occupants of Flat 31, No. 14, Samopalova, Maria and Samopalov, Lev Ustinovich.

The case was simple enough both in essence and ramifications, but savage and militant, with no foreseeable reconciliation.

Maria and Lev Ustinovich had once been husband and wife, but had separated some ten years before the war on account of an extreme rupture at the cultural level. The house manager understood this well and sympathized with Lev Ustinovich and respected his resolve and strong will, because for a quarter of a century now he himself had been oppressed by the low cultural level of his better half.

That was long ago and long forgotten, and now, of course, the former couple didn't even remember that they had once twined in tender embraces and forgotten themselves in fits of unrestrained mutual passion. Now they sat before Nikolaev and looked at one another with heavy stale ill-will. Maria, a cottage-industry worker, was stout and dark-faced, whereas Lev Ustinovich, manager of a hair-dressing salon, was the exact opposite— dessicated and fair.

At that time, ten years before the war, Samopalov had brought into the house one Zulphia, a woman of eastern origins, and begotten of her four boy-devils, and all those years Maria had battled along with Samopalov's first-born, her daughter Agrippina, whom she kept, raised and made into an assistant in her difficult domestic trade.

The essence of the dispute came back to Lev Ustinovich's complaint that Maria, who had formerly earned her living by inoffensive embroidery, had now acquired a loom, whose rattling did not create any conditions whatsoever for relaxation for Samopalov and his family. The arguments on both sides had already been exhausted, except for the main trumps which were kept in reserve, and the two sides were merely exchanging meaningless retorts.

"You're a slob, Lev Ustinovich," said Maria.

"And you, Maria, are a self-seeking, narrow egoist," countered Samopalov.

"Your Sulphidon makes more noise than my loom when she's bashing your head against the wall."

"My God!" choked Samopalov with indignation. "What slander! And I have forbidden you, Maria, to call Zulphia Sulphidon."

"And what about your kids bawling at night?" Maria wasn't letting up.

"The floors shake the way your Agrippina walks!" shouted Samopalov, stung.

"My Agrippina is like a turtle dove, as for you, Lev Ustinovich, you might pay attention to people's protests, clearing your throat of a morning in the toilet and making such noises it's impossible to go past into the kitchen."

"That's not true!"

"It is so!"

"Children!" called Samopalov, and instantly his four swarthy boys, the best gymnasts in No. 14, ran into the house manager's office.

"Agrippina!" shouted Maria and into the office swayed her incredibly plump fair-haired daughter, the dead spit of Samopalov.

"It's a disgrace, Lev Ustinovich," she blabbed, "the way you victimize Mother and me in communal matters, it's beyond endurance."

Samopalov's children by Zulphia, Ivan, Ahmed, Zurab and Valentin surrounded Agrippina, yelling, and the house manager Nikolaev couldn't make out a single word.

The irresoluble situation which had arisen in Flat 31 depressed Nikolai Nikolaevich beyond words, this great storm of passion merely saddened him, but God forbid that he should give the slightest indication of sorrow or alarm, after all he was the administrator, the law and the terror, the word and deed of Fonarnii Lane. How could he help these people, what could he rouse them to? At that time the term "peaceful coexistence" did not exist. The only thing he could do was put one of the Samopalovs in prison, but strange as it may seem, that didn't even enter his head. What could be done, what initiatives taken, on whom could he lean? As everybody knows, the role of the public at that time ws reduced to zero: it was necessary to act alone, to administer, divide and rule, with the whip and treacle cake, or whatever.

"Quiet, everybody!" he commanded softly, and the Samopalovs fell silent, because they knew that for all Nikolai Nikolaevich appeared slow moving, he could be tough and occasionally capricious.

"I order you from this day to cease dissension and quarrels," said the house manager severely, adding in a gentler tone with an inward smile. "After all, you are relatives."

"But what about that loom? The loom should be smashed!" burst in the hot-headed Ivan, but he was restrained by the more rational Ahmed.

"Comrade House Manager," began Samopalov, bringing out his hidden trump, "the loom, as I see it, is a typically capitalist means of production, and in our country, as I see it..."

"Ooooh, Lev Ustinovich! Oh, you so and so!" Realizing the point of his speech, Maria let fly, "and you don't hold on to your means and take clients at home, why, you shave the deputy minister in his flat, you rake it in on the side, and you want to do the dirty on a poor widow!"

"Just a minute, what sort of a widow are you?" reported an outraged Samopalov. "I seem to be still alive. None of my wives have been widows yet."

"Mama has a certificate from the co-op for the loom," wailed Agrippina in floods of tears.

"I won't give up the loom, certificate or no," declared Maria. "I'm a Soviet citizen and I'm not going to give up my beloved loom. I'll write to Stalin, our father."

"Don't you dare!" shouted the House manager at this juncture with unfeigned anger. "Don't you dare take Generalissimo Stalin's name in vain! What is this? As if Josif Vissarionovich could be bothered with your squabbles and your idiotic loom."

The quarrel subsided and the Samopalovs abandoned the office.

Nikolai Nikolaevich, brushing away melancholy thoughts, established some basic order in his place of work, closed the office and set off home. He too, like the Samopalovs, lived in No. 14, which had been built in 1910, and so was faced with tiles that gleamed in the sunset. The house had six stories, one main entrance with a bizarre canopy overhead, a working, if pre-revolutionary, lift, central heating, telephones, and other such conveniences. There were 36 flats in the house and 101 accountable tenants. In a word, this house was the pride of Fonarnii Lane, and indeed remarkable for the whole Arbat[4] area.

When he had finished his supper, read the "Evening Moscow" and fed his superb goldfish, Nikolai Nikolaevich sat down on the ottoman, drew the cornet-a-piston out of its case and called to his wife:

"Klasha, lock up!"

His wife, accustomed to such commands, locked the flat entrance without demur and fastened the chain. Nikolai Nikolaevich raised the instrument to his lips and softly, most tenderly, began to produce the melody "... And squadron by squadron, the cavalry-men tighten the reins and fly into battle."[5]

At this point Nikolai Nikolaevich's small secret had better be revealed. Before the war he was soloist in the Gorkii Park woodwind orchestra, and in the war years, despite breaking his neck to get into the front lines he was assigned to the orchestra at the front. Cornetist Nikolaev's playing won many a military commander by the purity of its sound and its major key quality, and so by the end of the war he had earned the rank of major. Guards major. On leaving the service he realized there was no way back, a Guards major couldn't, had no right to be a frivolous cornet-à-piston player even in the C.P.C.R. or the orchestra of the Bolshoi Theater. Having blotted out his past, Nikolaev appeared before the Raikom[6] and requested an administrative job. And so he became a house manager. Naturally, none of the inhabitants of Fonarnii Lane knew about Nikolai Nikolaevich's past, and those of them who heard the pure major notes of an evening assumed it was the radio.

True, occasionally Nikolai Nikolaevich would begin to stray into a minor key: such was the nature of the work, it would dispose anyone to melancholy reflections, even to philosophy. And then these very secret evening rehearsals became a source of Nikolai Nikolaevich's melancholy, a source of recollections of a bright, happy life, of that animated collective labor to which the rank of Guards major prevented him from returning.

Nikolai Nikolaevich was a high class musician and had achieved such a degree of unity with his instrument that sometimes the cornet-a-piston would begin to express those deep thoughts and feelings of its master to which house manager Nikolaev did not normally give rein, and which he at times did not even suspect in his make-up.

And so now it was with the aim of distracting himself from sorrow that Nikolai Nikolaevich began rendering the rollicking cavalry song, but slipped without noticing it into a queer and none too jolly improvisation.

"How did it happen, how can it be, why is there discord in the Samopalov fam-i-ly?" sang the cornet. "Poor, poor Stalin, my unhappy leader, beloved father, dear heart of iron."

It should be observed at this juncture that Nikolai Nikolaevich, in addition to the prevalent filial respect for Stalin and worship of his qualities of genius, experienced the most ordinary pity for the leader, i.e. he felt almost fatherly towards him, as he would toward a child of his own torn from its parents by inhuman destiny, or towards an orphan. Sometimes he had the feeling that the leader was tormented by his comrades-in-arms and ministers, and by the 220 million Soviet people plus all progressive mankind. Of course he was afraid of these feelings and suppressed them, but now and again they would break out via the cornet-a-piston.

"Dear people, you are not crocodiles, why then do you shun friendship and love? Aunty Maria, run your wretched loom a bit quieter, don't disturb others. Dear barber Samopalov, remember how tenderly you once caressed Maria, remember the child, share your living space,[7] always keep the laws of society. Don't write to Stalin, dear Maria, don't hinder the poor man thinking and creating. Have pity, my dear, on the standard-bearer of peace, our dearly beloved son and father"—sang the cornet.

"The theme of the leader is magnificent," said someone behind Nikolai Nikolaevich.

It would be difficult, no impossible to describe Nikolai Nikolaevich's state the following instant. His physical movements were extremely unbecoming: firstly, he dropped the cornet, secondly, he fell to the floor, thirdly, he farted, fourthly, he attempted to hide his instrument under the ottoman bolster and only fifthly and finally did he turn around.

Before him in an indecisive pose stood a man holding two string bags. Something dark dripped from the latter onto the parquet floor.

"What? What did you say?" exclaimed Nikolai Nikolaevich.

"Don't worry," said the man, "I merely said that you gave a very moving and original rendition of the leader theme. I have never heard it treated like that before."

"How do you know what I was expressing? What kind of paradox is this?"

"I just happen to understand and love music," replied the man with the string bags very seriously.

"Then you understand my cornet?" Nikolai Nikolaevich was still conducting this dialogue in rather high, almost falsetto tones.

"Yes."

"Are you a composer?"

"No."

"Who are you then?"

"Benjamin Fedoseevich Popenkov."[8]

Nikolai Nikolaevich was silent simply staring at the newcomer.

The latter stood before him, frail, unclean and stinking, in a soiled frayed lounge suit, which was however made of good pre-war "Champion" cloth, a field shirt under the jacket, minus a single medal or decoration, but wearing two pre-war badges—a "MOPR"[9] and a "Voroshilov gunner."[10] Nikolai Nikolaevich pinched himself hard on the behind, but all in vain, it was solid reality.

"Please understand," the silence was broken by the man called Popenkov, "what you were playing was very close to me. It was my life, my feelings, my sufferings. Take the Samopalovs, to whom the cornet appealed so movingly, I don't know them, but they must be wonderful, wonderful, *wonderful* people!" he cried, "but can't they really come to any agreement? And what you were playing about Stalin, that's right here"— his chin nodded towards the area of the heart.

"Something is dripping from your bag," said Nikolai Nikolaevich gloomily, all the strings in his soul ajangle.

"No wonder," Popenkov smiled meekly. "This one's meat"—he raised his right hand, "and this one's fish"—he raised his left hand. "Omnea mea mecum porto, or translated, all I have I carry with me."

"Are you just out of prison?" asked Nikolai Nikolaevich. He still hoped for salvation.

"No," replied Popenkov, "I haven't the slightest connection, not even family connection, with enemies of the people."

Nikolai Nikolaevich felt crushed, pitiful, almost naked, almost a slave.

"What can I do for you?" still frowning, grasping for his position, he asked.

"Nikolai Nikolaevich, Comrade Nikolaev," began Popenkov piteously, "I come to you not only as a man, not only as a musician, but as to a house manager. You are a wonderful, wonderful, *wonderful* man!" he barked.

Here he squatted down and looked up at Nikolai Nikolaevich from the deep hollows of his eyes, and Nikolai Nikolaevich was touched by the desert heat, so powerful was the sorrow in these eyes. The next instant Popenkov, leaving his string bags behind on the floor, leaped high into the air, even too high, rubbed his hands madly and landed.

"Nikolai Nikolaevich, I am asking for refuge, cover, a roof over my head in one of the houses entrusted to you."

"But you know about the passport system," mumbled Nikolai Nikolaevich plaintively, "and then where could I put you, even so they are occupied beyond capacity."

"Nikolai Nikolaevich, I'll lay my cards on the table, I'll tell you everything," Popenkov began hastily. "I have walked a long way here, I have been through a lot, I flew here, driven by loyalty and love for a certain person. For a year now... that is, I beg your pardon, for a week now I have been living down amongst the foundations of the Palace of Soviets. And now I have finally worked up the courage to come to him. My cards are on the table—I am talking about Deputy minister Comrade Z.! The fact is, dear Nikolai Nikolaevich, that I saved Z's life several times. I sacrificed myself for his sake, and he said 'Benjamin, come and live with me, you'll be my friend, my brother, a part of my very self.' And here I am, and what do I see? A wife, a young beauty, beauty, a *beauty!*" he cried, "antique furniture... I was very happy for him. But Z. didn't recognize me, more than that, he was even frightened of me. I don't understand how anyone can be afraid of me, a small pitiable man. In short, Z. is a marvellous, marvellous, *marvellous!*" he cried, "man, I see his point—responsible position, mental and physical hypertension, a young wife, and so on, but what am I to do now, because that was my last hope."

Popenkov squatted on his heels again and looked up at Nikolai Nikolaevich from below, and if the house manager had had any concept of the geography of our planet he would have compared the sorrow of his eyes to the ancient sorrow of Mesopotamia or the sun-scorched hills of the Anatolian peninsula. But since he had no such object of comparison, the intangible sorrow of the eyes affected him more powerfully than any learned geographer or historian.

"You say that you have suffered, that you have lived down in the foundations, and I still don't know where to put you," said Nikolai Nikolaevich in a shaky voice. "Of course you realize that I can't very well lean on Z., he's way above me."

"Yes, yes, me too," concurred Popenkov.

"He only lives here, you know, out of a sort of eccentricity, and because his wife likes the pre-revolutionary molded ceilings, essentially he lives here in Fonarnii Lane only out of democratism and I don't know that to do about you, Comrade Popenkov," Nikolai Nikolaevich was completely nonplussed.

"Don't feel awkward about it," Popenkov said encouragingly, "I'm not fussy, you know. Any leftover space would do. Your entrance, for example, is spacious and just fine..."

"The entrance would be impossible, the district inspector is very severe, you know. The yard-keepers I could manage, but the district inspector..."

"A-t-t-t-t-t- A-t-t-t-t-" Popenkov began thinking, clicking his tongue loudly, "A-t-t-t-t-... The lift! Your excellent spacious lift! It would suit me just fine."

"The lift..... is for general use," muttered Nikolai Nikolaevich.

"Well, of course," agreed Popenkov, straightening up. "Believe me, I won't disturb anyone. You can give me a camp-bed and I'll sit up in the lift only when I have checked that all are present, that all the birdies are in their little nests, and I'll be on my feet at six a.m. and the lift will be at everybody's disposal. In the event of any extreme nocturnal need, first aid, or say, a visit from our comrades from the organs[11] I will free the lift immediately, flit straight out. How about it? Well, Nikolai Nikolaevich? I can see you've come round already. Well, one last effort. Remember, dear friend, what the cornet-a-piston was singing. Dear people, you are no crocodiles, why then do you shun friendship and love..."

"Well, all right, I'll give you a camp-bed, but be so good as to remember that the lift is for general use," growled Nikolai Nikolaevich, who always growled like that when meeting someone halfway. "Let's go, Comrade Popenkov."

"Wait a moment!" exclaimed Popenkov. "Let's have a few moments silence. Moments like these should be captured."

Nikolai Nikolaevich, in a complete trance, as if he were under hypnosis, silently captured the moment.

Having done this, they went out into the hall. Klavdia Petrovna glanced out of the kitchen and froze, her mouth wide open, seeing her husband scramble up to the top cupboard after the camp-bed. Popenkov looked at her sorrowfully from the top of the ladder.

"Here is your camp-bed," growled Nikolaev. "But take note, it's only meant for one: the springs are weak."

"Nikolai Nikolaevich, you are a wonderful, wonderful, *wonderful*! man," Popenkov began his descent with the stretcher under his arm.

"Tell me, how did you get in?" Nikolaev asked after him.

Popenkov turned round.

"The usual way. Don't you worry, Nikolai Nikolaevich, I won't let on about your cornet. Not a whisper, silent as the grave. I understand that each of us has his little secrets, I for example..."

"Thank you, you needn't let me in on your secrets," said Nikolai Nikolaevich, gloomily, looking askance at the string bags, which were still dripping something.

When he had shut the door he laid into Klavdia Petrovna.

"Why on earth don't you shut the door, mother, when you're asked?"

"Kolia, dear, have a conscience, I locked it the moment you began to play, and fastened the chain."

"Then did he fly in the window or what?"

"That's true," gasped Klavdia Petrovna, "it couldn't have been through the window. Perhaps I forgot, got caught up with things in the kitchen. I'm getting old, Kolia, sclerosis... Who was he?"

"From the organs," growled Nikolai Nikolaevich to stop further questioning.

His wife was well-trained and said no more.

That evening on their way past into the lift several of the tenants noticed a sorrowful figure with two string bags and a camp-bed in the dark corner of the entrance hall, but some passed by without noticing. Popenkov acknowledged the tenants with a submissive nod. When the last tenant, the flighty Marina Tsvetkova, having adroitly given the slip to the officer who had seen her home, had taken the lift up to her floor, and when the officer had stopped capering around the entrance, railing against Maria's treachery, Popenkov brought the lift down, set up his camp-bed in it, ate a little meat, a little fish, and assumed a horizontal position. In this position he thought with a feeling of deep gratitude about the house manager Nikolaev, with kindly feelings about Maria Samopalova, whom he as yet knew only from the cornet song, with slight reproach about Deputy Minister Z., with some agitation of the latter's young wife, with a touch of playfulness about the fleet-footed Marina Tsvetkova, and then he sank into dreams.

His dreams were unchecked, almost fantastic, but we won't enlarge on them just yet, let us just say that if for most people sleep is sleep with or without dreams, for Popenkov sleep was a sort of orgy of dreams.

In the morning, at six sharp, Popenkov cleared out the lift and took up his position in the corner, submissively greeting the tenants as they left the house. So it was on the following day, on the third, the fifth and the tenth...

Naturally all kinds of rumors, conjectures, speculations got about, but they eventually got back to the house office and stopped there.

A conversation something like the following took place between Nikolaev and Deputy Minister Z.

"Listen here, Comrade Major," said Z., "this guy from the entrance, he hasn't said anything to you about me, has he?"

"He said that he saved your life more than once," replied Nikolaev.

"There are a lot of people who have saved my life, but I don't seem to remember this one," mused Z., "no, I definitely don't remember him."

"Perhaps he'll save it yet," suggested Nikolaev.

"Do you think so?" again Z. was thoughtful. "He couldn't be dangerous, could he? I'm not a nervous type myself, you know, but my policeman is agitated."

(Police sergeant Yurii Filippovich Isaev was on permanent guard on the Deputy Minister's landing.)

"I don't think he's dangerous," said Nikolaev, "what's dangerous about him? An unfortunate man, sensitive, understands... er... art."

"Then that's all right," Z. dismissed it with a wave.

Well that's about all, this is where the first chapter ends. It should only be said that everybody soon got used to Popenkov, and many were even inspired to sympathy. Soon he was admitted to some of the apartments. He was a good listener, he sympathized with people and a fair number of the inhabitants opened their hearts to him. True, the working class, headed by diver Fuchinian, looked askance at Popenkov and wouldn't let him anywhere near them.

The Building Inspector's Report

The double door to No. 14 opens outwards, is 3 meters 52 centimeters wide and 6 meters 7 centimeters high. The door is manufactured from the wood family known as "oak," has copper handles in the form of a reptile, "the snake," on both sides.

Above the door hangs a light in a colored metal grid, the grid has 24 cells, the bulb (100 w.) is working.

Note. The oaken surface of both sections of the door has a carved representation of the fruit of the vine, seriously damaged in the lower parts. Three centimeters from the external handle a three-letter inscription[12] carved out with a sharp instrument has been concealed by three parallel strokes by order of the house office; however, it can be deciphered under close examination.

Passing through the door we have before us an oval-shaped area, known as the main entrance hall, measuring approximately 178.3 meters. The figure is approximate, since it is as difficult to measure the square area of an oval as of a circle. The height of the dome-shaped ceilng of the "main entrance" is 16.8 meters at its highest point. The floor consists of a tiled mosaic of oriental, or more precisely Mauritian character (consultation at the Oriental Institute). The tile stock of the floor has been damaged, about 17.2% of the total number of tiles.

A light fitting in the form of an ancient Greek amphora with handles hangs from the ceiling by a metal cord (consultation with the A. S. Pushkin Museum).

This is not functioning and represents a danger to life and limb, on account of the worn nature of the cord, but in view of the absence of the requisite ladders (12 m.) in the house office, it cannot be removed for transfer to a museum.

Lighting of the "main entrance" is effected by means of four light fittings, two on each side, each having three light sockets. Of the twelve bulbs eight are functioning. The light is diffuse, dull yellow. The far right plafond is damaged (broken) on the left corner, thus directing the light into a niche on the left side of the door, about 1.25 meters from the latter. The niche has an arched top, is 2.5 meters high, 1.5 meters wide. Formerly the niche housed a hollow cast-iron sculpture of Emperor Peter I, of which only the 1.1 meter high boots, known as Wellingtons, remain (consultation with the journal *October*).

Color of the walls to a height of 1.6 meters is dark blue, oil paint mixed with turps. Above this point and all over the dome are fragments of badly damaged frescoes (1914 A.D.), that is curls, extremities, folds of garments, female mammary glands, etc., elements of Greek mythology (consultation with the journal *October*).

Note. To the right and the left on the dark-blue background of the walls are chalk inscriptions and drawings, erased by order of the house office, although the said inscriptions and drawings were not harming anybody.

Daytime lighting of the "front entrance" is effected by means of six windows with colored glass, three windows on each side. The windows rise to a point, are 4.5 meters high, 0.5 meters wide, situated 0.7 meters off the floor at intervals of 0.8 meters from one another. The panes on the left side reflect an oriental, more precisely a Japano-Chinese subject, that is: geishas, rickshas, water-carriers, teahouses, gunboats (consultation with the Soviet-Chinese Friendship Society).

The windows on the right hand side reflect a medieval Franco-Germanic subject, that is: knights, minstrels, fair ladies, animals, horses, sidearms (consultation with the Soviet-French Friendship Society). The lower section of the second left pane is reinforced by a sheet of ply 0.5 m x 0.7 m, the lower section of the first pane on the right is reinforced by a sheet of cardboard 0.5 x 0.9.

The area is heated—four central heating radiators, with three sections each, set along the walls.

At the far end of the oval-shaped area is a lift shaft housing a working lift. On the doors of the lift are four enamelled white plates 0.2 x 0.4 c with black letters. The signs say: "Look after the lift—it preserves your health," "Unload the children first, then yourselves," "Dogs prohibited," "The lift is not a lavatory!"

The inside of the lift is a box, area 4 sq. m., 2.5 m high, painted brown, containing a square mirror, unevenly broken in 1937.

To the right of the lift begins the first flight of a white-marble staircase, numbering thirty-eight steps, of which sixteen are damaged. At the very base of the stairs is a hollow cast-iron figure 1.25 high, absolutely unidentified by the specialists. In the figure's right hand there is a lamp, which several of the inhabitants attempt to use as a rubbish bin, when they know quite well that the lamp is fixed solid and can't be tipped up and what will happen if the rubbish reaches the top?

Part for Cornet-à-piston

Theme: Good day, capital, good day, Moscow! Good day, Moscow sky! These words are in everyman's heart, no matter how far away he is... Improvisations: Poor unfortunate, he lay in the foundations, suffered long years. He saved the Deputy Minister, only to be cast out by him, where then is gratitude? There is no justice, they can ruin the fledgling. Poor stinking wretched transient, who are you? Have you a residence permit,[13] have you a mother, have you a passport? Terrible fledgling, live in your lift, only keep tight about me. If you should tell, it will be dreadful for me, I shall be silenced forever. The terrible burden of authority oppresses night and day. A post in management is a great thing, a terrible thing...

Sudden end to the part: Morning meets us with coolness, the river meets us with the wind, curly head, why then do you not welcome the gay whistle's song?

Chapter Two

What had happened? What was wrong? There was banging and shouting on every floor, a nocturnal working bee in No. 14 Fonarnii. Sergeant Yurii Filippovich, stupefied with terror, pounded at Z.'s door, fell into the flat and began trembling in the Deputy Minister's arms.

"What's the matter, Yurii Filippovich?" asked Z., back only half an hour from a night conference. "What's happened?"

"I don't know, blessed father, I don't know, blessed mother... The banging and the shouts," muttered Yurii Filippovich.

Leaving his guard to his spouse, Z. dived for his cherished Browning.

Samopalov's children came spilling down from the sixth floor. Maria in her flight threw herself on Lev Ustinovich's neck. Zulphia clutched at him from the other side. Only Agrippina, duffer though she was, immediately armed herself with a coupling bolt ready to defend her mother's loom.

Doctor Zeldovich from the fifth floor emerged onto the landing already dressed in an overcoat and warm scarf, carrying a suitcase. His family likewise made ready in the space of a few minutes.

It had all started with that flighty Marina Tsvetkova galloping down four flights of the marble staircase like a frightened antelope and all but tearing off its hinges the door to Nikolai Nikolaevich's flat. At this time, it being the dead of night, Nikolai Nikolaevich was sitting in the lavatory, concealed from his family, and was playing his cornet. On the sly, almost inaudibly. The cornet piece was interrupted by the unbelievable godforsaken banging and crashing.

"Comrade Nikolaev!" yelled Tsvetkova.

"Him. Your! protégé! there! in the lift!.."

"What's the matter with him?" roared Nikolaev like a bear.

"In... convulsions!" shouted Tsvetkova, opening her already huge eyes.

"Save him, good people!" roared the cornet player in a panic.

The whole house was roused and everybody streamed downstairs, some in pajamas, some in dressing-gowns, some in underpants, in whatever came to hand. In one minute the vestibule was crammed with a buzzing crowd, resembling the Roman forum. Those who pushed nearer to the front could see Popenkov writhing on his camp-bed through the open doors of the lift.

"Doctor! Get a doctor! Comrade Zeldovich!" shouted people in the crowd.

Doctor Zeldovich steered a course through the corridor that had formed to the lift, and here the convulsions ceased, Popenkov lay quiet, his arms stretched out along his sides.

This unpleasant occurrence (the convulsions, the sharp attack) took place several months after Popenkov moved into the lift. Until then the life of the house had flowed comparatively peacefully, calmly, almost without a hitch, at any rate without any overt troubles.

As has already been stated, the inhabitants quickly got used to the submissive figure with the camp-bed, patiently standing in the darkest corner of the vestibule near the radiator. And the figure meanwhile was adapting to its new place of abode.

Above all he had to master the vestibule, to interpret its secret nocturnal life. In the dead of night Popenkov observed things very closely, silently, not interfering until he had completely got to the bottom of their contradictions.

The fact is, the oriental ornament was in direct and irreconcilable conflict with the ancient Greek amphora hanging directly above it. It would clink its tiles at night, changing the figures of its mosaic in order to create an indecent word, thereby offending the ill-mannered amphora for good, and the frescoes too, all these lumps of unbridled flesh, in short, the whole ancient world. Alas, all the ornament's efforts were in vain, either there was not enough time, or something else, just as with the ceiling's nightly attempts to organize the scattered parts of the body into one whole.

And there was ferment in the stained glass panels, a restrained simmering of passions. A flat Gothic figure, perhaps Roland or Richard the Lion Heart, being seated with fair ladies, was sending kisses to the geisha on the other side, who in turn had turned to the knight the enticing triangle of her naked back and was smiling over her shoulder, scorning utterly the samurai and water-carriers.

"Ojo-san, tai hen kirei des' ne," whispered the knight in Japanese.

"Arigato," replied the geisha, gently as a little bell. "Domo Arigato."

An enigmatic figure on the staircase (it would have been Diogenes, were it not for some likeness to Aladdin) kept straining to go out for a walk, but at his first movement the snake on the inside stretched and hissed, and the one on the outside beat its head furiously against the door.

Then naturally they were all devilishly interested in the luckless amphora, nobody knew what was inside it. The knights and samurai assumed that it was wine, and what man doesn't dream of wine? The fair ladies and the geishas were convinced the amphora contained a sweet-smelling substance and dreamed of massaging themselves with it. By morning speculation on the amphora had gone to extremes.

Only Popenkov knew for certain that there was nothing in the amphora but half a century of dust, thirteen desiccated flies, two spiders dying of starvation, and a "Herzegovina Flor" cigarette butt—goodness knows how that got there.

On the whole, this nocturnal life was not to his taste. He had some reason to suspect that if it went on much longer, there would be a general shift, and the samurais would dash for the fair ladies and the knights would get in amongst the geishas; the gunboats would land the "tommy" troops, the lad with the lamp would go out on the town, the ornament finally form its cherished word, the amphora would naturally be broken open; the snakes, God forbid, might find their way into his camp-bed and the world he intended to rule by virtue of being animate might collapse altogether. So one day, in the heat of the vestibule orgy, that is at five a.m., he sprang out of his camp-bed, scattered the already maddened ornament and leapt into Peter's boots.

Naturally everybody took fright, gasped, began whispering in corners as to who and what, what kind of a bird this was, but Popenkov hushed them, jumped up (somewhat strangely, since he jumped together with the boots), tore down the Greek amphora, smashed it to smithereens on the floor, and, back in his niche, proclaimed:

"There's your despicable filthy dream, there's nothing in it but dead flies and half-dead spiders, and I'll finish smoking the butt, 'Herzegovina Flor' doesn't lie around the floor. Is it understood now, who's boss?"

With these words he jumped out of the Wellingtons, picked up the butt and puffed away on it for a good hour, lying in the camp-bed.

They all fell silent and froze for ever and ever, even before his specific instructions, only the ornament arched obsequiously and attempted to crawl up and lick him on the foot in gratitude for his having dealt with the amphora, but Popenkov brushed it away with his heel and wouldn't let it near him.

In the morning Maria Samopalova was first down, she was off to the co-op to deliver her work.

"Well, well," she said when she caught sight of the broken amphora. She thought about it and gasped.

"The cord wore out, Maria Timofeevna, what can you do, time erodes even the most solid metal," remarked Popenkov philosophically.

"It could have come down on my head," Maria calculated.

"According to the probability theory, quite likely," concurred Popenkov.

"It could have slammed Lev Ustinovich," Maria screwed up her eyes.

"Easily," nodded Popenkov. "Imagine, one minute there was Lev Ustinovich, and the next he was finished."

"It could have crowned Nikolai Nikolaevich...."

"Not only him, it could even have been Deputy Minister Z.," Popenkov entered in enthusiastically.

"Yes, if one of the top bosses came to our house it could have crashed down on him," Maria went on speculating.

"Exactly. That would be a right disaster," Popenkov grew sorrowful.

"Anybody at all could have been killed," said Maria, summing up.

"You are quite right," agreed Popenkov.

"And what about you, you weren't hurt, Benjamin?" inquired Maria.

"I got by, Maria Timofeevna. I was sleeping peacefully, Maria Timofeevna, when suddenly I heard a crash, practically an explosion! Shades of the war, and I began shaking with horror. Surely not again? Surely the imperialists couldn't do it again... Do you understand?"

"I wouldn't put anything past them," growled Maria. "The light should have come down on Churchill's head, or Truman's."

"I subscribe to your sentiments," said Popenkov, opening the door for Maria. "It looks as if you are on your way to the co-op, Maria Timofeevna."

"I am delivering my work," replied Maria importantly. "It mightn't be much, but I do my bit for the state, not like your barbers. At a pinch a man can get by with a beard, but he can't manage without textiles. The other day I was walking past Kindergarten No. 105, they've got a bit of my embroidered linen on their window, it's real heart-warming."

"Permit me to have a peep at your work," asked Popenkov.

They went outside and Maria, for all she was very suspicious, unwrapped her bundle and showed him part of the linen. Popenkov, his arms folded on his breast, stared at the cloth.

"Why don't you say something?" Maria was surprised. Popenkov brushed that aside.

"Of course we are only handicraft workers, invalids," whined Maria, "we're a long way off these..."

"This is art!" suddenly exclaimed Popenkov fervently. "It's real art, Maria Timofeevna. You are a talented, talented, *talented* person," he cried out.

"Spontaneity, expression, fi-li-gree. You ought to go further. You could produce"—his voice dropped to a whisper—"old French tapestries."

"What tapestries? Are you out of your mind, Benjamin? You'll get me into a predicament," Maria was getting anxious.

"Don't worry, I'll explain everything. Let me come with you," he seized the bundle with one hand and Maria with the other. "I'll help you, I'll get the reproductions, and you and I will make tapestries. I don't need any kind of remuneration. I would just like people to have beautiful old tapestries."

He led Maria along the winding Fonarnii Lane, persuading her to take up old tapestries, simultaneously going into raptures over the charms of the lindens in flower, the flight of swallows (a keen dagger-like glance above), and the clear June day. From time to time he would jump into the air, rubbing his hands excitedly. Maria merely groaned under his pressure.

The reader is quite right to ask who is this Benjamin Fedoseevich Popenkov, where he came from, his cultural level, what he is by profession and so on and so forth. If he isn't given this information the reader is within his rights to assume the author is leading him by the nose.

I could fall back on some naive mystification and really lead the reader by the nose, but literary ethics above all, so I am forced to declare that I know nothing about Popenkov. Water in clouds is dark. I have the feeling that in the course of the narrative some kind of a portrait of this character will emerge, however approximate, but the story of his origins and various other data are most unlikely ever to float to the surface.

The first tapestry was naturally sold to antique-lover Zinochka Z., young wife of our good Deputy Minister. The tapestry was beautiful, although of course it had suffered from the effects of time, whatever you say, almost two centuries have gone by since it was produced by anonymous craftsmen in Lyons. A pastorale was depicted on it, slightly reminiscent of Bouché.

Zinochka actually gasped when Popenkov brought her this tapestry. So did the Deputy Minister, when he learnt what it cost.

"It's unthinkable!" he said, immediately calculating in his head that about two months wages would go on the acquisition of this object. "Zinochka, it's unthinkable, it smacks of bourgeois decadence."

"What are you talking about darling?" said Zina in astonishment and came towards him, her shape visible through a transparent negligee.

The Deputy Minister immediately flew into the abyss, the tenth wave closed over his head, a typhoon raged.

"Mind you, it's very valuable," he said, when some time had elapsed.

After the sale of the tapestry friendly relations were established between Popenkov and Zina. The Deputy Minister was hardly ever home, he lived for his department, and Zina naturally was bored, and in need of live human company. Occasionally in a state of misanthropy she would dispatch Yurii Filippovich to walk the dog and summon Popenkov up to talk about life, the sad nature of human existence.

"For goodness' sake, Benjamin Fedoseevich," she would say, reclining on the sofa in her dressing gown, with Popenkov sitting on the edge, "Here

I am, young, beautiful... I'm not ugly, am I?"

"How can you ask! How can you?" said Popenkov indignantly.

"No, I'm not fishing for compliments," Zina dismissed his protest with a wave of the hand, "it's only lack of confidence in myself, doubts, anxieties... You understand, I am young and not ugly, I've got everything—a beautiful apartment, money, my own car, foodstuffs, why should I be so unhappy, why aren't I satisfied with life? Perhaps I am a superfluous person, like Pechorin?"

"I understand you Zina, I am familiar with all that," said Popenkov sadly, gazing at the floor, "it's as if we were the same person. We are drawn to the heights. We are superior beings, Zina"—for an instant he raised his eyes and scorched Zinochka with the fire of Mesopotamia.

"In '43 I gave myself to a pilot," said Zinochka. "He was the first, he took me savagely, inhumanly. It happened on the river bank in a downpour, but he was like a tiger, like..."

"Like an eagle," prompted Popenkov, "after all, he was a pilot."

"He was a pilot then, now he's a Deputy Minister," nodded Zina sadly. "He's a friend of my husband's, he visits and drinks vodka with Z., he's changed."

Popenkov would get up, pace the carpet nervously, rub his hands, turn sharply to Zinochka... Ooh, how she appealed to him, ly-y-ing there unafraid.

Then there would be Yurii Filippovich's cough and the dog's bark. Zinochka would get up off the sofa, tell Popenkov all sorts of trivia to do with the delivery of antiques and see him to the door. Because of Yurii Filippovich and the dog, their meetings began to take on a sort of unnecessary ambiguity.

At night Popenkov would command the frescoes on the dome to move, to piece together the scattered parts of the body. He didn't give up hope of assembling Zina's tempting figure, but kept getting freaks, sympathetic enough to look at, but "typically not the real article."

Two people were much later than the rest coming home, No. 14's number two charmer Maria Tsvetkova and the Deputy Minister himself. In those days, as everybody knows, the windows in the ministries and departments shone all night in the center of sleeping Moscow.

Z. always entered the house energetically, slammed the doors hard, crossed the vestibule in military strides, waking Popenkov as he went.

"How is life for the young, Savior?"

Popenkov jumped up, opened the lift door, refrained from answering this question, which hurt his pride, but would ask humbly:

"Will you take the lift?"

"It won't be required," Z. would say and fly up to his first floor apartment on strong legs.

Tsvetkova would tap with her wedge-heeled shoes, the current season's model. She wore a white woolen coat, like Claudia Shulzhenko, and had a "Marika Rokk" hairstyle.

In the war years a girl like Tsvetkova was the dream of all the warring countries, that is, of all civilized mankind. She had something that disturbed and inspired hardened fighting men, that connected them with normal human life, and if this was symbolically labeled "Ludmilla Tselikova," "Valentina Scrova," "Wait for me, and I will return,"[14] and on the other side "Marika Rokk," "Zarah Leander...," "Lili Marlene," and in the sands of the Sahara and in the Atlantic "Deanna Durbin," "Sonia Henie," "It's a long, long way to Tipperary," in real life it was Maria Tsvetkova.

The war years were for her a time of tender power, of romance, sorrow and hope. Her boys, her beaus, were flying over Königsberg in night bombing raids, tramping the highways of Poland and Czechoslovakia, surfacing in submarines in the cold Norwegian reefs. By one such hero, actually the only one she had really loved, Tsvetkova had a daughter. The hero didn't return, he died after Germany's capitulation, somewhere near Prague.

Tsvetkova was still lovely in 1948, but her style had altered a fraction, almost imperceptibly. She continued to accept the attentions of officers, because their shoulder-straps and decorations reminded her of the not-too-distant past, and because "youth was passing," but as for civilian dandies in long jackets with box shoulders—they got zero attention and a pound of scorn.

The officers would see Tsvetkova home, she would get into the lift with bouquets of flowers, and tap one wedge heel as they went up, hum "The night is short, the clouds slumber," barely notice the camp-bed with Popenkov, and never react in any way to his compliments regarding her figure and general charms.

Whereas Popenkov added Tsvetkova to his dreams, practiced black magic on his dome and ornament, and in general, if we are to be quite honest, experienced great anger towards the human race.

That night Tsvetkova entered the vestibule tipsy and gay, covered in dahlias, poppies and other flowerbuds.

"Permit me a sniff," requested Popenkov and buried his face in the bouquet, almost touching Marina's breast with his bony nose.

"You really should visit the bathhouse, Popenkov," said Marina, "you smell most unpleasant. Would you like thirty kopeks for a bath? Here's thirty kopeks and a peony for good measure."

"How am I to interpret your gift?" asked Popenkov, stuffing the flower and the coin to his bosom. "As a sign of interest or a sign of pity? If it's pity, then I shall return it; pity lowers a man, and a man has a proud ring about him."

"Are you a man, then, Popenkov?" Tsvetkova showed naive surprise and pressed the button for her floor.

Popenkov shuddered with proud and powerful feelings he himself didn't fully understand.

"You are a flighty creature, Marina, I know everything about you," he said, getting a grip on himself.

"You don't know anything about me," Tsvetkova suddenly grew sullen, "and I'm not at all flighty, I'm very down to earth, and you don't know a thing about me."

They went up.

"I do know," said Popenkov.

"Ha-ha," said Tsvetkova, "you don't know anything. For example, you don't know who I'm in love with, which man I have adored from afar for a long time, I love Deputy Minister Z., so there!"

The lift came to a halt and Tsvetkova attempted to get out, but Popenkov pushed the ground-floor button, and down they went.

"What do you think you're doing?" asked Tsvetkova.

"Just this," giggled Popenkov. "But what about Zinochka Z.?"

"Zinka, that so-and-so heifer!" cried Tsvetkova. "When Z. moved into our house he liked me better than Zinka, but I dropped him, because he was a Deputy Minister so he wouldn't think that I loved him just because he was a Deputy Minister. Fool that I am!" she burst into tears and pressed the button for her floor.

Up they went.

"Curious, curious," pronounced Popenkov. "So you were seeing Z. then?"

"So we were seeing one another, what of it, so we went on trips together, but we haven't been seeing one another for a year now, and I don't want anything from him," Tsvetkova was still crying.

"Don't cry, my dear," said Popenkov, putting his arms around Tsvetkova and unobtrusively pressing the ground-floor button, "don't cry, unhappy, delightful, *delightful* woman," he cried, opening his eyes wide. "Unrequited love, how well I understand it, that's the story of my life, we are creatures with a similar destiny..."

Down they went.

"Let go of me, you foul-smelling fellow!" Tsvetkova suddenly came to and pressed the button for her floor. "Have you gone mad or what?"

She tried to struggle out of Popenkov's embrace, but his arms were like steel. She felt the incredible superhuman strength of his arms and was even afraid.

"Let me go!"

Down!

"And if it is exposed... haven't you thought?... the excesses?... Zinaida's wrath... and if it were made public?... What if I take it around the various departments... eh?"

Up!

"Let me go, you wretch! You nut... miserable booby," and slap across the face, "idiot... let me go, I won't be answerable for what I do... I... I work on the newspaper... as a secretary... I'll write a piece about you... What a scoundrel you are... let me go!... that's it..."

Down!

"In misfortune I... kreg, kreg, karusers chuvyt... hemorroids... how can I see?... fit, fit, rykl, ekl, a?"

Up!

"You nothing... you scourge, you animal! My tears are not over you! My lover was a pilot, a hero twice over! Get out of the way!"

Down!

"In the paper... about me?.. chryk, chryk,.. grym firaus ekl... in brackets... why not take pity... I ekl buzhur zhirnau chlok chuvyr... kuri-kuri... a weak organism..."

Up!

"Are you out of your mind? You're quite mad! Ha-ha-ha-ha-ha-ha-ha-ha-ha-ha-ha-ha! You can't fool me!"

Down!

"Lyk bruter, kikan, kikan, kikan..., pity and love... I thirst like an eagle... order... liton fri au, au... we'll fly away... fit, fit, rykl, ekl, a?... over the ruins over the houses... flowers, Marina... ekl..."

Down, down, she was no longer in control of her arms, her laughter had died away and her tears dried up, whereas the lift was as full of electricity as a Leiden jar, and kept falling, falling, then rocketed upwards into thick blackness, into a wretched sky, and she felt as if she herself.. any minute.. just like her beloved pilot or tankman.. the one who hadn't returned.. any minute would meet her end, but just then Popenkov crashed into the camp-bed and went into convulsions.

The women of No. 14 set up a rescue committee and organized a roster by the patient's bedside.

In the morning they brought semolina, cream and cottage cheese from a neighboring kindergarten.

Comrade Z., under pressure from his wife, sent a doctor from the Kremlin hospital and the latter held a consultation with Doctor Zeldovich. Yurii Filippovich ran to the chemist. Alarming the pharmacists with his uniform and the inscription *cito!*, he got the medicines without having to queue.

Lev Ustinovich shaved the patient gratis, and his children made no noise in the entrance, on the contrary, they tried to amuse Popenkov, reading him verses and singing him oriental songs.

Maria and Agrippina draped the lift with clean and artistic canvases.

"What will we do about the lift?" asked Nikolai Nikolaevich at a general meeting of the tenants.

"What about the lift? What is a lift, when there's a sick man in it?

Damn the lift!" replied the tenants as one man.

"So that's settled—the lift is out of action!" Nikolai Nikolaevich summed up, and his usually stern eyes softened.

So in No. 14 Fonarnii Lane the lift was put out of action. On that we could end the second chapter.

Recollections of Mikhail Fuchinian, a Diver

Everybody knows me, I'm Fuchinian, and anybody who doesn't, soon will, and anybody who doesn't want to know me can leave, and if they don't leave they'll get to know me, and these here are my friends, they're first rate young men and lads. Bottoms up! Away, lads!

Well, O.K., if anybody's interested, I can tell you about this type. Only mind you don't interrupt, those who are going to interrupt had better leave right away, or they'll run into trouble.

In short, here is my arm, check it yourselves, if you want. Well, how is my arm, in order! Biceps, triceps, all in place? The left one's the same, see! In short, before you is my whole humeral belt. On the whole, as you see, no weakling!

One evening the lads and I were sitting in the yard playing dominoes. Tolik, he was a driver at the Central Fish Cannery, had that very day scored about six kilo of dried fish, so as it turned out, we sent the boys for some beer. The boys dragged in two cases of beer and it was turning out a nice quiet evening. We sere sitting normally, having knocked off the same, we're gorging the dried fish, washing it down with beer and swapping experiences from the Second World War.

Then this booby Benjamin Popenkov appears. He squats down, picks away at the fish, someone poured him a beer, he's sitting there saying nothing. Nice and clean, not like in '48, smelling of "Flight" eau-de-cologne, in a tie, boots, no worries.

I disliked this little rat from the very beginning—if I were a cat, I'd have gobbled him up and that would be that, but I didn't show my feelings, because it's my principle to live and let live, the lads will tell you that.

But here I began to get mad just looking at him. Oh you unfortunate fellow, I think, you wretched, homeless creature, everybody's feeding you, everybody's sorry for you, they all throw something your way, and meanwhile you're making yourself comfortable, you damned rook. I just thought God grant that everybody set himself up as well as this wretch. True, he hasn't got a flat, but then he's got the whole of the vestibule at his disposal, he's put in screens there, the tenants have only got the narrowest passage from the stairs to the door, and I don't even mention the lift. Next question: our poor unfortunate has taken himself the best stacked woman in the whole lane and has a ball with her behind the screens, and how!—the whole house rocks. Next: Here am I, a diver, a highly paid worker, well, for my two-hundred and fifty I squirm around on the bottom of the Moscow River like a crab, while that bastard walks around up top in a suit the like I've never dreamed of, and the smells in the vestibule are so gastronomic, there's never anything like them in my place. If you look at it this way, there's an unfortunate devil walking around looking at everybody as if they all owed him something. It's a sort of hypnotism, like with magicians, such as the Kio brothers or Cleo Dorotti.

Well anyway, I got mad and I took a sharp turn towards trouble. Tolik Proglotilin was just recounting an operation on Tsemissk Bay, and Popenkov kept humoring him, nodding away with his beak. Here I interrupt Tolik and say:

"Why don't you share your wartime experiences, Popenkov? I suppose you were defending Tashkent? No doubt you struck a blow to the dried apricots?" He smiles, the cad, smiles a mysterious, contained, incredible smile.

"Ah, Misha," he says to me, "you know nothing about my war. Your war is over, but mine isn't. My war will be more terrible than yours."

Everybody fell silent, sensing there was going to be trouble, everybody knows I don't like my fighting past being insulted.

"Who could you fight, you sparrow, you chicken feed," I say, with my voice raised. "Women? You wouldn't have the strength for anything else, you tom-tit!"

But he keeps on grinning away, and suddenly he fixes his orbs on me, so that a blast of heat comes my way, like out of a ship's furnace.

"In the first place, Misha, I'm no sparrow or tom-tit, and in the second place, not everybody knows his real strength. Perhaps I am stronger than you, eh Misha?"

So. Like that. That's how it's going to be.

Then I lift my right arm, this very arm you see before you, and put my elbow on the table.

"O.K., strong man, let's put it to the test."

It's a real laugh, but he too places his wasted paw on the table, his pale, moderately hairy paw. The lads are bursting with laughter, because I am the champion at this caper, not just in Fonarnii Lane, but in the whole of the Arbat district, and for that matter I don't know who in the whole of Moscow could pin my arm to the table, except perhaps Grigorii Novak.

So we engaged, and gently, almost without trying I bent his paw down, but about ten centimeters from the table it somehow jammed. I doubled my pressure, to no avail. I trebled it, but it was no go. It was as if my arm were resting on solid metal, practically tank armor. I looked into his eyes, with their yellow fire. On his lips was an amiable smile. I quadrupled my efforts and at this point my arm, as if it didn't belong to me, moved upwards, and then down under the force of a pressure that just couldn't be human, it had to be mechanical, and there it was stamped to the table. Everybody was silent.

"He beat you by sheer nerve, Misha, sheer nerve," whispered Vaska Axiomov. "Have another go. Flex your muscles..."

"Quite right," says Popenkov, "It wasn't my muscle power that beat Misha, it was the superiority of my nervous system. If you like, we could have another go..."

We tried again—the result was the same.

We tried a third time—no go.

Here to tell you the truth, my temperament got the better of me—as you know, my father is of Armenian origin—and I leapt on Popenkov. I rolled him, I pummelled him, I spun him, I bent him, and suddenly I was pinned down by both shoulder blades, touché, and above me yellow fires, ugh!, his damned eyes.

"Nerves," said Tolik Proglotilin, "he's got nerves of steel. We've all got weak nerves, but they," indicating Popenkov with respect, "they've got nerves of steel."

A gentleman acknowledges defeat, and I did so, I slapped Popenkov on the shoulder (he practically collapsed) and sent for vodka.

Popenkov sat quiet and modest, I must say he didn't brag at all. We drank. To smooth it over the lads began singing songs of the war and pre-war years, different marching songs.

> Where the infantry can't pass
> Nor armored train race by
> Nor heavy tank crawl through
> The Steel Bird will fly.

"Here's our steel bird," said Vaska Axiomov, embracing Popenkov, "our very own real steel bird."

"Steel, all metal," continued Tolik Proglotilin affectionately.

And a new version was composed.

> Where Axiomov is not outstripped
> Where Proglotilin can't race by
> Nor Fuchinian crawl through
> The Steel Bird will fly.

Well, naturally, they all roared laughing. You only have to hold a finger up to our boys and they guffaw.

And here, brothers, something very strange took place, just like they describe in novels. Popenkov jumped up, began waving his arms around, just like a bird, his eyes burning feverishly, he became pretty terrifying, and began telling in some half-intelligible language:

"Kertl fur linker, I knew it, at last! Yes, I am a Steel zhiza, chuiza drong! Aha, we've got.. fricheki, klocheki kryt, kryt, kryt! In flight—the whistle and claw of their percators!"

We were all dumbfounded, looking at this freak, then suddenly he was silent, got embarrassed, smiled gently and squatted down.

"Not a bad trick I played on you, eh? A funny one, eh?"

Everybody breathed a sigh of relief and burst out laughing—"What a card! A steel bird, all right, what a nervous system!"

But he called me aside.

"Actually, Misha, I was after your hide," he told me softly.

I began to shake, and resolved to resist to the end, defend to the death.

"You couldn't help me to install some furniture tomorrow, I suppose?" he asked. "I can't manage alone, and my wife, you know, is a weak woman. You see, we have decided to furnish the place, as it is, it's like being on bivouac. It would be nice to have furniture for when our relatives come."

"Sure, Steel Bird," I said, to tell the truth relieved that my hide hadn't been required after all. "Sure, Steel Bird, we'll do whatever we can. I'll be along tomorrow with Vaska and Tolik." So that's how it was, chaps! We went on with what we were doing. Bottoms up! Salute. Oh yes, we carried the furniture in for him, and that evening he nailed up the main entrance. Since then the tenants have been using the back entrance.

The Doctor's Recollections.

I treated him many times, each time as if I were blindfolded, each time the diagnosis was completely unclear to me. In the end I began to think it was nothing to do with my treatment, the antibiotics or the physiotherapy that made him get better, it was just his own will, the same way as he got sick.

Each summons to him was agony for me, a concentration of all my spiritual strength, that is, all the strength of my higher nervous system. In the first place, I sometimes began to think that there was something powerful and mysterious about him, in his organism, something of the sort that completely contradicts my outlook as a Soviet doctor. In the second place, I noticed each time that this secret force plunged me into a state of absolute abulia, i.e. the absence of any voluntary reactions, into the torpid state of a domestic animal, merely awaiting orders and the lash.

One day he asked me to admit one of his relatives to the hospital for two weeks. This relative was a strapping seed bull, like a blacksmith. I examined him and naturally refused to hospitalize a perfectly healthy man. What on earth for, I thought, after all even the hospital corridors were crammed with critically ill patients, really in need of treatment.

"Try to understand, Doctor," Popenkov wheedled, "this man has traveled a long distance, he has spent a month in the foundations of the Palace of Soviets, he'll die if you don't save him."

"Not at all, Comrade Popenkov," I objected. "Your relative is in fine working condition. If he is tired from the journey, he can rest at your place. I observe that your vestibule has turned into a fairly comfortable apartment." At this point I permitted myself a grin.

That was in a very difficult time for we medicos, the winter of 1953. Just a short while before a group of professors had been arrested and charged with terrible crimes. All my life I admired these scientists, in point of fact they were my teachers, and I couldn't understand their logic. How could they leave the high road of humanism for the path of crime against humanity? Naturally I kept my thoughts to myself.

It was all aggravated by the fact that the crimes of these scientists ricocheted on all of us honest Soviet doctors. Some folk even developed a distrust of anything in a white coat. In the polyclinic where I conducted consultations once a week I had occasion to meet such instances of suspicion and also insulting comments, can you imagine, apropos of my nose. I never would have thought that a nose had anything to do with medicine.

One night as I lay in bed I heard the lift coming up. The lift in our building hadn't been used for several years, so this unusual and unexpected sound put me on my guard.

"You can't fry an omelette without breaking eggs," I thought and quickly got up and put on warm clothes.

There was a soft knock at the door, I calmly opened it, and on the landing stood Popenkov.

"I wanted to have a word with you, Doctor," he said, "I can't understand what's going on. Two days ago you gave me some medicine for my ears, and my liver played up. Forgive me, but for some time I have been noticing some strange things, fuchi melazi rikatuer, you prescribe something for the heart, and there's a sharp pain in the ureter, kryt, kryt, liska bul chvar, your vitamins cause severe vitamin deficiency. What is it all about? Can you give me an explanation?"

On my word of honor, he said all that to me.

"Yes, I see," I replied, "I am sorry, it won't happen again."

Next morning I took his relative to the hospital.

The Doctor's Consilium, Having Taken Place in the Summer of 1956.

"Yes, we must look the facts boldly in the face. There is still much in nature that has not been studied..."

"You will excuse me, comrades, perhaps you will think me mad, but..."

"Why did you stop? Go on!"

"No, wait a bit."

"Let's compare our data once more with the anthrocometry and the test data and x-rays of a homo sapiens."

"Nonsense, colleague! Perhaps you are assuming that normal anatomy and physiology can have somehow changed recently."

"Comrades, you will think I'm mad, but..."

"You've stopped again? Say it."

"No, I'll wait a bit."

"However, your data is so astonishing, that one inevitably begins wondering..."

"Doctors, let us remain within the bounds of science. Miracles don't happen."

"No, but that way we will never get out of the impasse."

"Comrades, I must be mad, but..."

"Well, say it!"

"Go on, say it!"

"Have your say!"

"... but could we not surmise that we have before us an airplane?"

"Imagine, the same thing occurred to me, but I couldn't bring myself to say it."

"Colleagues, colleagues, let us stay within the bounds..."

"... and yet I am convinced that before us is no homo sapiens, but an ordinary steel airplane."

"Let's not be too hasty, let's call in a construction engineer. I'll ring an engineer I know."

....

Tupolev arrived and was acquainted with the data.

"No, this is not altogether an airplane," he said, "although it has many features in common with a fighter-interceptor."

....

"Comrades, perhaps my train of thought will seem strange, but...??"

"... but would it be impossible to assume we have a bird before us?"

"I wanted to suggest it myself, but couldn't bring myself to."

"Let's not rush to conclusions, Doctor, let's call in an ornithologist."

....

Academician Bukhvostov arrived and was acquainted with the data.

"Although it has some similarities," he said, "it is not a bird. It can't be a bird with such obvious features of a fighter-interceptor."

....

"Might we not, Comrades—of course, this may throw us way off—but might we not, considering all the statements and summing up the opinions of authoritative specialists, and likewise the nature of the subject's behavior, his somewhat frequent use of sound combinations as yet unknown on earth, might we not assume, with all due caution, naturally, could we not tentatively assume that we are dealing with a completely new species with a unique combination of organic and inorganic features, could it not be assumed that in this given instance we are pioneers, might we not be dealing with a steel bird?"

"I ask you all to rise, I ask you all to remember that the records of this consilium are absolutely confidential."

Part for Cornet-à-piston

Theme: We were born to make fantasy fact, overcome distance and space... Improvisation: The doors are nailed up with rusty nails, what are we tenants to do about him? It's hard to get through the dirty back way, but still if we must we will go that way. As long as there's concord, peace, and splendor, and the fire regulations are observed. End of theme: ... Steel arm-wings gave us reason, and in place of a heart a combustion engine.

The Barber's Recollections

Our downstairs neighbor from the vestibule pinned me to the wall. "I beg your pardon," I say, "what's going on?" And he says: "kryt, kryt, fil burore liap," that is, in some foreign language. "And what if I have a go at you with the cut-throat?" Snap and the razor snapped. "Let me through," but he doesn't. "And what if I have a go at you with scissors?" Snap, and the scissors snapped. "And what if I give you a blow-wave?" "That—by all means," he says. "And what if I freshen you up with 'Flight' eau-de-cologne?" "By all means," he says. "And what about a face massage with nourishing cream?" "By all means," he says, and lets me through.

Chapter Three

The dreary necessity of battling on with the plot obliges me to try to reconstruct the chronological sequence of events.

In 1950, or maybe the year before or after, a quarrel of unusual force blew up between the Zs. It started, of course, on account of old French tapestries and other such objects from the time of Mme. Pompadour. The Deputy Minister was becoming impoverished teriffyingly fast, his wardrobe was wearing out, the food was deteriorating daily, all his salary and extra allowances, and even a certain portion of their rations went on antiques. It reached the point where Z. began hitting up his guard Yurii Filippovich for a "North" cigarette. That's what it had come to— descending from "Herzegovina Flor" to "North," somebody else's, at that.

"You know, Zinaida," said Z., "it's high time to put a stop to this. Our apartment has turned into a secondhand shop. It's bourgeois decadence and cosmopolitanism."

"You've no sensitivity, you're a ruffian, you're rusty," sobbed Zinaida. "I get no understanding from you, no flicker of interest. All you want to do is to wink at that vulgar Tsvetkova. I'm leaving."

"What has Tsvetkova got to do with it? Where are you going? Who to? God, what's going on?" wailed Z. The thought that Zinochka might deprive him of her embraces seemed incredibly awful, quite hellish. Incidentally he thought of the unpleasantnesses at work, of explanations in the party, of the whole complex of unpleasantnesses associated with a wife's departure.

"I am going to a man who speaks my language. To a man whose esthetic views concord with my own," announced Zinochka.

And she went downstairs, to the vestibule, to Popenkov, who had for ages been jumping in wild anticipation all over the squares of the ornament.

"Will you have me?" she asked dramatically.

"My love, light of my eyes, kuvyral lekur lekuvirl ki ki!" Popenkov danced in delight.

"How about that! I've toppled the Deputy Minister," he thought, beside himself with joy and animal optimism.

There was an immediate division of property, after which Z. was left in his rooms alone with a camp-stretcher, a bedside table, a battered wardrobe and a few books in his specialty. He was standing there at a complete loss, almost prostrate, when in walked Popenkov with the aim of delivering the final blow to k.o. the ungrateful Deputy Minister.

"As a man and a knight," he addressed himself to Z., "I am obliged to intervene on behalf of the unfortunate woman you have tormented and in addition to everything else accused of cosmopolitanism. Zinaida is not a cosmopolitan, she is a true Soviet citizen, whereas you, Comrade Z., would do well to remember those peculiar notions and doubts which you shared with your wife after disconnecting the telephone and tucking up in the blankets. Remember, I am in the know. By the way, Zinaida asked me to bring down this little cupboard. A woman can't exist without a wardrobe, and you'll get by without it. Adios."

Effortlessly lifting the huge wardrobe and shaking out Z.'s last few things, he departed.

All night long the vestibule was noisy, with the squeak of springs, incomprehensible throaty utterances, while on the first floor landing Z. and Yurii Filippovich suffered bitterly over a half-liter.

"We have been orphaned, you and I, Filippich," wept Z. "We are alone, Filippich... How shall we bear it?"

"Shut yourself off, Comrade Deputy Minister," advised the sergeant, "withdraw into yourself and think only of work..."

Quite understandably, from that night Z.'s career took a sharp downward turn.

Popenkov and his young consort gradually normalized their surroundings. Relatives frequently arrived to do their bit. Relative Koka helped with his hammer, relative Goga with his paint brush, relative Dmitrii turned out to be good at everything.

The vestibule was partitioned, creating two rooms, alcoves, boudoirs, and sanitary areas. Peter the Great's boots ended up in Popenkov's study. The Japanese theme adorned Zinochka's boudoir, intimately and yet delicately. The knights, Vikings and Novgorodians ended up in the sitting room, which must have greatly inspired visiting relatives as they frequently sang warlike songs together there.

Their diet improved constantly, Zinochka grew kinder, succulent, with milky-waxy, sugary-creamy ripeness. Her life was complete harmony, her inner world was ruled by subtropical calm, splendor, and magnificent peace.

Popenkov would appear in her boudoir always suddenly, purposefully, throwing from the threshold a daggerlike glance into the blue lagoons of her eyes, fling himself in, drown in delights, boiling furiously.

"You are my geisha!" he would cry out. "My courtesan! My Lorelei!"

In the winter of 1953 an important event took place in Moscow—J. V. Stalin died. The nation's grief overwhelmed No. 14 Fonarnii Lane too. Hollow groans could be heard there for several days. Up on the first floor two lone wolves, Yurii Filippovich and Deputy Minister, wept bitterly at night. The shrill desperate notes of the cornet-à-piston penetrated every apartment, taking advantage of the tragic freedom of those days.

Nikolai Nikolaevich Nikolaev all but perished in the scuffle on Trubnaia Square. Misha Fuchinian, Tolik Proglotilin and Vaska Axiomov just managed to drag him out of the sewerage hatch. These men organized a battle unit and somehow or other rescued the tortured inhabitants of Fonarnii Lane from the Trubnaia. So not one of them pushed through into the Hall of Columns.

Nobody, that is, except of course, Popenkov, who without himself knowing how, perhaps by supernatural means and without special effort or bodily harm found himself in the "holy of holies," saw everything in the greatest detail and even brought back as a souvenir a scrap of the mourning crepe from the chandelier.

The whole day after that he was preoccupied, absorbed in himself, he repulsed the relatives and even Zinochka, he stood in Peter's Wellingtons and thought and thought.

Well, he decided towards the end of the day, here is the result of half measures and running on the spot. The sad result, the consequence of an unnecessary masquerade. Fuchi elazi kompror, and kindly lie in a coffin. No, we will take another route, ru hioplastr, ru!

Then he took his lift up to the fifth floor and went into Maria Samopalova's flat, rattling his iron boots.

As he anticipated, Maria and Agrippina were sitting grief-stricken by their idle loom. Folding his arms on his breast, Popenkov mourned with them for several minutes in complete silence. Then he said his piece.

"Maria Timofeevna and you, Agrippina! Our grief is boundless, but life goes on. We mustn't forget our nearest, we mustn't forget the thousands waiting on us for joy, light, desirous of daily worshipping art. We must work. We must respond with labor!"

At this, Maria and Agrippina roused themselves and set the loom in motion. Popenkov stood for a while watching the next masterpiece emerge, then left quietly so as not to disturb the creative process.

Maria and her daughter had worked all these years, barely sleeping a wink. They understood perfectly the importance of their job—after all, Benjamin Fedoseevich's relatives, those disinterested culture-peddlers, were spreading antique French tapestries throughout the Far East and in Siberia, the Ukraine, the Trans-Caucasian and Central Asian republics.

Popenkov took the barber on himself, had a chat with him, expounding the importance of Maria's work. He had a chat with Zulphia, too, who soon afterwards set on her husband, demanding a small tapestry for their apartment, and forcing Lev Ustinovich to loosen the purse-strings.

After this purchase the Samopalov family's attitude to Maria became very respectful, moreover over the years all the members of the family had grown accustomed to the noise of the loom which now was perceived by them as something dear and familiar.

House manager Nikolaev marvelled: the squabbles in Flat 31 had stopped and so had the scandals and constant appellations to himself and Stalin. Mind you, the latter addressee, as everybody knows, soon dropped out of the picture, having tasted very little of the quiet life.

Nikolai Nikolaevich lived in constant terror. He was afraid Popenkov might unmask him to the tenants, show him up as a common cornet-à-piston player, not a frivolous musician, not a manager.

When they met he would adopt a superior dourness and show interest in the organization of his quarters.

"Well, how is it? Are you getting organized? Can you cope with the discomfort? Can I send you a metal worker?"

Popenkov would smile understandingly, tip him a wink and turn around conspiratorially.

"And how about you, Nikolai Nikolaevich? Are you still improvising? I'm keeping mum."

And Nikolai Nikolaevich would be lost, drop his domineering tone and crumple before Popenkov like a delinquent schoolboy before the headmaster.

"I put up with the discomfort, of course, Nikolai Nikolaevich. You know for yourself, the flat is like a thoroughfare. My wife's nerves are in a bad way."

And Popenkov would adopt his favorite pose, squatting on his haunches and looking up at Nikolai Nikolaevich with his burning gaze.

"But what can be done, Benjamin Fedoseevich, I can't think of anything, it's an entrance hall, after all," said Nikolaev.

'Hulo marano ri!" Popenkov exclaimed, jumped up and rubbed his hands wildly.

"What did you say?" Nikolai Nikolaevich began to tremble like an aspen leaf.

"I beg your pardon," Popenkov feigned embarrassment, "I meant to say that it will be no great misfortune if we decide to do away with the unnecessary extravagant vulgar so-called main entrance which was once used by jurors and other servants of the bourgeoisie and direct the stream of tenants through the so-called back entrance, which is really quite convenient and even a more expedient entrance."

"That of course... is of course reasonable," mumbled Nikolaev, "but the so-called back entrance is terribly narrow. With my size I can only squeeze through with a great effort, and in the event of somebody buying a piano or somebody's death, how would you carry in a piano or a coffin?"

"What are the windows for?" exclaimed Popenkov, but recollecting, burst out laughing. "But what am I saying—the windows are quite unacceptable to you... Wait, wait, the windows could easily be used for raising a piano or lowering a coffin. A bracket, a pully, a strong rope, that's all! Do you follow me?"

"A bold... a bold..." muttered Nikolaev, "a very bold solution to the problem, but..."

"You needn't worry about the rest, dear Nikolai Nikolaevich, I'll handle the tenants' reaction. Don't you worry yourself over anything, just keep on quietly making music, ha-ha-ha! Yes, I understand, I understand, I won't say a word, not a word!"

And so the main entrance was nailed up and the white marble staircase was walled up. Relative Goga made a really aristocratic candelabra for Zinochka out of the snake door handles. In the beginning the windows were used for getting in and out of the fashionable apartment, but later, when the tenants were used to the new regime, the front entrance was reopened, but only for the Popenkov family's private use.

And so the first stage was completed, and although it had taken quite a number of years, Popenkov was satisfied, went around serene and proud, but his eyes betrayed their former heavy yellow heat, the ancient dream and longing of Tamerlane.

Sometimes at night he would interrupt his delights and put a question to his spouse.

"Are you content with your fate, Zinaida?"

The fabulously magnificent Zinaida would stretch in servile languor.

"I am almost content, 99.9 percent content, and if you were to..."

"I understand your restless soul. I understand the magnitude of that .1 percent," he said and began to boil furiously, and then a little later asked again, "but do you understand me?"

Zinochka, now 99.99 percent content, replied:

"I think I understand you and the beauty of your dream. You, like a mighty spirit, have transformed this foul vestibule into a majestic palace, an esthetic temple to our fatal passion, and you are different from the gray drab men, the Deputy Ministers, and policemen, doctors, barbers and divers that I knew before you, you are a hurricane of fire and steel, a powerful and proud spirit, but sometimes, Benjamin, I am bewildered, I still cannot understand your mysterious words..."

"Which words....?" Popenkov laughed excitedly.

"Well, for example, the words which you utter in an excess of passion—bu zhiza hoku romuar, tebet felari..."

"... kukubu?" cried Popenkov. The dialogue was temporarily interrupted.

"Yes, those words, what do they mean?" Zinochka asked weakly afterwards.

"Ha-ha," Popenkov was euphoric, "but you know I am no ordinary man, and some of my characteristics are even different from those of a bird. I am the steel bird. That's our language, the language of steel birds."

"Oh, how fascinating! How exciting! A *steel* bird!" breathed Zinochka.

"Kukubu!" cried Popenkov.

Once more there was an interruption in the conversation.

"But are there any others? Are there more in the world like you?" Zinochka renewed the conversation.

"Not many yet, but not so few, either. Earlier attempts unfortunately fell through, in my opinion because of half-measures and running on the spot. Chivi, chivi zol farar, do you understand me?"

"Almost."

"For the time being we are forced to get around in jackets and shoes and lisp English, French or Spanish. I have to use the great and wonderful, truthful and free,[15] damn it, cuchumo rogi far! But never mind, the time will come! What strength I feel! What predestination! You know," he whispered, "I am the chief steel bird..."

"You are the chief! The chief! The chief!" breathed Zinochka.

"Kukubu!" cried Popenkov.

"Let me in on your plans, my steel bird," Zinochka cooed tenderly after a short pause.

Popenkov ran out of the boudoir and returned with the iron boots on his bare legs.

"I can do anything," he said, striding around the bed, "I shall arrange everything as I want it. First I shall complete my little experiment with this puny six-story house. I'll sit them all at looms, all these intellectuals. They'll all be weaving tapestries for me, all these Samopalovs, Zeldoviches, Nikolaevs, Fuchinians, Proglotilins, Axiomovs, Tsvetkovas..."

"Tsvetkova too?" Zinochka inquired drily. "I think Tsvetkova should be treated differently."

"Ha-ha-ha, you want to deal with Tsvetkova?" Popenkov laughed patronizingly. "By all means, pet."

"Thank you," Zinochka smiled secretively.

"What do you want to do with her? Fuchi elazi kompfor trandiratsiu?" asked Popenkov.

"Fuchi emazi kir madagor," replied Zinochka.

"Kekl fedekl?" Popenkov roared with laughter.

"Chlok buritano," giggled Zinochka.

"Mugi halogi ju?"

"Lachi artugo holeonon."

"Burtl?"

"Holo oloh, ha-ha-ha!" shrieked Zinochka madly, like a mare.

"Kukubu!" cried Popenkov.

A pause and silence, desire and lust, scuffling and profanation, loathing, rotting rebirth and self-generation, quivering, swallowing, absorption, expulsion, smothering, annihilation of a live, light, good person with the gait of a calf, the eyes of a young deer, with apple-breasts, with emerald eyes, with a little orange of a heart and a mysterious soul, annihilation.

And meanwhile the chapter comes to an end, and the years pass, certain individuals are growing old, some are growing up and see love and college, records, fame and earthly goods on soft pillows and sweaty fists, and nobody sees death, on the contrary, everybody sees scenes from life,

and nobody hears in his sleep the soft rumble of the apparently nonfunc-
tioning lift going up and down, even Doctor Zeldovich sleeps soundly now,
his warm things hidden in a trunk with naphthalene till winter.

The Night Flight of the Steel Bird.

a) Address to the Bronze Horseman.
   Whence did you think to threaten the Swedes?
   Tut-tut. And this city you founded to spite
   an arrogant neighbor? Tut-tut. Were all your deeds
   the fleet, Poltava, a window on Europe?
   Well, do you know who stands before you? I am
   the Steel Zhiza Chuiza Drong! I
   need no monuments, I myself am
   a flying monument. If I want,
   I devour, if I want, I pardon. I shan't
   pardon you, don't expect it. I will gobble you up, Peter Alexeevich.

b) Address to the monument to Yurii Dolgorukii.
   I shall devour your horse, make shashliks
   of your horse. To the "Aragvi" with your
   horse, to the kitchens! You I have already devoured.

c) Address to the monument commemorating a thousand years of Russia.
   What a date—a miserable thousand!
   What sort of creatures are these in cassocks, in
   cloaks, in armor, in jerkins, in
   frock-coats? I'll smelt you all and make
   a porridge of bronze, and here will be a monument
   to bronze porridge! and I will eat it.

d) Address to the monument to Abraham Lincoln.
   "Don't look down your nose, Abe! You freed
   the Negroes? Nothing to be proud of.
   No protests! to the rubbish heap!

e) Address to the monument to the Warsaw ghetto.
   Well, no need for discussion here! Everyone
   into the oven, and I've already eaten Mordechai Anilewicz.

f) Conversion to Earth Satellite and address to all mankind.
   This is Earth Satellite the Steel Bird
   speaking. All your artificial satellites
   I have already devoured. Honored comrades, a great
   surprise is being made ready,
   a big purge, a purge of the planet from
   the monuments of the past. There will be no past,
   there will be no future, and I have devoured the present
   already. Honored comrades, eat up monuments
   disciplinedly! Now you have one monument—the charming satellite, the Steel Bird. Make ready
   perches, a perch from each city, or I
   shall eat you up.

The Doctor's Recollections

He came to see me and complained about his appetite. His stomach actually was swollen and covered with blue lines. My appetite has disappeared, he said. Then take the matter to the police, I advised boldly. What about the digestion tract, he asked. Some rivets in the gut really had worked loose, there were bolts rattling around, and some welded seams had come apart. When all's said and done I'm no engineer and we're not living in some science fiction novel, but in ordinary Soviet reality, I announced to him and washed my hands of it. Very well, Zeldovich, you'll end up in here, he said and slapped his swollen belly. I opened the window and suggested he vacate the flat. He flew out of the window. His flight was heavy, sometimes he would fall, like a plane in air pockets, but then he would suddenly soar and disappear. Of course I realize I'll have to pay for my boldness, but the prospect of ending up in his stomach, in that steel bag, I tell you straight, I don't relish in the least.

The Building Inspector's Report

In the course of the years due to the rebuilding of the ground floor, and likewise due to the almost incessant rhythmic shaking in the righthand corner of the former vestibule the foundations of No. 14 are collapsing and the righthand corner sinking after the fashion of an Italian tower in Pisa (Consultation with the U.S.S.R.—Italian Friendship Society). Sewage from the new autonomous sewerage system is vigorously washing away the soil.

The situation is catastrophic, one could say, Help, good people! A representative for the foundation, the corner stone, declared in a private conversation that they can't hold out more than two months.

I hereby give warning and take this opportunity to state, on the basis of the above, that in the continuing absence of measures to organize a reprieve for No.14, which I love and adore, I relinquish my commission as building inspector and in a state of spiritual disharmony will put an end to myself by means of a hemp rope.

Part for Cornet-à-Piston.

Theme: A smell of crisp crusts floats out the windows, a flutter of hands behind the curtain....
Improvisation: The foundations are collapsing, clouds are gathering, it leans like a willow, our dear home. It has inclined like the tower in Pisa, it leaks, sewage at that. Young tenants, old heroes go on living in it, unsuspecting. There will be a disaster, my heart is thumping, my arms hang loose, there is grief in my gut...
End of theme: Help, good people!

Chapter Four

Coming back to a strictly chronological narrative, I must inform you that exactly eighteen years have passed since the beginning of this story. Every reader is aware of the changes that have taken place over that period in the life of society, so there's no need to elaborate on them. I shall continue my dreary task and weave the web of the plot, the web in which my heroes have been trapped without realizing it, and in which for the time being they are basking, their emerald tummies turned upwards to the caressing May sun.

One wonderful May evening the barber Samopalov's eldest son Ahmed, by now a very famous, almost fantastically famous young writer, one of those idols of the young that drive around in small "Zaporozhets"[16] cars and have the habit of turning up exactly where they are least expected, well, this same Ahmed Lvovich Samopalov was going to his home in Fonarnii Lane. Ahmed had recently smashed his "Zaporozhets" and sold it for scrap, so he was returning home on foot. He was excited by his battles in the Central Writers' club and was still passionately engaged in mental polemics with his opponents.

"It didn't come off, the old man didn't die," he thought. "Well then, all right, you're aligning, you come along, you vipers, sit and snigger, you crawl, and interfere with the game, right? And to finish it off you pit against me one of your well-trained scum, right? You think that he's got a strong attack and a good defense, don't you? You've got Ahmed Samopalov already buried, haven't you? I'll show you, I only need two serves to find his weak points, I see quite clearly that he won't get a twister into the right hand corner of the table. First I serve him a couple of strong hits from the right, he gets them, I foreshorten, he gets it, then I smash one into the right corner and even if by some miracle he gets it I immediately cut in from the left and he's done for, the point goes my way. Fine activists and geniuses when they can't even hold a racket correctly, poor little pricks!"

And here Ahmed suddenly gasped, shuddered, clutched at his heart, then his pulse, next closed his eyes, opened them again, and then pinched himself on the leg.

In the shadow on the other side of the street, in the blue marine ozone strode along a rare specimen of the human race, a long-legged, blue-eyed, tanned, sexy, fair, provocative girl. Ahmed began drumming to himself a militant literary anthem, because this specimen was the ideal, the idol, the clarion call of 1965 young Moscow prose, the secret dream of all "Zaporozhets" car owners, starting with Anatolii Gladilin.[17]

I don't know what it will be in the printed text, but I just numbered this page 88 in my manuscript. This was completely fortuitous, but significant, since 88 in the language of radio operators means love, as was proclaimed by the poet Robert Ivanovich Rozhdevstvenskii.

Ahmed Lvovich drummed the anthem and darted purposefully forward.

"Ninochka! What a surprise! Have you been back long? Did you see anyone from home?" he cried, feigning unprecedented and absolutely platonic delight.

"Hello, Ahmed Lvovich," said the girl awkwardly, slowing her pace, reddening and lowering her eyes.

"Popularity, blasted popularity, monstrous fame," raced wildly through Ahmed's head.

"Well, how are the folks there? How brown you are, how you've grown, you're a grown woman," he burbled affectionately, taking her by the elbow. "Have you been back long, Ninochka?"

"I beg your pardon, Ahmed Lvovich, but I'm not Ninochka, my name is Alia, I'm Alia Tsvetkova from across the landing," lisped the girl, "And I saw your folks this morning, Lev Ustinovich and Auntie Zulphia, and Auntie Maria, and Auntie Agrippina, and Zurab took me for a ride on his motorcycle... But I haven't seen *you* for about five days, Ahmed Lvovich."

It was quite understandable that she hadn't seen him for so long. Ahmed Lvovich hadn't slept at home for five days, he had been hanging around the literary scene, playing dice, "buru," "preference," "Fool," "King," "nines,"[18] ping-pong.

"Good God, so you're Alia then, Marina's daughter!" cried Ahmed. "What has happened to you in the last five days?"

"I've no idea what's happened," replied Alia. "You can see how I've changed in the last five days. Men won't leave me alone, and your brother Zurab takes me for a ride on his motorcycle every morning. Last week he wouldn't let me near his motorcycle, he wouldn't let me lay a finger on it," she sobbed.

"There, there, there, Alia, Alia, Aliechka, Aliechka," muttered Ahmed thinking: "If Zurab gets in the way I'll wrap his motorcycle around his head!"

They were already in Fonarnii Lane, and destiny herself skated towards them in the form of a jolly, purposeful old man on roller skates with a perky turned-up goatee, and with a long pole, by means of which he was lighting the luminescent lamps, as if they were the gas lanterns of blessed 19th century memory, and the lanterns lit up in the sun, which, like destiny, was sitting on the chimney of No. 14, dangling its thin legs in striped stockings, smoking and winking away, and the sky was blue, like their bright blue destiny, and without a single cross, a single fighter plane, an antediluvian blissful sky with small orange corners.

"Well, have you read any of my books?" Ahmed suddenly remembered his position in society.

"Of course I have," replied Alia. "We did them in school. Brovner-Dunduchnikov, our literature teacher, analyzed your books and really ran you down, but I told him I loved you."

"What?" exclaimed Ahmed, giving Alia's elbow a tight squeeze.

"I did, that's just what I said to him. I love Ahmed Samopalov's work because it treats the problem of alienation very interestingly. And then we had a joint conference about your work with Soft Toys Factory No. 4, and all the girls at the factory said that you give an interesting treatment of alienation, and Brovner-Dunduchnikov couldn't say anything. You might say it was only because of this common interest that I went to work at Soft Toys Factory No. 4 after I left school."

For the fourth time Zurab Samopalov's motorcycle dashed by, minus its muffler, expressing its indignation with the most dreadful din. Zurab himself ran after it in utter despair, in a state of dreadful oriental jealousy.

"So you love me?" Ahmed asked insinuatingly.

"On the whole, as a writer," said Alia.

With these words they entered the yard.

In the yard two members of the pensioners' council were sitting in the blazing sun—the former Deputy Minister Z. and Lev Ustinovich Samopalov, along with the janitor, Yurii Filippovich Isaev. They had for hours been discussing matters of literature and art.

"What I think about these abstract artists," said Yurii Filippovich, "is if you can't draw, then don't try, don't muck about. Personally I love painting and understand what's what. I used to draw myself once. I love Levitan's 'Eternal Peace,' now that's an outstanding watercolor. Have you ever noticed, comrades, how well it portrays vast expanse? And now we are conquering that expanse, that's why the painting is so good. Now your Ivan, Lev Ustinovich, is a real abstractionist, a formalist, an unreliable element. I don't know which way Nikolaev is looking, what he's thinking about in the House Office, when there are abstractionists under his nose speading their rotten influence on spiritually ripe young people."

"That's not true, Filipich, my Ivan is a figuratist!" objected Lev Ustinovich heatedly. "Of course, he does distort, he filters, so to speak, nature through his imagination, through his fantasy, but that's not formalism, Filipich, that's a search for new forms."

"A figuratist, you say?" Yurii Filippovich was indignant. "Just recently I posed for him, and how do you suppose he depicted me? A tiny forehead, a face like a fat blister, and a blue knife drawn on from the side, now what was that in aid of?"

"You shouldn't take offense, Filipich, he was portraying your inner self, not printing a photograph."

"Then my inner self is a fat blister?"

"That's right," concurred Samopalov.

"They should be pulled out by the roots, your figuratists!" bawled Isaev. "In other days they would have been struck down at the root and that would be that. Isn't that right, Comrade Zinoliubov?"[19]

"You must have Belinsky's times in mind, Yurii Filippovich? The times of the violent Visarrion?" Z. smiled gently.

"That's right, Comrade Zinoliubov! Precisely those times!" yelled the janitor.

"Not so loud," said Z., "a bit more gently, delicately. Don't forget, Yurii Filippovich, you have to tread carefully with talent, not all at once."

"What are you ranting about, Filipich," said Samopalov. "What are you cursing for? Why should you be losing sleep over my sons? We're all going to die soon, we'll be grains of sand in the stream of the universe."

"Philosophically correct," remarked Z.

"What did you say? You think I don't agree? Of course we'll soon be grains of sand in the philosophical whirlwind of the universe," said the janitor. "That's why we should let a few of them have what for before it's too late, strike at the roots of this whole fraternity."

"Easy, easy, Yurii Filippovich, gently, gently, be more cultivated," Z. admonished his former bodyguard.

And so the pensioners sat for hours on end, discussing issues of literature and art. Every week these issues were put on the agenda of the Pensioners' committee meeting, where opinions were recorded for posterity.

Meanwhile, at the bottom of the yard, the dominoes had been cast aside, and Fuchinian, Proglotilin and Axiomov were discussing questions of literature and art.

"Today I started up the machine, got a book, and I'm reading away," Vasilii Axiomov was telling the others. "Well, I'm reading this little book. Up comes the chief engineer. 'What are you reading, Axiomov?' I turned the book over and read the title. It turns out this book was written by our Ahmed Samopalov. *Look Back in Delight*, it was called. 'Do you like it?' asks the chief engineer. 'Pretty powerfully put together,' I say, 'the way he rips through the full stops and commas.' 'Crap!' yells Mitia Kosholkis from his machine. 'I know the book inside out,' he yells, 'it's utter crap.' Well, then all the boys begin talking at once. Some of them are shouting: 'he's out of touch with the people!' Others that: 'he *is* in touch with the people!' You can't make head or tail of it. The chief engineer says: 'Opinions are divided. Let's have a discussion. Stop the machines.' We stopped the machines and began discussing Ahmed's book. Our foreman Shcherbakov spoke from the synopsis. The director came and joined in. We've got a fiery director, he's easy to get going. We argued till lunchtime."

"I've read that book," said Tolik Proglotilin. "Yesterday the controller gave it to me together with my roster. Something funny happened. I'm driving around and the sergeant is sitting in his box reading. What are you reading, Sarge? I ask. He holds it up—it's *Look Back in Delight*. Pretty good, isn't it? I yell. Not bad, he says with a sour smile, you can see Bunin's influence, Robbe-Grillet's too. Just then a semi-trailer ran into the back of me. The drive got carried away with the book too. So we had a lightning reader's conference."

"I've read that book too," said Fuchinian. "Yesterday we were repairing a cable under Crimea Bridge, so I put it in my diving-suit. I put it inside my mask, in front of my eyes, I'm repairing the cable and reading away. To tell you the truth, chaps, I was engrossed. I didn't notice that the air tube broke. Ahmed really deals well with alienation of the individual."

"That's true. What's true is true," agreed Axiomov and Proglotilin. In short it was a peaceful warm spring evening. In three windows people were playing violins, in five more—the piano. One window was transmitting a number for cornet-à-piston via the radio. Furniture movers were unhurriedly hoisting up another two pianos on pulleys, one of them dangled for the moment at third floor level and the other was crawling up to the sixth. From Maria Samopalova's window the incessant tap of a loom floated down. Agrippina had hung several new old French tapestries in the yard and was beating the dust of labor out of them. The artist-figuratist Ivan Samopalov displayed his latest portrait in his window, the likeness of a man-bird shot with burnished steel, product of the figuratist imagination. A still captivating Marina Tsvetkova was training a mirror on ex-Deputy Minister Zinoliubov through the wild ivy shading her window.

Well, what else? Yes, the junior footballers were neatly hitting the ground floor windows. And a furious motorcycle burst into the yard. Zurab had finally got it saddled and begun circling the yard, from time to time shooting up onto the fireproof wall. And then the youngest Samopalov, Valentin, entered the yard in Texan jeans, flippers, and a mask, with an aqualung on his back, a transistor on his chest, a movie camera in his pocket, a guitar in his hands, playing big beat,[20] whirling a hula hoop and shooting an amateur movie through his pocket. And last of all, to everyone's surprise, Ahmed was kissing young Alia Tsvetkova under the arch, punctuating the kisses with vows of eternal love.

Doctor Zeldovich appeared under the arch. Catching sight of Ahmed kissing, he addressed him:

"Good evening, Ahmed. Good evening, Alenka. Here's a sweetie for you. You know, Ahmed, during an operation today we got to arguing about literature. We opened up an abdominal cavity and somehow got talking. Well naturally we remembered your *Look Back in Delight*. The surgical nurse was reading it in the operating room and she said she was mad about it. I gave you your due too, Ahmed, although I confess I did criticize certain shortcomings. Our anesthetist was completely on your side, but the patient we were operating on said that the book might well be interesting, but that it was harmful."

"He should have been given an anesthetic," said Ahmed disapprovingly.

"Just imagine, the strange thing was he was talking under anesthetic," said Zeldovich. "Anyway, we got into a discussion and decided to conduct the operation in two stages. The patient said he would marshal his arguments together with quotes for the second stage. But I beg your pardon, I am disturbing you. All the best. Every success."

Zeldovich was about to whisk through the back entry, but he bolted straight back out because Benjamin Fedoseevich and his wife Zinaida were coming out towards him.

Popenkov had changed little over the years, he had merely acquired stability, a slight heaviness and distinct imperiousness in his gaze. Zinaida reminded one of a festive cake. The instant they appeared the radio went off on the fifth floor and into the yard ran a breathless Nikolai Nikolaevich, pulling on his braces as he ran. Apologizing for being late he joined the Popenkovs and walked after them, just a little behind.

A tense silence immediately settled on the yard, if you ignore the kisses and intermittent whispering under the arch, the clatter of the motorcycle, the cries of big beat and the lowing of the frivolous artist.

"Cut off the Samopalov's water and power for the disrepectful formalist caricature," Popenkov threw over his shoulder.

Nikolai Nikolaevich made a note of it.

"How will we manage without water and power?" gasped Lev Ustinovich. "I've got a large family, Benjamin Fedoseevich, you know yourself, it won't be possible to have a shave or a haircut.."

"Why kumni tari huchi cha?" shouted an enraged Popenkov.

"What?"

"Why doesn't your son want to put his talent to the service of the people?" translated Zinaida.

"Benjamin Fedoseevich, what about my application? Have you looked into it?" he was addressed by Zinoliubov.

"The marriage to Tsvetkova?" grinned Popenkov.

"Chichi michi kholeonon," Zinaida whispered into his ear and burst out laughing.

"Quite so, marriage to Marina Nikitichna Tsvetkova," affirmed Zinoliubov. "The realization of an old dream. At one time you used to say that you had saved my life on several occasions, Benjamin Fedoseevich, and on one occasion you saved it indeed," with a sideways glance at Zinochka. "Now you have yet another opportunity."

"Kukubu with Tsvetkova? Chivilikh! Klocheki, drocheki rykl ekl!"

"Marriage to Tsvetkova? Never! In the event of insubordination we will cut off your power, water and sewerage," translated Zinaida, adding on her own account, "The sewerage, understand? Do you understand what that smells of, Comrade Zinoliubov?"

"He is forgetting Russian altogether, this Steel Bird," said Ahmed to Alia.

"Oh, damn *him*," said Alia. "Kiss me again please, Ahmed Lvovich."

The tour of the yard continued. Popenkov stopped in the center and began examining the walls and open windows of the building very carefully.

"Benjamin Fedoseevich, I meant to tell you yesterday," began Nikolaev carefully. "The fact is, Benjamin Fedoseevich, they have begun taking an interest in you."

"What? How? Where?" cried Popenkov. "Where have they begun taking an interest in me?"

"Up there," said Nikolaev significantly, indicating the sky with his thumb.

Popenkov dropped onto his belly and began crawling, twisting his head round like a guilty dog and poking out his tongue. Then he jumped up and slid around the yard on tiptoes, to tragic music that only he could hear.

"Assa," he whispered to himself, "assa, a dance to feast the eyes, oom-pa, oom-pa, oom-pa-pa!"

The whole yard followed with interest Popenkov's pirouettes, his jumps, the tragic clapping and dislocations of his hands, his fiery smiles, bows and equivocation towards the spectators, the top-like gyrations quivering to a stop.

Nikolai Nikolaevich, at first bewitched by the dance, almost expired in fright when Popenkov lay down on the asphalt. He ran to him, lay down alongside and whispered:

"Benjamin Fedoseevich, get up, my dear man! Don't torment me. They want to put you on the commission for decent living. They acknowledge your experience, Benjamin Fedoseevich, your grasp of the subject, your taste..."

Popenkov quickly jumped to his feet and shook himself.

"Why not, I'm willing!" he exclaimed. "I'll join the commission gladly. It's high time they put me on the commission, shushi marushi formazatron!"

"I'll introduce order into life," translated Zinochka.

"By the way, Nikolaev," Popenkov made a slow tour around the yard and motioned to the Zhek chief to follow him. "By the way, rufir haratari koblo bator..."

"Please, speak Russian," begged Nikolaev.

"It's time you understood," said Popenkov in irritation. "Very well. Well, it's like this. Tomorrow my relatives want to remodel the roof, make a hatch so I can get straight out of the lift onto the roof."

"What for?" asked Nikolaev in panic.

"What do you mean, what for? You know I occasionally use the lift to... to go for a ride. Sometimes I feel like having a sit on the roof."

"Of course I understand that," said Nikolaev, "I understand your desire, but the fact is, Benjamin Fedoseevich, that our building is in a very precarious state, almost a state of collapse. The building inspector gave me a report on it today, and I am afraid that an opening in the roof may finally shatter the foundations."

"Rubbish. Panic-mongering. It's high time the building inspector passed on to the next world," said Popenkov. "In short, the discussion is closed. Tomorrow my relatives make the hatch."

Suddenly a cry resounded over the yard.

"Citizens!"

And everybody looked up to see the building inspector standing on the fifth floor ledge. He was waving his hands to balance himself, like a large butterfly beating against an invisible window.

"Citizens!" he cried. "This is the third night I am unable to sleep, I can't eat, my teeth have worked loose, my strength is ebbing away... Citizens, our building is in a state of collapse! Take a look, can't you see it has become like the Italian tower in the city of Pisa? The foundations can't hold for more than a week. He told me that himself! Citizens, urgent measures are called for! Citizens, all my reports just get shelved!"

To stop himself falling the building inspector was making circular movements with his arms, but he didn't look like a bird, rather like an unfortunate butterfly, because he was wearing his wife's vast floral dressing gown, from under which his bare legs poked out.

Nobody noticed how Popenkov appeared on the ledge, they only saw him quickly sliding towards the building inspector.

"Citizens!" called the building inspector for the last time and was just then seized in the steel grasp of Popenkov, quick as a wink crushing the bold fabric of the dressing gown.

"Did you see the madman?" barked Popenkov to those below, scattering bolts of lightning from his burning eyes, dragging the limp body of the building inspector. "Citizens, he is mad! Nikulu chikulu gram, ous, suo!"

"There is no place in civilized life for madmen and panic-mongers!" cried Zinaida.

Popenkov clambered up the water pipe with the speed of light with the building inspector's body, clattered across the roof and disappeared through the dormer window.

The tenants, stunned and aroused, crowded round Nikolai Nikolaevich. What was it all about? What had happened? Was there any reason to evacuate? What had set the building inspector off?

"Citizens, remain calm, remain in your places," Nikolaev admonished them. "Of course there are certain grounds for concern, the foundations are in a pretty tense position, I talked to him, too, but disaster is projected only in the long range, somewhere at the end of the quarter, no sooner. Citizens, tomorrow I go to the regional housing office[21] to do battle, I shall return either on my shield, or with my shield. I would like your thoughts and hearts to be with me at that moment."

"What was that we heard, Nikolai Nikolaevich?" shouted Proglotilin. "Is Popenkov intending to smash the roof?"

"That way we won't make it to the end of the quarter, the shanty will collapse!" screamed Axiomov.

Fuchinian, his muscles flexed, jumped into the center of the circle.

"Fuchinian is here!" he shouted. "Everybody knows me—I am here! I will not permit it. The roof shall be whole! And we shall break the Steel Bird's wings. Vaska, Tolik, am I talking sense?"

"We'll carve the Steel Bird up into hair combs!" cried Vaska.

The tenants were in an uproar.

"Nikulu chikulu gram, ous, suo!" cried Zinaida Popenkova in a panic. "Nikolai Nikolaevich, what is going on? Crowd hysteria?"

"Citizens, quiet! Citizens, order," admonished Nikolaev. "The removal of part of the roof does not threaten instant disaster. Citizens, you must understand Benjamin Fedoseevich, enter into his position. Citizens, quiet. Citizens, let's talk it over."

But the crowd grew even noisier, aroused by the belligerent and assertive appearance of Fuchinian.

"It's all Popenkov's fault!" people shouted.

"He shakes the building in the most incredible fashion all night!"

"Evict him!"

"Open up the front entrance!"

'We're sick of it!"

"Away with the Steel Bird!"

"Citizens, I'll try to see Benjamin Fedoseevich on this matter," entreated Nikolaev. Nobody recognized the stern administrator. "I'll try to beat him down. Citizens, I practically promise that the roof will remain whole."

The sun set, the shadows thickened, but the tenants still did not disperse and in the buzzing crowd there was the flash of matches, the flicker of cigarette-lighter flames, cigarettes and eyes, the whole dark yard was an uneasy volatile flicker. Fuchinian, Proglotilin and Axiomov climbed up onto the roof via the fire escape. They had resolved to save it by means of their vigilant roster and readiness for any kind of battle, even to the death. The young Samopalovs, Zurab and Valentin, blockaded the back entrance. Ahmed and Alia Tsvetkova were called on to keep watch in the garden. Comrade Zinoliubov took up an observation post in Tsvetkova's apartment. Maria Samopalova and Agrippina declared a strike and went to bed for the first time in eighteen years. Lev Ustinovich got his cut-throat ready and armed Zulphia with the scissors. In a word, all the tenants did what they could in the collective protest against Popenkov's arbitrariness.

The night passed uneasily, people slept in bursts, kissed feverishly, smoked, and smoked, some of them drank, others made ready to evacuate, nobody knew what morning would bring.

Fuchinian, Proglotilin and Axiomov sat on the ridge of the roof, knocking over a bottle, they were elated, remembering bygone battles on the vast expanse between the Volga and the Spree. Several times it seemed to them that a dark body passed over them with a quiet reactive whistle, blocking out the stars, and then they regretted not having anti-aircraft artillery at their disposal.

The sun rose high, dragged itself out of the city's ravines, and hung over Moscow. The roof immediately got scorching hot.

At eight o'clock in the morning the self-defense brigade got the feeling there was someone below them in the attic. They quickly assumed their battle positions, tensed themselves, ready. Out of the dormer windows crawled Popenkov's relatives—relative Koka, relative Goga and relative Dmitrii. They were armed with axes, handsaws and hammers.

"Hello, lads! Sun-baking?" said relative Dmitrii to the self-defense brigade. "We are getting an early start to work."

"Now then boys, back down without any fuss!" commanded Fuchinian and advanced.

"Look Mitia," said Goga, looking down at the pavement, "it's a big drop. If anyone should accidentally get pushed, he'd be squashed flat as a pancake! What do you think?"

"He'd be like jelly," suggested relative Koka sadly.

"Liquid," relative Dmitrii summed up and began sawing the roof.

"Now we'll test out what would happen," said the self-defense brigade and rolled up its sleeves. The roof swelled and cracked under their first heavy step.

The relatives, abandoning their jests, also flexed their muscles and advanced. Their tattooed muscles swelled up to such an extent it seemed as though this was not three men moving, but a series of terrifying balloons; in a flick the narrow strings of pocket knives leaped out of their fists; bared gold teeth reflected the sun; so did signet-rings, bracelets, pendants, earrings and rings. In the blazing light of the morning sunlight, joyous death advanced on the self-defense brigade in foreign waistcoats and jackboots.

"Vaska, you get the one on the right! Tolik, the one on the left! And I'll get Goga the bad!" yelled Fuchinian and dashed forward.

There began the self-defense without arms. The relatives' Argentinian pocket knives swished through the air, but collected nothing. Fuchinian, Proglotilin and Axiomov, remembering their street fighting days, pulled at the relatives' legs and punched them on the noses. The relatives' tears and snot rose like fountains to the blue sky, but nevertheless knives are knives, and blood flowed, and they drove our lads to the edge of the roof.

Suddenly there was a crash to the rear of the relatives. The four Samopalov brothers were crawling along the roof, the writer, the artist, the motorcyclist and "big beat."

"Retreat!" ordered relative Dmitrii and jumped off first. Relative Koka and relative Goga flung themselves off after him.

The self-defense brigade leaned over in horror, imagining the conversion of these powerful organisms into pancake, jelly and liquid respectively. However, the relatives landed unharmed and took to their heels in different directions.

At eight hours thirty minutes the first crack appeared on the northern side of the building. Maria Samopalova leaned out through the crack and shouted to the whole of Fonarnii Lane:

"Fight, good people!"

At eight hours forty-five minutes all the inhabitants of No. 14 had gathered by the front entrance, as had the sympathetic occupants of neighboring buildings. Domestic animals, cats, Pomeranians, fox terriers, Great Danes, jumped out the windows onto the pavement. Siskins, canaries and parrots, which had been released from their cages, soared above the crowd. The emerald water of aquariums ran out of the water pipes, carrying veiltails, redfins and loaches. Shutters flapped, draughts blew through empty apartments, overturning pots of everlastings. There were groaning sounds. The tenants sighed over abandoned possessions, over everyday articles and expensive and cherished knick-knacks.

The building inspector bustled about the crowd in his wife's billowing dressing gown.

"Citizens!" he cried. "I have done some calculations. The building can hold another twenty-seven minutes. It's still possible to save a few things! We only need to open up the front entrance! Clean out the vestibule!"

"Open the front entrance!"

"Break down the the doors!"

"Bugger them!"

"But the suite, my good fellows, we've just bought it! We saved seven years for it, we hardly ate or drank!"

"Break it down!"

The doors were already bending under the force of the crowd, but inside Popenkov was calmly tying his tie, pinning a diamond into it, polishing his nails and getting into his iron boots.

"You'll think of something, won't you?" Zinaida was dashing about, bouncing like a push-ball. "You'll find a way out, my darling, my love, mankind's genius, my gigantic steel bird?? Zhuzho zhirnava zhuko zhuro?"

"Noki murloki kvakl chitazu!" replied Popenkov calmly. "Are you afraid of this crowd, my Lorelia? This pitiful crowd, these lice. Ten minutes work for a cyclone. Filio drong chiriolan!"

And wrenching out all the nails in one go, he flung open the door and stood in front of the tenants.

Silence fell. The building inspector, remembering yesterday's treatment, hid in the crowd.

"What are you all here for? What do you want?" asked Popenkov, his arms folded on his breast.

"We want to throw you out, Steel Bird," replied the bandaged and altogether heroic Fuchinian.

"Throw me out?" grinned Popenkov. "Now hear my conditions." And his eyes kindled with a distant secret and terrifying fire, sounds like a jet's exhaust issued from his throat. "Drong haleoti fyng, syng! Zhofrys hi lasr furi talot..."

We don't understand your language!" cried voices from the crowd. "Leave, comrade, while you still can!"

Popenkov switched to Russian with a visible effort.

"These are my conditions. Everybody returns to his apartment, is to get a loom, the looms will be here by evening and... to work! Is that understood? Naturally some sacrifices will have to be made. Some of you will be subjected to chiziolastrofitation. Chuchukhu, klocheki, drocheki?"

"If you want to take us on a 'get it—got it' basis," said Fuchinian, "then we want to take you on a 'get it—got it' basis. Got it?"

He advanced again, and they all advanced, and Popenkov suddenly actually realized that he was going to come off worst: the circle tightened, and the damned tin awning hung directly over him. Of course it would be possible to break through it, but in that instant somebody would grab him by his iron legs. There was practically no way out, and he almost burst into tragic laughter inside at such a ludicrous end to his great cause.

At one point there was suddenly complete silence, and in this instant the staccato clatter of approaching hooves reached them. The sound of hooves in Moscow is an out-of-the-ordinary occurrence, so they all turned round and saw a galloping white horse at the end of Fonarnii lane, and on it Nikolai Nikolaevich Nikolaev, head of ZhEK. It was nine hours fifteen minutes, Nikolaev was returning from the regional housing commission with his shield, and to boot on a white horse with a wide breast, round powerful croup, cunning pink eyes, a fringe fluttering like a holiday flag. Galloping unhurriedly, the horse recalled to mind an old-time caravelle, merrily sailing across a fresh sea beneath billowing white sails.

Drawing near and seeing the crowd at the entrance, the wide-open windows and branched cracks in the walls, Nikolai Nikolaevich pulled out from under his shirt a cornet-à-piston which glittered in the sun, and raised it to his lips.

"Dear citizens, sisters and brothers!" sang the cornet triumphantly. "The regional housing commission has allotted us a building! It's eight stories high, practically all glass, practically all plastic, I assure you! In a fabulous experimental area, a palace being erected for all to admire! Blue bathrooms adjacent lavatories and waste disposal units await you! A solarium each, a dendrarium each, a dining room each, a swimming pool each! Make ready, citizens, sisters and brothers, we are going to trot off toward happiness in a piebald caravan!"

"Hoorah!" the tenants all shouted, and, forgetting Popenkov, they dashed into their disintegrating dwelling for their belongings. Popenkov managed to dive into the lift.

At nine hours thirty minutes a wagon train, sent by the regional housing commission, drew up at the entrance. They were shaggy lively ponies, perkily chewing on their figured bits, pounding the asphalt with their strong little hooves. They were harnessed into small, but capacious carts, decorated with carved folk motifs.

At nine hours thirty-nine minutes the loading of goods and chattel was completed and the wagon train trotted cheerfully off down Fonarnii Lane. The hooves clattered, the little bells rang, colored ribbons and flags fluttered, harmonicas, guitars, transistors were playing, and at the head rode Nikolai Nikolaevich on a white horse with his cornet-à-piston. The long caravan wound through Moscow streets, headed for a new life, to New Cheriomukhy.[22]

At nine hours forty-four minutes No. 14 collapsed. When the brick dust had cleared the few who had stayed behind in Fonarnii Lane saw that only the lift shaft rose above the ruins. Soon after, the lift began ascending out of its depths. In it stood a completely withdrawn Benjamin Fedoseevich Popenkov. When the lift stopped at the top of its shaft, Popenkov opened the door, squatted on his haunches and froze, fixing his lifeless gaze on the boundless expanse. Nobody knows what he was thinking or what he saw in the distance. Nor is it certain whether he saw Zinaida bouncing like a push-ball along Fonarnii Lane.

For long months he sat on the carcass of the lift shaft quite motionless, like one of the chimeras of Paris's Notre Dame cathedral.

One day bulldozers appeared in Fonarnii Lane. Hearing the officious rumble of their engines, Popenkov roused himself, jumped and flew off over Moscow, over the lanes of Arbat, the blue saucer of Moscow's swimming pool, the big Kamennyi bridge... Two dark trails stretched out behind him. Then the wind dispersed them.

The End.

The Steel Bird's Farewell Monologue

Rurrro kalitto Zhiza Chuiza Drong! Chivilikh zhifafa koblo urazzo! Rykl, ekl, filimocha absterchurare? Fylo sylo ylar urar!

Shur yramtura y, y, y! Zhastry chastry gastry nefol! Nefol foliadavr logi zhu-zhu? Uzh zhu ruzh zhur orozh zhuro oleozhar! Razha!

Faga!

Lirri-otul!

Chivilozh zuzamaza azam ula lu? Luzi urozi klockek tupak! Z fftshch! Zhmin percator sapala! Sa1 Sa! La! Al! Spl! Vspyl sevel fuk zhuraru! Refo yarom filioran, otskiuda siplstvo any yna! Any, yna, any, yna, any yna, any! Pshpyl, pshpyl, pshpyl—vzhif, vzhif karakatal!

Chorus

and notwithstanding the flowers bloom and childhood lives on in every head and old age asks for a hand some depart thereto with a kiss and merge in passion in order to meet in heaven and butter on a fresh bun and berries in the morning dew in a jumble of shining dotted lines where can one find a cunning little face with berries on its lips in the streets the sentries evoke love with a guitar frost on the pavement morning voices promise us milk in the latest newspaper the usual reports of the doings of dolphins younger brothers in the light surface layers of the ocean tend for us shoals of tasty and delicate fish and each dreams of a ticket on an ordinary thousand-seater airplane to fly over the ocean with a greeting for the marine shepherds and later return to their old folk to their cunning little kids falls asleep so as to gallop on his creaky wooden horse through the forest across the clearings in the gleam of the spring morning of the spring summer and the autumnal winter of the summer spring and the wintry autumn of the wintry summer and the summery winter of the wintery spring and the summery autumn of the spring winter and the autumnal summer.

July 1965
Kalda farm

Translated by Rae Slonek

NOTES

1. In Russian *Fonar* means a lamp.
2. (small) fish.
Manager of ZhEK, the local housing office which is responsible for maintenance and overseeing of a number of blocks of flats, perhaps a whole street or square.
4. A central district of Moscow.
5. From one of the songs of the Civil War.
6. Raikom: the Regional Party Office, the highest instrument of local government.
7. Each Soviet citizen is entitled to a minimum amount of living space, currently 9 square meters for the head of a family, or single tenant, and 6 square meters for every additional member of the family.
8. Based on "popa," euphemism for "ass."
9. International Organization to aid fighters for the Revolution, founded in 1922 at the 21st Communist International Congress.
10. Voroshilov gunner. Voroshilov, a cavalry commander during the Revolution, was People's Commissar for Defense 1925-1934. With the militarization of sport in the thirties senior school students, tertiary students and young workers learned to shoot in Voroshilov Shooting Clubs. The "Voroshilov gunner" badge was awarded to those who attained a certain score in shooting competitions.
11. The K. G. B.
12. The Russian word for "prick."
13. Each citizen must obtain a residence permit and have the address stamped in his passport before taking up residence in a flat.
14. Famous wartime poem by K. Simonov.
15. Reference to Turgenev's well-known poem in prose on the Russian language.
16. The smallest Soviet-made sedan (a four-seater).
17. One of the fashionable young writers of the sixties, depicting positive Soviet youth. Also notable for innovative style (collage), using colloquial language and drawing on newspaper cuttings, excerpts from radio broadcasts, etc.
18. Card games.
19. Means "Zina-lover."
20. In English in the original.
21. The office responsible for issuing accommodations, and to which the ZhEK office is subordinate.
22. New area of Moscow with intensive housing development schemes.

Vasily Shukshin

SNOWBALL BERRY RED

This story begins in a corrective labor colony lying somewhat north of the city of N., in a region both beautiful and severe.

It was an evening after a working day. People had gathered in the club.

A broad-shouldered man with a wind-burned face came out onto the stage and announced:

"And now the former-recidivists' choir will sing for us the pensive song 'Evening Bells.' "

The members of the choir entered the stage one by one from the wings and arranged themselves into two groups: one large, one small. The choristers gave remote resemblance to being singers.

"Taking part in the 'bom-bom' group," the broad-shouldered man continued, pointing to the large group, "are those whose sentences are up tomorrow. This is our tradition, and we are honoring it now."

The choir began to sing. That is, they started up in the small group, but in the big one they bowed their heads until the required moment, when they rang out with feeling:

"Bom-m, bom-m..."

It is in the "bom-bom" group that we see our hero, Egor Prokudin, about forty years old, with cropped hair. He is making a serious effort; when it is time to "chime" he wrinkles his forehead and sways his round head, so as to make it seem that the sound of the bell is rolling and floating in the evening air.

Thus ends Egor Prokudin's current sentence. Ahead—is freedom.

In the morning, in the office of one of the superintendents, the following conversation took place:

"So tell me, how do you intend to live, Prokudin?" asked the superintendent. He had obviously asked this many, many times—the words came out so readily, like a prepared phrase.

"Honestly!" Egor hurriedly gave out in reply—also, one must suppose, prepared in advance, since the answer leaped out with such remarkable ease.

"That I understand... But how? What do you imagine you will do?"

"I plan to work in agriculture, citizen superintendent."

"Comrade."

"Huh?" Egor didn't understand.

"Now everyone is your comrade," the superintendent reminded him.

"Aha!" recalled Prokudin with pleasure. And he even laughed at his forgetfulness. "Yes, yes. I'll have many comrades!"

"And what exactly drew you to agriculture?" the superintendent inquired with genuine interest.

"Why, because I'm a peasant! That is, by birth. In general, I love nature. I'm going to buy a cow..."

"A cow?" The superintendent was astonished.

"A cow. With an udder like that." Egor made an outline with his hands.

"You don't choose a cow by its udder. Suppose it's young—then what sort of udder 'like that' would it have? Of course, if you pick an old cow, then it really would have an udder like that... But that's not the point. A cow should be...shapely."

"How is it done then, by the legs?" asked Egor deferentially.

"What?"

"Choosing. Do you choose a cow by its legs, maybe?"

"And why by its legs? By its breed. There are different breeds—such and such a breed... For instance, the Kholmogorsky and the..." But the superintendent didn't know any other breeds.

"I love cows," Egor reasserted vehemently. "I'll lead her into the barn...put her into her stall..."

The superintendent and Egor were silent for awhile; they stared at one another.

"A cow, that's good," agreed the superintendent. "Only...well, you can't spend all your time with a cow. Do you have some sort of trade?"

"I have many trades."

"For instance."

Egor thought for awhile, evidently selecting from the multitude of his pursuits the least...how to say it—the one least accommodating to felonious intentions.

"Metalworker."

The telephone rang. The superintendent picked up the receiver.

"Yes. Yes. And what kind of class was it? What subject? 'Eugene Onegin'? So, and who did they ask all the questions about? Tatiana? And what was it about Tatiana that they couldn't understand? What I'm saying is, why did they..." The superintendent listened for a while to the thin, clamorous voice in the receiver, glanced at Egor reproachfully. Then he barely nodded his head: it was all clear to him. "Let them... Listen to me: let them just knock off their clever heckling. What significance does that have—will there or won't there be any children?! As if the poem was written about that! Or else *I'll* come and explain it to them! You tell them... Okay, Nikolaev will come over immediately." The superintendent hung up that receiver and picked up another one. While he was dialing the number he remarked, annoyed, "Those wise guys... Nikolaev? They broke up the literature class of one of the women teachers: they began to ask questions. What? 'Eugene Onegin.' No, not about Onegin, about Tatiana—will she have any children by her old husband or won't she? Go and check it out. Okay? Those damned smart alecks!" The superintendent hung up the receiver. "They actually began to ask questions!"

Egor snickered, as he pictured to himself this literature class. "They just wanted to know..."

"Do you have a wife?" the superintendent interrupted sharply.

Egor pulled a photograph out of his shirt pocket and handed it to the superintendent. The latter took it and looked at it.

"Is this your wife?!" he asked, not hiding his amazement.

The photograph showed a rather pretty young woman, kind-looking, with clear features.

"Future wife," said Egor. He did not like it, that the superintendent had acted so surprised. "She's waiting for me. But I've never seen her face to face."

"How did it all come about?"

"Pen pal." Egor reached over and took the photograph. "I'll just take that..." And then he himself became lost in contemplation of the sweet, simple Russian face. "Baikalova, Lyubov Fyodorovna. What trustfulness in her face, eh? It's amazing, isn't it? She looks like she could be a cashier or something."

"And what does she write?"

"She writes that she understands all my trials... 'But,' she says, 'I don't understand how you took the notion to land up in prison.' Nice letters. They make you feel peaceful... Her husband was a boozer. She kicked him out. And even so, she didn't get bitter about people."

"And do you understand what you're getting into?" the superintendent asked quietly and seriously.

"I understand," said Egor, also quietly, and hid the photograph away.

"First of all, dress properly! Going off like that—and showing up like some riff-raff." The superintendent looked Egor over with dissatisfaction. "What sort of clothes...why are you dressed in that outfit?"

Egor was wearing boots, a Russian blouse with the collar on the side, a short jacket and some sort of peaked uniform cap—making him look either like a country truck driver or a sanitation worker—or possibly also like an amateur actor in costume.

Egor gave himself a cursory glance and grinned.

"This was the way I had to dress for my role in the play. And afterwards I didn't have time to change."

"Actors..." was all the superintendent said, and then he began to laugh. He was not a mean man, and he never ceased to be amazed at the unlimited inventiveness of the people he had to deal with.

And now here it was—freedom!

That is—a door slammed behind Egor and he found himself on the street of a small settlement. He took a deep, deep breath of the spring air, screwed up his eyes and twisted his head back and forth. He walked along for a bit and then leaned against a fence. An old woman carrying a handbag came by and stopped.

"Do you feel bad?"

"I'm okay, mother," said Egor. "It's good that I did time in the spring. One should always do time in the spring."

"Do time?" The old woman didn't understand.

"In prison."

Only then did the old woman realize with whom she was talking. She warily edged away and shuffled on. She looked at the fence beside her, then glanced back at Egor.

But Egor was holding up his hand at a Volga. The Volga stopped. Egor began to dicker with the driver. The driver at first would not agree to give him a lift, but then Egor took a wad of bills out of his pocket and flashed it... He walked over to get in next to the driver.

Just then the old woman who had talked with Egor approached him again. She had even taken the trouble to cross the street.

"I beg you to forgive me," she began, bowing to Egor. "But why exactly in the spring?"

"What, do time? Well, if you do time in the spring, you get out in the spring. Freedom and spring! What more does a man need?" Egor smiled at the old woman and declaimed: "Oh, my skies of May, and the long blue days of June."

"My lands!" The old woman was astonished. She straightened up and stared at Egor the way people stare at a horse in the city that's going right down the same street where cars are traveling. The old woman had a rosy, wrinkled little face and clear eyes. Without knowing it, she had given Egor a most pleasant and precious moment.

The Volga pulled away.

The old woman watched it leave. "Can you believe it? A poet—a regular Fet."

But Egor had completely given himself up to motion.

The settlement came to an end, and they leaped into open space.

"Do you happen to have any music?" asked Egor.

The driver, a young fellow, reached into the back with one hand and fetched out a transistor tape recorder.

"Turn it on. The button on the end."

Egor turned it on and some splendid music began to play. He leaned his head back on the seat and closed his eyes. He had waited a long time for such a moment. He had got tired waiting.

"Happy?" asked the driver.

"Happy?" Egor came back to consciousness. "Happy..." He seemed to be tasting the word to see how he liked it. "I'll tell you, kid, if I had three lives to live, I'd spend one in prison, give one to you, and live the third for myself. But since I only have one, then right now, of course, I am happy. And do *you* know how to be happy?" Egor was sometimes able out of fullness of feeling to ascend to the realm of beautiful but empty words. "You know how, right?"

The driver shrugged his shoulders, did not reply.

"Ah, that's a bad deal for you, son—if you don't know how."

"But what's there to be happy about?"

Egor suddenly grew serious, became lost in thought. That happened with him—he would suddenly for no reason fall to thinking.

"What's that?" asked Egor, from the depths of his thoughts.

"I said, what is there to be so all-fired happy about?" The driver was a sober fellow and rather dull.

"Well, that, brother, I don't know—what to be happy about," said Egor, returning with reluctance from his faraway inner world. "If you know how, then be happy; if you don't, then lump it. There's no use asking questions. But do you like poetry, for instance?"

The fellow again shrugged his shoulders vaguely.

"Well, see," said Egor with pity, "and you were expecting to be happy."

"No I wasn't."

"Well, you have to love poetry," Egor decisively ended this flaccid conversation. "Just listen to the kind of poetry there is in the world." And Egor began to recite, though with omissions, to be sure, because he had forgotten parts:

" . . . into the snowy whiteness
The strident terror heaves.
Thou hast come, my black destruction
Unafraid I rush to meet thee.

"O city, in your discord cruel,
You called us filth and liars.
And now the field in frozen sorrow...
"And something, something. I forgot a little there.
"Is choked by telegraph wires.

"There's another part I forgot. But it goes on:

"May your heart be pierced with pain
By this song of animals' rights!..
...As hunters torture a wolf,
While the beaters close in like a vise.

"The beast lies low, while deep in the brush,
A trigger will soon be pulled...
But a sudden leap... and the two-legged foe
Is ripped by the fangs of the wolf.

"My favorite beast, I salute you!
Though the knife you are certain to feel.
Like you I am everywhere hounded
By the menacing enemy steel.

"Like you I am always on guard—
And though the hunter's horn is loud,
With my final dying leap,
I will draw my enemy's blood.

"Deep in the fragile whiteness
I will fall and twist in the snow...
But this song of revenge for my death
Shall be sung on the other shore."[1]

Egor, stunned by the power of the words, sat silent for a time, staring ahead with his jaws clenched. There was a resoluteness in his gaze, intent on the far horizon, as though he himself had fearlessly thrown down such a challenge in the past and was unafraid to do so now.

"How was the poetry?" asked Egor.

"Good."

"Yes, good. Like you've just slugged down a glass of pure alcohol," said Egor. "And you say you don't like poetry! You're still young—you should be interested in everything. Hey, stop! I just saw some sweethearts of mine."

The driver did not understand what sort of "sweethearts" Egor was talking about, but he stopped.

Egor got out of the car. All around was an unbroken birch forest. And such a pure, white world against the still black earth, such luminescence!.. Egor leaned against a birch tree and looked around.

"Well, will you look at what we have here!" he said with quiet rapture.

He turned toward the birch tree and stroked it with the palm of his hand. "Hullo there! Ah, you look so... You're like a bride. Are you waiting for your groom? Soon, soon he'll come." Egor swiftly returned to the car. Now everything had become clear to him. He had to have some kind of release. And soon. Immediately.

"Step on it, kid. Put it to the floor. Or else my heart is going to jump out of my chest: I've got to do something. You don't have any alcohol with you, do you?"

"Hardly!"

'Well, keep rolling, then. How much did your music box cost?"

"Two hundred."

"I'll take it for three hundred. I like it."

When they reached the main city of the district, Egor commanded the driver to stop on the outskirts, before they had reached the house where his people would be. He paid off the driver generously, took his music box and, cutting across courtyards by a complicated route, walked to the "shanty."

The gang was in session.

A good-looking young woman was sitting with a guitar. Near the telephone, at which he stared stubbornly, sat a hulking bruiser with a face like a bulldog. Also sitting down were four young chicks with bare legs... A muscular young man strode about the room and kept glancing at the phone... In an armchair sat a fellow with protruding lips and stained teeth who was swigging champagne from a long-stemmed glass... Five or six other young men were scattered around the room—some smoking, others just sitting.

The room was dingy and ugly. Some sort of dark-blue wallpaper, torn and dirty, quite inappropriately called to mind by its color the spring sky, and this made that stinking, closed little world altogether unbearable and oppressive. Such habitations are called dens—an insult to animals.

They all sat as though in some sort of strange torpor. From time to time they glanced at the telephone. The room was heavy with tension. Only the young woman, so striking with her high cheekbones, ran her fingers lightly over the strings of her guitar and sang softly, beautifully, in a rather husky but tender voice:

"Snowball berry red,
Snowball berry ripe,
A little birdie told me
My sweetheart he had lied.

"My sweetheart he had lied,
Just wanted to be my lover.
When I would not give in,
He left me for another.

"And I..."

At the front door sounded a prearranged knock. Everyone started, as though they had heard a scream.

"Hush!" said Fat Lip with a slight lisp. He looked at everyone in amusement, remarking, "Nerves!" And with a glance he sent someone to open the door.

It was the muscular young man who went.

"Keep it on the chain," said Fat Lip. He put his hand into his pocket. And waited.

The muscular young man opened the door a crack. And then he quickly released the chain and looked around at everyone.

The door closed.

But suddenly from behind the door marching music blared out. Egor opened the door with a kick and marched into the room. Everyone jumped up from their places and tried to hush him.

Egor turned off the tape recorder and looked at them all in surprise.

They came up to him, greeted him, but all made an effort to keep quiet.

"Hey, Gore." (That was Egor's nickname—Gore.)[2]

"How ya doin'?"

"You got sprung, huh?"

Egor offered his hand, but could not figure out what was going on. A lot of his acquaintances were there—and others who were more than acquaintances: Lucienne (the girl with high cheekbones) for one, and Fat Lip for another. Egor was glad to see them. But what were they up to?

"How come you're all here together like this?"

"Some of our boys are knocking over a store," explained one, shaking hands with Egor. "They're supposed to call... We're waiting."

The girl with high cheekbones was especially glad to see Egor. She clung to his neck and covered him with kisses. Her eyes glistened with tears of unfeigned joy.

"Oh my Gore!.. I dreamed about you today."

"Well, well," said the happy Egor. "And what did I do in your dream?"

"You hugged me. Oh, so tight."

"Are you sure you didn't confuse me with somebody else?"

"Gore!.."

"Well, turn around, little son!" said Fat Lip. "You've become a real Cossack."

Egor went over to Fat Lip and they embraced reservedly. Fat Lip did not even stand up. He looked at Egor merrily.

"I remember a certain evening in spring," began Fat Lip. And everyone got quiet. "The air was somewhat damp, and there were hundreds of people in the train station. There were so many suitcases that it dazzled your eyes. The people were all excited—couldn't wait to get on their trains. Among these nervous and excited people sat one lonely person... He was sitting on his old-fashioned trunk and thinking bitter thoughts. A certain elegant young man went up to him and asked: 'And why do you grieve, good man?' 'Oh, woe is me! I'm all alone in the world and I don't know where to go.' Then the young man..."

The telephone rang. Again everyone started, as though shocked.

"Yes?" said the one who looked like a bulldog, feigning indifference. He listened for a long time, nodding now and then. "Everyone is sitting here. I'm not going to leave the phone. They're all here. Gore showed up... Yes. Just now. We're all waiting." Bulldog hung up the receiver and turned toward the others.

"They've begun."

They all began to fidget.

"Champagne!" ordered Fat Lip.

Bottles of champagne were passed around.

"How big is the job?" Egor asked Fat Lip.

"Eight grand," said the latter. "To your health!"

They drank.

"Luciene... sing something, to relieve the tension," asked Fat Lip. He was lean, calm and extremely insolent; very insolent eyes.

"I will sing about love," said the charming Lucienne. She tossed back her dyed hair and placed her palm with a flourish on the strings of her guitar. Everyone fell silent.

"Tittle-tattle, my magpie,
Spells of magic, eyes of night.
Those not gay and those in sorrow,
Go away now, out of sight.

"In the meadow, in the dark,
Love is free, and shining eye.
My heart is aching, lure me on,
Tittle-tattle, my magpie."

Again the telephone rang. At once a funereal silence descended.

"Yes?" said Bulldog, using all his strength to stay calm. "No, you called the wrong number. That's all right, don't worry about it. Yes, it could happen to anyone." Bulldog hung up the receiver. "She was calling the laundry, the bitch."

They began to fidget again.

"More champagne!" said Fat Lip. "Gore—whose greetings have you brought us?"

"Later," said Egor. "Let me just look at you all first. And here are all these young people I don't even know yet. I'll just have to introduce myself."

The young people respectfully shook hands with him for a second time. Egor, with a grin, attentively looked each of them in the eye. He nodded his head and said, "So, so..."

"I want to dance!" announced Lucienne. And she smashed her champagne glass on the floor.

"Lay off, Lucienne," said Fat Lip. "Don't start up with that, now."

"Go to the devil!" said Lucienne, half drunk. "Gore, our feature number!"

And Egor also dashed his wineglass to the floor.

And his eyes, too, began to flash.

"Okay, everybody, make a circle. Move it!"

"Cut it, Gore!" said Fat Lip, raising his voice. "You picked the wrong time!"

"But we can still hear the phone!" they shouted at Fat Lip from all sides. "Let them do their hop... What do you care? And besides, Bulldog is sitting right by the phone."

Fat Lip pulled out a white handkerchief, and, though late with the gesture, pretentiously waved it at them in the style of Pugachev.

Two guitars struck up a *barynia* folk dance.

Lucienne stepped out... Ah, how she danced! She really knew how, too. Not wildly, no, but precisely, lightly, with a fine sense of rhythm. She seemed to be hammering her crippled life into the grave with her heels, while her true self beat its wings like a bird trying to fly away. She put so much into her dance... She even became suddenly beautiful—sweet and natural.

Whenever Lucienne approached him, Egor would also dance, moving only his legs. He folded his arms behind his back, avoided fancy steps, did not prance like a goat—in short, he was also good. And they looked very good together. Their dance was imbued with something lasting and unforgettable.

"This is the moment my long-suffering soul was waiting for," said Egor with utter seriousness. Indeed, this was just what he had hoped for from his long-desired freedom.

"Wait, Egorushka, and I'll soothe your soul in another way, too," replied Lucienne. "Oh, how I will soothe it. And I will soothe my own soul, too."

"Soothe it, Lucienne, it's crying."

"I will. I'll press it to my heart like a little dove and say to it: 'Are you tired? Darling... darling... dearest, you're tired...' "

"Make sure that dove doesn't peck you," interjected Fat Lip into the sentimental conversation.

"No, it's not an evil dove," said Egor seriously, not looking at Fat Lip. And a grim shadow passed over his kindly face. But they did not stop dancing. They danced—and one wanted to watch them forever. The young people watched them anxiously, avidly, as though an ugly part of their lives, too, was being trodden into the grave—and afterward they would emerge into the bright daylight, and it would be springtime.

"It's weary in its cage," said Lucienne tenderly.

"It's crying," said Egor. "It needs a holiday."

"Switch it on its little head with a twig," said Fat Lip. "And that will calm it."

"What people, Egorushka, eh?" exclaimed Lucienne. "How wicked they are!"

"Well, Lucienne, to wicked people, we ourselves are wolves. But my soul, my soul... it's crying."

"We'll soothe it, Egorushka, we'll soothe it. I'm an enchantress and I'll put my spells on it..."

"Doves make good soup," said Fat Lip maliciously. He was thin as a knife blade, cool and terrible in his youthful insolence. His whole character was reflected in his eyes. His eyes glittered with malice.

"No, it's crying!" said Egor in a frenzy. "It's crying! It's smothering in there, so it's weeping." He tore open his shirt and stood in front of Fat Lip. The guitars suddenly fell silent. And the dance of Lucienne-the-enchantress suddenly came to a halt.

Fat Lip already had his hand in his pocket.

"Back to your old ways again, eh, Gore?" He spoke with an odd satisfaction.

"I'm telling you for the last time," said Egor calmly, wearily, as he buttoned his shirt. "Don't touch me on my sore place again. Next time you might not get your hand in your pocket in time. That's a warning..."

"I'll keep it in mind."

"Ahh," said Lucienne, distressed. "How tiresome. More blood, more corpses. Brr! Pour me some champagne, somebody."

The telephone rang. Somehow they'd all forgotten about it.

Bulldog lunged for the phone and grabbed the receiver. He put it to his ear—and dropped it almost at once, as though it were hot.

Fat Lip was the first to jump up. There was always an urgency about him, yet he was calm at the same time.

"They got burned," said Bulldog tersely in a horrified voice.

"Everybody split up!" commanded Fat Lip. "Spread out. And lie low for two weeks. Now!"

They disappeared one by one. This was something they evidently knew how to do. No one asked any questions.

"No two together!" added Fat Lip. "We'll meet at Ivan's place. No sooner than ten days."

Egor sat down at the table, poured himself a glass of champagne, drank it.

"What are you going to do, Gore?" asked Fat Lip.

"Me?" Egor thought for awhile before answering. "I think I might actually go into agricultural work."

Lucienne and Fat Lip stood over him in disbelief.

"What sort of agricultural work?"

But then Lucienne shook him. "What are you sitting there for? We've got to leave."

Egor started, got to his feet.

"Leave? Time to leave again?... When am I ever going to arrive, citizens? Where's my amazing music box?.. Oh, there it is. Is it absolutely necessary to go? Perhaps..."

"What are you talking about? In ten minutes they'll be here. They probably tailed our boys."

Lucienne walked to the door.

Egor was about to follow her, but Fat Lip laid a restraining hand on his shoulder and said quietly:

"Better not. Let's talk a minute. We'll all be seeing each other again anyway..."

"Are you going with her, or what?" asked Egor bluntly.

"No," said Fat Lip firmly, with seeming honesty. "Take off!" he barked at Lucienne, who had lingered in the doorway.

Lucienne glowered at Fat Lip and left.

"Take a rest someplace," said Fat Lip, pouring out two glasses. "Take a rest, old buddy—with King Kolka maybe, or Vanka Samykin. Samykin has a real cozy place. and look—don't hold it against me for... today. But, Gore... you know, Gore, you sometimes press my sore place, too, only you don't realize it. Well, drink up! To our next meeting! And now, goodbye. Don't be unhappy. Have you got enough dough?"

"Yeah, they made up a collection for me before I left..."

"I can throw in some more."

"Well, okay," Egor changed his mind.

Fat Lip took a roll of bills out of his pocket and peeled off a thick sheaf for Egor.

"Where are you going to be, then?"

"I don't know. I'll find somebody. But tell me, how could you have screwed up so bad, anyway?"

Just then one of the young fellows slipped into the room, white with fear.

"They've surrounded the whole block," he said.

"What are you doing here?"

"I don't know where to go... I wanted to tell you..."

"His horns don't even show yet," laughed Fat Lip. "What made you come back here? Ah, you sweetheart, my sweetheart, my little calf... Follow me, brothers!"

They left by a back entrance and ran along a wall toward the street, but they could hear the heavy footsteps of a patrol coming toward them. They changed direction—and again heard footsteps.

"Damn," said Fat Lip, without losing his enigmatic gaiety. "It looks like they've got us. What do you think, Gore?"

"Quick, in here!" Egor pushed his companions into some sort of recess in the wall.

The footsteps, coming from both directions, drew closer.

The beam from a powerful flashlight played along the wall to the right.

Fat Lip pulled out his revolver.

"Put it back, you fool!" said Egor sharply, angrily. "You psychopath. Maybe they won't even see us—but suddenly you're going to open fire!"

But I know those bastards!" exclaimed Fat Lip nervously. He was finally beginning to lose his cool.

"Look, I'll rush out and lead them away. I've got my release papers," said Egor quickly, peering about to see the best direction to run. "The papers have today's date on them, so I'm covered. If they catch me, I'll just tell them I panicked. I'll tell them I was looking for a woman, when I heard the whistles—and just lost my head. I'm off. Don't remember ill of me!"

And Egor dashed away from them, running blindly with all his might. At once from all sides whistles began to blow and running footsteps resounded.

Egor ran exultantly, like a kid... As he ran, he urged himself on and even hummed a song. He spotted a patch of light, threw himself in that direction, crawled over some pipes—and triumphantly burst into song:

"Hip, hip, hooray! Oh, nothing saw I, no one do I know..."

He had already got past the pipes, but behind him in the darkness they were running up very fast. Egor dove back into one of the wide ducts and froze.

Overhead footsteps boomed on the iron pipe...

Egor squatted, hunched over, smiled contentedly and hummed:

"Oh, nothing saw I, no one do I know..."

He had undertaken a rather dangeous venture. When the booming footsteps had subsided, even though it would have been possible just to stay there and outsit them, he suddenly rushed out and began running again.

Again they scrambled after him.

"Oh, nothing saw I, and no one do I know... No one do I know..." Egor sang to embolden himself. He hopped over a low fence, ran through some bushes: he had gotten into some sort of garden. A dog began to bark close by. Egor abruptly changed direction... Another fence. He leaped over it on the run and found himself in a cemetery.

"Hello!" said Egor. And began to walk quietly.

The hullabaloo behind him gradually veered off to the side.

"Damned if I didn't outrun them!" marvelled Egor. "Too bad it's not always like that. When you really *need* to escape, then you get caught, like some kid."

And again Egor was overcome by the joy of being free and of being alive.

"Oh, nothing saw I, and no one do I know," he sang once more. He turned his tape recorder on low and walked along looking at the inscriptions on the gravestones. A street curved around the cemetery and the headlights of cars rounding the bend would light up the crosses for a considerable time. And the shadows of the crosses, long and deformed, would sweep over the ground, the grave mounds, and the fences... It made a rather eerie scene. Suddenly Egor's music seemed totally out of place. He shut it off.

" 'Sleep in peace till the bright dawn,' " Egor managed to read. "'Merchant Neverov of the First Guild.' And how did *you* get here?!" Egor exclaimed. " '1890'—Ah, that explains it. Well, well—a merchant of the First Guild. 'Riding with wares on the road from Kasimov,'" Egor began to sing softly, but stopped suddenly. " 'To my dear, unforgettable husband, from his inconsolable widow,'" he read a little farther on. He sat down on a low bench for awhile... Then he stood up. "Well, friends, you have to lie here while I move on. There's nothing I can do about it... I'll go off on my own, like an honest John. There's got to be someplace where I can lay my head. There's just got to be, right? Right!" And he sang yet again: "Oh, nothing saw I, and no one do I kno-o-ow."

So he set out to look for a place to lay his head.

At the door of a wooden cottage on the very edge of town they yelled at him from inside:

"Go away! Or else I'll come out there and give you something to suffer about... I'll show you grief and suffering."

Egor was silent for a minute.

"Okay, come on out."

"I'll do it, too!"

"When you come out, tell me—is Ninka here or not?" Egor asked the man in a civil tone of voice. "But tell the truth! Because I'll find out, and if you've lied to me, I'll punish you severely!"

The man also fell silent. And then he, too, changed his tone of voice and said grumpily—but not threateningly:

"There's no Ninka here, I told you. Can't you understand that? All you loafers, hanging around every night..."

"How would you like to get singed a little?" Egor spoke his thoughts aloud, rattling the box of matches in his pocket. "Hah?"

There was a long silence behind the door.

"Just try it," the voice said at last—but now almost placatingly. "Just try to start a fire... There's no Ninka here, I'm telling you the truth. She's gone away."

"Where to?"

"Somewhere up north."

"Why the hell didn't you say that at the beginning, instead of barking at me like a damned dog? What's the problem, anyway?"

"Because your kind only bring trouble. That's why she had to go away, because of people like you."

"Well, think of it this way—she's in good hands now, they'll take care of her. Goodbye now. Take it easy."

In a nearby phone booth Egor got angry again.

"What do you mean, it's forbidden? Why?!" he roared into the receiver.

Someone gave him a long explanation.

"You're all diseased," said Egor, his voice trembling. "I'll make a bouquet out of you sons-of-bitches and stick you in the ground head first... You bastards!" Egor slammed down the receiver. He fell into thought. "Lyuba!" he said with exaggerated tenderness. "That's it! I'll go see Lyuba." And he spitefully pushed the door of the phone booth as hard as he could and strode off toward the train station. He spoke to Lyuba, his dear one, as he walked along:

"Ah, my darling... Lyubushka, my little dove. You're my little Siberian potato cake! I'll at least put on a little weight at your place, and let my hair grow out. Oh, you dear little cupcake!" Egor got more and more frenzied. "I'm coming to eat you up!" he shouted into the silence of the night. He didn't even look around to see if he had startled anyone with his noise. His footsteps echoed in the empty street; it was already freezing, and the cold asphalt rang out. "I'll smother you with my embraces! I'll tear you into pieces and gobble you up! And wash you down with home-brewed vodka. To the last morsel!"

Egor had just arrived at the village of Yasnoe on the local bus.

Lyuba stood on a little rise of ground waiting for him. He spotted her from a distance, recognizing her at once. His heart skipped a beat.

He walked up to meet her.

"Oh, man," he whispered to himself, in rapture. "She's absolutely gorgeous! Sweet as sugar and plump as a little bun. She's a regular Little Red Riding Hood."

"Hello," he said politely, affecting shyness, and extended his hand. "I'm Georgii." He warmly pressed her strong, countrywoman's hand. And, for good measure, he shook it as well, also warmly.

"And I'm Lyuba," she said. She looked at Egor evenly and somewhat thoughtfully. She was silent. Egor grew restless under her gaze.

"It's me," he said. He felt very stupid.

"I'm me, too," said Lyuba, and continued to stare at him calmly and thoughtfully.

"I'm not very handsome," said Egor inadvertently.

Lyuba burst into laughter.

"Let's go sit for awhile in the teashop," she said. "You can tell me about yourself."

"I don't drink," said Egor hastily.

"Oh, really?" Lyuba was sincerely pleased. She responded with complete simplicity and naturalness. Her innocence disconcerted Egor.

"Well, of course," he said, "I do take a drink in company. But I don't, you know, get plastered... I'm very temperate..."

"We'll just drink tea then. And you can tell me a little about yourself." She continued to gaze at her pen pal. She looked at him so strangely, that it seemed as though she was secretly laughing at herself, as if to say, astonished at her behavior: "You're a fool, aren't you? What have you gotten yourself into?" But she was obviously an independent woman—able to laugh at herself, yet did what she wanted anyway. "Let's go. Talk to me. You know, my mother and father—they're very strict—they say to me: don't come around here with your convict." Lyuba was walking somewhat ahead. As she said this, she turned around with a calm and cheerful look. "And I say to them: but he's a convict by accident. Through misfortune. That's right, isn't it?"

At the news that she had parents—and strict ones besides—Egor began to feel glum. But he didn't let it show on his face.

"Yes, yes," he said "intelligently." "It was all a matter of circumstantial coincidence, incredible bad luck."

"That's just what I told them."

"Are your parents Old Believers?"

"Why, no. What in the world made you think that?

"Well, they're strict... And there's something else they won't like. I smoke, for instance."

"Oh, heavens! My father smokes, too. Though my brother, it's true, doesn't smoke."

"So you have a brother, too?"

"Yes, we have a big family. My brother has two children—grown up already: his son is already studying at the institute and his daughter is finishing her tenth year in high school."

"Everybody studying... That's good," approved Egor. "Fine young people." He began to get a sour taste in his mouth from such kinfolk.

They stopped in at the teashop. They sat down at a little table in the corner. The teashop was crowded, people came and went continually... And they all looked Egor over with interest. This, too, made him feel ashamed and uncomfortable.

"Maybe we could get a bottle of something and go somewhere else," suggested Egor.

"What for? It's so splendid here... Oh, Nyura, Nyura!" Lyuba summoned the waitress. "Bring us something, dear... What should we get?" she said, turning to Egor.

"Make it red wine. Vodka gives me heartburn," said Egor, making a grimace.

"Red wine, Nyura!" Lyuba was making a rather puzzling impression, as though she were playing some sort of intellectual game. She played it calmly, gaily, as she studied Egor with curiosity. Had he guessed what was going on or not?

"Well, Georgii," she began, "tell me about yourself."

"Just like the third degree," said Egor, laughing weakly. But Lyuba didn't respond to that, so Egor got serious again.

"Well, what to say? I'm a bookkeeper. I was working in a supply house. The bosses, of course, were stealing... Suddenly—bang!—an audit. I was the one they reeled in. Naturally, I had to take the rap. Listen," said Egor, following Lyuba's example in using the intimate form of address, "let's get out of here. They all keep staring..."

"Oh, let them stare! What do you care? After all, you didn't run away..."

"Right here's my release papers!" exclaimed Egor, about to dig into his pocket.

"I believe you, I believe you, for heaven's sake! I only said what was true. All right? And how many years did you do, then?"

"Five."

"And so..."

"That's all... what else is there to say?"

"With hands like those—you're a bookkeeper? It's hard to believe."

"What? My hands?... Oh, well. They got that way from all the physical exercise I got while I was in..." Egor put his hands under the table.

"Hands like those would do better at breaking locks than keeping accounts," laughed Lyuba.

And Egor, rather disturbed, also gave a false little laugh.

"So what do you plan to do here? Are you going into bookkeeping again?"

"No!" said Egor with alacrity. "I'm never going to be a bookkeeper again."

"But what will you do, then?"

"I'll have to look around... But let me rein in my horses a little, okay, Lyuba?" Egor now gazed directly into the woman's eyes. "You want to run them full speed on the subject of work. But work is not something you rush into.[3] Let's drop that for awhile."

"But why have you been deceiving me?" asked Lyuba with equal directness. "The fact is, I wrote to your superior, and he replied that..."

"Ahh," sighed Egor, defeated. "So that's the way it is. And then he became relaxed, even cheerful. "Okay, then—whip the whole troika up the mountain. Pour me a drink."

And then he turned to his music box.

"And you wrote such nice letters," said Lyuba regretfully. "They were more like poems—genuine poems—than letters."

"Really?" Egor perked up. "You like them? Maybe I've been wasting my talents." He sang: "'He lost his youth and his talent behind those prison walls...' Let's have another one, Lyuba! 'Oh, those nights in prison, oh those nights of fire...'Another drink!"

"Why are you carrying on like that? Wait a minute... Let's talk."

"Oh, that damned superintendent—the craphead!" exclaimed Egor. "And he never said a word to me. Well, I showed up here as a law-abiding citizen, didn't I? A bookkeeper!" Egor roared with laughter. "Keeping accounts of consumer goods..."

"What were you intending to do, Georgii?" asked Lyuba. "You were lying to me... Does that mean you were going to rob me?"

"Jesus Christ Almighty! To come way the hell out here to Siberia to steal a couple of pairs of felt boots? You're insulting me, Lyuba."

"Well, what is it you want here, then?"

"I don't know. Maybe just find rest for my soul... But that's not it, either. Anyway, for me to find rest, that would be... No. I just don't know, Lyubov."

"Ah, Egorushka..."

Egor actually flinched and looked at Lyuba in fright—so much had she sounded like faraway Lucienne when she said his name that way.

"What?" he said.

"You really are like a horse on a mountain. You're exhausted. Your sides haven't started to heave yet, and you're not yet foaming at the mouth. But you'll surely drop. You'll drive yourself until you die. Is it true that you have no one? No relatives?"

"That's right—I'm just a poor little orphan. I wrote you that. Do you know my nickname? It's Gore—woe is me: my pseudonym. But let's not get into my private life, please. Forget that. I'm not a beggar yet. Maybe I'm not good for much, but I still know how to knock over a store. Sometimes I'm fantastically rich, Lyuba. It's too bad you didn't meet me during one of those times... Then you would have seen that I... completely detest that stinking money."

"You hate it, yet because of it you end up being crucified."

"It isn't because of the money."

"Well, why, then?"

'There's nothing else on this earth that I'm fit to be—except a thief." Egor said this with pride. He was feeling very much at ease with Lyuba. He had simply taken the notion to astonish her with something.

"Oy-ee!" said Lyuba. "Well, drink up and we'll go."

"Where?" asked Egor, surprised.

"To my house. You came to see me, didn't you? Or do you have another pen pal somewhere else?" Lyuba chuckled. She also felt very much at ease with Egor, very much...

"Wait," said Egor in confusion. "I thought we just made it plain that I'm not a bookkeeper..."

"That was certainly some profession you picked!" Lyuba shook her head. "Pig keeper would have been an even better one. You could have pretended that your pigs all got sick and they sent you to prison for it. You really don't act much like a swindler. More like a normal guy—even like one of our village types here. So, Mr. Pigkeeper, shall be go?"

"By the way," said Egor, with a touch of smugness, "for your information, I'm a truck driver of the second class."

"Do you have a licence?" asked Lyuba skeptically.

"My license is in Magadan."

"See, you're invaluable—even if your name does mean grief. That grief needs to be whipped out of you. Let's go."

"Typical peasant psychology, like driving a cart horse," said Gore. "Listen—I'm a recidivist convict, you little fool. I'd steal the pennies off a dead man's eyes. I..."

"Hush! I think you're a little tipsy, aren't you?"

"Right. But what's going on?" Egor came to himself. "I don't understand. Explain it to me, please. We're going to your house. Okay. But what then?"

"Stay at my house. Take a rest, even if only for a week... I don't have anything worth stealing anyway... Just relax for awhile... Then after that you can start breaking into stores again. Let's go. Or else people will say, 'She no sooner met him, than she turned him away at the door. Why did she invite him, then?' That's the way we are here! We're always minding each other's business... But for some reason I'm not afraid of you, I don't know why."

"Good. But your daddy might decide to give me a love-tap... with an axe. There's no telling what ideas he'll get about me."

"Don't worry about that. From now on, just trust me."

The Baikalovs' house was a large one, built of logs. Lyuba lived with her parents in one half of it; on the other side of a partition lived her brother and his family.

The house was situated on a high river bank. Beyond the far shore was a limitless plain. The Baikalovs were well set up, with a large yard surrounded by trim outbuildings and a bathhouse down on the river bank.

The old people happened to be cooking little meat pies in the kitchen when grandmother Mikhailovna caught sight of Lyuba and Egor out the window.

"Oh, lookee, she's bringing him!" she said in alarm. "Lyubka—and that jailbird!"

The old man pressed himself against the window.

"Now what sort of life will we live!" he said in a fit of temper. "He'll put his ways on us, like a knife in the heart. What has that girl brought down on us?"

They could see Lyuba telling Egor something as she pointed with her hand beyond the river, then looked around and pointed back, toward the village. Egor obediently turned his head, but he kept glancing at the house, at the windows.

Behind the windows there was total panic. The old people had never really believed that someone from a prison was going to visit them. Even though Lyuba had showed them Egor's telegram, they still didn't believe it. But now it had all turned out to be horribly true.

"Oh, that baneful wench!" the old woman wept. "But what could I do with that wanton girl?! I couldn't stop her no ways..."

"Don't let on that we're frightened," the old man instructed her. "We've seen such bandits before! It's Stenka Razin all over again."

"We're bound to greet him, though, aren't we?" said the old woman, after first giving the matter some thought. "Or what? My head's just all in a whirl, I can't think what to do..."

"Yes, we're bound. We'll treat him just like people, or else watch out—we'll lose our lives. All from our own daughter. Oh, Lyubka, Lyubka..."

Lyuba and Egor entered the house.

"Hello!" said Egor cordially.

The old people only nodded in reply and openly stared him up and down.

"Well, here's our bookkeeper," said Lyuba, as though everything were perfectly normal. "And he's not at all a highway robber, he only got in trouble because... because..."

"Because of a misunderstanding," prompted Egor.

"And how many years are they giving now for misunderstandings?" asked the old man.

"Five," said Egor tersely.

"Not enough. They used to give more."

"But just what sort of misunderstanding did he sit in prison for?" asked the old woman straight out.

"The bosses were stealing, and he was writing it off," explained Lyuba. "Well, have you asked all your questions? It's time to eat now—our guest has been on the road a long time. Take a seat, Georgii."

Egor uncovered his close-cropped head and sat down meekly on the edge of a chair.

"Sit down for now," commanded Lyuba. "I'll go heat up the bathhouse, and after that we'll eat." Lyuba went out. She seemed to have gone off on purpose, to let the three of them come to some kind of understanding with each other—by themselves. No doubt she was counting on her basically goodhearted parents.

"May I smoke?" asked Egor. He wasn't all that anxious—let them kick him out if they wanted to; but if they could get on peacefully together, it would be better—and more interesting. Of course, it wasn't simply for amusement that he wanted to settle in here, even if only for a short while. The thing was, he absolutely had to find someplace where he could hole up and get his bearings.

"Feel free," said the old man. "What do you smoke?"

"Pamirs."

"Those are cigarettes, aren't they?"

"Right."

"Give me one, I'd like to try them." The old man sat down next to Egor. And all the while he kept looking him over and staring at him.

They lit up.

"So what kind of misunderstanding was it you had again?" asked the old man, as though just in passing. "Did you go to hit somebody on the forehead and accidentally break his skull?"

Egor stared at the sly old man.

"Yes..." he said vaguely. "We bumped off seven people in one place, but we didn't spot the eighth. He got away. And that's how we got caught."

The old woman dropped a piece of stove wood on the floor and sat down on a bench.

The old man proved to be less naive and remained calm.

"Seven?"

"Seven. We cut their heads clean off, put them in a sack and lammed off..."

"Oh, my Lord and saints above," muttered the old woman, crossing herself. "Fedya..."

"Quiet!" commanded the old man. "One fool talks nonsense, and the other believes him... And you, mutt, watch your tongue in front of elderly people."

"Well, what kind of elderly people are you, to call me a bandit right off the bat? You hear that I'm a bookkeeper, and all you do is snicker. Okay, I was in prison, but what do you think—the only people in prison are murderers?"

"Who's calling you a murderer? But that bookkeeper business, you're also... you're just going too far with that... don't tell your lies here. Book-keeper! I've seen a passel of bookkeepers in my day, and they're all quiet types, with a sort of hang-dog look. Your bookkeepers are all four-eyed, with weak voices... and I notice they've all got turned-up noses, too. But what sort of bookkeeper are you? You—if they beat you on the head for six months, you still wouldn't feel it. Go tell Lyubka that bookkeeper business, she might believe you. But not me. As soon as you walked in here, I could tell right off—this one either beat somebody up or stole a truckload of lumber. Am I right?"

"You ought to get a job as a police inspector, pop," said Egor. "You'd be worth your weight in gold. Are you sure you didn't serve with Kolchak in your young years? Like maybe in the White counterintelligence?"

The old man blinked his eyes rapidly. Somehow he was thrown completely off balance, though he wasn't sure why. Egor's accusations had taken an ominous turn.

"What's that for?" he asked. "Why are you talking that way?"

"And why did you get so shook up? All I did was ask a question... Okay, another one: you never stole any grain from the kolkhoz fields during hard years?"

The old man, stunned by such an unexpected reversal, kept silent. He had been completely thrown off the condescending tone of voice he'd been using and could not find a way to reply to this upstart. Egor, of course, had pursued his interrogation precisely with this in mind. He had seen real masters of this technique in his life.

"You're having difficulty answering," continued Egor. "Well, never mind... We'll now ask a question of a different sort, closer to home, so to speak: do you often take part in the meetings here?"

"What sly tricks are you trying to pull now?" the old man asked at last. He was on the verge of really losing his temper. He was ready to counterat-tack profusely and angrily, but Egor suddenly jumped up from his chair, put on his uniform cap and began to stride around the room.

"See how cozy we've learned to live!" Egor rapped out, glancing sharply from time to time at the old man, who had remained seated. "The country is producing electricity, steam engines, millions of tons of cast iron... People work and strain with all their might. They literally drop from the effort; they eliminate all traces of sloppiness and stupidity in themselves, and they finally reach a point, you could say, where they are staggering from the exertion." Egor leaped on the word "exertion" and smacked his lips over it. "In the Far North people get old before their time and they have to go out and get themselves gold teeth... But at the same time there are other people, who, out of all the achievements of mankind, have chosen for themselves only a warm stove! Think of it! Really wonderful... They'd rather prop their feet up on the hearth than work in harmony with all those others who are killing themselves..."

"But he's been working since he was ten years old!" the old woman butted in. "He's been in the fields from childhood..."

"Rebuttals later," said Egor, cutting her short rather sharply. "We're all as nice as pie when our own interests are not at stake, when our own pockets, so to speak, are not touched..."

"I've been a Stakhanovite all my life!" the old man almost screamed. "I've got eighteen commendations!"

Egor stopped, surprised.

"Well, why did you sit there without saying anything?" he said in a different tone of voice.

"What do you mean? You didn't give me a chance to get a word in edgewise!"

"Where are the commendations?"

"Over there," said the old woman, also utterly bewildered.

"Over where?"

"There, in the cupboard, all put away."

"They belong on the wall, not in a cupboard! In the cupboard! Everybody keeps hiding everything in the cupboard..."

At that moment Lyuba walked in.

"Well, how are you getting along?" she asked cheerfully. Her cheeks had got all red in the bathhouse and her hair had worked loose from her kerchief... How pretty she was. Egor looked at her involuntarily. "Is everything okay? Nice and peaceful?"

"What a fire-eater you found!" said the old man with unfeigned delight. "Look how he's taken over here! A regular commissar!" he laughed.

The old woman shook her head and angrily pursed her lips.

Thus Egor made his acquaintance with Lyuba's parents.

He got acquainted with her brother Petro and his family somewhat later.

Petro drove into the yard in a dump truck... The sound of its raucous engine rattled the windowpanes for some time. Finally Petro got the truck parked, and the motor sputtered into silence. Petro stepped down from the cab. His wife Zoya came out to meet him. She was a sales clerk at the village store, an articulate butterfly of a woman, quick and bustling.

"He finally got here... Lyubka's, you know, pen pal," she said at once.

"Oh, yeah?" said Petro with mild curiosity. Petro was a strapping fellow, somewhat morose, constantly preoccuppied. "Well, what about him?" He kicked one of the tires of the truck, then another one.

"He says he was a bookkeeper—there was something about an audit, he says. But with that mug of his, he looks more like a bandit."

"Yeah?" said Petro, again rather lazily and incuriously. "So then what?"

"Oh, nothing. But we'll have to keep an eye on him for awhile... Go take a look at that bookkeeper! See for yourself! He'd stick a knife in you without a second thought, that bookkeeper."

"Yeah?" Petro continued to kick the tires. "You think so?"

"You just go take a look at him! Take a look and see what she found for herself! Go take a look—we're all going to live under the same roof with him now."

"Well, what of it?"

"Oh, nothing at all!" said Zoya, raising her voice. "We've got a daughter in school, that's what! Is that all you can think of to say, 'What of it?' You constantly leave us alone overnight, that's what! You and your 'What of it,' you stump. His wife and daughter are going to have their throats cut, and he won't even stir himself!"

Petro went over to the house, wiping his hands on a rag as he walked along. As to his wife's remark about not stirring himself, this was indeed characteristic of him: he was an extraordinarily calm, even phlegmatic man, though he was suffused with massive, capable strength. This strength could be sensed in every movement that Petro made, especially when he turned his head and stared with his rather small eyes—with a steady, steely, unblinking fearlessness.

"Now you can go with Petro," said Lyuba, as she set about getting Egor organized to take a bath. "But what can we give you to change into? What made you do that—to come a-courting, and not even bring an extra pair of underclothes? Well? What in the world were you thinking of, to turn up like that?"

"You're talking about prison!" exclaimed the old man. "Not a health resort. It even happens that they come out of health resorts stripped clean. Why, Ilyushka Lopatin—you remember—went to take a cure for radiculitis. It cost him a whole cow—and he came back without a kopek."

"Well, here's some of my husband's old things I just found. I hope they fit." Lyuba pulled out of a trunk a long white undershirt and a pair of drawers.

"What's this?" said Egor, not understanding.

"Clothes that belonged to my former husband," Lyuba stood there with the pair of drawers in her hand. "What's the matter?"

"Oh, no..." Egor was insulted. "I'm not some beggar who has to drag around in somebody else's old underwear! I've got money. I'll go buy some in a store."

"Where are you going to buy any now? The stores are already closed. But why the fuss? These have been washed..."

"Go ahead and take them," said the old man. "They're clean."

Egor thought it over for a minute, and took them.

"I'm sinking lower and lower," he muttered. "It's interesting even to me, what's happening to me. After awhile I'll probably even sing you a song: 'In the garden, in the garden—cabbages or flowers?' "

"Oh, go on now," said Lyuba, escorting him to the door. "By the way, Petro's not the tenderhearted type, so don't get upset: he treats everybody the same."

Petro was already taking off his clothes in the little dressing room of the bathhouse when Egor came down the riverbank.

"Will they let in people with shaved heads?" said Egor, tryng to be as cheeful as possible. He even stretched his lips into a smile.

"They let in anybody," said Petro, in the same unemotional tone of voice he had used with his wife.

"Let's introduce ourselves. I'm Georgii." Egor held out his hand. He kept smiling as he looked into Petro's somber eyes. In spite of himself, he wanted to be accepted by these people. He really felt it now. Was it on account of Lyuba, perhaps? "As I said—I'm Georgii."

"Okay, okay," said Petro. "Do you want us to kiss each other, too? So your name is Georgii. So what? Maybe I'll call you Zhora..."

"George, to you." Egor was left with his hand hanging in the air. He stopped smiling.

"What?" said Petro, perplexed.

" 'What?' 'What?' " repeated Egor heatedly. "Christ, I've been sucking around here like a beggar-whore all day!" He threw his underwear down on the bench. "The only thing I haven't done is wag my tail! What have I done to step on your toes, that you won't even shake my hand?" Egor was really agitated. He groped in his pocket for a cigarette, lit it, and sat down on the bench. His hands were almost trembling.

"What's up with you?" asked Petro. "What are you sprawling there for?"

"Go and wash," said Egor. "I'll go next. I've been in prison. Us convicts know our place. Don't worry about it."

"Oh ho!" said Petro. And he went into the bathing room without bothering to take off his shorts. Egor could hear him clattering around with the basins and the dipper...

Egor lay down on the bench and smoked.

"So that's the way it is!" he said to himself. "Just like a poor relation. Crap!"

The door of the bathing room opened and Petro glanced in at Egor out of a cloud of steam.

"What's the matter?" he asked.

"What do you mean?"

"Why are you lying there?"

"I'm just a foundling."

"Oh ho!" said Petro. And he went down into the bathing room again. He stayed there a long time, pouring water in basins, moving benches around... Finally he got impatient and opened the door again. "Are you coming or not?!" he asked.

"I've got release papers!" Egor almost yelled in his face. "Tomorrow I'm going to get the same kind of passport you have! Exactly the same, except for one little remark that no one will ever read anyway. Understand?"

"In just one minute I'm gonna shove your head in a bucket," said Petro expressionlessly. "And sit your ass on the hot stove. Without a passport." Petro was rather pleased at his own wit. He added, "But you have to show your release papers," and chuckled briefly.

"Well, this is a different conversation altogether!" said Egor. He sat up on the bench and began to get undressed. "If I don't watch out, I'll have to show you my high school diploma."

Meanwhile, Lyuba's mother and sister-in-law had driven Lyuba into the corner with their questions.

"Whatever made you take him to the tearoom?" shrilly queried the highly vocal Zoya, a woman given to hysteria. "Why, the whole village knows already: some jailbird came to see Lyubka! They all told me about it at work."

"Oh, Lyubka, Lyubka!..." her mother persisted in a quaking voice. "Tell him this, see: if you came here just to put on some fat and then afterward go into the world again, then—tell him—he should go away this very day and not shame you in front of everyone. Tell him, if he..."

"How could it be possible that he doesn't have a family someplace?

Think about it. He's not some kid of seventeen, is he? Use your head."

"Tell him this: tell him, if he means to do something bad, then he should just gather up his things and..."

"What things? All he needs to do is tighten his belt and he'll be ready to go," put in the old man, who until then had been silent. "What are you jumping on the girl for? What do you expect to get out of her? Let's just see what happens, see what sort of fellow he turns out to be. How in hell can she answer for him now?"

"Don't frighten me, for the love of Christ," was all that Lyuba could say to her mother and sister-in-law. "I'm already frightened. Do you think this is easy for me?"

"There! That's just what I'm trying to tell you!" exclaimed Zoya.

"Here's what to do, dearie... Are you listening, Lyuba?" the old woman continued with her pestering. "Tell him this: see here, my good man, go away today and spend the night someplace else."

"And where would that be?" asked Lyuba, feeling numb.

"In the village meeting hall."

"Phoo!" said the old man, disgusted. "Have you all gone completely off your rockers, or what? Look, you can't invite the guy here and then send him off to sleep at the village soviet. What a thing to do! It goes against Christ!"

"Tomorrow we can get a policeman to investigate him," persisted Lyuba's mother.

"What's to investigate? His face tells the whole story."

"I don't know," said Lyuba. "It seems to me that he's a good man. Somehow I can see it in his eyes. I already noticed it in a picture he sent me—his eyes—sort of sadlike. I don't care what you do to me—I feel sorry for him. Maybe I'm..."

Suddenly Petro leaped out of the bathhouse with a roar and rolled around on the damp ground, still holding a twig besom.

"He's boiling me!" yelled Petro. "He's boiling me alive!"

Egor ran out after him with a dipper in his hand.

They all ran out of the house toward Petro. The old man had an axe.

"Help! Murder!" screamed Zoya wildly. "Help, good people, murder!"

"Don't bellow like that," requested Petro in a pained voice, as he sat on the ground and rubbed his scalded ribs. "What's the matter with you?"

"What happened, Petya?" asked the sputtering old man.

"I asked this halfwit to splash on a dipper of hot water—to toss it on the hot stove—but instead he poured it all over me!"

"I couldn't believe my ears," said Egor, dismayed. "'How will he ever be able to stand it?' I think to myself. The water was hot as hell. I tested it with my finger—it was boiling hot! 'How can he tolerate it?' I wonder. 'Well,' I think, 'probably he's hardened to it. Probably his skin is all thick, like a bull's.' I had no idea I was supposed to throw it on the stove..."

" 'He tested it with his finger,' " mimicked Petro. "What are you, anyway—an absolute child? A little baby?"

"Well I thought you wanted to rinse yourself..."

"But I hadn't finished my steam bath!" bawled the always calm Petro. "I hadn't even washed myself!.. What would I want to get rinsed off for?"

"We'll need to smear some kind of grease on it," said Petro's father, inspecting the burn. "It's not all that bad. All we need is some sort of grease... Who's got some?"

"I've got some rendered mutton fat," said Zoya, and she ran off to the house.

"Okay, let's go back inside," commanded the old man, "before all kinds of people start showing up."

"But how could you have done that, Egor?" asked Lyuba.

Egor hitched up his shorts and again began to justify himself:

"Here's the way it happened, see: he had already got the room filled with steam so that you couldn't breathe, and then he calls out: 'A dipper of hot water!' Well, I think, he wants to balance the temperature somehow."

" 'Balance the temperature,' " mimicked Petro again. "What I ought to do is balance you—with a dipper on the forehead! What a halfwit—he scalded my whole side! And suppose the water had really been boiling?"

"I tested it with my finger..."

" 'With my finger,' he says. What you need is a good..."

"Okay, hit me on the forehead, then," pleaded Egor. "That'll make me feel better." He handed Petro a dipper. "Please. Hit me. I mean it..."

"Petro..." said Lyuba. "It was just an accident. Forget it now."

"Go on back to the house, for God's sake!" said Petro, now angry at everybody. "Look up there—people really starting to gather!"

In fact, there were six or seven curious neighbors standing at the Baikalovs' fence.

"What happened?" asked a man who had just come up.

"Petro, their son here, got drunk and fell on the stove," explained some old woman.

"Oy, oy!" said the man. "Is he still alive?"

"Sure, he's alive—look, he's sitting there, just coming to."

"I bet he really yelled!"

"Oh, how he yelled! My windowpanes even began to rattle!"

"Naturally he yelled..."

"Where did he get it, on his hind end?"

"What do you mean, hind end? You can see he's sitting down!"

"Yeah, that's right... He probably fell on his side. And who's that with him? What man is that?"

"He really must have got drunk!" marvelled the old woman.

It was long past midnight, and they were all still sitting up.

The old people, slightly tipsy, were talking and arguing with friends about their various common interests. There must have been above a dozen of the old folks gathered around the table. They chatted away, constantly interrupting each other, two or three always talking at once.

"Who did you say? Who did you say? No, no—she's the one who went way off to get married in... where was it? In Kraiushkino!"

"That's right. And who did she marry, again? It was..."

"Mitka Khromov. She married Mitka Khromov!"

"Right—Mitka."

"It was the Khromovs who were kulaks, had their property taken away..."

"Who'd you say got dekulaked? The Gromovs? Not on your life!"

"No, no, not the Gromovs, the Khromovs!"

"Oh, I thought he said the Gromovs. I was gonna say... I went off with Mikhailo Gromov to go lumberjacking in the taiga."

"And when old Khromov got dekulaked..."

"That's right—he used to have an oil press."

"Who had an oil press? Khromov? What are you saying? It was the Voinovs who had an oil press! Khromov's the one who drove in sheep herds from Mongolia. It was a felting machine that he had—and the Voinovs had the oil press. They were dekulaked, too. They came and got Khromov right out of his pasture. I recollect how they started to tear down his storehouse, looking for felt boots—that's where they made their felt. The whole village, I recollect, came to watch."

"Did they find any?"

"Nine pairs."

"Did they do anything to Mitka?"

"No, Mitka was already off on his own by then. Yes, that's right! He had already married Klanka. His father had set him up. Nothing happened to them. Even so, when they took his father away, Mitka moved off from Kraiushkino. It was too hard for him to live there after that."

"Wait a minute, which one of them got married in Karasuk?"

"That was Manka. And Manka's still alive. She's living in town with her daughter. It's hard for her now. I happened to meet her at the market. She's sorry she sold her house in the village. She says that while the kiddies—her grandchildren—were still little, they needed her to take care of them. But now they're all grown up and nobody needs her anymore. It's hard for her."

"That's how it is," said several of the old women at once. "When the children are little, you're needed, and when they grow up a bit, no one wants you anymore."

"It's all a matter of what kind of son-in-law you have... If he turns out to be an ingrate, then too bad for you..."

"Yes—the sort of husbands they marry nowadays... It's scandalous!"

Egor and Lyuba were sitting somewhat off to the side from the old people. Lyuba was showing him the family photograph album that she herself had made up and carefully preserved.

"And that's Mikhail," said Lyuba, pointing to her brother. "And that's Pavel and Vanya together. They were in the war together at first, but then Pasha got wounded. When he was all healed up, he went back. And that time he got killed. Vanya was killed last, in Berlin. His commanding officer sent us a letter... I feel the saddest over Vanya—he was always so cheerful. He took me around with him everywhere. I was little then, but I remember him so well... I still dream about him; he's always laughing. Look, he's laughing in the picture. And here's our Petro... Look how stern he is, and he was only... how old was he then? Eighteen? Yes, eighteen. he was captured, then our soldiers freed him. They beat him up bad in the camp... But otherwise he never got a scratch."

Egor raised his head and looked over at Petro. Petro was sitting alone, smoking. You couldn't tell he'd had anything to drink at all. He sat there like always, pensive and serene.

"And what I did today... splashed him. It was like the devil had pushed my hand."

Lyuba leaned over closer to Egor and asked him quietly and slyly:

"Are you sure you didn't do it on purpose? It's hard to believe that you..."

"What do you mean!" Egor exclaimed sincerely. "I really thought he wanted it on himself—that he was calling down fire on himself, as they say."

"But you're from the country, you said. You must know all about bathhouses. How could you have thought such a thing?"

"Well, people have different customs..."

"Well, I'm ashamed to say that I thought Petro had said something to you that you didn't like and you were only pretending to be dumb when you splashed him."

"What? No! I swear it!"

Petro, sensing that they were looking at him and talking about him, glanced over at them... He met Egor's eye and gave him a friendly grin.

"So, Zhorzhik, you were about to boil me?"

"I'm really sorry, Petro!"

"Never mind! Turn on your music one more time, will you? It's really good music."

Egor switched on his tape recorder. It blasted out with the same march tune that he had used to announce himself to the gang. It was a joyful and life-affirming march. It sounded strange here in the peasant cottage—it broke into the peaceful conversation with a sharp and somehow incongruous rhythm. But music is music: gradually the conversation at the table died down... And everyone sat and listened to the lively march.

Late at night, utterly quiet... The moon shone brightly through the windows.

They had put Egor in the same room with the old people, behind a flowered curtain through which the moonlight easily penetrated.

Lyuba was sleeping in the front room. The door to the room was open. In there it was also quiet.

Egor couldn't sleep. The silence was maddening.

He raised his head and listened intently... All was quiet—except for the old man's snoring and the ticking of the wall clock.

Egor snaked out from under the blanket, dazzling white in his drawers and long shirt, and silently stole into the front room. Nothing banged or creaked... The only sound was the cracking of a little bone somewhere in Egor's foot.

He was already at the door. He took another step or two into the front room, when suddenly in the silence Lyuba's sharp and not-at-all-sleepy voice rapped out:

"Okay, march right back to bed!"

Egor stopped dead. He said nothing for a moment.

"What's the matter?" he whispered in a hurt voice.

"Nothing. Lie down and go to sleep."

"I can't get to sleep."

"Lie down anyway... think about the future."

"But I just wanted to talk for a little while!" said Egor, starting to get angry. "I wanted to ask you a couple of questions..."

'We'll talk tomorrow. What sort of questions do you need to ask at night?"

"One question!" said Egor at last in an angry voice. "That's all..."

"Lyubka, grab something—grab a frying pan!" suddenly rang out behind him the voice of the old woman, also quite wide awake.

"I've got a pestle under my pillow," said Lyuba.

Egor went back to his bed.

"Oh, how he crept along on his tiptoes, the tomcat," the old woman went on. "He thought nobody was listening. But I heard everything, and saw him, too!"

"Honest John!" hissed Egor behind his flowered curtain. "Wanted to give his soul a rest! And his body! Honest John with his release papers!"

He lay back quietly... Then he turned over on his side.

"The damned moon! It's shining like a son-of-a-bitch." He turned over on his side. "They've taken up defensive positions against me! Who are they trying to protect, I wonder?"

"Come on now, stop your grumbling," said the old woman in a placating tone of voice. "He's got to grumbling and can't stop."

Suddenly Egor began to recite in a loud, clear, almost frenzied voice: "She wore a long underskirt of wide, red and blue stripes that looked as though it had been made from a theater curtain. I would have given anything to be in the front row, but the performance never took place." A pause. And then into the silence, from behind the curtain, a scholarly footnote followed: "Lichtenberg! 'Aphorisms'!"

The old man stopped snoring and asked anxiously:

"Who's there? What happened?"

"It's him over there, lying in bed and cursing," said the old woman in a disapproving voice. "He didn't get to sit in the front row, he says."

"It's not me that's cursing," exclaimed Egor, "but Lichtenberg!"

"I'll give you something to curse about," muttered the old man. "What the hell's going on?"

"It's not me!" exclaimed Egor in exasperation. "I was quoting Lichtenberg. And he wasn't cursing at all, he was being witty."

"Also, no doubt, a bookkeeper?" asked the old man, not without malice.

"He was a Frenchman."

"What?"

"A Frenchman!"

"Go to sleep, everybody!" said the old woman irritably. "We've all had our say now."

It became quiet. All that could be heard was the ticking of the clock on the wall.

And the moon stared in at the windows.

In the morning, after everyone had eaten breakfast and Lyuba and Egor were sitting alone at the table, Egor said:

"So now, Lyubov... I guess I'll go into the city and see about buying myself some clothes... and things. I need something to wear..."

Lyuba looked at him calmly, almost mockingly, but with a faint touch of sadness as well. She remained silent, as though she had understood more than what Egor had said to her.

"Go, then," she said softly.

"Why are you looking at me that way?" Egor found himself gazing at Lyuba as well, she looked so nice in her morning freshness. He felt a touch of alarm at the possibility of parting from her. And he also became sad. But that made him uncomfortable. He became agitated.

"What way?" she said.

"Don't you believe me?"

Lyuba was again silent for a long time.

"Do what your heart tells you to do, Egor. Why do you ask whether I believe you or not? Whether or not I believe you—that won't stop you from going."

Egor bent down his cropped head.

"I'd rather not lie, Lyuba," said Egor resolutely. "All my life I've hated it when I lied... And I do lie, of course—and that only makes life all the harder. I lie, and I hate myself for it. I even feel like I want to do away with myself, smash my life to bits. Only, I'd like to go out in style—with a smile on my lips and a glass of vodka in my hand. So right now I'm not going to lie. All I can say is that I don't know. Maybe I'll return, maybe I won't."

"Thank you for the truth, Egor."

"You're really nice," Egor burst out. Then he began to fidget and fret even more than before. "Ah, it's all a come-on. How many times have I said that to women! Slobbering over the words. Words are worth nothing! Why do people believe them?.. Look, here's what I'll do." Egor put his hand on Lyuba's hand. "I'll go off alone and search my heart. I have to do it that way, Lyuba."

"Do what you have to do. I won't say a word. But if you go away, I'll be sad. Really sad. Probably, I'll cry." At that moment tears came into her eyes. "But I won't say anything bad against you."

Egor became quite helpless: he could not bear to see tears.

"That's enough now, Lyubov. I have to go. It's too hard for me. I ask your forgiveness."

Egor stepped out into the wide expanse of a new field... It had not yet been plowed, and pointed little shoots of grass had just begun to break through. Egor strode along briskly, resolutely, stubbornly. That was the way he had gone through life—as he did through this field—resolutely and stubbornly. He would fall, then get up and again stride along. He would push on as though in that lay his only salvation, just to go and go, never stopping, never looking back, as though in that way he might escape from himself.

And suddenly behind him, as though out of nowhere, people began to appear. They would appear and follow along behind him, barely able to keep up. These were all his friends, shabby, crumpled men and women whose venality was revealed in their eyes. All were silent. Egor was silent, too, as he kept on walking. More and more people joined the throng behind him... they walked along that way for a long time. Then Egor stopped all of a sudden and, without glancing around, vigorously waved them all away and muttered angrily through his teeth:

"No more now! That's enough!"

He looked back. Only Fat Lip was there, striding up to meet him. He smiled as he walked along. And he kept his hand in his pocket. Egor clenched his teeth more firmly and put his own hands in his pockets... And Fat Lip disappeared.

... Egor stood by the road and waited to see whether a bus or some chance automobile might not come along and take him into the city.

In the distance a truck came into view.

Lyuba worked all that day in a daze... Her feelings kept getting the better of her. She unexpectedly confessed to her girlfriend, after they had finished the milking chores and were walking out of the cattle yard:

"You know, Verka, I've really got stuck on the guy..." She surprised herself by saying such a thing. "I can't help it! My heart has been aching and aching all day."

"Did he leave for good or not? What did he tell you?"

"He said he didn't know himself what he was going to do."

"Tell him to go to the devil. He's not worth spitting on! 'He doesn't know himself.' That means he's got a wife someplace. What does he say about that?"

"I don't know. All he says is that he has no one."

"He's lying, Lyubka—don't be a fool: take your Kolka back and live with him again. They all drink nowadays anyway! Who do you know that doesn't? Mine came home the day before yesterday... that worm!" And Verka, a lively little woman, confided in a whisper: "He came inside, and crack!—I conked him with a rolling pin! I even frightened myself! In the morning he gets up and says, 'My head aches, I must have bumped it someplace.' I say to him: 'You shouldn't drink so much!' " And Verka began to titter.

"But how did it happen in so short a time?" Lyuba continued to marvel at her own thoughts.

"What?" asked the puzzled Verka.

"How did I ever manage it, I say, in so short a time? Why, I saw him for only one day! How could it have happened? Is such a thing really possible?"

"What was he in prison for?"

"Burglary..." Lyuba looked at her friend helplessly.

"Out of the frying pan, into the fire," said the latter. "A drunkard for a thief. What a terrible fate, poor thing. Live alone, Lyuba. Maybe somebody halfway normal will turn up. And this other one—won't he take to stealing again? What then?"

"What then? They'll put him in jail again."

"Bite your tongue! Have you gone crazy, or what?"

"I just don't know what's happened to me. I've completely lost my head. It's disgusting even to me... And here my heart is aching and aching for him as though I've known him for a hundred years. And it's only been a day. It's true, he did send me letters for a whole year..."

"Well, they don't have anything to do there, so it's easy for them to write."

"But you should see what letters they were!"

"Love letters?"

"Oh no... All about life. He really must have seen a lot, that poor devil of a jailbird. When you read what he writes—it's enough to break your heart. I don't even know myself whether I love him, or pity him. All I know is that my heart is aching."

Meanwhile, Egor was attending to his affairs in the regional capital. The very first thing he did was buy some stylish duds.

He walked down the wooden sidewalk of the wooden provincial town: brand new suit, necktie and hat, hands in his pockets.

He stopped in at the post office, got a telegram blank, wrote down an address, a sum of money to be sent and a few words of greeting. He handed in the blank, leaned on the counter near the window and began to count out the money.

"Give the money to fatlip," the girl behind the counter read out. "Fatlip—is that someone's last name, perhaps?"

Egor thought for a couple of seconds and said:

"Absolutely correct, someone's last name."

"Well, why did you write it with small letters then? And what a funny name!"

"There's others that are worse," said Egor. "Down in the plant we had a guy named Pistonov."[4]

The girl raised her head. She was as cute as could be, with great big eyes and a little turned-up nose.

"So?"

"Nothing. His name, he said, was Pistonov." Egor was very serious, to go with the hat he was wearing.

"Well, that's a normal enough name."

"Yes, in general, quite normal." Egor agreed. And suddenly he forgot he was wearing a hat and grinned. And then he became rather self-conscious. "Excuse me, please," he said, sticking his head in the window, "see... I just got in town from the gold fields, and I don't know a single soul here..."

"So?" said the girl, not following him.

"Look, do you have a boyfriend?" asked Egor bluntly.

"Why do you want to know?" The cute little snubnose did not seem to be very put off and even looked up from her work to stare at Egor.

"What I had in mind was, maybe you and me could paint the town red together."

"Citizen!" the girl admonished, raising her voice sharply. "Mind your manners! This is a public place. Either send your money order, or get out!"

Egor crawled back out of the window. He was insulted. Why the hell had she looked up at him with her big eyes, then? Egor simply couldn't get it out of his head: one minute she was looking at him tenderly, and the next she was snapping his head off. What the hell was this phoney-baloney, anyway?

"Leading me on that way!" he grumbled indignantly. "'Citizen!' How am I 'citizen' to you? To you I'm comrade, and even friend and brother."

The girl again looked up at him with her big gray eyes.

"Back to work, back to work," said Egor. "Don't be making eyes all the time."

The girl hmphed and bent over the telegram blank again.

"And what a stupid hat he put on!" she could not refrain from remarking, not looking at Egor.

She handed him a receipt, also without looking at him. She put the receipt on the counter and turned to other matters, from which she absolutely refused to be distracted.

"Ah, these broads," raged Egor, as he left the post office. "You just wait! You'll be doing the dance of the little swans for me yet! Cracow style!" He strode off toward the railroad station restaurant. "The butterfly polka!" Egor kept working himself up. In his eyes appeared an uneasy glint that bore witness to the hurt that he felt. It pained him inside his chest. He quickened his step. "No, dammit, it's too much! These dames, these Little Red Riding Hoods... Watch out, because I'm going to put on a little figure-skating show in this town! I'm going to electrify the atmosphere in this place and open up a whorehouse!" After that he mumbled nothing but nonsense, anything that flew into his head: "Ta-rum-pum-pum, ta-rum-pum-pum, ta-rum-pum-pum-pum-pum."

In the restaurant he ordered a bottle of champagne, handed the sharp-looking waiter a twenty-five ruble note and said:

"Thanks. Keep the change."

The waiter was overcome.

"Thank you very much, oh, thank you..."

"It's nothing," said Egor, and motioned for the waiter to sit down for a minute. The waiter took a chair. "I've just got in from the gold fields," Egor went on, as he studied the obliging young fellow, "and I wanted to ask you... is there someplace around here where we could organize a nice little whorehouse?"

The waiter automatically looked around behind him...

"Well, I'm expressing myself rather crudely... I'm worried, because all this money is burning a hole in my pocket." Egor pulled out a rather thick wad of ten-and-twenty-five-ruble notes. "What say? I've got to use them up. What's your name, by the way?"

On seeing the money, the waiter began to lick his lips, but he restrained himself, held onto his dignity. He knew that people with dignity got paid more.

"Sergei Mikhailovich."

"Well, Mikhailych... I need a holiday. I've been up north a long time..."

"I think I can come up with something," said Mikhailych, after first putting on a thoughtful expression for a couple of minutes. "Where are you staying?"

"Nowhere. I just arrived."

"In all probability, something can be arranged... A nice little picnic, so to speak, in honor of your arrival."

"Right, right, right," said Egor, getting excited. "A cozy little cat-house. A nice private bordello... We'll have ourselves a party, right, Mikhailych? There was something about you I liked the minute I laid eyes on you! I thought to myself—here's somebody I can rumple up my money with."

Mikhailych broke into sincere laughter.

"What's so funny?" asked Egor.

"Hokay!" said Mikhailych gaily in English. "Got you."

Late that evening Egor was lying on a plush divan and talking on the telephone with Lyuba. Mikhailych was in the room, too, and a sharp-nosed woman with a wart on her temple kept walking in to consult with Mikhailych in a low voice.

"Hey! Lyubasha!" shouted Egor. "It's me! I'm in the military registration office. I didn't have time to get registered. What? It's late?... Well, they put in late hours here. Yes, yes..." Egor nodded at Mikhailych. "Yes, Lyubasha!"

Mikhailych opened the door of the room, slammed it noisily, and loudly stomped past Egor, shouting as he drew near:

"Comrade Captain! May I see you for a minute?!"

Egor nodded his head at Mikhailych in approval and continued to talk, while Mikhailych pretended to go off into gales of silent laughter.

"But, Lyubasha, what can I do? I'll probably have to stay overnight here. Yes, yes..." Egor listened for a long time, kept saying "yes, yes" while grinning proudly and happily at the play-acting Mikhailych. He even covered the mouthpiece once and said: "She says she's worried. She's been waiting for me."

"Wait, wait..." began the accommodating Mikhailych, but Egor stopped him with a glance.

"Yes, Lyubushka darling!... Just keep talking. I love to hear your beautiful voice. It gets me all excited!"

"He's too much!" whispered Mikhailych in feigned delight. "It gets him excited!" He began to laugh again, but rather hoarsely, unconvincingly, as he bared his gold teeth. He was trying as hard as he could, since Egor had promised to pay well for the party.

"Where will I spend the night? Oh, right here someplace, on the couch, I guess... It's okay, I can sleep anywhere—I'm used to it. Don't worry about it, now. Yes, my little darling, my little sweetheart!" Egor said this so sincerely and tenderly that Mikhailych even forgot to pretend to laugh. "I'll see you soon, dearest. So long, now. Here's a kiss for you... Okay, I understand, I understand. Goodbye."

Egor hung up the receiver and looked at Mikhailych strangely for a time—as though he didn't even see him. At that moment it was as if a tender, invisible hand were stroking Egor's face, which gradually lost its habitual look of hardness and truculence.

"Yes," said Egor, returning to himself. "Well, then, innkeeper, shall we get on with the orgy? How are things in back?"

"Everything's ready."

"Did you find me a dressing gown?"

"Yes, more or less... We had to borrow it from some old actor. Nobody had one!"

"Let's have it!" Egor donned the long, quilted robe which had several worn places. He looked down at himself.

"You can't get them anywhere anymore," said Mikhailych, trying to excuse himself.

"It's a good robe," approved Egor. "Well, have you followed all my orders?"

Mikhailych left the room.

Egor reclined on the couch with a cigarette.

Mikhailych returned and announced:

"The people have assembled for the orgy!"

"Let's go," nodded Egor.

Mikhailych flung open the door... And Egor in his dressing gown, just barely inclining his head, swept off like Caligula to debauch himself.

The "debauchers" were a strange group—most of them decidedly old. There were some women, but these were all remarkably homely and wretched-looking. They were all seated at a richly-laden table, staring at

Egor in bewilderment. Egor was noticeably taken aback, but quickly composed himself.

"Why is everybody so sad?!" said Egor loudly and cheerfully, as he proceeded to the head of the table. He paused, gazing at them all attentively.

"Yes, he said, the words tumbling out of him. "Tonight we'll tear out our sorrow by its tail! Pour the drinks!"

"Dear fellow," one of the guests addressed him, a middle-aged, almost doddering man. "Tell us, what are we celebrating here? Some special occasion, or what?"

Egor pondered for a moment.

"We are gathered here," began Egor softly, thoughtfully, as at a funeral, glancing at the bottles of champagne, "in order to..." And suddenly he raised his head and studied them all once more. Again his face was released from its harshness and tension. "Brothers and sisters," he said withs feeling, "my soul has just been shaken by a tender experience. I realize my beautiful words mean nothing to you, but let me say them, nevertheless." Egor spoke seriously, forcefully, even ceremonially. He even paced up and down, as far as the room would permit, continuing to look at them all. "Spring..." he went on. "Soon the little flowers will begin to bloom. The birch trees will turn green." Egor suddenly choked up completely and had to stop. He could still hear the sweetly natural voice of Lyuba, and this distracted him.

"It won't be long until Trinity Sunday," said someone at the table.

"You can go out now and walk and walk," said Egor, "through a little clearing deep into the woods, down into a ravine where a brook is bubbling... Am I making sense? Because I'm like a jerk!" Egor got genuinely angry at himself. and then the words began to pour out of him, loud and angry, as though a crowd of hecklers were standing in front of him. "You all took me for a fool, didn't you? Three hundred rubles, and I just threw it to the wind! But what if it just so happens that I love everybody today? I feel tender and loving today, like the most... like a cow that has just calved! So what if the orgy fell flat? Who needs it? Better off without it. But don't misunderstand me—I'm not stupid and I'm not a fool. And if anyone thinks he can do what he wants with me just because I'm tenderhearted— he'll get a surprise from me. Dear people! Let's love one another." Egor was almost shouting now and beating himself on the chest. "Well, why are we rustling around here like spiders in a jar? Do you know how easily they die?! I don't understand you..." Egor walked down the length of the table. "I don't understand! I refuse to understand! And I don't understand myself, either—because every night I dream about market stalls and suitcases. But no more! Go out and do your own thieving... I'm going to sit down on a stump and I'm going to sit there thirty and three years. I'm just joking. I feel sorry for you. I also feel sorry for myself. But if someone else were to pity me or stupidly fall in love with me, I would... I don't know, I'd feel sad, I couldn't stand it. I feel wonderful, and my heart is bursting—but I feel terrible, too. I'm frightened! It's a hell of a thing..." confided Egor quietly, unexpectedly in conclusion. He paused with bowed head, then looked kindly at everyone and commanded: "Everybody take a bottle of champagne! Have you got them? Okay! Unseal them now—and shoot off the corks all at once!"

Everyone responded, began to chatter... Amid the sounds of approval and general hubbub, the bottles exploded.

"Pour it out quick, before it bubbles over!" ordered Egor.

"Ah, right... it's gushing away. Give me a glass! Hey, friend, a glass. Hurry!"

"Hey, damn you!... You spilled some!"

"Spilled some?"

"Yes—a pity, it's so good."

"What cheerful stuff it is. Look, how it bubbles and boils! From the fermenting. They must keep it a long time."

"Well, of course! With this stuff they try to..."

"And listen to it fizz!"

"My dears!" said Egor, with genuine tenderness and pity. "I am happy that you have perked up and started to smile, that you like my champagne. I love you all more and more!"

They were all too embarrassed to look Egor in the face, with all that muddle-headed nonsense he was spilling out. They got quiet while he talked and stared at their wine glasses.

"Drink up!" said Egor.

They drank up.

"Down the hatch—again! Drink up!"

Again they perked up and began to jabber. It was certainly a strange celebration—and all for free.

"Ooh, it just keeps on fizzing and fizzing."

"But weaker now. The strength is gone."

"Yes, indefinite, sort of."

"Ah?"

"It looks like horse piss, but the taste of it, you can't tell what it is."

"It sticks in your throat, kind of... Does it stick in your throat, too?"

"Yes, it feels like it's foaming all away in there."

"Right, and it gets all up your nose, too! Drink up—it's good!"

"That's the proof that foams away like that."

"What do you mean, 'proof'? This stuff is no stronger than kvass. That's gas escaping, not 'proof.'"

"Okay, forget the champagne!" commanded Egor. "Now grab the bottles of cognac!"

"What's the hurry?"

"I want us to start singing some songs."

"That we can do!"

"Open the cognac!"

They opened it. Everyone did as he was told.

"Pour only half a glass each! You don't drink cognac in large amounts. And if anybody says that cognac smells like bedbugs, I'll hit him over the head with a bottle. Drink up!"

They drank up.

"Sing a song!" commanded Egor.

"But we haven't eaten yet..."

"They're starting in against me," said Egor, offended, and sat down. "Okay, then. Eat. All they want to do is stuff themselves. That's all they can think about..."

Some of the more punctilious guests put down their forks and stared in puzzlement at Egor.

"Eat, eat!" said Egor. "What's the matter with you?"

"But you should eat, too, or else you'll get drunk."

"I won't get drunk. You eat."

"Go to hell, then!" loudly protested a large, bald-headed man. "You invite us to a party and then you start criticizing us. But I know for myself—there's no way I can drink without eating, or I'll be under the table in a second. It's boring that way. Nobody wants to drink that way..."

"Well, eat then!"

Meanwhile, in the village, Lyuba's mother and father were pestering Lyuba with questions. They wouldn't let the poor thing alone.

"How could that be? Do you mean to say they don't close the registration office at night?" the old woman wanted to know.

Lyuba herself was lost in conjecture. She didn't know whether to believe that story about the registration office or not. Yet, she herself had talked with Egor, had heard his voice, listened to what he said... Even now, she couldn't stop talking to him in her mind: "Well, Egor, with you it's never boring. What are you up to now, I wonder?"

"Lyubka?"

"What?"

"What sort of registration office is that? You know very well all those places close up at night."

"Well, evidently not, since he said he was spending the night there..."

"A likely story! You can't believe what that one says."

"Here's what I think," said the old man. "They told him: 'Come here tomorrow at eight o'clock—sharp.' That's the way those army people are. And he decided it was better to spend the night in town than have to go all the way out there again tomorrow morning."

"That's exactly what he said," said Lyuba joyfully. " 'I'm going to spend the night here,' he said, 'on the couch.' "

"But all those official places close up at night!" insisted the old woman. "Are you both daft? How could they leave him alone there all night? He'd steal one of their rubber stamps for sure."

"Mama!"

The old man also curled his lip at such stupidity:

"What in hell would he need a rubber stamp for?"

"Well, it appears I can't say a word around here! No sooner say something, than they jump down your throat!"

Egor was organizing the debauchers into a choir.

"We'll start up a melody," he said, pulling at the bald man, "and you all over there, as soon as I wave my hand, you start singing 'bom-bom.' Okay, start:

"Those evening bells... Those evening bells..."

"Egor waved his hand, but the "bom-bom" group didn't respond.

"What's the matter with you?! I told you, as soon as I wave, you go 'bom-bom.' "

"But when you waved, you were still singing yourself."

"Just chime in anyway. I began to wail because I thought I was hearing church bells from long ago. I'm so homesick, I feel like I'm dying. So I started to sing real soft. But you just do your 'bom-bom' and don't worry about it... There's no way for you to know how sad I feel—that's not your problem."

"It's like someone in jail, pining like that," suggested Mikhailych. "Or a prisoner-of-war camp somewhere."

"What sort of churches do they have in prisoner-of-war camps?" someone objected.

"Why not? They've got churches over there, too. Not exactly like ours, of course, but all the same—a church with a bell. Right, Georgii?"

"Damn you all! All you know how to do is yammer!" said Egor, really angry now. "They start in talking and can't stop. I swear they've got diarrhea of the mouth!"

"Never mind. Let's start again. Don't get all worked up over it!"

"How can I keep from getting worked up, when I tell you something and you won't do it? Oh well, let's go now:

"Those evening bells... Those evening bells..."

"Bom... bom... bom." The bells in the tower rang helter-skelter and all off key, spoiling everything.

Egor waved his hands in disgust and went into the next room. He paused in the doorway and said despairingly:

"Sing anything you want. Don't get sore, but I can't take you all anymore. Just have a good time without me. Sing one of your own songs, why don't you?"

The "bom-bom" group, and all the others, too, fell into confused silence... But there was so much wine and fantastically tasty food on the table that their grief was short-lived—just enough to appease their consciences.

"What's with him?"

"You don't even know how to sing 'bom-bom'!" Mikhailych chided them all. "What's so hard about that?"

"Yeah, it came out off key..."

"That was Kirill's fault... He started too soon."

"Who started too soon?" said Kirill, insulted. "I sang normal—just like somebody was ringing a bell. I certainly know you can't hurry that up. Because a bell—first you have to swing it."

"Well, who came in too soon then?"

"Forget it! Why hash that over now? Let's have a good time—like he told us to do."

"It seems like we didn't deserve to be yelled at—because maybe I don't even know how to sing. How am I going to sing like some canary, if I wasn't even born with a good voice?"

Egor, disgruntled, was reclining on the couch when Mikhailych walked in.

"I'm really sorry, Georgii, that we didn't do it right—with the bells."

Egor was silent for a minute, then asked peevishly:

"And how come they were all so ugly?"

Mikhailych was completely dismayed.

"Well, look, Georgii—all the good-looking ones are married, with families. I only got the single ones—like you told me."

Egor sat for awhile longer. Gradually his face began to brighten. His heart seemed to beat faster, as though he were recalling some joyous thing.

"Can you get me a taxi?"

"Sure."

"To Yasnoe. I'll pay whatever he wants. Go ahead and call!" Egor got up, threw off the dressing gown, put his jacket on and straightened his tie.

"But why to Yasnoe?"

"I've got a friend there." And he again began to pace about in agitation. "My soul... I feel like turnpentine's been poured on it, Mikhailych. It's going to lead me off God knows where. As soon as it smells freedom, I have to get moving. Call the taxi! How many people did you collect?"

"Fifteen. Seventeen counting the two of us. What about it?"

"Here's two hundred for you. Give each of them a ten spot and you keep the rest. Don't cheat! I'm going to come back and check up."

"Georgii, I wouldn't do that!.."

Egor flew through the bright, moonlit night along the wide highway—toward the village, toward Lyuba.

"What am I doing? What am I doing?" Egor tortured himself. "What's the matter with me?" He was possessed by anxiety and excitement. He couldn't remember when he'd been so shaken up by a skirt.

"Well, what's the story on family life these days?" he asked the taxi driver. "What's the latest thing they're writing about it?"

"Writing where?" asked the confused driver.

"In general—in books."

"In books they write all sorts of things," said the taxi driver with a frown. "In books, everything's okay."

"And in life?"

"In life... What's the matter, don't you know how it is in life?"

"Bad, right?"

"Bad for who?"

"Well, you, for instance?"

The taxi driver shrugged his shoulders—very much like the fellow who had sold Egor the tape recorder.

"What's the matter with all of you!... Brothers, I swear I don't understand you. Why are you all so sour on life?" said Egor in amazement.

"What do you want me to do, giggle at you? What do I have to do to satisfy you?"

"Satisfy me! You'd better save that for your old woman!" And make sure you know how to do it, too. Or else you'll crawl up on her and she'll say: 'Get away from me, you smell like a goat!' "

The taxi driver began to laugh:

"Is that what they say to you?"

"No. I don't like the way goats smell, either... Say, roll the window down a little, will you?"

The driver glanced at Egor, but kept silent.

Egor again returned to his own thoughts, which he simply could not get straightened out. His head was all in a muddle—on account of this Lyuba.

They drove up to the big, dark house and Egor sent the taxi on its way. Suddenly he panicked. He stood at the gate with his bottles of cognac and didn't know what to do. He walked around the house and entered Petro's gate; he walked through the garden, went up on the porch and kicked the door with his foot. It was quiet for a long time, but then a door creaked, someone in bare feet came walking down the entrance hall, and Petro's voice called out:

"Who's there?"

"It's me, Petro. Georgii. Zhorzhik..."

The door opened.

"What do you want?" said the astonished Petro. "Did they kick you out, or what?"

"No, no... I didn't want to wake them up. Listen, did you ever drink any Remy Martin?"

Petro stood silent for a long time, gazing into Egor's face.

"Drink what?"

"Remy Martin. Twenty rubles a bottle. Shall we go hole up in the bathhouse with it?"

"Why the bathhouse?"

"So we won't disturb anybody."

"Let's just sit in the kitchen..."

"No, I don't want to wake anyone."

"Well, let me get some shoes on, then... And I'll bring out something to eat, too."

"Don't bother with that! All my pockets are full of chocolate—I stink of it, like some college girl."

Into the small dark world of the bathhouse a moonbeam made its way through a window and left a patch of light on the floor. Petro and Egor also lit a lantern. They sat down by the window.

"Why the hell didn't you come home?" asked Petro.

"I don't know. You see, Petro..." Egor started to say, but then fell silent. He opened one of the bottles and set it on the window sill. "Look— cognac. Twenty rubles a bottle! Can you believe it?!"

Petro pulled two glasses out of the pocket of his old riding breeches.

Neither of them said anything for awhile.

"I don't know what to say, Petro. I don't understand what's going on with me myself."

"Well, don't say anything, then. Pour me a glass of your precious stuff... I used to drink a little of this during the war. In Germany. It smells like bedbugs."

"It does not smell like bedbugs!" exclaimed Egor. "It's bedbugs that smell like cognac. Where do they get that, anyway, that it smells like bedbugs?"

"Maybe the good stuff doesn't smell, but the normal kind does."

The night drew on. The moon kept shining. The entire village was bathed in its pale, greenish, cadaverous light. All was quiet. No dog barked, no gate creaked. Such silence prevails in a village just before dawn. And in the steppe, too, when just at dawn the fog and the damp imperceptibly collect in the low places. Quiet and chill.

And suddenly in this silence there was heard from the bathhouse:

"I sit behind bars in the damp and the gloom..."

Egor sang first and then Petro joined in. It came out so unexpectedly beautiful, so sonorous and sad, that it made you want to cry:

"And feed a young eagle that lives in my cell—
My unhappy comrade who stretches his wings
And pecks at the meat that has brought him to hell..."

Early that morning Egor accompanied Lyuba to the dairy farm. He just fell in next to her and walked along. He was dressed in his fancy suit again and wearing his hat and tie. But he was rather quiet and pensive. Lyuba was overjoyed that he was walking with her—she was in a radiant mood. And the morning was lovely—cool and clear. It was springtime indeed, no doubt about it.

"Why so mournful, Egorsha?" asked Lyuba.

"Oh, just..." Egor mumbled vaguely.

"They hid away in the bathhouse," laughed Lyuba. "And they weren't even afraid! Ever since I was a little girl, you couldn't get me to go in there at night for anything!"

That surprised Egor:

"Why not?"

" 'Cause devils are in there! That's where they hatch out, in the bathhouse!"

Egor looked at Lyuba in tender amazement... And quite unintentionally he brushed his hand along her back.

"That's right: don't ever go in the bathhouse at night. Or else those devils... I know all about them!"

"When you drove up last night in the car, I heard you. I thought it was my saintly Kolenka coming home."[5]

"What Kolenka?"

"Why, my husband."

"Ah. And does he come back now and then?"

"That he does."

"Well? What do you do then?"

"I lock myself in the front room and sit there. He never comes when he's sober and when he's drunk I can't stand to look at him. He turns into a complete fool. It's disgusting. I begin to shake all over."

Egor's heart beat faster upon hearing these genuinely angry words. He could not bear despondency, spinelessness and abasement in people. Perhaps that was why he had been led so far off the beaten track in life, why he had always from early youth been attracted to people who were sharply drawn. Sometimes they were drawn with crooked lines—but always with sharp definition.

"Yes, yes, yes," said Egor, affecting sympathy with Lyuba. "It's a real affliction, with those alcoholics."

"Yes, an affliction!" affirmed the openhearted Lyuba. "But a very bitter one, with constant tears and cursing."

"An out and out tragedy... Oy, oy!" said Egor in surprise. "Look at all the cows!"

"The dairy farm... This is where I work."

Egor stood as though rooted to the ground upon seeing the cows.

"Look at them... those cows," he repeated. "Look, they saw you, didn't they: They're all excited. See how they roll their eyes at you..." Egor fell silent. Then all at once, in spite of himself, he began to talk in a rush. "All I can remember from my whole childhood is my mother and our cow. We called the cow Manka. One spring, in April, we let her out of the fence so she could pick up old hay on the road. You know, it drops off the carts in the winter and then shows up along the roads and fences when the snow melts in the spring. Well, somebody stuck a pitchfork in her belly. She had gone inside somebody's fence—a few people still had some hay. They punched a hole in her—she came home dragging her guts on the ground."

Lyuba stared at Egor, much struck by the artless narrative. It was apparent that Egor was sorry he had come out with this story. He was displeased with himself.

"Why are you looking at me?"

"Oh, Egorsha..."

"Forget it," said Egor. "It's just words. Words aren't worth anything."

"You didn't make the story up, did you?"

"No, no! Why should I? But you shouldn't take people so seriously. Listen to them, but take what they say with a grain of salt. You're too trusting..." Egor looked at Lyuba and again tenderly, solicitously, hesitantly stroked her back. "Have you really never been deceived by anyone?"

"No—who would ever do that?"

"Hmmm." Egor gazed into the clear eyes of this woman and grinned. What a nightmare—all he wanted to do was touch her and look at her all the time.

"Oh, look, the director of the sovkhoz is coming," said Lyuba. "He must have been at our cow barn." She became quite animated and smiled broadly, without even fully realizing it.

Walking toward them came a well-nourished, sturdy-looking fellow, still rather young—perhaps about the same age as Egor. He walked with a firm, proprietary stride, looked with curiosity at Lyuba and her—who was he? her husband? a friend?...

"Why are you smiling all over your face like that?" said Egor in unpleasant surprise.

"He does a good job of running things. We respect him. Hello there, Dmitry Vladimirovich! Have you come by to see us?"

"Yes, I have. Hello!" The director firmly shook Egor's hand. "You aren't one of the replacements, are you?"

"Dmitry Vladimirovich—he's a chauffeur," said Lyuba, not without pride.

"Oh, yes? Good. Can I put him behind the wheel right away? Does he have a license?"

"He doesn't have his passport yet," Lyuba's pride vanished.

"Too bad. He could have come with me right now. My own driver was called up by the military registration office for some reason. I'm afraid he'll be gone a long time."

"Oh, Egor!" said Lyuba, getting all excited. "Why don't you go with him? You'll get to see our district and have a chance to look around."

And that animated excitement, those absurd words—about "getting to see the district"—induced Egor to do something that five minutes earlier he would have laughed at the very thought of.

"Let's go," he said. And he went off with the director.

"Egor!" Lyuba shouted off after him. "You'll be eating dinner at a tearoom somewhere! Where will you be... Dmitry Vladimirovich, you'll have to suggest a place to him, because he doesn't know where to go."

Dmitry Vladimirovich laughed.

Egor looked back at Lyuba for a minute, then turned around and followed the director, who had been waiting for him.

"Where are you from?" asked the director.

"Who, me? From around here. Your district—the village of Listvianka."

"Listvianka? We don't have any such village."

"What do you mean? Sure you do."

"No we don't. I know my district."

"That's strange... What happened to it?" Egor didn't like the director: smug and sleek. The smug part especially rubbed him the wrong way. He couldn't stand smug people. "There was a village called Listvianka here. I remember it well."

The director looked at Egor thoughtfully.

"Well, could be," he said. "Probably it burned down."

"Yes, it probably burned down. Too bad—it was a nice little village." So you're going to come along with me?"

"Yes. That's what we decided, if I understood you correctly."

And so they drove off over the wide-open fields of the giant sovkhoz— a state farm worth a million rubles.

"Why did you start off with me that way?"

"What way?"

"Pretending you were some local yokel. Why?"

"I don't like it when people start right in on your biography. What's a biography?—just words that anyone can make up."

"How do you mean? How is it possible to 'make up' your biography?"

"How? Like with me for instance: I don't have any documents except for one paper, and nobody knows me around here—so I just say whatever I please about myself. If you really want to know, I'm the son of a public prosecutor."

The director gave a laugh. He didn't like Egor, either: too irrationally belligerent, somehow.

"What's the matter? I'm wearing a hat and tie, aren't I?" Egor glanced at himself in the mirror. "Why couldn't I be a prosecutor's son?"

"I'm not going to ask for any documents. I'm even letting you drive without a licence. But what shall we do if we run into a police inspector?"

"You're the boss."

They pulled up at the apiary. The director jumped lightly out of the vehicle.

"I'll just be a minute. Or if you want to, you can come with me. The old man will give you some honey."

"No, thanks." Egor had also got out. "I'll just stay here... and admire the view."

"Look all you want." And the director went off.

Egor indeed began to admire the view. He gazed all around, and then he walked over to a birch tree and touched it.

"Well? Are you starting to get green yet? It won't be long now... You'll be able to put your clothes on. You must be tired of standing there naked. Soon you'll look beautiful—all dressed up."

The old beekeeper came out of his hut.

"Why don't you come on in?" he shouted from the stoop. "Come in and have a glass of tea!"

"Thanks anyway, pop. I don't feel like it."

"Well, look around then." And the old man went back inside.

Soon the director came out, accompanied by the old man.

"Drop in more often," the latter said politely. "Drink some tea for the road. You pass by here a lot."

"Thanks, dad, I appreciate it. Time to go now."

They drove off.

"Look," said the director, putting a package of some kind down between the seats. "This is interesting stuff—propolis, a sort of glue used by bees."

"For curing stomach ulcers?"

"Right. Have you had ulcers, then?" the director turned towards him.

"No, I've just heard about the stuff."

"Yes. Well, one of our men got an ulcer. I'm trying to help him—a good man."

"They say it really works."

A village came into view up ahead.

"Let me out at the club," said the director, "and then go to Sosnovka—seven kilometers from here—and pick up the brigade leader Savelev and bring him here. If he's not at home, ask where he is and find him."

Egor nodded.

He let the director out at the club and drove off.

Men and woman, boys and girls all began to gather at the club. Some of the older people came up, too. They were getting ready to have some sort of meeting. They surrounded the director and he said something to them in his usual confident and self-satisfied manner.

The young people had gathered off to the side, where they were also holding a lively conversation. They frequently broke into laughter.

The old men stood smoking by the fence.

Large banners had been hung across the front of the clubhouse. Everything pointed to a familiar celebration.

The clubhouse was new, just recently built: near the foundation lay a pile of bricks and the bed of an old dump truck containing hardened cement.

Egor drove up with the brigade leader Savelev and went off to find the director. They told him the director was already in the club, sitting on the stage at the table reserved for the presidium.

Egor walked across the main room where the sovkhoz workers were sitting, climbed up on the stage and walked around behind the director.

The director was conversing with some broad-shouldered man and shaking a piece of paper. Egor touched his sleeve.

"Vladimirych..."

"Well? Did you bring him? Good. You can go now."

"No, it's not that..." Egor called the director off to the side, and when they had got to where no one could hear them, he said: "Can you drive a car yourself?"

"Sure. What's the problem?"

"I can't do it anymore. You'll have to drive back yourself. I'm not up to it. And there's no way I can make myself do it. That I know."

"But what's the matter... Did you get sick, or what?"

"I just can't drive people around anymore. I agree—I'm a fool, irresponsible and politically backward... I'm just a worthless ex-con—a *zek*—

but I still can't do it. I feel all the time as though I'm laughing at you. It would be better if I drove a dump truck. Or a tractor! Okay? Don't be sore at me. You're a good guy, but... The thing is, I really feel bad right now, so I'm going." And Egor quickly stepped down from the stage. As he walked across the auditorium, he berated himself for having prattled away like a fool to the director. He'd become a regular chatterbox... all that apologizing. But why apologize? Just tell him I can't, and that's the end of it. But no, he'd had to go and explain, and justify himself and even slobber about his "backwardness." Phooey! Egor had a rancid taste in his mouth. This was the way you became an ass-kisser—little by little. By going up and looking them in the eye... Tfoo! What a bitter pill to swallow!

The director, meanwhile, was watching Egor as he walked across the room. He didn't fully understand what had happened. That is, he understood nothing.

Egor passed through a little wood on his way back.

He came out into a clearing, crossed it, and entered another wooded area where the trees were thicker.

Then he walked down into a little ravine where a brook was bubbling. He stopped above the brook.

"I knew you had to be here!" he said.

He stood there for a long time, then jumped over the stream and climbed up the hill on the other side...

And there spread out before his eyes was a birch grove: the entire numerous family of trees seemed to run up and greet him.

"Ah, you!" he said.

And he walked into the grove.

He strolled among the birches... He took off his necktie and tied it around one of the most beautiful, one of the whitest and most graceful trees. Then he noticed a high stump right next to it and placed his hat on it. He stepped back and admired them from the side.

"What a pair of squares!" he said. And he walked on farther. But for a long time he kept looking back at this natty couple, smiling the while. He felt a lot better now.

Back at Lyuba's house, Egor walked from one corner of the room to the other, completely lost in thought. He was smoking. From time to time he would suddenly begin to sing: "Tell me, pretty maidens, why do you love the handsome lads?" Then he would stop singing and stand still, gazing out the window or staring at the wall... And then he would start pacing again, seized once more by fretful impatience—as though he had just about made up his mind about something, but couldn't make the final decision for the life of him. He kept stewing and stewing and fretting.

"Don't worry yourself to death, Egor," said the old man. He was also pacing the room—over to the door and back, braiding unbleached thread into a trot line. He threw the line through an old mitten. "It's no worse to be a tractor driver. Probably even better. Look at all the money they make now!"

"I'm not all that worried."

"I'll be done braiding this soon. Then when the water clears a little we can go down and set out the trot line. That's something I really like to do."

"Yeah, me, too. Nothing I like better than setting out trot lines."

"Right. Some people would rather use a seine. But a seine, I don't know... They get caught too easy, and after a while you get worn out with the damned thing, untangling it, tossing it out again—it takes up too much time."

"Yeah, it's not easy casting those nets... 'Tell me, pretty maidens...' Will Lyuba be back soon?"

The old man looked at the clock.

"She should get back home soon. Right now they're delivering the milk. As soon as they get that done, she'll be home. Listen, Gore—don't hurt her. She's our last one. Somehow you always worry more over the baby. When you have kids of your own, you'll remember what I'm telling you. She's a nice girl, a good girl—but she's had all this bad luck. Her husband turned out to be a drunk, and we only barely managed to get rid of him."

"Yeah... These alcoholics are a complete disaster! Whenever I see one, I want to put every last one of those devils in prison! Give each of 'em five years, right?"

"Well, prison's a little harsh, isn't it? But maybe for a year someplace"—the old man brightened—"in strict isolation—I'd go for that. Put all of them there together in one heap."

"And will Petro be back soon?"

"Petro? He ought to be home soon, too... Let those drunks sit there for awhile and think things over."

"Sit—nobody would mind that! Let them do a little work!" said Egor, adding wood to the fire.

"You're right! Let them go in the forest and chop trees!"

"No, down in the mines! In the forest—out in the fresh air—any fool would agree to that. No, it has to be the mines! The pits! The bottom of the shaft!"

At this point Lyuba walked in.

"Well, look who's here!" exclaimed Lyuba in surprise. "I thought they'd be gone till dark—and here he is back already."

"He left off driving the director," said her father. "Don't yell at him, though—he explained why. He gets sick when he drives a passenger car."

"Let's go talk for a bit, Lyuba," said Egor. And he led her into the front room. He seemed to have made up his mind about something.

Just then Petro drove into the yard in his dump truck and Egor walked out to meet him. He didn't get to tell Lyuba what had got him so upset.

Lyuba watched from a window while Egor and Petro talked for quite some little time; but then Egor beckoned to her and she went running out. Egor clmbed up into the cab of the dump truck and got behind the wheel.

"Are you going far?" called out the old man. He had also seen Petro hand over the truck to Egor and realized that Egor and Lyuba were evidently getting ready to drive off.

"I don't know... Egor has to go someplace," Lyuba barely had time to say as they drove off.

"Lyubka!" shouted the old man, wanting to add something, but Lyuba had already slammed the door.

"What is that Zhorzhik up to?" the old man wondered aloud. Everything's gone to hell with us now, never know what's going on..."

And soon he went over to his son's half of the house to find out where Egor had taken his daughter.

"There's a village called Sosnovka," Egor explained to Lyuba in the truck as they drove along—"nineteen kilometers from here."

"I know Sosnovka."

"An old woman called Kudelikha lives there. She lives with her daughter—but the daughter had to go to the hospital."

"Where did you learn all this?"

"Well, I just found out—I was in Sosnovka today. But that's not the point. This guy I know, see, he asked me to go see her and find out about her children—if they're still alive, where they live and so on."

"And why does he want to know all that?"

"Well—she's some kind of relation to him, an aunt or something. But here's what we'll do: when we get there, you go in... No, we'll go in together, but you ask her the questions."

"Why?"

"Let me explain things first and then you can ask questions!" Egor almost shouted. He was obviously very agitated.

"All right, Egor. But just don't shout at me, okay? I won't ask anymore. So then what?"

"You have to talk to her, because if she sees that a man is asking her questions, then she'll guess that, you know—he was in prison with her son—I mean her nephew. And then she'll start asking all kinds of questions. But my friend warned me that I mustn't tell her he's in prison... Whew! It's complicated. Anyway, do you understand now?"

"I understand. But what excuse can I give her for asking all the questions?"

"We'll have to think of something. For instance, you're from the village soviet. No, not from the soviet, but the district... what is that again, where they give out the pensions?"

"The district social security department."

"Right, social security. You tell her you're from that office and you're checking up to see how the old people are getting along. Ask her where her children are, and if they write to her. Okay?"

"Okay. I'll do it the way you want."

"Don't be too abrupt with her."

"I'll do it right, you'll see."

Egor fell silent. He was unusually serious and intent. He forced a smile and said:

"Don't be offended, Lyuba, but I don't feel like talking now, okay?"

Lyuba touched his hand with hers.

"Don't say anything more. Do what you know you have to do. I won't ask any more questions."

"And I'm sorry I shouted at you, added Egor. "I don't like it myself when people yell at me."

Egor drove along at a good clip. The road followed the edge of a forest. The dump truck bounced heavily as the wheels rolled over bared roots and stumps. Lyuba clung to the door handle as the truck jolted along. Egor gazed straight ahead, his lips firmly compressed, his eyes narrowed almost to a squint.

They pulled up to a roomy log house. It had a Russian stove, benches, and a pine floor that had been scrubbed, scraped and scrubbed again. A simple table with a painted top. In the holy corner, an ikon of St. Nicholas.

The old woman Kudelikha peered and peered at Lyuba and Egor through her half-blind eyes... Egor was wearing dark glasses.

"Why have you covered your eyes, sonny?" she asked. "Can't you see with them?"

Egor shrugged his shoulders vaguely, said nothing.

"Well, Granny," said Lyuba, "they've sent me around to find out all about you."

Kudelikha sat down on the bench and folded her brown, withered hands over her apron.

"Well, what do you want to know? They pay me twenty rubles..." She looked up at Lyuba trustingly. "What else?"

"And where are your children? How many did you have?"

"I had six, dear. One still lives with me—Nyura, and three are out away... Kolya's in Novosibirsk, he's a train engineer. Misha's there, too—

he builds houses. And Vera's in the Far East. She got married out there, husband's in the service. She just sent me a photograph of the whole family. The grandchildren are already getting big. There's two of them—a boy and a girl."

The old woman fell silent, wiped her mouth with the edge of her apron, nodded her little, birdlike head, sighed. She was plainly accustomed to wandering far back in her memories. She was there now, no longer noticed by her guests. But then she came to herself again and looked at Lyuba, said something just to break the awkward silence. After all, they seemed to be concerned about her...

"So... They're alive, you see." And then she stopped talking again.

Egor was sitting on a chair by the door. He seemed to have turned to stone, never moved a muscle while the old woman talked, just stared at her.

"And the other two?" asked Lyuba.

"Well, those... I just don't know if they're alive, bless their hearts, or if they passed away long ago." The old woman again began to nod her tiny, wrinkled head, in an effort to compose herself and keep from crying. But tears began to fall on her hands and she quickly wiped her eyes with her apron.

"I just don't know. They went out into the world during the famine time... Now I don't know where they are. Two more sons... two brothers... And I don't know anything about them."

A heavy silence descended in the house... Lyuba couldn't think of anything else to ask. She felt sorry for the old woman. She glanced at Egor. He sat there like a statue, still staring at Kudelikha. And his whole face, with those dark glasses, also seemed to have turned into stone. Lyuba began to feel very strange.

"That's all right, Granny." She completely forgot she was from "the social security" and went over to the old woman, sat down next to her in the most simple and natural way, as she knew how to do, put her arm around her and cuddled her. "You just wait, dear. Don't cry. There's no need to cry. You'll see. They'll still be found. We just have to look for them!"

The old woman obediently wiped away her tears and nodded her head.

"Maybe they'll be found... Thank you. Are you from peasant people yourself? You seem so natural, like."

"Yes, indeed I am. And we must certainly try to find your sons..."

Egor stood up and went out of the room.

He walked slowly across the entryway. He stopped at the front door and ran his hand over the doorpost. It was smooth and cold. He leaned his forehead against it and stood as if frozen. He stayed that way for a long time, gripping the doorpost with his hand until his fingers turned white. Lord—if only he were still able to cry in this life—things would be a little easier. But not a single tear moistened his eye. Only his cheekbones turned to stone and his fingers were squeezing whatever they could with all their strength. And there was nothing else that could have helped him in this awful moment—not tobacco, not vodka—nothing. Nothing would have done him any good. He suffered openly, groaned aloud in torment; he felt as though his soul was being seared in a slow fire. Over and over he repeated to himself, like a prayer: "That's enough! Stop it now. That's enough!..."

Egor heard Lyuba's footsteps coming, swung away from the doorpost and stepped down from the low front stoop. He walked away quickly along the fence, glancing back at the house. He again fell into concentrated thought as he walked around to the other side of the truck, kicked at the tires... He took off his glasses and stared at the house.

Lyuba came out.

"Lord, how sorry I felt for her," she said. "She just broke my heart."

"Let's go," commanded Egor.

They turned around... Egor glanced at the house for the last time and then drove off.

They were both silent. Lyuba thought sadly about the old woman.

After they had driven beyond the village, Egor stopped the truck, laid his forehead against the steering wheel and tightly closed his eyes.

"What's the matter, Egor?" asked Lyuba, frightened.

"Wait a minute... I want to stop here for a minute," said Egor with a catch in his voice. "You know... she broke my heart, too. That's my mother, Lyuba. My mother."

Lyuba gasped quietly.

"What were you thinking of, Egor? How could you not tell her?"

"It's not the right time," said Egor almost angrily. "I need a little more time... But I'll tell her soon. Soon."

"What do you mean, you need time! We're going to turn around right now!"

"I can't now!" shouted Egor. "I have to at least let my hair grow out... I want to at least look like a human being." Egor put the truck into gear. "I sent her some money," he added, "but I'm afraid she'll go off to the village soviet with it and demand to know who it's from. She might even not take it. I beg you, Lyuba—go by and see her tomorrow, say something to her. Think of something. Right now I just can't. Not right now. My heart would crack in half."

"Stop the truck," ordered Lyuba.

"Why?"

"Stop."

Egor stopped.

Lyuba leaned over and embraced him, as she had just embraced his mother, tenderly and capably... She laid his head on her breast.

"Oh, God!... Why are you like this? Why are you both so loveable?" She burst into tears. "What am I going to do with you?"

Egor freed himself from her embraces and coughed a few times in order to clear his throat. He put the truck into gear and declared in a near frenzy of joy:

"Don't worry, Lyubasha!... Everything will turn out all right! I'll put my head on the block if I have to, but you'll have a good life with me, I swear it."

When they got back home Petro met them at the fence.

"He's obviously worried. About the truck," guessed Lyuba.

"But why? I told him..."

Lyuba and Egor climbed down from the cab and Petro approached them.

"He showed up again here... your..." Petro broke off, speaking in his customary reluctant manner.

"Kolka?" said Lyuba in unpleasant surprise. "How dreadful! What does he want? He's torturing me to death, that whining slob..."

"Maybe I'll just go and get acquainted with him," said Egor, glancing at Petro. Petro barely nodded his head.

"Egor!" said Lyuba in alarm. "He's certain to be drunk. He'll start a fight. Don't go, Egor!" Lyuba moved to stop him, but Petro held her back.

"Don't be afraid," he said. "Hey, Egor..."

Egor turned around.

"There's three more waiting for you, behind the fence. Keep on your guard."

Egor nodded and went into the house.

Lyuba struggled with all her might to free herself, but her brother held her tightly.

"But they're going to beat him up!" said Lyuba, almost crying. "What's wrong with you? Let me go, Petro!"

"Who are they going to beat up?" said Petro calmly in his deep voice. "Zhorzhik? It won't be so easy to whip him. Let them talk for a bit... And then your Kolya won't be coming around here anymore. Let him understand that once and for all."

"Ah," said Kolya, stretching his mouth into a forced smile. "Here's the new master." He got up from the bench. "While I'm the old one." He walked up in front of Egor. "We need to have a little talk." Kolya was not so much drunk as hung over. He was a tall fellow, rather good-looking, with intelligent blue eyes.

The old people looked fearfully at the "masters"—the old one and the new one.

Egor decided not to dally. He immediately grabbed Kolya by the collar and dragged him out of the house...

He led him with difficulty onto the porch, then pushed him off it.

Kolya fell down. He hadn't expected they would begin so soon.

"If you ever show up around here again, you piece of carrion... This here was your last visit," said Egor from above. And then he started to walk down the steps.

Kolya scrambled up from the ground and began agitatedly to threaten Egor: "First let's get away from here. Follow me, now... Come on, now, you dog! Come on, now!"

They were already on the other side of the fence. Egor was walking ahead, Kolya following. Kolya kept making nervous threatening moves, once pushed Egor from behind. Egor looked back and shook his head reproachfully.

"Keep going, keep going," repeated Kolya, his voice shaking.

The three Petro had warned Egor about came up to meet them. "Not here," commanded Egor. "Let's go on farther."

They walked on. Egor again found himself in front.

"Listen," he said, stopping. "Let's walk together, so it won't look like you're leading me to the firing squad. They're watching us..."

"Keep moving, keep moving," repeated Kolya, hardly able to contain himself.

They walked on for a short way.

When they reached a high wattle fence, where they were less visible from the road, Kolya no longer restrained himself and leaped on Egor from behind. But Egor quickly twisted to the side and tripped Kolya. Kolya again ignominiously fell down. Then one of the others came to the attack, but Egor smashed his fist into the fellow's stomach. That one sat down. The other two stood dumbstruck by this turn of events, but Kolya jumped up and ran over to the fence to break loose a long stake.

"Okay, you dog!" said Kolya, choking with anger. He pulled out the stake and rushed at Egor in a rage.

Egor knew from long experience that a man almost never completely forgets himself—always, even at the last possible moment, he somehow manages to consider the consequences. If he kills you, it means he meant to do it. He will seldom kill you by accident.

Egor stood with his hands in his pockets and looked at Kolya. Kolya ran head-on into that calm—that somehow ominously calm—gaze.

"You won't have time to hit me with it," said Egor. He paused for a second, then added sympathetically: "Kolya..."

"Why are you threatening me? What have you got to fight with?" shouted Kolya, still trying to bluff. "A knife, maybe? Okay, take it out, then! Take out your knife!"

"You shouldn't drink so much, you jerk," said Egor with sympathy.

"You tore the stake loose, but now your hands are shaking so much you can't hold it. Don't ever come to this house again."

Egor turned around and walked back. He heard someone make a move toward him from behind—no doubt Kolya—but the others stopped him:

"Let him go! The piece of shit. Some jerk from the city. We'll take care of him some other time."

Egor neither stopped nor turned around.

Egor was plowing a furrow for the first time in his life.

He stopped the tractor, jumped to the ground, and walked along the freshly plowed furrow, quite amazed at himself: was this really his own work? He kicked a lump of dirt with his boot and grunted with satisfaction.

"Well, well, Zhorzhik. There's no doubt about it—if you keep on this way, you'll become a real shock-worker!" He gazed out over the steppe, breathed in the vernal smell of the new earth and closed his eyes for a minute. He stood there without moving.

When he was a kid he had loved to listen to telegraph poles. He would press his ear to the pole, close his eyes, and listen to the humming of the wires—a sensation that always stirred him deeply. He never forgot it: that eerie humming sound, as though it came from another world—from the devil knew where. If you shut your eyes even more tightly and entered that powerful, resonant sound with your whole being, then it would seem to be coming from within you—from somewhere in your head, or your chest—it was hard to say where. It was scary, but fascinating. How strange it was: that part of his life had been quite long and varied, yet the things from it that he remembered well were so few: the cow Manka, the birch saplings he and his mother would chop down for stove wood... But these precious memories still lived within him, and when his life became unbearably oppressive, he would recall that far-off village, the birch forest on the river bank, and the river... This did not make things any easier for him, it only made him feel a deep sense of loss and sadness, and his heart would ache in a different way—with sweetness as well as pain. And now, when such calm seemed to emanate from the freshly plowed field, when he could feel the warm sunshine on his head, and he was able to rest from his ceaseless running, he could not understand how it could ever happen—that he would stop his running for good and find peace. Was that really possible? In his heart was the premonition that his days of rest would be short.

Egor again surveyed the steppe. He would be sorry to lose this too. "What kind of freak am I," he thought involuntarily, "that I don't know how to live! God damn it! You have to live! Is life good? Yes, it's good. So enjoy it then, be happy!" Egor drew a deep breath.

"You could live for a hundred and forty years, breathing air like this," he said. And only now did he notice a birch copse at the edge of the field. He walked toward it.

"Ah, my beauties, standing here all by yourselves at the edge of the field. Well, have you got what you were waiting for? You've finally turned green..." He caressed one of the trees. "What pretty dresses! Oh, my little brides, what beautiful clothes you've put on—but you stand here saying nothing. You could have shouted and called me, but all you did was get dressed up and stand there. But now I've finally seen you. You're all beautiful. I must go back to my plowing now. But I'll be right nearby, and I'll visit you again sometime." He walked some distance from the birches, looked back and laughed: "Look at them, standing there like that!" And then he returned to his tractor.

As usual, he talked aloud as he walked along.

"If I stand around with you, I'll never become a shockworker. And the thing is... Well, it's all the same to you, anyway—and I really must work hard from now on. That's the way it is." And Egor began to sing:

"Snowball berry red,
Snowball berry ripe,
A little birdie told me,
My sweetheart he had lied.
My sweetheart he had lied,
Just wanted to be my lover..."

Still singing, he climbed into the cab and put the huge iron mass into motion. He continued to sing, but the song could no longer be heard over the roaring and clanking of the tractor.

In the evening they all ate supper together—the old people, Lyuba and Egor.

Some nice songs were playing on the radio and they were all listening to the music.

Suddenly the door opened and an unexpected guest appeared: a tall young fellow—the same one who had come rushing back the night of the police raid.

Egor was rather taken aback.

"Oh ho!" he said. "We have a guest! Sit down, Vasya!"

"Shura," corrected the guest, smiling.

"Oh yes—Shura! I keep forgetting. I keep mixing you up with Vasya, remember him? That big guy—the first sergeant..." Egor chattered on while making an effort to regain his composure: the guest was indeed most unexpected. "Shura and I were in the service together," he explained. "Under the same general. Sit down, Shura, eat supper with us."

"Sit down, sit down," invited Lyuba's mother as well.

And her father even moved over on the bench to make room: "Here, sit down."

"Thanks, no, I can't, I have a taxi waiting for me. I just need to tell you something, Georgii. And give you something..."

"Now you just sit down and eat!" insisted Egor. "The driver will wait for you."

"No, I can't," Shura glanced at his watch. "I have to catch a train..."

Egor got up from the table. He kept on chattering away, so that Shura would have no opportunity to let something slip from his tongue. Egor, who hated empty and trivial words himself, nevertheless knew how to confuse people by inundating them with a stream of words. Sometimes he did the same thing when he himself was confused.

"Well, tell me, do you ever meet any of the guys? Man, we really had the good times, didn't we? I still dream about those days in the army. Well, let's go. What do you want to give me? I guess it's in the taxi. I wonder what it is the general sent me. What do I have to do, sign for it? Did you come here direct, or did you have to change trains? Well, let's go, then..."

They went out.

The old man fell silent. All he could think about, with his honest peasant mind, was one thing.

"Say," he said, "how much does it cost to go riding around in a taxi? What do they get for each kilometer?"

"I don't know," said Lyuba distractedly. "Ten kopeks." She had sensed something very unfriendly in this guest.

"Ten kopeks? Let's see, ten kopeks times thirty-six versts... how much is that?"

"Well, that would be thirty-sixty kopeks," said the old woman.

"Don't be an idiot!" exclaimed the old man "Ten versts, that would already be one ruble. And thirty-six would be three-sixty—that's how much it is! And three-sixty and three-sixty is seven-twenty. That's seven-twenty just for the round trip from town. And I used to work a whole month for seven-twenty..."

Lyuba couldn't stand it anymore and also got up from the table.

"I wonder what they're doing out there?" she said and left the room.

She went out into the entryway and saw that the outside door was open. She could hear Egor and Shura talking. She froze.

"You tell him that. Got it?" said Egor harshly, angrily. "Remember what I said and tell him."

"I'll tell him—but you know him..."

"I know. But he knows me, too. Did he get the money?"

"Yeah."

"Okay. You guys and me are quits. If you come looking for me, I'll get the whole village after you." Egor laughed shortly. "I wouldn't advise it."

"Gore... Don't get pissed off at me now, I'm only doing what he told me. He said, 'If he's out of money, give him some.' So here—take it."

And Shura, evidently, handed Egor a packet of bils. Egor must have taken the money and hit Shura in the face with it—once, again, a third time. And then he said quietly, through his teeth:

"You son-of-a-bitch—you were right. I did get pissed off."

Lyuba made a deliberate noise and then walked out onto the porch. Shura was standing there with his hands at his sides, his face white...

Egor handed him the money and said in a quiet, almost hoarse voice: "Here you are. I'll be seeing you, Shura. Be sure to give them my regards. Do you remember what I told you?"

"I remember," said Shura. He gave Egor one last glance, full of evil promise, and went to the taxi.

"Well, well," said Egor as he sat down on the step. He watched the cab turn around... He followed it down the road with his eyes and then glanced up at Lyuba.

Lyuba was standing above him.

"Egor..." she started to say.

"Never mind," said Egor. "Just some old business of mine. Debts, you might say. But they won't come here anymore."

"I'm afraid, Egor," confessed Lyuba.

"Of what?" said Egor in surprise.

"I heard that when you try to... quit a gang... well, they..."

"None of that now!" said Egor sharply. "None of that," he repeated. "Come on, sit down now and don't talk about that ever again. Sit down..." Egor took her hand and pulled her down. "Why are you standing behind me like that? That's not nice, to stand behind somebody's back. It's impolite."

Lyuba sat down.

"Well?" asked Egor cheerfully. "Why then do you grieve, my pretty dawn?[6] What we need to do is sing a song!"

"Lord, I can't sing now..."

Egor ignored her.

"Come on I'll teach you... I know a real good song." And Egor began to sing:

　　　　"Snowball berry red,
　　　　Snowball berry ripe..."

"Oh, I know that!" said Lyuba.

"Okay then, sing along with me. Now...
　　　　Snowball berry..."

"Egor!" beseeched Lyuba. "Please, for the love of Christ, tell me they're not going to do anything to you."

Egor clenched his teeth and said nothing.

"Don't be angry, Egorushka. Why are you acting that way?" And

Lyuba burst into tears. "Why is it you can't understand me? I've been waiting and waiting for happiness—and now it's going to be taken from me... What's the matter with me? Have I been cursed? Will I never be allowed to find joy in life?!"

Egor put his arm around Lyuba and wiped away her tears with the palm of his hand.

"Don't you believe me?" he asked.

"Believe, believe... what does that mean when you don't want to talk? Just tell me, Egor. I won't be afraid. Maybe we can go away somewhere..."

"Oh, no!" howled Egor. "Are you sure you want me to be a shock-worker? I'll tell you the truth, Lyuba, I'll never make it this way. I just can't bear it when people cry. I can't bear it. Have pity on me, Lyubushka."

"Okay, I'm sorry. Everything's going to be all right, then?"

"Everything's going to be all right," said Egor carefully and precisely. "I'll swear by anything you want, by all that's holy. Now let's sing a song." And he began:

"Snowball berry red,
Snowball berry ripe..."

Lyuba joined in and they sounded just terrific together, really beautiful. For a minute she forgot everything and became calm.

"A little birdie told me,
My sweetheart he had lied.
My sweetheart he had lied,
Just wanted to be my lover.
When I would not give in,
He left me for another."

Petro watched them from behind the fence.

"Write down the words for me," he said mockingly.

"Oh, Petro," said Lyuba in an offended voice. "You've ruined our song."

"Who was that that came to see you, Egor?"

"Just a friend of mine. Are we going to heat up the bathhouse?" asked Egor.

"Sure we are. Come here a minute, I've got something to tell you."

Egor walked over to the fence. Petro leaned over and said something quietly in Egor's ear.

"Petro!" shouted Lyuba, "I know what you're up to. I know. After the bath!"

"I asked him to take a look at the jet in my carburetor," said Petro.

"I'm just going to see what's wrong with the carburetor," said Egor. "Probably needs to be blown out."

"I'll carburetor you! After the bath, I said." And with these final words, Lyuba went into the house. She felt much calmer, but just the same a worrisome fear had crept into her heart. It was the sort of persistent fear familiar to women in love.

Egor climbed over to Petro's side of the fence.

"Brandy—that's shit," he said. "I prefer either champagne or Remy Martin."

"But you just try this."

"I have—and everything else, too. One thing I rather like, for instance, is whisky and soda..."

They continued their conversation as they walked toward the bathhouse.

Now Egor was sowing the field that he had plowed earlier. That is, he was driving the tractor and towing a seeder, upon which stood a young woman with a trowel who saw to it that the seed was spread evenly.

Petro drove up in his dump truck, which had been modified to carry seed. Egor helped him fill the seeder. They talked briefly:

"Are you going to eat dinner here or at home?" asked Petro.

"Here."

"I can take you back if you want. I have to go home anyway."

'That's okay. I brought everything with me... Why do you have to go back?"

'The motor started missing. It's undoubtedly the carburetor jet."

They laughed, recalling the "carburetor" they had "blown out" together that last time in the bathhouse.

"I've got another one at home. I've been keeping it ready."

"Do you want me to take a look and see if something else is making it miss?"

"Nah, just a waste of time. I know it's the carburetor jet. It's been giving me trouble for a long time. I just hated to throw it out. But now I'll change it."

"Well, I'll see you." And Egor returned to his tractor. Petro left to distribute seed to the other sowers.

... Egor was distracted momentarily from the instrument panel, glanced ahead, and noticed in the distance that a Volga had stopped near his little birch grove at the edge of the field. Three people stood near the car. Egor stared hard at them... and finally recognized them. They were Fat Lip, Bulldog and the tall fellow. And Lucienne was in the car. Lucienne was sitting in the front seat; the door was open. Although her face was hidden, Egor recognized her from her skirt and legs. The men stood by the car, waiting for the tractor.

Nothing had changed in the world. The day was warm and clear, the birch copse at the edge of the field stood all green and freshly washed from yesterday's rain... The soil gave off such a rich odor, such a rich, thick, damp smell, that it made one feel slightly dizzy. The earth had assembled all its vernal forces, its living juices, and was getting ready again to bring forth life. And the faraway dark-blue stripe of forest, a cloud above it, white and fleecy, and the sun high aloft—all of this was life, spilling out everywhere, concerned about nothing, afraid of nothing.

Egor throttled back very slightly... He leaned down and picked out a wrench—not too heavy a one, but one he could handle deftly—and stuck it in the pocket of his trousers. He glanced down to see if it was visible under his jacket. You couldn't tell it was there.

When he drew even with the Volga, Egor stopped the tractor and turned off the engine.

"Galya, go eat dinner," he said to his helper.

"But we've only just filled up the seeder," said Galya uncomprehendingly.

"Never mind. Just go. I've got to talk with my comrades here—from the central committee of the trade union."

Galya set out toward the brigade shack, just barely visible in the distance. She turned around two or three times to look at the Volga, at Egor...

Egor also glanced across the field unobtrusively... Two other tractors with seeders crawled along the far side; their steady rumble somehow did not disturb the silence of the vast bright day.

Egor walked over to the Volga.

Fat Lip began to grin while Egor was still quite a ways off.

"Look how dirty he is!" exclaimed Fat Lip with a smile. "Take a look at him, Lucienne!"

Lucienne climbed out of the car and looked seriously, unsmilingly, at the approaching Egor.

Egor walked awkwardly through the soft plowed earth. He looked at his guests. He did not smile.

Only Fat Lip smiled.

"By God, I never would have recognized you!" he continued in his mocking tone. "If I had just run into you someplace, I never would have known who you were."

"Please don't touch him," said Lucienne suddenly in her husky voice, looking demandingly, even angrily, at Fat Lip.

While Fat Lip was all agog with a kind of vengeful joy.

"Lucienne! What are you saying! He's the one that shouldn't touch *me*! Tell him not to touch me! Or else he's liable to hit me on my damned neck with his holy fist..."

"Don't touch him, damn you!" Lucienne blurted out. "You'll be dead yourself soon, so why..."

"Shut up!" hissed Fat Lip. And his smile was gone in an instant. It was obvious—you could see it in his eyes—that his vindictive impotence had turned to black rage: the man was permanently deaf to any suggestion of justice. If he had no one to bite, he would turn like a snake and bite his own tail. "Or else I'll lay you out next to him—and put your arms around him. I'll add another statute to my list of offenses: desecration of corpses. What the hell difference does it make to me?"

"Please, I beg you," said Lucienne, after a pause. "Don't touch him. It will soon be all up with us, anyway—let him live. Let him plow the earth—he likes it."

"For us it's the end—but he's going to plow the earth?" Fat Lip smiled, showing his rotten teeth. "Where's the justice in that? Did he do less than we did?"

"He got out of the game... He has his release papers."

"He hasn't got out yet." Fat Lip again turned toward Egor. "He's still on his way."

Egor was still walking toward them, his boots continually sinking into the soft earth.

"He's even got a new walk now!" said Fat Lip with delight. "Like a real working man."

"Like a proletarian," mumbled the dull-witted Bulldog.

"Like a peasant—what do you mean 'proletarian'?"

"But the peasants are also the proletariat!"

"Bulldog! You only got through the fourth grade. Go read *Murzika*— and wipe your mouth, you're drooling.[7] Hey, good boy, Gore!" Fat Lip loudly greeted Egor.

"And what else did they say?" Lyuba asked her parents in alarm.

"Nothing else... I told them how to get out there..."

"To Egor?"

"Well, yes.."

"Mother of God!" screamed Lyuba, and ran out of the house.

Just then Petro drove up to the fence.

Lyuba waved at him to stop.

Petro stopped.

Lyuba jumped into the cab, said something to Petro. The dump truck backed up, turned around and immediately sped off, bouncing and crashing over the potholes in the road.

"Petya, dear brother, faster, faster! Oh Lord, I knew in my heart this would happen!" Tears rolled down Lyuba's cheeks. She didn't wipe them away, didn't even notice them.

"We'll make it," said Petro. "I just left him a little while ago..."

"They were just here... asking about him. And now they're already out there. Faster, Petya!"

Petro squeezed everything he could out of his humpbacked bogatyr.

The group that had been standing near the Volga moved toward the birch grove. Only the woman remained at the car—even crawling inside and slamming shut all the doors.

The group had not quite reached the birch trees when it stopped. They were evidently talking something over... Then two of the group stepped aside and returned to the car. The other two—Egor and Fat Lip—went into the birch grove and were soon hidden from sight.

... At that moment Petro's dump truck came into view far down the road. The two standing near the Volga gazed at the truck. They realized the truck was headed for them, shouted something in the direction of the trees. Immediately one man—Fat Lip—came running out of the grove, concealing something in his pocket. He also saw the dump truck and ran to the Volga. The Volga tore away and rapidly gathered speed as it shifted into higher gear...

... The dump truck pulled up to the birch copse.

Lyuba leaped out of the cab and ran toward the trees.

Walking slowly out to meet her, holding one hand over his stomach, came Egor. He staggered, clutching at the trees with his other hand. And on the white birches bright-red stains appeared.

Petro, seeing that Egor was wounded, jumped back into his truck, intending to chase down the Volga. But the Volga was already far away. He began to turn around.

Lyuba took hold of Egor's arms and supported him.

"I'll get blood on you," said Egor, wincing from the pain.

"Hush, don't speak." Lyuba was strong. She took him in her arms. Egor was about to protest, but another wave of pain passed over him. He closed his eyes.

Petro rushed up, took Egor carefully from the arms of his sister and carried him toward the truck.

"It's okay, it's okay now," he rumbled softly. "This is nothing... Men had bayonets run right through them during the war and still lived. In a week you'll be jumping around..."

Egor shook his head weakly and took a breath—the pain had subsided slightly.

"In there... the bullet..." he said.

Petro glanced down at him, at his white face, clenched his teeth and said nothing. He quickened his step.

Lyuba jumped into the cab first. She took Egor's hands. She held him in her lap, with his head resting on her breast. Petro cautiously put the truck into motion.

"Be patient, Egorushka darling. Soon we'll be at the hospital."

"Don't cry," said Egor quietly, not opening his eyes.

"I'm not crying."

"Yes, you are... your tears... on my face. Don't cry..."

"I won't, I won't..."

Petro spun the wheel this way and that, trying to avoid the bumps. But all the same the truck jolted. Egor winced in agony and groaned a couple of times.

"Petya..." said Lyuba.

"I'm doing the best I can. But I don't dare slow down. There's no time."

"Stop," said Egor.

"Why, Egor? We have to go as fast as we can."

"No... it's over. Take me... down... from the truck."

They lifted him out, placed him on the ground, on a shirt.

"Lyuba," called Egor, searching for her in the sky with unseeing eyes. He lay on his back. "Lyuba..."

"I'm here, Egor. I'm right here, see?..."

"Money..." Egor strained to get out his last words. "In jacket.. share it... with my mother..." A single tear squeezed out from under Egor's closed eyelids, rolled down his scalp toward his ear, hung there a minute, detached itself and fell into the grass. Egor was dead.

And there he lay, a Russian peasant on his native steppe, not far from home... He lay with his cheek pressed to the earth, as though he were listening to something that only he could hear. That was how he had listened to the telegraph poles in his childhood.

Lyuba fell on his breast and quietly, terribly, wept.

Petro stood above them looking down and also cried, without making a sound.

Then he raised his head, wiped away his tears with the sleeve of his jersey.

"No!" he said, letting out his breath, so that all his frightening strength could be felt. "They're not going to get away!" He circled around Egor and his sister and, not looking back, ran heavily toward the dump truck.

The truck gave a roar and rushed out over the open steppe, away from the main road. Petro knew perfectly every road and cart track in the region; he had suddenly come to the conclusion that it was possible to intercept the Volga by cutting across its path. The Volga would have to make a wide sweep around the forest that was visible in the distance as a dark blue band on the horizon... But passing through the forest was a lumber road used for hauling out timber on tractor sledges during the winter. Now, after the rain, the lumber road littered with branches and brush might even be better for the truck than the muddy main road. But the Volga, of course, would never go in there—and how could they know anyway where the road led?

... Petro intercepted the Volga.

The dump truck lurched out of the forest before the beige beauty was able to slip past. Its hopeless position immediately became apparent: it was too late to turn around, because the truck was racing toward it head on; and it was impossible to squeeze past the truck, because the road was too narrow. As for turning off the road: on one side was the forest, and on the other plowed ground soaked with yesterday's rain—out of the question for the small city vehicle. Yet that was the only chance the Volga had—to pull off into the field at full speed and try to jump back onto the road after it had passed the truck. The Volga turned off the hard road and immediately its rear wheels began to spin and skid. It slowed down to a crawl, though the engine roared at top speed. At this point Petro bore down on it. No one in the Volga even had time to jump out. The great toiler dump truck, like an infuriated bull, crashed into the side of the car, turned it over and reared up on top of it.

Petro climbed down from the cab...

From out of the field, jumping down from their tractors, people who had seen what happened came running up.

1973

Translated by Donald M. Fiene

NOTES

Original Russian: "Kalina krasnaia," *Nash sovremennik*, 4 (1973), 86-133. Reprinted in *Izbrannye proizvedeniia v dvukh tomakh* (1975), Vol. 1, pp. 417-492, and in *Kinopovesti* (1975) with only a few minor changes.

1. Egor is reciting a poem by Sergei Esenin written in 1922. The first stanza, which Egor omits (he also omits the fourth) is:

Mir tainstvennyi, mir moi drevnii,
Ty, kak veter, zatikh i prisel.
Vot, sdavili za sheiu derevniu
Kamennye ruki shosse.

(My secret world of bygone days,
You're cowering now like the dying wind.
The countryside's been strangled
By the highway's stony arms.)

The destruction of ancient rural culture by urban encroachment was a frequent theme with Esenin, as with Shukshin. The poetic line quoted two pages earlier by Egor, "Oh, my skies of May, and the long blue days of June," is also from Esenin (and not from Afanasy Fet as the old woman's remark might seem to imply). The line in Russian is: "Mai moi sinii! Iiun' goluboi!" It is from "Snova p'iut zdes', derutsia i plachut," 1923.

2. *Gore* in Russian means "grief, sorrow, woe, misfortune..." It has two syllables in pronunciation: Gor-ye. The hero's full name is Georgii, pronounced Gi-or-gi, with both G's hard; the version of the name he usually goes by, Egor, is pronounced Yegor. He is also referred to by such diminutives as Egorsha, Egorushka, Zhora and Zhorzhik. He even identifies himself once as "Dzhordzh" using the English pronunciation (spelled here: George).

3. Shukshin's phrase here is: "Rabota ne Alitet" (Work is not Alitet). This is a reference to the colorful hero of a popular two-volume novel about a far northern Siberian horseman of the Chukchi tribe by Tikhon Z. Semushkin: *Alitet ukhodit v gory* [Alitet flees to the mountains] (1947-48).

4. The name Pistonov rather remotely suggests *pizda,* "cunt."

5. Kolenka is a diminutive of Nikolai, hence "saint" Nikolai (or Nicholas).

6. Egor is borrowing some words from a popular song. What he says is: 'Chto zakruchinilas', zoren'ka iasnaia?" (literally: Why have you begun to grieve, clear dawn?"). The actual title of the song is: "Chto zatumanilas', zoren'ka iasnaia?" ("Why have you become foggy, clear dawn?").

7. *Murzika*: monthly illustrated magazine for young school children.

Sasha Sokolov

A SCHOOL FOR FOOLS

*To the retarded boy
Vaitis Dantsin,
my friend and neighbor*

Then Saul, who is also called Paul,* filled with the
Holy Ghost, set his eyes on him, and said, O full of all
subtilty and all mischief, *thou* child of the devil, *thou*
enemy of all righteousness, wilt thou not cease to
pervert the right ways of the Lord?

Acts, 13, 9-10

To drive, to hold, to run, to offend,
to hear and to see, to turn and to breathe,
to hate and to depend,
and to endure.

*A group of infinitives which, in
Russian, are exceptions to certain rules*

Not a line in all the marked and singular lineaments of
his face which was not, even in the most absolute
identity, *mine own!*

Edgar Allan Poe, "William Wilson"

Savl and Pavel are the Russian forms of Saul and Paul. [Trans. note]

Chapter One   *Nymphea*

All right, but how do you begin, what words do you use? It makes no difference, use the words: there, at the station pond. At the *station* pond? But that's incorrect, a stylistic mistake. Vodokachka would certainly correct it, one can say "station" snack bar or "station" news stand, but not "station" pond, a pond can only be *near* the station. Well, say it's near the station, that's not the point. Good, then I'll begin that way: there, at the pond near the station. Wait a second, the station, the station itself, please, if it's not too hard, describe the station, what the station was like, what sort of platform it had, wooden or concrete, what kind of houses were next to it, you probably recall what color they were, or maybe you know the people who lived in the houses near that station? Yes, I know, or rather I knew, some of the people who lived near the station, and I can tell something about them, but not now, later sometime, because right now I will describe the station. It's an ordinary station: signalman's shack, bushes, ticket booth, platform (wooden), squeaky planks, nails sticking up all over and you shouldn't go barefoot. There were trees around the station: aspens, pines, a variety of trees, you know, a variety. The station itself was a normal station, but what was beyond the station was regarded as something really fine and extraordinary: the pond, the high grass, the dance platform, the grove, the rest home and other things. Ordinarily people went swimming in the pond near the station in the evening, after work, they would arrive on commuter electrics and go swimming. No, first they would go their separate ways to their dachas. Weary, breathing heavily, wiping their faces with handkerchiefs, swinging briefcases and shopping bags. Do you remember what was in the shopping bags? Tea, sugar, butter, salami; fresh fish with whipping tails; macaroni, buckwheat, onions, prepared foods; more rarely, salt. They would go to their dachas, drink tea on verandas, put on pyjamas, and take walks—arms behind their backs—through the orchards, and glance into the fire barrels full of efflorescent water, astonished by the multitude of frogs—which were hopping through the grass everywhere—and play with children and dogs, and play badminton, and drink kvass from refrigerators, and watch television, and talk to their neighbors. And if it was not yet dark, they would set out for the pond in groups—to go swimming. Why didn't they go to the river? They were afraid of the whirlpools and main channels, the wind and the waves, the deep spots and bottom reeds. And maybe there just wasn't any river? Maybe. But what was it called? The river did have a name.

Basically, every path and trail in our district led to the pond. Poor, narrow, virtually nonexistent paths stretched from the most distant dachas situated at the forest fringe. They barely glowed in the evening, glimmering, while the more significant paths, pounded down long ago, trails so beaten that there could be no question of any weeds growing on them at all—trails of this kind glowed clear, white, and even. This is at sunset, yes, naturally, at sunset, only right after sunset in the dusk. And so, one merging with the other, all paths led in the direction of the pond. Finally, several hundred meters from the shore, they united in one excellent road. This road ran through some meadows before penetrating the birch grove. Look back and admit it: wasn't it nice in the evening, in the gray light, to ride into the grove on a bicycle? It was nice. because a bicycle is always nice, in any weather, at any age. Take Pavlov, for example. He was a physiologist, he did various experiments on animals and rode a bicycle a lot. In a certain textbook— you of course remember the book—there is a special chapter on Pavlov. First come pictures of dogs with some sort of special physiological pipes sewn into their throats, and it is explained that the dogs got conditioned to receiving food when a bell was rung, and when Pavlov did not give them food, but just rang the bell for nothing, the dogs got excited and their saliva started to flow—quite amazing. Pavlov had a bicycle, and the academician rode around on it a lot. One ride is shown in the textbook too. Pavlov is old there, but hale and hearty. He rides along, observing nature, and there's a bell on the handlebar—like in the experiments, exactly the same kind. Moreover, Pavlov had a long gray beard, like Mikheev, who lived, and perhaps still lives, in our dacha settlement. Mikheev and Pavlov—they both loved bicycles, but the difference is this: Pavlov rode a bicycle for pleasure, at leisure, but for Mikheev the bicycle always meant work, that was the kind of work he did: delivering mail by bicycle. Of him, of the postman Mikheev—but maybe his name was, is, and will be Medvedev?— one has to speak separately, he has to be allotted some separate time, and one of us—you or I—will definitely have to do this. Incidentally, I think you know the postman better, since you lived at the dacha much more than I, although if one were to ask the neighbors they would surely say it's quite a complicated question and that it's almost impossible to figure out. The neighbors will say, we did not keep very close track of you—that is, of us,—and in general what kind of weird question is that, why do you suddenly need to clarify something absurd, what difference does it make who lived there longer, that's frivolous, they'll say, you'd do better to get to work: it's May in your garden, and apparently the trees have not been spaded, and you surely like to eat apples; and even wind-driver Norvegov, they'll remark, —even he's been digging in his little garden since morning. Yes, he's digging, we'll reply—one of us—or we'll say in chorus: yes, he's digging. Instructor Norvegov has the time for that, and the desire. Besides, he has a garden and a house, but us—we have nothing like that—no time, no garden, no house. You have simply forgotten, we haven't lived here in this settlement for a long time, probably nine years. We sold the dacha after all—up and sold it. I suspect that as the more loquacious, gregarious person you'll want to add something to this, to rehash everything, start explaining why we sold it and why, from your point of view, we did not have to sell, and how the point isn't that we *could* not have sold, but that we *should* not have sold. But we'd better get away from them, we'll leave on the very first train, I don't want to hear their voices.

Our father sold the dacha when he was pensioned off, although the pension turned out to be so large that the dacha postman Mikheev, who has dreamed of a good new bicycle all his life, but who cannot ever save enough money, not because he's a spendthrift exactly, he's simply thriftless—so when he learned from our dacha neighbor, the prosecutor's crony, the kind of pension our father was going to get, Mikheev almost fell off his bicycle. The postman was riding placidly past the fence around our neighbor's dacha—by the way, do you remember his name? No, can't recall like that all at once: a bad memory for names, but then what's the sense in remembering all these first names and last names—right? Of course, but if we knew his name it would be nice to tell it. But we can think up some arbitrary name, names—no matter how you look at it—are all arbitrary, even if they're real ones. But on the other hand, if we give him an arbitrary name people can think we're making up something here, trying to fool someone, delude them, but we have absolutely nothing to hide, this is about a man who was our neighbor, a neighbor everyone in the settlement knows, and they know that he was one of the prosecutor's cronies at work, and his dacha is ordinary, not very fancy, and it was probably just talk about his house being made from stolen brick—what do you think? Eh?—what are you talking about? What's wrong with you, aren't you listening to me? No, I'm listening, only it just occurred to me that there was probably beer in those containers. In what containers? In the big ones in the neighbor's shed, there was ordinary beer in them—what do you think? I don't know, I don't remember, I haven't thought about that for a long while. And at the moment when Mikheev was riding past our neighbor's house, the owner was standing on the threshold of the shed and examining the container of beer in the light. Mikheev's bicycle rattled violently as it jounced over the pine roots sticking up through the ground, and the neighbor could not help hearing and recognizing Mikheev's bicycle. And having heard and recognized it, he walked quickly to the fence to ask if there were any letters, but instead—surprising even himself—he informed the postman: the prosecutor—said the prosecutor's crony—have you heard? He's gone on pension. Smiling. How much did they give him? responded Mikheev, not stopping, but just braking slightly—how much money? He looked back in motion, and the neighbor saw the postman's suntanned face had no expression. The postman, as always, looked calm; the only thing was that his beard, with pine needles sticking to it, was waving in the wind: in the wind born of the speed, in the swift bicycle wind; and it would certainly have seemed to the neighbor—had he been only a little of a poet—that Mikheev's face, blown by all of the dacha crosswinds, itself emanated wind, and that Mikheev was that very person who was known in the settlement as The Sender of Wind. To be more precise, *who was not known.* No one had ever seen this person, possibly he did not exist at all. But in the evenings, after swimming in the pond, the dacha dwellers gathered on their glassed-in verandas, sat down in their wicker armchairs and told each other all kinds of stories, and one of them was the legend of The Sender. Some asserted that he was youthful and wise, others that he was old and stupid, a third party insisted that he was of middle years, but retarded and uneducated, and a fourth party that he was old and sagacious. And there was also a fifth party which declared that The Sender was young and decrepit, a fool—but a genius. It was said that he appears on one of the sunniest and warmest days of summer, rides a bicycle, whistles with a nut-wood whistle and does nothing but send wind to the locale through which he is riding. What they had in mind was that The Sender sends wind only into a locale where there are all too many dachas and dacha dwellers. Yes, indeed, and ours was precisely that kind of locale. If I'm not mistaken there are three or four dacha settlements in the area of the station. And what was the station called?—I just cannot make it out from the distance. The station did have a name.

This is zone five, ticket price thirty-five kopeks, the train takes an hour twenty northern branch, a branch of acacia or, say, lilac blooms with white flowers, smells of creosote, the dust of connecting platforms, the smoke looms along the track bed, in the evening it returns to the garden on tiptoe and listens intently to the movement of the electric trains, trembles from the rustling noises, and then the flowers close and sleep, yielding to the importunities of the solicitous bird by the name of Nachtigall; the branch sleeps, but the trains, distributed symmetrically along the branch, rush feverishly through the dark like chains, hailing each flower by name, dooming to insomnia the following: bilious old station ladies, amputees and war-blinded traincar accordion players, blue-gray linemen in sleeveless orange tops, sage professors and insane poets, dacha irregulars and failures— anglers for early and late fish, tangled in the spongy plexus of the limpid forest, and also middle-aged islander buoy-keepers whose faces, bobbing over the metallically humming black channel waters, are alternately pale and scarlet, and, finally, the dockmen, who think they hear the sound of an unfastened boat chain, a splash of oars, a rustle of sails, and then, throwing over their shoulders buttonless Gogolian overcoats, emerge from their dock-houses and stride across porcelain shoreline sands, and dunes, and grassy embankments; the faint, still shadows of the dockmen are cast on the reeds and the heather, and their home-made pipes gleam like maple stumps, attracting astonished moths; but the branch sleeps, flower petals closed, and the trains, lurching across switches, will not awaken it for anything, will not brush from it a drop of dew—sleep sleep branch smelling of creosote wake up in the morning and flower make the profusion of petals bloom into the eyes of the semaphors and dancing in time to your wooden heart laugh in the stations sell yourself to passersby and to those departing weep and keen naked in the mirrored coupes what's your name I'm called Vetka I'm Vetka acacia I am Vetka of the railroad I am Veta pregnant by the tender bird called Nachtigall I am pregnant with the coming summer and the crash of a freight here take me take me my blossoms are falling and it costs very little at the station I cost no more than a ruble I am sold by tickets and if you wish travel without paying there will be no inspector he is sick wait I will unbutton myself see I am all snow white so shower me shower me all over with kisses no one will notice the petals they are not visible on white and I am sick of it all sometimes I seem to myself simply an old lady who has spent all her life walking across red-hot engine slag on the roadbed she is aged appalling I don't want to be an old woman dear no I don't want to I know I will soon die on the rails me me it hurts me it will hurt me let go when I die let go these wheels are coverd with oil your palms what are your palms in can those be gloves I told a lie I am Veta chaste white branch I flower you have no right I dwell in gardens don't shout I'm not shouting it's the train coming tra ta ta shouting what's this tra ta ta what tra who there ta where there there there Veta willows willows branch there outside the window in that house tra ta ta tum of whom of what of Vetka oars of wind tararam trailer tramway *tramway ay* even good ticks tick its lee lethe there is no Lethe no Ay-colored Lethe for you a hue like Alpha Veta Gamma and so on which no one knows because no one would teach us Greek it was an unforgivable mistake on their part it's because of them we cannot sensibly enumerate a single ship and the running Hermes is like unto a flower but we scarcely understand this that the other Cape Horn blow horns but naturally beat drums tra ta ta question is that a conductor answer no a constrictor why are you shouting there you feel bad it seemed like that to you I feel good it's a train coming forgive me now I know precisely it was a train coming but you I know I was dozing and suddenly heard something like someone singing clickety clak clickety clak clickety clak de dum de dum netto brutto Italia Italian person Dante person Bruno person Leonardo artist architect entomologist *if you want to see flying with four wings step into the moats of the Milan fortress and you will see black dragonflies* a ticket to Milan even two for me and Mikheev Medvedev I want dragonflies flying in willows on rivers in moats uncut along the main railway of the Veta constellation in the thickets of heather where Tinbergen himself born in Holland married a colleague and soon it became clear to them that *ammofila* does not find the way home the same way *filantus* does and of course you beat a tambourine someone in the train tambour-platform there tum ta tum ta tum tum there a simply merry song is being performed on a reed pipe on the Vetochka branch of the railroad tra ta tra ta ta a cat married a cat married Tinbergen's cat dancing up and down nightmare witch she lives with an excavator operator never lets one sleep at six in the morning sings in the kitchen cooking him food in pots the fires flame burning boil the pots aboiling have to give her some name if the cat Tinbergen she will be witch Tinbergen dances in the hall from earliest morn and doesn't let one sleep sings about the cat and probably behaves very affectedly. But why "probably?" Haven't you ever seen her dancing? No, it seems to me I have never ever seen her. I have lived in the same communal apartment with her for many years now, but the point is that the witch Tinbergen is not at all the old woman who is registered here and who I see in the mornings and evenings in the kitchen. That old woman is a different one, her surname is Trachtenberg, Seina Solomonovna Trachtenberg, a Jewess, on a pension, she is a lonely pensioner, and every morning I say to her: good morning, and in the evening: good evening, she replies, she is a very plump woman, she has red hair flecked with gray, curls, she is such a sixty-five year old, we scarcely speak to her, we simply have nothing to talk about, but from time to time, approximately once every two months, she asks to borrow my record player and plays the same record on it every time. She doesn't listen to anything else, she hasn't got any other record. And what is the record? I'll tell that in a minute. Let's suppose I am coming home. From somewhere or other. I should note that I know in advance when Trachtenberg is going to ask for the record player, several days ahead I foresee that soon now, quite soon, she will say: listen, my dear, be nice, how about your record player? I walk up the stairs and I can feel it: Trachtenberg is already standing there, behind the door, she is in the hall, waiting for me. I enter boldly. Boldly. I enter. Good evening. Boldly. Evening's good, my dear, do me a favor. I get the record player out of the cabinet. A pre-war record player, bought sometime and somewhere. By someone. It has a red case, it's always covered with dust because although I wipe up the dust in the room the way our good and patient mother taught me, my hands never reach the record player. I haven't wound it up myself for a long time. In the first place I have no records, and in the second the record player doesn't work, it's wrecked, a spring broke a long time ago and the turntable doesn't turn, believe me. Sheina Solomonovna, I say,—the record player doesn't work, you know that yourself. That's not important, answers Trachtenberg,—I need only one little record. Oh, just one, I say. Yesyesyes, smiles Sheina, her teeth are basically gold, she wears horn-rimmed glasses and powders her face—one little record. She takes the record player, carries it off to her room and locks the lock. And in about ten minutes I hear the voice of Yakov Emmanuilovich. But you didn't say who Yakov Emmanuilovich is. You mean you don't remember him? He was her husband, he died when you and I were about ten, and we lived with our parents in the room where I now live alone, or you live alone, in short—one of us does. But still—who precisely? What's the difference? I am telling you a very interesting story, and you're starting to pester me again, and I don't pester you after all, I thought we agreed once and for all that there is no difference between us, or do you want to go *there* again? Excuse me, in the future I will try not to cause you unpleasantness, you understand, not everything is right with my memory. And you think mine is all right? Well, excuse me, please excuse me, I didn't want to distress you. So then, Yakov died from medicine, he poisoned himself with something. Sheina really tormented him, demanding money, she seemed to imagine her husband was hiding a few thousand from her, but he was an ordinary druggist, a pharmacist, and I'm sure that he didn't have a penny. I think Sheina's demands for money were a way of poking fun at him. She was some fifteen years younger than he and as she said sitting on the benches in the yard she betrayed him with Building Superintendent Sorokin, who had only one arm, and who later, a year after the death of Yakov, hanged himself in the empty garage. A week before this he had sold the captured automobile which he had brought back from Germany. If you recall, the people on the benches liked to talk about why it was Sorokin needed a car, he couldn't drive it anyway, he wasn't about to hire a chauffeur. But then it all became clear. When Yakov went away on business trips or had all-night shifts on duty in the drugstore, Sorokin would take Sheina into the garage, and it was there, in the car, that she betrayed Yakov. What a blessing, they said on the benches, what a blessing to have one's own car, and it turns out he didn't even want to ride around in it: he'd come to the garage, lock it from inside, turn on the lights, put back the seat—and there you go, have all the fun you like. Well, they said in the yard, it's too bad he's armless. Describe our yard, what did it look like then, such-and-such a number of years ago. I would say it was more a junk heap than a yard. Stunted linden trees, two or three garages, and behind the garages—mountains of broken brick and all kinds of rubbish in general. But mainly there were old gas stoves lying around, three or four hundred of them, they had been brought into our yard from all of the neighboring buildings right after the war. Because of these stoves there was always a kitcheny odor in the yard. When we opened the ovens, the doors to the ovens, they screeched terribly. And why did we open the doors, why? It strikes me as strange you don't understand why. We opened the doors *in order to* slam them with a bang immediately. But shouldn't we get back to the people who lived in our neighborhood, we knew a lot. No, no, so boring, I'd like to talk a bit about some other things now. You see, in general in our mind something is wrong with time, we don't understand time properly. You haven't forgotten how once many years ago we met our teacher Norvegov at the station? No, I haven't, we met him at the station. He said that an hour earlier he had left the reservoir, where he had been fishing for mosquito grubs. And it is true he had a fishing pole and bucket with him, and I managed to get a glimpse of some sort of creatures swimming in the bucket, but not fish. Our geographer Norvegov had also built a dacha in the region served by this station, only on the other side of the river, and we visited him often. But what else did the teacher tell us that day? Geographer Norvegov told us more or less the following: young man, you have probably noticed what fine weather has been holding in our area for many days in a row now; do you agree that these respected dacha dwellers of ours do not deserve such luxury? Doesn't it strike you, my youthful comrade, that it's time for a storm to break, a tempest? Norvegov looked at the sky, shading his eyes from the sun with his hand. And it will break, my dear fellow, and how it will break—the pieces will fly up every back alley! And not just any old time, today or tomorrow. Bye the bye, have you thought about this seriously, do you believe it?

Pavel Petrovich *was standing in the middle of the platform*, the station clock showed two fifteen, he had on his usual light cap, all covered with little holes, as if eaten by a moth or repeatedly punched by a ticket-collector's punch, but in reality the holes had been put in at the factory so that the buyer's head, in this case Pavel Petrovich's, would not get sweaty during the hot times of the year. And moreover, they thought at the factory, dark holes on a light background—that did mean something, it was worth something, it was better than nothing, that is, better with holes than without them, or so they thought at the factory. All right, but what else did our teacher wear that summer, and generally during the best months of those unforgettable years when we lived at the same station he did, though his dacha was located in the settlement on the other side of the river, and ours was in one of the settlements which were on the same side as the station? It is rather difficult to answer that question, I don't remember precisely what Pavel Petrovich wore. It would be simpler to say what he didn't wear. Norvegov never wore shoes. In the summer at any rate. And that hot day on the platform, on the old wooden platform, he could easily have gotten a splinter in his foot, or both of them at once. That could have happened to anyone, but not to our teacher, he was so small and fragile, and when you saw him running along a dacha path or the school corridor, it seemed to you that his bare feet did not in the least touch the earth, the floor, and when he was standing there in the middle of the wooden platform that day, it seemed he was not standing there at all, but suspended over it, over its fractured planks, over all its burnt matches and butts, thoroughly sucked popsicle sticks, cancelled tickets and dried-up—and therefore invisible—gobs of passenger spit of various qualities. Allow me to interrupt you, it's possible there is something I've understood incorrectly. Do you mean Pavel Petrovich went barefoot even in school? No, apparently I went too far, I meant he went barefoot at the dacha, but perhaps he didn't put on shoes in town either, when he was going to work, and we simply didn't notice it. And maybe we did notice, but it wasn't too obvious. Yes, somehow not too, in such cases a lot depends on the person himself, and not on the people who are looking at him, yes, I recall, not too obvious. But however it was during school terms, you definitely know that in the summer Norvegov went without shoes. Precisely. As our father noted one day, lying in the hammock with his newspaper in his hands, why the hell would Pavel need shoes in hot spells like this! It's only we official drudges, father went on, who never give our feet any rest: if not boots then rubbers, if not rubbers then boots—and that's the kind of torment you go through all your life. If it's raining outside—then you have to dry off your shoes, if the sun's shining—that means be careful they don't crack. And the main thing is every day in the morning you have to mess around with shoe polish. But Pavel is a free man, a dreamer, he's going to die with his feet bare. He's an idler, your Pavel—our father said to us—that's why he's a barefoot tramp. All his money's in his dacha probably, up to his neck in debt, and he keeps on going there—to go fishing, loafing about on the shore, what kind of dacha-dweller is he anyway? His house is worse than our shed, but to top things off he put a windvane on his roof, just think of it—a windvane! I ask him, the fool: why, I say, why the windvane, all it does is squeak. And he replies from there, the roof: why there's a lot of things can happen, citizen prosecutor, for example, he says, the wind keeps blowing and blowing in one direction and then suddenly changes. That's all right for you, he says, I see you read the newspapers, they write about it there of course; about the weather, that is, but, you know, I don't subscribe to anything, so that for me a windvane is an absolutely essential item. You know, he says, you learn from the papers right off if something's not right, but I'll be using the windvane to get oriented, which is much more precise, more precise than that it's impossible to be—our father told us, lying in his hammock with his newspaper in his hands. Then father climbed out of the hammock, strode off—hands behind his back—amid the pines oozing hot resin and sap from the earth, picked and ate several strawberries from a strawberry bed, looked up at the sky, where at the moment there were no clouds, no planes, no birds, yawned, shook his head and said, with Norvegov in mind: well, he should thank God I'm not his principal, I'd make him dance, he'd learn about the wind from me, the wretched boob, the tramp, the miserable windvane. The poor geographer—our father felt not the slightest respect for him, that's what not wearing shoes gets you. True, around the time we met Norvegov on the platform, to him, i.e., Pavel Petrovich, everything seemed to indicate, it made no difference if our father respected him or not, inasmuch as around this time he, i.e., our instructor, did not exist, he had died in the spring of the year such-and-such, that is, some two years before our meeting with him on that same platform. So as I was saying, with us something is not right about time, let's get it straight. He was sick for a long time, his illness was painful and prolonged, and he knew perfectly well that he would soon die, but he didn't let on. He remained the most cheerful, or to be precise, the only cheerful person in the school, and there was no end to his jokes. He would say that he felt so skinny that he was afraid some chance wind would blow him away. The doctors, laughed Norvegov, forbid me to get closer than half a kilometer to windmills, but the forbidden fruit is sweet: I am drawn to them irresistibly, the ones right by my house, on the wormwood hills, and a time will come when I can no longer resist. In the dacha settlement where I live they call me wind-driver and windvane, but tell me, is it so bad to pass for a wind-driver, especially if you're a geographer? Why, a geographer has to be a wind-driver, that's his specialty—don't you think so, my young friends? Don't give in to depression—he shouted fervently, waving his arms,—isn't that right, live at full bicycle speed, get tan and go swimming, catch butterflies and dragon-flies, the ones with the most colors, especially those magnificent Blacks and Yellows that are so numerous at my dacha! What else? Know this, my friends, there is no happiness on earth, nothing of the sort, nothing like that at all, but then—Lord!—there is, finally, peace and freedom. The contemporary geographer, like, incidentally, the electrician, the plumber, and the general, lives only once. So live in the wind, young folk, lots of compliments to the ladies, lots of music, smiles, fishing trips, vacations, knightly tournaments, duels, chess matches, breathing exercises and other nonsense. And if you are ever called a wind-driver, said Norvegov, rattling the box of matches he had found so loudly it could be heard all over the school,—don't feel offended: that's not such a bad thing. For what do I fear in the face of eternity if today a wind ruffles my hair, freshens my face, puffs the sleeves of my shirt, blows through my pockets and tears at the buttons on my jacket, but tomorrow—destroys the unneeded old buildings, rips out oaks by the roots, stirs and swells the reservoirs and scatters the seeds of my garden all across the earth,—what do I fear, geographer Pavel Norvegov, an honest suntanned man from suburban zone five, a modest pedagogue, but one who knows his business, whose skinny but nonetheless commanding hand turns the hollow globe made of fraudulent papier-maché from morning to night! Give me time—I'll show you which of us is right, some day I'll give your lazy, squeaky ellipsoid such a whirl that your rivers will back up, you'll forget your false books and newspapers, your own voices, names, and ranks will make you vomit, you will forget how to read and write, you will want to babble and whisper like aspen leaves in August. An angry crosswind will blast away the names of your streets and back alleys and the asinine signs, and you will want the truth. You lousy cockroach tribe! You brainless Panurgian herd, crawling with bedbugs and flies! You will want the great truth. And then I will come. I will come and bring with me the ones you have murdered and humiliated and I will say: there is your truth for you, and retribution against you. From horror and sorrow the obsequious pus which pollutes the blood in your veins will turn into ice. Fear The Sender of Wind, you sovereigns of cities and dachas, cower before the breezes and crosswinds, they engender hurricanes and tornadoes. I tell you this, I, geographer of the fifth suburban zone, the man who turns the vacuous cardboard globe. And saying this, I take eternity as my witness—isn't that right, my youthful assistants, my dear contemporaries and colleagues, isn't that right?

He died in the spring of the year such-and-such in his little house with the windvane. That day we were supposed to take our last exam in a class, his class as it happened, geography. Norvegov promised to come by nine, we gathered in the hall, and waited for the teacher until eleven, but he did not come. The principal of the school, Perillo, said the exam would be postponed until the next day, inasmuch as Norvegov had apparently fallen ill. We decided to visit him, but none of us knew the instructor's city address, so we went to the teachers' room to Assistant Curriculum Director Tinbergen, who secretly lives in our apartment and dances in the entrance hall in the morning, but whom neither you nor I have ever seen, for all one has to do is boldly fling open the door from our room into the hall and you will find yourself—fling it open boldly!—in the moat of the Milan fortress and you are watching flying on four wings. The day is extremely sunny, and Leonardo wearing an old wrinkled tunic is standing by an easel with a drawing pen in one hand and a bottle of red India ink in the other, and putting some sort of diagrams on a piece of Whatman paper, sketching leaves of the sedge which has totally overgrown the damp and silty bottom of the moat (the sedge comes up to Leonardo's waist), making sketches of ballistic machines one after the other; and when he gets a little tired he takes a white entomological net and catches black dragonflies in order to study the structure of their retinas properly. The artist looks at you sullenly, he always seems to be dissatisfied with something. You want to leave the moat, return to your room, you are already turning around and attempting to find a door covered with leatherette in the perpendicular wall of the moat, but the master manages to restrain you by the arm, and looking into your eyes he says: homework assignment: describe the jaw of a crocodile, the tongue of a hummingbird, the carillon of the Convent of Novodevichy, describe the bird cherry's stem, Lethe's circumflexion, the tail of any loca!

dog, a night of love, the mirages over hot asphalt, the clear noonday in Berezovo, the face of a flibbertigibbet, the pits of Hell, compare a termite colony with a forest anthill, the dolorous destiny of leaves—with the serenade of a Venetian gondolier, and transform a cicada into a butterfly; turn rain into hail, day—into night, give us this day our daily bread, change a vowel sound into a sibilant, prevent the crash of a train whose engineer is asleep, repeat the thirteenth labor of Hercules, give a passer-by a light, explain youth and old age, sing me a song about how where the bee sucks there suck I, turn your face to the north, to the high courts of Novgorod, and then tell how a yardman finds out if it's snowing outside if the yardman sits in the vestibule all day chatting with the elevator operator and doesn't look out the window, because there is no window, yes, tell precisely how he does this; and moreover, plant the white rose of the winds in your garden; show it to your teacher Pavel, and if he likes it—give teacher Pavel the white rose, pin the flower to his cowboy shirt or his dacha boater, do something nice for the man who is departing into nowhere, delight your old pedagogue—the jovial man, the jester, the driver of winds. O Rosa, the teacher will say, white Rosa Windova, dear girl, sepulchral flower, how I want your untouched body! On one of the nights of a summer embarrassed by its own beauty I await you in the little house with the windvane beyond the blue river, address: dacha locale, zone five, find postman Mikheev, ask for Pavel Norvegov, ring the bicycle bell repeatedly, wait for the rowboat from the misty shore, light up a signal fire, don't be depressed. Lying at the top of the steep sandy slope in a rick of hay, count the stars and weep from happiness and anticipation, remember a childhood which was like a juniper bush covered with fireflies, a Christmas tree trimmed with incredible whimsy, and think of what will come to pass toward morning when the first electric train is going by the station, when the people of the plants and factories awake with their hungover heads, and spitting and cursing the components of their engines and machines, they stride intemperately past the ponds near the station to the station beer-stands—green and blue. Yes, Rosa, yes, teacher Pavel will say, what is going to happen to us that night will be like a flame consuming an icy waste, like a starfall reflected in a fragment of a mirror which has suddenly fallen from its frame in the dark, forewarning its owner of imminent death. It will be like a shepherd's reed pipe, and like music which is yet unwritten. Come to me, Windy Rose, can it be that your old teacher, striding across the valleys of nonexistence and the tablelands of anguish is not dear to you. Come, to ease the trembling in your loins, and to soften my sadnesses. And if your instructor Pavel does say this—Leonardo says to you—inform me about it the very same night, and I will prove to everyone on earth that *in time nothingness is in the past and future and it contains nothing from the present, and in nature it borders on the impossible, from which it follows, pursuant to what we have said, that it has no existence, inasmuch as there would have to be emptiness present where nothing is supposed to be,* but nevertheless—continues the artist,—*with the help of windmills I can produce wind at any time.* And a last assignment for you: this device which looks like a gigantic black dragonfly—see it? It stands on a grassy slope—*try it tomorrow over the lake and be sure to put on a fur strip as a belt so that if you fall you won't drown.* And then you answer the artist: dear Leonardo, I'm afraid I cannot do your interesting problems, except for the problem connected with a yardman's finding out if in fact snow is falling outside on the street. I can answer this question for any examination committee at any time just as easily as you can produce wind. But unlike you I will not need a single windmill. If the yardman sits in the vestibule from morning to evening and chats with the elevator operator, and if there are *yok* windows, which in Tatar means *no*, the yardman determines if on—or to be more precise, over—the street, or onto the street it is snowing, by the snowflakes on the hats and collars which hurriedly enter the vestibule from the street, hastening to meetings with superiors. They, the ones who have snowflakes on their clothing, are usually divided into two types: well dressed and badly dressed, but it's amusing that snowflakes fall equally on both the former and the latter. I noticed this when I worked as yardman in the Ministry of Agitation. I got all of sixty rubles a month, but then I made a detailed study of such fine phenomena as snow-fall, leaf-fall, rain-fall, and even hail-showers, which of course none of the ministers or their helpers can say of themselves, even though they all got several times more per month than I. So I make a simple deduction: if you are a minister you cannot do a proper study and understand what is happening in the street and in the sky, because even if you have a window in your office, you have no time to look out: you have too many receptions, appointments, and telephone calls. And if the doorman can easily learn about snow-fall from the snowflakes on visitors' hats, you, the minister, cannot, for the visitors leave their outer clothing in the cloakrooms, and if they do not leave it, by the time they wait for the elevator and go up the snowflakes have time to melt. That's why it seems to you, the minister, that it's always summer outside, but this is not so. Therefore, if you want to be a smart minister, ask the yardman about the weather, call him on the telephone in the vestibule. When I worked as yardman in the Ministry of Agitation, I spent long periods sitting in the vestibule and chatting with the elevator operator, and the Minister of Agitation, knowing me as an honest, diligent fellow employee, would call me from time to time and ask: is this yardman so-and-so? Yes, I would reply, so-and-so, I've been working for you since such-and-such a year. Well this is Minister of Agitation so-and-so, he would say, I work on the fifth floor, office number three, and third on the left in the corridor, I have a job for you, stop by for a couple of minutes if you're not busy, it's quite urgent, we'll talk about the weather. Oh, by the way, not only did I work in the same ministry as he, we also were, and possibly still are now, dacha neighbors, in the dacha settlement that is, the Minister's dacha is catty-corner from ours. To be on the safe side I used two words here: *were* and *are*, the latter meaning *to be*, present tense. I did so because—although the doctors maintain that I got well long ago—to this day I cannot be precise and make definite judgments about anything that is in the slightest degree connected with the concept of *time*. It would appear to me that we have some sort of misunderstanding and confusion about it, about time, not everything is what it should be. Our calendars are too arbitrary: the numbers that are written there do not signify anything and are not guaranteed by anything, like counterfeit money. For example, why is it customary to think that the second of January comes right after the first, and not the twenty-eighth right away? And in general can days follow each other, that's some sort of poetic nonsense—a line of days. There is no line, the days come whenever one of them feels like it, and sometimes several come all at once. And sometimes a day doesn't come for a long time. Then you live in emptiness, not understanding anything, quite sick. And other people are sick too, but they keep quiet. I would also like to say that every person has his own special calendar of life not resembling anyone else's. Dear Leonardo, if you asked me to make up a calendar of *my* life, I would bring you a sheet of paper with a multitude of dots on it: the whole sheet would be covered with dots, just dots, and every dot would stand for a day. A thousand days—a thousand dots. But don't ask me which day corresponds to this or that dot: I don't know anything about that. And don't ask during what year, month or age of my life I made up my calendar, for I do not know what these words mean, and you yourself, pronouncing them, do not know either, just as you do not know a definition of time the truth of which I would not doubt. Be humble! Neither you nor I nor any of our friends can explain what we mean when we discuss time, conjugate the verb *to be*, and divide life into yesterday, today and tomorrow, as if these words differed from each other in meaning, as if it had not been said: tomorrow is just another name for today, as if it had been granted us to comprehend even a small portion of what happens to us here in the closed space of an explicable grain of sand, as if everything that happens here is, exists,—really, in fact *is, exists*. Dear Leonardo, not long ago (just now, in a short time) I was floating (am floating, will float) down a big river in a rowboat. Before this (after this) I was often (will be) there and am well acquainted with the area. It was (is, will be) very good weather, and the river—quiet and broad, and on shore, on one of the shores, a cuckoo was cuckooing (is cuckooing, will be cuckooing), and when I put down (will put down) the oars to rest, it sang (will sing) to me of how many years of life I have left. But this was (is, will be) stupid on its part because I was quite certain (am certain, will be certain) that I will soon die, if I have not died already. But the cuckoo did not know about that and, one must suppose, my life interested it to a much smaller degree than its life did me. So I put down the oars, and counting what were supposedly my years, asked myself several questions: what is the name of this river drawing me to its delta, who am I, the one being drawn along, how old am I, what is my name, what day is today and what year is it, in essence, and also: the boat, here's the boat, an ordinary boat—but whose? and why precisely a boat? Esteemed master, these were such simple but agonizing questions that I couldn't answer a one and decided that I was having an attack of the same hereditary disease from which my grandmother suffered, my former grandmother. Don't correct me, I intentionally used the word *former* here instead of *deceased*, agree that my choice sounds better, softer and not as hopeless. You see, when grandmother was still with us, sometimes she lost her memory, it usually happened when she looked at something extraordinarily beautiful for a long time. And therefore on the river I thought: it's probably too beautiful around, and so, like grandmother I have lost my memory now and am not in any state to reply to my own commonplace questions. Several days later I went to Doctor Zauze, who was treating me, and consulted him, asking for advice. The doctor told me: my little friend, you should know that you undoubtedly have the same thing your grandmother had. To hell with the countryside, he said, stop going there, look what you've lost there. But doctor, I said, it's beautiful there, beautiful, I want to go there. In that case, he said, taking off or perhaps putting on his glasses, I forbid you to go there. But I didn't obey him. In my opinion he's one of those greedy people who like to be in good places themselves and would like to keep anyone besides themselves from going there. Of course I promised him not to go anywhere outside the city, but I did go as soon as I was let out, and I lived at the dacha the remainder of the summer and even part of autumn until they started making fires for fallen leaves and part of the fallen leaves had floated down our river. During those days it got so beautiful that I could not even go out on the veranda: all I had to do was look at the river and see the many-colored forests on the other side, the Norvegov side, and I'd begin to cry and couldn't do anything with myself. The tears flowed spontaneously, I couldn't say no to them, and inside I was disquieted and feverish (father demanded that mother and I return to the city—and we did), but what had happened on the river, that time in the boat, did not repeat itself—not that summer, or that autumn, or in general ever again after. Obviously I can forget things: an object, a word, a name, a date, but only then, on the river, in the boat, did I forget everything at once. But as I realize now the condition was nevertheless not grandmother's, it was something else, my own, perhaps something not yet studied by doctors. Yes, I could not reply to the questions I had asked myself, but understand this: it did not mean loss of memory at all, that wouldn't cover any of it. Dear Leonardo, it was all far more serious, to wit: I was in one of the phases of disappearance. You see, a man cannot disappear momentarily and totally, first he is transformed into something distinct from himself in form and in essence—for example, into a waltz, a distant, faintly audible evening waltz, that is, he disappears partially, and only later does he disappear totally.

Somewhere in a glade a wind orchestra assumed position. The musicians sat down on the fresh stumps of pine trees, and put their sheet music in front of them not on music-stands but on the grass. The grass is tall and thick and strong, like lake rushes, and it supports the music without difficulty. You probably don't know this, but it's possible there is no orchestra in the glade, but you can hear music from beyond the forest and you feel good. You feel like taking off your shoes, socks, standing on tiptoe and dancing to this distant music, staring at the sky, you hope it will never end. Veta, my dear, do you dance? Of course, my sweet, I do so love to dance. Then allow me to ask you for a turn. With pleasure, with pleasure, with pleasure! But then mowers appear in the glade. Their instruments, their twelve-handled scythes, glitter in the sun too, not gold like the musicians', but silver, and the mowers begin to mow. The first mower approaches a trumpeter, and lifting his scythe in time to the playing music, with a quick swish he severs the grassy stems upon which the trumpeter's music rests. The book falls and closes. The trumpeter chokes off in mid-bar and quietly goes away into a bower where there are many cool springs and all kinds of birds are singing. The second mower advances to the French horn player and does the same thing—the music is still playing—that the first did: cuts. The French horn player's book falls. He gets up and goes off after the trumpeter. The third mower strides expansively up to the bassoon: and his book—the music is still playng but it is getting softer—falls too. And then all three musicians, noiselessly, single-file, go to listen to the birds and drink the spring water. Soon—the music is playing *piano*—they are succeeded by the cornet, the percussion section, the second and third trumpets, and also the flutists, and they are all carryng their instruments— each carries his own, the entire orchestra disappears into the bower, and although no one touches his lips to the mouthpieces, the music continues playing. Now *pianissimo*, it lingers in the glade, and the mowers, shamed by this miracle, weep and wipe their wet faces with the sleeves of their red Russian shirts. The mowers cannot work—their hands tremble, and their hearts are like the mournful swamp frogs—but the music continues to play. It lives independently, it is a waltz which only yesterday was one of us: a man disappeared, transposed into sounds, and we will never find out about it. Dear Leonardo, as for the incident with me and the boat, the river, the oars, and the cuckoo, obviously I too disappeared. I turned into a nymphea then, into a white river lily with a long golden-brown stem, or to be more precise put it this way: I *partially* disappeared into a white river lily. That way's better, more precise. I remember well, I was sitting in the boat, the oars at rest. On one of the shores a cuckoo was counting the years of my lfe. I asked myself several questions and was all ready to answer, but I couldn't and I was amazed. And then something happened to me, there, inside, in my heart and in my head, as if I were turned off. And then I felt that I had disappeared, but at first I decided not to believe it, I didn't want to. And I said to myself: it's not true, this is just an illusion, you are a bit tired, it's very hot today, take the oars and row, row home. And I tried to take the oars, I stretched out my hands toward them, but nothing happened: I saw the grips, but my palms did not feel them, the wood of the oars flowed through my fingers, past the phalanges, like sand, like air. No, on the contrary, I, my former and now no longer existing palms, let the wood flow through like water. This was worse than if I had become a ghost, because a ghost can at least pass through a wall, but I couldn't have, there would have been nothing to pass through, and there was nothing left of me. But that's not right either: something was left. A desire for my former self was left, and even if I was incapable of remembering who I was before the disappearance, I felt that then, that is, *before*, my life had been fuller and more interesting, and I wanted to become the same unknown, forgotten what's-his-name again. The waves beat the boat to shore in a deserted spot. After taking several steps along the beach I looked back: there was nothing resembling my tracks on the sand behind. And in spite of this I still did not want to believe. It could be a lot of things, one, it could turn out that all this was a dream, two, it's possible that the sand here is extraordinarily firm and I, weighing a total of only so many kilograms, did not leave tracks in it because of my lightness, and, three, it is quite probable that I hadn't even gotten out of the boat onto shore yet, but was still sitting in it and, naturally, I could not leave tracks where I had not yet been. But next, when I looked around and saw what a beautiful river we have, what wonderful old willows and flowers grow on this shore and the other, I said to myself: you are a miserable coward, and becoming an inveteratre liar, you were afraid that you had disappeared and decided to fool yourself, you're inventing absurdities and so on, it's high time you became honest, like Pavel, who is also Savl. What happened to you is certainly no dream, that's clear. Further: even if you didn't weigh as much as you do, but a hundred times less, your tracks would still have been left in the sand. But from this day forth you do not weigh even a gram, for you no longer are, you simply disappeared, and if you want to be convinced of that turn around and look at the boat again: you will see that you are not in the boat either. But no, I replied to my *other* self (although Doctor Zauze tried to prove to me that supposedly no *other* me existed, I am not inclined to trust his totally unfounded assertions), true, I am not in the boat, but then there is a white river lily with golden-brown stem and yellow, faintly aromatic stamens lying in the boat. I picked it an hour ago at the western shores of the island in the backwater where such lilies, and also yellow water-lilies, are so numerous that one doesn't want to touch them, it is better to just sit in the boat and look at them, at each individually or all at once. One can also see there the blue dragonflies called in Latin *simpetrum*, quick and nervous water-striding beetles resembling daddy-longlegs, and in the sedge swim ducks, honest-to-goodness wild ducks. Some mottled species with nacreous shadings. There are gulls there too: they have concealed their nests on the islands, amid the so-called weeping willows, weeping and silvery, and not once did we manage to find a single nest, we cannot even imagine what one of them looks like—the nest of a river gull. But then, we do know how a gull fishes. The bird flies rather high over the water and peers into the depths, where the fish are. The bird sees the fish well, but the fish does not see the bird, the fish sees only gnats and mosquitoes which like to fly right over the water (they drink the sweet sap of the water-lilies), the fish feed on them. From time to time a fish leaps from the water, swallowing one or two mosquitoes, and at that instant the bird, wings folded, falls from on high and catches the fish and bears it in its beak to its nest, the gull's nest. True, the bird occasionally fails to catch the fish, and then the bird again achieves the necessary altitude and continues flying, peering into the water. There it sees the fish and its own reflection. That's another bird, thinks the gull, very similar to me, but different, it lives on the other side of the river and always flies out hunting along with me, it goes fishing too, but that bird's nest is somewhere on the reverse side of the island, right under our nest. It's a good bird, muses the gull. Yes, gulls, dragonflies, water striders and the like—that's what there is on the western shores of the island, in the backwater, where I picked the nymphea which is now lying in the bottom of the boat, withering.

But why did you pluck it, was there some necessity for that, you don't even like to pick flowers—I know—you don't even like to, you only like to stare at them or cautiously touch them with your hand. Of course, I shouldn't have, I didn't want to, believe me, at first I didn't want to, I never wanted to, it seemed to me that if I ever picked it something unpleasant would happen—to me or to you, or to other people, or to our river, for example, it might evaporate. You just uttered a strange word, what did you say, what was that word—*eshakurate*? No, you're imagining things, hearing things, there was no such word, something like that, but not that, I can't remember now. But what was I just talking about in general, could you help me to recapture the thread of my discussion, it's been broken. We were chatting about how one day Trachtenberg unscrewed a handle in the bathroom and hid it somewhere, and when the custodian came he stood in the bathroom for a long time just staring. He was silent for a long time, because none of it made sense. The water was running, making noise, and the bathtub was gradually filling, and then the custodian asked Trachtenberg: where's the faucet handle? And the old woman answered him: I have a record player (That's not true, I'm the only one who has a record player), but no faucet handle. But there's no faucet handle in the bathtub, said the custodian. That's your problem, citizen, I don't answer to you—and she went into her room. And the custodian went up to the door and started knocking, but neither Trachtenberg nor Tinbergen opened to him. I was standing in the entrance hall and thinking, and when the custodian turned to me and asked what to do, I said: knock, and it shall be opened unto you. He started knocking again, and Trachtenberg soon opened to him, and he again expressed his curiosity: where's the handle? I don't know, objected old Tinbergen, ask the young man. And with her bony finger she pointed in my direction. The custodian observed: maybe that kid doesn't have everything upstairs, but it strikes me that he's not so stupid as to unscrew the faucet handle, you're the one who did that, and I'll complain to Building Superintendent Sorokin. Tinbergen burst out laughing in the custodian's face. Ominously. And the custodian went off to lodge his complaint. I just stood there in the entrance hall meditating. Here, on the hat-rack, hung an overcoat and head-gear, here stood two containers used for moving furniture. These things belonged to the neighbors, i.e., Trachtenberg-Tinbergen and her excavator. At least the greasy, eight-pointed cap was his definitely, because the old woman wore only hats. I often stand in the entrance hall examining all of the objects on the hat-rack. It seems to me they are benevolent and I feel at home with them, I'm not afraid of them when no one is dressed in them. I also think about the containers, wondering what wood they are made of, how much they cost, and what train, on what branch, brought them to our town.

Dear student so-and-so, I, the author of this book, have a pretty clear picture of that train—a long freight. Its cars, for the most part brown, were covered with scrawls in chalk—letters, ciphers, words, whole sentences. Apparently workers wearing special railway uniforms and caps with tin cockades made their computations, notes, and estimates on some of the cars. Let's suppose the train has been standing on a stub for several days and no one knows when it will start up again or where it will go. And then a commission comes to the stub, examines the seals, bangs hammers on wheels, peeps into the axle-boxes, checking for cracks in the metal and to see if anyone has mixed sand in the oil. The commission squabbles and swears, its monotonous work has long been a bore, and it would take pleasure in going on pension. But how many years is it to pension?—penses the commission. It takes a piece of chalk and writes on anything at hand, usually on one of the boxcars: year of birth—such-and-such, work seniority—such-and-such, therefore such-and-such a number of years to pension. Then the next commission comes to work, it is deep in debt to its colleagues on the first commission, which is why the second commision doesn't squabble and swear, but tries to do everything quietly, without even using hammers. This commission is sad, it too takes chalk from its pocket (here I should note in parentheses that the station where this action takes place could never, even during two world wars, complain about a lack of chalk. It had been known to have shortages of: sleepers, handcars, matches, molybdenum ore, semaphores, wrenches, hoses, crossing barriers, flowers for decorating the embankments, red banners with the requisite slogans commemorating events of varying qualities, spare brakes, siphons and ashpits, steel and slag, bookkeeping records, warehouse logs, ashes and diamonds, smokestacks, speed, cartridges and marijuana, levers and alarmclocks, amusements and firewood, record players and porters, experienced scriveners, surrounding forests, rhythmical timetables, drowsy flies, cabbage soup, oatmeal, bread, and water. But there was always so much chalk at this station that, as indicated in the telegraph agency's announcement, it would require such-and-such number of trains each with such-and-such payload capacity, to carry away from the station all of the potential chalk. More accurately, not from the station, but from the chalk quarries in the area around the station. The station itself was called *Chalk*, and the river—the misty white river with chalky banks—could have no other name than the *Chalk*. In short, everything here at the station and around was made out of this soft white stone: people worked in chalk quarries and mines, they received chalky rubles dusted with chalk, they made the houses and streets out of chalk, they whitewashed with chalk, in school the children were taught to write with chalk, chalk was used for washing hands, cooking pots and teeth were cleaned and scrubbed with chalk, and, finally, when dying, people willed that they be buried in the local cemetery where instead of earth there was chalk and every grave was decorated with a chalk headstone. One would have to think that the settlement of Chalk was singularly clean, all white and neat, and cirrus or cumulus clouds pregnant with chalky rains constantly hung over it, and when the rains fell the settlement got even whiter and cleaner, that is, absolutely white, like a fresh sheet in a good hospital. As for the hospital, it was here too, a good one and big. In it the miners suffered their illnesses and died, sick with a special disease which in conversation among themselves they called "the chalky." Chalk dust settled in the workers' lungs, penetrated their blood, their blood became weak and anemic. The people paled, their pellucid white faces glowed in the murk of the night-shift hours, they glowed against the background of pillows on which they would die, and after that the faces glowed only in the photographs of family albums. The snapshot would be pasted on a separate page and someone from the household would carefully draw a box around it with a black pencil. The frame came out solemn, if uneven. However, let us return to the second railroad commission which is getting chalk out of its pocket, and—let us close the parentheses) and writes on the car: so much for Petrov, so much for Ivanov, so much for Sidorov, total—so many chalk rubles. The commission moves along, writing on some of the boxcars and flatcars the word *checked*, but on others—*to be checked*—for it is impossible to check them all at once, and there is after all a third commission: let it check the remaining cars. But besides the commissions there is *noncommission* at the station too, or to put it another way, people who are not members of commissions, they stand outside them, employed at other jobs, or they don't work here at all. Nevertheless, they are among those who cannot resist the desire to take a piece of chalk and write something on the side of a boxcar—wooden and warm from the sun. Here comes a soldier wearing a forage cap, he heads for a boxcar: *two months to demob*. A miner appears, his white hand produces a laconic: *scum*. A D-student from fifth grade, whose life is perhaps harder than all of ours put together: *Maria Stepanna's a bitch*. A woman station laborer in an orange sleeveless jacket, whose duty is to tighten the nuts and clean out the viaducts, throwing the waste onto the rails below, knows how to draw a sea. She draws a wavy line on the car, and truly, a sea is the result, and an old beggar who doesn't know how to sing or play the accordion, and hasn't yet managed to buy a hurdy-gurdy, writes two words: *thank you*. Some drunk and scraggly guy who has accidentally discovered that his girfriend is being unfaithful, in despair: *Three loved Valya*. Finally the train leaves the stub and rolls along the railways of Russia. It is made up of cars checked by the commissions, of clean words and curse words, fragments of someone's heartaches, memorial inscriptions, business notes, idle graphical exercises, of laughter and curses, howls and tears, blood and chalk, of white on black and brown, of fear of death, of pity for friends and strangers, of wracked nerves, of good impulses and rose-colored glasses, of boorishness, tenderness, dullness and servility. The train rolls along, Sheina Solomonovna Trachtenberg's containers on it, and all Russia comes out onto windswept platforms to look it in the eye and read what has been written—the passing book of their own life, a senseless book, obtuse, boring, created by the hands of incompetent commissions and pitiful, misled people. After a certain number of days the train arrives in our town, at the freight station. The people who work at the railroad post office are worried: they have to inform Sheina Trachtenberg that the containers with her furniture have finally been received. It's raining outside, the sky is full of storm clouds. In the special postal office at the so-called border of the station a one-hundred-watt bulb burns, dispelling the semidarkness and creating comfort. In the post office there are several worried office workers wearing blue uniforms. They worriedly make tea on a hot plate, and worriedly they drink it. It smells of sealing wax, wrapping paper, and twine. The window opens onto the rusty reserve lines, where grass is sprouting up among the sleepers and some kind of small but beautiful flowers are growing. It is quite nice to look at them from the window. The vent in the window is open, therefore certain sounds which are characteristic of a junction station are quite audible: a lineman's horn, the clank of air hoses and buffers, a hissing of pneumatic brakes, the dispatcher's commands, and also various types of whistles. It is nice to hear all this too, especially if you are a professional and can explain the nature of each sound, its meaning and its symbolism. And of course the office workers of the railroad are professionals, they have many railway kilometers behind them, in their time they have all served as heads of postal cars or worked as conductors of those same cars, a few of them on international runs even, and as they are wont to say, they've seen the world and know what's what. And if one were to show up and ask their supervisor, is it so...

Yes, dear author, that's right: go see him at home, ring the vibrant bicycle bell at the door—let him hear that and open. Whom tum tum tum lives here supervisor so-and-so's here open up we've come to ask and be given an honest answer. Who is it? Those Who Came. Come tomorrow, today it's too late, my wife and I are sleeping. Wake up for the time has come to tell the truth. About whom? about what? About the fellows in your office. Why at night? At night sounds are easier to hear, the cry of a baby, the moan of a dying man, the flight of a nightingale, the cough of a trolley constrictor: wake up, open up, and answer. Wait, I'll put on pyjamas. Put them on they suit you very well very nice check you make them or buy them? Don't remember, don't know, have to ask my wife, mama, Those Who Came would like to know about the pyjamas made or bought if so where and how much yes made no bought it was snowing and cold we were coming back from the movies and I thought well now my husband isn't going to have warm pyjamas this winter looked into the department store and you stayed on the street to buy bananas there was a line for them and I wasn't in any special hurry looked first at carpeting and signed up for a meter and a half for a meter seventy-five for three years from now because the factory was closed for repairs and then in the men's section undergarments I saw those pyjamas right away and some Chinese shorts with a top sort of shaggy but I just couldn't decide what's better in general I liked the underwear better cheap and a good color one could sleep in them and wear them underneath at work and wear them around home but then we live in a coummunal apartment with neighbors you know how it is in the hall or in the kitchen you can't go out there but in pyjamas it would be decent and even nice so then I signed up for the pyjamas I return to the street and you're still waiting for the bananas I say to you give me I say some money I signed up for pyjamas and you say but I don't need them probably some kind of junk no I

say not junk at all but a very decent import item with wooden buttons go on
look for yourself and in front of you there's some middle-aged woman
wearing a plastic raincoat standing in front of you with earrings so plump
so gray she turned around and says are you going go don't be afraid I'll be
standing here the whole time if anyone says anything I'll say you were
behind me and as for the pyjamas you're wrong to argue with your wife I
know those pyjamas a very worthwhile buy they'll be last week I bought
that kind for the whole family bought father bought brother bought
husband and sent some to a brother-in-law in Gomel he's in school studying there so don't think just buy and put an end to it because next time
you'll have to look all over town to sign up for the same pyjamas and they'll
tell you come in at the end of the month you'll come in at the end of the
month and they'll tell you they had them yesterday so don't even stop to
think say thanks to your wife and I'll hold the line never fear and then you
say well all right let's go in and look we enter the store and I ask how you
like them and you shrug and say I don't know the devil only knows not bad
only the check is kind of odd and I think the bottms are a bit tight you say
and the saleslady hears it a youngish one nice and proposes what do you
mean try them on use the little booth that's what they're here for not for me
I took the pyjamas they were hanging on a wooden hanger we went behind
the curtain there three big mirrors when you started to undress snowflakes
or rather not snowflakes but waterdrops sprinkled right against all the
mirrors and I stuck my head out from behind the curtain and I shout to the
saleslady miss do you have some sort of cloth and she but what do you need
it for and I say have to wipe the mirror and she but what happened did it get
sprinkled yes a little after all it's snowing outside and it's so warm here in
your store that it all melted then she got a yellow flannel cloth from under
the counter there she says and asks later well have you tried them on and I
say no still trying it on yet I'll tell you when everything's ready and then you
glance in and give your advice maybe the pants really are too narrow and
tight I look and you're already wearing the pyjamas and you're turning
around in various directions even squatting once or twice to check the
crotch well how are they I ask and you keep muttering somethng about the
pants being a bit tight and somehow the check is disturbing not Russian I
should think not I say it's an imported item and I'll call the saleslady for her
advice but just at that time she has a load of customers she replies in a
minute in a minute but doesn't come and doesn't come then you say I'll go
out to her myself but I don't let you what's wrong with you there are people
around it's embarrassing and you say so what if there are people haven't
they ever seen any pyjamas they all each of them has ten pairs himself
what's so scary about that you say aren't we people ourselves and you go
out of the booth and ask the girl well how do they fit and she like they were
tailored for you very good even take them you won't be sorry only one
hundred fifty sets left in that size by tonight there won't be any left they're

going fast then you inquire it seems to me the pants are a little too tight it just seems like that to you the girl replies but that style is the most fashionable now a long jacket and sort of wide but the pants the reverse but if you want you can get them altered let out in places but now for example in the jacket I would do the reverse take it in because the jacket really is a trifle wide in the waist but your wife will do it or take it to a seamstress and she asks me do you have a machine at home yes only not so good I used to have a Singer foot model my mother's and when my daughter got married I gave it to her not sorry of course but still I do regret it a little but it's essential for my daughter too they have a little one now occasionally one thing or another has to be made for him of course let my daughter do it on the Singer and we'll buy ourselves another one a new completely electric one but it's hard to work on it either it's a bad one or I'm not used to it the seams it makes are uneven it'll break the thread but better it than going to a seamstress the time would be extensive and expensive so that naturally we'll alter them at home and the girl says of course you'll alter them at home spend one evening at it but they'll come out so well that they'll last more than a year and she asks you and what about you do you like them you smiled even a little embarrassed I think and normal pyjamas you say what's so special then the girl says to you and you probably work on the railroad you and I exchanged glances as if to ask how did she guess and I ask her the question how did you find that out I'd be interested to know very simple she replies your husband has on his head a uniform cap with a hammer and adjustable wrench on it and my brother works on trains too he serves the commuter lines sometimes he comes in the evening and tells all about his work where what wreck occurred where what is interesting I even envy him every day something new but it's always the same thing here nowhere to escape are you going to take them she says then I ask her to please wrap up the pyjamas for us and I'll go pay for them right now and she says first you go pay for them and then I'll wrap them up right away I went to pay at the cashier's booth there was a line and you took off the pyjamas in the dressing booth and I see you're already taking them to her on a hanger she started to wrap a ribbon around them even to tie them up not true mama not true I remember everything it was twine and I thought like at work we pack packages and retie parcels we always have whole rolls and skeins of it never ends as much as you want good twine it was twine there in the store there at the girl's there where we work ahead of schedule don't worry stop in drop by check ring the bicycle bell any time we'll look at the twine we'll read the Japanese poets Nikolaev Semyon knows them by heart and reads a lot in general the clever fellow.

A one-hundred-watt bulb burning, the odor of sealing wax, string and paper. Outside the window—rusty rails, small flowers, rain, and the sounds of a junction station. Cast of characters. Supervisor So-and-so, a man who hopes to be promoted. Semyon Nikolaev, a man with an intelligent face. Fyodor Muromtsev, a man with an ordinary face. These, and Other Railway Workers are sitting at a common table, drinking tea with rolls. Those Who Came are standing by the door. Boss So-and-so speaks: Nikolaev, Those Who Came have come, they would like to hear some poetry or prose from the Japanese classics. S. Nikolaev, opening a book: quite by chance I happen to have with me Yasunari Kawabata, who writes: "Are there really such cold spells here? You are all heavily bundled up. Yes, sir. We're all wearing winter things already. It's particulary cold at night when the clear weather sets in after a snowfall. It must be below freezing now. Below freezing already? Yes, it's cold. Whatever you touch is cold. There were intense cold spells last year too. Down to twenty-some degrees below freezing. And was there a lot of snow? On the average the snow cover was seven or eight *shaku*, and after intense snowfalls more than one *jo*. It'll probably start to fall soon. Yes, it's just the time for snowfalls, we're waiting. There was snow not long ago, it covered the ground, but then it melted, got down to almost less than a *shaku*. You mean it's melting now? Yes, but you can expect snowfall any time now." F. Muromtsev: now there's a story for you, Semyon Danilovich, isn't it something! S. Nikolaev: it's not a short story, Fyodor, it's an excerpt from a novel. Supervisor So-and-so: Nikolaev, Those Who Came would like some more. S. Nikolaev: if you like, at random then: "The girl was sitting, beating a drum, modestly and sedately. I was watching her back. She seemed very close, in the next room. My heart beat in time with the drum. A drum so enlivens table-talk!—said the forty-year-old woman, also watching the dancer." F. Muromtsev: how about that, eh? S. Nikolaev: I'll read some more, here is the verse of the Japanese Zen poet Dogen. F. Muromtsev: Zen? that's incomprehensible, Semyon Danilovich, but you didn't give his birth and death dates, please do so if it's not a secret. S. Nikolaev: forgive me, I'll recall in a moment, yes, they are 1200-1253. Supervisor So-and-so: only fifty-three years? S. Nikolaev: but what years they were! F. Muromtsev: what were they like? S. Nikolaev, rising from his stool: "Flowers in the spring, a cuckoo in the summer. And in the autumn—the moon. Cold clean snow in the winter." (He sits down.) That's all. F. Muromtsev: that's all? S. Nikolaev: that's all. F. Muromtsev: somehow that's not much, Semyon Danilovich, eh? A bit too little? Perhaps there's something else, maybe it got torn off? S. Nikolaev: no, that's all, it's a special form of poem, there is long poetry, epics for example, and there are shorter ones, and there are quite short ones, a few lines, or even one. F. Muromtsev: so that's it, now I see: if one were to take it comparatively: rolling stock covers different distances, right? S. Nikolaev: sure, yes it does. F. Muromtsev: and the trains are different too. There are such long ones that the end never seems to come as you wait to cross the track, but there are short ones (he bends down the fingers on his hand), one, two, three, four, five, yes, five, we'll say, five cars or flats—that good enough? that's laconism too, right? S. Niko- laev: basically, yes. F. Muromtsev: so there, I've got it straight. What did you say: cold clean snow in the winter? S. Nikolaev: yes, in the winter. F. Muromtsev: that's very precise, Tsuneo Danilovich, we've always got enough snow in the winter, in January no less than nine *shaku*, and at the end of the season it's towards two *jo*. Ts. Nikolaev: maybe not two, one and a half would be more precise. F. Muromatsu: what do you mean one and a half, Tsuneo-san, when it's a solid two everywhere. Ts. Nakamura: how should I put it, it depends on where you look, if on the lee side of a stump, of course, but much less in the open, one and a half. F. Muromatsu: well, what difference does it make, one and a half, Tsuneo-san, why argue? Ts. Nakamura: look, the rain still hasn't stopped. F. Muromatsu: yes, it's raining, not very good weather. Ts. Nakamura: the whole station's wet, nothing but puddles around, and who knows when it'll dry up. F. Muro- matsu: it's better not to go outside in slop like that without an umbrella— it'll soak you. Ts. Nakamura: last week at this time the weather was exactly the same, the roof started to leak at my house, it soaked all the *tatami*, and there was no way I could hang them up outside to dry. F. Muromatsu: too bad, Tsuneo-san, this kind of rain is no use to anyone, it's just a bother. True, they say it's very good for the rice, but rain like this brings nothing but unpleasantness to a man, particularly a city man. Ts. Nakamura: my neighbor hasn't been able to get out of bed for a week because of this rain, he's sick, coughing. The doctor said that if it continues to pour much longer he'll have to send my neighbor to the hospital, otherwise he'll never get better. F. Muromatsu: there is nothing worse than rain for a sick person, the air gets humid and the sickness intensifies. Ts. Nakamura: this morning my wife wanted to go to the store barefoot, but I asked her to put on *geta*, after all, you can't buy health at any price, and nothing's easier than getting sick. F. Muromatsu: correct, sir, the rain is cold, one shouldn't think of going out without footwear, on days like these we should all take care of ourselves. Ts. Nakamura: a little *sake* wouldn't do us any harm would it? F. Muromatsu: no, but just a tiny bit, one or two cups, that would enliven the table-talk no less than a drum. Supervisor So-and-so: Those Who Came are interested in the fate of certain containers. S. Nikolaev: which ones exactly? Boss So-and-so: Sheina Trachtenberg's. F. Muromtsev: Those Who Came, we're worried, have to write a postcard, they're standing out there in the open, rain, they'll be soaked through, have to write her, here's a form, there's the address. Semyon Danilovich, you write it.

Dear Sheina Solomonovna,—I read, standing in the entrance hall, which at that time seemed almost huge, because there were no containers yet,— dear Sheina Solomonovna, we the workers of the railroad post office herewith inform you that over our entire town, and also over its surrounding areas, a prolonged pre-autumnal rain has been observed. It's wet everywhere, the settlement roads are awash, the leaves of the trees are engorged with moisture and yellowed, and the wheels on the trains, the boxcars and sleepers, have gotten extremely rusty. Days like these are hard on everyone, especially on us, the men of the railways. And nevertheless we have decided not to get thrown off our good working rhythm, we are fulfilling our plan, striving to stick strictly to the usual timetable. And the results are there for everyone to see: in spite of the depth of some puddles, which here at the station has reached two or three *shaku*, in recent times we have dispatched no fewer letters and parcels than was done in the same period last year. In conclusion, we hasten to inform you that two containers have arrived at the station in your name, and we request that you make arrangements for their removal from the yard by our office as promptly as possible. Yours truly. Why did you tell me about that, I wouldn't like to think you capable of reading other people's mail, you've disappointed me, tell me the truth, maybe you invented the incident, after all I know how you love to make up different stories, when I'm talking to you I invent a lot too. *There*, in the hospital, Zauze made great fun of us for being such dreamers. Patient so-and-so, he would laugh, honestly speaking, I have never met a person more healthy than you, but your trouble is this: you are an incredible dreamer. And then we answered: in that case you cannot keep us here so long, we demand immediate release from the *here* which is under your supervision. Then he immediately got serious and asked: well, all right, let's suppose I release you tomorrow, what do you intend to do, what will your occupation be, will you go to work somewhere or return to the school? And we replied: to the school? oh no, we'll go to the country, for we have a dacha there, though more accurately, it's not ours as much as our parents', it's unimaginably beautiful there, at one-twenty, awaiting the wind, the sand and the heather, a skiff on the river, spring and summer, reading in the grass, light lunch, skittles, and a deafening multitude of birds. Then comes autumn, the whole countryside vaporous, no, not fog and not smoke, but exquisite sailing gossamer. In the morning there is dew on the pages of the book we left in the garden. Walking to the station for kerosene. But, doctor, we give you our word of honor that we won't drink beer at the green stand by the pond where the dam is. No doctor, we don't like beer. You know, we've thought about you too, you could probably come for a few days too. We'll set it up with father, and we'll meet you with the special bicycle, the one with the side-car. You know, an old bicycle, and on the side there's a side-car from a small motorcycle. But the side-car probably won't be there: we don't yet know where to get a side-car like that. But we do have the bicycle. It's in the shed along with the kerosene barrel and two empties, sometimes we yell into them. There are boards in there too, and some garden tools and the grandmother chair, that is, no, forgive us, that's wrong, father always asked us to say it the other way: grandmother's chair. More polite that way, he explained. One day he was sitting in that chair, we were sitting beside him on the grass reading various books, yes, doctor you're up on things, you know it's hard for us to read the same book for very long, first we read a page from one book and then a page from another. Then one can take a third book and read a page from it too, and only then go back to the first book. It's easier that way, you don't get as tired. So we were sitting on the grass with sundry books, and in one of them there was something which at first we didn't understand at all, because it was quite an ancient book, no one writes in that language any more, and we said: papa, would you please explain something to us, we don't understand what it says here. And then father tore himself away from his paper and asked: well, what have you got there, some more rubbish? And then we read aloud: *And Satan asked God for holy Russia in order to incarnadine it with martyred blood. A good idea, Devil, it pleases us for our world to suffer for Christ's sake.* For some reason we remembered these words, generally we have a bad memory, you know, but if we like something we remember it right away. But father didn't like it. He jumped out of his chair, snatched the book away from us and yelled: where did this come from, where did it come from, the devil take you, what fool gibberish! And we replied: we were taking a ride on the other side of the river yesterday, our teacher lives there, and he inquired what we were doing and what we were reading. We said that you had given us several volumes of a certain contemporary classic. Our teacher laughed and ran to the river. Then he came back, water dripping from his big freckled ears. Pavel Petrovich told us: dear colleague, how glorious it is that the name you uttered not more than a minute ago dissolved, dissipated in the air like road dust, and that those syllables will go unheard by the one whom we call The Sender, how good it is, dear colleague, isn't that right, otherwise what would happen to that remarkable old fellow, in his fury he would undoubtedly fall off his bicycle and then there wouldn't be a stone left of our esteemed settlements when he got through, and by the way, that wouldn't be such a bad thing anyway, because it's high time. As for my moist ears, which you are studying so attentively, they are wet because I washed them in the waters of the reservoir you see before you, in order to cleanse them of the nastiness of the aforementioned name and to meet my forthcoming state of nonbeing with purity of soul, body, thought, language, and ears. My young friend, pupil and comrade,—our teacher said to us,—whether it's the bitter treasury of folk wisdom or sweet adages and dicta, whether it's the dust of the bedamned or the dismay of the beloved, the sacks of bums or Judas's sums, whether it's movement *from* or standing *by*, the lies of the defrauded or the truths of the defamed, whether war or peace, whether stages or studios, taints or torments, whether darkness or light, hatred or pity, in life and beyond it—whether it's any of these, or anything else, you have to make good sense of it. There is something to be said for doing so, not much perhaps, but something. Here and there, or everywhere, something happens, we cannot say with certainty what exactly, since so far we do not know the essence of the phenomenon, or its name, but, dear pupil and comrade so-and-so, when we have elucidated and discussed this together, when we have elucidated the cause and defined the effect, our time will have come, the time to say our piece—and we will say it. And if it should happen that you are the first to make sense of this, inform me immediately, the address you know: standing by the river at the end of day when those bitten by snakes are dying, ring the bicycle bell, or better—ring the peasant scythe, saying: the scythe is lithe in the dew of morn, make hay while the sun shines, or: along came a spider and sat down beside her, and where are you now, and so on, until the suntanned teacher Pavel hears, and doing a dance, comes out of his house, unties his boat, jumps into it, takes the home-made oars in his hands, rows across Lethe, gets out on your side, embraces you, kisses you, says kind and mysterious words, receives, but no, does not read the sent letter, for he, your teacher, is not among the living, that's the trouble, that's the rub, not among the living, but you—you go on living, until you die, rock beer in barrels and children in carriages, breathe the air of the pine groves, run through meadows and gather bouquets—O, flowers! how wondrously beautiful you are, how wondrously beautiful. Taking leave of this world, I yearned to see a bouquet of dandelions, but my wish was not granted. What did they bring to my house in my final hour, what did they bring? They brought silk and crepe, dressed me in an execrable double-breasted jacket, took away my summer hat, punched all over with a checker's punch, put on some sort of pants, junky—don't argue—junky pants for fifty sweaty rubles, I never wore that kind, they're repulsive, they stick, my body can't breathe or sleep, and the tie—!—they tied a polka-dotted tie around my neck, take it off immediately, open me and at least take off the tie, I'm no bureaucratic rat, I never—understand—I'm not your kind, I'm not your kind—never wore any tie. Preposterous, preposterous wretches, left to live, sick with chlorosis and deader than I, you pooled your funds for the funeral, I know that, and bought all this scaramouche trumpery, but how dare you dress me in the vest and metal-buckled leather shoes of a kind I never wore in my life, oh, you didn't know, you imagined I make five hundred sweaty rubles a month and buy the same useless rags that you do. No, you scalawags, you failed to defame me alive and you'll have no more success when I'm dead. No, I'm not one of yours, and I never made over eighty, and not your kind of rubles, unbesmirched by the lies of your disgusting theories and dogmas, beat me as I lie dead if you must, but take this off, give me back my hat, punched all over with a constrictor's punch, give back everything you've confiscated, a dead man is supposed to get his things, give me my cowboy shirt, my sandals in the style of the Roman Empire period when the aqueduct was built, I will put them under my balding head because—to spite you—I am going to go barefoot even in the valleys of nonbeing and my pants, my patched up pants—you have no right, I'm not wearing your crap, turn your trash over to the second-hand shop, give the money back to those who contributed, I don't want a kopek from you, no, I don't want any, and don't tie that tie on me, or I'll spit my blistering poison spit into your worm-eaten mugs, leave geography teacher Pavel Petrovich in peace! Yes, I am shouting and I will go on shouting without sleep, forever—I will shout of the sublime immortality of the sublime teacher Savl, my desire is for you to find me violently repulsive, I will burst into your dreams and your reality like a hooligan bursting into class during a lesson, burst in with bloodied tongue, but implacable. I will shout to you of my unassailable and beautiful poverty, so do not try to cajole me with gifts, I don't need your sweaty rags and your pussy rubles, and stop that music, or I'll drive you mad with my shout, the shout of the most honorable of the dead. Hear my order, my cry: give me dandelions and bring me my clothes! And to hell with your snotty funeral music, ram pikes up the rears of that dipso orchestra. Malodorous rubbish, mausoleum tumblebugs! Clog the gullets of the requiem lovers, away from my body, or I'll rise up and drive you all away with my damned school pointer, I—Pavel Petrovich, teacher of geography, most prominent turner of the cardboard globe, I am leaving you in order to come, let me go!

Thus spake teacher Pavel, standing on Lethe's bank. From his cleansed ears dripped river water, and the river itself streamed slowly past him and past us along with all its fishes and flat-bottomed boats, with its ancient sailing ships, its reflected clouds, its unseen and future drowners, with the roe of frogs, and duckweed, and tireless water striders, the torn fragments of nets, someone's lost grains of sand and gold bracelets, with empty tin cans and ponderous Monomakh caps, with fuel oil slicks and the almost invisible faces of ferrymen, with bones of contention and pears of despondency, and with little pieces of rubber tubing for caps, without which you can't ride a bicycle, for you can't pump up the tire if you don't put this kind of rubber cap over the valve, and then all is lost, because if you can't use your bicycle it's as if it didn't exist, it virtually disappears, and without a bicycle there's nothing to do at the dacha: you won't be able to go for kerosene, roll down to the pond and back, be at the station to meet Doctor Zauze, who has arrived on the seven-o'clock train: he stands on the platform, turning around, looking in all directions, and you're not there, even though you agreed you would not fail to meet him, and there he stands waiting, and you don't come because you can't find a good valve cover, but the doctor doesn't know about this, although it is beginning to dawn dimly on him: my patient, he conjectures, probably has something wrong with his velocipede, most likely it's the valve cap, the usual thing, those valve caps are really a pain, too bad I didn't think to buy two or three in town, you would have had enough for the whole summer—muses the doctor. Excuse me, please, but what did Pavel Petrovich say to us when giving us the book which so displeased our father? Nothing, the teacher said nothing. Well in my opinion he said: a book. Or even: here's a book. Or even more: here's a book for you, said the teacher. And what did father say about the book when we reported our conversation with Pavel to him: Father didn't believe a word we said. Why, you mean we weren't telling the truth? No, it was the truth, but you know our father, he doesn't believe anyone, and when I said something about that to him once he replied that the whole world is made up of scoundrels and nothing but scoundrels, and if he were to believe what people said, he'd never have become the town's chief prosecutor, and at best he'd be working as a building superintendent like Sorokin, or a dacha glazier. And then I asked father about the newspapers. What about the newspapers?—he responded. And I said: you're always reading newspapers. Yes, I do, he replied, I read newspapers, and so what. Isn't it true that there's nothing written there?—I asked him. Why do you say that, said father, everything is written there, whatever is needed—is written. And if, I asked, something is written there, then why read it: it's scoundrels that write it. And then father said: what scoundrels? And I replied: those who write. Father asked: write what? And I replied: the newspapers. Father was silent and looked at me, and I looked at him, and I felt a little sorry for him, because I saw how disconcerted he was and how two big flies, like two black tears, crawled across his wide white face, and he couldn't even swat them because he was so disconcerted. Then he said to me softly: get out, out of my sight, you son of a bitch, get out of here. This took place at the dacha. I rolled my bicycle out of the shed, tied my butterfly net to the frame and rode out along the path in our garden. In our garden the first apples were ripening, and it seemed to me I could see a worm curled up in each of them, tirelessly chewing our, that is, father's, fruit. And I thought: autumn will come and there will be nothing left in the garden to pick, nothing but rot. I rode on, and still hadn't reached the end of the garden, but there was no end to it, and when the end appeared, I saw the fence and the gate before me, and mama was standing at the gate. Good day, Mama,—I yelled, you're at home from work so early today! My goodness, what work?—she countered, I haven't been working since you started school, almost fourteen years now. Oh, really,—said I, I guess I must have simply forgotten, I've been rushing around the garden too long, all these years probably, and a lot has slipped my mind. You know, there are worms in the baffles, or rather, in the apples, in our garden, we have to think of something, some remedy, otherwise there'll be nothing but garbage left and there'll be nothing to eat, nor even to cook for jam. Mother glanced at my butterfly net and asked: what's wrong, have you quarrelled with father again? I didn't want to upset her, so I answered this way: a little, Mama, we were chatting about Fyodorov, Ivan, the first Russian printer, I expressed the conviction that he—a, bee, see, dee, ee, ef, gee, zee, and so on, but father didn't believe me and advised me to go butterlfy hunting, and so I'm going. Good-bye, mama,—I shouted, I'm going to be alone, going for some meadow chanterelles, long live summer, spring and the flowers, great thoughts, the mightiness of passion, and also love, kindness, and beauty! Ding-dong, bing-bong, tick-tock, toock-toock, scrip-scrape. Not so long ago I enumerated these sounds, they are my favorite sounds, the sounds of a blithe bicycle flying along a dacha path and the whole settlement already swathed in the gossamer of tiny spiders, even if the real fall was far away. But it made no difference to the spiders, good-bye, mama, don't be sad, we'll meet again. She yelled: come back!—and I looked around: mother was standing at the gate anxiously, and I thought: nothing good will come of it if I go back: mother will undoubtedly begin to weep, make me abandon my bicycle seat, take me by the hand, and we will return to the house through the garden, and mother will start to reconcile father and me, which will take several more years, and life—which in our and neighboring settlements is customarily measured in increments of so-called *time*, days of summer and years of winter—my life will stop and it will stand still like a broken bicycle in a shed which is full of discolored old newspapers, and wooden blocks and rusted pliers lie around. No, you didn't want to be reconciled with our father. That's why when mother shouted after you *come back!*—you didn't go back, although you were somewhat sorry for her, our patient mother. Looking around you saw her big eyes the color of dried grass, tears were slowly coming to life in them and they reflected some tall trees with astonishing white bark, the path along which you were riding, and you yourself with your long skinny arms and thin neck, you, too—in your unstopping motion *away*. To a bystander beaten down by the chimeras of the eminent mathematician N. Rybkin, compiler of many textbooks and anthologies of problems and exercises, a man without imagination, without fancy, you would have seemed at this moment boring bicycle rider blank charting a path from point A to point B, in order to surmount an assigned number of kilometers and then to disappear forever in a cloud of parching roadway dust. But I, initiated into your elevated designs and aspirations, I know that on the aforementioned day, a day marked by uncommonly sunny weather, you were a different kind of bicycle rider, one intransient in time and space. Irreconcilability with surrounding reality, staunchness in the battle against hypocrisy and sanctimoniousness, unbending will, firmness in achieving set goals, exceptional principles and honesty in relation to your comrades—these and many other remarkable qualities set you above the usual type of bicycle rider. You were not only and not so much a bicycle rider as a bicycle-rider-*man*, a velocipede-citizen. Really, I'm somehow embarrassed to have you praising me like this. I'm sure that I don't deserve these eloquent words. It even strikes me that I was wrong that day, I probably should have gone back at my mother's call and calmed her, but I rode on and on with my butterfly net, and it made no difference to me where or how I went, it simply felt good to ride, and as I usually do when no one hinders my thinking, I simply thought about everything I saw.

I recall that I turned my attention to someone's dacha and thought: there's a dacha, two stories high, someone lives there, some family. Part of the family lives there all week, and part only on weekends. Then I saw a small two-wheeled cart, it was standing at the edge of a grove, alongside a hay rick, and I said to myself: there's a cart, various items can be carried in it: earth, gravel, suitcases, pencils from the pencil factory named in honor of Sacco and Vanzetti, raw chalk, the fruits of mango trees, apfelstock, ivory scrimshaw, shingles, collected works, rabbit cages, ballot-boxes and trash cans, fluffy things and the contrary—shot, stolen washbasins, tables of ranks and artifacts from the time of the Paris Commune. And in a moment someone will return and start hauling hay in the cart, it's a very handy cart. I saw a little girl, she was leading a dog on a leash—a simple, ordinary dog—they were headed toward the station. I knew that in a moment the girl would come to the pond, she would swim and wash her ordinary dog, and then a number of years would pass, the girl would become a grown-up and start to live a grown-up life: get married, read serious books, hurry and be late to work, buy furniture, talk on the telephone for hours, wash stockings, cook food for herself and others, go visiting and get drunk on wines, envy neighbors and birds, follow the weather reports, wipe away dust, count kopeks, expect a child, go to the dentist, have shoes repaired, please men, look out the window at passing automobiles, go to concerts and museums, laugh when something isn't funny, blush when embarrassed, weep when she feels like weeping, cry out from pain, moan at the touch of her beloved, gradually turn gray, dye lashes and hair, wash hands before supper and feet before bed, pay fines, give receipts for translations received, leaf through magazines, meet old acquaintances on the street, speak at meetings, bury relatives, bang dishes in the kitchen, try smoking, retell the plots of movies, be impertinent to superiors, complain of migraine again, take a train out to the country to collect mushrooms, betray her husband, run from store to store, watch honor guards, love Chopin, pass on idiotic gossip, be afraid of gaining weight, dream of a trip abroad, contemplate suicide, curse out-of-order elevators, save up for a rainy day, sing ballads, expect a child, save old photographs, get promotions at work, scream from terror, shake her head critically, grouse about the incessant rain, regret what has been lost, listen to the latest news on the radio, catch taxis, go to the south, raise children, stand in lines for hours, grow irremediably old, dress in fashion, curse the government, live through inertia, drink medicine, curse her husband, be on a diet, go away and come back, put lipstick on, desire nothing more, visit parents, consider it all over and velveteen (worstedcambricsilkchintzmorocco) very practical, be on the sick-list, lie to friends and relatives, forget about everything on earth, borrow money, live the way everyone lives, remember the dacha, the pond, and the simple, ordinary dog. I saw a pine singed by lightning: yellow needles. I imagined that stormy July night. At first it was quiet and muggy in the settlement, and everyone was sleeping with open windows. Then a storm cloud appeared secretly, it shrouded the stars and brought with it the wind. The wind gusted—across the entire settlement shutters and doors banged shut, and there was a tinkling of broken glass. Then, in total darkness, the rain began to roar: it soaked the roofs and the gardens, the chaises and mattresses and hammocks, sheets, children's toys, primers—and everything else which had been left out in the yards. People woke up in the dachas. Turned on, and immediately turned off, the lights, walked from room to room, looking out the windows and talking to one another: well look at that storm, well look at it pour. Bolts of lightning flashed, apples ripened and fell to the grass. One bolt of lightning struck right here, no one knew where exactly, but they agreed that it was someplace right in the settlement, and those who didn't have lightning rods on their roofs swore to themselves that tomorrow they would get them. And the lightning struck the pine which lived at the edge of the forest, without setting it on fire, just singeing it, and at that instant the entire forest was lit up, along with the dachas, the station, and the railroad branch. The lightning blinded the moving trains, silvered the rails, whitened the sleepers. And then—oh, I know—then you saw the house in which *that* woman lived, and you left the bicycle by the fence and knocked at the gates: toock-toock, my dear, toock-toock, I've come, your timid, your tender one, open and receive me, open and receive me, I don't ask anything of you, I'll just look at you and go away, don't drive me away, just don't drive me away, my dear, I think about you, I weep and I pray for you.

No, no, I won't tell you anything, you have no right to question me about my personal affairs, you shouldn't have anything to do with that woman, don't persist, you fool, you sick person, I want nothing to do with you, I'll call Doctor Zauze, he can take you *there* again, because I'm sick of you and disgusted with you, who are you, why do you pester me with your questions, stop it, better stop it or I'll do something to you, something bad.

Don't pretend that you don't know who I am, if you call me insane then you are just as insane because I am you yourself, but you won't be able to see that woman for two or three months, and when we are released, I'll go to that woman and tell her the whole truth about you, I'll tell her that you're not as old as you claim to be, but only such-and-such an age, and that you're a student in the school for fools not of your own volition but because you weren't accepted at the normal school, you're sick, like me, terribly sick, you're practically an idiot, you can't memorize a single poem, so let that woman throw you over, leave you to stand alone in the dark commuter platform, yes, on a snowy night, when all the lights are broken and all the trains have gone and I'll tell her: the guy who wants you to like him is not worthy of you, and you cannot be with him, because he can never be with you as with a woman, he is deceiving you, he is a crazy snotnose, a bad student in the special school, incapable of learning anything by heart, and you, a serious thirty-year-old woman, you should forget him, abandon him on the snowswept platform at night and give preference to me, a real man, an adult male, honest and healthy, for I would like this very much and I have no difficulty memorizing any poem or solving any problem in life. You're lying, that's base, you won't tell her that because there's no distinction between you and me, you are exactly the same, the same kind of stupid and incompetent person and you're in the same class with me, you've simply decided to excuse yourself from me, you love that woman, but I'm in your way, but nothing will come of it for you, I'll go to her myself and tell her the whole truth—about you and about me, I'll confess that I love her and would like to be with her always, a whole lifetime, even though never once have I tried to be with a single woman, but, probably, yes, of course, for her, for this woman, that's not important, for she is so beautiful, so intelligent—no, it doesn't mean anything! and if I don't dare to be with her as with a woman, she will forgive me, after all that's not necessary, not essential, and this is what I'll say about you: soon a person who somewhat resembles me will come to you, he will knock on the door: toock-toock, he will ask you to abandon me alone on the snowswept platform, because I am sick, but please, please, I will say, don't believe him, don't believe any of it, he is counting on being with you himself, but he has no right to do that, because he is much worse than me, you'll realize that right away, as soon as he shows up and starts talking, so don't believe him, don't believe, because he *is not* in this world, he doesn't exist, he has no existence, is not, no him, no, dear, only I, I alone came to you quiet and radiant, kind and pure, that's what I'll say to her, and you, you, who are not, remember: nothing will come of it for you: you love that woman, but you don't know her name, how will you get to her, you brainless fool, you nullity, you wretched student of the special school! Yes, I do love the woman, I certainly love her, but you are deluded, you are certain that I don't know her, or where she lives, but I do know! Do you understand me? I know everything about her, even her name. you cannot, you should not know that name, only I know her name—I alone in the whole world. You've erred: Veta, her name is Veta, I love the woman whose name is Veta Acatova.

When our dachas are veiled in dusk and the heavenly dipper, tipped over the earth, spills out its dew on enchanting Lethe's banks, I emerge from my father's house and walk quietly through the garden—quietly so as not to awaken you, the strange person who lives beside me. I slink along my old tracks, through the grass and the sand, trying not to step on the glowing fireflies or the sleeping *simpetrum* dragonflies. I go down to the river, and my reflection smiles at me when I untie my father's boat from the gnarled white willow. I smear the oarlocks with thick dark water dipped from the river—and my path is quieter than the flash of stars vanishing into the past, my path lies around the second bend, to the Land of the Lonely Nightjar, bird of the good summer. My path is neither too short nor too long, I will compare it to the path of a tarnished sewing needle stitching a wind-severed cloud. Now I float on, rocked by the waves of phantom ships, now I pass the first bend and the second, and shipping the oars I stare at the shore: it floats to meet me, rushes rustling and a good duck voice quacking. Good evening, Shore of the Lonely Nightjar, it's I, vacationing student So-and-so of the special school, allow me to leave my father's boat by your remarkable cane rushes, allow me to pass along your paths, I would like to visit the woman called Veta. I ascend the high hilly shore and stride in the direction of a high and solid fence behind which one can divine a house with whimsical wooden turrets at the corners, but one can only divine it is there; in fact, on such a dark night among the tight interlacings of acacias and other tall bushes and trees one cannot distinguish either the house itself or the towers. Only on the second story, in the attic, is there a light, clearly and greenly shining to me as I walk, the lamp of Veta Arcadievna, my mysterious woman Veta. I know a place where one can easily clmb through the fence, I climb through it and hear her simple ordinary dog running across the high grass of the yard toward me. I get a piece of cut sugar out of my pocket and give it to the shaggy, yellow dog, she wags her tail and laughs, she knows how I love my Veta, and would never bite me. And now I approach the house itself. It is a very large dacha, there are many rooms in it, it was built by Veta's father, a naturalist, an old scientist whose name is world-renowned, who in his youth attempted to prove that the so-called *galls*—swellings on various parts of plants—were nothing but the dwelling places of harmful insect larvae, and that for the most part they, the *galls*, were caused by the bites of various wasps, mosquitoes and elephant beetles which deposit their eggs in these plants. But he, Academician Acatov, was believed by hardly anyone, and one day some men in snowy overcoats came to his house and took the Academician away somewhere for a long time, and somewhere there, where precisely is not known, they beat him in the face and stomach so that Acatov would never again dare to assert all this nonsense. And when they released him it turned out that many years had passed, and he had aged and started seeing and hearing poorly, while the swellings on various parts of plants remained, and all these years, as the men in the snowy overcoats became convinced, the harmful larvae really were living in those swellings, which is why they, the swellings, that is, no, the men, or maybe both the swellings and the men together, decided to release the Academician, and also give him an incentive award so that he could build himself a dacha and quietly, without intrusions, investigate the galls. Acatov did just this: built a dacha, planted flowers on his land, got a dog, kept bees, and studied galls. And right now, the night of my arrival at the Land of the Lonely Nightjar, the Academician is lost in one of the bedrooms of the mansion, sleeping, unaware that I have come and am standing under the window of your daughter Veta and whispering to her: Veta Veta Veta it is I special school student so-and-so respond I love thee.

.

Chapter Two   *NOW: stories written on the veranda*

THE LAST DAY. He was leaving for the army. He realized that the three years would not pass quickly for him: they would be like three northern winters. And it didn't matter where they sent him to serve, even to the south—no matter what, each of the three years would become an incredibly long snowy winter. He was thinking this now, as he was going to see her. She didn't love him. She was too good to love him. He knew this, but his eighteenth birthday was not long past, and he could not help thinking of her every minute. He noticed that he was thinking about her constantly, and rejoiced that he wanted nothing from her, which meant he really loved her. This state of affairs had lasted for two years; he was surprised that he didn't want to think about anything else, and that it didn't bore him. But in general, he reasoned, he should be done with it. Today he was being sent off to the army, and tomorrow he would go somewhere far away, for three winters, and there he would forget everything. He wouldn't write her a single letter: she wouldn't answer anyway. Now he will go to her and tell her everything. He had been terribly stupid. In the evenings he had wandered under her windows till very late, and when the windows went dark, for some reason he would keep standing there and standing there, staring at the dark glass. Then he would go home and smoke in the kitchen until dawn, flicking the ashes onto the worn floor. From the window he could see the small night yard with the summerhouse in it. There was always a lantern on in the summerhouse, and a board with the sign "Summer Reading Room" hung under it. At dawn the pigeons went winging. Striding along on the chilly mornings of that call-up autumn, he sensed an odd weightlessness in his body, and in his mind this commingled with the inexplicability of everything that he knew and felt. At times such as these he asked himself many different questions, but usually found answers to none—he would go to the house where she lived. She would emerge from the porch at half past seven and always pass through the yard hurrying, and he would watch her from a plywood summerhouse, which also had a hanging lantern and the same kind of sign—"Summer Reading Room." A stupid sign, he thought, stupid, in the summer no one reads in this summerhouse. Thinking this, he followed the girl at a distance at which she couldn't hear or sense him behind her. Now he was remembering all this, and he realized that today was the last day that he could see the girl, the yard where she lived, and the Summer Reading Room in this yard. He goes up to the second floor and knocks at her door.

THREE SUMMERS IN A ROW. Her father and I—we worked at the same theater. Her father was an actor, and I worked as a stagehand. Once after a performance he took me home with him, treated me to some foreign wine and introduced me to her. The two of them lived on the second floor of a yellow two-story barracks. From the window of their room you could see another identical barracks and a small cemetery with a church in the middle of it. I've forgotten the name of the actor's daughter. But even if I remembered her name now, I wouldn't tell: what business is it of yours. So then, she lived in the yellow barracks at the edge of town and was the daughter of an actor. It's quite possible that you have nothing to do with her. But then you don't have to listen. No one's making anyone do anything. And seriously, as far as that goes you don't have to do anything at all—and I won't say a word to you. Only don't try to find out her name, or I won't tell any of this story at all. We met for three winters and three summers in a row. She would often come and sit through whole performances in the half-empty theater. I watched her, standing behind the holey curtain—my girl always sat in the third row. Her father played bit parts and didn't appear more than three times during the whole show. I knew that she dreamed of her father getting a bigger part at least once. But I guessed that he would not get a good part. Because if an actor hasn't gotten a decent part in twenty years, he won't ever get one. But I didn't tell her that. I didn't tell her that when we were strolling through the city's late evening and very wintery streets after performances, running after trolleys which were screeching around corners, in order to get warm; nor on rainy days when we went to the planetarium and kissed in the empty dark hall beneath the artificial starry sky. I didn't tell her that the first summer, nor the second, nor the third, when her father went away on tour, and on rushed nights we took walks in the small cemetery around the church where lilac, elders and willows grew. I didn't tell her that. Nor did I tell her that she wasn't pretty, and that probably there would be a time when I would not take walks with her. Nor did I tell her about the other girls whom I used to meet or whom I met at this same time on other days. I told her only that I loved her—and I did. But perhaps you think one can love only pretty girls, or you think that when you love one you can't go out with others? Well, I already told you—you don't have to do anything at all in your life, including not walking with a single girl in the world—and I won't say a word to you. But that's not the point. I'm talking about her, not you. She was the one I said I loved. And if I happen to meet her now, she and I will go to the planetarium or to the cemetery which is overgrown with elder, and there, as many years ago, I will tell her about that again. Don't you believe me?

AS ALWAYS ON SUNDAY. And the prosecutor could not stand relatives. I was putting in some window glass for him, and here came a tribe of relations to his dacha, and he walked around the yard all sort of white, with a newspaper under his arm. He was white like the places in the newspaper where nothing is written. And everyone in the dacha settlement and in the village beyond the meadow knew that he couldn't stand relatives or disorder, because wherever there's disorder there's drinking. He always puts it that way. I heard him myself. I was putting in the glass and that's what he said to his wife then. And his wife is an interesting one too. How many times I put in glass for her, and repaired the stove and fixed up the shed, and never once did she give me refreshments. Money she gives, but when it comes to booze always zero. I'll do any job. I clean out people's outhouses, but never had to for the prosecutor. His wife wouldn't let me. No reason for you to get filthy, she says, I'll do it myself. And it was true. Once in the spring I'm putting in the glass, and she takes the special shovel from the shed and starts carrying shit to around the trees. Later she stopped doing this and asked me to put a lock on the outhouse so it would be locked for the winter, so that neighbors wouldn't carry any of it away free. Otherwise they'll carry it off, she says, and why for free: it's hard to get fertilizer now, she says. Of course, I put in a lock, and later their neighbor, the prosecutor's crony, asked me for the key to the prosecutor's lock. Well, he gave me some refreshments, everything the way it's supposed to be done. So I got him the key, of course. Only later in the manager's office I hear a conversation to the effect that the prosecutor's outhouse had been cleaned out while the prosecutor was away in the city. And what was it to me—I was just putting glass in the manager's office, that's all. There's enough work in this settlement to last me a whole lifetime. In the winter all sorts of trash live in the dachas—they knock out glass, wreck the stoves, and all the better for me. As soon as the snow melted away my work started up. And then the prosecutor called me to fix the glass. Our country folks had busted out all his windows over the winter. Even in the attic. And they'd broken in the roof over the veranda besides. That's my job too. When there's time I'll fix the roof. But this particular day I'd been putting in glass since morning. The prosecutor's reading his newspaper while lying in the hammock, drowsing off and waking back up from time to time. At the same time, his wife is digging a huge pit in the middle of the yard. Why, I ask. I'll make channels, she says, from all over the yard to this pit, so that all of the rains will be mine. O.K., I think, dig away, and I'll go on putting in the glass. And the prosecutor, I say, is drowsing off or waking up or getting out of his hammock to go over to the fence and chat with his neighbor and crony. What's going on, Comrade Prosecutor, says the prosecutor's crony, are your windows down to zero? Sure are, the prosecutor replies, in the winter the winds here are probably strong—and the wind knocked them out. By the way, the prosecutor's crony says, I hear someone cleaned out your outhouse recently. Yes, says the prosecutor, they cleaned it out—damned vandalism. Too bad, the prosecutor's crony says, unpleasant. And he himself was the one, the son of a gun, he was the one who cleaned it out. That crony of a prosecutor, he was a funny guy. Comes to the dacha all dressed normal, but soon as he comes right away puts on some sort of nightcap, tricks himself out in all kinds of rags, galoshes on his feet, and a rope for a belt, and the galoshes tied with rope. O.K., I think, tie away, and I'll go ahead and put in the glass. But this evening, you shit-stealer, I'm going to get three rubles off you. And if you don't cough it up, I'll have to report it all to your comrade, the prosecutor. The prosecutor, he can't stand disorder you know. Or relatives. And they happened to show up just in time for supper. The prosecutor—he's gone all white, I say, even stopped reading his newspaper. Walks around his yard stomping on dandelions. He looks like a dandelion himself—round and white like empty newspaper, but he's got plenty of relatives—about nine had arrived for supper. All of them laughing it up, got games going on the grass right away, sent off the prosecutor's son to the store right away. Well, this time we got in with them too. Fine people they were. One was a conductor in the city, one a chauffeur, and two were elevator operators. Also one coach, and also an excavator operator. And he had his daughter with him. Everything worked out well between her and me. And the weather just happened to be dry—as always on Sunday.

THE TUTOR. The physics teacher lived on a sidestreet. When I was a young girl, I went to his place for lessons twice a week. We studied in a small room in a semibasement where the teacher lived with several relatives, but I never saw them and don't know anything about them. Now I'll talk about the teacher himself, and also about how he and I studied during that stiflingly hot summer, and what kind of odor there was in the sidestreet. The sidestreet had a constant and strong odor of fish, because somewhere near was a store called "Fish." The crosswinds blew the odor through the sidestreet, and the odor came through the open window to us in the room where we were looking at obscene postcards. The tutor had a big collection of these postcards—six or seven albums. He made a special point of frequenting the various train stations in the city and buying whole sets of such photographs from some people. The teacher was heavy, but handsome, and he was not too old. When it was hot he perspired and turned on the table fan, but it didn't especially help, he perspired anyway. I always laughed about it. When we got tired of looking at postcards, he would tell me jokes; it was a peaceful, lighthearted time for the two of us in the room with the fan. He would also tell me about his women. He would say that at various times he had had many different women: big ones, small ones, various ages, but he still had not decided which, after all, were best—big ones or small ones. Because, he would say, everything depends on one's mood. He would tell how he was a machine-gunner in the war, and then, at seventeen, he became a man. The summer when he was my tutor I reached my seventeenth year too. I didn't go on to school, and because of this I really got it from my parents. I flunked physics and went into a hospital to become a nurse. The next year I applied for an institute where you didn't have to pass physics—and I got in. True, later on they expelled me, during my second year, because they caught me in the dormitory with a guy. He and I weren't doing anything, we were just sitting and smoking, and he was kissing me, and the door to the room was closed. But when they started knocking we didn't open for a long time, and when we did open up no one believed us. Now I work as a telegraph girl at the station. But that's not important. I haven't seen my tutor for almost ten years. How many times I've run past or ridden the trolley past his street and not once dropped in. I don't know why it happens in life that you just can't do something uncomplicated but important. I've been passing quite close to that building for several years. Always thinking about my physics teacher, remembering his funny postcards, the fan, the gnarled wooden cane which he would use to look important, even to go out to the kitchen to check the teakettle. Finally, not long ago, when I was feeling sad, I did drop in. I rang twice, like before. He came out, I said hello, he also said hello, but for some reason he didn't recognize me and didn't even invite me into his room. I asked him to try to remember me, reminded him how we had looked at postcards, told him about the fan, about that summer—he didn't remember anything. He said that at one time he really did have many students, boys and girls, but now he hardly remembered anyone. The years pass, he said, they pass. He had gotten a little old, my physics teacher.

A SICK GIRL. One can spend the nights on the veranda during July—it's not cold. And the big sad moths hardly bother me: they can easily be driven off with cigarette smoke. In this story, which I am writing on a July night on the veranda, the subject will be a sick girl. She is very sick. She lives in the next dacha along with a man whom she considers to be her grandfather. Grandfather drinks heavily, he's a glazier, he puts in glass, he is no more than fifty, and I don't believe he's her grandfather. Once when I was spending the night on the veranda as usual, the sick girl knocked for me. She came through the gate in the fence which separates our small lots. Came through the garden and knocked. I turned on the light and opened the door. Her face and hands were covered with blood—the glazier had beaten her, and she had come to me through the garden for help. I washed her, put iodine on her cuts and gave her some tea. She sat with me on the veranda until morning, and it seemed to me that we had managed to talk about many things. But in fact we were silent almost all night, because she can hardly talk, and her hearing is very poor due to her illness. In the morning, as always, it got light, and I walked the girl home along the garden path. In the country, and in Moscow too, I prefer to live alone, and the paths around my house are barely visible. That morning the grass in the garden was white with dew, and I regretted not putting on my galoshes. We stood by the gate for a moment. She tried to say something to me, but couldn't, and in her misery and sickness she began to weep. The girl turned the latch, which like the whole fence was wet with autumn mist, and ran off to her own house. And the gate was left open. Ever since then we've been good friends. Sometimes she comes to see me and I draw or write her something on Whatman paper. She likes my drawings. She studies them and smiles, and then goes home through the garden. She walks, brushing the apple branches with her head, looking back, smiling at me or laughing. and I notice that after every visit she makes my paths get better and better marked. I think that's all. I've got nothing more to tell about the sick girl from next door. No, it's not a long story. Not long at all even. Even the moths on the veranda seem bigger.

IN THE DUNES. It's nice to meet a girl whose mother works on the dredging barges: if someone asks, you say bluntly—she works on the dredging barges. Then everyone envies you. They were deepening the channel; watery sand kasha came up from the bottom through special tubes twenty-four hours a day. This watery mass went onto the shore and gradually sand dunes formed around the cove. Here you could lie out to get a tan even in the windiest weather—if the sun shone at all. I would go to the island on my motorcycle every morning and stand on the highest dune and twirl my faded plaid shirt over my head. As soon as she noticed me from the barge she would get into a big leaky boat that was tied to the barge and quickly row to shore. Here were our dunes, only ours—because it was my girl's mother who had deposited these merry shifting hills. And the summer was like a picture postcard, smelling of river water, willow and the resin of the coniferous forest. The forest was on the other side of the cove, and on the weekends people would relax there with badminton sets. And the Sunday couples would row up and down the cove talking in blue boats. But no one disembarked on our shore, no one except us tanned themselves on our dunes. We lay on the hot, very hot sand and went swimming or raced each other, and the barge constantly rumbled, and a stout woman wearing blue overalls would walk up and down the deck examining the machinery. I watched her from afar, from the shore, and I always thought that I was really lucky—I had met a girl whose mother lived and worked on that remarkable thing. In August the rains began, and we built a lean-to out of willow branches on the dunes, although, you understand, the rain wasn't the whole point. The lean-to stood right at the water. In the evenings we would light a fire, which reflected the cove, illuminating various floating pieces of wood. Well, at the very end of the summer we had a quarrel, and I never went to see her again after that. It was devilishly sad that fall, and the leaves rushed through the town as if demented. Still too short, right?

DISSERTATION. The professor spent his research leave in the country. He was writing his doctoral dissertation in chemistry: he would make notes from books and fool around with test-tubes, but everything was dominated by an astonishingly warm September. Besides that, the professor loved beer, and before supper he would go into his shed in the depths of the garden. There, in the shed, in the corner, in the coolness, stood the beer barrel. Using a rubber tube the professor would siphon a little beer out into a five-liter receptacle and return to the house, trying not to spill the liquid. A distant relative of his wife made his lunch for him: she had dropped in from somewhere very far away a month ago like a bolt from the blue, or like a relative of his wife, but the professor's wife herself had died long ago, and so far there had not been anyone else. It should be noted that breakfast and supper were made by this same relative of his wife, but usually this happened in the mornings and evenings respectively. In the afternoon the professor would stroll through the dacha settlement or go fishing in the pond beyond the birch grove. There were no fish in the pond, and as a rule the professor failed to catch anything. But this didn't bother him, and so as not to return home empty-handed, he would pick the late field flowers on the edge of the woods and make up some pretty nice bouquets. When he returned to the dacha he silently handed the flowers to the distant relative whose name he could never remember, and kept forgetting to ask. The woman was about forty years old, but she loved signs of attention as much as at twenty, and in the mornings she did calisthenics behind the shed. The professor didn't know about this, but even if the glazier-neighbor, who knew about it perfectly well, having often seen it from behind his fence, even if the glazier had told the professor about it, there is no way he would have believed it, and in any event he wouldn't have gone spying. However, one day at dawn he had an unexpected urge for some beer, and on tiptoe, so as not to make noise, he went to the shed, and while the beer was pouring out through the tube, out of the barrel into the receptacle, the professor was standing at the spider-webbed window and he saw his wife's relative in a scanty bathing suit, flailing her arms, and hopping and squatting on his garden grass. After breakfast the professor did not go to work, he spent his time on some trivia: he got two rusty bicycles out of the attic, fixed them and pumped them up, and then ironed his suit and rode down to the station for some wine. Besides wine he bought sprats and grapes and he helped his relative make lunch. After lunch the professor talked about what fine weather had been holding for two weeks now, what blue cornflowers were growing in the grove, and what fine rusty bicycles he had gotten out of the attic. That evening they went for a ride. Along the highway. On bicycles. They returned late—with flowers on the handlebars. On the relative's head there was a wreath. The professor had woven the wreath for her himself. This was a surprise for her, because she didn't know that he knew how to weave wreaths and repair bicycles. But then the professor hadn't known that his, in essence, relative was jumping up and down on his garden grass. Every morning. In a scanty swimsuit. Flailing her arms.

THE LOCALE. The railroad passes close by, and the yellow electric trains run past the lake. Some trains go to the city, and others away from the city. But this is a suburban area. And therefore even in the sunniest weather everything here seems unreal. Down the railway line, beyond the right-of-way fences, the city begins with big buildings, and in the other direction, beyond the lake, there is a pine forest. Some call it a park, others a forest.

But in fact it is a forest-park. These are the suburbs, and it seems as if one can't see anything distinctive around. At one time this locale was considered a dacha area, but now the dachas have become simply the old wooden houses of the suburbs. The houses smell of kerosene and quiet middle-aged people live in them. A one-track branch of the railroad goes close to the forest-park. The branch leads to a dead-end—trains don't come in here. The rails have rusted, and the sleepers have rotted. There are some brown cars in the dead-end at the edge of the forest-park. Repair workers live in these cars. They have temporary permission to live in the suburban area, and all of them have big families. Every repairman knows that there aren't any fish in the swampy lake nearby, but on their hours off they all go to the shore with fishing poles and try to catch something. One of the workers, who lives in the third car from the forest-park, has a daughter of eighteen. She was born here, in the car, and she likes a young man from the city who comes to the forest-park with his friends fairly often to play soccer on the trash-strewn fields. He's a good lad, he courts the repairman's daughter, and he has already dropped in on them for tea a few times. He likes these little cars at the dead-end too. You know, maybe he'll marry the repairman's daughter soon and start spending even more time here. The wedding will be on a Sunday, dances will be arranged on the lake shore, and all will dance—everyone who lives in the brown cars at the dead-end.

AMID THE WASTELANDS. A door slammed upstairs, on the third floor, and I was left alone. The wind blew in from the wastelands, through the opened door and into the hall, and here on the staircase it was a little warmer than outside in the street. I lit up and went out into the yard where the linen of the inhabitants of this building was drying on the lines. Pillowcases, sheets, and blanket-covers were inflated by the wind. I sat down on a bench wet with dew: in front of me loomed an improbably long five-story building: I've never seen such a long building; the shadow of the building ended at my feet. I was illuminated by the helpless September sun. Clouds as flabby as the muscles of old men moved across the sky, and behind my back stretched the infinite suburban wastelands, so infinite that even the ash-heap of the city was lost amid them and only the unpleasant odor reminded one that the city existed. The cigarette which I was smoking quickly ended in the wind, and I didn't have any more, so I decided to go to a store. But I didn't know where a store was. I didn't know anything about this place in general, there were no familiar faces, or familiar streets, I didn't know, and didn't want to know what the woman who had agreed to help us was doing with my fianceé. The woman lived and treated people in this long monotonous building. Passing through the shaded courtyard, I went around the building to the left and came out on the asphalt road. New buildings similar to this one stood all around. Perhaps I was a little afraid of these buildings. But I wanted to smoke and I went to a store, pretending that I had nothing to do with them. And that's the way it was really, I was just a little afraid of them: they looked at my back and eyes from a distance, and there wasn't anyone around. But soon I caught up with a girl. She was carrying two net bags full of groceries, and I decided that she would know where to buy cigarettes. I hailed her and asked. She said she'd show me to the store so I wouldn't get lost. The wind was blowing. The wastelands stretched out behind the buildings. Near the buildings wind-blown bed linen was slapping on lines. Across the wastelands, eating the seeds of grasses, huge flocks of sparrows rustled. The girl seemed every thin, something was wrong with her eyes, but I couldn't figure out what exactly, and then I realized: she was crosseyed. She showed me the way and kept explaining which things were located where in this area, but to me it was quite uninteresting and unnecessary. She went into the store with me, waited for me to buy the cigarettes, and said that she wanted to walk me to the station where she worked as a telegraph operator. I don't have to go on the electric, I said, I don't have to. The girl went away. Not far from the store a milk truck was doing business. Middle-aged but talkative women wearing old-fashioned overcoats were standing in line. Each of them had a can and all of them, despite the cold wind, were talking nonstop. One chubby one who had already bought milk walked away from the truck, and I saw her slip and drop the can. The can fell onto the asphalt, the milk spilled out, the old woman fell too, rolling. She had on a black overcoat, she sat there all covered with milk, trying to get up. The line stopped chattering and looked at her. I stood there looking too. I probably would have helped her, but my hands were full: in one there was a cigarette, and in the other a match. I lit up and walked back to the building where they were doing something to my fianceé and which from a distance looked me intently in the eyes.

EARTH WORKS. The coffin hung on the tooth of the scoop, wobbling over the trench, and everything was normal. But then the lid opened and everything fell out into the bottom of the hole. At that point the excavator climbed from his cabin and examined the coffin and saw that there was a little glass window cut in the head of the coffin, and in the coffin lay some plastic boots. And the excavator was very sorry that there was no way to repair those boots, otherwise he would have undertaken the job. But the boots turned out to be very bad ones, and the sole of one of them flopped off as soon as he tried it on. The threads had rotted, and the sole with its plates immediately flopped off, and the top was too tight. So the mechanic-excavator threw the boots away even though he really needed some new footwear badly. But the excavator was more disappointed by something else. The machine operator wanted to look at a skull, because he had never managed to see a real skull in his whole life, never mind touch one with his hands. True, from time to time he touched his own head or his wife's head and imagined what it would be like if you removed the skin from his or his wife's head, and you had a real skull. But to do that you'd have to wait who knows how long yet. And the excavator couldn't stand waiting for anything very long. He loved to do everything that came into his head immediately. So, now, when the machine operator was digging up the coffin, he immediately decided to shake everything out of it and find the skull. He wanted to see what happened to the skull of a man who had died long ago and lay for many years, looking out the coffin window. Yes—reflected the machine operator, descending into the grave on a ladder—yes, now I'll have a good skull, otherwise a person can go on living and living and never have anything like it. Of course, I have a bad head, and really it's not so often there's enough free time to palpate it properly. Besides, when you feel your own head, it gives you hardly any pleasure—you need a bare skull, someone else's, without any skin on it, so that you can put it on a stick, or set it wherever you need to. What luck! Now I'll pick through the rags, chuck the bones and take the bare skull—in its natural state. You can't let such moments in life pass you by or else you turn around and someone else is putting your skull on a stick and walking around the street with it, scaring anybody he wants. The machine operator peered under the lid lying on the sand, then crawled out of the trench and peered through the window into the coffin, and then peered not through the window, but simply into the coffin the way people usually look into a coffin when the coffin is hanging on the tooth of a scoop, and the one who is looking is standing on the edge of the grave. But there was no skull in the coffin or under the lid on the sand. Ain't no skull—said the excavator to himself—ain't no skull here, the skull's missing, and maybe there wasn't ever one here—they buried just the torso, eh? But no matter what there ain't no skull, and I can't put it on a stick and scare anybody I want. It's the other way around, now anybody can scare me with a skull, a real one, or his own. What bum luck!—the excavator said to himself.

THE GUARD. Night. Always this cold night. His work is night. Night is his livelihood and what he hates. In the day he sleeps and smokes. He never loads the rifle. What reason is there to load it when it's winter and there's no one around. No one—winter, fall or spring. And no one in the actor's houses either. These are the actors' dachas, and he is the dacha guard. He has never been in a theater, but once his partner told him that his son was going to school in the city, and that he went to the theater. The partner's son: he comes to visit his father on weekends. But no one comes to visit him. He lives alone and smokes. Before his shift he takes the rifle to the guard box and then walks along the little streets of the dacha settlement all night long. Today and yesterday there was a lot of snow. The streets are white. The trees, especially the pines, are too. They are white. The moon is dim. The moon can't break through the clouds. He smokes. He looks from side to side. He stands at each intersection for a long while. It's very dark. It will never be light in this settlement in the winter. In the summer it's better. In the evenings the actors drink wine on their verandas. That is, if summer comes. But summer never comes, the verandas and their dim stained glass windows are locked and empty. They freeze all the way through, they get piled with snow. And every third evening, after working for two, he takes his unloaded rifle and walks. Past the windowed dachas. He walks without paths, without shells, without smokes. He is going to get something to smoke, to the outskirts of the settlement where the store is. The store is always empty. The spring on the door is a strong one. An aging woman works there. She is kind, because she gives credit. In the icy cold he doesn't remember her name. Why her, this woman, he wonders. I can get along without her, he thinks or can I? No, I can't. Without her I wouldn't have anything to smoke. He laughs softly. It's cold, he continues thinking, it's cold. Dark. He sees the woman shut the shutters on her store and head home for bed. There she goes. I'm standing here, he says to himself, I'm smoking, and she's walking past. Do I want to smoke? No, I'm smoking because she's going away. That's all, she's gone. Now alone till morning. A cat runs by. There used to be a lot of them in the settlement. They lived under the porches of the houses. His partner used to shoot his rifle at them. It's cold. No cats. He walks on again, looking at the actors' houses. Snow on top. So it'll be warm. As long as there's no wind. There is a light on one veranda. The actors don't come in the winter, he thinks. Tracks on a plot of ground. A fence broken in one place. Two fence staves lie in the snow, criss-crossed. He has never loaded it, and he's not going to now either. He'll walk up and take a look, see what's up. He approaches. A shot. As if from afar, in the forest. No, much closer. Ah, someone's shooting from the stained glass windows. Hurts a lot, my head hurts. Sure would like a smoke. He falls face down in the snow. He isn't cold any more.

NOW. He came back from the army before his hitch was up, after the hospital. He served in the rocket units, and one night he came under powerful radiation, at night, during a practice alert. He was twenty. On his way home, he sat in the restaurant of the half-empty train for a long time, drinking wine and smoking. The pretty young woman who was traveling in his compartment was not in the least embarrassed about undressing before

going to bed, standing in front of the door mirror, and he saw her reflection, and she knew that he saw it and smiled to him. The last night of the
trip she invited him into bed with her, below, but he pretended that he was
asleep, and she guessed this and laughed softly at him in the darkness of the
small and stuffy compartment, and at that moment the train shrieked and
flew through the black snowstorm, and the suburban train stops con-
fusedly nodded their dim lights to him as he passed. The first two weeks he
sat at home—leafing through books, looking through old photographs,
grade school pictures even, trying to decide something for himself and
endlessly quarrelling with his father, who had been retired on a big military
pension and didn't believe a word he said and considered him a malingerer.
The mustering-out pay which the regiment paymaster had issued him came
to an end, and he had to look for a job. He wanted to be a driver at the
neighboring hospital, but there, in the hospital, they offered him something
else. Now, after the army, at the end of the snowy winter, he had become a
janitor in the hospital morgue. He was paid seventy rubles a month, and
that was enough money for him, because he didn't go out with girls: all he
did was drive to the park occasionally, to ride the rollercoaster and watch
people he didn't know dancing, through the transparent walls of the dance
hall. Once he noticed a girl there whom he had once gone to school with.
She had come to the park with some fellow in a sports car, and the janitor,
concealed in the murk of large trees, watched them dance. They danced for
half an hour, then slammed their car doors and rolled deeper into the park
along the little illuminated streets. And a few weeks later, in May, they
brought to the morgue a man and a woman who had been crushed in an
automobile somewhere outside of town, and he didn't recognize them at
first—but finally he did recognize them, though for some reason he just
couldn't recall her name, and kept looking at her and thinking about how
three or four years ago, even before the army, he had loved this girl and
wanted, very much wanted, to be with her constantly, but she did not love
him, she was too pretty to love him. And now, thought the janitor, it was all
over, over, and it was impossible to know what the future would bring...

Chapter Three   *Savl*

But Veta does not hear. The night of your arrival in the Land of the Lonely Nightjar, Veta Arcadievna, a thirty-year-old teacher in our school, the strict teacher of botany, biology, and anatomy, is in the town's best restaurant dancing and drinking wine with some young, yes, relatively young, man, a gay, intelligent and generous fellow. Soon the music will end—the drunken drummers and fiddlers, pianists and horn-players will quit the stage. Lights dimmed, the restaurant will count its final guests, and the relatively young man whom you have never and will never see in your life, will take your Veta away to his apartment, and there he will do anything he wants with her. Stop, I understand, I know, there, in his apartment, he will kiss her hand and then, right after that, he will take her home, and in the morning she'll come here to the dacha, and we can meet, I know: we'll meet tomorrow. No, that's wrong, you probably don't understand anything, or you're pretending you don't, or you're simply a coward, you're afraid to think about what will happen to your Veta there, in the apartment of the man you will never see, but of course you would like to have a look at him, or am I wrong? Naturally I would like to make his acquaintance, we could all go somewhere together, the three of us: Veta, he and I, to some town park, to the old town park with the rollercoaster, we would ride it and chat, it would surely be interesting, I say: interesting, it would be interesting, the three of us together. But maybe the man is not as intelligent as you say, and then it would not be so interesting, and we would be wasting the evening, it would be a failure of an evening, that's all, nothing more than that, but at least Veta would realize that I'm much more interesting than he is, and we would never meet him again, and on the night of my arrival in the Land of the Lonely Nightjar she would always come out at my cry: Veta Veta Veta it is I special school student so-and-so come out I love you just as before. Believe me: she always came out to my cry, and she and I would be together in her garret until morning, and afterwards when it started getting light, cautiously, so as not to awaken Arcady Arcadievich, I would go down to the garden on the outside spiral staircase and go back home. You know, before leaving I usually petted her ordinary dog, and I used to play with it a little so it wouldn't forget me. That's nonsense, our teacher Veta Arcadievna never came out to your call, and you were never in her garret, either during the day or at night. I watch every move you make, you know, that's what Doctor Zauze advised: if you notice that the one whom you call *he* and who lives and studies together with you is going off somewhere, trying to be unnoticed, or if he simply runs away, follow him, try not to lose sight of him, stay as close to him as possible, find a way to get so close to him as to virtually merge into one with him, your acts becoming his, do it in such a way that a time comes—such a moment will certainly come—that you unite with him in a single whole, a single being with inseparable thoughts and aspirations, habits and tastes. Only in this way, Zauze asserted, will you achieve peace and freedom. And so wherever you went, I followed you, and from time to time I managed to merge with you, your acts becoming mine, but you drove me away as soon as you noticed this, and again I got worried, even terrified. I was afraid of, and in general am afraid of, many things, only I try not to let on, and it strikes me that you are no less afraid than I. For example, you're afraid I'll up and start telling you the truth about what that relatively young man did with your Veta in his apartment the night of your arrival. But I'm going to tell about it anyway, because I don't like you, because you don't want to merge with me, my acts becoming yours, as the doctor advised. I'll also tell you what other young and not-so-young men did to your Veta in their apartments and hotels during those nights when you were sleeping at your father's dacha or in the city or *there*, after the evening injections. But first I have to convince you that you were never in the attic of Acatov's dacha, even though sometimes you did run away to the Land of the Nightjar late at night. You looked at the illuminated windows of the mansion through a crack in the fence and dreamed of entering the park, striding along the path—from the gate to the front porch, I understand you, striding along the path, easily, unselfconsciously, and, striding, to kick two or three of last year's acorns, pick a flower from a flowerbed, sniff it, stand by the gazebo a while—like that, looking all around with a slight squint of deep all-comprehending eyes, then to stand under a tall tree with a starling in it, to listen to the birds—I understand you quite well, I would take great pleasure in doing the same myself, and even more: striding along the path of Acatov's garden (or park—no one knows which it is better to call their lot and everyone calls it whatever occurs to him), I would play with their fine ordinary dog and I would knock at the front door: toock-toock; but now I will confess to you: I, as, incidentally, you too—we are afraid of that big dog. And if we weren't afraid of it, if, let's suppose, it didn't even exist—could we permit ourselves to do all that, is it only because of the dog that we cannot knock at the door?—that's my question to you, I would like to talk about it some more, the theme is one I find terribly absorbing. It strikes me you are dissembling again, is this all really so interesting, you're talking my head off, you don't want me to tell you the whole truth about Veta, about what those young men who you'll never see did to her in their apartments and hotel rooms well why tell me finally why you or why I why we are afraid to talk about that to each other or each to himself in all this there is so much truth why why why yes you know much but you know if I know nothing and you nothing we know nothing about that yet or we no longer know what can you tell me or yourself if neither you nor I ever had any woman we don't know in general what it's like we are just guessing we can guess we just read just hear from others but the others don't really know anything either once we asked Savl Petrovich if he had had women this was at school there at the end of the corridor behind the narrow door where it always smells of smoke and cleanser both in the washroom and the toilet Savl Petrovich was smoking he was sitting on the windowsill it was between classes no after classes I had stayed after class to do the next day's lessons no they made you stay after class to do the next day's lessons in math we're bad students they told mama especially in math it's very hard you get tired it's very bad bad to the point of pain some of the problems for some reason they give too many lessons one has to outline and think they make you do too much Savl Petrovich for some reason they torture us by holding up examples they say that supposedly some of us when we finish school will enter an institute and some of us a few of us part an occasional one of us will become engineers but we don't believe it nothing of the sort will happen for Savl Petrovich you yourself can guess you and the other teachers we will never become any engineers because we are all terrible fools isn't that so isn't this a special school that is not specially for us why do you deceive us with these engineers who needs all that but dear Savl Petrovich even if we did all of a sudden become engineers that's not needed no it shouldn't happen I don't agree to it I would petition to be in the commission I have no desire to be an engineer I will sell flowers and postcards and monkeys-on-a-string on the street or I'll learn shoe-repair, to saw plywood with a fret-saw but I will not agree to work as an engineer until the formation of the very main very biggest commission here one which will straighten out the matter of time isn't that so Savl Petrovich we have a time disorder and is there any sense in working at any serious matter for example belaboring blueprints with blue ballpoints when time is all messed up that's no good at all very strange and stupid you know that yourself of course you and the other teachers.

Savl Petrovich was sitting on the windowsill smoking. The naked bottoms of his feet were resting on the radiator for the steam heat or, as this device is also called, the battery. Beyond the window lay autumn, and if the window had not been covered with a special white paint, we would have been able to see part of the street, along which a moderate northwesterly wind was blowing. Foliage floated in the wind, puddles rippled, passersby, dreaming of turning into birds, precipitantly pushed home in order to prattle with neighbors about the poor weather. In short—it was the usual autumn, the middle of autumn, when the coal has already been brought to the school-yard and unloaded from trucks, and an old man, our stoker and guard, whom none of us called by name, since none of us knew his name, inasmuch as determining and remembering that name made no sense, because there is no way our stoker could have heard and responded to that name, inasmuch

as he was deaf and dumb—and he had already lit the boilers. It got warmer
in the school, although as several teachers remarked, shivering and hunching up their shoulders, it was still windy, and—one thinks—Savl Petrovich
was right to occasionally go into the bathroom to warm the naked bottoms
of his feet. He could have warmed them in the teachers' room, and in class
during lessons, but apparently he didn't want to do this too openly, with
people around, despite everything he was a bit bashful, mentor Norvegov
was. Maybe. He was sitting on the windowsill with his back to the painted-
over window, facing the stalls. The naked bottoms of his feet were on the
radiator and his knees were pulled high, so that the teacher could rest his
chin on them comfortably. And looking at him, sitting that way, from the
side, in profile were: a publisher's logo, ex libris, the series book after book,
the silhouette of a youth sitting on the grass or the bare ground with a book
in his hands, a dark youth against the background of a white dawn,
dreamily, a youth, dreaming of becoming an engineer, a youth-engineer if
you like, curly-haired, rather curly-haired, book after book, reading book
after book against a background, free, ex libris, at the publisher's expense,
one after the other all the books in a row, very well-read, he is very
well-read, your lad—this to our kind and beloved mother—Vodokachka,
teacher of the subjects literature and Russian language written and oral
told mama too well-read even, we wouldn't recommend everything all at
once, particularly the Western classics, that's distracting, it overloads the
imagination, makes one arrogant, lock them up, no more than fifty pages a
day for middle elementary school age. The Boy from Uzhum, The Childhood of Tioma, Childhood, A House on the Hill, Vitya Maleev, and now
this: life is given to man only once, and you have to live it so as to. And also:
to seek and to strive, to find and not to surrender, forward to meet the
dawn, comrades in the fight, we'll clear a path with bayonets and shot—the
songs of the Russian revolutions and civil wars, hostile whirlwinds, dark
eyes, pack up your troubles, all together, heave ho, and then we would
recommend music lessons, any instrument, in moderation, therapy, so it
won't be awfully hard, beyond this, you know, it's a period of maturation,
this age, well, say the *bayan*, or, say the accordion, the violin, the piano-
forte, and even more forte than piano, they began: ee-ee-ee barcarolle three
quarter flat don't confuse the treble clef with a fiddler's mushroom half-
poison boil them ee-ee-ee to the clank of the railroad cars to the station
which is on the same branch as ee-ee-ee according to Veta willows are
disturbing the sleepy passengers you weep in the train car from love from
the unnecessary things in life mama it's raining out do we really have to go
out in such slop oh my dear a little music won't do you any harm we did
agree after all the maestro will be waiting today it would be awkward it's
Sunday, then we'll drop in on grandmother. The station, bushes, noonday,
very damp. However, there's winter too: the platform snowcovered, dry
snow, crunchy and sparkling. Past the market. No, first the viaduct with

the squeaky ice-covered steps. Squeaky, mama. Careful, the way up ee-ee-ee when you see a passing freight below covered all over with chalk graffiti or a clean express with starched-collar curtains try not to look down or you'll get dizzy and fall your arms flailing on your back or face down and the sympathetic passersby who haven't managed to turn into birds will surround your body and someone will raise your head and start slapping your cheeks the poor lad he probably doesn't have any heart it's avitaminiosis anemia a woman in a peasant dress the owner of the baskets holds the accordion and his mama where's his mama he's probably alone taking music lessons look he's got blood on his head of course he's alone God what happened to him nothing now he's now I Veta I'm alone I beg you to forgive me your boy your tender student looked too long at a freight covered all over with chalk graffiti its cars were written on by commissions but after years and after some distances your timid so-and-so will come to you overcoming the storms which pound at man like the spiky fire of silver and he will play on a barcarolle a wild czardas and God grant he not go out of his mind from the extracurricular passion turning him to ashes toock-toock hell Veta Arcadievna ee-ee-ee here're some chrysanthemums even if they're wilted and faded still what is going to happen will make up totally for everything when will that be? Ten years or so, perhaps. She is forty, she's still young, in the summer she lives at the dacha, swims a lot—and table tennis, ping-pong. And me, and me? Let's count up now. I'm twenty-eight, I finished the special school long ago, and the institute and became an engineer. I have a lot of friends, I am in fine health and saving up money for a car—no, I've already bought one, saved up and bought it, savings bank, savings bank, we'll turn your kopeks into rubles. Yes, that's it precisely, you've been an engineer for a long time and you read book after book, sitting on the grass whole days at a time. Many books. You've gotten very intelligent, and the day is coming when you'll realize that it's impossible to postpone it any longer. You get up from the grass, shake out your trousers—they are beautifully pressed—then you bend down, gather all of the books in a pile and take them to the car. There, in the car, lies a jacket, a good one, a blue one. And you put it on. Then you examine yourself. You are of superior height, much taller than now, approximately so many *shaku* more. Besides that, you're broad in the shoulders, and your face is almost handsome. Precisely *almost*, because some women don't like men who are too handsome, isn't that so? You have a straight nose, languid blue eyes, a stubborn willful chin and strongly compressed lips. As for your forehead, sometimes it is extraordinarily high, as, for example, it is right now, and dark locks of hair cascade down upon it in thick shocks. Your face is smooth, you shave. Having examined yourself, you get behind the wheel, slam the door and you leave the sylvan locale where you have spent so much time reading books. Now you are going straight to her house. But the chrysanthemums! you have to buy them, you have to stop somewhere, buy them at the market. But I don't have a centavo with me, I'll have to ask mother: mama, the thing is that a girl in our class died, no, of course not, not right in class, she died at home, she was sick for a long time, several years, and didn't come to class at all, none of us students had ever seen her, except in photographs, she was simply on the roll, she had meningitis, like so many people, so then she died, yes, it's terrible, mama, terrible, like so many people have, so then she died and she has to be buried, no, naturally, no, mama, you're right, she has her own parents, no one can make anyone bury other people's children, I was just saying this: she has to be buried, but it's not customary to do that without flowers, it would be awkward, you remember, even Savl Petrovich, whom the teachers and parents' committee disliked so much, even he had a lot of flowers, and now our class has decided to take up a collection for a wreath for this girl, several rubles per person, or more accurately this way: whoever lives with his mama and papa gives ten rubles, and anyone who lives only with his mama or only with his papa, he gives five, so you see I have to give ten, please give me ten and be quick about it the car is waiting for me. What car?—asks mama. And then I will answer: you see, it's happened that I bought a car didn't pay much but even so I had to go into debt. What debt—mama will wave her arms—where did you get any money at all! And she'll run to the window to look out in the yard where my car will be standing. You see, I'll answer calmly, while I was sitting on the grass and reading book after book, my circumstances developed in such a way that I was able to finish school and later the institute, forgive me, please, mama, I don't know why but it seemed to me it would be a pleasant surprise for you if I didn't tell you all at once but somehow later, after some time, and now the time has come, and I am informing you: yes, I became an engineer, mama, and my car awaits. Then how much time has passed—mother will say—you mean to tell me you didn't go to your school this morning with a briefcase, and that it wasn't today that I saw you off and ran after you on the stairs almost to the first floor to shove some sandwiches into your overcoat pocket, and you jumped down three steps and yelled that you weren't hungry, but that if I kept forcing these sandwiches on you you would sew your mouth shut with thick thread?—you mean that didn't happen today?—our poor mother will say in amazement. And we, what will we tell our poor mother? We must tell her the following: alas, mama, alas. True, here it is essential to use the half-forgotten word *alas*. Alas, mama, the day when you wanted to put the sandwiches in my overcoat pocket I refused because I was not altogether well—that day passed long ago, now I've become an engineer, and my car awaits. Then our mother will burst into tears: how the years fly, she'll say, how quickly children grow up, you no sooner turn around than your son is an engineer! But then she'll calm down, sit on a stool, and her green eyes will grow stern, and her wrinkles, especially the two deep vertical wrinkles etched beside her mouth, will become even deeper and she will inquire: why are you deceiving me, you just asked for money for a wreath for a girl who was in your class, and now you're maintaining that you graduated from school and even the institute long ago, do you mean to say you can be a schoolboy and an engineer simultaneously? And besides that, mama will remark sternly, there isn't any car in the yard, if you don't count that truck by the garbage cans, you've made this all up, no car is awaiting you. Dear mama, I don't know if one can be an engineer and a schoolboy together, perhaps some people can't, some are unable, some haven't been given the gift, but I, having chosen freedom, one of its forms, I am free to act as I wish and to be whoever I want either simultaneously or separately, can it be you don't understand this? And if you don't believe me, then ask Savl Petrovich, and although he hasn't been among us for a long time, he will explain everything to you: we have a problem with time—that's what you'll be told by the geographer, the man of the fifth suburban zone. And as for the car—don't get upset, I just fantasized a little, it really isn't there and never will be, but then always, from seven to eight a.m., every day of every year, in full gale or fair weather—the garbage trust's trusty truck will be guarding the garbage cans in our yard, bedbuglike, green as a fly. What about the girl, inquires mama, did the girl really die? I don't know—you have to answer—I don't know anything about the girl. Then you must walk quickly to the hall where your coat is hanging on the coat-rack, the jackets and hats of your relatives too—don't be afraid of these things, they're empty, no one is wearing them—and your coat is hanging there. Put it on, put on your cap and fling open the door onto the stairs. Run from the house of your father without looking back, for if thou lookest back thou willst behold the grief in thy mother's eyes, and you will have a bitter taste as you race across the frozen ground to the second shift at school. As you race to the second shift, you realize you didn't do your homework for today either, but to the hostile question of how this happened, as you stare out the window at the parting day—the town's streetlights aflare, dangling over the street like mute bells with their clappers torn out—answer whichever teacher asks, answer with dignity and don't be embarrassed. Answer: since I consider myself an enthusiastic competitor in the entomology competition announced by our esteemed Academy, I devote my leisure to the collection of rare and semi-rare lepidoptera. Well, so what, the pedagogue will interpose. I dare say, you continue, that my collection will hold considerable scientific interest in the future, which is why, without fear of the materials or time sacrificed, I deem it my duty to supplement it with unique new specimens: so don't ask why I didn't do my homework. Since it's winter what kind of butterflies can you be speaking of, asks the pedagogue with mock surprise, what's wrong—are you crazy? And you respond with unshaken dignity: in the winter one can speak only of winter lepidoptera, those which are called snow butterflies, I catch them in the countryside—in the forest and the field, in the mornings primarily—to the second of the questions you posed my reply is this: the fact of my existence is of no surprise to anyone, otherwise they wouldn't keep me in this damn school along with others who are fools. You're being impertinent, I'll have a talk with your parents. To which the answer should be: you have a right to talk to whomever you like, including my parents, only don't express your doubts about the winter butterflies to anyone, you'll become a laughing-stock and be made to study here with us: there are just as many winter butterflies as summer ones, remember that. Now, put all your folios and folders into your briefcase and slowly, with the tired gait of an aging entomologist, coughing, leave the auditorium.

I know: you're like me—we never liked the school, especially since the day our principal Nikolai Gorimirovich Perillo introduced the slipper system. In case you don't recall, this was the name of the procedure which obliged pupils to bring slippers with them, moreover, you had to carry them not simply in your hands, and not in briefcases, but in specially made cloth bags. Right, in white bags with pullstrings, and on every bag, in Chinese black, was written the name of the pupil to whom the bag belonged. It was required to write, let's say: *Student so-and-so 5 "U" class*, and below that, but in larger letters, it was obligatory to put: *slippers*. And still lower, but even larger: *special school*. Well of course I remember the time well, it started suddenly one of those days. N. G. Perillo came to our room during class, he came gloomily. He always came gloomily, because, as our father explained, the principal's salary was low and he drank a lot. Perillo lived in a one-story annex which stood in the schoolyard, and if you want I'll describe both the annex and the yard for you. Just describe the yard, I remember the annex. Our red brick school was surrounded by a fence made of the same brick. An asphalt drive led from the gate to the front entrance— there were some trees beside it, and flower beds. Along the facade you could see several sculptures: in the center were two small old chalk men, one wearing a plain cap, the other a military forage cap. The old men stood with their backs to the school and their faces to you, as you race along the drive to the second shift, and each of them had one arm thrust forward—as if they were pointing to something important taking place there, in the stony barrens in front of the school where once a month they made us run cross-country conditioning relays. To the left of the old men a sculpture of a little girl with a small deer was whiling away its time. The girl and the deer were also shiny white, like pure chalk, and they too were looking at the barrens. And to the right of the old men stood a little bugler boy, and he would like to play the bugle, he knew how to play, he could play anything, even an extracurricular czardas, but unfortunately he didn't have a bugle, the bugle had been knocked out of his hands, or more accurately, the white plaster bugle had been broken in transit and the only thing protruding from the boy's lips was the support for the bugle, a piece of rusty wire. Allow me to correct you: as far as I remember, there really was a little white girl standing in the schoolyard, but the girl had a dog, not a deer, she was a chalk girl with an ordinary dog; when we rode our bicycle from point A to point B, this girl with the short dress and the dandelion in her hair was on her way to go swimming; you say that the chalk girl stands (stood) in front of our school and looks (looked) at the barrens where we run (ran) cross-country conditioning relays, but I tell you: she looks at the pond where she'll soon be swimming. You say she's petting a deer, but I tell you the girl is petting her ordinary dog. And you didn't tell the truth about the little white boy: he's standing but he isn't playing the bugle and although some sort of metal is protruding from his mouth, he doesn't know how to play the bugle, I don't know what the metal is, maybe it's the needle he uses to sew his mouth shut so as not to eat his mother's sandwiches wrapped in his father's newspaper. But the main thing is this: I maintain that the little white boy is not standing, but sitting—it is a little dark boy sitting against the background of a white dawn, book after book, on the grass, it is a little boy engineer whose car is waiting, and he is sitting on his base just exactly the way Savl Petrovich sat on the windowsill in the bathroom, warming the bottoms of his feet when we go and enter furiously, carrying in our briefcases entomological notes, plans for the transformation of time, many-colored nets for catching snow butterflies, and the six-foot-long handles of these beautiful devices stick out of the briefcases, catching the corners and the smug portraits of the scholars on the walls. We walk in furiously: dear Savl Petrovich, this terrible school is getting impossible, they give a lot of homework, the teachers are almost all fools, they aren't a bit smarter than us, you know, something's got to be done, there has to be some decisive step—perhaps letters here and there, perhaps boycotts and hunger-strikes, barricades and barracudas, tympani and tambourines, burned rolls and gradebooks, a large-scale auto-da-fe embracing all the special schools of the world, look here in our briefcases we have nets for catching butterflies. We'll break the poles off our own nets, catch all the really stupid people, and put these nets on their heads like dunce caps, and then we'll beat their hateful faces with the poles. We'll arrange a fabulous mass-scale civil execution, and then those who tormented us in our idiotic specschools for so long will have to run conditioning relays by themselves—through the stony barrens, and they will have to solve problems about bicycle riders, and we, the former students, liberated from our slavery to ink and chalk, we will get on our dacha bicycles and race along the highways and byways, occasionally greeting in motion girls we know wearing short skirts, girls with ordinary dogs, we will become the suburban bicycle-riders of points A, B, and C, and let those damned fools, damned fools that they are, solve problems about us and for us, the bicycle-riders. We will be bicycle-riders and postmen like Mikheev (Medvedev) or like the one whom you, Savl Petrovich, call The Sender. All of us, the former idiots, will become Senders, and it will be beautiful. Remember, once upon a time you asked us if we believe in this person, and we said that we had no idea what to think about the matter, but now when the incandescent summer has given way to dank autumn, and passersby, heads hidden in their collars, dream of turning into birds, now we hasten to declare to you personally, dear Savl Petrovich, and to all other progressive pedagogues, that we do not doubt the existence of The Sender, as we do not doubt that the future full of bicycle-riders and bicycle-rider-senders lies ahead. And today, from here, from our disgusting men's toilet with the bespattered windows and the floors which never dry, we shout to the whole wide world: long live the Sender of wind! Furiously.

Meanwhile our thin and barefoot teacher Savl is sitting on the windowsill, looking at us, touched as we boom this greatest of oratorios, and when its final echo reverberates through emptied rooms and corridors which still stink of the classes, when it does this and flies out into the autumn streets, teacher Savl will pull some little scissors from the chest pocket of his shirt, he will cut his toenails, look at the stall doors, all covered with obscene words and decorated with idiotic drawings, and: how much that is vulgar—he'll say—How much that is ugly we have in our restroom, O God—he'll note—how cynical we are, we the people of the special school. Is it impossible to select more exalted, profound and tender words instead of these vile and alien ones? O people, teachers and pupils, how fatuous and filthy you are in your ideas and your deeds! But are we the ones to blame for our idiocy and animal lust, are our hands the ones that scribbled on the doors of the stalls? No, no!—he will exclaim—we are nothing but weak and helpless servants and non-servants of our Principal, Kolya Perillo, and it is he who has inspired us with debauchery and weakmindedness, and it is he who did not instruct us to love tenderly and profoundly, and his hands are the ones which guide ours when we are drawing on the walls here, and he is to blame for our idiocy and our lust. O vile Perillo—Savl will say—how loathsome you are! And he will weep. We shall stand there at a loss as to what to say to calm him, our genius of a teacher and man. We shall stand on the tiled floor, shifting from one foot to the other, and the wet filth left by the second shift will ooze underfoot and slowly and quite imperceptibly begin to seep through our canvas slippers, which our poor mother spent such a painfully long time in line to get. One evening, an evening of one of those days: Mama, Perillo came to our classroom gloomily today. He erased everything the teacher had written on the board, erased it with a rag.

Attention—he, the principal, said in the stillness—from this day forth this special school with all of its chemicals, Faraday lamps, volleyballs, inkwells, blackboards, chalkboards, maps and pirozhki and other fancy-wancies is declared to be the Great Fatherland Mathematician Lobachevsky Model Shockwork Special School, and it goes over to the slipper system. The class got noisier and noisier, and one boy—I don't remember his name, or maybe I simply don't understand it, or maybe I was this boy myself—this boy began to cry out, for some reason he cried out at great length, like so: a-a-a-a-a-a-a-a! Sorry, mama, I realize there's no need to demonstrate precisely how the boy cried out, especially since father is napping, it's enough to say that a boy cried out, I could say that he shouted very loudly and unexpectedly, and there's no need to demonstrate that he shouted like so: a-a-a-a-a-a-a-a! In doing this he opened his mouth wide and stuck out his tongue, and it seemed to me that he had an exceptionally red tongue, the boy was probably ill, and it was the beginning of an attack—that's what I thought. I have to note, mama, he really does have a very long red tongue with violet spots and veins, as if the boy drank ink, it's really amazing. It was as if he were sitting at the ear-throat-nose doctor's and the doctor asked him to say his "ah," and the boy opened his mouth and is diligently saying, or rather, shouting: a-a-a-a-a-a-a-a! He shouted for a few minutes, and everyone looked at him, and then he stopped shouting and quite quietly asked, addressing the principal: Ah, what does that mean? And at that point everyone remembered that the boy stutters, that sometimes the shift from vowel to consonant comes hard to him, and he gets stuck on the vowel and shouts, because he feels ashamed. And so today he shouted like that: a-a-a-a-a-a-a-a! He wanted to ask the principal: ah, what does that mean—that's all. And finally he asked and Principal Perillo replied through his teeth: the slipper system is an arrangement whereby every pupil buys slippers and brings them to school in a special sack with pull-strings. Arriving at school, the pupil removes his usual footwear and puts on the slippers he has brought, and the emptied bag is filled with his usual footwear and he hands this to the lady in the cloakroom along with his coat and hat. Am I explaining it comprehensibly?—asked the principal, looking blankly to the ends of the earth. And at this point the boy began shouting horrendously again, this time it was another sound: o-o-o-o-o-o-o-o!I won't do it any more, mama, I'll just finish. And at this point the boy shouted: o-o-o-o-o-o-o-o!—and then he got it out: oh, that's nice. Perillo was ready to leave now, when we, that is, he and I, the other, we stood up and declared: Nikolai Gorimirovich, we are appealing to you personally and in your open and honorable person to the entire administration as a whole with a request to allow us to carry one bag for two people, inasmuch as it would be twice as hard for our mother to sew two bags as one. To which the principal, exchanging glances with the teacher, as if they knew something that no one else knew, as if they knew more than we did, replied:

each student of the Great Fatherland Mathematician Lobachevsky Model Shockwork Special School must have his own bag with pull-strings—one bag apiece. And as long as you consider that there are two of you, you must have two bags—no more, no less. If you imagine that there are ten of you, then get ten bags. Curses!—we said loudly and furiously—it would be better if we didn't exist at all, then you wouldn't pester us with your damned bags and slippers, poor mama, you'll have to sew two bags, sitting up till late at night, whole nights through, at your sewing machine, stitching—tra-ta-ta, tra-ta-ta—through, through the heart, yes it would better if we turned into a lily forever, into the *nymphea alba*, like that other time, on the river, only forever, to the end of life. Furiously. Principal Perillo took a wadded handkerchief from his inside jacket pocket and carefully wiped the freckled, rubicund bald spot mushed into his skull. He did this to conceal his dismay, he was dismayed, he didn't expect the presence of such infuriated pupils in the school. And he said gloomily: student so-and-so, I didn't imagine that there were people here capable of losing my trust in them to the extent that you have just done. And if you don't want me to expel you from the school and pass your documents along to *that place*, *there*, sit down at once and write an explanatory note about this lost trust, you must explain everything to me, and particularly your stupid pseudo-scientific theory about turning into a lily. Having said this, Perillo turned, clicked his heels militarily—in the school it was said that the principal had served in the same batallion as Kutuzov himself—and exited, slamming the door. Enraged. The whole class looked in our direction, stuck out a red poisonous tongue, aimed slingshots, and giggled, because the whole class, like all the others in the specschool—is stupid and barbarous. The idiots, they are the ones who hang cats on the fire escape, they are the ones who spit in each other's faces during the long recesses and take jam pirozhki away from each other, they are the ones who secretly urinate in each other's pockets and trip each other, they are the ones who twist each other's arms and gang up on weaklings, and they are the idiots who scribbled all over the doors to the stalls.

But why are you so angry with your comrades—says our patient mother to us—aren't you like them? If you were different, better than them, we wouldn't send you to study in the specschool. O, you can't imagine what a joy it would be for me and your father! Lord, I would surely become the happiest of mothers. No, mama, no, we are totally different people, and we have nothing in common with those crumbs, we are incomparably superior, better than them in all respects. Naturally, it might seem to the uninitiated that we are the same, and in terms of general academic progress there is no one worse than us, we aren't capable of remembering a single poem all the way, still less a fable, but on the other hand, we do remember things which are more important. Not long ago Vodokachka explained to you that we, your sons, have a so-called selective memory, and that is quite right, mama, this kind of memory allows us to live as we wish, for we remember only what is necessary to us, not what is necessary to those cretins who insolently take it upon themselves to teach us. You know, we don't even recall how many years we have already spent in the specschool, and sometimes we forget the names of school objects, or objects in general, not to mention your formulas and definitions—those we don't know at all. Once, a year or three ago, you found us a tutor in some subject, perhaps mathematics, and as it happens we usually went to his place for lessons, and he got a certain number of rubles for each lesson. He was a sweet and knowledgeable pedagogue, and during approximately the second lesson he informed us: young man—no, I'm mistaken, he used an odd inverted form of expression: man of youth; man of youth, you are unique, the sum total of your knowledge of this subject is zero. When we came for the third lesson, he left us alone in the apartment and ran to the store for some beer. It was summer, hot, we came from the dacha for lessons, it was unbearable, mama. The tutor said to us: ah, hello, hello, man of youth, I kept waiting and waiting—wiping his hands—it's hot for it's summer, did you bring the money? Give it here, I've been waiting, not a kopek, stay here, I'll hop down for some beer, make yourself at home, do some drawing or something, feed the guppies, the light in the aquarium has burned out, the water is murky, but when the fish swims up to the glass, you can observe and examine it, yes, by the way, take a look at Fishman too, he's on the shelf, it's an exercise book, an exercise book of problems, I recommend number such-and-such, singularly interesting, a bicycle rider is riding along, can you imagine that? He goes from point to point, a most interesting situation, the heat out is impossible, I've been waiting, not a kopek in the whole house, the neighbors are all in the South, absolutely no one to borrow from, in general, I'm off, make yourself comfortable, do whatever you like, only don't raid the icebox, there's not anything in it anyway—it's empty, and so, for beer, for beer, and again for beer, so it won't be frightfully painful. Absentmindedly. No, concentrating. Turning around in front of the mirror. When the tutor came back with the beer—thirty bottles, mama—he asked us if we knew how to play chess. We do, we replied. Just that day we had invented a new piece, called the rookinghorse, which could move corner to corner or not go at all, that is, skip a move and stay in place. In this case the player simply says to his partner, the rookinghorse moves, but in reality the rookinghorse stands as if nailed to the ground and looks blankly to all the ends of the earth, like Perillo. The tutor was terribly pleased by the idea of a new piece, and later when we would come to his house he would often sing to the tune of the "Children of Captain Blood": rookinghorse, rookinghorse, smile on. And drink beer, and we never did any work on our subject, we played chess and beat our tutor fairly often. So we don't have a bad memory, mama, it is, rather, selective, and you shouldn't be upset. And at this point the three of us, sitting in the kitchen, heard our father's voice and realized that he was no longer drowsing in his armchair, but moving along the corridor, flopping his houseslippers and rattling the fresh evening newspapers. He was taking a long time, walking tiredly and coughing—that was precisely his voice, it was this in which his voice was expressed. Good evening, papa's wearing pyjamas, don't be concerned that they're old, sometime mama will make or buy you some new ones, and Those Who'll Come will inquire: make them or buy them, make them or buy them, make them or buy them? Your prosecutor-father is very large: when he stands in the kitchen door wearing his checked pyjamas he fills the entire entrance, he stands there and asks: what's going on, what are you shouting here in my house, what's wrong with you, are you crazy? I thought your dumb relatives had come again, a hundred of them at once. What the hell is this, anyway! Can't you keep it down a little, you've let your brat get hopelessly out of hand, things are perfectly clear with him—straight F's. No, papa, that's not the basic thing, you understand, the rookinghorse has slipped into my dreams the way a man's red fist slips into a leather glove, and he has, the poor fellow, a selective memory, the rookinghorse has. What rubbish is this, I don't want to hear your delirium—father said to me. He sat down on a stool, and it might seem that at any second it would collapse under the weight of this endlessly exhausted body, and he shook a sheaf of newspaper pages to straighten them, and used his fingernail to mark some notice under the heading *advertisements*. Listen—he addressed mother— to what it says here: wanted to buy, a winter dacha. What do you think, should we sell our house to this character, he's probably a swindler and a rascal, some foreman or collective farm director, and he's got money of course, otherwise he wouldn't bother running an ad. I was just sitting and thinking—continued father—why the hell do we need that hovel, there's nothing good out there: the pond is filthy, the neighbors are all bums and drunkards, and think what the upkeep alone costs. But the hammock— said mama—how glorious it is to lie in the hammock after a hard day, why you know you love to do that. I can hang the hammock up in the city too, on the balcony—said father—true, it'll take up the whole balcony, but then not a single relative will turn up there, on the balcony, and that's the main thing, I'm sick and tired of maintaining a dacha for your relatives, do you understand this or not? Sell it, and everything's here, and no taxes, or glass repairers, or roof repairers and what-not for you, especially since my pension is not sky-high, eh? Whatever you think best—said mama.

And then I—this time it was precisely me, and not that fellow from the

same class who stutters so painfully—then I bellowed at my father: a-a-a-a-
a-a-a-a! I bellowed more loudly than ever before in my life, I wanted him to
hear and understand what the cry of his son meant: a-a-a-a-a-a-a-a! wolves
on the walls even worse on the walls there are people, people's faces, they're
the hospital walls that time when you are dying quietly and terribly a-a-a-a
huddled up in the fetal position faces which you have never seen but which
you will see years later these are the preludes to death and life for it has
been promised to you that you will live in order to be able to sense the
reverse movement of time and to study in the specschool and feel infinite
love for your teacher Veta Vetka of acacia a fragile woman in tight
stockings which susurrate when she walks a girl with a tiny birthmark near
her exquisite and provocative mouth, a dacha girl with the eyes of a
light-hearted doe a stupid slut for sale from the suburban electric platform
over which there is a viaduct and clock and humming wires in the snowy
wind snowy wind and higher up a-a-a-a flashing young stars and storms
flashing through summers—am I late? excuse me, for God's sake, Veta
Arcadievna, I was seeing my mother off, she was going to her relatives for a
few days, to another town, but then I suppose you're not interested, to be
honest, I don't even know what to do so that things will be interesting for
you, well, now, I thought, let's go for a ride somewhere, let's say to the park
or a restaurant, you're probably cold, button up, why are you laughing, did
I really say something funny, come on, stop, pleae, what? you'd like to go
to the dacha? but we sold the dacha long ago, we have no dacha, because
father retired, let's go to a restaurant, yesterday I got some money, not too
much, but some, I work in a certain ministry now, what do you mean, no
I'm not an engineer, what? I can't hear, an electric is coming, let's move
away from the edge, why did I write you this note? curses, I can't answer
like this all at once, we really have to have a little chat, sit down somewhere,
let's go to a restaurant, all right? what? on the electric? of course, there's no
stop here, this is an out-of-town locale, more precisely, a suburban one, I
will tell you everything along the way, it's all very important, imagine,
there was a time, probably rather a long time ago, I used to come here, onto
the snowswept platform, together with my mother, you probably know,
don't you, you face in the direction the train's headed, and the cemetery is
on the left, my grandmother is buried there—ee-ee-ee-ee-ee—just as they
do now, electric trains used to go by, freights, expresses—careful, mama,
don't slip—or was that a different platform? they all look so much alike—
the wide white cemetery, but first comes the market, the market, we have to
buy sunflower seeds there, the women are wearing peasant kerchiefs, it
smells of cows and milk, long tables and stalls, several motorcycles at the
entrance, workers in blue aprons are unloading a truckload of boxes, from
the crossing with its barrier and striped watchman's box one hears a
raucous whistle, two dogs are sitting by the butcher shop, along the fence is
a queue for kerosene, a horse which has brought a cistern, and snow is

falling onto the horse from the tree under which it is standing, but since the horse is white the snow on its crupper is virtually unnoticeable. Also a water hydrant, and around it iced wet spots, strewn with sand, also—butts thrown into the snowbank, also—an invalid wearing a padded jacket, sellers of dried mushrooms on strings. A wagon wheel leaning against a garbage bin. Mama, will we drop in on grandmother or go straight to the maestro? To grandmother—replies mother—first of all to grandmother, she's waiting, we haven't been to see her for a long time, it's simply bad, she might think we've completely forgotten about her, straighten your scarf and put on your gloves, where's your hanky, grandmother will be unhappy about the way you look. Pass the iron gates with their protuberant cast-iron decorations, buy a bouquet of paper flowers—they are sold by a blind crone next to the church, go out into the central walkway, then turn to the right. Keep going until you see the white marble angel in the form of a young woman. The angel stands behind the blue fence surrounding the grave, its fine big wings folded behind its back and its head down: it listens to the train whistles—the line passes a kilometer from here—and mourns for my grandmother. Mama searches for the key to the fence, that is, to the padlock which locks the fence, the wicket gate in the fence. The key is in there somewhere, in mother's nice-smelling purse—along with a compact, perfume bottle, lace hanky, matches (mama doesn't smoke, of course, but she carries matches just in case), national identity card, roll of paper twine, along with a dozen old trolley tickets, lipstick and change for the road. For a long time mama cannot find the key and she gets upset: well where is it, Lord, I know perfectly well that it was here, you mean we aren't going to get to visit grandmother today, what a shame. But I know that the key will certainly be found, and I wait calmly—no, not true, I'm upset too, because I'm afraid of the angel, I'm a little afraid of the angel, mama, it's so gloomy looking. Don't say silly things, it's mournful, not gloomy, it's mourning grandmother. Finally the key is found, and mama starts trying to open the lock. It doesn't work right away: wind has blown snow into the keyhole and the key won't go in, so mama presses the lock into her palm to warm it, and the snow in the keyhole melts. If this doesn't help, mama bends over the lock and breathes on it, as if trying to melt someone's frozen heart. Finally the lock clicks and opens—a motley winter butterfly, which was resting on an elder branch, is frightened and flies to the neighboring grave; the angel just shudders, but doesn't fly away, it stays with grandmother. Mama mournfully opens the gate, walks up to the angel and looks at it for a long time—the angel is covered with snow. Mama bends down and gets a fir whiskbroom from under the bench: we bought it one day at the market. Mama sweeps the snow from the bench, then turns around to the angel and brushes the snow from its wings (one wing is wrecked, broken) and its head, the angel frowns unhappily. Mama takes a small shovel—it stands behind the angel's wing—and cleans the snow from grandmother's mound.

The mound under which grandmother is. Then mama sits down on the bench and takes a handkerchief from her purse to wipe away her coming tears. I stand alongside, I don't especially want to sit down, mama, not especially, thanks, no, I'll stand. Well—says mama to her mother—well, here we are again, hello my dear, you see, it's winter again, aren't you cold, maybe I shouldn't have taken away the snow, it would be warmer, hear that, the train is going by, today's Sunday, mama, there are a lot of people in church, at home—at this point the first tears slip down my mama's cheeks—at home everything is fine, my husband (mama uses my father's name) and I don't quarrel, everyone's healthy, our son (mama uses my name) is in such-and-such a class, he's doing better in school. Not true, mama, not true, I think, I'm doing so poorly in school that if not today then tomorrow Perillo will expel me, I think, and I will start selling paper flowers like that old crone, I think, but I say aloud: grandmother, I try terribly, terribly hard, I'll definitely graduate from the school, please don't worry, and I'll become an engineer, like grandfather. I can't say anything else, because I have a feeling I'm going to burst out crying in a second. I turn away from grandmother and look along the walkway: at the end, by the fence, a little girl is playing with a dog—hello, girl with the ordinary dog, I see you here every time, do you know what I wish to impart to you today, I'm deceiving my former grandmother, somehow it's awkward for me to disappoint her, and I am not telling the truth, none of us imbeciles will ever become engineers, the only thing any of us is capable of is selling postcards or paper flowers like that old crone by the church, and probably not even that: there is certainly no way we will ever learn how to make that kind of flower, so we won't have anything to sell. The girl departs, taking away the dog. I notice that the butterfly, which is now resting three paces from me on the bend of a fresh branch, is spreading its wings, getting ready to fly. I throw open the gate and run, but the butterfly notices me before I manage to cover it with my hat: it disappears among the bushes and crosses. Up to my knees in snow I run after it, mournfully, trying not to look at the photographs of those who are dead; their faces are illuminated by the setting sun, their faces smiling. Dusk descends from the heavenly deeps. The butterfly, after flitting here and there, vanishes utterly, and you remain alone in the middle of the cemetery.

You don't know how to get back to your mourning mother, and you head in the direction of the train whistles which you can hear—towards the line. An engine, blue smoke, a whistle, some kind of clicking inside the mechanism, the blue—no, black, hat of a mechanic, he has his head out the cab window, looking ahead and to the sides, he notices you and smiles—he has a moustache. Raises his arm, apparently to where the controls and signal handle are. You guess that in a second there will be another whistle—the engine will scream, come to its senses, jolt and pull the cars along, begin to emit steam and, increasing speed, blow smoke. Softly, hunched in clumsy constraint from its own inexplicable power, it will roll across the bridge, and vanish—melt away, and never from this day forth will you find consolation for this loss: where can you ever find another—an engine as black as a rook, the moustachioed mechanic—and where will you ever again see these—exactly these, not others—battered little patched-up cars, brown and sad and squeaking. It will vanish—melt away. You will re-member the sound of the whistle, the steam, the eternal eyes of the engineer, you will wonder how old he is, where he lives, you will wonder—and forget (vanish—melt away), you will recall someday but be unable to tell anyone else about it—about everything you saw: the engineer and the engine and the train that they both took away over the bridge. You won't be able to, people won't understand, they'll look at you strangely: what's so unusual about trains. But if they understand—they'll be amazed. It will vanish—melt away. Crow-engine, engine-crow. Engineeer cars rocking on their springs, the cough of couplings and airhoses. A distant route, playing-card houses just outside the right-of-way barriers—government ones and private ones, with frontyard gardens and ordinary apple or-chards, in the windows—the lights of the blinking darkness, all around a life unknown and incomprehensible to you, and people whom you will never meet. Vanish—and melt away. Standing in the lengthening dusk—hands in the pockets of your gray spring coat—you wish the train a fast night on the rails, you wish all its stokers, trackmen, and engineers well, you want them to have a good night on the rails where there will be: the somnolent faces of stations, the hum of signal arrows, steam-engines which drink from the T-shaped water hoses of the watertowers, dispatchers' cries and curses, the odor of the car platforms, the odor of burned coal and clean bed linen, the odor of cleanliness, Veta Arcadievna, of clean snow—in essence, the smell of winter, its very beginning, that's what is most im-portant—you understand? My God, student so-and-so, why are you shouting so loudly, it's quite embarrassing, the whole car is looking at us, can't we discuss all this quietly. Then you get up, go to the center of the car, and raising your arm in salutation you say: citizens, suburban passengers, I beg your pardon for talking too loudly, I'm very sorry I behaved badly; in school, in the special school where I once studied, they taught us something quite different, they taught us to speak quietly, no matter what the subject was, I have tried to behave exactly this way all my life. But today I am incredibly upset, today is an extraordinary case, today, or rather, for today I arranged a meeting with my former teacher by writing her an emotional note, and then my teacher came to the windswept platform in order to see me after such-and-such a number of years, and there she sits now, in our electric train car, on that yellow electric bench, and everything that I am telling her now and that I will tell her—everything is extraordinarily important, believe me, that's why my voice sounds a little louder than usual, thank you for your attention. Excitedly. You want to return to Veta, but at this point someone puts a hand on your shoulder. You turn around: before you is a stern woman of more than forty, almost gray-haired, wearing glasses with thin gold frames, the woman had green eyes and vertical, painfully familiar furrows by her mouth. You look carefully—it is your patient mother. For a solid hour she has been looking all over the cemetery for you: where did you go, you repulsive child, why did you head for the trains again, she thought that something had happened to you, it was already quite dark. Reply simply and with dignity: dear mama, I saw a winter butterfly, I ran after it and so I got lost. Let's go right now—mother is angry—grandmother is calling you, she asks to be shown how you learned to play the accordion, play her something mournful, sad—do you hear? and don't you dare refuse. Grandmother, can you hear me? I will play you a piece by Brahms called the "Potato," but I'm not sure I've learned it very well. I take the accordion—the instrument is standing in the snow of the walkway in its black case. I remove the case and sit down on the bench. It's evening at the cemetery, but the white angel—it's right nearby—is quite visible as I sit with my accordion three quarter. The angel spread its wings and instilled mournful inspiration in me: ee-ee-ee—one two three, one two three, in a garden girls were walking, wa-a-lking, one two three, one two three, don't cry mama, or I'll stop playing: granny's fine now, you don't have to get upset, one two three, one two three, wa-a-lking, she had a selective memory too, grandmother did, wa-a-lking. Remember how the accordion sounds in the chill cemetery air in the early evening when the sounds of the railroad come from the direction of the railroad, when the violet trolley sparks cascade off the distant bridge at the very edge of town, corruscating through the bare elder branches, and when from the store in the market—you remember this well too—workers use carts to carry away boxes full of bottles? The bottles clank and ring metallically, the horse stamps its hooves on the frozen cobblestones, and the workers shout and laugh—you won't learn anything about those workers, and they won't learn anything about you either—so, do you remember how your Barcarolle sounded in the chill cemetery air in the early evening? Why are you asking me about that, it's so unpleasant for me to remember that time, I am tired of remembering it, but if you insist, I will reply calmly and with dignity: at such moments my accordion sounds lonely. May I be permitted to ask the following question, one detail interests me, I intend to check your, and simultaneously my, memory: in those years when you or I, when we visited our grandmother with our mother to play her a new piece on the accordion or to give a brief plot summary of some story we had just read from the series book after book—was our teacher Norvegov still alive in those years or had he already died?

You see, the years which we are now discussing dragged quietly for rather a
long time, they dragged on and on, and in that time our mentor Savl
managed both to live and to die. What do you mean, that he lived first, and
then died? I don't know, but in any case he died right in the middle of those
long dragging years, and it was only at the end of them that we encountered
the teacher on the wooden platform of our station, and that some sort of
water creatures splashed around in the barrel at Norvegov's. But I don't
understand in precisely which end of the years in question our encounter
took place—in the earlier or the later. I will explain to you, once in some
scholarly journal (I showed our father this article, he leafed through it and
immediately threw the entire journal off the balcony, and moreover, when
throwing it off, repeatedly shouted the word *Acatovism*) I read the theory
of a certain philosopher. There was a preface to it, it said the article was
being printed for porpoises of discussion. The philosopher wrote that in his
opinion time had a reverse side, that is, that it moved not in the direction
we suppose it should move, but in reverse, backwards, because everything
which was—all this is just going to be, he said, the real future is past, and
that which we call the future has already passed and will never be repeated,
and if we are incapable of remembering the past, if it is concealed from us
by the shroud of an imaginary future, it is not our fault, but our misfortune, because all of us have amazingly weak memories, in other words, I
thought, reading the article, like you have and I have, like you and I and
our grandmother have—selective. And I also thought: but if time is
rushing back, that means everything is normal, therefore Savl, who died
precisely at the time when I read the article, therefore Savl still *will be*, that
is, will come, will return—he is all ahead, as a fecund summer is ahead, full
of magnificent water nymphs, a summer of rowboats and bicycles, a
summer of butterflies, a collection of which you finally assembled and sent
off to our respected Academy in a big box used for some imported eggs.
You appended to the parcel the following letter: "Dear Sirs! More than
once and more than twice orally (on the telephone) and in writing (by
telegraph) I have requested confirmation of the rumors that an academic
entomological competition, named after one of the two chalk men standing in the courtyard of our special school, is taking place. Alas, I have
received no reply. But since I am a passionate collector and at the same
time (which has a backwards flow) one selflessly devoted to science, I
consider it my duty to proffer for the exalted perusal of your scholarly
council my modest collection of night and day butterflies, among which
you will find both summer and winter ones. The latter, apparently, are
particularly interesting, inasmuch as—in spite of their numerousness—

they are scarcely ever observed in nature or in flight, a fact which yours truly has already made reference to in talks with specialists, among others with Academician A. A. Acatov, who reacted very favorably to the present collection, now composed of more than ten thousand specimens of insects. I request that you inform me of the results of the competition at this address: the railroad, the branch, the station, the dacha, ring the bicycle bell until it is opened unto you." You sealed the envelope, and before putting it on top of the butterflies in their egg box, you wrote on the reverse side of the envelope: with greetings fly, return with reply—across it, from corner to corner on the diagonal, in huge letters. This is what our teacher of Russian language and literature, nicknamed Vodokachka, taught us, even though if you were to look for a person less resembling a watertower both externally and internally you couldn't find anyone better than our Vodokachka. But the point wasn't in the similarity, but in the fact that the letters which compose the word itself, or more accurately, half of the letters (read every other one, starting with the first)—are her initials, the teacher's: V. D. K. (Valentina Dmitrievna Kaln—that's what she was called). But two letters are still left over—*ch* and *a*—and I've forgotten how they're supposed to be decoded. In the minds of our classmates they could mean anything you like, but no decodification other than the following was acknowledged: Valentina Dmitrievna Kaln—the human-arquebus. It's funny, but Kaln didn't look any more like a human-arquebus than like a watertower, but if anyone were ever to ask you to give her, Vodokachka, a more precise nickname—although it's incomprehensible why and to whom it could occur to do such a thing—you would certainly fail to find one. Even though the teacher didn't look in the least like a watertower—you would say—still in some inexplicable way she recalls the word itself, the combination of letters of which it is made up (was made up, will be made up)—V, O, D, O, K, A, Ch, K, A.

Chapter Four   *Skeerly*

Now allow me to clear my throat, look you straight in the eye and pinpoint one detail from your cover letter. In it you said something to the effect that Acatov himself had reacted very favorably to our collection, but I don't recall us ever talking to him on this theme—generally we never did actually meet him, we saw him only from afar, usually through the crack in his fence, but how we dreamed of one day walking down Acatov's garden path, knocking on the door to his house, and—when the old man opened—of saying hello and introducing ourself: student of your daughter so-and-so, a beginning entomologist, would like to discuss a few problems with you and so forth. But not once did we dare to knock on the door to his house, inasmuch as—or was it for another reason—a big dog lived in the garden. Listen, I don't like it when you call my collection—*our* collection, no one gave you any such right, I assembled my collection alone, and if we should ever merge into one, our acts identical, this act is not going to have any relation to butterflies; so there, now about the talk with Acatov: it's true, I was not deceiving the Academy, I really did talk to him. One summer, at the dacha, on a Sunday when father had had us sitting since morning rewriting the lead articles from newspapers, so that we would have a better understanding of internal and external *polyticks*. I decided that you would get along fine here without me. I waited for the moment: you put aside the pen, turned away to the window and began examining the structure of the lilac flower—I left the table noiselessly, put on father's cap—it was hanging on a peg in the hall—and took a cane—it belonged to one of our relatives, who had it about five years earlier. On the station platform five years earlier, in the evening. Our mother to the relative: I hope you had a good rest here with us, don't squash the strawberries, wash them, greetings to Elena Mikhailovna and Vanyusha, come together, pay no attention, he's just nervous, works a lot, scads of cases, gets tired, but you know basically he's kind, yes soft and kind deep down, but sometimes he does lose control, so do come, do come, only don't argue with him, wait, where's your cane, oh, how unfortunate, what's to be done. Anxiously. Let's go back, there'll be another electric. The relative: come on, it's not worth it, don't worry, if it were an umbrella it would make sense, it's getting ready to rain, thanks for the berries, I appreciate it and we'll come again for the cane, just think, a cane is rubbish, as they say, happiness doesn't depend on canes, so long, here it comes. However, since that time the relative hasn't come, and the cane was on the veranda until the very day when I took it and set off to the neighboring settlement to visit the naturalist Acatov: toock-toock (the dog runs up and sniffs me, but today I'm not afraid of it), toock-toock. But no one opens the door to the house. And then again: toock-toock. But no one responds. You walk around the house on the thick grass, you peer through the windows to check and see if the house does have the large wall clock with the chimes, which by your reckoning definitely has to be there, so that it can cut dacha time into chunks with its pendulum—but all of the windows are curtained. Fire barrels are dug into the ground at the corners of the house—these are filled with rusty water and some sort of lackadaisi-cal insects live in them. Only one barrel is completely empty, it contains neither water nor insects, and a happy thought occurs to you: to fill it with your shout. Long do you stand there, bent over the dark cylindrical abyss, running over in your selective memory the words which best reverberate in the emptiness of empty chambers. Such words are not numerous, but there are some. For example, if—thrown out of class—you are running through the school corridor when classes are in progress, and deep in your core a desire is born to shout in such a way that your shout will freeze the blood of your mendacious and debauched teachers, so that interrupting their speeches in mid-word they will swallow their tongues and be transformed—to the amusement of the idiot-students—into pillars of chalk, or pillarettes (depending on their height), you can't think up anything more delightful than the cry: bacilli! What do you think, mentor Savl?

Dear student and comrade so-and-so, whether sitting on the windowsill in the restroom, standing at the map in front of the class with a pointer in my hand, playing preference with a few colleagues in the teacher's room or in the boiler-room, I have rarely been witness to the kind of ultramundane terror which your mad cry caused the pedagogues and the students, and even the deaf-mute stoker, for it was said somewhere by someone: deaf man, the time will come and you will hear. Did I not see the capacious shovel with which he tirelessly hurls coal into the insatiable, hellish furnaces during the cold seasons, did I not—I ask—see the capacious shovel fall out of the hands of the miserable old man when the time of your cry came, the time for the deaf to hear, and he, turning to me with his face besooted and horrible in the dancing flecks and reflections of the flame, his ulcerated and unshaven face, he acquired for a moment the gift of speech, and right after you, shaking his hung-over head, he shouted—no, he bellowed the same word: bacilli, bacilli, bacilli. And so vast was his anger, and so powerful his passion, that the fire in the furnaces was extinguished by his bellow. And did I not see the teachers of their special school, who are used to a lot, turn pale and the cards, the playing cards that they were holding in their hands turned into leaves of a forest willow, which has the ability to draw out pus, and they, the pedagogues, moaned in horror. And did I not see the faces of your fellow pupils, which are infinitely obtuse anyway, become even more obtuse from your shout, and all of them opened their mouths—even the most capable of them and those who seemed almost normal, suddenly opened their mouths in an answering, albeit mute, cry, and all the dolts of the specschool howled in a monstrous, deafening chorus, and sick yellow saliva flowed from all these frightened psychopathic mouths. So don't ask me in vain what I think about your fierce and spellbinding shout. O, with what rapturous effort and pain I would shout, if it were my lot to shout even half of your shout! But it isn't my lot, how weak I am, your mentor, before your talent, given from on high. So shout then—most capable of the capable, shout for yourself and for me, and for all of us, deceived, defamed, dishonored and stupefied, for us, the idiots

and holy fools, the defectives and schizoids, for the educators and educa-
tees, for all those to whom it has not been given and whose salivating
mouths have already been shut, or will soon be shut, for all those who have
been innocently muted, or are being muted, tongues torn out—shout,
intoxicated and intoxicating: bacilli, bacilli, bacilli!

In the emptiness of empty chambers there are a few other words which will
reverberate fairly well too, but having gone over them in your memory, you
realize that not one of the ones known to you suits this situation, for in
order to fill the empty Acatov barrel, a uniquely special new word is
essential, or several words, inasmuch as the situation strikes you as exceptional. Yes, you say to yourself, here we need a shout of a new type.
Some ten minutes pass. There are a lot of grasshoppers in the Acatovs'
garden. They hop through the warm amber grass, and each hop is swift and
unexpected, like a shot from a specschool slingshot. The fire barrel beckons
you with its emptiness: this emptiness, and the stillness abiding in the
garden and the house and the barrel, soon became unbearable for you, a
person who is energetic, decisive and efficient. That's why you don't want
to reflect further on what to shout into the barrel—you shout the first thing
that comes into your head: I'm Nymphea, Nymphea!—you shout. And the
barrel overflows with your incomparable voice, releasing its surfeit into the
beautiful dacha sky, towards the tops of the pines—and the voice rolls over
the stuffy dacha mansards and attics which abound in all kinds of junk,
over the volleyball courts where no one ever plays, over the hutches
containing thousands of fattened rabbits, over garages redolent of gaso-
line, over verandas with their toy-bestrewn floors and smoking kerosene
lamps, over the gardens and heather barrens surrounding the dacha settlements: eya, eya-eya-eya-yayayaya-a-a! Your father, resting in the hammock in his yard, gives a start and awakens: who's shouting there, damn
him, mother, I heard your spawn bellowing somewhere in the pond, didn't I
tell him to do some work. Father rushes into the house and looks into our
room. He sees you sitting at the desk diligently—the diligence is expressed
in the way you bend your closely cropped head to the side and contort your
back absurdly, as if you had been smashed apart, yes, as if someone had
thrown you onto the rocks from a lofty cliff, and then come and smashed
you some more, using the adjustable pincers which clamp red hot ingots—
writing. But father sees only what he sees, he doesn't know, doesn't guess,
that it is only you sitting at the desk, while at this moment the other you is
standing beside Acatov's barrel, revelling in your soaring shout. Looking
around, you notice by the shed a rather old man in a torn, white robe, like a
doctor's. The man has a rope for a belt, there is a cocked hat of yellowed
paper on his head and on his feet—look carefully at what he has on his feet,

that is, how he is shod—on his feet—I can't see very well, after all he is relatively far away—on his feet, it seems, he has overshoes. Maybe you're wrong, maybe they're sneakers instead of overshoes? The grass is too high, if it were cut down I could make a more definite statement about his footwear, but this way—you can't make it out, but hold it, now I see: they're galoshes. Well, well, now look at that, I don't think that man has any pants, I don't mean specifically at this moment he hasn't any, but that specifically at this moment he hasn't any, in other words, he's not wearing any pants. Not so unusual, it's summer now, and aren't a robe and galoshes sufficient for summer; wearing pants, if you're going to put on a robe too, would be hot, inasmuch as a robe is practically an overcoat, to some degree it's an overcoat, an overcoat with no lining, or the other way around, a lining with no overcoat, or just a light coat. And if the robe is white, medical, it can also be called a light medical coat, and if the white robe doesn't belong to a physician, but, let's suppose, to a scientist, boldly call this robe a light scholarly duster, or laboratory jacket. You're explaining it all correctly, but we still don't know whom the robe belongs to, the robe on the man who is wearing the galoshes or more simply: who is it standing there by the shed so old and quiet—wearing the paper cocked hat and white duster, with galoshes on his bare feet, who is he? You mean you haven't recognized him, it's Acatov himself, who once declared to all the world that strange swellings—the galls—are caused by such-and-such, which was extremely precipitous on his part, even though as you see justice conquered and after such-and-such and such-and-such, which it has long been unacceptable to mention, the academician lives quietly in his dacha, and you, who have turned up here for a talk, are filling his fire barrel with your shout. And the academician, who in his intent wariness resembles a stooped little tree, asks you in a high-pitched and agitated human voice: who are you, I'm afraid of you, are there a lot of you? Be not afraid, sir—you say, trying to be as suave as possible in your manner and speech— I am quite alone, absolutely, and if anyone else turns up, don't believe him when he says he is me too, it's not like that at all, and obviously you can guess what the trouble is; when he comes I'll hide in the logpile, and you, you lie to him, lie, I implore you, say you don't know anything, no one was here, he'll look around a bit and then take off, and we shall continue our talk at leisure. But why were you shouting into the barrel like that—Acatov inquires curiously—what prompted you? Putting his palm to his ear, he adds: but talk louder, my hearing's not so good. Sir, allow me to approach you through this high grass. Come on, I don't seem to be afraid of you anymore. Hello. Hello. Dear Arcady Arcadievich, the essence of the matter is that I catch butterflies. Aha, butterflies, and have you caught many? Snow butterflies or in general?—you answer the question with a question. Snow, naturally—says the academician. Such-and-such a number—you say—I am collecting a collection, at the present time it includes the genera such-and-such and such-and-such. A-ah, how marvelous—Acatov says in surprise—but why so loud, I can't stand shouting, collect quietly, for God's sake. His face, wrinkled and tawny, like a pear in compote, goes pale from irritation. However—he continues—you'll go on shouting anyway, no matter what happens, I know, it's the fate of your generation, you're young, after all, from the looks of you you're not more than sixteen. Oh no, sir, you are in error, I'm way past twenty, I'm thirty, you see, after all, I have a hat and a cane. So, all right, listen—Acatov interrupts you—may I consult with you? Animatedly. At your service, sir, I'm all ears. The other day—the academician looks around and lowers his voice almost to whisper—I invented a new invention, follow me, it's in the shed, I've locked up the house and live in the shed now, it's easier, you take up less space. It was an ordinary shed, the sort of which there are many in our dacha locale: the ceiling is the reverse side of the roof, the walls are made of unplaned boards, as is the floor. What did you see inside the shed when you walked in and took off your footwear and left your cane, so as not to track in dirt? A table, a chair, a bed, and a pile of books on the windowsill are what I saw there. And up over all of this, squinting from the white winter sun—wearing a raccoon coat—snowdrifts and snowswept forest in the background—radiant, soaring, reigning supreme—is your incomparable Veta, teacher of biology, botany, anatomy—and on her amazing face, which was overwhelming, like a stifling noose, there was nothing which would remember you or which spoke to you one-to-one, O, Nymphea, her face was the face for anyone who ever looked upon it, and it was promised to many—but can it be that in that terrible, irreversible multitude, indistinguishable in the darkness of hotel rooms and apartments, can it be that there was a place for you among them too, you, the deficient dolt from the special school, you who, in a frenzy of tenderness and ecstasy, turned into the flower which you yourself had picked, can it be that you, who desired it infinitely more times than any of the others, that you too were among them?! Lord sir what an astonishing photograph she is like alive here that is no I'm mistaken a stylistic mistake I wanted to say like real like during class beautiful and inaccessible who took that when why I don't know anything some scroundrel with a camera who is he what is his relation to her here or elsewhere a legion of questions. Now then, I invented a certain invention: you see, an ordinary stick, eh? it would seem. Yes yes it would seem sir it would seem I come here fairly often in the winter too but I come alone without any of your photographers I don't have any acquaintances with cameras, she should it would seem have informed me that such and so and so and she was going to the Land of the Nightjar by car with a certain engineer a degree candidate an art historian a director a bookkeeper dammit she got photographed against a snowdrift background at the dacha she could have said something like we didn't even drop in so as not to have to clear the snow from the paths we walked for half an hour and returned to town after all I would have believed it. But that is a most profound misapprehension, observe, youth, I move it from one vertical position to another vertical position, or to put it another way—I turn it upside down, and now what is revealed to our astonished gaze? I am howling sir howling for I have been betrayed I Nymphea 'tis I bald weak flatfooted with a high forehead like on a real cretin and a face old from doubts look I am absolutely awful my nose is all covered with disgusting blackheads and my lips puffed forward and flattened as if I were born of a duck and it makes no difference that once upon a time in the flower of my crucial age I learned to play on a mother-of-pearl three quarters barcarolle that didn't help me nevertheless it is excruciatingly painful. We see an ordinary nail, hammered into the top of our stick, it was hammered in head first, and its pointed end is staring at us like a deadly steel stinger—but have no fear, youth, I will not aim it in your direction, I will not cause you any piercing wound, but I will direct it at any paper which pollutes my dacha lawn, and I will stab it with my unique invention, and when they, the papers, are collected in sufficient quantity on the tip, I will remove them from the nail, as a *bogatyr* removes the enemies he has run through from his lance, and I will cast them into the abyss of the garbage pit which is in the corner of my garden—that is my invention, which allows me, an old man, not to abandon the ranks of unbending warriors: because of my ailments I cannot bend down and pick up a piece of paper, but thanks to an ordinary stick with a nail I fight for cleanliness without bending; so then, inasmuch as you seem to me an uncommonly decent person, I will allow myself to ask you advice, to wit: is there, in your view, any sense in taking out a patent and patenting this stick?

Restraining the indignant birdlike shriek which is surging in your tonsillitic throat between unremoved glands: dear Arcady Arcadievich, I have the greatest respect for your invention, however, at the moment I need *your* advice—and even more than you need mine, yours is a question of ambition, while mine—excuse me, I am talking like in a novel and so I feel somehow embarrassed and ridiculous—my question to you is one of an entire life. Hold it, hold it, I'm starting to be afraid of your presence again, do you really intend to ask me about something important, let me sit down, do you really need something from an aging, half-blind dacha resident, and after all, who are you to be asking me questions, and stop shouting in my beautiful barrel too. I won't do it any more, sir, I'm prepared to explain everything, I live in the neighborhood, at my parents' dacha, and it's so beautiful around here that an unpleasant thing happened to me once, but about that later, the main thing is that I hate a certain woman, a Jewess, Sheina Tinbergen, she is a witch, she works as the assistant principal in our

school, she sings about the cat, well you probably learned the song when you
were a little boy: tra-ta-ta, tra-ta-ta, Cat was looking for Tomcat, wants to
wed Cat Catovich—oh, by the way, remember what the cat's name was, sir?
A moment, youth—Acatov rubs his pulsating blue temples, straining his
memory—the tomcat's name was Trifon Petrovich. Right, however, that's
not the thing that interests me either, to the devil with Trifon Petrovich,
he's a common excavator, let's talk about Sheina herself instead. Imagine
her, the lame crone, moving through the vast empty hall dancing (every
other light is off, the second shift has run home, and only I have been left
after school to do the next day's lessons), and as I stand at the end of the hall
or go forward to meet her, holding a polite bow of the head at the ready, I
get even more nauseated than in my sleep after injections. No, she never did
me any harm, and I talk to her only about the record player; and although it
hasn't worked for a hundred years and there is no way it should play, when
Sheina takes it into her room and turns it on, it plays like new. More
precisely, it doesn't play, but talks: the old lady spins a record of her late
husband's voice, he hanged himself because she was betraying him with
Sorokin in the garage, or no, Sorokin hanged himself, and her husband,
Yakov, he poisoned himself. I see—responds Acatov—but what sort of
text is recorded there, on the record? Ah-a, there now, that's just it, the
main thing—there, on the record, the late Yakov reads *Skeerly*. Forgive
me, youth, I've never heard of that before. A nightmarish thing, sir, I won't
even repeat...but, briefly it goes like this: you see, *Skeerly*—is the name of a
fairytale, a horrific children's fairytale about a bear, I can't exactly...basi-
cally, in the woods there lives a bear, it would seem nothing out of the
ordinary, it would seem! But the trouble is that this bear is an invalid, a
cripple, he's minus one leg, but how all this happened is a mystery, all that's
known is that the leg is gone, a hind leg I think, and in its place the bear has
a wooden prosthetic device. He, the bear, cut it out of the trunk of a linden
tree with an ax, and when the bear walks through the woods the screech of
the prosthetic device is distantly audible, it screeches as in the name of the
fairytale: *skeerly, skeerly.* Yakov does a good imitation of the sound, he
had a screechy voice, he worked as a pharmacist. Another character in the
fairytale is a little girl, who is apparently made of chalk, she's afraid of the
bear and never leaves home, but one day—the devil knows how this
happened—the bear pounces on her anyway and carries her off in a
special—wicker, I think—basket to his lair and does something with her
there, exactly what is unknown, it's not explained in the fairytale, it ends
with that, it's terrible, sir, one doesn't know what to think. When I recall
Skeerly—even though I try not to remember it, it's better not to remember—it occurs to me that the girl might not be a girl, but a certain
woman acquaintance of mine, with whom I have close relations, you
understand, of course, you and I are no longer children, and it occurs to me
that the bear is not a bear either, but some man I don't know, a man, and I

can almost see him doing something there in a hotel room with my acquaintance, and the accursed *skeerly* resounds repeatedly, and I get sick with hate for the sound, and I suppose that I would kill that man if I knew who he was. Thinking about the *Skeerly* fairytale is painful for me, sir, but since I rarely do my homework, they often keep me after school to do the lessons for the next day and the day before, and after I'm left alone in the classroom, I usually go out to take a walk in the hall, and when I go out I encounter Tinbergen there, and when I see her drawing nigh, with a crippled but also sort of merry, dancing gait, and I hear the melancholy— like the call of the lonely nightjar—squeak of her prosthetic device, then, spare me, sir—I cannot help thinking of the fairytale *Skeerly*, because the sound is exactly the same as the one in the hotel, and she herself, the graybearded witch with the sleepy face of an old woman who has died but then been forced to awaken and live, she, in the crepuscular light of the deserted hall with its shimmering parquet floor, she herself is the *Skeerly*, the embodiment of all that is saddest in this story of the little girl, although to this day I can't figure out what was going on, and why it was all like this, and not some other way.

Yes, youth, yes, I have no difficulty understanding you. Thoughtfully. Something similar happened to me once, something of the sort happened in my youth, of course I don't remember what it was specifically, but to one degree or another everything was like your case. But—Acatov suddenly asks—what school are you in, I can't make sense of this, after all you are already past twenty, you are thirty, what school? The special, sir. Ah, so that's it—says the academician (you both leave the shed and you look back at her photograph for the last time)—and what is the specialty of your school? By the way, if it is difficult or awkward for you, or if it's a secret—don't answer, I'm not forcing you, there is scarcely any need for your answer, as there isn't for any question, we're talking quite casually, after all this is not an examination at Oxford, understand me properly, I was simply curious, I asked just to ask, so to speak, as part of the delirium, any of us has a right to pose any question and anyone has a right not to answer any question, but, unfortunately, here—here and there, every- where, there are still a lot of people who haven't assimilated this truth, *they* made me answer every question they asked, *they*, in the snow-covered... But I'm not *them*—continues Acatov, whipping shut his white scientific duster, open and shut—and don't answer me if you don't feel like it, we'll sit silently instead, look around, listen to the song of summer, etc., no, no, don't answer, I don't want to know anything about you, as it is you've come to seem so *sympatico* to me, that cane and hat go with your face as- tonishingly well, only the hat is a trifle large, you probably bought it to grow into. Yes, precisely, to grow into; but I would like to answer, there is nothing awkward about it at all: the school where I study specializes in mental defectives, it's a school for fools, all of us who study there are abnormal, each in his own way. Just a moment, I've heard something about just such an institution, someone of my acquaintance works there, but who exactly? Perhaps you mean Veta Arcadievna, she works in our school, handling such-and-such and such-and-such. Well, of course! Veta, Veta, Veta coquetta and curvetta—Acatov sang, without any melody, absent-mindedly snapping his fingers. What a wondrous song, sir! Rubbish, youth, a family jingle, a trifle from earlier years, innocent of meaning or melody, forget it, I fear it will debauch you. Never, never—anxiously. What? I said I'll never forget it, I really like it, I can't do anything; yes, there is a certain difference in age between us, but, how can I define this best, formulate it—there's more which unites us than disunites us, you ask what it is I'm talking about, but in my opinion I am expressing myself with utmost clarity, Arcady Arcadievich. The common factor to which I just alluded is an attraction to all that you and I as men of science call living nature, everything that grows and flies, flowers and swims—in fact this is the purpose of my visit to you—not only butterflies, although I (my word of honor) have been catching them since childhood and won't ever stop catching them until my right arm dries up and drops off, like the arm of the artist Repin, and I came to you not in order to shout into the barrel, although I am inclined to see exalted meaning in this occupation, and I will never give up shouting into barrels and with my shout I will fill the emptiness of empty chambers until I have filled them full, so it won't be excruciatingly painful, however, I am digressing again, to be brief: I love your daughter, sir, and am prepared to do anything for her happiness. Moreover, I intend to marry Veta Arcadievna as soon as circumstances allow. Triumphantly, with dignity and a slight bow.

Poor Acatov, this was so unexpected, I'm afraid you upset the old man a bit, surely you should have prepared him better for this kind of conversation, for example, you could have written two or three warning letters, informed him of your arrival in advance, called him or something like that, I'm afraid that you behaved tactlessly, and moreover, it's dishonorable to do what you did: you had no right to ask for Veta Arcadievna's hand alone, without me, I will never forget her either and in some inexplicable way everything that grows and flies joins me to her too, we too, she and I also have in common everything that grows and flies, you know that, but naturally you didn't tell Acatov anything about me, about the one who is much better and more deserving than you, and for that I hate you and I'm going to tell you how a certain person, indistinguishable in the obscurity of a hotel corridor, leads our Veta to his room, and there, there... No wait I'm not guilty at all you were staring at the lilac petal you were rewriting the article I left my father's house by chance I didn't dream I would succeed nothing might have worked out I only wanted to see Acatov about the butterflies I would certainly have told him everything about you and your vast superhuman feeling which I you know this yourself which I so respect I would have told him that it wasn't just me alone but that there are two of us and I did tell him about that in the beginning I would have said sir yes I love your daughter but there is a person who being incomparably more deserving and better than me loves her a hundred times more fervently, and although I am grateful to you for a positive resolution of the question, it is obvious that this other person should be invited too, undoubtedly he will appeal to you even more, if you want I'll call him, he's here, not far, in the neighboring settlement, he had intended to come, but was somewhat busy, he has some work, some urgent copying (what is he, a copyist? no, no, of course not, it's just that there are people, or more accurately, one person, who makes him copy things out of newspapers, he has to do that, otherwise it wouldn't be very easy for him to live in that house), and besides that, he got to staring at the lilac petals, and I decided not to distract him, let me call him—I would have said to the academician, if the resolution of the question had turned out to be positive. Do you mean Acatov refused you? Only you better tell me the whole truth, don't lie, or I'll hate you and complain to our mentor Savl: dead or alive, he never put up with sneakiness or bias. I swear to you by the name which flames in our hearts that from this day forth I, student of the special school so-and-so, nicknamed Nymphea Alba, a man of exalted aspirations and ideals, fighter for eternal human joy, hater of callousness, egotism and sadness, no matter where manifested, I, heir to the finest traditions and utterances of our pedagogue Savl, I swear to you that my lips will never be besmirched by a single word of falsehood, and I will be pure as a drop of dew born on the banks of our enchanting Lethe in the early morn—born and flying to moisten the brow of our little chalk girl Veta, who is sleeping in the garden so many years in the future. O, speak on! How I love thy utterances, full of power and eloquence, inspiration and passion, bravery and intellect, speak, hurrying and swallowing the words, we still have to discuss many other problems, and there is so little time, probably no more than a second, if I understand correctly the meaning of the aforementioned word.

Then Acatov (no, no, I myself figured that he would laugh, make fun of my hat, or rather father's, and of the fact that I'm not very handsome, more than that, ugly, and despite this I was asking for the hand of such an incomparable woman) simply looked at me, lowered his head and stood there pondering something, most likely our conversation, my confession. If up to my last words he had looked like a little stooped tree, during this time—right before my very eyes—he came to look like a stooped little tree which has dried up and ceased to feel even the touch of the grass and the wind: Acatov was pondering. Meanwhile I was reading the newspaper headlines on his cocked hat and examining his wide, loose scientist's duster—out of which, like a clapper from a bell, hung Acatov's thin and veiny legs, the legs of a thinker and an ambitious person. I liked his duster, and I thought that I would have worn the same kind with pleasure, if I had an opportunity to buy one. I would have worn it everywhere: in the garden, in the orchard, at school and at home, in the shade of the trees across the river, and in the long distance postal *diligence* when out the window one could see rain and villages floating past, covered with straw, ruffled up like wet hens, and when my soul is wounded by human sufferings. But until— until I become an engineer—I don't have a duster, I wear ordinary pants with cuffs, made out of hand-me-downs from my prosecutor father,with a four-buttoned, double-breasted jacket and shoes with metallic buckles—in school and at home. Sir, why are you silent, can I have offended you somehow, or do you doubt the sincerity of my words and feelings for Veta Arcadievna? Believe me, I would never lie to you, a man, a father of the woman I adore, don't doubt that, please, and don't be silent, otherwise I will turn and leave, to fill with my shout the emptiness of our dacha settlements—a shout about your refusal. O no, youth, don't leave, I will be lonely, you know, I have no hesitation about accepting your every word on faith, and if Veta agrees I will have no objection. Have a chat with her, talk to her, after all you haven't opened up to her yet, I guess she doesn't suspect a thing yet, and what can we decide without her agreement, you un- derstand? We can't decide anything. Thoughtfully with difficulty selecting words selecting words seeking them with his eyes beforehand in the dry grass where somehow dissatisfied grasshoppers are hopping and every one is wearing a green dress coat conductors selecting words in the grass. Sir, I will not conceal the fact that indeed I have not yet had a talk with Veta Arcadievna, there simply hasn't been time; although we meet fairly often, our talks usually touch on other things, we speak mostly about matters of science, we have a lot in common, that's as it should be: two young biologists, two natural scientists, two scholars, who *sew promise.* But aside from that—on both sides—something quite special is maturing—has ma- tured already—the communality of interests is being supplemented by another communality. I understand you perfectly, youth, when I was your age something similar happened to me, to me and a certain woman, we were naive, good-looking and we lost our heads. Dear Arcady Arcadievich, I intend to make one other simultaneous confession to you. You see, I'm not absolutely sure that Veta Arcadievna likes me as a man, it's possible that the communality of which I spoke is, from your daughter's point of view, based only on philanthropy, what I mean is that she loves me only as a human being, I don't insist this is so I'm just hypothesizing out of a fear of seeming ridiculous, I wouldn't want to find myself in an awkward position. But inasmuch as you are Veta Arcadievna's father and you know her tastes and character far better than I, I make so bold as to ask you: in your opinion am I handsome enough that Veta Arcadievna will like me as a man too, somehow I'm vaguely worried that I'll seem somehow uninteresting to her. Look examine me carefully, is this so in reality, or am I just imagining it. Are my features so ugly that even the most elevated of all feelings attainable by man would not improve my face and my build? But for God's sake don't lie, I beg of you. What nonsense—answers Acatov—you're quite normal, quite, I imagine there are a lot of young women who would agree to go through life arm and arm with you—and who would never regret it. The one thing I would advise you as a scientist is to use your handkerchief more often. Purely arbitrary I know, but how it ennobles, distinguishes, and lifts a personality over the muck of circumstances and your contemporaries. True, at your age I didn't know this either, but then I did know a lot of other things, I was getting ready to defend my first dissertation and marry the woman who subsequently became Veta's mother. By that time I was already working, I had worked a lot and had earned a lot—and you? Yes, by the way, how do you propose to arrange your family life, on what basis, are you aware of the kind of responsibility which lies on you as the head of the family? That's very important. Sir, I could hardly help anticipating that you would ask such a question, and I was ready for it long before I came to visit you. I understand perfectly well what you mean, I know everything already, because I read a lot. I found out a few things even before our conversation with our geographer Norvegov, but after we met him in the restroom one day and had a frank discussion about everything, almost everything became comprehensible to me. Moreover, Savl Petrovich gave me a book to read, and when I read it I understood every last thing. What is it that you understood?—asks Acatov—share it with me.

Savl Petrovich is sitting on the windowsill with his back to the painted glass, and his face to the stalls; the bare bottoms of his feet rest on the radiator, and his knees are pulled up so that it's easy for the teacher to rest his chin on them. Ex libris, book after book. Staring at the stall doors, all scribbled with hooligan words: how much that is vulgar, how much that is ugly we have in our restroom, how impoverished our feelings for woman are, how cynical we are, we the people of the special school. We don't know how to love tenderly and powerfully, no—we don't know how. But dear Savl Petrovich—standing before him wearing white canvas slippers, on the malodorous tile, I object—in spite of not even knowing what to think or how to calm you, the best teacher in the world, I consider it essential to remind you of the following: after all, don't you, you yourself, you personally—don't you love one of my fellow classmates powerfully and tenderly, the chalk girl Rosa. O Rosa Windova—you said to her one day—dear girl, sepulchral flower, how I desire your untouched body! And you also whispered: on one of the nights of a summer embarrassed by its own beauty I await you in the little house with the windvane beyond the blue river. And also: what happens to us that night will be like a flame consuming an icy waste, like a starfall reflected in a fragment of a mirror which has suddenly fallen from its frame forewarning its owner of imminent death, it will be like a shepherd's reed pipe and like music which is yet unwritten. Come to me, Rosa Windova, isn't your old teacher, striding across the valleys of nonexistence and the tablelands of anguish dear to you. And also: come, to ease the trembling in your loins, and to soften my sadness. But, my dear fellow, I did say or perhaps only will say those or similar words to her, but since when have words ever meant anything? Only don't think that I was being hypocritical (will be hypocritical), that's not characteristic of me, I am incapable of that, but there are times when—and some day you will be convinced of this yourself—times when a man lies, without suspecting it. He is sure he's telling the truth, and sure that he's doing what he promised. This happens most often in childhood, but then in adolescence too, and then in one's youth and old age. This is what happens to man when he is in a state of passion, for passion is like unto madness. Thanks, I didn't know that, I'll mull it over, I had only a suspicion of that—of that and a lot of other things. You understand, I'm worried by a certain circumstance, and today, here, after classes, when it's damp and windy outside and the second shift of future engineers has gone home, finishing off the smushed sandwiches from their briefcases (the sandwiches have to be eaten, in order not to disappoint their patient mothers), I intend to impart to you, Savl Petrovich, certain information which, probably, will strike you as improbable, it might make you disillusioned with me. I have long intended to ask your advice, but I kept putting off the conversation every day: too many quizzes, much too much tiresome homework, and even if I don't do it, the awareness that I should depresses me. It's exhausting, Savl Petrovich. But now the time has come when I want to and can inform you. Dear teacher! in forest cottages lost in the fields, in long distance postal *diligences*, at bonfires the smoke of which creates coziness, on the banks of Lake Erie or—I don't remember precisely—Baskunchak, on the ships of the Vigel class, on the roofs of European omnibuses and in the Geneva Bureau of Tourist Information and Better Family Living, in the thicket of heather and religious sects, in parks and gardens where there are no places to sit on the benches, behind a stein of beer in the mountain inn *At the Cat*, on the front lines of the first and second world wars, tearing across the green Yukon ice on dogsleds, racked by gold fever, and in other places—here and there, dear teacher, I have pondered what woman is, and how to behave if the time ever came to act, I pondered the nature of convention, and the peculiarities of the fleshly in humans. I have thought about what love is, and passion, and eternity, what it means to give in to desire and what it means not to give in to it, what lust and carnality are; I have reflected on the details of copulation, dreaming of it, for from books and other sources I knew that it gave pleasure. But the trouble is that in none of these places, or anywhere else, did I once in my whole life happen to *be with,* or to put it more vulgarly—*sleep with* a woman. I simply don't know what it's like, I would probably be able to, but I can't imagine how to begin all that, or, mainly, with whom. Obviously some woman is necessary, and it would be best if she were someone you've known for a long time, who would prompt you in case something went wrong, in case something didn't work out right away; you need a very kind woman, I've heard it's best if she's a widow, yes, for some reason they say a widow, but I don't know a single widow, except Tinbergen, but after all she's the assistant principal, and she has Trifon Petrovich (but only I have the record player), and I don't know any other women—only Veta Arcadievna, but I wouldn't want to with her, for I love her and intend to marry her, those are different things, I absolutely never think—I force myself not to—about her as a woman, I realize that she is too beautiful, too upstanding, to permit herself anything with me before the wedding—isn't that so? True, I also know some girls from class, but if I started courting one of them, for example, the girl who died not long ago from meningitis and for whose wreath we took up a collection, I'm afraid Veta Arcadievna wouldn't like it very much, that sort of thing gets noticed immediately: in a small collective, in view of one's fellow students and the teachers—it would be obvious in no time, Veta would realize that I intended to betray her, and she would have a perfectly reasonable grievance, and then our marriage might be upset, all hopes would collapse, and we have nurtured them so long! A few times, Savl Petrovich, I have tried to strike up the acquaintance of women on the streets, but apparently I don't know the approach, I'm not elegant, my clothes are ugly. In short, nothing came of it, they shooed me away, but I won't conceal that one day I almost managed to strike up an acquaintance with an interesting young woman, and although I can't describe her, inasmuch as I don't remember her face or her voice or her walk, I will go so far as to assert that she was extraordinarily beautiful, like most women.

Where did I meet her? Probably in the movies or the park, or, most likely, in the post office. The woman was sitting there behind the window and cancelling envelopes and postcards. It was the AllUnion PanUniversal Day for the Defense of the Nightjar. That morning I had promised myself I would spend the whole day collecting stamps. True, I didn't have a single stamp at home, but I did find a matchbox label with a picture of a bird which all of us should defend on it. I realized that this was the nightjar, and set off for the post office so they would cancel it for me, and I took an immediate liking to the woman sitting there behind the window. You told our teacher that you can't describe the woman; in that case at least describe the day on which your encounter occurred, tell a story about what it was like outside, and what the weather was like, if, naturally, this doesn't put you out any. No, no, there's nothing particularly complicated about that, and I'd be happy to meet your request. That morning the clouds were scudding across the sky more swiftly than usual, and I saw white cotton batting faces appearing and dissolving in each other. They were floating and colliding with each other, their color mutating from gold to lilac. Many of those whom we call passers-by, smiling and squinting from the diffused but still powerful sunlight, were observing the shifting clouds just as I was, and like me they sensed the approach of the future, heralds of which were these *untutored* clouds. Don't correct me, I'm not mistaken. When I go to school or the post office for them to cancel the matchbox label with the picture of the nightjar it is easy for me to find, both in my surroundings and in my memory, things, phenomena—and I enjoy thinking about them— which it would be impossible either to give as homework or to memorize. No one is capable of memorizing: the sound of rain, the aroma of night violets, premonition of nonexistence, the flight of the bumblebee, Brownian motion and many other things. All of this can be studied, but *memorized*— never. In the same category are rainclouds and stormclouds bursting with turbulence and future tempests. Besides the cloudy sky that morning, there was the street, cars with people in them were going by, and it was really hot. I could hear the uncut grass growing on the lawns, baby carriages screech- ing in the courtyards, the clanging of garbage can tops, elevator doors slamming in the entranceways, and in the schoolyard the first shift students were running invigorating wind sprints headlong: the wind bore me the beating of their hearts. I heard from somewhere very far, perhaps from the other side of town, a blind man wearing dark glasses the lenses of which reflected the dusty foliage of the weeping acacias and the scudding clouds and the smoke creeping from the brick stack of the offset printing factory, ask people walking by to help him across the street, but no one had time and no one stopped. I heard two old men in a kitchen—the window onto the sidestreet was open—chatting (the subject was the New Orleans fire of 1882), cooking meat and cabbage soup: it was the day when the pensions were paid; I heard the bubbling in their pot, and the bookkeeper counting out cubic centimeters of expended gas. I heard, in the other apartments of this and neighboring buildings, the pounding of printing and sewing machines, the darning of socks, and magazine files being leafed through, I heard people blowing noses and laughing, shaving and singing, closing their eyelids or, from lack of anything to do, drumming their fingers on tautly stretched glass, imitating the sound of slanting rainfall. I heard the silence of deep apartments whose owners had gone to work and would return only towards evening, or who wouldn't return because they had gone into eternity; I heard the rhythmical rocking of pendula in wall clocks and the tick of various brands of watches. I heard the kisses and whispers and close breathing of men and women unknown to me—you will never understand anything about them—doing *skeerly*, and I envied them, and dreamed of meeting a woman who would allow me to do the same with her. I was walking along the street reading, in order, the signs and advertisements on the buildings, although I long since knew them by heart, I had memorized every word on the street. Left side. REPAIR OF CHILDREN'S CONSTRICTORS. In the show-window—a poster boy dreaming of becoming an engineer, he is holding a large model of a glider in his hand. POLAR REGION FURS. In the show-window a white bear, a skin with open maw. MOVIE-LEAFFALL-THEATER. The day will come and we will come here together: Veta and I; which row do you prefer?—I'll ask Veta—the third or the eighteenth? I don't know—she'll say—it makes no difference, pick any. But then add: but I do like to be close, take the tenth or seventh, if it's not too expensive. And I say reproachfully: What silliness, my dear, money is no object, I'm ready to give everything if only it makes you feel good and comfortable. BICYCLE RENTAL. After the movie we have to rent two bicycles. The girl who rents the bicycles is blond and smiley, with an engagement ring on her right hand, seeing us, she laughs: finally some customers, it's odd, a warm spell like this but no one wants to go riding, it's simply odd. Nothing odd about it—I say cheerfully—with weather like this the whole town's gone out to the country, after all today's Sunday, everyone's been out at the dachas since early morning, and everyone there has his own shed with his own bicycle in it, we intend to go to the dacha now too, on your bicycles, straight along the highway, at our own speed: it's probably stuffy on the electric in spite of the ice cream. Look out—warns the girl—be careful, there's a lot of traffic on the highway, stay close to the shoulder, obey the signs, don't exceed the speed limit, pass only on the left, caution—pedestrian crossing, the traffic is regulated by radar and helicopters. Of course, we'll be careful, we have no reason to lose our heads, especially now, a week after the wedding, we had been hoping for so long. Ah, so that's it—the girl will smile—so this is your honeymoon trip. Yes, we've decided to take a little ride. That's what I thought when you came in—newlyweds: you suit each other awfully well, congratulations, it really pleases me, I got married myself not so long ago, my husband is a motorcycle racer, he has a great motorcycle, we ride really fast. I like races too—Veta says, holding up her end of the conversation—and I would like my husband to be a motorcyclist too, but unfortunately he's an engineer, and we don't have a motorcycle, we only have a car.

Yes—I reiterate—unfortunately only a car, and it's a used one, but in principle I could buy a motorcycle too. Of course, do buy one—smiles the girl—buy one and my husband will teach you how to ride, it doesn't strike me as too complicated, the main thing is to release the clutch in time and regulate the radiator. And then Veta will propose: you know what, why don't you and your husband drop in on us next week, come on the motorcycle, our dacha is located right on the water, the second clearing to the left, it'll be a lot of fun, we'll have dinner, drink some tea. Thanks—the girl will reply—we'll definitely come, I'm going to have some leave time starting day after tomorrow, only tell me what kind of cake you like: crow's feet or holiday, I'l bring one for tea. Better holiday, yes, and if it's not too much trouble, pick up a kilogram or two of truffles at the same time, I'll pay you back right away. Oh, come, what do you mean money! FISH-FISH-FISH. WILD-BULLFINCH-GAME STORE. Aquariums with tritons and green parrots on perches. REGIONALHISTORYMUSEUM. Show some curiosity, study your region, it's a useful thing to do. ASP—Agency for Secret Portage. SHOVELS. And I read the word "shovel" as "love" on the store. FLOWERS. BOOKS. A book is the best present, all that is best in me I owe to books, book after book, love books, they refine and ennoble one's taste, you look into a book and it's clear as mud, a book is man's best friend, it decorates any interior, exterior, fox terrier, a riddle: a hundred jackets but none with buttons—what's that? the answer: a book. From the encyclopedia: the *Bookmaking in Russia* article: bookprinting in Russia began under Ivan Fyodorov, popularly known as the first-printer, he wore a long library duster and a round cap knitted from pure wool. And then the ship's cook Ilya gave him a book: take this and read it. And through the cover of meagre needles, moistening the pale moss, the hail capered and bounced like pellets of silver. Then also: I approached the appointed place—all was darkness and whirlwind. When the smoke cleared there was no one on the square, but along the river bank strode Burago, the engineer, his socks flapping in the wind. I'm saying only one thing, general, I'm, saying only one thing, general: what's this, Masha, have you been gathering mushrooms? I often sent back doom with nothing more than a signal cannon. At the beginning of July, at a particularly hot time, toward evening, a certain young man. And you—say, eh, youuu! Are there any white ones? There are. Tsop-tsop, tsaida-braida, eenie meenie miney moe. Shine, shine, stars in the sky, freeze, freeze tail of a wolf! Right side. BOATS-UMBRELLAS-CANES, all in the same store, so you can buy everything without messing around. FASHION SHOP, building on the left. SALAMI. Some get salami, and now some like it hot on a bun! HABERDASHERY-KNITTED GOODS. PARK OF REST the fence stretches for twenty and a half parsecs. And only after it ends—POST OFFICE. Hello, may I put a cancellation on my stamp, or more accurately, may I have it put on for me, or even better: what do I have to do so that with your help I can get a cancellation put on my stamp, cancelling it. Give it here, show me, what kind of stamp is this, boy, it's a matchbox. I know, I simply didn't think it would make any difference to you, there's a nightjar depicted here too, look. She glanced at it and smiled: you have to steam off the label. All right, fine, I'll steam it, I don't live far, it strikes me I'll be able to persuade mama to let me put the teakettle on (mama, may I warm up the teakettle? you want some tea? since when do you drink tea before school, how can you drink tea when it's time for supper. The point is mama, that it's necessary to use steam to unstick the label. Steam? Steam that's what they said at the post office. O, Lord, you've made up something again, what post office, who said, why, what label, you'll steam off your face!), but I'm not positive—couldn't that be done in the post office, one day I happened to see (the window was open) you drinking tea in the room where the parcels and tube mailers are, you were drinking from an electric teakettle, there were several women and one man wearing an overcoat, you were laughing. Yes, true—she said—we do have one, come here, boy.

And you followed her down a long corridor hung with naked lightbulbs and it smelled of a real post office: sealing wax, stickum, paper, twine, inks, stearin, casein, overripened pears, honey, squeaky boots, cremebrulee, cheap comfort, vobla, bamboo shoots, rat droppings, the tears of the senior clerk. There was a medium-sized chamber at the end of the corridor, as if crowning it: thus a river is crowned by the lake into which it empties. In this chamber were racks of parcels and tube mailers, addressed there and here, the window was barred, and on the table in the center of the room was the argent glow of an electric teakettle with a striped cord ending in a plug. The woman stuck the plug into the socket, she sat down on a chair and you sat on another—and you both started waiting for it to boil. I know you well: by nature you are fitful, you don't have anough perseverance either at home or school, you're still too young, and therefore you can't abide another person's silence, prolonged pauses in a conversation, they make you ill at ease, not yourself, in a word, you cannot endure passivity, inaction, or silence. Right now, if you were the one in this post office room you would fill it with your shout just the way you fill the empty school auditoriums, rest rooms, and hallways during your leisure time. But you're not alone here, and although the indescribable howl that is being generated in the depths of your being is splitting you apart, and is ready to burst out at any instant, splitting and cracking you like an early April bud and turning you completely into your own shout—I Nymphea Nymphea Nymphea, eya-eya-eya, ya-ya-ya, a-a-a—you cannot, you have no right to frighten this nice young woman. For if you do shout, she will drive you away and won't put the cancellation on the nightjar, don't you shout here no matter what, in the post office, otherwise you won't have the collection of which you have dreamed for so long, a collection consisting of a single cancelled stamp. Or label. Control yourself, distract yourself, think about something else, something mysterious, or start a conversation which doesn't oblige you to anything with this woman, all the more so that, as I understand it, you liked her right away. All right, but how does one begin, with what words, I've suddenly forgotten how one is supposed to begin conversations which do not oblige one to anything. Very simple, ask her if you can ask her a question. Thanks, thanks, right away. Can I ask you a question? Of course, boy, of course. Well, what now, what do I say next? Now ask her about postal pigeons or about her work, find out how things are with her in general. Yes, that's it: I would like to find out from you how things are here with you in the poached office, no, I mean the post office, the postal posterior postnatal postscript post mortem. What's that, the post office? All right, boy, all right, but why does that interest you? You, no doubt, have postal pigeons, right? No, why? But then where would postal pigeons live if not here on your posts? No, we don't have any, we have postmen. In that case you know postman Mikheev or Medvedev, he looks like Pavlov and he rides a bicycle too, but don't expect to see him out that window, he doesn't ride here, not in town, he works in the country, in the dacha settlement, he has a beard—so you've never been introduced to him? No, boy. Too bad, if you had you and I could enjoy chatting about him and you wouldn't be bored with me. Well I'm not bored as it is—answers the woman. Now that's great, so you do sort of like me, I have some business with you, if I'm not mistaken: it occurred to me to strike up a friendship with you, and even more than that, my name is such-and-such, what's yours? What a funny one—said the woman—so funny. Don't laugh, I'll tell you the whole truth the way it really is, you see, my fate is decided: I'm getting married, very soon, maybe yesterday or last year. But the woman who is to become my wife—she is extremely moral, you know what I mean? and there is no way she will agree to the wedding. But I need it very much, it's essential, otherwise my inhuman shout will drain out like blood. Doctor Zauze calls this condition a posterior nerve core fit, therefore I have decided to ask you to help me, to do me a certain favor, a kindness, it would be extremely kind of you, after all, you are a woman, I imagine you'd like to shout from your postal nerve core too, so why shouldn't we gratify our velleities together, don't I appeal to you at all, I've tried so hard to make you like me! You can't imagine how I'm going to miss you after we've unstuck the label and you do the cancellation and I go back, to the house of my father: I will find no consolation anywhere. Or maybe you already have someone with whom you gratify your velleities? My God, what business is it of yours—says the woman—you've got a lot of nerve. In that event I am ready right now to prove that I am superior to him in all respects, even though you've already admitted as much. Isn't it clear that my intellect is the quintessence of suppleness and logic, is it not a fact that if there is only one future engineering genius in the whole world—I'm the one. And I am the one who will tell you a story right now, yes, something that'll bowl you over. Here. Let me present to you, in my own words, the composition which our Vodokachka passed last week. I will begin at the very beginning. *My Morning. A composition.*

The whistle of the shunting train sings "cuckoo" at dawn: a shepherd's pipe, a flute, a cornet-a-piston, a child's crying, doodlelee-dey. I wake up, sit on the edge of the bed, examine my bare feet, and then look out the window. I see a bridge, it is totally empty, it is illuminated by green mercury lights, and the lampposts have the necks of swans. I see only the roadway part of the bridge, but all I have to do is walk out on the balcony and the whole bridge will open up before me, its entire gantry—like the spine of a frightened cat. I live with my mama and papa, but sometimes it happens that I live alone, and my neighbor, old Trachtenberg—or more likely Tinbergen, lived with us in our old apartment, or she is going to live at the new one. I don't know what the other parts of the bridge are called. Under the bridge is the railroad line, or to put it better, several tracks, several transport tracks, a certain number of identical tracks of identical gauge. In the mornings the witch Tinbergen dances—danced, will dance—in the hall, humming the song about Trifon Petrovich, the tomcat and excavator. She dances on the red mahogany containers, on their upper surfaces, near the ceiling, and beside them too. I have never seen it, but I've heard. Near the ceiling. Across them—hither and thither—goes the "cuckoo"—shaking on all the switches. Tra-ta-ta. She beats out the rhythm with maracas. She pushes and pulls the brown boxcars. I hate the shaggy crone. Wrapped in rags, long hooklike nails protruding, furrowing her face with the wretched wrinkles of centuries, club-footed, she frightens me and my patient mother in the daytime and at night. And at dawn—she starts singing—and then I wake up. I love that whistle. Doodelee-dey?—it asks. And after waiting a moment, it answers itself: da-da-da, doodeley-dey. She was the one who poisoned Yakov, the poor man, man and pharmacist, man and druggist, and she's the one who works in our school as curriculum director of the studies section, a section of the studies section of respect section of arsenic. Thus, in drawing conclusions about my morning one may say that it begins with the cuckoo cry, the sound of the railroad, the loop railroad. If one were to look at the map of our town, where the river and the streets and the highway are shown, it appears that the loop road is strangling the town, like a steel noose, and if, after begging permission of the constrictor, you were to get on a train going past our home, in one day this freight train will make a full circle and return to the same place, the place where you boarded it.

The trains which go past our home move along a closed—and therefore infinite—curve around our town, which is why it is virtually impossible to leave our town. There are only two trains which work on the loop line: one goes clockwise, the other counterclockwise. In this relation it is as if they mutually destroy each other, and at the same time destroy movement and time. So goes my morning. Tinbergen gradually stops stomping through the young bamboo groves, and her song, vigorous, self-satisfied and merciless as old age itself, dies away in the distance, beyond the coral lagoons and only the booming and drumming and tambourining of the cars which surge across the bridge destroys—and that rarely—the quiet of our apartment. It vanishes—melts away.

A beautiful, beautiful, beautiful composition—Savl says. We hear his resonant, mist-covered pedagogical voice, the voice of the region's leading geographer, the voice of a farsighted guide, fighter for purity, truth and filled-up spaces, the voice of the intercessor for all of the insulted and bloodied. We are here again, in the cleaned men's restroom, where often it is so cold and lonely that steam streams from our blue student lips—symptom of breathing, phantom of life, a fair indication that we still exist, or that we have gone to eternity, but, like Savl, we will return in order to perform or complete the great deeds begun on earth, to wit: receipt of all and sundry academic prizes, a large-scale auto-da-fé involving all special schools, the ac-quisition of a used automobile, marriage to the teacher Vetka, the thrashing of all the world's idiots with the poles of butterfly nets, the improvement of selective memory, the smashing of the skulls of chalk old men and women like Tinbergen, the capture of unique winter butterflies, the cutting of the stout threads in all sewn-shut mouths, the establishment of a new kind of newspaper—papers in which not a single word would be written, the abolition of windsprints, and also the free distribution of bicycles and dachas at all points from A to Z; moreover—the resurrection of mentor Savl accompanied by his reinstatement in work in his special field. A beautiful composition—he says, sitting on the windowsill, warming the bottoms of his feet on the steam heating radiator—how late we discover our students, what a pity that I didn't discern your literary talent earlier, I would have persuaded Perillo to excuse you from literature classes, and you could have done whatever you liked in the leisure that resulted—you understand me? anything you like. Thus you could have tirelessly collected stamps with pictures of the nightjar and other flying birds. You could have rowed and swum, run and jumped, played red rover and mumbledy-peg, gotten tempered like steel, written poetry, drawn on the asphalt, played paper-rock-scissors, muttering the charming and incomparable: scissors cut paper, paper covers rock, rock breaks scissors—

no don't talk and are you coming to the ball? Or sitting in the forest on a tree toppled by a storm, quickly and in an undertone, having in mind no one and nothing, repeat to yourself the time-tested tongue-twister: higgledy-piggledy, three Japs went willikers—Yak, Yak-Tsidrak, Yak-Tsidrak-Tsidroni; higgledy-piggledy, three more Japs went willikers—Tsipa, Tsipa-Dripa, Tsipa-Dripa-Limponponi; they married each other: Yak to Tsip, Yak-Tsidrak to Tsipa-Dripa, Yak-Tsidrak-Tsidroni to Tsipa-Dripa-Limponponi. O, there are so many things there are to do on earth, my youthful comrade, things which one could do instead of the stupid, stupid writing done in the literature classes! With regret for what is impossible and lost. With sadness. With the face of a man who never was is or will be. But, student so-and-so, I'm afraid you won't escape those lessons, suffering terrible pain you will have to memorize bits and pieces of the works which in our country are called literature. You will read our prostrate and mendacious monsters of the pen with revulsion and sometimes you will find it impossible to go on, but once you have passed through the forge of this unhappiness, you will be hardened, you will rise over your own ashes like the phoenix, you will understand—you will understand everything. But, dear teacher—we object—didn't the composition which we retold to the woman at the post in our own words convince you that even as it is we have long understood that there's absolutely no need for us to pass through any kind of literary forge? Unquestionably—answers our mentor—I realized it from your first words, it's true you don't need a forge. I was speaking of the necessity of a forge—which for you is apparently a false necessity—only so as to somehow console you as you ponder the impossibility of being excused from classes in the aforementioned subject. Would you believe it, it wasn't so long ago I could have easily persuaded Perillo to offer you voluntary attendance of all classes in general, you no doubt know the kind of authority your humble servant enjoyed in teachers' circles—in the school and in the ministry of people's edufaketion. But since something happened to me—what precisely I still don't completely understand, I have been deprived of everything: flowers, food, tobacco—did you notice I've stopped smoking?—women, my railway pass (the constrictor assures me that my paper expired long ago, but there is no way I can buy a new one, inasmuch as they also deprived me of my salary), amusements, and, the main thing—authority. I simply can't imagine how this can be: no one listens to me—neither the teachers at pedagogical meetings, nor the parents at the PTO meeting, nor the students in class. They don't even cite me as they used to. Everything is happening as if I, Norvegov, no longer existed, as if I had died. And here Savl Petrovich filled the restroom with a soft flickering laughter. Yes, I am laughing—said he—but through tears. Dear student and great friend Nymphea, something has definitely happened to me. Formerly, not so long ago, I knew precisely what it was, but now it seems to have slipped my mind. To use your terminology, my memory had become selective, and I'm particularly happy we've met here, at point M, inasmuch as I am counting on your help. Help me, help me remember what happened. I've asked people about it, but no one could—or did they want to?—explain anything to me. Some simply didn't know the truth, some knew but concealed it: they quibbled and lied, and some simply laughed in my face. But as far as I know, you will never lie about anything, you are incapable of lying.

He fell silent, his voice no longer filled the emptiness of space, and the sounds of the evening city became more distinct. Someone large, polyped, and infinitely long, like the prehistoric dinosaur which later turned into the snake, was walking past the school outside, slipping on the bare ice, whistling a Schubert serenade, coughing and cussing, asking questions and answering them for himself, striking matches, losing hats, hankies, and handbags, squeezing in his pocket a recently purchased exerciser, looking at a watch from time to time, eyes running over the pages of the evening papers, making conclusions, looking at a pedometer, losing and finding the way, analyzing the system of house numbers, reading signs and billboards, dreaming of acquiring new plots of land and of ever-increasing profits, recalling the deeds of days gone by, suffusing the surrounding air with the odor of cologne and crocodile purses, playing on a harmonica, stupidly and nastily sniggering, envying the fame of the dacha postman Mikheev, desiring untried possession and knowing nothing about us, mentor and students, chatting here in the melancholy confines of M. This someone, polyped, like a prehistoric dinosaur, and as unending as medieval torture, kept walking and walking, knowing neither weariness nor peace, and still couldn't get all the way past, because it could never get all the way past. Against the background of its movement, against the background of this unceasing, susurrating striding, we listened to the trolley whistles, the squeal of brakes, the hissing created by the slippage of the trolleybus contact antennae along the electric wires. Then came hollow blows, caused by the quick impact of a wood mass on the galvanized mass of ordinary tin: probably one of the special-schoolers, who didn't want to return to the home of his father, was methodically pounding a stick on the water pipes, attempting to play a nocturne on the flute of the pipes—as a sign of protest against everything. The sounds which were generated inside the building, however, were the following. In the cellar worked deaf-mute stoker so-and-so—his shovel scraping against the coal, the boiler doors screeching. An old lady was washing the floor in the hall: the brush with the wet rag wrapped around it would plunge rhythmically into the bucket, choke, slosh onto the floor and noiselessly moisten a new section of dry surface—the swimming of a rubious steed, the waltz of a man with a cold, *skeerly* in a filled bathtub. Along another hall, a floor higher, walked the curriculum director Sheina Solomonovna Trachtenberg, her prosthetic device was thumping and squeaking. It was empty and quiet on the third floor, and on the fourth, in the so-called auditorium, a rehearsal of the combined choreographic ensemble of the town's special schools was going wild: fifty idiots were getting ready for some new concerts. Now they were rehearsing the dance ballad "Boyars, Here We Are": they were singing and yelling, stomping and whistling, snorting and grunting. Some were singing: Boyars, she's a dummy, young folks, she's a dummy. Others were promising: But we'll teach her, Boyars, but we'll teach her, young folks. The tympani banged with metallic disdain, slowly unwinding, the oboes crawled along, a bass drum with a goat's face drawn on the side was thumping, a sharp-winged pockmarked piano was in a convulsive fit of hysterics—skipping notes, hitting wrong notes, and swallowing its own keys. Then an ominous pause came to the fourth floor, and within a second, if we understand this word correctly, all of them, the dancers and the singers in chorus, intoned, bawled the Hymn of Enlightened Humanity, at the initial chords of which anyone who possesses ears must put aside whatever he is doing, stand up, and tremorously attend. We barely recognized the song. Passing through all the barriers, it did reach point M, but the bannisters, the steps and the stairwells, the sharp corners at the turnings, distorted and disfigured its inflexible members, and it reached us bloodied, snowswept, in the torn and filthy dress of a girl whom someone forced to do everything they wanted. But amid the voices performing this cantata, among the voices which meant nothing and were worth nothing, among the voices mingling in that senseless, meaningless, voiceless noisy clot of sound, among voices doomed to oblivion, among the incredibly commonplace and off-key voices, there was one voice which came to us as the embodiment of purity, strength and triumphant mortal grief. We heard it in all its undistorted clarity: it was like unto the flight of a wounded bird, it was a dazzling snowy color, the voice sang white, white was the voice, buoyant the voice, buoyant and melting, melted the voice. Piercing through everything, despising everything, it would rise and then fall, in order to rise. The voice was naked, stubborn, and filled with the loud pulsating blood of the singing girl. And there were no other voices there, in the auditorium, only her voice was there. And—do you hear it?—Savl Petrovich said in a whisper, a whisper enchanted and ecstatic—do you hear that, or is it my imagination? Yes-yes-yes, Savl Petrovich, we hear Rosa Windova singing, the dear girl, sepulchral flower, the best contralto among the defectives of all the schools. And from this day forth, if—to the question: what are you doing here, here in the restroom?—if you reply to us: I am resting after classes, or: I am warming the bottoms of my feet—we will not believe you, you splendid, but sly, pedagogue. Because now we understand it all. Like an ordinary schoolboy with a crush, you are waiting for the rehearsal to end, and she will descend from the auditorium along with the other damaged and still-born children—she, the one with whom you have arranged a rendezvous on the back stairs in the right wing where there isn't a single unbroken lightbulb left—it's dark, so dark, and smells of dust, where the discarded gym mats are piled in a heap on the landing between the second and third floors. They are ripped, sawdust is spilling out of them, and there, precisely there, this is what happens: come, come, how I want your untouched body. Ecstatic whisper. Only careful, someone might hear—the Chechens wander all around. Or to be more precise: watch out for widow Tinbergen. All night long, sleeplessly and tirelessly, she wanders from floor to floor of the sealed, sagely silent school for fools. Starting at midnight the only thing you will hear in the building is footsteps—ee-ee-ee, one-two-three, one-two-three. Humming, muttering, witchlike chants, waltzing or tap dancing, she moves through the halls and the classrooms and the stairways, hanging down in the stairwells, turning into a buzzing dung fly, pivoting on the steps, clacking her castanets. Only she, Tinbergen, and only the clock with the gilded pendulum in Perillo's office: one-two-three—at night the entire school is the lonely night pendulum, cutting the darkness into even, softly-dark slices, into five hundred, into five thousand, into fifty, according to the number of students and teachers: for you, for me, for you, for me. You'll get your share in the morning, at dawn. In the frosty morning, which smells of a wet rag and chalk, when handing in your shoes in bags and putting on your slippers—along with your claim check—you'll get yours. So take it easy there on the mats.

Therefore, says our teacher Savl to us, I am listening to you attentively, the truth and only the truth. you are obliged to open my eyes to verity, let me recover my sight, raise my lids. A huge nose, like a Roman legion soldier, flat, gravely compressed lips. His whole face is coarse-cut, and perhaps coarse-chopped, from white marble with rose veins, a face with merciless wrinkles—the consequence of a sober evaluation of the earth and the men on it. The grim look of a Roman legion soldier marching in the front ranks of an unbending legion. Armor, a white cloak trimmed with the fur of the purple Italianate wolf. His helmet studded with evening dew, brass and gold clasps here and there—misted over, but flashes from the near and far fires flaming along the Appian Way nevertheless make the armor and the helmet and the clasps glitter. All that is happening here is spectral, grandiose and terrible, because it has no future. Dear Savl Petrovich, obeying your unforgettable commandments—they pound at our hearts like the ashes of Klaus—we have in fact attained one of the highest of human qualities, we have learned how never to lie about anything. We note this without false modesty, for in the conversation here with you, our teacher, you become our conscience and our happy youth—it would be out of place. But, mentor, no matter how elevated the principles by which we guide ourselves in relation to other people, they, the principles, will in no way take the place of our repulsive memory: as before it is selective, and it's very unlikely we shall be able to shed light and raise your heavy lids for you. We scarcely remember what happened to you either, after all, a lot of time has passed—or will pass—since. True, answers Savl, quite a bit, true, quite a bit, not unlikely, more truly, a lot. But nevertheless, do try, strain your amazing, albeit repulsive memory. Help your teacher, who is suffering in his ignorance! A drop of dew dripped from the washbasin faucet and dropped into the rusty, thousand-year-old basin in order, following the dark slimy sewer pipes, and bypassing the sediment tanks and prize-winning modern filters, to slip quietly into the grief of the river Lethe as someone's serene soul; Lethe, moving backwards, bears out your boat and you, transformed into a white flower, onto a white sandbar; for an instant the drop will cling to the mandolin-shaped blade of your paddle and again drop triumphantly into Lethe—it will vanish—it will melt away—in a second, if you properly understand the meaning of the word, it will gleam immortally in the inlet of a just-built Roman aqueduct. Leaf-fall September, such-and-such a date, of such-and-such a year B.C., Genoa, the Palace of Doges. A birchbark pictograph rolled into a tube. Beloved Senator and Legion Soldier Savl, we hasten to inform you that we, your grateful students, have finally remembered some details of the event which happened to you sooner or later, the one which so disturbed you. We have managed to strain our memory and now, it would seem we can guess precisely what happened, and we are prepared to raise your clanked-shut lids for you. We hasten to inform you that Principal N.G. Perillo, incited to do this malicious deed by S.S. Trachtenberg-Tinbergen, relieved you of your position at your own request. That's impossible—objects Norvegov— I did nothing that could...why? for what? on what grounds? I don't remember anything, tell me. Anxiously.

Chapter Five   *Testament*

It was one of the days of that enchanting month when early in the evening Saturn, soon to descend below the horizon, can be seen in the Western part of the sky in the constellation Taurus, and during the second part of the night bright Jupiter stands out in the constellation Capricorn, and toward morning, markedly lower and to the left, in the constellation Aquarius,

Mars appears. But above all it is when the racemosa in our school's lilac garden blossoms dizzyingly: and we, the fools of several generations, are the ones who planted it, much to the envy of all the smart people who pass by in the street. Esteemed Savl Petrovich, allow us to note here that we, the prisoners of the special school, slaves of the Perillo slipper system, deprived of all rights to a normal human voice and therefore forced to explode in an inarticulate uterine shout, we, pitiful gnats entangled in the stiff spider nets of the class schedule, nevertheless, in our own way, in our stupid way, we love it, our hateful special, with all its gardens, teachers and cloakrooms. And if someone were to propose to us that we transfer to a normal one, an ordinary school for normal people, and inform us that we had gotten better and become normal—no, no, we don't want to, don't force us out!—we would weep, and wipe away the tears with our cursed slipper sacks. Yes, we love it, because we are used to it, and if we ever, after spending several so-called years in each class, if we ever graduate from it with its graffiti-covered black and brown desks, we will be terribly dismayed. For in leaving it, we would lose everything—everything that we had. We would be left alone, and lonely, life would toss us to its corners, through the crowds of the smart ones who are striving to attain power, to attain women, cars, engineer's diplomas, but we—utter fools that we are—we don't need anything of the sort, we have but one wish: to sit in class, look out the window at the wind-torn clouds, paying no attention to the teachers, except for Norvegov, and await the white-white bell, which is like an arm-ful of racemosa during that dizzying month when you, Savl Petrovich, geographer of the highest level, quickly—if not to say *headlong*—enter our class for the last lesson in your life. Barefoot. Warm spell. Warm wind. When the door is flung open—the windows, the frames of the windows—open out. Warmth wafts in. Pots of geraniums are strewn across the floor, smashed to smithereens. Glistening rain worms wriggle in the clods of black earth. Savl Petrovich, and you—you laugh. You laugh, as you stand on the threshold. You wink at us, recognize every one of us, to the last man. Hello, Savl Petrovich on a warm Thursday in May, wearing a sport shirt with sleeves rolled up, pants with wide cuffs, a summer hat with a multitude of holes poked in it by a conductor's punch. Hello, devils, sit down, come on, nuts to these absurd ceremonies, because it's spring. By the way, have you noticed how the whole man is invigorated when caught up in the fresh breath of spring, eh? All right, I'll find a some way to tell you about it. But right now we shall begin the lesson. My bosom friends, today according to the plan we have a discussion of mountain systems, Cordilleras or Himalayas or something. But who needs all that, who needs it, I ask you, when across our entire beloved earth run automatic machines whose wheels splash the taut water of puddles, thus spattering all of our sweet little girl-friends wearing their short little skirts in the streets. Poor babies! The drops fly right up into their most secret spots even, way above the knees—

do you understand what I'm trying to say? Merrily, hitching up his sail-cloth pants and doing a little dance by the map of both hemispheres, which suggest gigantic blue glasses without rims. Student so-and-so, do me a favor, enumerate some women's names for us, the way I taught you, in alphabetical order. One of us students—now, from the distance, I can't see exactly who—gets up and speaks in a rapid semi-whisper: Agnes, Agrip-pina, Barbara, Christina, Galina... Yes—you repeat with the smile of a person who is touched—Leocadia, Valeria, Yulia, thank you, sit down. My faithful friends, how happy I am to attest my respect for you today, a spring day. Spring: it's not like your winter, when my yard is isolated, blanketed by the sad snow, the sleighbell rang out. Now there's a story. On the Island, on a night crossing, I took three bottles of cliquot and toward morning of the next day I was approaching the desired goal. All was darkness and whirlwind. No, on the contrary, today we will devote our efforts to a desert incarnadined with the blood of seals. Student so-and-so, I behold some-thing terrible: of the three windows which give onto the open sky, only two are open, so open the third one too! Thanks. Today I will tell you a story which I found in a bottle of cliquot on the bank of the dacha river Lethe. I have called this story *The Carpenter in the Desert.*

My bosom friends, in the desert there lived a carpenter, a great master of his craft. When the occasion arose he could build a home, a dome, a carousel, a swing, knock together a mailing crate or any other kind. But the desert, in the words of the carpenter himself, was empty: no nails, no boards. *Esteemed legionnaire Savl, we are obliged to put the following fact to you immediately: no sooner did you utter the words no nails no boards, than it seemed to get dark and gloomy for an instant in the St. Laurence Mars Flame Orebearer University, where you are giving your regular lecture, it seemed to us that someone's shadow—a bird or a pterodactyl or a heliplane—fell across the podium, replacing the sun. But then immediately went away.* Some people—you continued, as if having noticed nothing—will say: that's not true, there is no place where there isn't at least a board or two and a dozen nails, and if one looks around carefully, one can find material anywhere for a whole dacha with a veranda like all of us have, as long as the desire to do something useful hasn't disappeared, as long as one has faith in success. But I, angry, will reply: the carpenter really did manage to find one board, and then a second. Besides that, he had had one nail in his pocket since times of yore, the master was saving it just in case, a lot can happen in a carpenter's life, many are the uses to which a carpenter can put a nail, for example, scratching a line, marking drill holes, and so on. But I should add: in spite of the fact that the carpenter had not lost his desire to do something useful, and he believed in success to the end, the master could not find more than the two ten-millimeter boards. He had walked and ridden the whole desert over on his small zebra, studied every shifting dune and each gully overgrown with scrawny halogetons, he had even ridden along the seashore, but—the devil take it!—the desert gave him no material. *Mentor Savl, we're afraid, it seems the shadow was just here again—just a second ago.* One day, exhausted by his quest and the sun, the carpenter said to himself: all right, you have nothing to build a home, carousel or crate with, but you do have two boards and one good nail—so you at least have to make something out of this small quantity of materials, after all a master cannot sit on his hands. Having said this, the carpenter placed one of the boards across the other, got the nail out of his pocket, and took a hammer from his tool box, and he used the hammer to pound the nail into the point where the boards intersected, thus firmly joining them: the result was a cross. The carpenter took it to the summit of the highest sand dune, set it up vertically there, pounding it into the sand, and he rode away on his small zebra, in order to admire his cross from a distance. The cross was visible from almost any distance, and the carpenter was so happy about this that from joy he turned into a bird. *Very, very scared, dear Savl, the shadow again loomed across your podium, loomed and dissolved, loomed and dissolved, dissolved, the shadow of a bird, that bird, or not a bird.* It was a huge black bird with a straight white beak which emitted abrupt cawing sounds. *Savl Petrovich, could it be the nightjar? The cry of the nightjar, the cry of the nightjar, protect the nightjar in its habitat, by the reeds and the hedges, hunters and huntsmen, grasses and shepherds, watchmen and signalmen, tra-ta-ta, tra-ta, ee-ee-ee-ee.* The bird flew up and perched on the horizontal bar of the cross, sitting there and watching the movement of the sands. And some people came. They asked the bird: what's the name of the thing you're sitting on? The carpenter replied: it's a cross. They said: we've got a man with us here that we'd like to execute, could we crucify him on your cross, we'd pay a lot. And they showed the bird some grains of rye. *Beloved Senator and Legionnaire Savl, look, for all our sakes, look out the window, it seems to us that someone is sitting there, on the fire escape railing, perhaps the nightjar, perhaps he's the one that's casting a shadow on your podium?* And they showed the bird several grains of rye. Yes, said the carpenter, I'm agreed, I'm happy that you like my cross. The people went away and after a time returned, leading on a rope behind them some skinny and bearded person, to all appearances a beggar. *O, Mentor, you don't hear the mute and anxious outcry of our class, alas! Again: look back in fear! There, outside the window, on the fire escape.* They went up to the summit of the sand dune, stripped the rags off the man and asked the black bird if he had nails and a hammer. The carpenter replied: I have a hammer, but not a single nail. We'll give you nails, said they, and soon they brought many—big ones and bright ones. Now you must help us, said the people, we're going to hold this man, and you pin his hands and his feet to the cross, here are three nails for you. *Attention, Captain Savl, off the starboard bow—a shadow, order a broadside, your spyglass is fogged over, ulalum is nigh.* The carpenter replied: I think it's going to be bad for this man, it'll be painful for him. However that may be, objected the people, he deserves punishment, and you are obliged to help us, we have paid you, and will pay more. And they showed the bird a handful of wheat grains. *Woe unto you, Savl!* Then the carpenter decided to be crafty. He says to them: can't you see that I'm an ordinary black bird, how can I pound in nails? Don't pretend, said the people, we know perfectly well who you are. You are a carpenter after all, and a carpenter must pound nails, that's the work of his life. Yes, replied the carpenter again. But I am a master craftsman, not an executioner. If you have to execute a person, crucify him yourself, that's not for my hands. Stupid carpenter, they laughed, we know that in your miserable desert you haven't got a single board or one nail left, therefore you cannot work and you are suffering. A little more time—and you will die of inactivity. If, however, you agree to help us crucify the man, we will bring you much choice building lumber on camels, and you will craft yourself a home with a veranda, like all of us have, a swing, a boat—everything you want. Agree to it, you won't be sorry. *How sorry you will be, mentor, that you heed not our mute advice—look out the window, look!* The bird thought for a long time, then flew down from the cross and turned into a carpenter. Hand me the nails and hammer—agreed the carpenter—I'll help you. And he quickly pinned the hands and feet of the condemned man to his cross, while they, the others, held the wretch. The next day they brought the carpenter the promised goods, and he worked a great deal and with pleasure, paying no attention to the large black birds which flew in with the blue dawn and pecked at the crucified man all day, and only that evening flew away. Once the crucified man called the carpenter. The carpenter mounted the sand dune and asked what the man needed. He said: I'm dying, and I want to tell you about myself. Who are you?—asked the carpenter. I lived in a desert and was a carpenter—the crucified man replied with difficulty—I had a small zebra, but almost no boards or nails. Some people came and promised to give me the needed material if I helped them crucify a carpenter. At first I refused, but then I agreed, for they offered to give me a whole handful of wheat grains. Why did you need grain—the carpenter said in surprise as he stood on the sand dune—can it be that you know how to turn into a bird too? *Why don't you look out the window, mentor, why?* Why did you use the word *too*—replied the crucified carpenter—O foolish man, do you really not yet realize that you and I—are one and the same carpenter, don't you realize that on the cross which you have created in the name of your sublime carpenter's craft, you have crucified yourself, and when they were pinning you down, you pounded in the nails yourself. After saying this, to himself, the carpenter died.

Finally, our good mentor, finally, having heard our disaster warnings, finally you are looking around. But it's too late, teacher: the shadow which starting with a certain moment—*no nails, no boards*—has been disturbing our minds, is no longer sitting on the fire escape railing and is not looming over the podium—and it is not a shadow, and not a nightjar, and not the shadow of the nightjar. It is the directress Tinbergen, hanging down on the other side of the window, which is wide open to the sky. Clad in rags bought secondhand from a train-station gypsy, in an old crone's knitted cap, from under which closely cropped Medusa serpents protrude, flecked with platinum gray, she hangs there outside the window, as if dangling from a rope, but in fact she is hanging there without the help of outside forces or objects, simply using her witch's powers, hanging like a portrait of herself—filling the window frame, covering the entire opening, hanging there because she wants to hang there, hovering. And without coming into the classroom, without even stepping on the windowsill, she will scream at you, incomparable Savl Petrovich, tactlessly and unpedagogically paying no attention to us, frozen and chalky from agitation, she will scream, baring those rotten metallic teeth of hers: sedition! sedition! sedition! And then disappear, Mentor Savl—are you crying, you, with a rag and piece of chalk in your hand, you, standing there at the board, which in English is called *blackboard*? They were eavesdropping on us, eavesdropping, now they'll fire you on their own, only on what basis? We'll write a petition! My God—this is you talking now, Norvegov—do you really imagine I'm afraid of losing my job? I'll manage, I'll get by somehow, I don't have long to go. But, my friends, it's very painful to part with you, the future and past ones, with Those Who Came, and who will go away, bearing with them the great right to judge, without being judged. Dear Mentor, if you believe that we, who have appeared in order to judge, will ever forget your steps dying away in the hall and then on the stairs, you are in error—we will not forget. Almost soundless, your bare feet have left an imprint in our brain and frozen there forever, as if you had imprinted them in asphalt softened by the sun, walking across it to the triumphal ceremonial march of the Julian calendar. It is a bitter thing for me to recall this story, sir, I would like to have a moment of silence together with you in our garden. If I may I'll sit down there in that wicker chair, so as not to tromp pointlessly on the grass, wait a moment, I'll continue soon. When I return.

As you walk onto the bridge, notice the railings: they are cold and slippery. And the stars are flying. The stars. The trolleys are cold, yellow, unearthly. The electric trains below will request permission to pass the slow freights. Descend the stairway to the platform, buy a ticket to some station, where there is a station snackbar, cold wooden benches, snow. There are several drunks at the tables in the snackbar, drinking non-stop, reciting poetry to each other. This is going to be a cold, numbing winter, and during the second half of the December day this station snackbar will be the same way. It will be under demolition by the concertinas and poetry inside. People will be singing wildly and hoarsely. *Drink your tea, sir, it'll get cold.* About the weather. Mainly, about dusk. In the winter in the dusk, when you are little. Dusk is coming. It's impossible to live, and impossible to walk away from the window. Tomorrow's lessons are not in any of the known subjects. A fairytale. Outside it's dusk, snow the color of blue ashes or the wing of some sort of pigeon. Homework isn't done. Dreamy emptiness of the heart, of sunny linkages. The melancholy of all man. You are little. But you know, you already know. Mama said: that'll pass too, childhood will pass, like an orange trolley rattling across the bridge, showering cold fiery sparks which barely exist. A tie, watch, and briefcase. Like father's. But there'll be a girl, sleeping on the sand by the river—just an ordinary girl wearing a clean, tight, white swimsuit. Very pretty. Almost pretty. Almost unpretty, dreaming of field flowers. In a sleeveless blouse. On the hot sand. It'll get cold when dusk sets in. When it's evening. A steamer happens by: the whistle causes her simple eyelashes to quiver—she looks up. But you still don't know if—if she's the one. All covered with lights, the steamer leaves its cozy foam to the care of the night. But it's not yet night. An incoming surge of violet waves. By the shore, deep, there are springs. This water can be drunk, by leaning over. The lips of the dear, tender girl. The rumble of the steamer, the plash, the flickering lights recede. On the other shore, chatting with a chum, someone lights a fire to make tea. They laugh. One can hear their matches striking; who you are, I don't know. The mosquitoes spend the night in the tops of the pines, in their crowns. The very middle of July. Later they'll descend to the water. It smells of grass. Very warm. This is happiness, but you still don't know about it. So far you don't know. The bird is a corncrake. The night ebbs and flows, solicitously turning the millstones of the heavenly mill. What is that river called? The river has a name. And the night has a name. What will you dream? Nothing. You'll dream of the corncrake, the nightjar. But you don't know yet. Almost unpretty. But incomprarable, because she's the first. A wet salty cheek, silence invisible in the night. My dear, how impossible you are to make out in the distance. Yes, you'll find out, you'll find out. The song of years, the melody of life. All the rest is un-you, all the others—are alien. Who are you yourself? You don't know. You'll only find out later, stringing the beads of memory. Consisting of them. You will be all memory. The dearest, most evil and

eternal. Pain trying for a whole lifetime to get out of the sunny entangle-
ment. But what about the girl? Don't rattle the page, don't rustle it. She's
sleeping. Morning. *I stood in the wind lonely and abandoned, like a
church. You came and said that golden birds do exist.* Morning. Dew
disappearing underfoot. A brittle willow. The sound of a bucket borne to
the river, the soundlessness of a bucket borne away from the river. The dust
of silver dew. The day taking on a face. Day in its flesh. Love day more than
night, folks. Smile, try not to move, this is going to be a photograph. The
only one which will survive after everything that is going to happen. But so
far you don't know. Later—such-and-such a number of years in a row—
comes life. What's it called? It's called *life*. Warm sidewalks. Or the other
way around—one's swept by snow. It's called *the town*. You rush out of a
doorway wearing high clacking heels. You have a nice figure, it's early in
the morning, you're surrounded by perfume and the nimbus of a Parisian
hat. Clacking. Chil-dren and birds begin to sing. Around seven. Saturday. I
see you. You I see. Clacking all over the courtyard, all over the Boulevard
with its unblossomed lilacs. But they will blossom. Mama said. Nothing
else. Only this. Though there is more. But now you know. You can write
letters. Or simply shout, going insane from your dream. But that'll pass too.
No, mama, no, that will remain. Wearing heels. Is she the one? She. The
one? She. The one? She. Tra-ta-ta: right through. The whole town smells of
that perfume. and it's too late to speak, consumed. But one can write
letters. Saying *farewell* at the end every time. My love and my joy, if I die
from illness, madness or sadness, if before the time allotted me by fate is up,
I can't get enough of looking at you, enough joy in the dilapidated mills on
the emerald wormwood hills, if I don't drink my fill of the transparent
water from your immortal hands, if I don't make it to the end, if I don't tell
everything that I wanted to tell about you, about myself, if one day I die
without saying farewell—forgive me. Most of all, I would like to say—and
to say it before a very long separation—to say what you have long known
yourself, of course, or what you are just surmising. We all make surmises
about it. I want to say that there was already a time when we were
acquainted on this earth, you no doubt remember. For the river has a
name. And now we've come again, we've returned in order to meet again.
We are Those Who Came. Now you know. Her name is Veta. Veta.

Lad, what's wrong? Are you asleep? Hey! No, how could that be, I just
retreated into myself for a bit, but now I've returned... Don't worry, Doctor
Zauze calls it dissolving in the environment—it happens fairly often. A
man dissolves as if he had been put in a bathtub full of sulphuric acid. One
of my comrades—we are in the same class together—says that he got a
whole barrel of acid somewhere, but maybe he's lying, I don't know. In any

case, he intends to dissolve parents in it. No, not all parents in general, just his own. I don't think he likes his parents. So, what, sir, I imagine they are harvesting the fruits which they themselves sowed, and it is not for you and us to decide who is right here. Yes, lad, yes, not for you and me. Shaking his head, clicking his tongue, buttoning and immediately unbuttoning the buttons on his duster. Stooped and wooden and dry. But let's return to the sheep, sir. One day during that same remarkable month a rumor spread through the specschool that you, Savl Petrovich, had been fired as if by magic. Then we sat down and wrote a petition. It was laconic and severe in style; it said: To the School Principal, N. G. Perillo, A Petition. in connection with pedagogue-geographer P. P. Norvegov being fired at his own request, but in fact not—we demand the immediate surrender of the guilty parties by prison transfer convoy. And the signatures: respectfully, student so-and-so and student so-and-so. The two of us made our appearance together, pounding and knocking, slamming every door in the world. We made our appearance, furiously, and Perillo was sitting in his armchair relaxing and gloomy, in spite of the fact that it was still the morning of his middle years, a hale and hearty morning full of hopes and *planctons* for the future. In Perillo's office the clock with the gilded pendulum was rhythmically cutting nonexistent time into units. Well, what have you written?—said our director. You and I—we started searching for a petition in our pockets but couldn't find anything for a long time, and then you—precisely you, and not me—got a crumpled sheet of paper out from somewhere behind your back and put it on the glass before the Principal. But it was not the petition—I immediately realized it wasn't the petition, because we wrote the petition on a different kind of paper, on beautiful crested paper with watermarks and several special seals, on petition paper. But the sheet which lay on Perillo's glass now—glass reflecting the safe, the barred window, the chaotic foliage of the trees outside, the street going about its affairs, the sky—was ordinary lined notebook paper, and what you had written on the sheet—and it most certainly was you who wrote it—was not a petition but that old note explaining lost faith, about which I managed to forget a hundred years ago, I would never have written it if it hadn't been for you. That is, I hasten to underline that you wrote it, and that I never had anything to do with it. Woe unto us, Savl, we were betrayed by a third party, all was lost: the petition vanished, and it was beyond our strength to recreate the text, we had already forgotten it all. We recall only that during this whole time Nikolai Gorimirovich's face—after he started to read the explanatory note—became somehow different. Of course, it continued to be gloomy, inasmuch as it could not not be gloomy, but it also became something else. There was a nuance. A shade. Or like this: it was as if a slight wind had blown across the Principal's face. The wind did not take anything away, it only added something new. A sort of special dust. We probably wouldn't be mistaken in saying: Perillo's face became gloomy and special. Correct, now this was a special face. But what was Perillo reading—Savl asks with interest—what did you do there, my friends? I don't know, ask *him*, he was the one who wrote it, *the other*. I'll tell you right away. Here's what was there. As your humble correspondent has already informed the Italian artist Leonardo, I was sitting in the boat, not holding onto the oars. A cuckoo was counting my years on one of the banks. I had asked myself questions, several questions, and was already prepared to answer, but I could not. I was surprised, and then something happened inside me—in my heart and in my head. As if I had been turned off. And at that instant I felt that I had vanished, but at first I decided not to believe it. Didn't want to. And I said to myself: it's not true, it just seems like it, you're a little tired, it's very hot today. Get busy, and row, row home, to Syracuse, enumerate the Taurian ships. And I tried to grasp the oars, and stretched my hands out to them. But it didn't work. I saw the handles, but couldn't feel them with my palms. The wood of the oars flowed through my fingers like sand, like air, like immobile, nonexistent time. Or vice versa: I, my former palms, were flowed round by the wood, as if by water. The boat was washing to shore in a deserted spot. I walked a certain number of steps along the beach and looked back: there was nothing resembling my tracks left in the sand, and in the boat lay a white water lily, called by the Romans Nymphea Alba, that is, white lily. And then I realized that I had turned into it and no longer belonged to myself, or the school, or you personally, Nikolai Gorimirovich—to no one on earth. From this time forth I belong to the dacha river Lethe, which streams against its own current at its own desire. And—long live The Sender of Wind! As for the two slipper sacks, ask my mother, she knows everything. She'll say: that'll pass too. She knows.

Mama, mama, help me, I'm sitting here in Perillo's office, he's calling *there*, for Doctor Zauze. I don't want to, believe me. Please come, I promise to do everything you want, I give my word. I'll wipe my feet at the door and wash the dishes, don't give me away. Better yet, I'll start going to the maestro again. With pleasure. You see, in the course of these few seconds, I've rethought a lot of things, I've come to realize that in essence I love all music inordinately, especially the accordion three-quarter. Ee-ee-ee, one-two-three, one-two-three, ee-one, ee-two, ee-three. On the Barcarolle. Come on, we'll go visit grandmother again, we'll talk, and from there—straight to the maestro, he lives quite close, you remember. And I give my word that I'll never again spy on you. Believe me, it makes no difference to me what you do there with him, there, in the tower, on the second floor. Go ahead—and I—I will be memorizing the czardas. And when you come back down the skeerlying stairs, I'll play it for you. Sextets or even scales. And please, don't worry. What business is it of mine! We've all been grownups for a long time—you and maestro and me. Isn't it reasonable for me to understand. And could I ever carry tales? Never, mama, never. Come on and tell me, when did I ever tell papa anything—even once. No. Go ahead and do it, do it, and I'll be memorizing the czardas. Imagine it, how it'll be when we go again. Sunday, morning, and papa is shaving in the bathroom. I am cleaning my shoes, and you are making our breakfast. An omelette, fritters, coffee with cream. Papa is in a splendid mood, yesterday he had a difficult meeting, he said that he was devilishly tired, but then everybody got what they deserved. That's why as he shaves, he is humming his favorite Neapolitan song: After a bit of a trip, a hole in her hip, in a Neapolitan port, Gianetta set the rigging; before weighing anchor, all sailors went ashore, whirlagigging. Well, what's happening, are you going for your lesson?—he asks after breakfast, though he knows better than us that yes we are going for the lesson. Yes, papa, yes, music. How is he, your one-eyed fellow, I haven't seen him for a long time, is he minstrelizing as usual, composing all sorts of hibbeldy-dibbeldy? Of course, papa, what else has he to do, after all he's a handicapped veteran, he has loads of free time. Oh I know these veterans—papa smirks—these veterans ought to be loading barges, not sawing on fiddles, if it were up to me they'd do some sawing to a different tune, the no-count Mozarts. But—you remark, mama—he doesn't play the violin, his main instrument is the horn. All the more—says papa—if it were up to me, he'd blow the horn where one's supposed to. It'd be better— continues papa, wiping up the remains of the fried eggs with a piece of bread—it'd be better if he washed his socks more often. What have socks got to do with this—you answer, mama—we're talking about music; naturally, everyone has his weaknesses, the man is a bachelor, he has to do everything all by himself. There you are—says papa—you go ahead and wash his socks for him if you feel sorry for him, just think of it—we've found a genius so great that he's incapable of washing his socks! Finally we go out. Well, get going—papa sends us off, standing on the threshold—get going. He is wearing his favorite and only pyjamas and has a bundle of newspapers under his arm. His big face—it is virtually wrinkleless—gleams and shines from the recent shave. I will do some reading—he says—careful with that accordion, don't scratch the case. The electric is full of people— everyone going somewhere off to their dachas. There's absolutely no place to sit, but as soon as we appear, everyone looks around at us and they say to each other: let the mother with the boy through don't get in their way, sit the mother and the boy with the accordion down, seat them, let them sit down, they have an accordion. We sit down and look out the window. If the trip to my lesson happens to take place on a winter day, outside we see horses hitched to sleighs, we see snow and various tracks in the snow. But if it happens in the autumn everything outside is different: the horses are hitched to carts or simply wandering through the meadows by themselves.

Mama, I'm sure the constrictor is going to come in a moment. How do you know? That's not for sure. you'll see, just wait. Tickets—says the constrictor, coming in. Mama opens her purse, she searches for our tickets, but can't find them for a long time. Upset, she pours out all of the small things which there are in the handbag onto her knees, and the entire car looks on as she does so. The car examines the things: two or three handkerchiefs, a bottle of perfume, lipstick, a notebook, a dried cornflower in memory of something that happened long ago, a case for glasses, or, as mama calls it—an eyecase, keys to the apartment, a pincushion, a spool of thread, matches, a compact and the key to *grandmother*. Finally mama finds the tickets and holds them out to the approaching constrictor, a fat man wearing a special black greatcoat. He turns the tickets in his hands, languidly checks their color, languidly closes one eye, and he punches it with a punch, which looks like: sugar tongs, a barber's hair-clippers, a dynamometer, tiny tongs, tooth-pulling tongs, a "beetle" flashlight. Noticing the accordion, the fatty languidly winks at me and asks: a Barcarolle? Yes—I say—a Barracuda, three quarters. We're on the way to his lesson— adds mama, upset. The whole car is listening, slightly rising from the yellow lacquered benches, trying not to let a word slip by. The teacher is waiting for us—continues mama—we are a little late, didn't make the nine o'clock, but we'll make up lost time on the way from the station. We'll walk a little faster than usual, my son has a very talented pedagogue he's a composer true he's not quite well the front you know but very talented and he lives completely alone in an old house with a tower you yourself understand it's not too comfy at his place and sometimes it's a mess but what does that matter if we are talking about the fate of my son you see the teachers advised that we give our son a musical education at least an elementary one he doesn't have a bad ear and then we found this teacher we have a friend and he recommended him to us we are very grateful they were together at the front our friend and the teacher have been friends for many years now by the way if you have a son and he has an ear if you'd like I could give you the address an honest man and a remarkable musician a specialist in his craft one can only bow down to him he doesn't charge much if it had to be earlier for you an agreement could be reached and he'd come to your house it's not hard for him all the more that for you too it would be cheaper here I'll write down your address. No need—languidly says the constrictor— nuts to all that music and a Barcarolle alone costs who knows what. Wrong, wrong, mama answers after all the accordion can be bought in a second-hand store and it's not in the least expensive there and can one think about money if one is talking about the fate of one's son in the final analysis you could get a loan here I'll have a talk with your wife we women always understand each other better yet my husband and I could loan you the money if not the whole amount then at least part of it you could gradually repay us we would trust you you can after all. No need—answers the constrictor—I'd be glad to borrow from you, but I don't want to bother with all that music, why the teacher alone costs who knows how much, and besides that I don't have a son anyway, no son, no daughter, no, so excuse me, thanks. Languidly. The constrictor walks away, the people in the car sit down in their places and present their tickets. When we exit from the train and descend from the platform I look back: I see the whole car staring after us. Going along minding our own business, we are reflected in the eyes and glass of the train as it gathers speed: my medium-height mother in the brown spring jacket with the collar of a sick steppe fox, mama in a scaly, hard-looking hat, made from no one knows what, and wearing shoes; and I—skinny and tall, in a dark duster with six buttons, made out of my prosecutor father's greatcoat, in an awful wine cap, shoes with clips and galoshes. We fly further and further from the station, dissolving in a world of suburban objects, noises and colors, with each movement penetrating further and further into the sand, the bark of the trees, we mingle with the sunrays, we become optical illusions, inventions, children's amusement, a play of light and shadow. We burst into the voices of the birds and people, we attain the immortality of the nonexistent. The maestro's house stands on the edge of some annexes, calling to mind a ship made of matchboxes and blocks. You see the maestro from afar: he is standing in the center of a glassed-in veranda, in front of a music stand, practicing on a smallish flute which on some other days seems to be a telescope; moreover, he is wearing a black eye bandage, like a pirate captain. The garden is filled with black wind-twisted trees, and across the lake, touched by the elegant melody, boats float glassily in the Sunday sky's cold and larsh luminescence. Good day, maestro, here we are, we've come again, to learn. We have missed music so much, and you and your garden. The doors of the veranda are flung open, the captain moves unhurryingly to meet us. Mama, look at your face! Can the wind from the lake have changed it so? Now, right now. Mama, I can't keep up with you. Now. Now we step across the threshold of the house and are submerged in its peculiar architecture, absorbed in its halls and stairways and floors. Here we go in. One. Two. Three.

Excuse me, sir, I seem to have digressed rather far from the essence of our conversation. What I wish to say is that Savl Petrovich is sitting on the windowsill with his back to the window as before. The naked bottoms of his feet rest on the radiator, and the teacher, smiling, is talking to us: yes, I remember quite well that Perillo wanted to fire me on request. But after thinking it over he gave me a probationary period—two weeks, and so as not to get kicked out of work I decided to show myself at my best. I decided to try very very hard. I decided not to be late to school, I decided to buy and wear some sandals, I swore to conduct the lessons strictly according to the plan. I would have given away half of the dacha summer to someone, if only I could remain with you, my friends. But then the very thing that I keep asking you about happened. I don't remember—you understand? I don't remember what took place during my probationary period, apparently right at the start. All that I know is that it happened on the eve of the regularly scheduled examination. Student so-and-so, do me a favor, help me. Every day my memory is getting worse and worse, getting dull, like table silver which lies unused in the buffet. So breathe on this silver and wipe it with a flannel cloth. Savl Petrovich, we reply, standing on the Dutch tile—or whatever else these tiles are called—Savl Petrovich, we know, now we know, we remember, only don't worry. But I'm not worried, Lord, just tell me, please, tell me. Anxiously. Savl Petrovich, this might be extremely unpleasant news for you. Come on—the teacher urges us—I'm all ears. Well, you see, the thing is that you yourself wanted to know what happened, you informed us about it yourself at the time. Yes, yes, of course, that's what I'm saying: my memory is like unto silver. So listen. That day we were supposed to take the last examination in some class, your class in fact, geography. It was set for nine o'clock, we gathered in the classroom and waited for you till twelve, but you never came. Clicking his heels at the corners, Perillo appeared and said that the examination was being postponed until the next day. Some of us surmised that you were sick, and we decided to visit you. We went off to the teachers' commons room, and Tinbergen gave us your city address. We set off. The door was opened by some woman, extraordinarily pale and gray. To be frank, we have never met such a chalky woman. She spoke barely audibly, through her teeth, and she was dressed in a nondescript duster the color of a sheet, without buttons and without sleeves. Most likely it was not even a duster, but a sack, sewn from two sheets, in which only one hole had been cut—for the head—you understand? The woman said she was your relative, and asked what message there was. We replied that that wasn't necessary, and inquired where we might find you, Savl Petrovich, how, we said, can we see you. And the woman says: he doesn't live here now, he lives outside of town, at his dacha, because it's spring. And she offered to give us the address, but, thank God, we know your dacha, and we decided to set off immediately. Wait—interrupts Savl—by that time I really had moved to the dacha already, but you went to the wrong apartment, because there couldn't have been any such woman in my apartment, all the less a relative, I have no relatives, even male ones, my apartment is always empty from spring to fall, you mixed up the address. Possibly, Savl Petrovich—we say—but for some reason the woman did know you, after all, she wanted to explain how to get to your dacha. Strange—replies Savl pensively—what was the apartment number, do you remember? Such-and-such, Savl Petrovich. Such-and-such?—the teacher asks again. Yes, such-and-such. I'm very concerned—says Savl—I don't understand any of this. I'm very concerned. Where could the woman have come from? Well, did you happen to notice if there, by the door, on the stairwell landing—was there a sled there? There was, Savl Petrovich, a child's sled, yellow, with a strap made from a wick for a kerosene lamp. Right, so, right, but, my God, what woman? And why gray-haired, why in a duster? I don't know any such women, I'm very concerned, but—continue. Crushed. And so we set out to your dacha. The morning was already ending, but despite that, the nightingales, countering the trains, went on singing harmoniously all along the railroad, in the bushes outside the right-of-way fences. We stood on the connecting platform eating ice cream and listening to them—they were louder than anything in the world. We don't imagine, Savl Petrovich, that you have forgotten how to get from the station to your dacha, and we won't describe the road. We must only remark that there was still melted cold water in the roadside ditches, and the young leaves of the plantain were hurriedly drinking it, in order to survive and live. One may also make reference to the fact that the first people had already appeared in the garden plots: they were burning trash fires, digging in the earth, pounding hammers, and warding off the first bees. Everything in our settlement that day was precisely the same as on the corresponding day last year and all the past years, and our dacha stood drowning in the joyous six-petaled lilacs. But there were now some different dacha folk in our garden, not us, inasmuch as by this time we had sold our dacha. Or maybe hadn't yet bought it. Here nothing can be asserted with confidence, in this given case everything depends on time, or vice versa—nothing depends on time, we could be mixing up everything, it may seem to us that that day was then, but in actuality it falls in a completely different period. It's really terrible when things keep getting combined without any system. That's right, that's right, now we aren't even in a position to maintain with certainty if we had, our family had, any dacha, or if we had and do have it, or if we just will have it. A certain scientist—I read this in a scientific journal—says: if you are in the city and at a given moment you think that you have a dacha in the country, it doesn't mean that it is there in fact. And vice versa: lying in a hammock at the dacha, you cannot seriously believe that the city, where you intend to go after supper, does in fact exist in space. Both the dacha, and the city, between which you race all summer—writes the scientist—are only fruits of your somewhat disordered imagination. The scientist writes: if you want to know the truth, then here it is: you have *nothing* here—no family, no work, no time, no space, nor you yourself, you have made this all up. Agreed—we hear Savl's voice—as far as I can recall, I've never doubted that. And here we said: Savl Petrovich, but nevertheless something *is*, this is just as obvious as the fact that the river has a name. But, what, what specifically, teacher? And he answers: my dears, you might not believe me, your goatish, retired drummer, cynic and troublemaker, wind-driver and windvane, but believe the other person in me—the indigent citizen and poet who came in order to enlighten, to cast a spark into hearts and minds, so that people would be enflamed with hatred and a zeal for freedom. Now I shout with all my blood, the way one shouts of vengeance to come: there is nothing in the world, there is nothing in the world, there is nothing in the world—except The Wind! And The Sender—we asked. And The Sender too—replied the teacher. Water rumbled in the bowels of the unpainted radiators, outside strode the inexorable, indestructible polyped street, our stoker and guard rushed from one open boiler to another in the basement, with a shovel in his hand, muttering, and on the fourth floor the quadrille of fools boomed like cannon, shaking the foundations of the entire establishment.

So, our dacha stood drowning in the six-petalled lilac. But other people were bustling around in our garden now, not us, or possibly, it was us nevertheless, but rushing past ourselves towards Savl's we didn't recognize ourselves. We went down to the end of the street, turned left, and then—as often happens—right, and found ourselves on the edge of an oats field, beyond which, as you know the waters of the dacha Lethe stream and the Land of the Nightjar begins. On the road which bisects the oats field we ran into the postman Mikheev, or Medvedev. He was slowly riding his bicycle, and although there was no wind, the postman's bear was swept back in the wind, and from it—clump after clump—clumps of hair were flying as if it were not a beard but a cloud doomed by a storm. We said hello. But sullen—or just sad?—he didn't recognize us and didn't answer, and he rolled along in the direction of the water-tower. We looked after him and: have you seen Norvegov? not turning around, the embodiment of the postmanbicyclist, a monolith, a slave pinned dead to his saddle, Mikheev shouted hoarsely as a raven one word: *there*. And his hand, separating from the handlebar, made a gesture which subsequently was immortalized in a multitude of ancient ikons and frescoes: it was the hand witnessing goodness and the hand which gives, the inciting hand and the calming hand, the arm bent at the elbow and wrist—palm turned up to the flawlessly shining sky, the entire gesture serene and restrained. And this hand pointed *there*, in the direction of the river. O friends—interrupts Norvegov—I am glad that you ran into our esteemed postman on the way to see me, that's considered a good omen in our parts. But I'm getting anxious again, I want to go back to the conversation about that woman, I expect some new details from you. Tell me whom or what you could compare her to, give me a metaphor, a simile, otherwise I am unable to imagine her very distinctly. Dear retiree, we could compare her to the cry of a night bird embodied in human form, and also to the bloom of a withering chrysanthemum, and also to the ashes of burned-out love, yes, to ashes, to the breath of the breathless, to a phantom, moreover: the woman who opened unto us was grandmother's chalk angel, the one with the broken wing, the one—well, you probably know. So that's it—responds Savl—I am beginning to suspect the worst, I am in despair, but that cannot be, after all here I am chatting with you normally, I can hear your every word, I feel, I perceive, I see, and nevertheless it's as if, as it were, as follows from your descriptions...no, I still have the right not to believe it, not to acknowledge it, to say—no, isn't that right? Decisively. With disheveled gray hair. Gesticulating. Savl Petrovich, where the oats field ends—Lethe begins almost immediately. Its bank is rather high and precipitous, it consists for the most part of sand. Pine trees jut up on the very summit of the precipice, on a grassy flat. The other bank and the entire river are quite visible—upstream and downstream from this square. The river's color is a deep blue; it pushes its clean waters along solicitously, leisurely. As for its width, about that it would be best to ask those rare birds which. They fly out and do not return. Approaching the precipice we immediately saw your house—as always, it stood on the other bank, surrounded by foliage, with flowers swaying and teeming dragonflies. There were swifts and swallows too. And you, Savl Petrovich, you yourself were sitting by the water, with several fishing lines in, rods resting on special slingshot-like sticks. There were bites now and then, and the little bells attached to the saplings would tinkle and awaken you from noonday dreaming. You would awaken, hook and drag out the next grouse, or rather, gugdeon. No, no—remarks the geographer—I never once managed to catch a single fish, there simply aren't any fish in our Lethe, it was the tritons biting. I must say that they are not a bit inferior to crucian or perch, even better. Dried, they recall the taste of vobla, quite nice with beer. Sometimes I would sell them at the station: take a whole bucket and sell them, there, beside the beer stand. It used to be they'd dry out right before your eyes as you were carrying them, right there in the bucket, if it was hot, of course. And then we approached the precipice, saw you, sitting on the opposite sand, and when we said hello: hi, Savl Petrovich! are they biting? how do you do—you replied from the other bank—not much today, it's burning hot. We fell silent for a bit, one could hear Lethe flowing backwards. Then you asked: and you, my friends, why aren't you in class, why are you out strolling? No, no, Savl Petrovich, we have come for you. Did something happen in school? No, no, nothing, or rather, the following—it so happened that you didn't come for the examination today, mountain systems, rivers and other things—geography. Now how about that—you replied—but I can't today, don't feel so very well. What do you have, tonsils? Worse, boys, much worse. Savl Petrovich, wouldn't you like to come over to our side, you have a boat, but we don't have anything here, although our boat is here, the oars are locked in the shed, we have a present for you, we brought a cake. Dig in yourselves, friends—you said—I have no appetite at all, and besides I don't like sweets, thanks, don't be shy. All right—said we—we'll eat it right now. We untied the box, cut the cake into two equal parts with a penknife and started eating. A motorized barge went past, linen hanging on ropes on the deck, and an ordinary little girl swinging on the swing on deck. We waved the cake box-top to her, but the girl didn't notice because she was looking up at the sky. We quickly ate the cake and asked: Savl Petrovich, what should we tell Tinbergen and Perillo about when you'll *be*? I don't understand, can't hear—you replied—let the barge get past. We waited for the barge to get by, and said again: what should we tell Trachtenberg about when you'll *be*? Don't know how things will work out here, boys, the point is that obviously I won't come at all, say that as of this Tuesday I'm not working there any more, I'm quitting. But what is this, Savl Petrovich, we're very sorry, we'll miss you, this is unexpected. Don't grieve—you smiled—there are plenty of qualified pedagogues in the special without me. But from time to time I'll fly in, look in, we'll see each other, chat a bit, the devil take it. Savl Petrovich, but would it be possible for us, the whole class, to visit you on the other side next week? Come ahead, I wait joyously, only warn the others: no snacks are needed, complete loss of appetite. But what is your sickness, Savl Petrovich? It's not a sickness, friends, it's not a sickness—you said, standing up and rolling down the pants rolled up around your knees—the thing is that I *died*, you said—yes, still and all I did die, dammit, I died. Of course, your medicine is crap, but in these cases it's always precise, no mistakes, the diagnosis is a real diagnosis: *died*—you said—it's damn maddening. Irritatedly. Just as I thought—says Savl. Sitting on the windowsill, warming the naked bottoms of his feet on the radiator—when you mentioned the woman who opened the door, I immediately had a kind of bad premonition. Well it's clear, now I remember everything, she was a certain acquaintance of mine, or more likely even a relative. So what happened next, student so-and-so? We went back to town, went to school and told everyone what had happened to us, or rather, you. Immediately everyone was somehow aggrieved, the faces of many went dead and they cried, especially the little girls, especially Rosa... O Rosa!—says Savl—poor Rosa Windova. And then came the funeral, Savl Petrovich. You were buried on Thursday, you lay in the auditorium, a great many people came to pay their last respects: all the students, all the teachers, and almost all the parents. You see, they loved you awfully much, especially us, the specialschoolers. You know what's interesting: a huge globe was placed at the head of your coffin, the biggest one in the school, and those who served in the guard of honor took turns rotating it—it was beautiful and solemn. Our wind orchestraa played the whole time, five or six fellows, there were two horn, and the rest were drums, big ones and little ones, can you imagine that? Speeches were made, Perillo wept and swore that he would get the Ministry of People's Edufaketion to get the school renamed in honor of Norvegov, and Rosa—you know?— Rosa read some astonishing and beautiful poetry to us, she said she hadn't slept all night and wrote it. Really? But I somehow vaguely...can you remember at least a line or two? Just a second, a second, it seems, roughly like this:

I slumbered yesterday to the sound of seven winds,
So sepulchral and cold, to the sound of seven winds.
And Savl Petrovich died to the sound of seven winds.
I cannot sleep at home now to the sound of seven winds.
A god continues howling to the sound of seven winds.
And someone's walking very close, through snow and winds,
Walking toward my voice, and he whispers something to me,
And straining to reply, I called to him by name—
He came unto my gloomy tomb,
And suddenly he knew me.

O Rosa—says Savl in agony, my poor little girl, my tender one, I knew you, I recognized you, I thank you. Student so-and-so, I beg of you, take care of her for me, for our ancient friendship, Rosa is very sick. And please remind her not to forget, to visit me, she knows the way and the address. I still live in the same place, on the opposite bank, where the windmill is. Tell me, is she doing as superbly as before? Yes, yes, nothing but A's. And at this point we heard a rumbling, howling, screeching on the fourth floor, and then down the whole front stairs—from top to bottom—this meant that the rehearsal was over and rushing down, emptying out of the auditorium and towards the street. The fools of the choreographic ensemble careened to the cloakrooms in an instant, the entire idiotic mass, spitting in each other's faces, hallooing, grimacing, distorting their bodies, tripping each other, grunting and giggling. When we again turned our faces towards Savl Petrovich, he was no longer with us—the windowsill was empty. And outside the window strode the inexorable polyped street.

What a sad story, lad, how well I understand your feelings, the feelings of a student who has lost his favorite teacher. Something similar happened, by the way, in my own life. Would you believe it, I didn't become an Academician overnight, I had to lose more than a dozen teachers first. But still—continues Acatov—you promised to tell me about some book, your pedagogue apparently gave it to you that time. That slipped my mind totally, sir. He gave me that book during another meeting, either earlier or later, but with your permission, I'll tell you now. Savl Petrovich was sitting there again, on the windowsill, warming his feet. We had entered pensively: dear mentor, you probably know that the feeling which we have for our teacher of biobotany Veta Arcadievna are not void of sense and basis. Apparently our wedding is not on the far side of the mountain, with your permission to say so, systems. But we are utterly naive about certain delicate matters. Couldn't you, simply speaking, tell us how one has to do that, after all you had women. Women?—asks Savl again—yes, as far as I can remember, I did have women, but there's a catch here. You understand, I can't explain anything sensibly, I no longer know myself precisely how that goes. As soon as it's over, you immediately forget everything. I don't remember a single woman of all those I had. That is, I remember only the names, faces, and clothes they were wearing, their individual utterances, smiles, tears, their anger, but on the subject you are asking about, I will say nothing—I don't remember, I don't remember. For all of that is structured rather on feelings than on sensations, and in any event certainly not on common sense. And feelings—well, they are somehow transitory. And I'll make just one remark here: every time *it* is precisely the same as it was the previous time, but simultaneously it is totally different and new. But no time is like the first time, the only time with the first woman. But I won't say a word in general about the first time, because there's absolutely nothing to compare it to, and we still haven't invented a single word that one can say about it and not be saying nothing. Ecstatically. With the smile of one who is dreaming about the impossible. But here's a book for you—continued Norvegov, pulling a book from inside his bosom—I have it merely by chance, it's not mine, someone gave it to me for a couple of days, so you take it, read it, maybe you'll find something there for yourself. Thanks—we said, and went to read, reading. Sir, that was a fine translated brochure by a certain German professor, it was about the family and marriage, and as soon as I opened it everything immediately became clear to me. I read only one page, opened at random, approximately page such-and-such—and then immediately returned the book to Savl, inasmuch as I understood everything. And what precisely, lad? I understood precisely how my life with Veta Arcadievna would go, what its bases would be. It was all written there. I memorized the whole page. This is what was printed there: "He (that is, I, sir) was away for several days. He missed her, and she (that is, Veta Arcadievna) him. Should they (that is, we) conceal this from each other as is often done—as a result of incorrect upbringing? No. He returns home and sees that everything is very nicely cleaned (Arcady Arcadievich, you will certainly be hanging in our living room, that is, your full-length portrait, this evening it would be decorated with flowers). As if by the way she says, "Your bath is ready. I've already put out your linen. I've already taken mine." (Can you imagine that, sir?) How marvelous that she is happy and in anticipation of love has already prepared everything for it. "He desires her, but she desires him too, and she gives him to understand this with no false modesty." You understand, sir? *desires* me, Veta *desires desires* with no false.... I understand, lad, I understand. But you haven't grasped my idea quite accurately. I had something else in mind. I was hinting not so much about the spiritual and physiological bases of your relationship, as at the material ones. More simply put, what do you intend to live on, what are the means, what is your income? Let's suppose within a short time Veta does consent to marry you, well, what then? do you intend to go to work or school? Bah! So that's what you are worried about, sir, though I did surmise that you would ask about that too... But, you see, I will probably graduate from our specschool in a very short time, apparently as a correspondence student. And I will immediately enter one of the divisons of some engineering institute: like all of my classmates, I dream of becoming an engineer. I will quickly—if not to say *headlong*—become an engineer, buy a car and so forth. So don't worry, I would appreciate it if you accepted me as a potential student, no less. If you like, if you like, but in that case what of all your discussion of butterflies? You told me about a large collection, I was certain that a young colleague of promise was standing before me, and here it turns out that for the last hour I have been dealing with an engineer of the future. O, I made a mistake, sir, becoming an engineer is the dream of that *other* one, the one who isn't here now, although he may glance in here every minute or so. Me—not for anything, it would be better to do the humblest work, to be the apprentice of some bleak cobbler, to be a Negro of advanced age, but an engineer—no, not for anything, and don't even ask me to. I have decided resolutely: only to be a biologist, like you, like Veta Arcadievna, for my whole life—a biologist, and mainly in the area of butterflies. I have a little surprise for you, Arcady Arcadievich, in a day or so I intend to ship my collection off to the Academy entomology competiton, several thousand butterflies. I've already prepared the letter. I trust that success will not make me wait long, and am confident that my future accomplishments will not leave you indifferent either, and that you will rejoice together with me. Sir, sir, just imagine, it's morning, one of the first mornings which find Veta and me together. Somewhere here, at the dacha—at yours or at ours, it makes no difference. Morning, full of hopes and happy premonitions, a morning which is marked by the news of my being awarded the Academy prize. The morning which we will never forget, because—well, I don't have to explain to you precisely why: can a scientist be allowed to forget the instant when he first tasted fame! One of those mornings....

Student so-and-so, allow me, the author, to interrupt you and tell how I imagine to myself the moment when you receive the long-awaited letter from the Academy, like you, I have a pretty good imagination, I think I can. Of course, go ahead—he says.

Let's suppose it's one such morning—let's suppose it's one Saturday in July—the postman named Mikheev, or perhaps Medvedev (he is rather old, obviously not under seventy, he lives on his pension and also the half salary he receives in the mail for distributing newspapers and letters, for being deliverer of telegrams and various messages which, by the way, he carries not in the usual postman's bag, but in a bag extraordinary for a postman—his bag—an ordinary shopping bag made of black leatherette—not on a strap across his shoulder, but on the usual handstrings, slipped over his bicycle handlebars), thus, one Saturday morning in July postman Mikheev stops his bicycle alongside your house and, oldmanishly, in a pensioner's awkward way, hops off into the bitter roadside dust, the yellow roadside dust, the light and flying dust of the road, and presses the rusty button of his bicycle bell. The bell strives to ring, but there is hardly any sound, since the bell is virtually dead, because many of its crucial internal gears are extremely worn down, they've abraded each other in the course of long service, and the tiny hammer fastened to the spring is virtually immobilized by rust. But nevertheless, this morning as you sit on the open veranda, which is enveloped in your father's merrily chirping garden, you hear the croak of this dying bell, or more accurately, you don't hear it, but sense it. You go down the veranda steps, you stride across the merry, bee-filled garden, you open the gate, see Mikheev, exchange greetings: hello, postman Mikheev (Medvedev). Hello, he says, I've brought you a letter from the Academy. Here, thanks, you say, smiling, although there is no point to your smile, since your smile won't change anything either in your everyday relations or in the fate of the suntanned old postman, as it hadn't been changed by thousands of other smiles, smiles precisely like this, smiles which didn't oblige anyone to anything, ones which he encountered every day at hundreds of dacha and even non-dacha gates, doors, exits and breaks in the fence. And you can't help agreeing with me, you un-der-stand all this perfectly well yourself, but the custom of polite gestures, which you have been urged to observe since childhood in school and at home, func-tions independently, apart from your consciousness: saying to Mikheev, here, thanks—you take a yellow envelope out of his aging, veined hand and—you smile. During one moment of your brief meeting, your tradi-tional, i.e., unnecessary dialogue, unnecessary to either of you but some-how essential ("Hello, postman Mikheev," "Hello, I've brought you a letter from the Academy," "Here, thanks"), during one hour of merry, light blue boats slipping, slipping across the river Lethe, which is invisible from here, and across other invisible rivers, his hand—blue and speckled with age and ugly from birth—holds out a yellow envelope to you and slightly touches your hand—young, dark from tan, and essentially free of wrinkles. Can it be—you reflect during that second—can it be that my hand will get like that someday too? But you immediately set yourself at ease: no, no, it won't, after all I run conditioning wind sprints in school, Mikheev didn't. That's why his hands are like that—you conclude, smiling. "Here, thanks." "You're welcome," Mikheev (Medvedev) murmurs indistinctly and without a smile, suburban distributor of letters and telegrams, deliverer of messages and newspapers, an old man, pensioner-postman, somber bicyclist with the usual extraordinary bag on his handlebars, a pensive man, gloomy and bibulous. Not looking back at you or the garden full of bluebirds, and just as awkwardly as he had dismounted a minute ago, he mounts his bicycle and, clumsily pedaling, takes his, or rather others', letters in the direction of the rest home and watertower, in the direction of the settlement outskirts, flowering meadows, butterflies and silver hazelnut trees. He's slightly hung over, he should probably hurry up the delivery of the remaining literature and letters, even if they're all bad ones, and then head home, mix a small quantity of water and spirits—his old lady works as a janitress in the local hospital, and this substance never gets used up at home, though it is put to good use—and after snacking on a slightly salted tomato from an oaken tub (in the cellar where it stands there are spiders, cold, germinating potatoes, and a smell of mould), go off somewhere among the pines, among the rowan trees, or among those hazelnut tress beyond the watertower, and sleep in the shade till the sun stops parching. When a postman is past seventy there's no need for him to go riding around all day in heat like this, he's got to rest too! But there are still some letters in the bag: someone is writing someone, someone isn't too lazy to reply, even though they have to borrow an envelope from a neighbor every time, buy a stamp, remember an address and walk through the heat to find a box. Yes, there are still a few letters left, and they have to be delivered. and there he goes now, in the direction of the watertower. The path, barely marked out in the uncut grass, goes uphill, and Mikheev's feet, which are shod in black shoes with high heels, almost like women's, slip off the pedals now and then, and when this happens the handlebars stop submitting to the letter carrier, the front wheel tries to stand against the motion of the other parts of this uncomplex machine, the wheel gives a skid, during which its spokes cut off the tops of some dandelions—the white seed parachutes are swept up and slowly descend on Mikheev (Medvedev), bestrewing the old mailman as if they intended to impregnate his black felt and wool hat and side-buttoning shirt, which is no doubt very sticky in this kind of weather. The little parachutes also descend on his pants, which are made of rubberized cloth, and one leg of which—the right—is pinned above Mikheev's ankle by a light linden clothespin so that the material, contrary to expectation, won't get caught in the gear mechanism—chain, small sprocket connected to the back wheel by means of a bushing, large sprocket with pedal mechanisms welded to it—otherwise Mikheev would immediately tumble into the grass and flowers, spilling all the letters as he did so. They would be caught up by the wind and taken across the river, into the backwater meadows: it had already happened, or it could happen, and therefore—it was as if it had happened—and what could an old mailman do then except take a boat from the ferryman and cross over, cross the river, capture and collect his, or more precisely, others', letters. Because somehow people do find time to write, there are still those who have the patience for this, but not to consider that all it takes is for Mikheev to fall off his bicycle one fine morning, and all their idiotic scribblings, all these contratulatory postcards and so-called urgent telegrams can go flying across the river—not a one of them ever thought about that even once, for each person tries not to fall himself, from his own bicycle, and then of course they don't care about an old letter carrier who hasn't known anything all his life except delivering their wretched scrawls from house to house. The wind—Mikheev (Medvedev) tells himself in an undertone—the wind is just in the upper air somehow, nowhere else, it's blowing up a rain. But that's not true: there is no wind of either lofty or lowly sort. And it will be at least a week before rain pours down on the settlement, and all that time it will be fair and windless, and the daytime sky will be coated blue Whatman paper, and the night sky—black carnival silk studded with big glistening stars of multicolored foil. As for Mikheev—he's just deceiving himself now, he's just sick of this heat, these letters, this bicycle, these indifferently polite addressees who always smile when they greet him at the gates to their gardens with their throbbing, ripening apples, and he, Mikheev, wants to give himself hope of at least some change in this stiflingly hot, boring and monotonous dacha life which, it would seem, he belongs to, but in which he scarcely takes part, although everyone who has his house here or on the other side of the river knows Mikheev by sight; and when he comes on his ancient velocipede with the soundless bell, the dacha people he meets smile to Mikheev, but he looks them over, gloomily or sadly, or in an old man's pensive way, as if admiring them, and then rolls on silently—towards the station, or the wharf, or—as now—on the watertower. Silently. Mikheev is nearsighted, he wears rimless glasses, from time to time he lets a beard grow and from time to time he shaves it off, or maybe, it is shaved off by the wind, but both with the beard and without, in the minds of the dacha folk he is a singular specimen—elderly dreamer, amateur of bicycle riding, and master of postal manipulations. The wind—he continues lying to himself—there'll certainly be a storm by nightfall, a thunderstorm, it'll ruffle up all the gardens, they'll be wet and ruffled, and the cats—ruffled and wet: they'll hide in the cellars, under the porches of the dachas, flood all these samovars boiling on verandas along with the smoky kerosene lamps, it will flood the mailboxes on the fences, and all the letters that are now lying in his sack, and which he will soon distribute to the boxes, will turn into nothing, into empty sheets of paper, words washed away or turned into gibberish, and the boats— these idiotic, rag-tag rowboats used by the loafers from the rest home and the dacha boaters—these boats, upside down, will float along in the current to the sea itself. Yes—muses Mikheev—the wind will turn this whole garden-samovar life upside down and conquer the dust at least temporarily. "Dust"—the pensioner suddenly recalls something he once read somewhere—"the breeze will build silver keels out of dust!" That's it, out of dust, Mikheev analyzes, and precisely, keels, that is, keels for boats, keeled boats, ergo, and not flatbottomed ones—may they all be empty. If only the wind would hurry up and come. "Wind in the fields, wind in the poplars," Mikheev cited, again in his mind, at the point where the path bends to the right and goes a bit downhill. Now to the bridge itself, across the ravine where burdock grows in abundance and snakes no doubt live, one can leave the pedals alone and give one's feet a rest: let the legs hang freely, jouncing on either side of the frame, not touching the pedals, and let the machine roll on by itself—to meet the wind. The Sender of Wind?—you wonder of Mikheev. You no longer see him, as they sometimes said, he's disappeared around a turn—melted in the July dacha heatwave. Bestrewn with the flying seeds of dandelions, risking with every meter of his bicycle's rush the loss of those summer postcards written from nothing to do, with his old man's veined hands, he is now rushing forward to meet that of which he has dreamed. He is full of cares and anxieties, he has virtually been thrown overboard from dacha life, and this he does not like. Poor Mikheev—you think—soon, soon your woes will leave you, and you yourself will become a metallic head-wind, a mountain dandelion, the ball of a six-year-old girl, the pedal of a highway bicycle, universal military service, the aluminum of aerodromes, the ashes of forest fires, you'll become smoke, the smoke of rhythmical food and textile factories, the screech of viaducts, the pebbles of the sea shores, the light of day and the pods of prickly acacias. Or—you'll become the road, part of the road, a stone of the road, a roadside bush, a shadow on the winter road you'll become, you will be eternal. Happy Mikheev. Medvedev?

I think you told about our postman beautifully, dear author, and it wasn't a bad description of the morning when the letter was received, I certainly wouldn't have been able to do it so graphically, you're very talented, and I'm glad that it was you who took upon yourself the work of writing about me, about all of us, such an interesting story, I really don't know anyone else who could have done it so successfully, thanks. Student so-and-so, your high evaluation of my humble work pleases me very very much, you know, of late I have been trying hard, I write several hours a day, and the rest of the hours—when I'm not writing, that is—I meditate about how to write better the next day, how to write so that all future readers will like it, and, above all, naturally, you, the heroes of the book: Savl Petrovich, Veta Arcadievna, Arcady Arcadievich, you, the Nympheae, your parents, Mikheev (Medvedev), and even Perillo. But I fear that he, Nikolai Gorimirovich, won't like it: still and all he is, as they used to write in novels, *a little too* tired and gloomy. I suspect that if my book comes into his hands he'll call your father—as I recall, he and your father are old army buddies, they served together with Kutuzov himself—and he'll say: do you know, he'll say, about the pasquinade that's been made up about us? No, the prosecutor will say, what's it like? Anti-us, the director will say. And who's the author?—the prosecutor will ask curiously—give me the author. Writer so-and-so—the director will report. And I'm afraid that after that there will be great unpleasantnesses for me, up to and including the most unpleasant, I'm afraid they'll immediately ship me off *there*, to Doctor Zauze. That's right, dear author, that's precisely the area where our father works, the area of unpleasantnesses, but why do you insist on having your real name indicated on the title page, why don't you take a *mynoduesp*? Then they wouldn't be able to find you even if you're right under their noses. Generally speaking, not a bad idea, I will probably do that, but then I will feel uncomfortable before Savl: daring and irreproachable, the geographer moved openly against everyone, infuriated. He might think badly of me, decide perhaps that I'm not good for anything—neither as a poet, nor as a citizen, and his opinion means a great deal to me. Student so-and-so, please advise me how to handle this. Dear author, it seems to me that though Savl Petrovich is not with us, and apparently is no longer thinking about us, nevertheless it would be better to act the way he himself, our teacher, would have acted in the analogous situation, he wouldn't have assumed a pseudonym. I see, and thank you, and now I want to find out your opinion about the name of the book... Everything would seem to indicate that our narrative is approaching its end, and it's time to decide what title we will put on the cover. Dear author, I would call your book A SCHOOL FOR FOOLS: you know, there is a School for Piano Playing, a School for Playing the Barracuda, so let it be A SCHOOL FOR FOOLS, some readers will be surprised: it's called A SCHOOL, but the story is about only two or three students, and where, they'll argue, are the rest, where are all those youthful characters, astonishing in their variety, in which our schools today are so rich! Don't worry, dear author, let your readers know, yes, tell them bluntly that student so-and-so asked you to let them know that in the whole school, except for the two of us, and maybe Rosa Windova, there is absolutely nothing of interest, there is no astonishing variety in it, everyone there is an awful fool, say that Nymphea said that you can only write about him, because it is only about him that you should write, inasmuch as he is so much superior to and more intelligent than the rest, which even Perillo admits, so when speaking about the school for fools it's sufficient to tell about student so-and-so—and everything will instantaneously become clear, just pass that on, and in general why are you concerned about who says or thinks what out there, after all the book is yours, dear author, you've a right to do with us, the heroes and titles, as you like, so, as Savl

Petrovich remarked, when we asked him about the tort—dig in: A SCHOOL FOR FOOLS. All right, I agree, but still, just in case, let's fill a few more pages with a chat about something related to the school, let's tell the readers about a botany lesson, for example, after all they are conducted by Veta Arcadievna Acatova, for whom you have so long cherished these feelings. Yes, dear author, I'll be glad to, it pleases me so much, I suppose that it won't be long before everything will finally be resolved, our inter-relations are becoming more and more sharply defined, as if they weren't relations, but a boat floating along the bemisted Lethe on an early morning when the fog is breaking up and the boat keeps getting closer, yes, let's write a few more pages about my Veta, but I, as so often happens, I can't figure out how to begin, with what words—prompt me. Student so-and-so, it seems to me it would be best to begin with the words: *and then*.

And then she came in. She came into the biology department office, where two skeletons stood in the corners. One was artificial, but the other—real. The school administration purchased them in a specialized store called SKELETONS, in the center of our city, moreover, the real ones there cost far more than the artificial ones—that's understandable, and it's hard to function outside this *efemoral* framework. One day, as we were passing SKELETONS together with our kind, beloved mother—this was shortly after the death of Savl Petrovich—we saw him standing in the show window, where samples of wares were displayed along with the hanging sign: *Skeletons from the Population Received Here*. You remember, autumn was setting in, the whole street was shrouded in long mousquetair cloaks, and it had been splattered with mud by the wheels and hooves of frozen phaetons and disheveled drozhkys, and no one talked about any-thing but the weather, regretting the lost summer. And Savl Petrovich—unshaven and skinny—stood in the showcase wearing just his sport shirt and sail pants, turned up to his knees, and externally the only concession to autumn were the galoshes on his bare feet. Mama saw the teacher and her hands flurried up in their black knit gloves: Lord, Pavel Petrovich, what are you doing here in such bad weather, you have no face on, all you're wearing is a shirt and pants, you'll catch your death of pneumonia, where's your nice warm good suit, and your covert coat, the farewell gifts we gave you, and the hat that we all took such a long time picking out together, the entire parents' committee! Ah, dear mama—replied Savl, smiling—don't you worry, for Allah's sake, everything'll be all right with me, better take care of your son, look, he's already got a runny nose, and as for the clothes I have this to say: to hell with them, a pox on them, I can't stand them, they choke me, they pull in one place, they pinch and crush, don't you under-stand? All of this stuff was alien, unearned, not purchased with my own money—so I sold it. Careful—Norvegov took mama under the arm—the omnibus will splatter you, get away from the edge. And why—she asked trying to free herself from his touch as quickly as possible, and she made this too obvious—what are you doing here, by such a strange store? I have just sold my skeleton—said the teacher—I sold it in advance, bequeathed my skeleton to our school. But why—mama asks in surprise—isn't *that* very costly to you? Very, dear mama, very costly, but one has to earn one's daily bread somehow: if you want to go on living, you have to know how to make do, isn't that so? You must know that I'm no longer on the school payroll, and you won't make ends meet for very long if you have to get by on just private lessons: just think about it—are there so many failures in my subject in today's schools? All right, all right—said mama—all right. And mama didn't say anything else, we turned around and walked on. Good-bye Savl Petrovich! When we get like you, that is, when we don't exist any more, we'll bequeath our skeletons to our beloved school too, and then whole generations of fools—straight A-students, B-students, and D-students—will study the structure of human bonery from our un-mouldering remains. Dear Savl Petrovich, is that not the shortest route to the immortality for which we all so fervently yearn when we find ourselves alone with ambition! When she came in, we rose and stood in front of the skeletons, so that she couldn't see them, but when we sat down, the skeletons remained standing and she saw them again. That's right, they always stood—on black metal tripods. Admit it, you love them a little, especially that one, the real one. Well I'm not hiding the fact, I really did love them and still do, to this time, after many years, I love them because they somehow exist on their own, they are independent and calm in all situations, especially the one in the left corner whom we call Savl. Listen, what were those incomprehensible words you just uttered—*to this time, after many years*—what do you mean, I don't understand, what are we—do you mean we aren't in the school any more, aren't we studying botany, running strengthening wind sprints, carrying white slippers in little bags, writing explanatory notes about lost faith? Perhaps not, perhaps we're not writing, not running and not studying, the school has been without us for a long time, either we graduated with honors, or we were expelled for stupidity—I don't remember now. Good, but then what did you and I do all those years after school? We worked. Oh-ho, but where, as what? O, in the most varied places. First we worked in the prosecutor's office with father, he took us on there as pencil sharpeners, and we sat in on many judicial hearings. In those days our father had initiated a case against the late Norvegov. But what was it, can the teacher have done something wrong? Yes, in spite of the new law about windvanes, prescribing the destruction of the same when located on roofs and in the yards of private houses, Savl didn't take down his windvane and our father demanded the court and lay assessors try the geographer under the most severe article. He was tried in absentia and sentenced to supreme punishment. Damn it, but why didn't anyone intercede for him? Here and there people learned about the Norvegov case, there were demonstrations, but the sentence remained in force. Then we worked as yard-men in the Ministry of Agitation, and one of the ministers often called us in to his office in order, over a cup of tea, to consult about the weather. They respected us, and we were in good repute and considered valuable members of the collective, for no one else in the Ministry had faces as frightened as ours. They were getting ready to promote us, transfer us to elevator duty, but at that point we made a certain declaration, at the wave of a wand, and on the recommendation of Doctor Zauze we entered Leonardo's studio. We were students in his studio in the moat of the Milan fortress. We were only humble students, but how much that celebrated artist owed to us, students so-and-so! We helped him observe flying on four wings, we mixed clay, carried marble, built projectiles, but mainly we pasted cardboard boxes and guessed rebuses. And one day he asked us: youth, I am working on a certain woman's portrait right now and I've already finished painting it except the face; I'm in a quandary, I'm old, my imagination refuses to work the way it used to, advise me, what, in our opinion, should the face be like. And we said: it should be the face of Veta Arcadievna Acatova, our favorite teacher, when she enters class for the day's lesson. That's an idea, said the old master, so describe her face for me, describe it, I want to see this person. And we describe it. Soon we quit Leonardo's: got bored, eternally having to grind colors, and there's nothing that would get your hands clean. Then we worked as controllers, conductors, switchmen, inspectors of railroad postal divisions, janitors, excavators, glaziers, night watchmen, ferrymen on the river, druggists, carpenters in the desert, haulers, stikers, as starters, or rather—captives, or more precisely, as sharpeners of pencils. We worked there and here, here and there—everywhere there was a possibility of laying on, that is, using our hands. And wherever we came, people said of us: look, there they are—Those Who Came. Greedy for knowledge, daring lovers of truth, heirs of Savl, his principles and declarations, we were proud of each other. Our life all those years was extraordinarily interesting and full, but during all its vicissitudes we never forgot our special school and our teachers, especially Veta Arcadievna. We usually imagined her at the moment when she entered class, when we were standing looking at her, and everything that we knew about anything else before this became totally unnecessary, stupid, stripped of sense—and in an instant flies off like a husk, a rind, or a bird. Why don't you tell exactly what she looked like when she came in, why not give, as Vodokachka says, a letter-of-recommendation portrait? No, no, impossible, useless, that will just overburden our talk, we'll get tangled in definitions and subtleties. But you just reminded me of Leonardo's request. Then, in his studio, we, it seems, did manage to describe Veta. Managed, but our description was laconic, for then too we could not say anything more than what we said: dear Leonardo, imagine a woman, she is so beautiful that when you look into her eyes you cannot say *no* to your joyous tears. And—thanks, youth, thanks—replied the artist—that's sufficient, I already see that person. Good, but in that case at least describe the biology room and us, those who at first were standing, and then sat down, tell briefly about those of our classmates who were present at the lesson. The stuffed birds were there, the aquariums and terrariums were there, the portrait of the scientist Pavlov riding a bicycle at the age of ninety hung there, hanging, there were pots and boxes with grasses and flowers on the windowsills, including plants very ancient and distant, some from the Chalk Age. Moreover—a collection of butterflies and herbariums, gathered by the efforts of generations. And we were there, lost in the bushes, cushes and shoots, amid the microscopes, the falling leaves and colored plaster casts of human and inhuman innards—and we studied. Please enumerate the ships that were on the river rolls—or, to be more exact, now tell about us, those sitting there. Right now I don't recall any of the names, but I do recall that among us there was, for example, a boy who if challenged could eat several flies in a row, there was a girl who would suddenly stand up and strip naked because she thought she had a pretty figure—naked. There was a boy who kept his hand in his pocket for long periods of time, he couldn't help it, because he was weakwilled. There was a girl who wrote letters to herself and answered them herself. There was a boy with very small hands. And there was a girl with very large eyes, with a long black braid and long lashes, she was a straight-A student, but she died approximately in the tenth grade, soon after Norvegov, for whom she had joyous and tormented feelings, and he, our Savl Petrovich, loved her too. They loved each other at his place in the dacha, on the shores of enchanting Lethe, and here, in school, on the discarded gym mats on the landings of the back stairs, to the thump of Perillo's methodical pendulum. And, possibly, it was precisely this girl that we and teacher Savl called Rosa Windova. Yes, possibly, but possibly such a girl never existed, and we invented her ourselves, just like everything else in the world. That's why when your patient mother asks you: and the girl, did she really die?—then: I don't know, about the girl I know nothing—is what you must answer. And then she walked in, our Veta Arcadievna. Up on the platform, she would open the class-register and call on someone: student so-and-so, tell us about rhododendrons. He would begin to say something, to talk, but no matter what he said and no matter what other people and scientific botany books said about the rhododendrons, no one could ever say the main things about rhododendrons—do you hear me, Veta Arcadievna:—the main thing: that they, the rhododendrons, growing every minute somewhere in Alpine meadows, are far happier than we, for they know neither love, nor hate, nor the Perillo slipper system, and they don't even die, since all nature, excepting man, is one undying, indestructible whole. If one tree somewhere in the forest perishes from old age, before dying, it gives the wind so many seeds, and so many new trees grow up around it on the land, near and far, that the old tree, especially the rhododendron—and a rhododendron, Veta Arcadievna, which is probably a huge tree with leaves the size of wash basins—doesn't mind dying. And the tree is indifferent, it just grows there on the silvery hill, or the new one does, after it has grown up out of its seeds. No, the tree doesn't mind. Or the grass, or the dog, or the rain. Only man minds and feels bitter, burdened as he is with egotistical pity for himself. Remember, even Savl, who devoted himself entirely to science and its students, said, after dying, it's damned maddening.

Student so-and-so, allow me, the author, to interrupt your narrative again. The thing is that it's time to end the book: I'm out of paper. True, if you intend to add two or three more stories from your life, I'll run to the store and buy several more packages right now. With pleasure, dear author, I'd like to, but you won't believe it anyway. I could tell about our marriage to Veta Arcadievna, about our great happiness together, and also about what happened in our dacha settlement one day when The Sender finally got down to work: that day the river overflowed its banks, flooded all the dachas and carried off all the boats. Student so-and-so, that is extremely interesting and it strikes me as totally believable, so let's go get the paper together, and along the way you tell my everything in order and in detail. Let's go—says Nymphea. Merrily gabbing and recounting pocket change, slapping each other on the shoulders and whistling foolish songs, we walk out into the polyped street and in some miraculous manner are transformed into passersby.

Translated by Carl R. Proffer

Yury Trifonov

THE EXCHANGE

In July Dmitriev's mother, Ksenya Fyodorovna, became seriously ill. They took her to Botkin hospital where she spent twelve days suspecting the worst. In September they operated on her and the worst was confirmed, but Ksenya Fyodorovna, thinking that she had ulcers, felt better, began to walk soon after, and in October was sent home weighing more and firmly convinced that things were on the mend. It was at that moment, after Ksenya Fyodorovna came back from the hospital, that Dmitriev's wife began the business about an exchange: she had decided to move in as quickly as possible with her mother-in-law, who lived alone in a nice twenty-by-sixteen room on Profsoyuznaya Street.

Dmitriev himself had raised the idea of moving in with his mother many times. But that had been long ago, at a time when the relationship between Lena and Ksenya Fyodorovna had not yet assumed the form of such hardened and solid enmity that it had now, after fourteen years of Dmitriev's marriage. He had always run up against Lena's firm opposition, and the idea had come up less and less over the years. And then only in moments of irritation. It had turned into a portable and comfortable *handy object*, a weapon in minor family skirmishes. When Dmitriev wanted to get Lena for something, accuse her of egotism or callousness, he would say: "And that's why you don't want to live with my mother." When Lena felt the need to taunt or to hit a sore spot, she would say: "And that's why I can't live with your mother, and never will, because you are the very image of her, and one of you is enough for me."

At one time all this had bothered and distressed Dmitriev. On account of his mother he had harsh words with his wife, driven to extreme animosity because of some malicious witticisms made by Lena; on account of his wife he let himself in for a painful "clearing of the air" with his mother, after which his mother didn't talk to him for several days. He stubbornly tried to throw them together, reconcile them, settle them together at the dacha; and once he bought them both vouchers for the Riga seashore, but nothing ever really came of it.

Some barrier stood between the two women, and they could not overcome it. Why it was like that he did not understand, although he'd often thought it over in the past. Why two intelligent women, respected by all—Ksenya Fyodorovna was the senior bibliographer of a major academic library; Lena translated English technical texts, she was an excellent translator, everyone said, and she had even taken part in the compilation of some special textbook of translation—why had two good women who dearly loved Dmitriev, also a good person, and his daughter Natashka, stubbornly cultivated mutual hostility which had grown harder with the years?

He was upset, amazed, racked his brains, but then he got used to it. He got used to it because he saw that the same thing had happened to all of them—they had all gotten used to it. And he soothed himself with the truism that there is nothing wiser or more valuable in life than peace, and that one must protect it with all one's strength. Therefore, when Lena suddenly began to talk of an exchange with the Markusheviches—it was late in the evening, supper had long been over, Natashka was sleeping—Dmitriev was frightened. Who were the Markusheviches? Where did she find them? A two-room apartment on Malaya Gruzinskaya. He understood Lena's simple secret thought, and his comprehension made fear pierce his heart and he grew pale, then bent over, unable to raise his eyes to Lena.

Since he was silent Lena continued: they would be sure to like his mother's room on Profsoyuznaya; the location would suit them because Markushevich's wife worked somewhere near Kaluga Gate, and they would probably have to add a premium for their room. Otherwise you wouldn't get them interested. One could of course try to exchange their room for something more worthwhile, that would be a third exchange, nothing so terrible about that. Must act energetically. Do something every day. The best thing would be to find an agent. Lucy knew an agent, a little old man, very nice. True, he couldn't give anybody his address or telephone number; he would just suddenly appear out of nowhere, such a conspirator, but he was supposed to make an appearance at Lucy's soon, she owed him money. That's the rule: never give them money in advance....

As she was talking, Lena made the bed. There was no way he could look her in the eye: now he wanted to, but Lena stood first sideways, then with her back to him, but when she turned and he glanced straight into her eyes, which were nearsighted, with enlarged pupils from the evening's reading, he saw—resolution. She'd probably been preparing for this conversation for a long time, maybe since the first day she'd found out about his mother's illness. Then it had come to her. And while he, terror-stricken, was running around to the doctors, calling the hospitals, making arrangements, being miserable—she had been considering, mulling it over. And now she'd found some Markusheviches. Strange that he felt neither anger nor pain now. Only something flashed by—about the ruthlessness of life. Lena wasn't the thing, she was a part of this life, a part of the ruthlessness of life. Besides, does one get angry at a person who is deprived, for example, of an ear for music? Lena had always been distinguished by a certain spiritual—no, not deafness, that would be too strong—by a certain spiritual imprecision, and this characteristic was further intensified whenever another even stronger quality of Lena's came into action: the ability to get her own way.

He latched on to what was handy: why did they need the agent if the apartment on Gruzinskaya had already been found? The agent's needed if it's necessary to change rooms. And to speed the whole process in general. She wouldn't pay him a kopek until she had the order in her hand. It doesn't cost so much, a hundred rubles, one hundred fifty maximum. That's how it is! She assessed his gloominess in her own way. Such a refined soul, such a little psychologist. He said that it would be better if she'd waited until he'd started this conversation himself, and if he didn't that meant it wasn't necessary, not at all, that this wasn't the time to think about it.

"Vitya, I understand. Forgive me," said Lena with an effort. "But...." (He saw that it was hard for her, but that she was going to get it all out.) "In the first place, you began this conversation already, didn't you? You started it many times. Secondly, this is necessary for all of us, most of all for your mama. Vitka, my dearest, I understand you, I feel for you like no one else does, and I say: it's necessary! Believe me...."

She embraced him. Her arms hugged him tighter and tighter. He knew: this sudden love was genuine. But he felt irritated and he moved her away by the elbow.

"You shouldn't have started it now," he repeated sullenly.

"Well, all right, so I'm sorry. But I'm not worrying about myself, really, really...."

"Be quiet!" he almost screamed in a whisper.

Lena went over to the turkish mattress and continued making the bed in silence. Out of the chest at the head of the mattress she took the thick, plaid tablecloth which usually served as a pad under the sheets, but which was occasionally used for its proper purpose on the dinner table; on top of the tablecloth she lay the sheet which had puffed up and lay not too evenly, so Lena bent over, stretching her arms out in front, to reach the far side of the mattress—her face reddened from it, and her belly hung down very low and seemed very big to Dmitriev,—she smoothed out the tucked-under corners (when Dmitriev made the bed he never smoothed the corners), then she threw two pillows on the bed in the direction of the chest, one of which had a case that was less fresh than the other; that pillow belonged to Dmitriev. Taking the two blankets out of the chest and putting them on the mattress, Lena said in a trembling voice:

"It's as if you're blaming me for tactlessness, but word of honor, Vitya, I was really thinking of all of us.... Of Natashka's future...."

"Oh, how can you!"

"What?"

"How can you talk about it at all right now? How can your tongue work? That's what amazes me." He felt that the irritation was going to grow and break out into the open. "For God's sake, you've got some kind of spiritual defect in you. A kind of underdevelopment of feelings. Something, forgive me, *subhuman*. How can you? The thing is that *my mother* is sick and not yours, right? And if I were in your place...."

"Talk softer."

"In your place I would never first...."

"Softer!" She waved her hand.

They both listened. No, everything was quiet. Their daughter was sleeping behind the screen in the corner. Behind the screen there stood a little desk at which she did her homework each evening. Dmitriev had played carpenter and had hung a bookshelf over the desk, and put in electricity for the lamp—he had made a special little room behind the screen, the "cell" as it was called in the family. Dmitriev and Lena slept on a wide turkish mattress of Czechoslovakian make, luckily purchased some three years before, which was an object of envy among their acquaintances. The mattress was by the window, separated from the "cell" by a carved oak buffet which had come to Lena from her grandmother,—a ridiculous thing which Dmitriev had many times suggested selling, Lena also not being against the idea, but his mother-in-law had objected. Vera Lazarevna lived not far away, two buildings from them and came to Lena's almost daily on the pretext of "helping Natashenka" and "making things easier for Lenusha," but in actual fact with one sole aim—to unforgivably interfere in someone else's life.

In the evening when they were lying on their Czech bed—which turned out to be not very durable, quickly getting rickety and squeaking with every move—Dmitriev and Lena always listened a long time for sounds from the "cell," trying to figure out whether their daughter had gone to sleep or not. Dmitriev would call, checking, in an undertone: "Natash! Hey, Natash!" Lena would go up on tiptoe and look through the crack in the screen. Some six years earlier they'd gotten a nurse who had slept on a cot here in the room. Their neighbors, the Fandeevs, had objected to her sleeping in the hall. The old lady suffered from insomnia and was possessed of the keenest hearing; all night long she would mutter something, groan, and listen: a mouse was scratching, a cockroach was running, someone had forgotten to turn off the faucet in the kitchen. When the old lady left, something like a honeymoon began for the Dmitrievs.

"She was doing physics till eleven again," said Lena in a whisper. "We'd better get someone.... Antonina Alexeevna has a good tutor."

The fact that Lena had shifted the conversation to Natashka's problems and had submitted to all of Dmitriev's insults, let them pass by—which was not like her—signified that she definitely wanted to make up and bring things to an end. But Dmitriev didn't want to make up yet. On the contrary, his irritation grew stronger because he suddenly realized what was Lena's chief tactlessness: she talked as if everything were predetermined, and as if it were also clear to him, Dmitriev, that it was all predetermined, and that they understood each other without words. She talked as if there were no hope. She had no right to talk that way!

It was impossible to explain all that. Dmitriev jumped up from the chair with a jerk, grabbed his pyjamas and towel, and without saying a word practically ran out of the room.

When he returned after a few minutes, the bed was ready. There was a smell of perfume in the room. Lena was combing her hair, in an unbuttoned robe, standing in front of the mirror, and her face expressed indifference, and if you please, even well-screened resentment. But the smell of the perfume gave her away. This was a call, an invitation to a truce. Holding the flap of her robe with one hand at her chin and the other at her stomach, Lena, with a quick businesslike step, and not looking at Dmitriev, walked past him into the hall. He again remembered the lines of poetry he'd been muttering all the time these past days: "O Lord, how perfect are Thy deeds...." Closing his eyes, he sat down on the mattress. "He thought, the sick man...." He sat like that for several seconds. He knew that in the depths of her soul Lena was satisfied, the most difficult thing had been done: she'd spoken. Now to lick the wound; it wasn't a wound though, but a small scratch which it had been absolutely necessary to make. Like an internal injection. Hold on to the cotton pad. A little painful, but it's so that later everything will be fine. It's very important that *later everything be fine*. But he didn't shout, didn't stamp his feet, he just blurted out a few irritated words, went into the bathroom, washed up, brushed his teeth, and now he would sleep. He lay down in his place near the wall and turned his face toward the wallpaper.

Lena came back quickly, clicked the lock on the door, swished her robe, rustled a fresh nightshirt and turned out the light. No matter how hard she tried to move lightly and be as weightless as possible, the mattress began to crack under her weight, and Lena, on account of this crackling, started to whisper with something like drollness, even:

"Oh God, what a nightmare...."

Dmitriev was silent, he didn't move. Some time went by and then Lena put her hand on his shoulder. It wasn't a caress, but a friendly gesture, perhaps an honest acknowledgement of her guilt even and a plea to turn over. But Dmitriev didn't stir. He wanted to get to sleep right away. With a vindictive feeling he was enjoying the fact that he was sinking into immobility, into sleep, that he didn't have time to forgive, explain in whispers, turn over, show generosity, he could only punish for insensitivity. Lena's hands began to stroke his shoulder gently. The final surrender! With shy touches she was sorry for him, she begged forgiveness, made excuses for her callousness of soul, for which one could find justification, however, and appealed to him for wisdom, goodness, and that he find in himself the strength to pity her. But he didn't give in. Something unsettled in him kept him from turning and embracing her with his right arm. Through the approaching drowsiness he saw the porch of the wooden house, Ksenya Fyodorovna standing on its highest step, wiping her hands with a crumpled waffle-weave towel, her slow look directly into Dmitriev's eyes, past the light brown head, past the blue silk dress, he heard the muffled voice: "Sonny, have you given it careful thought?" Muffled because it was from far away, from an icy May day when everyone was very young, Valka went to swim, Dmitriev lifted a 70-pound weight, Tolya rushed off on his "Wanderer" for wine, wrecked a fence on the way, police came, and later, on the cold veranda with the light of a lantern wavering in its glass, Lena cried, was miserable, embraced him, whispering that never, no one, it was for life, that it didn't matter at all. In the morning his mama got on the motorbike, hung a little milk can on the wheel and went to the station for milk and bread. Her misfortune: to say exactly what came into her head. "Sonny, have you given it careful thought?" What could be more ineffectual than that absurd and pitiful phrase? He couldn't think about anything. May with its icy winds tearing off the tender barely born leaf,— that's what they were breathing then. Mama was studying English, just so, for herself, so she could read novels, and Dmitriev was getting ready for graduate school, so they both studied with Irina Evgenievna together and suddenly stopped when Lena appeared. Mama tapped the veranda glass with the umbrella tip—it wasn't late, about seven in the evening: "Get up! Irina Evgenievna's waiting!" Dmitriev and Lena, hiding under a roomy quilt, pretended they were sleeping. The umbrella tapped indecisively two more times, then cones crunched under shoes—mama left in silence. She didn't want to study English any more herself, and had lost interest in the detective novels. Once she heard Lena, laughing, mimic her pronunciation. And from that, from that country veranda with the small-paned windows, began what it was now impossible to set right.

Lena's hand displayed persistence. In fourteen years that hand had also changed—before it had been so light, so cool. Now, when her arm lay on Dmitriev's shoulder, it pressed down with no little weight. Dmitriev, without saying a word, turned over on his left side, embraced Lena with his right arm and moved her closer, sleepily suggesting to himself that he had the right to, he'd already been asleep, had had dreams, and maybe he was even still asleep. At any rate, he said nothing, his eyes were closed, just like those of a man who was really sleeping, and during the moments when Lena really wanted him to say something to her, he continued to be silent. Only later, when he'd really fallen into a deep sleep, at about two in the morning, he mumbled something inarticulate in his sleep.

Dmitriev had turned thirty-seven in August. Sometimes it seemed to him that everything was still ahead.

Such surges of optimism came in the mornings when he suddenly awoke fresh, with inadvertent cheerfulness—the weather had a lot to do with it—and, opening the vent window he would begin to wave his arms in rhythm and bend and unbend at the waist. Lena and Natashka got up fifteen minutes earlier. Sometimes Vera Lazarevna would appear early in the morning to walk Natashka to school. Lying with closed eyes he heard how the women shuffled, moved around, exchanging words in a loud whisper, clattering the dishes, and Natashka would grumble: "Kasha again! Don't you have any imagination?" Lena reacted with her usual morning wrath: "I'll show you imagination! Sit as you should!" And his mother-in-law would growl: "If other children had what you have...." That was a deliberate lie. Other children had the same things and a lot more even. But on those mornings when Dmitriev awoke, gripped by that incomprehensible optimism, nothing irritated him. From the height of the fifth floor he looked out onto the square with the fountain, the street, the column holding the trolley schedule, and a dense crowd around it, and further on, the park, the multi-storied building against the horizon and sky. On the balcony of the next building, very close by, twenty meters away, a young unpretty woman in glasses appeared in a short, carelessly tied houserobe. She squatted down and did something with the flowers which stood in pots on the balcony. She touched and stroked them, checked under their leaves, lifted up some of the leaves and sniffed them. Because she was squatting, her robe opened and her large bluish-white knees became visible. The woman's face was the same shade as her knees, bluish-white. Dmitriev watched the woman bending and unbending at the waist. He watched her from behind the curtain. Why was inconceivable— he didn't like the woman at all,—but the secret observation of her inspired him. He thought about how all was not yet lost, thirty-seven—that's not forty-seven or fifty-seven and that he still could achieve something.

Pattering down the hall in turmoil, accompanied by Lena's cries: "Did you take the bags? Don't run across the street! Attention, children, attention!..."—Natashka and the Fandeevs' Valya, a sixth-grader, left the house at 8:30. The staircase shook under their jumps. Dmitriev slipped into the bathroom, locked himself in, and in three minutes a light knock interrupted his meditations: "Viktor Georgievich, today's Friday, I've got to do laundry, I implore you—hurry up!" This was the voice of their neighbor Iraida Vasilievna, who Dmitriev's mother-in-law didn't speak to, and with whom Lena maintained chilly relations, but Dmitriev tried to be proper, protecting his objectivity and independence. "All right!" he answered through the noise of the water. "It will be done!" He shaved quickly, turning on the water heater and rinsing the brush under the hot stream, then washed his face over the old yellowed washstand with the broken corner—it was supposed to have been replaced a long time ago, but the Fandeevs didn't give a damn what kind of washstand they washed up over, and Iraida Vasilievna begrudged the money—and soon, gently whistling, with the papers in his hand which he had had time to get from the box on his way to the bathroom, he returned to his room. The table was still loaded down with the dishes after Natashka's and Lena's recent meal. Now Lena was hurrying: she left ten minutes after Natashka, and his mother-in-law took upon herself the morning service of Dmitriev. Dmitriev didn't especially like it, and his mother-in-law waited on him with little enthusiasm—it was her little matutinal sacrifice, one of those inconspicuous feats which make up the entire life of the toilers who have the self-abnegating nature of Vera Lazarevna.

Sometimes, Dmitriev noticed, Lena just tried to act like she didn't have any time, but in fact she would have had plenty of time to make his breakfast, but she purposely relinquished this mission to her mother: as if in order that Dmitriev be in some way, if only for a minute, obliged to his mother-in-law. She was even capable of whispering in his ear in passing: "Don't forget to thank Mama!" He thanked. He saw through all these subterfuges in the regulation of family ties and, depending on his mood, would either pay no attention to them or quietly get irritated. Vera Lazarevna always responded in her usual way to quiet irritation—with the tenderest malice. "My, how quickly Viktor Georgievich freed the bathroom! What a hero!" she said smiling, and wiped a place on the oilcloth for Dmitriev with a damp kitchen towel. "Which means our neighbor asked you to...." Lena cut her off decisively: "What does our neighbor have to do with it? Vitya always washed up fast." "That's what I say, a hero, a military style hero...."

On that early October morning there was dark blue beyond the window, the room filled with the light reflected by the yellow bricks of the building opposite, and the voice of Vera Lazarevna was not audible. At first glance, having barely unglued his eyes, Dmitriev unconsciously—because of the sun and the light—felt joy, but in the succeeding second remembered everything, the blue darkened, and beyond the window a relentlessly clear and cold autumn day had set in. Before breakfast neither he nor Lena said anything to each other. But after Dmitriev had called up Ksenya Fyodorovna—he called his sister Lora's at Pavlinovo, where his mother now lived, and Ksenya Fyodorovna related in a cheerful voice that late yesterday Isidor Markovich had come by, found her condition fine, pressure normal, suggested that she go into some Moscow area sanitorium by the first snow, and then followed questions about Natashka's affairs, how were her eyes, had she improved on her C in physics, were they giving her raw ground carrots, the most effective food for eyes, and what was happening about Dmitriev's business trip,—he experienced sudden relief, just like an ebbing of pain from his head. All at once it seemed like maybe everything would come out all right. Mistakes can happen, the most incredible mistakes. And with this pathetic joy and fleeting hope, he returned to the room after the telephone conversation—Natashka had already run off, and Lena was hurriedly sewing something, half dressed in a skirt and a black slip with naked shoulders—and passing Lena he lightly slapped her on the bottom and asked amiably:

"Well, how's your mood?"

Lena abruptly answered drily that she was in a bad mood.

"What's the matter with you?" said Dmitriev, affected by the fact that his amiability was answered so drily. "What's it from?"

"As far as I'm concerned, I've got more than enough reason. Mama's sick."

"Your mother?"

"You think only yours can get sick?"

"And what does Vera Lazarevna have?"

"Something very serious with her head. She's been on her back for two days, I didn't tell you yesterday, but this morning she called.... Some kind of brain spasms."

Lena finished the sewing, put on the blouse and went over to the mirror, looking at herself superciliously. The blouse was short-sleeved, which wasn't attractive—Lena's arms were heavy at the top, her summer tan had gone, her skin had little white bumps showing through. She should only wear long sleeves, but it would be imprudent to tell her that. Such restraint—not a sound about her proposal of yesterday! Maybe she was ashamed, but more likely there was a certain arrogance in it: she had been accused of tactlessness, of a lack of delicacy, those very traits, as it happened, which she found most unpleasant in other people, and she had swallowed this injustice, had even asked forgiveness and somehow abased herself. But now she'd be silent. Why always be in the wrong? No, now you're already asking—you won't get anything out of me. Besides that, her mind's not on that, she's worried about her mother's illness (Dmitriev was ready to bet a hundred rubles to one that his mother-in-law had her usual migraine. Lord, he'd learned to read that book until he was blind!). But Dmitriev didn't have enough time to enjoy that last thought full of smugness before Lena stunned him. Completely prosaically, peacefully, she said:

"Vitka, I'm asking you—talk with Ksenya Fyodorovna today. Just warn her that the Markusheviches may look at her room, and the key has to be gotten."

After a silence he asked:

"When do they want to look at it?"

"Tomorrow or the day after, I don't know exactly. They'll call. And if you go to Pavlinovo today, don't forget, get the key from Ksenya Fyodorovna. Put the kefir in the refrigerator please, and the bread in the bag. Or else it'll dry out from you leaving it out all the time. Bye!"

Waving in a friendly way, she went out into the hall. She slammed the entrance door. The elevator buzzed. Dmitriev wanted to say something, some vaguely anxious thought had dawned on the threshold of his consciousness, but didn't quite dawn, and he, having made two steps after Lena, stood in the hall and then returned to his room.

There was not a trace left of the early dark blue. When Dmitriev went out to the trolley stop there was a fine drizzling rain, and it was cold. The last few days had been rainy. Isidor Markovich was right, of course—he's an experienced surgeon, an old hand, they invite him for consulations in other cities—his mother must be taken out of the city, but not into the same influenza damp. But if he advises a Moscow area sanatorium that means he doesn't see any immediate threats—that's it! And for the second time this morning Dmitriev timidly thought that maybe everything might turn out all right. They would make the exchange, receive a good separate apartment, would live together. And the sooner the exchange was made the better. For his mother's well-being. Her dream would be realized. It would be psychotherapy, the healing of the soul! No, Lena was sometimes very wise, intuitively, womanlike—suddenly it dawns on her. Really, that's possibly the only brilliant means of saving a life. When the surgeons are powerless other forces come into play.... And that's what not one professor could do, no one, no one, no one!

Dmitriev could think of nothing else standing at the trolley stop in the drizzling rain, and after, making his way inside the car, among the wet raincoats, briefcases which knocked against the knees, the coats smelling of damp cloth, and he thought about it running down the dirty subway steps, slippery from the rainy slop brought in by thousands of feet, and standing in the short line for the cashier to change a fifteen-kopek piece into five-kopek pieces, and again running down even further along the steps, and throwing the five into the slot of the turnstile, and walking along the platform ahead with quick steps so as to get a seat in the fourth car, which would stop exactly opposite the archway leading to the stairway to the connecting passage. And he was still thinking about it when the shuffling crowd carried him along the long hall where the air was stifling, and it always smelled of damp alabaster, and when he stood on the escalator, squeezed himself into the car, looked over the passengers, the hats, the briefcases, bits of newspapers, plastic envelopes, the flabby morning faces, the old man with the household bags on his knees, going to shop in the city center—any one of these people might be the saving variant. Dmitriev was ready to shout at the whole car: "Who wants a good room, twenty by sixteen?..."

At a quarter of nine he got out of the cave and onto the square, at five of he crossed the alley and, overtaking the cars standing by the entrance, entered a door beside which hung, under glass, the black plaque "IOGA."

On this day they were deciding the question of the business trip to Golishmanovo in the Tumenskaya district. The trip had already been confirmed back in July, and none other than Dmitriev was supposed to go. Pumps were his domain. He alone was responsible for this business, and he alone really understood it, unless you counted Snitkin. Dmitriev had started a conversation with him the week before, but Pasha Snitkin, a cunning, wise operator (in the office they called him "Pasha Snitkin-with-the-world-on-a-string," because he had never done one single job on his own, but was always able to fix it so that everybody helped him), said that unfortunately he absolutely could not go—also due to family reasons. He was probably lying. But it was his right. Who wanted to go in bad weather, in the cold, to Siberia? It was awkward for Snitkin to refuse, and he burst out with irritation: "Didn't you say that your mother had gotten better?"

Dmitriev didn't start to explain, he just waved his hand: "Now, better...." And Pasha had always inquired about Ksenya Fyodorovna's health so attentively, gave the phone numbers of doctors, in general expressed his sympathy, and Dmitriev was for some reason completely sure of his agreeing. But why? Why should he be? Now it was clear that this sureness had been stupidity. No, they're not pretending when they express sympathy and ask with moving carefulness: "Well, how are things at home?"—it's just that that sympathy and carefulness have sizes, like shoes or hats do. You should never stretch them too much. Pasha Snitkin was transferring his daughter to a music school, and the only one who could deal with this troublesome business was he himself—not the mother or the grandmother. And if he went away in October on a business trip, the music school would definitely fall through for this year, which would cause a deep trauma in the girl and the moral destruction of the whole Snitkin family. But my God, can one really compare them—a person is dying and a girl is entering music school? Yes, yes. One can. They are hats of approximately the same size—if a stranger is dying and your very own daughter is entering music school.

The director was waiting for Dmitriev at 10:30. Cocking his head to one side and looking Dmitriev in the eye with a sort of shy wonder, the director said:

"So what are we going to do?"

Dmitriev answered:

"I don't know. I can't go."

The director was silent, touched the skin of his cheeks and chin with his wide white fingers, as if checking to see whether he'd shaved well. His glance became thoughtful. He was really thinking very hard about something and even began to hum a tune unconsciously.

"Mm yes.... What to do, Viktor Georgievich? Um? And if it's for about ten days?"

"No!" said Dmitriev abruptly.

He understood that he could stand like a rock and they couldn't budge him. Only he shouldn't explain anything. And the director, after thinking it over, spoke the name of Tyagusov, a young fellow who'd finished the institute a year ago, and who, it seemed to Dmitriev, was a complete booby.

Not long ago Dmitriev would have started to protest, but now he suddenly felt that all this had no significance. So why not Tyagusov?

"Of course," he said. "I'll spend two days with him and explain everything to hm. He'll manage. Bright guy."

After he got back to his room on the first floor, Dmitriev worked an hour and a half without unbending, preparing the documentation for Golishmanovo. Even though earlier he had not believed that they'd make him go, the thought of the trip had weighed upon him, had been just one more little weight added to all his other burdens, and now when they'd removed the weight he experienced a relief. And he thought hopefully that today, maybe, would be a lucky day. Like all people who are oppressed by fate, Dmitriev cultivated superstition: he noticed that there were lucky days when success followed success, and on those days you had to try to deal with as many things as possible, and there were bad luck days when not a damn thing went right no matter what you did. It looked like a lucky day had begun. Now to borrow money. Lora had asked that he bring at least fifty rubles. On Isidor Markovich alone they'd spent—four times fifteen—sixty rubles this month. But where to get it? Such a crummy thing—borrowing money. But he had to do it today, since today was already a lucky day.

Dmitriev began to think of who he could hit for it. Almost everyone, he remembered, had complained that they had no money, that they'd used it up over the summer. Sashka Prutyov had gotten a cooperative apartment, and was totally in debt himself. Vasily Gerasimovich, the colonel, partner in games of preference and fishing trips, Dmitriev's constant rescuer, had suffered a tragedy—he'd left his wife, and it was awkward to ask him. Dmitriev's friends at the CSM (Club of the Semi-Married), to whom Dmitriev turned in moments of despair when he fought with Lena, were people of little resources—their fortune consisted of someone with a car, with a motorboat, a camping tent, bottles of French cognac or White Horse whiskey, bought by chance in Stoleshnikov and kept for any special occasions of the house on the bookcase—and they could lend you no more than twenty-five rubles, forty at the most, but he had to get no less than 150. Of course there was the ultimate possibility, the limit of torment: to ask his mother-in-law. But that would mean going downhill. Dmitriev could have forced himself to take it, but Lena took such things very badly. She knew her mother better. All at once it came to Dmitriev—it was the same thought which had vaguely come before and which now suddenly cut through— how was he going to tell his mother about the exchange? After all, she knew perfectly well how Lena had felt about the idea and now for some reason she had suggested moving in together. Why?

Just considering all this made Dmitriev sweat. He went out into the hall where there was a telephone on a stand, and called Lena at work. Usually it was not easy to get through to her. But he was lucky (a lucky day!): Lena happened to be in the office and she picked up the phone. Dmitriev hurriedly got out his doubts in one long confused sentence. Lena was silent, then asked:

"This means what, that you don't want to tell her?"

"I don't know how. I couldn't suggest it to her—you understand?"

After another silence Lena told him to call her again in five minutes on another phone where she could speak more freely. He called. Now Lena talked loudly and energetically:

"Say it like this: say that you really want it, but I'm against it. But you insisted. That is despite me, clear? Then it'll be natural and your Mama won't think anything of it. Put it all on me. Only don't overdo it—just some hints..." Unexpectedly she began to talk in a changed, flattering voice: "Excuse me please, just a minute, I'm leaving now! So everything's clear? Yes, Vitya, Vitya! Talk to somebody there in your office who's accomplished an exchange successfully, you hear? Bye!"

What Lena said was, of course, correct and cunning, but anguish gripped Dmitriev's heart. He was incapable of going back into the room right away, and he wandered along the empty hall for a few minutes.

He didn't go find anyone or find anything out before lunch, but after lunch he went up to the third floor to the economists. As soon as he opened the door, Tanya saw him and came out. Not asking anything, she looked at him fearfully.

"No, nothing bad," he said. "Maybe even a bit better. Tan, do you know, has anyone here made an exchange? Exchanged apartments?"

"I don't know. I think Zherekhov. Why?"

"I need some advice. We have to make an exchange, urgently, you understand?"

"You?"

"Yes."

"You want..." her face reddened, "to move in with Ksenya Fyodorovna?"

"Yes, yes! It's very important. It'd take a long time to explain, but it's absolutely essential now."

Tanya was silent, hanging her head. There was a lot of gray in the hair which had fallen over her face. She was thirty-four, still a young woman, but in the last year she'd gotten to look a lot older. Maybe she was sick? She'd gotten very thin: the slender neck stuck out of the collar, in the thin face only the eyes—good ones—shone out of the millet-colored freckled pallor in their habitual fright. This fright was over him, for him. Tanya would have been a better wife for him probably. It had begun three years ago, had lasted one summer and had ended itself when Lena and Natashka came back from Odessa. No, it hadn't ended, it had dragged out in a thin thread, it broke for months, for half a year. He knew that if one were reasoning sensibly, she would have been a better wife for him, probably. But you know, sensibly, sensibly.... Tanya had a son, Alec, and a husband with the strange last name of Toft. He had never seen him. He knew the husband loved Tanya very much, had forgiven her everything, but after that summer three years ago, she could no longer live with him, and they separated. He was very sorry that it turned out that way, that the husband became unhappy, quit his job, left Moscow, and Tanya also became an unhappy person, but there was nothing to be done about it. Tanya wanted to leave IOGA, so that she wouldn't have to see Dmitriev every day, but getting away turned out to be very difficult. Then she gradually reconciled to it all, and learned how to meet Dmitriev calmly and talk with him as an old friend.

Dmitriev suddenly perceived what she was now thinking: this means— that's all, never.

"Well, what can I do?" he said. "You see, this would be a kind of chance, a hope. It was my mother's dream to live with me."

"What are you talking about? She probably wasn't dreaming about this."

"I know."

"Oy, Vitya.... Well, have a talk with your Zherekhov. I'll call him now. Only he's a big mouth, keep it in mind." Suddenly she asked: "Do you need any money?"

"Money? No."

"Vitya, take it. I know what being sick means. My aunt was sick for eight months. I set aside 200 rubles for a summer coat, but as you see, the summer's over and I didn't buy anything. So I can give it to you till spring with absolutely no trouble."

"No, I don't need money. I have some."—He frowned. What else: borrow from Tanya! Suddenly he laughed. "Really, what a strange sort of day! One after another...."

"We'll go to my place after work, and I'll give it to you, all right?"

After a silence he said:

"I'm lying, I haven't got any money. But I don't want to take it from you."

"Fool!" She lightly slapped him on the cheek.

Dmitriev saw that she was glad. As they walked to the doors of the room Zherekhov was in she even took him by the hand.

"Leonid Grigorievich!" called Tanya. "Can I see you for a minute?"

Zherekhov, a small, affable old man, completely bald, with white, even false teeth, very kindly and willingly began to recount how he'd made an exchange. Dmitriev didn't know Zherekhov very well, but he'd noticed that the latter was kindly and affable with everyone—probably because, finding himself at pitiful retirement age, the old man was fighting for his place and wanted to have the best relations with everyone. Because of this, he told the story at unbearable length and detail. Someone went abroad, someone was in a desperate situation. Someone had to pay. None of this was right. But then Zherekhov exclaimed suddenly, and his light blue old man's eyes widened from the flood of benevolence:

"Yes. That's who you should see—Neviadomsky! You know Alexei Kirillovich? From KB-3? It was the same story with him, he also made an exchange because..." Zherekhov lowered his voice, "the mother-in-law was hopelessly sick. She had an excellent room, almost twenty-five meters, somewhere in the city center. But Alexei Kirillovich lived at Usachevka. Everything had to be done very fast. And he succeeded terrifically! He'll tell you. True, he had connections at the local Housing Commission. So in a word, like this: he·succeeded in making the exchange, made repairs in the apartment—he was forced to do it by ZHEK[1]—he moved his mother-in-law, got the personal account, and the old lady died three days later. Can you imagine? The poor guy, he went through a lot that winter, I remember. Almost took to his bed. But now he's got an exceptional apartment, like a general's deluxe. Loggias, two balconies, lots of all kinds of secondary cubic capacity. He's even growing tomatoes on one balcony. You drop by, drop by, he'll tell you. Wish you success!"

Zherekhov benevolently nodded, moving back, backed into the room with his seat. While he talked, Tanya stood beside Dmitriev and inconspicuously held onto the end of his little finger.

"Go downstairs at 6:00, and we'll go immediately," she said in a whisper.

"You understand I've got to go to Lora's in Pavlinovo. My mother's expecting me. She's at Lora's now."

He knew he was dealing a blow to certain hopes of Tanya's, but it was better to say it right away.

"Well, all right. Do what you have to." Everything immediately left an impression on her face: it darkened.

"No, and besides that...."

"I understand! You really think I do not understand! I won't hold you for a second. You'll get the money and then—be off."

Nodding, she walked quickly away from him down the hall. Not long ago, a year back, her tall figure was something exciting for Dmitriev. Especially at those times when she was walking away from him, and he looked after her. But now there was nothing left. It had all disappeared somewhere. Now she was just a tall, thin, very long-legged woman with hennaed hair in a bun on a slender neck. And still, every time he looked at her, he thought that she would have been the best wife for him.

Dmitriev returned to the office and sat over the papers for half an hour—his thoughts turned around the same thing: mother, Lora, Tanya, Lena, money, the exchange—and he saw that he'd have to leave work earlier, or else he'd get to Pavlinovo much too late. Tanya lived in an out-of-the-way place, a worse one you couldn't imagine—Nagatino. Dmitriev went to the little office of Varvara Alexeevna, his superior, and said that if it was possible, he'd like to leave today at five. Varvara Alexeevna agreed. Everyone in the office knew what was going on in Dmitriev's life and acted with understanding: every week, once or twice he could leave work early. Once even, it was such a sin, he ran to the Moskva department store under this pretext and bought a uniform for Natashka. Dmitriev went up to the third floor again and told Tanya to ask to leave at five. Then he went in to see Neviadomsky, also on the third floor.

Dmitriev decided to go to Neviadomsky after hesitation. Relations between them were cool—through the fault of a friend of Dmitriev's who, it's true, hadn't worked at IOGA for half a year. Neviadomsky had had some kind of scandal with this friend at the local trade union committee. And they stopped speaking to each other. And when Neviadomsky met Dmitriev in the company of this friend, he—at the same time—didn't say hello to Dmitriev either, and out of solidarity with his friend Dmitriev acted exactly the same way. However, when Dmitriev and Neviadomsky met alone, they greeted each other totally correctly, although a little coolly, and even exchanged two or three phrases. All this was utter nonsense, and Dmitriev decided to ignore it and go. And if Neviadomsky really has connections, will he share them?

Neviadomsky, a lean dark-haired man with a blackish-reddish curly little beard, raised his eyebrows in surprise when Dmitriev, stopping by the office, asked him for "a brief audience." At a small table in the corner there were two smashing away at chess, moving the figures about very quickly. Neviadomsky was standing by them, watching. The favorite occupation of the "Kabetrishniki" [project researchers] was chess, they played blitzes, five-minute ones, but among the "Kabedvash-niki" ["projdevelopers"] ping pong flourished. The battles took place during the lunch hour, but sometimes they borrowed from work time, especially towards the end of the day. Neviadomsky, after saying: "Just a minute! I'll come!"—continued to observe the players. The latter were slamming the figures around the board with the speed of automatons, until one cried, "Oh damn!"—and with a blow of the hand tipped over his king. Neviadomsky began to laugh maliciously and said:

"As that Balda said by way of reproach: if only you hadn't been so interested, priest, in the cheap price!"[2]

After this, he moved toward the door with the expression of the malicious smile on his face, but, meeting Dmitriev with a glance, he wiped off his smile and again his brows rose in surprise. Dmitriev began to clumsily put forward his request, or more precisely, to hint at his request, cloaked in hurried and inconsequential mumblings. Neviadomsky had to guess it: he was being requested to share his advice on how to behave in circumstances familiar to him. But Neviadomsky didn't guess. His blackish-red curly beard rose higher, his eyes looked more and more cold, and it seemed to Dmitriev, more haughty.

"Excuse me, I don't exact-ly understand...."

"I'll explain right now. The problem is that the causes prompting you and me.... In a word, we're in the same situation...."

"What do I have in mind?" Dmitriev felt how his neck and cheeks were flooding with color. "This is what I've got in mind: I've got to make an exchange as quick as possible too. So I wanted to consult you about how it's done, generally? What do you start with?"

"What do you start with? What do you mean—what do you start with? With the exchange bureau, of course. You pay three rubles and make an announcement in the bulletin."

"But you understand, that if a person is seriously ill, very seriously, and every hour is dear...."

"But you can't start any other way. With the exchange bureau, I don't know any other routes,"—Neviadomsky stuck a thumb into his nostril and began with concentration to extricate something from there. Obviously he was tensely trying to figure out whether it was worth it or not to let Dmitriev in on his *connections*. He decided: not worth it. "I didn't have any other ways."—Suddenly Neviadomsky chuckled. "You know, you've reminded me of the stupidest story! When I was a student, my father died. Two or three months went by...."—While he related this, he continued to extract something from his nose with his thumb.—"And a neighbor unexpectedly dropped by, an unknown man from another building entrance, and he says, 'My father died and I heard yours died not long ago too. So I've come to make your acquaintance and to ask you to share your experience.' What kind of experience? What? How? I, of course, courteously got rid of him."

"And I've got to take this too," thought Dmitriev, feeling numb. Turn around, leave, but he continued to stand there looking at the blackish-red beard. "There are tomatoes on the mother-in-law's grave. It's all the same. And this too. And there will be more of it."

"If you want it, I've got the number of one Adam Vikentievich, an agent. I could look for it...."

Overcoming his numbness, Dmitriev turned and walked away down the hall. At five he and Tanya went out onto the square and there—rare occurrence!—an empty taxi turned up. Dmitriev whistled, they jumped in and drove off. The alleyway was filled with a crowd moving in one direction toward the subway. The factory shift had just ended. The taxi moved slowly. People glanced into the cab, someone knocked on the roof with their palms. When they passed the subway and escaped onto the avenue,

Dmitriev began to talk about Neviadomsky with malice.

Tanya took him by the hand.

"Why are you being so malicious? Don't do it. Stop it...."

He felt how her calm and joy poured into him. Tanya, smiling, said: "We are all very different. We are people.... My cousin's little son died. This was incredible grief, of course, suffering, and along with it a kind of passionate love for children, especially sick ones. She was sorry for them all, tried to help as much as she could. And I have an acquaintance whose son also died, of leukemia. That woman hated everyone so much, she wished everyone dead. She gets happy when she reads in the paper that someone's died...."

Tanya moved closer. She put her head on his shoulder and asked: "Is it all right? It doesn't bother you?"

"It's all right," he said.

They traveled by way of the outskirts, through the new areas. Dmitriev told about Ksenya Fyodorovna. Tanya asked about her with compassion—this was sincere, Dmitriev knew, she felt sympathy for his mother. And Ksenya liked Tanya—they'd seen each other once or twice in summer, in Pavlinovo.... Tanya held his hand in hers, sometimes she softly tickled his palm with her finger. Tanya's caresses were always somehow schoolgirlish.

Without taking his hand away, he gave the details about his mother: what Zurin said, what Isidor Markovich said. Tanya began to laugh:

"Oh, what a rotten dame! She lends money and pesters with tendernesses, right?" She suddenly knocked against his cheek with her nose, snuggled. "Forgive me, Vitya.... I can't...."

He stroked her head. For a long time they rode in silence. They went past the Varshavka.

"Well, what's the matter?" he asked.

"Nothing. I can't...."

"What?..."

"I'm sorry for you, for your mother.... and for myself at the same time."

Dmitriev didn't know what to say. He simply stroked her head and nothing more. She began to sniffle, he felt dampness on his cheek. Then she moved away from him, turned and began to look out the window. Finally the embankment flashed by, they took the bus route past some factories, along a solitary, long stone fence. Near a beer stand there was a dense black crowd of men. Some of them, singly and in pairs, with mugs in their hands stood at some distance. Dmitriev felt like his throat was dry—he wanted to have a drop of something, to get his spirits up. "I should ask," he thought, "Tanyushka used to have stuff around. Anything would do."

The new sixteen-story building stood on the edge of a field. The road went in a detour, around the field.

"Right here," said Tanya.

Dmitriev remembered quite well that it was here. The last time he'd been here was about a year ago.

"Will you have the car wait?" asked Tanya.

Of course he would have it wait. But his usual timidity—he saw that Tanya passionately didn't want that—made him answer:

"Yes, O.K., let it go. I'll find one there."

"Of course, you will!" said Tanya.

They went up to the eleventh floor. Tanya lived alone with her son in a large three-room apartment. That poor devil Toft had constructed this ship in the coop building, and had just enough time to move into it when everything happened. At that time Alec was at camp, Toft was somewhere in Dagestan—he was a mining engineer—and Tanya lived alone in empty unfurnished rooms which smelled of paint. There were newspapers on the floors. In one room there stood a huge couch, and nothing more. And Dmitriev's love was inseparable from the smell of paint and fresh oak floors, as yet not polished once. Barefoot, he slapped over the newspapers into the kitchen and drank water from the tap. Tanya knew a lot of poetry and liked to recite it in a soft voice, almost whispering it. He was astonished at her memory. He himself didn't remember, if you please, even one poem by heart—just occasional quatrains. "You are still alive, my old one, and so am I, greetings to you by and by." But Tanya could whisper for hours. She had something like twenty notebooks, from her student days, where in the large clear handwriting of the A student was copied the poetry of Marina Tsvetaeva, Pasternak, Mandelstam, Blok. And so in moments of rest, or when there was nothing to talk about and it got sad, she would begin to whisper: "O Lord, how perfect are Thy deeds, thought the sick man..." Or: "Take your palm from my breast, we are wires under current."

Sometimes when he got tired of the monotonous murmuring of her lips he would say: "All right my love, take a rest. Why is it that your Khizhnyak doesn't say hello to Varvara Alexeevna?" After a pause she answered sadly: "I don't know." All of her resentments were momentary. Even when she could have taken offense for good reason. For some reason he was convinced that she *would never fall out of love with him.* That summer he lived in a state he had never experienced before: love toward himself. An incredible state! One could have defined it as the condition of usual bliss, for its strength consisted in its constancy, in the fact that it lasted weeks, months, and continued to exist even when everything was already over.

But Dmitriev didn't think about why: why did he have this bliss? Why him exactly—a not very young, heavy man with an unhealthy color in his face, with the eternal smell of tobacco in his mouth? It seemed to him that there was nothing puzzling about it. That was how it should be. Generally, it seemed to him that he had just joined in that normal, truly human condition, which people should—and would in time—always be in. Tanya, the opposite, lived in constant fear and a kind of passionate bewilderment. Embracing, she would whisper, like she did the poetry: "Lord, for what? For what?"

She didn't ask for anything or about anything and he didn't promise anything. No, not once did he promise. Why should he promise if he definitely knew that no matter what she *would never fall out of love with him*. It simply came into his head that she would have been the best wife for him.

New furniture had appeared in the rooms—in one room there was a breakfront and a round polished table, in the other—a half-empty bookcase. But as before, the parquet hadn't been polished and it looked sort of dirty. Alec came out of the room, noticeably taller, a pale freckled creature of about eleven, with glasses on his thin little nose. He held his head slightly tilted back and to the side, perhaps because he wasn't well, or perhaps he could see through his glasses better. This set of the head and his small compressed mouth gave the boy an expression of superciliousness.

"Mom, I'm going to Andrusha's. We're going to trade stamps," he announced in a squeaky voice, and rushed through the hall to the door.

"Wait! Why didn't you say hello to Viktor Georgievich?"

"Hi," Alec threw over his shoulder, not looking.

Hurrying, he unlocked the lock and jumped out, slamming the door.

"Be back no later than eight!" Tanya yelled to the closed door. "The young man doesn't shine in the manners department."

"He's probably forgotten me. I haven't been here for a long time, after all."

"And even if a stranger came? Doesn't one have to say hello?" Tanya went into the big room, opened the side door of the breakfront and said: "He didn't forget you."

She took a rolled newspaper from under a pile of clean linen, unrolled it and gave Dmitriev a bundle of money. He stuck it in his pocket.

"Well go," said Tanya. "You haven't got any time."

He suddenly pulled out a chair and sat down at the polished table.

"I'll sit a bit. I'm sort of tired." He took off his hat, touched his head with his palm. "My head aches."

"Do you want to eat? Could I get you anything?"

"Is there anything to drink?"

"No.... Wait!" Her eyes shone with happiness—"It seems to me that there's a bottle of cognac left someplace, which we didn't finish drinking. Remember, when you were here last time? I'll take a look right now!"

She ran into the kitchen and brought in the bottle a minute later. There were about a hundred grams left at the bottom.

"Now we'll have some hors d'oeuvres. One minute!"

"What do we need hors d'oeuvres for?"

"Just a second, just a second!" Again she rushed headlong into the kitchen.

Dmitriev got up and went to the balcony doors. There was a wonderful view from the eleventh floor of the stretching field, the river, and the village of Kolomenskoe, the cupolas of its cathedral visible. Dmitriev thought of how he could move into this three-room apartment tomorrow, see the river and the village in the morning and evening, breathe in the field, go to work on the bus to Serpukhovka, from there on the subway, it wouldn't take so long. Tanya carried in sprats, two tomatoes, bread and butter on a crystal dish, and wine glasses. He poured half a glass for himself, and the rest for Tanya. She always drank very little, she got drunk quickly.

"What are we drinking to?" asked Tanya.

"To everything going well with you."

"Well, all right! No. Not to that. Everything will go well with me anyway. Let it be to everything going well for you. All right?"

"O.K." It was all the same to him. He'd already drunk up, and was chewing on a tomato. He grunted, "The tomatoes are from the grave of Neviadomsky's mother-in-law, aren't they?"

"Because, Vitya," she said, "it's not likely that things are ever going to go well with you. But suppose, all of a sudden, they do? To that then."

He didn't think to ask what she had in mind. Superfluous conversations. After the cognac it got warm and he ate the tomato with pleasure and looked at Tanya, who was hunched over in a reverie, leaning on the table with her elbows, gazing at the corner of the room.

"Don't slouch!" he said, paternally slapping her lightly on the shoulder blades.

Tanya straightened up, continuing to gaze at the corner of the room. On her stupefied face, with the red spots due to the cognac on her cheekbones, suffering was distinctly visible. For one moment he pitied her very sharply, but then he remembered that somewhere far and near, through all of Moscow, on the shore of this same river, his mother was waiting for him, his mother who was experiencing the sufferings of death, but Tanya's sufferings belonged to life, so—what was there to pity her for? There is nothing in the world except life and death. And everything that is dependent on the first is happiness, and everything dependent on the second is the destruction of happiness. And there is nothing else in this world. Dmitriev got up with a jerk, with sudden haste, exactly as if someone strong had grabbed him and pulled him by the arms, and saying, "Bye! I've got to run!"—bolting with quick steps down the hall to the door. Tanya didn't have time to say anything to him. Maybe she didn't want to say anything to him.

Dmitriev went by bus to the subway—there was of course no taxi around at all—transferred twice and came out on the last station of the new line. A fine snow was drizzling down. Moscow was far away, its large buildings were white against the horizon, but here was a field torn up by foundation pits, pipes lay on the damp earth, and a line of people waiting for the trolley stood by a pillar on the highway. The sky was full of clouds, arranged in layers—on the top something motionless and dark-violet was thickening, lower light, crumbly clouds were moving, and lower still there flew on the wind a kind of white cloudy rag, like wisps of steam.

About forty years earlier, when Dmitriev's father Georgy Alexeevich had built a house in the settlement of Red Partisan, this place, Pavlinovo, was considered a dacha-resort area. It was a resort, and until the revolution they came here by horse train from the point. In the 30s the boy Vitya, a mediocre student, but diligent bike-rider, fisherman, and player of "501," devourer of Sienkiewicz, and Gustav Emar, came here on summer days, on the squeaky old bus which left at hourly intervals from the cobblestoned Zvenigorodskaya Square. It was always stuffy in the bus, the windows didn't open, it smelled of sackcloth. Waste lands flashed by, orchards, little villages, an ice-house, a radar field, a school with a white brick fence, a church on a knoll, and suddenly the arc of the mill-pond opened and the heart of the boy Vitya tightened. The road from the bus-stop went through pines, past unpainted fences black from rain, past dachas hidden by lilac bushes, sweetbriar, and elder with their small-paned verandas showing through the green. You had to walk for a long time along this road, the tar ended, then there was the dusty high road, to the right there was a pine grove on a little hill with a spacious clearing—in the 1920s a plane crashed there and the grove had burned down—and to the left the fences continued to stretch out. Behind one of the fences, in no way camouflaged by young bushes, there stuck up a log building of two stories and a basement, not at all similar to a resort house, but more to a trading post somewhere in the forests of Canada, or to a hacienda in the Argentine savannah.

The building had been built by a cooperative, with the resounding name of "Red Partisan."[3] Georgy Alexeevich wasn't a red partisan; his brother Vasily Alexeevich, who was a red partisan and an OGPU[4] worker, and the owner of a two-seater sports Opel, had invited him into the co-op. The third brother, Nikolai Alexeevich, lived in a little dacha nearby. Also a red partisan, he'd worked for Vneshtorg and had lived for months at a time in both Japan and China. From China he'd brought the game of mah-jongg—a mahogany box containing 144 stones (bamboo on one side, ivory on the other) placed on four little pull-out shelves. At first the grownups gambled for money at Mah-jongg, then when the grownups got bored or couldn't take it anymore, the game passed into the possession of Nikolai Alexeevich's children, and the whole crowd of the Pavlinovo children's commune. Nothing was left of those evenings with the phonograph music

("The weary sun tenderly said farewell to the sea"), with the loud conversation of the two deaf red partisans who were always arguing about something on the second floor, the clack of the Chinese stones on Nikolai Alexeevich's veranda. It's not just people who disappear in this world, it turns out, but whole nests, tribes with their environment, conversation, games and music. They disappear completely, so that it's impossible to find their traces. Although Lora was still left there in Pavlinovo. But besides Lora there was no one—not one single person. Of the brothers, the eldest, Georgy Alexeevich, died first. Instantaneous death from a stroke—they called it apoplectic stroke then—occurred right on the street one sweltering day.

Dmitriev remembered his father poorly, in fragments. He remembered a dark mustache and beard, gold-rimmed glasses and a very thin, yellowish tussore shirt, soft to the touch, with flakes of tobacco, a fat belly under it, and constant chuckling at all people and things. Georgy Alexeevich was a railway engineer, but his whole life he'd dreamed of leaving that job and taking up writing humorous stories. It seemed to him that this was his calling. He always went walking with a notebook in his pocket. Dmitriev recalled how quickly and easily his father composed funny stories—they went walking in the evening to the garden to water the cucumbers and saw how Marya Petrovna, the aunt of one of the red partisans, was trying to knock down her nephew Petka's ball from a pine tree. First she threw a stick, the stick got stuck; then she began throwing her shoe, and the shoe got stuck too. While they were walking to the garden, his father told Dmitriev a killingly funny fairy tale about how Marya Petrovna hurled her other shoe at the pine, then her blouse, belt, skirt; all this hung on the pine, and Marya Petrovna, naked, sat beneath, and then Uncle Matvei came running and started to throw his shoes and pants. A few days later his father came from town and brought with him a journal in which his story "The Ball" was printed. Georgy Alexeevich made fun of his brothers, whom he considered none too bright, and as a joke called them "woodchoppers." He himself had graduated from the university, but his brothers hadn't even managed to finish high school: the civil war was raging, tossing one to the Caucasus, the other to the Far East. Sometimes talking with his mother he marvelled: "And how is it they send such woodchoppers abroad when they can't say two words in any other language?" He further reproached his brothers for greed, for the fat life, mocked their Chinese stones, their eternal fussing with the car on days off—he always added a "Zh" when referring to his brother's Opel.[5] And in Kozlov, aunts related to them went hungry, dying one after another; their nephews had no means of getting to Moscow. Only Georgy Alexeevich helped as much as he could.

Sometimes the brothers would have quarrels—for months at a time he didn't visit them, or they him. His mother considered that Marianka and Raika were to blame for the quarrels and all the brothers' subsequent misfortunes, since they were contaminated by the petty-bourgeois mentality, but things didn't come out so sweet for them later on either, the poor things.

Generally, his father had been the best one, more intelligent than his brothers, a rather good man. But unlucky. He died early, didn't have time for anything. What was preserved of his notebooks, in which there had been so much that was funny, wonderful? They had gone, just like all the rest. Also gone was Raika, Nikolai Alexeevich's wife, who'd been a beauty at one time, and the main fashion plate of the Red Partisan settlement. Gone too was the sandy slope on the river bank where in the mornings, very early, there used to be excellent fishing. After eight o'clock the fish left here—the river passenger boat began to rumble between its moorage and the village, and the motorboats came out. You had to cross over to the other bank, there were quiet inlets there where fish hid, but sitting in the hot sun was unbearable—there was neither tree nor bush, just a naked meadow with stiff weeds.

Dmitriev jumped off the bus one stop before he should have. He wanted to walk to the place where his favorite slope had once been. He knew that now there was a concrete embankment there, but the fishermen still came anyway. New fishermen, from five-story buildings that were beyond the bridge. It was very convenient for them—they came by trolley.

He went down the stone steps—everything was done solidly, as in a real city park—at the bottom he walked along the concrete slabs which rose about six feet above the water level. You could walk along the river like that almost to the house itself. There was no crawling along the shore now. Every spring chunks of the bank crumbled down, sometimes along with the benches and pines.

The sky sparkled on the wet slabs, and not one fool was around. But no, there was somebody sitting there, off in the distance, and Dmitriev slowly walked up to him. The water seemed very clean, undirtied, but dark—autumn water. Dmitriev stopped behind the fisherman's back and began to watch the float. He watched for about five minutes, with increasing anxiety and a kind of sudden weakening of the spirit, thinking of how hard it was going to be to say it. Impossibly hard. With Lora too. What could he do? They would all understand, of course. However, it was possible that his mother wouldn't if one were to present the matter exactly as Lena had suggested, his mother was very unsophisticated—but Lora would understand it all right away. Lora was sharp, perspicacious, and didn't like Lena at all. If his mother, despite all of Lena's unfriendliness, had all the same made peace with her, had learned to pay no attention to this, forgive that, Lora's dislike had grown stronger over the years—on their mother's account. She once said: "I don't know what kind of person one would have to be to treat our mother without respect." True, friends loved Ksenya Fyodorovna, her colleagues respected her, her apartment neighbors and Pavlinovo dacha neighbors esteemed her because she was benevolent, compliant, ready to come to your aid and sympathize. But Lora didn't understand.... Oh, she didn't understand, she didn't! Lora hadn't learned to look beyond what lay on the surface. Her thoughts never bent. They always stuck out and pricked like horsehair from a poorly sewn jacket. How could one not understand that you don't dislike people just because of their vices and you don't love them on account of their virtues!

It was all the truth, the real truth: his mother was constantly surrounded by people in whose fates she constantly *took part.* For months some elderly people she barely knew had been living in her room, friends of Georgy Alexeevich's, and some old ladies who were even more decrepit, his grandfather's friends, and some casual acquaintances from vacation houses who wanted to get to the Moscow doctors, or provincial boys and girls, children of distant relatives who had come to Moscow to enter institutes. His mother tried to help all of them absolutely disinterestedly. But why should she help? All ties had been lost long ago, and she was worn out. But still—with shelter, advice, sympathy. She liked to help unselfishly. But to put it more exactly: she liked to help in such a way that God forbid any profit should come out of it. But the profit was this: in doing good deeds to be always conscious of being a good person. And Lena, sensing his mother's slightest weakness, said about her in moments of irritation: the hypocrite. And he would fly into a rage. He would yell: "Who's a hypocrite? My mother's a hypocrite? How dare you say that...." And —it would begin, get rolling.... Neither his mother nor Lora knew how he got violent on their account. Of course they guessed about a little of it, they'd been witnesses to some of it, but in full strength—with the whole battery of insults, Natashka's crying, the no talking for days on end, and at times even a little physical violence—this was unknown to them. They considered, Lora with especial firmness, that he'd quietly betrayed them. His sister one day said: "Vitka, how Lukianized you've gotten." Lukianov was the last name of Lena's family.

Dmitriev suddenly decided that he had to think through something important, definitive. He didn't have the strength to walk to the house, so he delayed it a minute.

He sat down not far from the fisherman, on a wooden box—also someone's fishing gear—which had lain there a long time, getting brown and damp all the way through. As soon as Dmitriev sat down, the box began to list slightly, and he had to lean very firmly on his legs to maintain balance. On the opposite bank, where there had been a meadow at one time, they were now making a huge beach, with cabanas, reclining chairs, and refreshment stands. The recliners were piled into two stacks, but for some reason two recliners still stood right by the water, making a spot of dim blue on the dark gray sand. Everything on that shore was dark gray, the color of cement. Beyond the beach a young grove of birches curled, planted some ten years before, and beyond the grove towered the mountains of housing in foggy white blocks, along which stood two especially tall towers. Everything on that shore had changed. Everything had "gotten Lukianized." Every year something changed in its details, but when fourteen years passed, it turned out that everything got Lukianized—finally and hopelessly. But perhaps that wasn't so bad? And if it happens to everything—even the shore, the river and the grass—does that mean maybe that it's natural and that's how it should be?

The first year Dmitriev and Lena had to live in Pavlinovo. Lora, then still without Felix, was living in Moscow with Ksenya Fyodorovna, the dacha was empty and Dmitriev and Lena wanted to be alone. But they didn't succeed even so. The dacha apartment at Pavlinovo had been unoccupied for a long time. The roof was leaking, the porch was rotting. The cesspool gave the most trouble—from time to time it overflowed, especially when it rained, and an unbearable stench spread throughout the entire area, blending with the smells of the lilac, linden and phlox. The inhabitants had come to terms with this blending of smells long ago, and it had become an inevitable characteristic of dacha life for them, and with it the thought that it was pointless to repair the cesspoool, that it cost incredible money, which none of them had. The village had grown poor, the inhabitants were not what they had been—the former owners had died off, they'd all faded from sight, and their heirs, widows and children, lived a rather hard and not at all dacha-like life. Petka, for example, Marya Petrovna's nephew and the son of a Red professor,[6] worked as a simple truck driver at the lumber center. And Valerka, Vasily Alexeevich's son, Dmitriev's cousin, got mixed up with trash and became a thief and landed somewhere in the camps. Some of the heirs, wearied by the dacha extortions and looking ahead—the city was coming—sold their shares, and totally strange people appeared in the village, who had no relation at all to red partisans. And only the birches and lindens, planted forty years ago by Dmitriev's father, a passionate gardener, grew into a mighty forest, chocked with foliage, and proudly gave notice to the passersby who looked through the fence that everything in the village was bubbling, flowering, thriving as it should.

And then suddenly Ivan Vasilievich Lukianov, Lena's father, who came by to call on the youngsters and to be a guest for the day, said that Kalugin, the master plumber who had fixed the pipes in the settlement for thirty years, was a swindler and a no-good, and that he, along with the sewer man, who was invited regularly to come pump out the pool, was robbing the red partisans and that it was possible to make the repair of the pool quickly and cheaply. Everyone was stunned. They collected the money. Ivan Vasilievich brought the workers, and in a week the repair was finished. The heirs of the red partisans were very afraid that Kalugin, offended, would quit the settlement, leaving them at the mercy of fate, but Ivan Vasilievich managed it so that the old sot didn't get offended by anyone, but was even filled with respect for Ivan Vasilievich and began to call him "Vasilich."[7]

Lora, with her way of speaking right out, remarked that this was probably because Kalugin had sensed a kindred spirit in Ivan Vasilievich. Where had he gotten the workers? Where had he gotten the bricks? The cement? Obviously underhanded. Through not exactly noble means. His mother was indignant: "How do you know? What right have you to so rudely slander someone without proof?"

"Well, I don't know, I don't know, Mama. Maybe I'm mistaken." Lora smiled mysteriously. "It was just a supposition. We'll see."

And Ivan Vasilievich really was a powerful man. His main strength was his connections, old acquaintances. In six months he had put in a phone at the Pavlinovo dacha. Ivan Vasilievich was a tanner by profession, he had begun with a master in the town of Kirsanov, but already by 1926, when they made him director of a factory—a crummy little factory requisitioned from a Nepman[8] in Marina Grove,—he was moving along the administrative line. When Dmitriev first met him, Ivan Vasilievich was already quite old and heavy. He suffered from short breath, had had a stroke and all kinds of misfortunes, such as being fired, party penalties, reinstatement, appointment with a raise, the slanders and libels of various rats who aimed to ruin him, but as he himself admitted, "As far as those moments were concerned, I was saved by only one thing: I was on the alert."

The habit of constant distrust and unremitting vigilance had insinuated itself so much into his nature that Ivan Vasilievich displayed it about the slightest trifles. For example, he'd ask Dmitriev before going to bed at night: "Viktor, did you put the hook on the door?"—"Yes," replies Dmitriev, and listens as his father-in-law slips down the hall to the door to check. (This was later, when they lived in the Lukianovs' apartment in the city.) Sometimes Dmitriev got so fed up that he'd yell: "Ivan Vasilievich, why are you asking, for God's sake?"—"Don't you get insulted, precious man, I do it automatically, with no evil intention." It was amusing that the same distrust for each and every one—first of all for the people living side by side—infected Vera Lazarevna too. Sometimes she'd telephone from somewhere and ask for Lena. Dmitriev would say that Lena wasn't home. In a little while there'd be another call, and Vera Lazarevna, changing her voice, would ask for Lena. And what comic scenes would occur sometimes in the evening when his mother and father-in-law would feed each other medicine! "What did you give me, Ivan?" "I gave you what you asked for."—"But what, what exactly? Say it!"—"You gave me diabasol?"—"Yes."—"Sure?"—"Why are you bringing up this question?"—"Tell you what: please bring me the container you got it out of,—for some reason it seems to me that this isn't diabasol...."

There was a time when such conversations heard in passing soothed Dmitriev, as did his father-in-law's manner of expressing himself: "In this respect, Ksenya Fyodorovna, I'll give you the following axiom." Or like this: "I was never my father's technical executor, and I demanded the analogical from Lena." They laughed silently about it. His mother called her new relative "the learned neighbor"—behind his back of course—and considered that he was not a bad man, in some ways nice even, although of course not at all of the intelligentsia, unfortunately. Both he and Vera Lazarevna were of a different breed—those "who know how to live." Well, it wasn't so bad to get related to people of a different breed. Inject fresh blood. Profit from someone else's abilities. Those who don't know how to live begin to oppress each other after living together—by their noble inability itself, which they are secretly proud of.

After all, could Dmitriev or Ksenya Fyodorovna, or anyone else of the Dmitriev relatives, have organized and carried through the repair of the dacha as dashingly as Ivan Vasilievich? He'd lent the money for all that music too. Dmitriev and Lena went away their first summer, to the south. When they returned in August the old little rooms were unrecognizable— the floors shone, the frames and the doors sparkled with white, the wall-papers in all of the rooms were expensive, with embossed patterns, green in one room, blue in another, brick-red in the third. True, the old furniture, which was wretched, and had been bought by Georgy Alexeevich a long time ago, was still there. It hadn't been noticeable before, but now it struck the eye: what shabbiness! Some iron bedsprings on a sawhorse instead of a bed, tables and cupboards of painted plywood, a wicker trestle bed, another wicker object, impossibly dilapidated. Lena of course took all of the junk out of the large room with the green wallpaper where the young couple was installed, and bought a few very simple but new things: a mattress with legs, a student desk, two chairs, a lamp, some curtains, and brought in two rugs from the other rooms—old rugs, but very good ones, Bokharas, one for the wall, the other for the floor. Dmitriev was amazed: how wonderfully things had changed! Even his mother said: "See what taste Lena has! We lived here so long and not once did we think of hanging that rug on the wall. No, she's got very fine taste!"

Vera Lazarevna and Ivan Vasilievich settled into the middle room temporarily, the blue one, for August and September, to help Lenochka, who was already expecting a child. Ksenya Fyodorovna lived in the small brick-red room and now and then Lora stayed over. It was then that Lora's tedious romance with Felix began, and she wasn't interested in the dacha. Their grandfather, Ksenya Fyodorovna's father, was still alive, and he also was a guest sometimes—he slept in the connecting room on the trestle bed. Strange to remember it. Could it have realy been like that: everyone sitting together on the veranda at the big table, drinking tea, Ksenya Fyodorovna pouring, Vera Lazarevna cutting the pie? And she called Lora *Lorochka* at one time, and arranged for her to have her best dressmakers. It had been like that, for sure. It had been, it had been. Only it didn't stay in his memory, it rushed past, vanished, because he couldn't live for anything, or see anyone but Lena. There was the south, sultriness, hot Batum, old lady Vlastopulo, from whom they rented a room next to the bazaar, an Abkhazian he'd fought with over Lena, on the embankment at night, the Abkhazian had tried to pass a note to Lena in a restaurant. They sat there with no money, only cucumbers to live on, they telegraphed to Moscow, Lena lay naked and black on the sheet with no strength, and he ran to sell the camera. And then all of it continued on, although it was different, Moscow, he was already working—one wild summer flew with momentum—again Lena lay like a mulatto on the sheet, again there was bathing at night, races to the shore, a cooling meadow, conversations, discoveries, tirelessness, suppleness, fingers ashamed of nothing, lips always ready for love. And besides that her devilish powers of observation! Oho, how she could pick up the weak or the funny things. And everything pleased him, he was struck by everything, astonished, registered it.

He liked the facility with which she made friends and became intimate with people. This was exactly what he lacked, as it happened. Especially remarkable was the way she succeeded in making *necessary* acquaintances. She'd hardly settled in Pavlinovo when she already knew all the neighbors, the police chief, the watchmen at the wharf, and was on familiar terms with the young directress of the sanatorium and the latter gave Lena permission to have dinner in the sanatorium dining room, which was considered the height of comfort in Pavlinovo, and a success almost unattainable by mere mortals. And how she scratched Downstairs Dusya, who lived in the semibasement, when the latter appeared with her usual arrogance, to demand that they clean their own, the Dmitrievs', shed, which it was true Downstairs Dusya had used as her own for the past ten years! Downstairs Dusya flew from the porch as if the wind had knocked her down. Dmitriev was delighted, and whispered to his mother: "So, how do you like it? This isn't how it was with us milksops, is it?" But all his secret delight quickly passed because he knew that there wasn't and couldn't be a woman more beautiful, intelligent, and energetic than Lena, therefore—why be delighted? It was all natural, in the order of things. No one had such soft skin as Lena. No one could read Agatha Christie so entertainingly, at the same time translating from English into Russian. No one could love him like Lena. And Dmitriev himself—that remote thin one with the absurd curly forelock—lived stunned and stupefied, as during heat, when a man can't think well, doesn't want to eat or drink, and just dozes off, lying in bed half asleep in a room with draped windows.

But once in the evening, at the end of the summer, Lora said: "Vitka, can we talk?" They went off the porch, down to the road, and while they were in the square of light which fell from the veranda, they walked in silence until they were in the shadow of the lindens. Lora, laughing unsurely, said: "Vitya, I wanted to talk about Lena, all right? It's nothing really, don't worry, just little things. You know I'm in favor of her, I like her, but the main thing for me is that you love her." This introduction offended him right away, because the *main thing* was not at all that he loved her. She was wonderful by herself, unrelated to him. And already on guard, he prepared to listen further.

"I'm surprised by certain things. Our mother would never say it herself, but I see it.... Vitka, you won't take offense?"—"No, no, what do you mean! Go on."—"Well, this is really nonsense, trivial—that Lena took all our best cups, for example, and that she puts the bucket by Mama's door...." ("Lord!" he thought. "And Lorka's saying this!") "I didn't notice it," he said aloud. "But I'll tell her."—"You don't have to! And I shouldn't have pointed it out to you."—Lora again laughed somehow abashedly. "That's all you needed, to be told every bit of nonsense! But I scolded Mama. Why not simply say: 'Lenochka, we need the cups, and please don't put the pail here, put it there.' I said that today, and I don't think she got offended at all. Although it's very unpleasant to talk about such trivial things, believe me. But something else jarred me—for some reason she took Father's portrait from the middle room and put it in the connecting room. Mama was very surprised. You should know about this because it's not some domestic trifle, but something else. In my opinion it's just tactlessness." Lora was silent and for a while they walked, not saying anything. Dmitriev ran his open palm over the lilac bushes, feeling how the little sharp twigs were pricking him. "Well, all right!" he said finally. "As far as the portrait goes, I'll tell her. Only listen: what if you happened to come into a strange house, Lora? Wouldn't you commit some involuntary tactlessnesses, slips?"—"It's possible. But not that kind. Generally we shouldn't be silent, but should speak out—I think that's correct—and then everything'll turn out right."

He told Lena about the portrait, not that night but the next morning. Lena was amazed. She'd taken down the portrait only because she needed the nail for the wall clock, and there had been absolutely no other meaning in her action. It seemed odd to her that Ksenya Fyodorovna didn't tell her about such a trivial matter herself, but sent Viktor as an ambassador, which gave the trivial matter exaggerated significance. He remarked that Ksenya Fyodorovna hadn't talked to him about this at all. But who had said it? At this point he blurted out from stupidity—how much would be "blurted out" from stupidity later on!—that Lora had spoken. Lena, reddening, said that his sister had apparently taken upon herself the role of rebuking her: sometimes independently, sometimes through a third person.

When Dmitriev returned from town that day it was unusually quiet in the apartment. Lena didn't come out to meet him right away, but appeared a few minutes later and asked the unnecessary question: "Shall I warm your dinner?" Lora had gone to Moscow. His mother didn't come out of her room. Then Vera Lazarevna appeared, dressed in town clothes, powdered, with beads on her powerfully jutting chest, and said, smiling, that she and Ivan Vasilievich thanked them for the hospitality, and were waiting for him to say goodbye. Ivan Vasilievich would arrive soon with the car. Through the door, which was opened for a second, Dmitriev saw that his father's portrait was hanging in its former place. He wondered: why so suddenly? They had wanted to live there all of September. Yes, but some business had come up—with Ivan Vasilievich at work, and she had household chores, had to make jam, and in general—haven't your dear guests tired you out.... Ksenya Fyodorovna came out to say goodbye to the relatives—she had a dispirited look—and invited them to come again. Vera Lazarevna didn't promise to, "I'm afraid we won't manage it, dear Ksenya Fyodorovna. Really, there are so many concerns of all possible sorts. So many friends want to see us, they're also inviting us to their dachas...."

They left, and Dmitriev and Lena went to the dacha next door to play poker. Late that night, when Dmitriev returned, Ksenya Fyodorovna called him into her room with the brick-red wallpaper, and said that she was in a rotten mood and that she couldn't get to sleep because of this business. He didn't understand: "What business?"—"Well, because they left."

Dmitriev had drunk two glasses of cognac at the neighbors', was slightly excited, wasn't thinking clearly. Waving his hand, he said with annoyance: "Oh, nonsense, mother! Is it worth talking about?"—"No, but Lora is uncontrolled. Why did she start all this? And you passed it on to Lena for some reason, she—to her mother, there was the stupidest conversation.... Complete absurdity!" "And because you don't go around moving portraits!" said Dmitriev, hardening his voice and shaking his finger with severity. Suddenly he felt himself to be in the role of family arbitrator, which was sort of pleasant even.—"Well they left, so fine. Lena said absolutely nothing to me, she's a smart lady. So don't get upset and sleep quietly." He gave his mother a smack on the cheek and left.

But when he went to Lena and lay down beside her, she moved away to the wall, and asked why he'd stopped in at Ksenya Fyodorovna's room. Sensing danger of some sort, he began to make excuses, said that he was tired of conversations and wanted something else entirely, but Lena, alternating between severity and caresses, got what she wanted to know out of him anyway. Then she said her parents were very proud people. Vera Lazarevna was especially proud and touchy. The problem was that she'd never been dependent on anyone in her whole life, therefore the slightest hint at dependency was taken badly by her. Dmitriev thought: "How is it she's not dependent, since she never worked and lives as a dependent of

Ivan Vasilievich?"—but he didn't say it out loud, but just asked how they'd infringed on Vera Lazarevna's independence. It turned out that when Lena related the conversation about the portrait to Vera Lazarevna, the latter simply oohed: Lord, did they really think they'd had any pretensions to that room? Dmitriev didn't understand something here at all: "Have pretensions? Why have pretensions?" Besides that, he wanted something else. It ended with Lena making him promise that he'd call Vera Lazarevna from work the next day, and gently, delicately, not mentioning the portrait or insults, invite them to Pavlinovo. Of course, they wouldn't come, because they were very proud people. But he should call. To clear his conscience.

He called. They arrived the next day. Why had he remembered this ancient business? Later there was a lot that was worse, blacker. Well, probably because the first was engraved forever. He even remembered what dress Vera Lazarevna was wearing when she arrived the next day, and with a look of unshakable worth—proudly and vainly looking before her—ascended to the porch, carrying a boxed torte in her right hand.

Then there was the matter of his grandfather. The same autumn that Lena was expecting Natashka. Oh, grandfather! Dmitriev hadn't seen his grandfather for many years, but there had smoldered in his heart for an incalculably long time the splinter of childhood devotion. The old man was so alien to any kind of *Lukianovableness*—he simply didn't comprehend a lot of things—that it was of course crazy to invite him to the dacha when those people were living there. But then no one understood that, or could foresee it. It was impossible not to invite their grandfather, he'd recently come back to Moscow, was very sick, and needed a rest. In a year he got a room in the Southwest.

His grandfather said to Dmitriev, marvelling: "Some worker came today to move the couch, and your marvellous Elena, and no less marvellous mother-in-law, used the familiar 'you' to him in a friendly way. What does it mean? Is it accepted now? To the father of a family, a man of forty?" Another time he started a funny and unbearably tiresome conversation with Dmitriev and Lena because they'd given the salesman in the electronics store—and made merry when they told about it—fifty rubles so he'd put aside a radio for them. And Dmitriev couldn't explain any of it to his grandfather. Lena, laughing, said: "Fyodor Nikolaich, you're a monster!" His grandfather wasn't a monster, he was just very old—seventy-nine—there were very few such old men left in Russia, and of jurists who'd graduated from Petersburg University still less, and of those who'd been involved in revolutionary activities, had been in prison, exiled, fled abroad, worked in Switzerland and Belgium, been acquainted with Vera Zasulich—there were no more than one or two in all. Perhaps his grandfather, in a sense, was a monster after all.

And what kind of conversations could he have with Ivan Vasilievich and Vera Lazarevna? No matter how they exerted themselves, both sides found nothing in common. Ivan Vasilievich and Vera Lazarevna were absolutely disinterested in his grandfather's past, and his grandfather understood so little of modern life that he couldn't report anything useful, and so they acted with indifference: just an old man. He shuffled along the veranda, smoked cheap, stinking cigarettes. Vera Lazarevna usually talked with his grandfather about his smoking.

His grandfather was small in height, dried up, with bluish-copper tanned skin on his face, and stiff hands rough and disfigured by hard work. He always dressed neatly and wore a shirt and tie. He polished his boyish little shoes, size eight, to a shine and liked to take walks along the shore. There was one Sunday, the last hot one in September, when everyone got together for a walk—a strain had already appeared in their conversations, no one needed this excursion, but somehow it was agreed: they gathered at the same time and strolled along together.

There were loads of people around that day. They bumped against each other in the woods, on the shore, they sat all over the benches: some in sports clothes, some in pyjamas, with children, dogs, guitars, and fifths on newspaper. And Dmitriev began to get ironical about the contemporary dacha residents: the deuce knows, he said, what kind of public this is. But before the war, he remembered, others with beards, in pince-nez, strolled here.... Vera Lazarevna unexpectedly supported him, saying that before the revolution Pavlinovo was also a marvellous resort area, she'd been a little girl here at her uncle's. There had been a restaurant with gypsies, called "The Riverside," they'd burned it down. Generally solid people had lived here: stock market speculators, businessmen, lawyers, artists. Over there in the clearing, Chaliapin's dacha had stood.

Ksenya Fyodorovna was interested: who was her uncle? To which Vera Lazarevna answered: "My papa was a simple worker, a furrier, but a very good, qualified furrier, they ordered expensive things from him...."— "Mamochka!"—laughed Lena. "They ask you about your uncle, and you tell about your father." The uncle, it turned out, had a leather goods shop: purses, suitcases, briefcases. On Kuznetsky, on the second floor, where there is a woman's dress shop now. During NEP there had been a leather goods store there, but no longer her uncle's because uncle had disappeared in 1919, during the famine time. No, he hadn't run away, hadn't died, he'd just disappeared somewhere. Ivan Vasilievich interrupted his spouse, remarking that these autobiographical facts weren't too interesting to anyone anyway.

And at that point, grandfather, till then silent, suddenly began to speak. "So, dear Vitya, just imagine, if your mother-in-law's uncle had lived to the time when the beards and pince-nez strolled here, what would he have said? Probably: what kind of public, he'd say, is in Pavlinovo now! Some riffraff in Tolstoi blouses and pince-nez.... Ah? Wouldn't he? And even earlier there used to be an estate there, the landowner ruined himself, sold his house, sold his land and fifty years later some heir would drop by here in passing, out of a sad interest, would look at the merchant's wife, the bureaucrat's wife, at the gentlemen in bowlers, at your uncle,"—grandfather bowed to Vera Lazarevna, "who rolled up in a cab and thought: 'Foo, filth! Well, this bunch of people are just trash!' Ah?" he laughed. "Wouldn't he?"

Vera Lazarevna remarked with a certain astonishment: "I don't understand, why trash? Why talk like that?" Then grandfather explained: contempt is stupidity. One doesn't have to be contemptuous of anyone. He said this for Dmitriev, and Dmitriev suddenly saw that his grandfather was in some degree right.... In some way which touched close to him, Dmitriev. Everyone grew thoughtful, then Ksenya Fyodorovna said no, that she couldn't agaree with her father. If we refuse to be contemptuous, we derpive ourselves of our last weapon. Let this feeling be inside us, absolutely invisible from the outside, but it should be there. Then Lena, giggling, said: "I agree completely with Fyodor Nikolaich. How many people are conceited about who knows what, myths, chimeras. It's so funny."—"Who exactly, and what are they conceited about?" asked Dmitriev in a half-joking tone, although the direction of the conversation had begun to disturb him slightly. "Who knows," said Lena, "you want to know everything, don't you?"—"Conceit and quiet contempt are two different things," pronounced Ksenya Fyodorovna, smiling. "That depends on who's looking," answered Lena. "I hate honor in general. In my opinion there's nothing more repulsive."—"You take a tone—as if I were proving that honor is something beautiful. I don't love honor either."—"Especially when there's no basis for it. Built on empty space...."

And so from this, from an innocent altercation, developed the conversation which concluded with Lena's heart attack that night, the call for the ambulance, cries from Vera Lazarevna about egotism and cruelheartedness, with their hurried departure by taxi the next morning, and then Ksenya Fyodorovna's departure and the silence which came over the dacha when two were left: Dmitriev and the old man. They walked by the lake, talked for a long time. Dmitriev wanted to have a conversation about Lena with his grandfather—her departure worried him—to curse her for her nonsensicality, her parents for idiocy, and maybe damn himself, or somehow pick at the wound; but his grandfather didn't utter a word either about Lena or her parents. He talked about death, and how he wasn't afraid of it. He'd carried out what he'd been appointed to do in this life, and that was all. "My God, I wonder how she is there? What if something serious happens suddenly, to her heart?"

His grandfather talked about how the past and his whole endlessly long life didn't interest him at all. There was nothing stupider than looking for ideals in the past. He only looked ahead with interest, but unfortunately saw little.

"Should I call or not?"—thought Dmitriev.—"Anyway, no matter what her condition is, that doesn't give her the right...."

He called in the evening.

His grandfather died three years later.

Dmitriev came to the crematorium straight from work, and looked stupid with his thick yellow briefcase in which there were several cans of saira [a popular fish from the eastern USSR], bought by chance on the street. Lena loved saira. When they entered into the crematorium's premises from the street, Dmitriev quickly went to the right and put his briefcase on the floor in a corner, behind a column, so no one would see it. And repeated mentally, "Don't forget the briefcase." During the funeral ceremony he remembered about the briefcase several times, looked at the column, and at the same time thought that his grandfather's death had turned out to be not as awful an experience as he had supposed it would. He was very sorry for his mother. Supporting her under her arms was Aunt Zhenya on one side, Lora on the other, and his mother's face, white from tears, was new somehow: simultaneously very old and childish.

Lena came too, sniffled, wiped her eyes with a handkerchief, and when the moment of farewell came she suddenly began to sob in a loud low voice, seized Dmitriev's arm and began to whisper that his grandfather had been a good man, the best of all the Dmitriev relatives, and how she loved him. That was news. But Lena sobbed so sincerely; real tears were in her eyes, and Dmitriev believed. Her parents also appeared at the last minute, in black coats with black umbrellas; Vera Lazarevna even had a black veil on her hat and they managed to throw a bouquet of flowers into the coffin, as it was lowered into the cellar. Then Vera Lazarevna said in amazement: "How many people there were!" That's why they came, out of old people's curiosity: to see whether there were a lot there to see him off. To Dmitriev's amazement a lot came. And the main thing was that there had come creeping from somewhere, in no small number, those who had seemed to disappear; but no, those strange old men were still alive, old lady smokers with angry dry eyes, a few of whom Dmitriev remembered from childhood. One hunchbacked old lady with a myopic ancient face, who his mother said had been a desperate revolutionary, a terrorist, and had thrown a bomb at someone, came. This hunchbacked lady gave the speech over the casket. In the courtyard, when everyone came out and stood in bunches, not dispersing, Lora came up and asked if Lena and he were going to Aunt Zhenya's, where the friends and relatives were gathering. Until that minute, Dmitriev had considered that they were going to Aunt Zhenya's without fail, but now he wavered: there was the possibility of choice in Lora's question itself. That meant that both Lora and his mother supposed that he, if he so desired, could not go, i.e., that it wasn't necessary for him to go because— suddenly he understood it—in their eyes he no longer existed as a part of the Dmitriev family, but as a different thing, connected with Lena, and maybe even with those in the black coats with the black umbrellas; and they had to ask him like an outsider.

"Are you going to Aunt Zhenya's?" The question was casually asked, but how much it signified! Among other things: "If you were alone, we wouldn't have asked. We always want to see you, you know. But when we have grief, why have strange people around? If it's possible, it'd be better to do without them. If it's possible, but—whatever you want...." Dmitriev said that most likely they would not go to Aunt Zhenya's "Why? You go!" said Lena. "I don't feel so well, but you go. Of course, go!" No, he wouldn't go, Lena had a bad headache. Lora nodded understandingly, and even smiled at Lena with sympathy and asked whether she should give her some aspirin. "Yes!" said Dmitriev. "I forgot my briefcase!" He went back to the crematorium's premises, where a new deceased was already lying in a coffin on a pedestal, around which a thin group of people were huddling, and on tiptoe he walked behind the column. After getting his briefcase he stopped, to be alone for a minute. The feeling of irrevocability, of being cut off, which comes at funerals—one thing had irrevocably gone, cut off forever, and now continues the other, but not that, something new, in other combinations—was the most tormenting pain, even stronger than the sadness about his grandfather. His grandfather had been old after all, he was due to die, but along with him disappeared something not directly connected with him, existing separately: threads of some kind among Dmitriev and his mother and sister. And this disappearance was revealed so implacably and right away, a few moments after they came out of the heavy floral smell into the air. Lora calmly agreed to his not going to Aunt Zhenya's, he came to terms with her calmness easily. And only his mother, turning halfway around, made a weak farewell gesture with her hand, and he suddenly felt that he'd added a pain to her, so he rushed to catch up—rushed internally for a moment,—but it was already too late, ir- revocable, it had been cut off; Lena pulled him to the taxi to go home.

Along with his mother, Lora, Felix, Aunt Zhenya and other relatives, there was Lyovka Bubrik. Maybe he'd been there earlier, but Dmitriev noticed him only when they came outside. Lyovka was hatless, dark, tousled, and his glasses were blindingly bright. He didn't come up to Dmitriev, but nodded from a distance. Lena asked in a whisper: "Why's Bubrik here?" Dmitriev, stifling a feeling of unpleasant surprise, said: "Well, so? He's related somehow. Second cousin twice removed."

This was the first time Dmitriev had seen Lyovka Bubrik for several months after that tedious story with the Institute. And he immediately remembered that his deceased grandfather had censured him on account of Lyovka. There had been a conversation in which his grandfather had said: "Ksenya and I expected you to become something else. Of course nothing terrible happened. You're not a bad man. But not wonderful."

He'd known Lyovka since childhood, they'd gone to school at the same institute. Not friends "you couldn't separate with water," but friends connected by the ties of home and family. Lyovka's father, Dr. Bubrik, who'd taken care of Dmitriev even in infancy, was the brother of Aunt Zhenya's husband, who died during the war. So Lyovka was an unrelated nephew of Aunt Zhenya's. Right after the Institute Lyovka went to Bashkiria and worked there for three years in industrial surveying, while at the same time Dmitriev, who was older, and had gotten his diploma a year earlier, stayed to work in Moscow at the gas factory, in the laboratory. They'd offered him various enticing odysseys, but it had been difficult to accept them. His mother wanted him very much to go to Turkmenia, to Dargan-Tepe, because it wasn't far from Lora's native Kunia-Urgench— some 600 kilometers, a trifle!—and the brother and sister could have met over a cup of kok-chai tea and have been homesick together. Natashka was born weak, she was sick, Lena was sick too, she had no milk so they found the wet-nurse, Frosya, the school cleaning lady who lived in the barracks near Tarakanovka, Dmitriev went there in the evenings for the bottles. Sure, Dargan-Tepe! Yes, and there was to be no Dargan-Tepe. There were dreams in the morning, in the silence when he awoke with the unexpected cheerfulness and thought: "It would be nice if...." And it all rose up before him, so transparent, clearcut as if he'd gone up a mountain on a clear day and looked down from it. "Vitya," said Lena (or "Vitenka," if it was a period of serenity and love),—"Why are you fooling yourself? You can't go away anywhere from us. I don't know whether you love us, but you can't, you can't! You're late. It should have been earlier...." And embracing him, she looked into his eyes with the dark blue caressing eyes of a witch. He was silent because these were his own thoughts, which he was afraid of. Yes, yes, he was too late, the train had left. Four years had gone by since he'd finished the Institute, then five, seven, ten went by. Natashka became a schoolgirl. The English Special School on Utiny Lane, the object of lust, envy, the measure of parental love and *putting yourself out to get it.* Another school district, almost unthinkable. And no one but Lena would've had the strength. For she gnawed on her desires like a bulldog. Such a nice-looking lady-bulldog with short straw-colored hair, and an always pleasantly tanned, slightly dark face. She didn't let up until her wishes—right in her teeth—turned into flesh. A great trait! Wonderful, amazingly decisive in life. The trait of real men.

"No expeditions. Not for longer than a week"—that was her wish. A poor simple-hearted wish with dents in it from iron teeth. Lena's other wish, which occupied her during the course of several years, was: to get into IICI. Oh, IICI, unattainable, beyond the clouds, like Everest! Conversations about IICI, telephone calls in connection with IICI, tearful despair, flashes of hope.

"Papa, did you talk with Grigory Grigorievich about IICI?"— "Lenochka, they called you from IICI!"—"From where?"—"From

IICI!"—"Oh, my God, from the personnel section or just Zoika?" Two
friends, ideally situated in life, worked in IICI—the Institute of International Coordination of Information. Finally she succeeded. IICI
became flesh and crunched in her teeth like a well-cooked chicken wing.
Convenient, it was piece work, beautifully located,—a minute's walk from
GUM[9], and her own boss was one of the friends she had studied with at the
Institute. Her friend gave Lena as much to translate as she asked for. Later
on, they had a fight, but for about three years everything was "okay."
During their lunch break they ran to GUM to see if they'd put out some
blouses. On Thursdays they showed foreign films in the original language.
But unfortunately Lena couldn't get Dmitriev's dissertation done for him.
At that time Dmitriev was getting 130 at the laboratory, but an acquaintance of his from the Institute, from the same class—a little gray guy,
but a big worker, clever Mitri, who'd denied himself everything and didn't
even get married ahead of time—received twice that because he'd sat
through his dissertation on his lead rear. Lena wanted Dmitriev to become
a Ph.D. terribly. Everyone wanted it. Lena helped him with English, his
mother approved, Natashka spoke in a whisper at night, and his mother-in-
law grew quiet, but after half a year he gave up. Probably because of that:
the train had left. He didn't have the energy, every night he came home with
a headache, and with one desire—to tumble into bed. And he did tumble in
if there wasn't anything worthwhile on television—soccer, or an old
comedy. And after giving in, he began to hate all the dissertation junk, he
said it was better to receive the honest 130 rubles than to torture himself
and overtax his health and humble himself before the necessary people.
And now Lena looked at it the same way and contemptuously referred to
the Ph.D.s of their acquaintance as smart operators and sly foxes. At this
time, as never more opportunely—but perhaps inopportunely—Lyovka
Bubrik showed up with his request about the Institute of Oil and Gas
Apparatus, abbreviated IOGA.

Lyovka couldn't find work for a long time after he returned from
Bashkiria. Then he found IOGA. But he had to find a way to get in. Neither
he nor anyone else would've gotten into IOGA if Ivan Vasilievich hadn't
called Prusakov. Then he went to see Prusakov himself, in an official car.
Prusakov was holding the job for someone else, but Ivan Vasilievich
pressed and Prusakov agreed. In the end it wasn't Lyovka's father-in-law
who went, but Dmitriev's! True, on Lyovka's behalf. That was true.
Because Lena had asked her father, she was sorry for Lyovka and his wife,
that fat hen Innochka. Then Innochka made a big mess when they were all
guests at mutual friends', and cried: "You're an awful person!" But Lena
had been ready for all of this and held on staunchly and coolly. Their
friends said that Lena held on magnificently. She took everything on
herself and said that Dmitriev hadn't wanted it, but she'd insisted. "I'm
guilty, only me, don't blame Vitka! You'd have wanted us to live on 130 and

Vitka to kill three hours on the road?"

Of course, that's how it was. The thought first came to her when Ivan Vasilievich came and told what kind of job it was. And Dmitriev really didn't want to do it. He didn't sleep for three nights, he wavered and worried but gradually that which it was impossible to think of, which was not the thing to do, turned into something inconsequential, diminutive, well-packed like a capsule you had to—it was necessary even, for your health—swallow, despite the nastiness it contained inside. There is no one who doesn't notice the nastiness after all. But everyone swallows the capsules. "I respect Lev," said Lena, "and I even love him, but for some reason I love my husband more. And if papa, an old man who can't bear to be obliged, got ready and went...."

They should have told them right away, but they didn't have the nerve—they dragged it out, kept quiet. They found out from someone else. And how they cut them off: they didn't come, they didn't call. The devil knows, maybe they were right, but it isn't done that way either: you come, you talk nicely, you find out why and how. And when they met at friends', Bubrik turned up his nose, but Innochka yelled like a fishwife. So the hell with it, forget it. And it was only after about four or five years—it was Ksenya Fyodorovna's birthday, winter, the end of February—that the whole story was stirred up again. His mother and grandfather had pestered Dmitriev about it before, but not very spitefully, because they correctly considered that Lena had started everything. And what kind of demand is there on Lena? You had to reconcile yourself to Lena as with bad weather. But then, on his mother's birthday....

It was as clear as if it were now. They go up the stairs, stop at the door. Natashka holds the presents, a box of candy and a book in English, Thackeray's *Vanity Fair*, and Lena is leaning with her shoulder against the door and with closed eyes whispers as if to herself, but of course to Dmitriev: "Oh, my God, my God, my God. God...." Look, she says, what ordeals I go through for your sake. And he begins to seethe as usual. Lena doesn't like to go to her mother-in-law's. Each year she has to force herself more. What was there to do? Well, she doesn't like to, she can't, can't stand it. Everything irritates her. No matter how nicely they fed them, no matter how kindly they conversed, it was useless: like heating the street. Dmitriev talks tenderly to his daughter, purposely, hugging her: "So, little monkey, are you happy that we've come to grandma's?"—"Uh-hunh!"—"You like to come here?"—"I like to!" But Lena, smiling, adds: "I like to, say, but I've got to go to bed early. And little papa, say, don't stay too long so that we've got to drag you from the table by force. Say, we should get up and go at 9:30."

Everything would have been avoided then if it had not been for that fool Marina, his cousin. As soon as he glimpsed her red physiognomy at the table over the pies and wafers, he immediately understood: it's going to be bad. Lena was much smarter than she was, but in some ways they were similar. And whenever they met at family gatherings, there was always some sort of cockfight started between them. Sometimes they fought out in the open, other times they pricked slyly, so that you wouldn't notice it from the sidelines. Like water polo players, who hit each other with their legs under water, which the spectators don't see. At night Dmitriev would suddenly be stunned: "Why did your cousin taunt me all evening?"—"What do you mean, taunt?"—"Didn't you hear it?"—"What exactly?"—"Well, even what she was saying about women of the East? About their behinds and legs?"—"But after all, you're obviously not a woman of the East, are you?"—"Oh! What point is there in talking to you...."

And then in February,—he remembered every last word for some reason—it all started with the most innocent underwater bumps. He remembered it because it was the last time Lena was ever a guest at his mother's. Since that time, never. It had been five years, and not once. Ksenya Fyodorovna would come to visit her niece, but Lena never went to her. "How are you, Marina? Everything the same with you?"—"Of course! And you? Still working at the same place?" These phrases, said with a smile and within the boundaries of the rules, in actuality meant: "So, Marina, as before, no one's bit? I'm sure no one's bit, and never will bite, my dear old maid."—"But that doesn't upset me because I live the creative life. Not what you do. After all, you work, but I create, I live by creation." At that time Marina was working as an editor in a publishing house. Now somewhere in television. "Have you published anything good lately?"—"We've published a few things. What kind of fabric is that you've got? Did you get it at GUM?" Here were resilient kicks underwater: "What creative work are you babbling about? Have you personally edited even one good book, put it out?"—"Yes, of course. But there's no sense in talking about it with you, it couldn't interest you. Mass production's what interests you." There were some arguments about poetry, about worldwide philistinism. Marina liked this subject a lot and didn't let a chance slip to trample on philistinism. Oh, the philistines! When she was boiling on account of those who didn't recognize Picasso or the sculptor Erzu, something curled up in her mouth and even seemed to sparkle.

Everything hateful that for Marina was connected to the word "philistinism" was contained for Lena in the word "phoniness." And she declared that "all that's phoniness." Marina was amazed: "Phoniness?"—"Yes, yes, phony."—"Loving Picasso is phony?"—"Of course, because those who say they love Picasso usually don't understand him, and that's phoniness."—"My God! Hold me back!" laughed Marina. "It's phony to love Picasso! Oy-oy-oy!" Both of their faces were burning, their eyes blazed with an unjoking brilliance. Picasso! Van Gogh! Sublimation! Acceleration! Paul Jackson! What Paul Jackson? It doesn't matter, because it's phony! Phony? Phony, phony. No, you explain then: what do you call phony?

Well, everything that's done not from the heart, but with an ulterior motive, with the desire to show oneself in the best light. "Aha! That means you are being phony when you visit Aunt Ksenya on her birthday and you bring her candy?"

Lena, after glancing at Viktor with a smile in which there was almost triumph (I predicted it, but you insisted, so take it, enjoy it!), said that her relations with Ksenya Fyodorovna weren't the best but she'd come to wish her well not out of phoniness, but because Vitya had requested it. Something along those lines. Then there was a gap. The guests said goodbye. His mother stumbled along. Aunt Zhenya began to talk about Lyovka Bubrik, why—no one knew. She always wanted to do things right, but it always came out the opposite. His mother said: a disgraceful story, and she couldn't believe for a long time that Vitya could behave like that. "Ah, you consider me guilty for everything? And your Viktor had nothing to do with it?"—"I'm not justifying Viktor."—"But still,—me?"—Lena's cheeks were covered with a stormy flush and Ksenya Fyodorovna's face showed granite features.

"Yes, sure, I'm capable of everything. Your Viktor's a good boy, I corrupted him." Aunt Zhenya spoke, shaking her benevolent gray head: "Dear Lena, you yourself explained it that way to Lyovochka, I remember it very well."—"What I explained doesn't matter! I was worried about my husband. And you don't have, you don't have...."—"Stop yelling!"—"And you're a traitor! I don't want to talk with you." Grabbing Natashka, she walked away from the table. "Why do you always keep quiet when I'm being insulted?" And—onto the stairs, out into the frost, forever. He ran downstairs and slipped on the frozen puddle. Lena and Natashka were stupidly bounding away from him to the bus, the door closed, and he didn't know where else to go, what would be. He couldn't go anywhere. When his home was destroyed he couldn't go anywhere, to anyone. No, she had gone to his mother's one more time after that February—there had been no way out of it, Ivan Vasilievich was laid up with a stroke and his mother-in-law was spending her days and nights with him; but Dmitriev and Lena were hot for a trip to Golden Sands—and there was no one to leave Natashka with. In Bulgaria they took walks in sweaters, and loved each other very strongly. In the daytime the room got very hot even though they opened the curtain, the shower water was warm. And they had never loved each other so strongly.

Dmitriev stood in front of the house and looked at the single lighted window—the kitchen. The second floor and the left side of the building were dark. At this time of the year no one lived around here. Lora was doing something in the kitchen. Dmitriev saw her head lowered over the table, the black hair with the gray streaks, which shone under the electric bulb, the tanned forehead—the yearly five months in Central Asia had made her almost an Uzbek. From the darkness of the garden he viewed Lora just as if on a luminous screen, as a strange woman—he saw her lack of youth, the diseases earned through years of life in the tents, saw the rough anguish of her heart, now gripped by one anxiety.

What was she doing there? Ironing or something? He felt that he couldn't say anything to her. At any rate today, now. The hell with all that! Nobody needed it, it wouldn't save anyone, it would just bring sufferings and new pain.

Because there is nothing dearer than a kindred soul.

When he went up the steps of the porch his heart was thumping. Lora was cutting the newspaper on the table into long strips with the scissors. Felix came in with a basin which contained paste. Dmitriev began to help them. First they sealed the window in the kitchen, then they moved to the middle room. His mother had gone to sleep at six o'clock, but she would probably wake up soon. At about four thirty it had gotten bad, the pains had started, Lora had been very frightened and wanted to call an ambulance, but his mother said it was useless, that she should call Isidor Markovich, or the doctor from the hospital. She took the papavirin and the pains went away. What was the matter? Their mother was very depressed. Such a sudden worsening. The first since the hospital. She says it's just exactly like it was in May: pains exactly as strong and in the same place.

They conversed in an undertone.

"I called you at four!"

"Yes, and everything was all right. But an hour later...."

Felix, humming something, was stuffing an old nylon stocking into a crack between the folds of the frames with a kitchen knife; Lora spread strips of newspapers with paste and Dmitriev pasted them. Then they sat down to tea. They listened for sounds from their mother's room the whole time. Lora's eyes were pitiful, she answered irrelevantly, and when Felix went out of the room she whispered quickly:

"I'm begging you: he's going to start about Kunia-Urgench, so say you're definitely against it.... That you can't...."

Felix came back with a black packet in which there were photographs. Still humming, he began to show them. They were color pictures of the Kunia-Urgench excavations: crocks, camels, bearded men, Lora in trousers, a quilted jacket, Felix squatting, with some old men, also squatting. Felix said that they had to leave at the end of November. At the very latest—the beginning of December. They had to be there by the fifteenth, like a bayonet. Lora said he'd be there, be there, just not to get worried. She'd let him go. Of course he must go, eighteen people were waiting. Collecting the photos and sticking them into the black packet—his fingers trembled slightly,—Felix said that Lora, unfortunately, had to go too.

Because eighteen people were waiting for her as well.

"We agreed: first you go...."

"How can you conceive of that?"

The glasses were bouncing on Felix's big nose, and he raised them up with a special sort of movement of his cheeks and brows.

"And how do you concieve of it all?"

"But there's Vitya, I believe, her son...."

"Well, that's enough! Vitya, Vitya. It doesn't matter about Vitya.... We can't talk about this today."

Felix stuck the packet into the pocket of his bike jacket, headed for the door into the other room, but stopped at the doorway.

"And when do you plan to discuss it? We have to send a telegram to Mamedov."

Lora waved her hand again, more energetically, and Felix disappeared, closing the door. Lora said that Felix was very good, loved mama, mama loved him, but sometimes he was dense. Sometimes it seems pathological to Lora. There are things it's impossible to explain to him, and then one simply had to say categorically: such and such, you say, and nothing else! And then he's resigned himself. He can't argue. Dmitriev should have said that he can't stay with mama, and then he'd stop being so tiresome. And how could Dmitriev stay, really? Take mama to his place? Move to Profsoyuznaya? Lena would never agree to either of these choices. It was important to Felix to go to Kunia of course, to her as well, all very true, but what could they do?

In Ksenya Fyodorvna's room it was still quiet as before. Felix took the coal bucket and stamped across the veranda and down the stairs to the shed. He made a clatter with the shovel, getting the coal. Dmitriev said that he could of course try to exchange the two rooms for a two-room apartment—which he'd tried to do before—so as to live with his mother, but that was a whole story. Not so simple. Although there was at the moment such a possibility right now.

He didn't want to say it, but it somehow said itself, comfortably and appropriately. Lora looked at Dmitriev slightly surprised. Then she asked:

"Is this idea Lena's or something?"

"No, mine. My old idea."

"Only don't report *your idea* to Felix, all right?" said Lora. "Because he'll grab it. And mama doesn't need this at all. When she's in such bad shape, to go through something else.... I know: everything'll be fine at first, noble, and then the irritation will start. No, it's an awful idea. A nightmare. Brr, I can imagine!" And Lora convulsed her shoulders with an expression of momentary fear and aversion. "No, I'll be with mama, I don't go anywhere, and Felix will manage somehow."

Felix returned with the bucket of coal. You could hear how quiet he was being so as not to awaken Ksenya Fyodorovna, scrabbling with his hands in the bucket, taking out the coal pieces and with care putting the pieces on an iron leaf in front of the stove. A slight clanging of the iron damper. Lora grinned wanting to say something, but she remained silent.

"What is it?" asked Dmitriev.

"No, nothing. I often wondered, by the way: why don't you get yourself a co-op apartment? It's not so expensive. The relatives would help. They love their granddaughter so much...." Her face was smiling, but there was spite in her eyes. This was the old familiar Lora face from years ago. They'd often fought in childhood, and Lora, enraged, was capable of hitting with anything that came to hand—a fork, a teapot.

"What are you talking about in there?"—asked Felix from the kitchen. He sensed something in Lora's voice.

"I'm saying: why don't Vitya and Lena build a co-op apartment? A little one, two rooms. Right?"

"We don't need any apartment at all,", said Dmitriev in a choked voice. "We don't need it, you understand? In any case *I* don't need it. I, me! I don't need a damn thing, absolutely not a damn thing. Other than our mother to be well. She's always wanted to live with me anyway, you know that, and if it could help her now...."

Lora covered her face with her palms. Only her lips remained visible: they were worrying, compressing. Dmitriev thought in despair: "Idiot! Why am I saying this? I really don't need anything...." He wanted to throw himself at his sister, embrace her. But he continued to sit there, chained to the chair. Felix, standing in the doorway, with a distracted look, looked now at his wife, now at his wife's brother. He walked like a master among these rooms—an unfamiliar squab in a bike jacket with slant pockets, something jackdawish, round, alien, in squeaky house slippers with inner soles—among the rooms in which Dmitriev's childhood had passed. He looked upon the crying sister in bewilderment, as upon disorder in the house, like a buffet door left open for some reason. Dmitriev muttered:

"Felix, get out for a minute!"

The man in the bike jacket got out. Dmitirev went up to Lora and with awkwardness tapped her on the shoulder:

"Come on, stop...."

She shook her head, she didn't have the strength to raise it....

"As you wish, as you wish.... If she wants it—all right...."

In precisely a minute Felix's voice was behind the door: "Can I come in, friends?"

He came in with an envelope.

"Today, see here, came a message from Ashirik Mamedov. The poor guy's asking if he should buy sleeping bags on our share. This is at Chardzhu, at the base of the Guber. He's got the money, but we have to answer fast: to have him get them or not. By telegraph."

He hummed and squeaked his inner soles, standing near Lora's chair with the envelope in his hand. They heard a sound from Ksenya Fyodorov-na's room. Dmitriev rushed to the door on tiptoe; he immediately saw his mother's face was different.

"Well, do you see this ugliness?" said Ksenya Fyodorovna in a weak voice, trying to get up.

A book that had been lying on the blanket slipped to the floor. Dmitriev bent over: it was the same *Doctor Faustus*, with the bookmark after a hundred pages.

"I talked to you this morning!" said Dmitriev in a kind of fervent reproach, as if this fact were extremely important for his mother's condi-tion and the whole course of the illness.

"How is it now, Mama?" asked Lora. "Here's the medicine. And put in the thermometer."

Ksenya Fyodorovna sat a moment on the bed, not moving, with an expression of deep concentration—she penetrated into herself with all her feelings. Then she said:

"But now it's as if...."—she carefully extended her hand and took the cup of water from Lora. She bent a little forward.—"It's as if there's nothing there. Foo, such nonsense!" She smiled and made a sign to Dmitriev so that he'd sit on the chair next to the bed. "Still, it's an awful filthy thing, this ulcerous disease. I'm indignant, I want to write a protest. To demand the complaint book. Only from whom? From the Lord God or something?"

"Is it comfortable for you lying like that?" asked Lora. "Move over a little closer here. Now hold the thermometer, and then I'll bring tea. Give me the hot water bottle."

Lora went out. Dmitriev sat down on the chair.

"Yes, Vitya! It's good that you came," said Ksenya Fyodorovna. "Lora and I were arguing today. On that chocolate bar. See the drawing from your childhood? Over there on the windowsill. Lorochka found it in the green cupboard. I think you drew it in the summer of '39 or '40, but Lorochka says it was after the war. When that one was living there, what was his name? Well? Such an unpleasant guy, with the eastern name. I forget, tell me yourself."

Dmitriev didn't remember. He also didn't remember the drawing. All which had to do with his art work was cut out forever. But his mother cherished these memories, and for that reason he said: yes, '39 or '40. After the war the figured fence was no longer in existence because they'd burned it. Ksenya Fyodorovna asked about Dmitriev's business trip, and he said that as it happened, today it had been decided that he wasn't going.

Ksenya Fyodorovna stopped smiling.

"I hope it wasn't because of my illness?"

"No, they just put it off. What does your illness have to do with it?"

"Vitya, I don't want the most minor of your affairs to be upset.

Because business before everything. For what? All old ladies are sick, that's their profession. We lie around a bit, groan a bit, get up on our legs, but you lose precious time and wreck your job. No, that's not the way. For example, what's tormenting me now...."—she lowered her voice,—"is Lorochka. She lies to me without compunction, says that it's not necessary to go this year; Felix hems and haws, answers evasively. And I know what's going on with them! Why do they do that? Am I really a helpless old lady that can't be left alone? Nothing of the sort! Of course there may be relapses like today, even strong pain, I'll admit, because the process works slowly, but in principle I'm getting better. And I'll get better alone beautifully. Aunt Pasha will come. You're near, there's a telephone—Lord, what problems are there? There is Marinka, of course, there is Valeriya Kuzminichna, who with pleasure...."—she became silent because Lora came into the room with the tea.

"Mama, don't get excited," said Lora. "Let Vitka talk and you listen. Why are you so excited?"

"Certain people make me indignant when they tell falsehoods."

"Ah! Well. Give me the thermometer...."—Lora took the thermometer. "Normal. Vitka, don't make mother get excited, you hear? Or I'll chase you out. And come have supper in ten minutes."

When Lora left, Ksenya Fyodorovna began to whisper about the same thing again: how to fix it so that old people could be sick quietly, and then nothing would get disturbed with the children. As always, his mother spoke half-jokingly, half-seriously. Dmitriev began to get a little annoyed. Why talk about it so much? These were pointless conversations. You couldn't change anything anyway. Then Dmitriev was called to the phone. Lena was asking if he was coming home, or if he was going to spend the night in Pavlinovo. It was already after eleven. Dmitriev said he'd stay there. Lena instructed him to give warm greetings to Ksenya Fyodorovna, and asked if he'd taken the key. He answered "Good night,"—and hung up the receiver.

This applied only to him. He alone could decide: to ask for the key or not to. About an hour and a half before bedtime, he seized a minute when Ksenya Fyodorovna was alone and said:

"There's still one other possibility: we could make an exchange, settle with you all in one apartment—then Lora would also be independent...."

"Make an exchange with you?"

"No, not with me, but with someone else, so you could live with me."

"Ach, that? Well, of course I understand. I wanted to live with you and Natashenka very much...." Ksenya Fyodorovna became silent. "But now—no."

"Why?"

"I don't know. I haven't had the desire to for a long time."

He sat, stunned.

Ksenya Fyodorovna looked at him calmly, and closed her eyes. It looked as if she were going to sleep. Then she said:

"You already made an exchange, Vitya. The exchange has occurred...." Again silence fell. With eyes closed, she whispered some gibberish: "It was a long time ago. And it always happens, every day, so don't be surprised, Vitya. And don't be angry. Just like that, unnoticeably...."

After sitting there a while he got up and left on tiptoe.

Dmitriev went to be in the room in which he'd lived with Lena at one time, that first summer. As before, the carpet hung there on the wall, nailed up by Lena. But the beautiful green wallpaper with the embossed drawing had noticeably faded and grown worn. Falling asleep, Dmitriev thought about his old watercolor: a bit of garden, a fence, the porch of the dacha and the dog Nelda on the porch. The dog had looked like a sheep. How could Lora have forgotten that after the war there was no Nelda? After the war he'd drawn like mad. Was never separated from his sketch pad. The pen and ink things came out especially well. If only he hadn't failed the exam, and hadn't thrown himself in misery into the first thing that came along, no matter what—chemical, oil, the food industry.... Then he began to think about Golishmanovo. He saw the room in the barracks where he'd lived last year for a month and a half. And he thought of how Tanya would have been the best wife for him. Once in the middle of the night he awoke and heard Felix and Lora talking in undertones.

In the morning Dmitriev left early while Ksenya Fyodorovna was still sleeping. He gave Lora the hundred rubles. Lora said it was very handy. They had breakfast in a hurry and he ran to the trolley. It was a dark dawn. The night rain ran off the trees in the garden. At the stop there were two men standing slightly apart, and a big German shepherd sitting on the ground. Who he belonged to was unclear. The empty trolley stopped, they all got in, and after everyone else the shepherd unexpectedly jumped in. The dog was big-bellied, it jumped heavily and sat down on the floor near the ticket dispenser. Two people, frightened, went up ahead, but Dmitriev stayed there in indecision. The shepherd looked out the window. It needed something in the trolley. Dmitriev thought that the driver perhaps might take it far away and it would get lost. After all, no one would understand what it was doing and why it was on the trolley. At the next stop, when people were dashing from the door, Dmitriev got out and called: "Come out, come out!"—and the dog jumped down obediently and sat on the ground. And Dmitriev managed to jump back on. Through the glass of the departing trolley he saw the dog, who was looking at him.

Ksenya Fyodorovna called Dmitriev at work two days later and said that she agreed to move in together, but that all she asked was that it be fast.

The whole drag started. The Markusheviches, of course, passed it up, many others did too, and then there appeared an expert on the sport of biking and everything was accomplished with him in the middle of April. Ksenya Fyodorovna wasn't so bad. They even had a housewarming, relatives came, the only ones that weren't there were Lora and Felix, who hadn't returned yet from their Kunia, where as usual, they were sticking around until the big summer heat started. But their troubles didn't end there: they still had to transfer both personal accounts to the name of Dmitriev, which turned out to be no less burdensome than the exchange. First the executive committee refused because the claim hadn't been correctly composed and some papers were lacking. The old geezer, Spiridon Samoilovich, the agent, who'd always boasted that the jurist of the regional housing section was his close acquaintance, turned out to be a plain liar. The jurist didn't even say hello to him when they ran into each other face to face. But this jurist was the major screw in the matter, because the claimants aren't called to the meeting, and the decision is only carried out on the basis of the jurist's conclusions and the presented documents. At the end of July, Ksenya Fyodorovna became sharply worse, and they took her to that same hospital which she'd been in almost a year before. Lena managed to get a second hearing of the claim. This time the jurist was inclined properly and all the documents were in order: a) the document affirming family relations, i.e., witness about Dmitriev's birth; b) a copy of the orders given out at one time for the right to occupy floor space; c) extracts from the building records; d) copies of the financial personal accounts given to ZHEK in which OZHK[10] requested that the executive committee satisfy the request that the personal accounts be united. Well, this time the decision was favorable.

After Ksenya Fyodorovna's death, Dmitriev had a high blood pressure crisis, and he spent three weeks in the hospital strictly confined to his bed.

What could I say to Dmitriev when we once met at mutual friends' and he related all this to me? He didn't look too well. He'd somehow gotten older all at once, and turned gray. Not yet an old man, but already middle-aged, with the flabby cheeks of an old uncle. I can remember him still a boy at the Pavlinovo dachas. Then he'd been a fat boy. We called him "Vituchni." He's three years younger than I and in those days I was closer to Lora than to him. Not long ago they took away the Dmitriev dacha as well as all the surrounding dachas, and built the "Stormy Petrel Stadium," and Lora and her Felix moved to Zyuzino, into a nine-story building.

1969

Translated by Ellendea Proffer

NOTES

1. ZHEK. Housing-exploitation office, which is in charge of the material and political well-being of a given group of apartment houses. The Zhek office checks to see if all persons living in a given place are properly registered, etc.

2. Balda. A quote from Pushkin's verse "Fairytale about the Priest and His Workman Balda."

3. Red Partisan. That is, partisans on the Bolshevik side during the Russian Civil War.

4. OGPU. Acronym for the secret police.

5. Opel/Zhopel. Adding "zh" makes the car name sound like "zhopa," meaning "ass."

6. Red professor. Again, one who supported the right side early.

7. Vasilich. Using just the abbreviated patronymic is both familiar and honorific; thus Lenin is called "Ilych."

8. Nepman. From "New Economic Policy" (NEP), a period in the 20s when limited capitalism was reintroduced.

9. GUM. The state department store near the Kremlin in Moscow.

10. OZHK. Acronym for the General Housing Commission.

Andrei Bitov

LIFE IN WINDY WEATHER

To Alexander Kushner

Finally they moved.

He was as usual struck by how overgrown the garden had become and how the lot itself seemed to have shrunk, and the dacha, hidden by undergrowth, seemed less bulky than it had last year. The trees, recently small, now reached to the windows of the second floor. The dacha, still unfinished, had already begun to get dilapidated, the frame, not yet trimmed, had gotten still blacker, and the entire dacha, which had stuck out so awkwardly and tastelessly before, now seemed to have made itself at home, to have taken root, and for the first time he liked it.

The doors opened poorly, and it was half-dark inside, like evening. The windows were shielded on the outside by winter shutters, and the sunlight, piercing through the cracks, clearly delineated one board of the shutters from another and just as neatly drew lines along the floor.

"Alyosha, if you don't need me anymore, I'll go," his father said uncertainly, and by the tone of his voice Alexei knew that his father was vacillating between staying to help him get settled and not really feeling much like staying. "I'd like to go back while the traffic is still light...."

"Of course, go ahead," said Alexei, carefully stepping on a strip of sunlight. "Thanks for bringing us."

As he accompanied his father to the car, he thought that the dacha, which would probably never be finished, somehow corresponded perfectly to this "limousine," which would never be a decent car. If his wife's parents had a sort of country house, then his father had a sort of car. In this way there was established a sort of balance.

The car finally started and his father drove off.

Alexei went back to the house. His wife was cooking cereal for their son. He was standing up in his crib, and he stamped his bare foot and joyfully held out his stocking to no one in particular. Alexei thought about the simple and for him unusual things which had to be done: undoing the shutters, chopping firewood, heating the house,—and something stretched his mouth toward his ears in that kind of smile which arises somehow apart from our own will, which we cannot restrain.

He did not sleep soundly that night, as always in a new place. He woke up early, and he was so free that he even felt at a loss. His wife, as in town, was busy with their son and had even more to do than usual. But he found himself with so much time that it was hard to get through it all. The move to the dacha was for him a real resettlement: all the parameters of his existence had changed, and the most important of these was time. As he lounged about, he turned on the radio: the announcer was giving the program for the day, and the thoroughness with which he stated the time made Alexei smile ironically. He looked at his watch—it had stopped. "Moscow time is zero hours, zero minutes, zero seconds," Alexei said.

Distances too had changed. Suddenly he no longer had to be somewhere by a specified time, he no longer had to wait for buses, which sometimes were late and sometimes didn't open their doors,—he was now totally independent in his movements, and distances which in town were inescapably connected with some means of transportation could here be traversed only on foot. In this sense he had suddenly become the owner of his own personal means of transportation—if he wanted to he went, if he didn't he didn't; he left his terminal when he had a good mind to, and in all this he was independent. After loitering about the house a bit and lighting the stove for his wife, he went out to take a walk and broke trails to the lake and the store, marvelling all the while at this new means of movement, and when he again found himself at home it was, as before, early: in town he would still be sleeping. This excessive amount of time stretching out before him made him wary. "Okay, I can finally get down to work...," he said uncertainly, and with unusual care, not regretting the time, even somehow wishing that it would race by with its usual speed and would stop being so very relative, he set about preparing a working place for himself.

He chose the second floor, which was not yet finished, and carried up a table, a chair, and his simple equipment. During this time again no time passed at all. As before, it was like a becalmed sea which he had to sail across, but he seemed to have forgotten how to sail.

He sat down at the table, and he got bored. He couldn't imagine a better place to work in, but he didn't feel like working. The four windows looked out in all four directions of the compass. They were level with the treetops, and the branches probably would have knocked against the glass if they had not been kept back by the small balconies; the branches perhaps knocked against the balusters of the balconies, but he couldn't hear it.

So he sat, thinking hostilely about his work, when he suddenly discovered that the weather outside had turned bad. The wind forcefully swooped down on his study; everything began to creak, to squeak; it felt as if a sailing ship had just set out, plunging through the water. The first large drops hit the north window; a real squall swooped in with them; the leaves of the trees which had covered the windows turned inside out like an umbrella, turned silver, and seemed to be streaming. Alexei gladly yielded to the feeling that his study was actually taking off into the air, and then it was no longer the wind but the study which raced along with such speed that it cleaved the air and caused the wind to rush by,—trees, forests, mountains flashed past the windows, merging together into an indistinguishable strip. The study howled in the gusts, and merging with it, he felt its stress, the straining of all its rafters, columns, piles, which Alexei called to himself first masts, then musical strings, as he called the whole of it first a ship, then an organ. The bad weather filled his abode with a kind of special coziness, and he wouldn't have wanted to change anything, to adjust anything in it. The jutting ribs of the house, the slag underfoot, the spiderwebs everywhere, and the clumps of dusty rubbish—everything seemed just as it ought to be.

Suddenly the wind fell, the foliage stopped flashing past the window, and a heavy shower clattered on the roof. Alexei raised his head and as if for the first time saw that there was no ceiling above him—just the roof. In places it rose in sharp angles, in places descended in obtuse arches (as he called them to himself), and then his entire dwelling took on the appearance of a cathedral, which merged in his mind with the image of the organ... But the study no longer howled, since the wind had stopped, and the roof simply jingled under the blows of the shower; the shower turned out to be a huge hailstorm; Alexei went over to the window and saw the hailstones jumping about on the floor of the balcony and said to himself that they were the size of eggs, chicken eggs, although they were no larger than bonbons. The sounds changed around him, and along with the jingling of the roof slating above him he heard other, brisk, sounds, rather like a ripping sound, and looking around, he saw water dripping from the roof into little rusty tin cans placed here and there about the room. A feeling of constancy and stability came upon him as he looked at these little cans standing here, just as they had in past years exactly in the places where the roof was leaking. The sense of all this could have become the beginning of his work, but drops began to fall onto his table, on his papers, infrequent drops, but large ones. He wandered about the second floor with the table in his hands, trying it out in various corners, but in these too there were some small leaks. He sought a waterproof spot by trial and error, by touch as it were, and had just about found one when he heard his wife, who had just discovered the rain, cry out from down below. She had apparently been sleeping until now, and she cried out that something of hers outside in the yard would get wet. Alexei went downstairs, muttered to her, "You always leave everything outside," and went out into the yard. But it had already stopped raining, and Alexei came out just in time to see it suddenly come to a stop: to see the newly colored swollen leaves swaying, each leaf more separate than before the rain; to see each leaf suddenly begin to stir in the still, thick air, and as if coming alive, bend down and straighten up its back and roll a large diamond drop off itself like a heavy burden; to see it breathe with joy and relief and offer itself up to a ray of sun which had just broken through and seemed, like the leaves, to be glowing with health.

In this way the days flowed by. Time was motionless, yet the days passed. And it was strange, looking back, to see how many of them had already passed. And he couldn't get at all used to the fact that the passage of time could be seen only by looking back and only in large sections, whereas at any present moment it was motionless. But as for work, he just couldn't get anything done. When he went to bed he couldn't understand where the time had disappeared to.

Whereas in town he woke up every morning with a feeling that yesterday evening had not been entirely normal, that is, he had chattered about God knows what, something superfluous or personal, had done some awkward and shameful things (what, exactly, he couldn't quite recall, as if he had been drunk); whereas every morning his first feeling was one of shame at the previous evening, and while dressing he immediately brushed this feeling aside and it disappeared, and then the day followed, bustling and unthinking, right up to the next "not-entirely-normal-evening," and just a brief spark of awareness had to flare up the next morning and fade away as he pulled on his trousers,—whereas in town everything was just like that, in the country everything was quite different.

In the country, on the contrary, in the family circle, in the sun, air, and water, he outwardly relaxed, grew younger, and in general began to look better. It was peaceful here, he managed very sensibly either to complete his affairs or lay them aside—specifically so as in the country at least, to be able to live peacefully and work on what he considered it his duty to work on.

At the same time, now that he had finally escaped from the city, where he labored, cursing its bustle, knowing in minutest detail and loving to expose all its nuances, now that he was able to do all those things he couldn't usually do, somehow instead of joy and activity he felt only a kind of significant emptiness which he had nothing to fill with, because now he didn't feel like doing the things he had planned on filling it with, for which he had been trying to create this emptiness. And besides, he had to some extent gotten tired of the eternal struggle and bother with himself, and consequently he found it boring by now to berate himself for laziness and idleness, to denounce, to flagellate himself, and nevertheless still not move a muscle, and then after all this to think about the whole complex—and so he didn't think about it.

At times he even felt a certain satisfaction at this state of affairs. Consciously he had already understood for a long time (this was very like the way he felt and understood the fuss and bustle, these understandings were directly related) that the main thing is simply *to live*, to be alive, and therefore no matter what your condition is—fruitful or unfruitful—as long as you are *alive*, not benumbed, and trying to accomplish things...but what does it mean to try to accomplish things: if you're not alive you won't accomplish anything anyway.

This state of idleness revealed to him, for example, that he had a son. Floundering about in the sea of time, he stayed home more and more and constantly saw his son nearby, a being so completely alive that it made him ashamed of all that was lifeless in himself, and especially of such a lifeless thing as the establishment and then the living through of this very lifelessness in himself. Such a taking-stock and comparison of himself with his son occurred in town too when, worn out by the fuss and bustle and unhappy after bothersome meetings and conversations which were so long that they caused him to lose all touch with reality, he would suddenly find himself at home and would see his son, whom he had not remembered once all day, break into a joyful smile at his arrival. At such times he felt simultaneously a kind of meaningful ebb and flow: an ebb away from his day, a flow toward his son. But in town this always happened somehow in passing, it didn't enter his consciousness, his feelings, he just somehow quickly got used to it: well, so, he's home and here's his son—nothing surprising in that... And the usual insane evening would begin.

But in the country, whether because he saw more trees and living things—cows and horses, calves and foals—, or whether the air was healthier, or whether he stayed home more and spent more time with his son, he began to look at his son differently.

He would be thinking about his son and suddenly he would understand things for which he had somehow, without noticing it when it had happened, lost his taste or sensitivity, things unusually simple and eternal in their simplicity: joy and pleasure, for example. Sometimes, bored by his idleness and thinking about the city, he would suddenly hear some foolish cooing sound from his son and he would turn around and see his outstretched hand and his face lit up with joy at the mere fact that they saw and recognized one another... Then Alexei felt his lifeless cloud fly away from him and something amazingly happy and light unfold in his breast, something which can be called many things and can be called love. He was truly grateful to his son for so generously sharing his life with him, for radiating life, and the unconsciousness of this gift did not detract from Alexei's gratitude, but rather confirmed it. He would be filled with amazement, a naive and simple amazement, when he watched his son. And as he came closer to the truth of this primitive nature and to belief in it, it was without the least bit of even goodnatured self-mockery that he had such thoughts as: How did he get to be like that? He's alive and already has everything? Hands, and eyes, and even ears? And he looks like his father?

The knowledge of how children come into being did not damp his feelings, he discarded this knowledge as not explaining anything, and then the phenomenon of his son amazed him even more—where was he from? No really, if you think it through to the end, where was he from? Or the helplessness and weakness of his son struck Alexei: the fact, for example, that it would take nothing at all to kill him, you could do it with one finger and there's the end of life in this little body!—how does so much life find room in such a small body? He was amazed at the youth of his son, at the tenderness of his skin—what a used-up piece of junk he was in comparison with his son! And the exactions of weakness struck Alexei: if it happens, for example, that his son needs something, simply needs it, wants it, he doesn't doubt in the least that everyone will obey him, will submit to him, while his son's dependence on them, his parents, is only imaginary: in actual fact the parents are dependent on him, obey him and fulfill his wishes, serve him.

Every day Alexei went for walks with his son, pushing him in his stroller. His son was already trying to walk, and once Alexei took him out of the stroller. His son stood on the ground for the first time. Alexei slowly pushed the stroller and his son held onto it and for the first time walked down the street with his father. It was windy, which made the sky seem high and the sun unusually small and distant. The couple they bought milk from was turning hay in a meadow, and either their children or grandchildren, or the children or grandchildren of summer residents, were turning somersaults in the hay; a train rumbled in the distance. And Alexei walked more slowly than he had ever walked before because for the first time, side by side with him, for some reason raising his unsteady little legs high, walked his son. And perhaps just because he was walking so slowly Alexei heeded and absorbed everything around much more intensely, minutely, palpably than usual, as if the life around him or in him had become much more concentrated at every foot of the way: every breath, every starling house, or bush, or chip in the dust of the road... And suddenly his son became unusually excited, and forgetting that he could not yet walk without support, he abandoned the stroller and stepped off to the side. He stretched his hand out to what he saw before him and said all the words he knew: "Mama, papa, wawa, goo, all." "All, all, all!" he said joyfully, pointing to what he saw. He saw a cat running across the road: an unfamiliar creature, but a living one. It was an uninteresting cat, plain and sedate; it had obviously lived a long time on this earth and was completely unaffected by his son's radiance. It neither stopped nor quickened its pace; it was not in the least affected by such rapt attention, and surprising Alexei by the constancy and measuredness of its movements it disappeared into the bushes on its own business. Alexei managed to pick up his son, who had taken the step so selflessly in the joy of learning. And suddenly he felt and understood his son as never before and remembered something long past and long forgotten about himself.

Truly, he had never seen so much life, joy, and pleasure so completely and fully embodied that they, and not flesh, seemed to be the basic material essence of his son's being. And then Alexei was even more amazed as he discovered in this so joyful babbling, in these so clear and loving eyes, not joy at all, but sadness, a sadness placed there by nature itself, simultaneous along with the joy.

In this way the son was helping his father to sail across time and come to land at evening.

Still, the fact that he was doing nothing tormented him terribly. He would remember then the bustling city, which he had so recently cursed, as a place full of life, a place outside of which he couldn't accomplish a thing. Then he would feel like going into town (though he wasn't always concretely aware of this, since it contradicted his summer schedule). And then unfinished matters would somehow all by themselves begin to be recalled, perhaps not very significant matters, but all the same, until he got them done they would give him no peace and he would not enjoy his freedom because of these trifles. And then he would begin (and this was almost activity) to make little lists of these matters, large and small, which kept cropping up and piling up, gladly and even lovingly including the merest trifles. He would rewrite these lists in various sequences: by importance, by time, by convenience of itinerary. He would elaborate points and make remarks in parentheses: "mustn't forget to ask," "mustn't forget to say," "pretend you forgot." After which he would remember one more thing, perhaps the most important of all, and would have to rewrite the list again to insert this matter in its proper place.

He would play around with these lists for a while and then begin to explain to his wife that he absolutely had to make a trip into town. His wife of course said he didn't need to go, that he already had so little time for relaxation and work, that this was all just a waste of time. He realized that her words were just, even recognized his own words in hers, and he began, as was completely natural, to get irritated, and like a child he rebelled not against the meaning of the words but against the logic by which they had arrived at these words; it was the logic which seemed especially unfounded and unjust, and irritated him more than anything else. They argued each point and then each went his own way: his wife to take care of the house, he to lie somewhere in the sun. But then, like people who love each other and know each other too well, they forgot their quarrel. Neither argued any longer about the trip to the city, at some point or other it simply began to be talked about as something already understood; the day was set, his wife gradually remembered more and more new errands: what to buy, what to bring from home,—the list grew and became much too large to be completed in one day's trip. But this didn't bother either one of them, because it was somehow clear to both that there was really nothing to take care of, that he simply needed to go to the city in order to see once more that everything there was bustle and delirium, and then to return satisfied, charged up, and perhaps begin to do something.

What always happened, though, was this. In town he would manage to get some item on his wife's list done and half of his own and return cheerful and raring to go and sit down to work the next day. Only the next day he didn't sit down to work, didn't get himself moving. This impulse to get moving, for which town was supposed to be the external stimulus, just completely faded away.

When all this became a steadily and clearly recurring cycle, Alexei became unbearable. Whereas in the city he was calm and balanced in the mornings (that was when yesterday appeared to him as something vague, half-forgotten, and insane), now it was the other way around. He would calm down only toward evening, and after involuntarily oversleeping he would wake up an irritable crank, almost sick—and his wife would bear the brunt of it. This was apparently a substitute for the work which he should have started each morning. And only towards evening, when the day was almost over and he could calmly live with the thought that there was no use starting anything anymore today, better to start tomorrow, "sleep on it,"—only then did he become the very nice person that he was in reality. In the morning and afternoon, though, he was a real fury (a fury because he was irritable in an unmasculine way), and everything seemed part of an evil design: any little trifle—his socks, his razor, matches—opposed him, hid somewhere; sharp corners appeared where they had never been before; something would fall; something would squeak; mosquitoes attacked him by surprise everywhere; little persecutions, dirty tricks, annoyances were stuffed into every little nook and cranny; everything stealthily carried on an absurd guerrilla warfare with him. Everything raised protest, hatred, and anger in him.

By the end of the day the abundance of irritations, recollections, associations, thoughts, and ideas would leave him tired out. And then— here the only thing lacking would be some act of reckless despair, just throwing up his hands and giving up on the whole thing—he would pull from his store of ideas one, arbitrarily selected, carelessly toss it about, savor it a bit, and present it to his wife at teatime, getting overly excited and agitated in his need to somehow rid himself of these feelings. His idea would be pretty good, but it wouldn't solve anything. While in general it would be on a rather high level, it was nevertheless on a scale with those in most idle conversations: the conversations of neighbors, of his wife's relatives, or of his father. As a rule some external impulse would give rise to an idea, a political one for example; then he could generalize and attack, extinguish his creative ardor, and calm himself down. He would hardly be making any real effort and would once more come to a halt on that difficult ascent towards work and come sliding back down the slope, so that tomorrow he would be able to pass and overcome the same moment of inertia and then ascent as yesterday and the day before, perhaps even gradually immersing himself in the matter inch by inch, but again coming no nearer to actually reaching his goal. He would take up the newspaper, look at it as if nothing were there, and say, for example:

"It's not quite clear what sort of meaning they've attached now to the word 'formalism.' I still understand it in its everyday sense that's forgotten now—'He's a formalist in matters of honor,' for example. If you can't pay a debt at cards—then it's a bullet in the head. That is, a strict adherence to certain principles, rules, forms, which are presented to us, nurtured in us, exist before us—an adherence which is often contrary even to common sense. In this case formalism is something conservative which has existed for a long time and become permanent and static. Academicism, then, is the highest degree of formalism. There cannot be formalism in something newly formed, something that has just come into being—this is a new form. Perhaps they're using 'formalism' for 'unjustified form,' or, as they say, for form which doesn't correspond to reality? But if one literally compares art with reality, that is compares them formally, then art has always been completely conventional and has never been a copy of reality. Not to mention the fact that art itself is reality anyway... Take even such an obvious phrase, for example, as: 'Ivan Ivanovich thought such-and-such and such-and-such,'—that is just such a conventionality! Almost an abstraction. Who knows what he was thinking!... In and of itself true art has not only never aspired to conventionality, but has always been most anxious to avoid it. To free oneself from the shackles of conventionality, of ossification, is precisely what one can call formalism, to free oneself and come closer to the living truth—this is the mechanism by which new forms are born. It is simply a liberation from forms which are past, confining, or incapable of expressing what is new—an emancipation, an escape into open space, a coming closer to that which is alive. Calling this formalism is just like calling black white."

The idea would sometimes be intelligent, sometimes stupid; sometimes precise, sometimes not so precise; sometimes original, sometimes unoriginal; on the average—well, an idea. Having expounded it, he would gradually regain his sense of time and place; the room which had blurred while he spoke would come back into focus, and the objects become clearly visible. He would nervously look at his wife's face and read approval of the idea in it, then he would calm down and feel a certain pleasant drainedness, as if he had done some real work. Having closed up shop for the day, as if having rounded up the whole unruly herd of his thoughts into the enclosure and lowered the bar with a clang, and for the last time having looked back over his shoulder at all that motley mess, that bellowing, bleating mass, he would return, tired and satisfied, to his hut to sleep, to remember nothing until morning.

One day he awoke and at that precise moment his petty, irritable splintered world fell on him and entered into him. This happened before there was even any concrete reason for it, as if this petty irritation stood at the head of his bed, watched over him, kept guard, waited for him to open his eyes and his soul. At night this irritation apparently slept, all curled up next to his slippers like a domestic pet. Alexei felt tired and desperate. "I'll go into town," he said. "When?" asked his wife. "Right now."

They argued—but these days it didn't do any good to argue with him: they shouted—and his son began to cry, and they stopped talking. Finally his wife wanted to be left alone and Alexei got permission to go to town with the absolute condition that he bring from home the night table which his wife couldn't live without. In this way the permission was rather more like an order to bring the night table than permission, and this conciliated his wife. Alexei was already feeling as if he were in the city, and even an order to bring back the sideboard couldn't have deterred him.

But as it happened, just as he was about to leave for the station his father unexpectedly arrived and brought with him the very night table in question. And so on the one hand he didn't need to go in by train, which was always so crowded, but on the other his wife no longer agreed to his going since the night table had already been brought and no new errand had come up. His wife again said that he had no reason at all to go and that she really ought to check out why he kept spending so much time in town. This was a mistake because he was in the clear and now he had a good reason to get all upset and quarrel with her. The advantage was on his side. His wife lost the skirmish.

He left feeling relieved. The quarrel had eased his tension. He felt a pleasant emptiness inside following his spasm of irritation. They left for the station along the rough country road. A strong wind raced along the rails to the city. The car waddled like a duck, and the wind outstripped it. He saw the train platform, from which the wind seemed to have blown all the people. A train had just left. The picture was sad and chilly; it calmed one. For some reason he imagined a girl standing on the platform with her back to the wind, imagined her figure: her dress pressed to her back by the wind, the bubble of her skirt blown forward, her hair streaming in front of her. It wasn't his wife. He didn't choose any face for her. There was in fact no such girl, but there certainly might have been, so he wasn't imagining anything extraordinary. A kind of bittersweet feeling filled his mouth at the whole picture and at the image of the girl in the wind, a feeling which fully corresponded to a general bittersweet sensation he was experiencing and which he called to himself to "acerb."

He could already recall the quarrel very calmly. It's strange, he thought, how easily and convincingly I dispelled her suspicions, even though I didn't try to prove anything, since I really don't have anything to prove—I'm not seeing anyone. And how unsure and difficult it would have been if I hadn't been blameless at the moment. The main thing is that there are the same grounds for suspicion in both cases. But if I had had something to hide, it would have seemed unconvincing to me the way I go to town just to go, and I would have begun to spin tales in order to hide something, but I really would be giving myself away.... All life with people seemed to Alexei to be a structure of suspicion and ignorance, and he pictured this structure as composed of interconnected rods, like steel fittings, or like a thick net in which the threads going in one direction are suspicions and the cross threads are ignorance, and when these threads intersect, in the knots... He got confused, the image didn't work any further. No, we really don't know anything about one another, continued Alexei, we could live together for a hundred years and still not know, only make guesses; our deductions are merely castles in the air, and these castles... It only seems as if these castles refer to other people, but they're really about oneself. We do, of course, know really—but almost nothing with total certainty. And we keep wanting that total certainty, we keep on trying to find out for sure, and from this mechanism arises doubt—from our trying to make sure for ourselves, trying to feel it. Situations are stereotyped and repeat themselves endlessly, every one of them can be interpreted different ways, each one can arouse suspicion, and only one in a hundred has any basis for suspicion. Because of that one percent we suspect all one hundred percent. If we could be cynical with a machine-mind cycnicism, then we would never be found out. We always give ourselves away, always call suspicion on ourselves, even though we could dissolve our guilt in the sea of those very situations when we weren't guilty. and we wouldn't even have to lie. But that's not the way people are... He again recalled the quarrel and thought that his wife hadn't really seriously suspected anything, that she even knew for sure that he was going into town just to go. She had said it without cause, just to insult him... After all, insults are always unfounded. She had no grounds, but what about a reason? He sensed perhaps that there was a reason, but was afraid to think about it. And after all, if there really had been something going on in town, thought Alexei, digressing, and if she had really known about it, then she wouldn't have said anything to him, she would have let him go without a quarrel, would have held off, gathered proof, and there would always be too little proof, and she would have kept on waiting for that next, decisive piece of evidence which would make everything clear, but this decisive piece of evidence would never turn up and would not even exist...poor woman!

Suddenly the car seemed to wake up and jerked forward, stopped swaying—they had come out onto the highway. People passed them, coming from the village heading toward the station, and Alexei was amazed at how many kept coming and coming, yet no one at all was on the platform. His father also cheered up on the smooth road, felt freer behind the wheel. A dog ran toward them and his father said:

"Have you ever noticed how all animals run a bit sideways?"

"Yes, I've noticed," said Alexei and could feel the tone of dissatisfaction in his voice which always appeared in conversations with his father. In this case he was a bit irritated by his saying "all animals," since it was not "all animals" but one dog that had run by. But he caught this mild irritation in himself and was already mulling over the irritation and condemning himself for it. Of course his father always talked somewhat unnaturally, that is, he talked not because he had something to say but just to make conversation, and this, moreover, was always colored by a certain intellectuality and emotionality of tone which was bound to be irritating. But now he often felt that his father really couldn't talk any other way and that in his inconsequential conversations there was a rather terrifying loneliness which made him try, in his inability to communicate, to retain at least the symbol of communication. Alexei glanced cautiously at his father, and suddenly saw how very old his father was, and a painful sense of resemblance, kinship, of the inevitability of likeness passed through him like a slender needle.

"Alyosha," his father said, wanting to talk. But the son was silent and his father had to begin again, had to overcome the awkwardness of having nothing in particular to begin with, since he didn't know what to say to his son so as to make the conversation arise naturally; so he said: "You know, it suddenly occurred to me, I don't know why..."

Alexei, continuing to note that day's feelings for his father, was touched by this maneuver and said to help him (which he would never have done another time):

"What occurred to you?"

"Have you ever heard the name Viksel?"

"No."

"How can that be? He's a famous scientist. A corresponding Member of the Academy?" he said questioningly. But his son seemed not to have heard the question and the father continued: "We studied together. I hadn't seen him for thirty years, and then I ran into him the day before yesterday... He's a big man now." His father sighed and again paused for his son's answer.

His son hummed something to himself and remained silent.

"Well, and now," his father said with a sigh, "he's in communications. Head of the institute. His institute has become extremely important now..." His father's face took on a mysterious look. "Because in this war it won't be the first day that will be most crucial, but the second..."

Alexei smiled ironically.

"And why's that?"

"Well, you see," his father answered, coming alive, "I didn't know this myself, I read it somewhere recently." His father's voice began to flow smoothly, almost like a lecturer's. "You see, the primary blow will be delivered on the first day, and then on the second day the war itself, strictly speaking, will begin, and then..." His father paused meaningfully, and then like water breaking through a dam his words began to flow still more easily and rapidly. "Communications will be the most important and difficult thing of all, since it will be difficult from a practical point of view to command not only the army, but a platoon as well—so everything depends on communications! Because there may be as much as several kilometers between soldiers..."

"That's silly, papa," said Alexei amiably and softly, amazing himself at his tone and at the fact that today he wasn't getting all worked up at such talk, although usually it took a whole lot less to make him flare up and get impertinent with his father.

"Why so?" asked his father, half-attacking, half-defending himself. He looked perplexed, as if he didn't know whether to feel insulted already or whether to force his son to say something obviously insulting.

"Why," his son answered calmly and affectionately, "would you need these communications on the second day when on the first no one would be left alive anyway?"

This was not like the usual course of such conversations—no squabbling had arisen—and his father was flustered.

"Well, if that's so...," he agreed uncertainly. And he fell silent. He was half-glad that his son was so restrained and polite today, and half-sorry that no conversation had ensued.

They drove for a while in silence. His father tried to think of a new topic, and not finding one, took up his most pointed and cunning subject: his son's work and affairs. Alexei continued to think about his father with the same sadness and tenderness and was not at all irritated (and this was a complete exception to the rule) when his father stepped into his field and began to weave hostile absurdities. Yet usually Alexei could not endure opinions of unqualified people, especially of his relatives and least of all of his father—it was out of some twisted thirst for communication that his father would say these things which were so important to Alexei simply to say them, even deliberately say them. And Alexei thought: why does Father deliberately say these things? After all, he always gets upset when his son gives him an impertinent reply, and Alexei always does get impertinent at such talk, like a little boy. The main thing is, his father knows all this; he is, after all, an intelligent man... And as he thought about all this Alexei began to understand better his father's awful loneliness. Namely, that over the long years the sweet feeling of insult had in its own way become dear to his father. "And just what have I said this time? No one ever..." And after this his father would almost be able to stop thinking about things, to shed his responsibility and train his blindness to a fine point.

Alexei thought about all this while his father told him in a calm voice things which always irritated him and led to quarrels... Alexei thought that these constant squabbles occurred only with his father, and not with others, precisely because of their closeness and lack of indifference to each other, because of his desire for equality between them. It's simple and easy with those you're indifferent to only because, justifiably or not, you set yourself above them—you feel an inexplicable superiority, and so you forgive them. Or rather, you ignore them. But his father is not his equal, so he's got to be forgiven. This was a childish atavism, this desire for equality. There could be no equality here. There was rather a reverse equality, a different dependence—one of father on son; and perhaps there had always been this very dependence. "And it's the same with me and my son," thought Alexei, "exactly the same..."

They were driving through a forest, and the road was quiet, there was no breeze: it felt like a warm summer day—and suddenly they drove out into an open space. There were fields, ploughed lands; he caught a brief glimpse of a bumpy country road next to a barn standing askew, and an emaciated, wild-eyed cow looked askance from a roadside ditch; further on the fields stopped suddenly, there were meadows and scanty shrubs blown about by the wind, and nothing more, not even any cars coming from the opposite direction. The wind cleared the horizon and a deep blue forest, the height of grass, rose in the distance with a strange clarity. Alexei lazily looked out the window and thought how unusally close and comprehensible this inexpressive wasteland felt to him. An affectionate, cool, calm feeling settled in Alexei when his glance, without straining, slid along this smooth space and encountered almost nothing to linger over. His glance was like a slender, suddenly animated thread which connected him with nature, and two scale weights hung on the thread of his glance: he himself and the wasteland—on one level, in complete balance... The grass touselled by the wind, the rusty little puddle in the grass, the solitary crooked little pine bent over it—all were dear to Alexei. His glance kept moving, never clinging to one thing—he felt spacious, it was like a deep sigh. The slow, indiscernible gradation of shades of green, blue, gray, the elusive pale beauty of the wasteland entered Alexei and filled him with a melancholy joy, a pleasant, vague regret. It was this cool beauty which now seemed to him to be the most authentic kind of beauty. This had not been so even recently, he thought, just recently I might have said: what a dull place! And he felt somehow surprised as he recalled that just five minutes before they passed a lovely pine grove like the ones Shishkin loved to paint, and Alexei had not even noticed it, just as he had never noticed the wasteland before. Alexei thought how little experience and how much effort were needed in order to perceive vivid beauty, to perceive what is usually meant by beauty. He remembered the sharp colors of the South which had so delighted him at one time—and now they seemed so lifeless, inauthentic, like paper flowers. "I am a northerner," he thought almost proudly. "If I ever go someplace for a vacation, I'll go to the tundra... I really must go to the tundra in the spring!" he said to himself excitedly, and he cheerfully straightened up on the car seat and glanced sidelong at his father.

Although before his father had habitually and unconsciously started quarrels with his son, he was now suddenly glad that no quarrel had occurred, and was grateful to his son for this and loved him. It was pleasant for his father to be sitting behind the wheel of his own car, earned by his own work, even though it was a small car—but then not everyone had one, especially now. How outrageous of them to raise the price: just think, a "Zaporozhets," just an old junkheap, and still... But here he was behind the wheel of his own car and next to him was his son, no one could say that his son had achieved little in his life. I was still just a kid when I was his age, didn't think about much of anything, while he's such a talented man, and well-known... And it was obvious how pleased he was to have heard in that one sentence Alexei had addressed to him the word "Papa," and how much he would like to hear it more often. "And here I am waiting for the time when my son will say 'Papa' to me," Alexei was thinking, "I need that as much as he does..." The father was flattering his son and in doing this it was again obvious how well he actually knew what irritated his son and what pleased him. Because once again he was saying unnecessary things which in principle should be unacceptable to his son, only now these things pleased his son. His son understood that the conversation had not changed at all in the way it worked, but now he thought: what can you do, the form of father's conversation is so unsuccessful, but its essence is the most beautiful thing in the world—love.

So they drove along the windy clear wasteland, and the forest remained on the horizon like a low deep brush. When the highway began to bear left the forest began to get closer, to grow; hills appeared and the road went up and down. They came to a long straight rise and could no longer see anything. When they got to the top they found themselves at a railroad crossing. The barrier was up; the switchman's hut looked through its red window at the sunset; in the distance below the rails disappeared around a bend in a curve that resembled a sabre: a train might appear any time on its blade,—and there was no one in sight. The wind rose again here with new strength and tossed the grass and shrubs in all directions; it slapped against the windows like a hail of slaps in the face... This crossing destroyed one's sense of time and seemed drawn-out. And Alexei looked about now in the same way that he had looked at the empty platform at the beginning of the suburbs.

Then, looking above the forest with the feeling inspired in him by the crossing, with the picture opening before it and the wind rushing all about it, looking about sadly and lazily, he suddenly saw something rising over the forest which he had never seen before, yet which seemed so familiar—a silent puffy ring on a slender gray stalk opening out like a bud and a fire, thick as kasha, slowly turning about within it. His father wouldn't be able to see it as his eyes were glued to the road, and the son, in a voice which amazed even himself by its strange calm, a calm which itself produced fear, said, "It's war, Father."

Now they would have to brake sharply, turn around, and rush back, away from the city, to get his wife and son... Alexei imagined how the four of them would drive and drive along empty roads, going further and further away from the dead city... But no, the shock wave would reach them at this crossing, they would not even have time to turn around. And the car would fly like a speck of dust and they would no longer feel anything inside this speck of dust... The radius of destruction... Or maybe they would have time to stop and jump out, fall face down in a ditch at the side of the road. Whirling about in the air, their "limousine" would take off above them, or the hut from the crossing would float past above them, maintaining its orientation in space with uncertain ease, and only then would they crawl out of the ditch into a strange and empty silence which even in daylight would create a feeling of eternal darkness, as if parts of the earth were gone... But no...

Alexei's daydream passed instantaneously and calmly. At another time it had occurred repeatedly, so by now it had lost its sharpness, was habitual and did not frighten him. At one time it had been agonizing: during periods of prolonged, forced separations it had meant the destruction of everything dear to him in his distant home city and his own empty, useless preservation. But now, suddenly feeling the edge of the usual crater hollowed out by this once agonizing daydream, he lightly slid into it: comfortably, without lingering over it in his consciousness, several pictures passed before him in a single moment—and that was all... They were driving in the same car, along the same road. If he had stopped his daydream, focussed on it, then the only thing that would have struck him in it would probably have been its banality, and his strongest feeling would have been relief at the thought that nothing is actually written on our faces and that at least some of our stupidities remain hidden and we don't have to blush over them... But now the car was coming out of the forest, which they had seemed to rush through surprisingly quickly. Because the forest had lain so blue so long on the horizon, because it had taken them so long to get to it, it felt as if the forest should have been more endless... And they found themselves already at the fork in the road by the automobile inspection post, and turning left again they began to enter the suburb.

His father passed the inspection post all scrunched down as usual, trying to make himself unseen, and when the red motorcycles grazing at the side of the road remained where they were he livened up, straightened up, became unnaturally dashing, cursed the inspection "cops," and hitting on one of the other habitual targets for his too frequent and therefore harmless abuse, he continued to talk about them in an excited tone of voice that demanded sympathy and censure on the part of his son; his son easily and readily agreed with him and said yes, that's true, since the subject of conversation made no difference to him. The father was again grateful to his son, glanced sideways at him deferentially, as if evaluating his son, seemingly again and again noting with pleasure that his high evaluation was in no way excessive, but if anything underestimated... Alexei saw his father in the rearview mirror looking at him and tried to look nonchalant and important.

"You're getting gray already," his father said. (This phrase always signified a final peace and gratitude and for some reason always pleased his son.)

"Yes," his son said carelessly, "I have been gray for a long time."

In this visit to town, as in all the others, Alexei didn't get anything done and felt especially strongly how senseless and unnecessary were the supposed affairs which had brought him there. All day he rushed from place to place, found one person in and another out, met someone else just to set the next (also unnecessary) meeting, and suddenly, or so it seemed, found himself in a long narrow room with almost no furniture, among strangers. It was dark outside, Alexei should have returned to the dacha long ago, his wife would be getting nervous and annoyed there, and there was absolutely no point in his being here... Three good-looking girls, strangers to him, were sitting on the floor with mats, their expressive legs crossed; a tall fellow, also a stranger, was pushing buttons on a tape recorder; one other fellow, the host, he at least was an acquaintance—a schoolmate he hadn't seen in ages, so of course he would come across him today—he wandered about the room, now turning off the light so that only the green eye of the tape recorder remained on, now turning the light on again so that everybody squinted in confusion and looked unnaturally pale; and the only bottle of vodka had been drunk up; and all the cigarettes were gone... Alexei sat in his corner on a pile of books feeling strangely sad, and just couldn't budge from his place even though he should have left long ago for the dacha, just sat there as if waiting for something. His sadness was almost shameful yet sweet, and it reminded him of something—he didn't know just what, as if he were at one of those first school parties with girls. Lonely—but unable to leave. The host again turned on the light and got out an air pistol from somewhere. They started target-shooting—the target was the cover of a German magazine—there was a dinosaur on the cover. Alexei suddenly got unusually interested, and with childish excitement grabbed the pistol: "Give it to me! Give it to me!"—and then he just couldn't hand it over to anyone else: "One more shot! Just one more!" "You know," his friend laughed, "that's just the way it was with me... When I first got this pistol I shot from morning to night, till I was utterly worn out. Wasted all my time on it. If only someone had taken it away from me!.." "Lend it to me," said Alexei with childish fervor. But his friend immediately refused and wouldn't let him have it. Alexei wouldn't give in: "No, lend it to me. Just for a while. I'll give it back... Just for a few days and then I'll give it back... You were planning on coming out to the dacha anyway, you can get it back then..." His friend finally seemed to tire of the argument and, coldly raising his eyebrows, he agreed. Alexei immediately grabbed the toy and left, hardly saying goodbye.

When he arrived at the dacha he didn't show his wife the pistol—he went to bed. And the next morning he took it up to his study on the second floor, hiding it in his shirt. Alexei admired it for a long time and then opened the barrel, enjoying the opposition of the spring of the cock and the coolness of the steel. He put in a lead pellet and shot at the rusty can standing on the floor. He hit it. He kept shooting for a long time at the little cans placed about in case of rain. The cans jangled and jumped, the pellets glanced off in various diretions. Alexei placed one can on top of another and then another on top of them, and the cans rolled around on the floor.

His wife quietly stole up to him, attracted by the strange sounds. She was surprised. She joined him in the shooting.

Alexei crawled around the floor picking up the pellets. They kept rolling away and disappearing. Each time they shot, fewer of them remained.

Thus the day passed.

On the next day Alexei shot for a while again in the morning until he could find only one pellet. He shot it—and there were none left.

Alexei went downstairs and aimlessly wandered around the yard. Again he went upstairs, again he took up the pistol and looked at it for a long time, stroking its lustreless, burnished surface. Looking out the north window he pensively raised the pistol to his temple. The barrel immediately found a place for itself, falling into a sort of recess which seemed made for it. He suddenly remembered the humorous words of his platoon commander: "Every man has a natural recess in his shoulder for a rifle butt." With a bemused chuckle he lowered the pistol, and for a moment more he continued to feel the cold circle on his temple. Alexei opened the barrel and cocked the pistol without a pellet. Again he laid it to his temple and slowly pulled the trigger. There was a hollow little bang and Alexei felt a slight pain. "A toy," he thought dully, turning the pistol about and staring at it with surprise and mistrust. "A toy pistol... And my toy temple." His glance slid over to the pile of clean paper. "And my toy desk." Alexei looked up at the roof. "And a toy house." A spider fell from above and began to sway in front of his nose, dangling up and down. "A toy spider," Alexei said aloud.

Alexei got up and wandered around his second floor for a long time with the pistol hanging in his slackened hand. He stuck the pistol under a pile of rags in the corner, looked at the pile with seeming satisfaction, and then immediately forgot completely about it.

To his wife's surprise Alexei suddenly became quiet and even-tempered. He wandered about the house more absent-minded than usual and didn't answer questions right away, as if answering to a call from a distance. When he bumped into something he didn't even get mad, just smiled absent-mindedly and guiltily. The variety of projects he thought of tormented him and he just couldn't decide which to take up first. And if he forced himself by great effort to settle on just one thing chosen at random, he still didn't know where to begin; too many things rose up before him, too many things filled his head to the bursting point—and so all his tormenting idleness suddenly turned out to be extremely full. At times he would be distracted from all this and then would begin to feel a tenderness for everything, would begin to live. This joy would be communicated to his wife, too, and they would feel unusually grateful to one another.

When he finally sat down at his desk it was Saturday, getting on toward evening. It didn't work out though because relatives came on Saturday to spend the day on Sunday. He was already feeling feverish, thoughts teemed, and despairing of ordering them, he finally steeled himself, jumped in, as if into cold water,—and it turned out that there really wasn't such chaos, the chaos turned to strength, everything was becoming ripe, indispensable, unique, and he was swimming, swimming...when something made him look out the window and he saw his smiling relatives coming up the path. He looked at them without recognition, as if remaining invisible to them, but they had already seen him and were waving. When he heard the commotion and exclamations below and he knew that he too should be standing in the doorway greeting them, his thoughts began to scatter and became disorderly again. For a brief moment he tried to force them back, restrain them, not let them go—but they scattered. He felt this physically, as if in his brain, in his cranium, a thought was crawling away...and giving up trying to restore any of them, he hurriedly went downstairs.

He stood in the doorway, smiling affectionately and quietly to everyone, while his relatives unburdened themselves in the passageway of all their bags and bundles and exchanged some rather unclear and too joyful exclamations with him and his wife. "Well, how's the work coming?" was all he made out. It was his father-in-law who said that to him. "Not bad," Alexei said ironically. But his irony was devoid of venom, he wasn't irritated now—and this too was the result of his period of idleness, when he had convinced himself that he was in no way better than anyone else, and his occupation was the same as everyone else's, and there was no call to make a cult of it. In addition, the feeling remained that now he had finally begun and would continue no matter how much he was interrupted, that his work had gotten underway. Basically everything was fine, although physically he didn't feel too well: he had a fever and the small of his back ached—his unslaked desire. Well, what of it, they're not to blame, they would have come anyway—he had forgotten...

Having put down their things, they went into the house.

Alexei conversed with his father-in-law on phenological and political subjects, made tea ("Where did you learn to make such marvelous tea!" his mother-in-law said ecstatically), paid attention to his guests: the duty of hospitality was his—and he fulfilled it. There was some confusion as to who were the guests and who the hosts: the owners of the house had come as guests, and he, a guest in their home, received them now as host. Whether because of this or because they were relatives, but not blood-related, life in the house turned into a cumbersome and distorted ritual.

All the rest of Saturday was taken up with tea drinking. They all poured for one another, handed each other saucers and spoons, here, do try this cookie or have some of this candy; from time to time someone took the teapot to be refilled with hot tea and this provided a brief respite, a halt, and then it all began again with renewed vigor. It became even harder to tell who was whose guest. But then, fortunately, it was time to go to bed.

Sunday was something else again. A disguised war was waged in the kitchen, near the baby's crib, and outside in the yard. The whole thing was made more complicated and confused by etiquette, politeness, and the friendly way they treated each other: all this served as a kind of battle shield or fortification—the Trojan horse with a communal apartment placed inside it, noisy squabbling baked into a sweet dough. Breakfast went off comparatively easily, but only because dinner lay ahead, for which all forces were being martialled. With the approach of the dinner hour the war moved into battle, the battle into a bloody slaughter. Their son, to whom everyone gave such loving attention, sometimes fell into the dense encirclement where they kept tearing him away from one another, cooing to him all the while, and at other times he was abandoned by everyone and found himself with no supervision at all. It was precisely because of this that no one was nearby when he got into his mother's powder, scattered it about, smeared it on himself, and ate some of it. Then mother and daughter, wife and mother-in-law, mother and grandmother—all quarreled a bit about who was to blame.

Finally dinner too passed, the relatives began to get ready for the return to town, and Alexei, tired and sated, afraid of the impending final battle known as "preparations for the road," simply fled, explaining that his son had not yet had his stroll.

He put his child in the stroller and pushed him about the village. Outside the gates of his own home it immediately seemed to him that it was still Saturday and no relatives had come or would be coming. Again he felt in himself that trembling which he had experienced yesterday on his second floor, that world which had arisen in him then, had pulsed, had come alive, had seized him and borne him away—he joyfully felt the same smooth swaying and as always thought with surprise and ecstasy that it hadn't broken off, hadn't stopped, that it could still happen to him. He tenderly thought about his wife, the dacha, and his relatives, and he glanced at his son. The latter sat in the stroller: fat, grasping the hand rails, looking at the world. What was he thinking about? He does, after all, think... "There are three things," thought Alexei, "which no one knows about, and everything that we know about them is only what we or other people have imagined and then affirmatively repeated so many times in the form of opinions that they seem real... Those three things are what, and more important, how a child thinks, because he cannot yet talk and when he can he won't remember how he thought; what a man thinks in his last moment, when life is coming to an end in him and he can no longer tell anyone anything; and thirdly, and this at every stage of life, what does a man—any man, Mr. Ivan So-and-So Ivanov—what does this man think who is someone else and not you..." Alexei pushed the stroller along the uneven, awkward side streets and he wasn't so much looking and seeing for himself as he was watching how his son looked and saw. Even though he didn't know what his child was thinking, it seemed to him as if an absolutely certain link was being established between them. And furthermore, it was he who was the subordinate one in this relationship, not his son, it was he who saw through his son's eyes. His vision had seemed sharper since yesterday, but now with his son, with his son's eyes, everything seemed even more sharply focussed.

He took his son around the village as if around a huge ABC book... They would see a stream and he would say to his son: "See, a stream?" His son would look at the stream, and Alexei would say, "This is a stream," and it really was a stream. He would say to his son, "There's a goat," and it really was a goat. He would say to his son, there's a tree, a boy, a house,—and it all really was just what he said it was. Alexei would not have been able to explain just then what was going on and what was happening to him. He felt a kind of genius in this nominative simplicity of things and words, and he felt as if he were on some higher threshhold beyond which everything truly begins, and that few had probably ever stood on such a threshhold of a new logic, a new thought process, a new world. He saw a cow. "There's a cow, and there's her son—a calf," this was all so; and further on, beyond the cow, lay a swampy meadow with such smooth young greenery that it seemed like something one could not touch, like an emanation perhaps. In the meadow strange little flowers in the form of white cotton balls were growing as if they had just surfaced onto the green, thick, and yet airy surface. The meadow was empty, and only somewhere in the center a small boy, made still smaller by the distance, stood bent over, apparently picking these white flowers; but from the distance it looked as if he wasn't picking flowers but was stroking the meadow's surface, which was as impalpable as the sky. He stood there, apparently barefooted, not afraid to get his feet wet, and not afraid of falling through: there was, after all, a quagmire under the covering there—he was apparently too light; and beyond the meadow stretched an embankment, and a locomotive raced, chugging along, piping its tune with amusing diligence, now hiding behind bushes, now reappearing; it worked like a fussy old man, looking small in the distance, and behind it stretched an endless line of cars which seemed oddly not to coincide with its hurry. Even though it was far away everything was clearly visible, as always happens on these last windy days—each car or platform was visible. Alexei felt like counting the cars and was too lazy to count them, and he didn't. Here was the meadow, the boy, the train... And all this was really so—the meadow and the boy and the train, and the cow with her calf, and he with his son... All this for a prolonged moment fell into a straight line and formed a kind of axis, and this was perhaps the greatest truth of all those that he so persistently sought and had sometimes found. The seemingly accidental symmetry by which his son stretched out his arm in the direction of the train, and the cow chewed its cud standing with its head in the opposite direction in which the train was going, and the meadow, and the boy stroking the meadow, and finally the train—and all of this as if lying on one axis which coincided with his gaze and the wind, united by the cupola of the sky, as by a legate, and brought to a completion within him, Alexei—all of this and the seemingly endless continuation of the axis beyond visible bounds—the feeling of this symmetry was one of the happiest feelings. It was a pinnacle, a summit, an explosion, and in the next moment, whether the train left or the boy moved from his place or the cow...the axis fell apart, and Alexei felt a blissful emptiness: he existed now in the greenery of the meadow, in the boy in the meadow, in the train moving away, in the sky, in his son, in each and every thing. His life exploded, sprayed out, and seemed to flow away and fill everything with meaning and life. He felt like a god, nowhere and in everything, embracing and permeating the world.

He suddenly found himself standing by a meadow he had seen a thousand times before, holding the stroller while his son babbled something. Then as if by the reversal of a film strip in which they play back an explosion, where all the fragments fly back and the smoke and flame flow back, thicken, and disappear like a genie into a bottle and only a smooth space remains as if nothing had exploded, Alexei separated himself off into a tiny point in space and felt as if he were drunk. He turned back, pushing before him his likeness, his eyes, his joy; he opened the gate and walked along the path in the garden; and he came alongside a flowerbed—of all flowerbeds this one was the most accidental. It was about the size of a plate, and nestled right next to the path, because it had only just been made and hadn't been planned at all. His mother-in-law, his wife's mother, his son's grandma, had made it today on some unclear inspiration, repeating all the while, "My grandson's flowerbed, my grandson's flowerbed." It was sentimental, but sentimentality toward children had ceased to seem reprehensible to Alexei when his own child had appeared, and on the contrary was somehow right and understandable. They came up to the flowerbed and Alexei said, "Here is a flowerbed, it's your flowerbed, these are your flowers..." He paused, squatted down, bent towards himself a yellow flower with pendant buds and couldn't remember its name. He bent it over so it would be closer to his son: his son immediately stretched out his arms to the flower, his little hands, his little finger-petals, his little petals, petal to petal—he reached out and then hesitated, not sure whether to touch it. Alexei was moved by this desire and fear, by these hands, and he said, "Here's a little flower, it's just like you, it's your brother..." He wasn't quite sure if he was right to call the flower "brother," and he muttered, "it's your sister..." Suddenly he had the feeling that someone was watching him, a feeling which destroyed and broke up everything, and he pretended that he had bent over in order to take his son out of the stroller, and when he straightened up with his son in his arms he saw his friend smiling to him from the porch and then recalled with consternation that he himself had invited him to come.

"I'm not alone," said his friend and pointed to the veranda, where Alexei saw his wife. He didn't understand, but then saw a girl, whom he recognized as an old acquaintance, looking out from behind his wife, and she smiled and waved to him. He and his friend went over to the others on the veranda, Alexei gave his son to his wife, and while everyone talked excitedly back and forth in greeting he thought about how he had known them separately, the two friends, but had never seen them together, and what could it mean that they had arrived together now? And it seemed to him that they hadn't "just happened to meet on the platform." His son started crying because of all the strangers and the unusual noise, his wife said they should go up to Alexei's study and that she would join them as soon as she had fed their son and put him to sleep.

They went upstairs and everyone was delighted with his second floor—his study with the spiderwebs; his friend was openly flattering him, although with a friendly coarseness, while the girl expressed herself in a way he would like most: without saying anything she simply glanced about with approval and satisfaction, as if she had already thoroughly and with interest thought about it all, about Alexei and his country abode, and was now pleased that everything was just as she had thought it would be and had not disappointed her; and Alexei, looking at everything through their eyes, was pleased both with his study and with himself.

Although Alexei mainly addressed his friend, and the girl was silent, she kept coming more and more to his attention. From time to time he watched her take something from his table and examine it, then put it back, or watched her listening to the conversation, or moving about carefully, avoiding the cobwebs, or watched her smile. There was in her simultaneously a kind of freedom and embarrassment which lent to her presence here a shade of personal concern that was more than just curiosity, and this concern flattered Alexei. And there was in her movements a sense of acceptance of the whole place, Alexei included, that made her presence here seem to him at once natural and eternal, as if she should stay and his friend should leave. The fact that Alexei had never seen them together and had not heard about them aroused in him a child's sense of the presence of lovers, a long-forgotten and mysterious feeling. He used to feel this way, for example, when his older brother had company and Alexei would sit quietly in a corner and try to figure out which beautiful girl was with his brother, and in general who was with whom, and when they would send him to bed and he couldn't sleep, but would listen to the noise from the next room and remember the girl who had come up to him, "Is this your brother? What a nice boy..." and had stroked his head; he didn't sleep and figured out how much younger he was than she and whether he could marry her when he grew up, and came to the conclusion that of course he could, that a seven-year difference is nothing. Or another feeling, when he was a bit older and was ready for love—a feeling he would suddenly get from two people sitting at a table—not the kind who noisily emphasize their liaison and find that pleasurable, but two quiet people who sat apart, who had a secret, a collusion, a telepathy, and Alexei had no proof of this, but it was so. Such a bond between two people in a sea of lives, each separate from the other, seemed to him in his childhood such an impossible, higher, inaccessible happiness, and he felt all this now—not as strongly, but something like a glimmer of his childhood feeling, and there was something genuine in it.

Moreover, as he watched her it began to seem to him that he had once been with her, that there had been something between them, and a compact hung between Alexei and her over his friend. This feeling was pleasant, somewhat troubling, because he really began to recall a bare room, and twilight, and an ashtray made out of a can on the window sill. Had it happened or not? Perhaps he had dreamed it? But no, it hadn't happened, he wouldn't have forgotten it; most likely he'd made it up... But no, a kind of agreement, some kind of thread stretched between them, and both felt it, he knew it and she did too. But all the same it wasn't just empathy, there was something with a touch of recollection, and he just couldn't put his finger on it.

They chatted for a while in his study and then went out onto the balcony. The low sun illuminated them on one side. The long slanting shadows of the railings arranged their geometry on the floor. The wind which had blown strongly for three days shook the trees, but the balcony was on the side away from the wind and it wasn't windy there, it was just continually sensed: heard and seen. And they sat on the sun-warmed boards and continued their conversation about something or other. His friend was relating something. Alexei listened and didn't listen to him. His wife joined them, having finally gotten their son to sleep. But this didn't interrupt Alexei's feelings, it even strengthened them. The bond between him and the girl was not broken, he felt its pull, and he felt something unusual and slightly romantic in the fact that they had made no visible efforts to support it, had done nothing specifically directed toward it; there were no glances, no poses, and a feeling rather like gratitude arose in him for the fact that she made not a single movement which would break their thread. And it was good that there was no growing excitement or tension, everything remained undisturbed, their bond grew stronger as if apart from their desire, and it was even as if they tried to subdue it. And this gave rise to a feeling of ease and naturalness in him, of something very rare after which you would feel no repentance or shame. As if everything had already happened, but only ease and gratitude remained in consequence, and seldom had he felt such ease—never, in fact.

They conversed pleasantly about this and that. About schoolmates and acquaintances, who had seen whom, although no one had seen anyone: it was vacation time. About various things, what seems like what in the light of today's events, although nothing was like anything, and there were no events: it was vacation time.

They had already run out of conversation and gradually began to feel awkward, to look silently at the view from the balcony—which was not, however, very interesting—when his friend said that here she, meaning his girlfriend, was trying in vain to hide from everyone the lovely songs she had brought along with her. Sing them, sing them, they begged her. "I'm not hiding them, I'll sing them," said the girl. And she sang simply and naturally, even interestingly, seeming to take advantage of the fact that she really had no voice and using that to good effect. Alexei was deeply moved, because he decided that she was singing for him. And so he hardly remembered anything of the three or four songs which really were good. Only the beginning of one of them. This song even distracted him from his sweet fantasies. The two-syllable words at the end of each line were sung with a double stress which made the words sound broken up, like splintered pieces of word-goblets and word-cups. This imparted to the song an even wilder quality than the strange text, the elusive motif, and the lack of rhyme.

Such a mighty tem-pest
Fell upon our is-land,

> Tore from homes the roof-tops,
> Like foam from milk too fro-thy.

The songs were sung—they again fell silent. And when his son started screaming below, they jumped up almost joyfully, gladly stretching and moving their legs, and without any transition from the silence began to talk too loudly and animatedly.

His son immediately calmed down when he saw the people. It turned out that he had been screaming simply because he wanted company. He got company and now he treated even the strangers cordially. He walked about the room going from person to person, or rather, didn't walk, but seemed to fall out of one person's arms and into another's, because between the time that one person let him go and another caught him he had to take only one independent step, and down he went.

And so, as he was enjoying himself together with his son, Alexei suddenly turned around, as if someone had called him, and caught the gaze of the girl. He immediately felt that her gaze hid in it a certain nuance, and because she had apparently been watching Alexei for a long time and now glanced away too quickly, as if it were giving her away, this nuance became an absolute certainty to Alexei—and he became embarrassed. He leaned back on the couch; his head receded into the twilight: from here he could observe and come to himself.

He felt a kind of childishly despairing sinking feeling each time he looked at the girl (now she tried hard not to look at him, and this, of course, gave Alexei renewed confirmation), and he felt a childish resolve to do something as yet unknown even to himself, something sweet in its non-fatal, savory peril. Because of this he could not have felt freer, more unfettered, and he continued to lie there, hiding his head in the shadows. Then he discovered something that would save him: it was a piece of fluff, like dandelion fluff, which had stuck to his knee. "For good luck,"—he remembered this omen from Pioneer camp days. The fluff suggested an action, and the action freed him of his awkwardness: he set the fluff on his extended finger, glanced at the girl as if hinting at what his wish was, and carefully blew. The fluff flew up to the ceiling; it was clearly visible and disappeared only right at the ceiling, merging with the chalky surface. Alexei persistently scrutinized the empty air and suddenly discovered the fluff lower than where he had expected to find it,—it was falling at a measured pace. Then his son noticed it too: he squealed and stretched out his hand, started to talk incomprehensibly. "Just think," said Alexei with simple pride, "such a little thing, a little piece of fluff, and he already notices it..." He caught the fluff and blew it again...

Whether everyone, like Alexei, saw the fluff through the eyes of childhood, or whether his son had communicated his view of things, everyone was unusually carried away. The fluff flew up sharply and fell, now merging and disappearing, now becoming visible, as it marked out in the air an invisible striped pattern of light and shade. Alexei looked about with a foolish expression on his face, and then the one to discover it first yelled, "There it is, over there!" Each time his son saw the fluff he became even more excited; confusion and perplexity fell like a blind over his face when he lost it from sight, and an even stronger excitement then replaced this perplexity. This intensifying of feelings in his son from repetition, rather than the quieting down which Alexei felt corresponded to human nature, pleasantly surprised him. The fluff again disappeared. "There it is! I see it!" Alexei recognized the girl's voice, was distracted, and suddenly saw everything from a detached point of view. In this light his son remained the same to him. The rest, supposedly adults, sat with half-opened mouths and vague smiles; their looks crossed, joining somewhere in the center of the room at an almost invisible and immobile point, and they were very tense, as if they were at a seance where the movement of the fluff was communicated by a common telepathic effort. There was such enthusiasm on their faces that they seemed possessed, almost ecstatic, as if they were testing fate, as if they were betting a fortune... Because he saw them all seeming to reveal themselves in their most defenseless and absurd essence, Alexei felt the abasement, gratitude, and awkwardness of the voyeur. He caught the fluff and held it back. For a moment those present seemed to return to reality, and when he noted the first gleam of recognition he said, "After all, we are adults..." Everyone laughed without embarrassment, and then realized that he had exaggerated, as always, and as always this was unpleasant to him. "Well, we have to go now," said his friend, and this "we" cut Alexei to the quick and sobered him up.

...He went with them to the station to see them off, feeling bored and depressed. But everything happened as it had to happen: from the very beginning it was clear they would leave together, but Alexei felt injustice and hurt in the fact that here they were leaving together, they would arrive in town where they would go somewhere and stay together... Alexei felt something like jealousy, but he wouldn't have admitted it to himself. He felt even sadder because it was beginning to seem as if he himself had thought up the whole thing about the meaningful bond between himself and her, that there had been nothing of the sort, that she in any case hadn't felt any of this, and he perhaps had given himself away by some absurd gestures; and she all the while had been laughing at him, and when she was alone with his friend they would laugh at him together... This was humiliating—to have to change one's perception so sharply: just before he had been experiencing a radiant feeling, another feeling from childhood, long-forgotten.

And so they silently made their way to the station. The wind nudged them from behind and urged them on. The air was amazingly transparent—all the distances seemed outlined. The red sun lay on the horizon and permeated everything through and through, as if piercing objects in its way. Several long, narrow clouds seemed stuck into the sun, like red arrows or red feathers. A withered tree near a warehouse for construction equipment, a misshapen snag, looked eerie and beautiful—black on the red sunset—so beautiful that it would be tasteless in a picture. Actually it was a cold day, a cold wind was blowing, and perhaps for this reason there were no people there at all, and those who were there had frozen immobile in the wind, and it seemed that it was precisely they who created the feeling of desertedness, and if they hadn't been there, the feeling wouldn't be. The wind raced along the tracks, chased chips and rubbish from where the freight cars were unloaded, and also—and this seemed endless to him when he saw it—the wind chased a large piece of cardboard with ragged edges: the wind turned it over, the piece stood up, stopped still for a moment, then slapped against the embankment and rolled on, raising dust; then it turned over again and for a short but seemingly very prolonged moment it stopped still and tremblingly opposed the wind. As before they were silent as they stood now on the platform. The train came and they shook hands; for some reason his friend thrust his hand out first (the pistol jutted out stupidly from under his arm), and then she gave him hers. And somehow she gave him her hand and squeezed his and looked at him as if he were still being a fool, but there had been something, there would be something, and he felt a pang and tried to restrain himself, but couldn't—his eyes clouded over and he saw only dimly, and was afraid he might blink out a tear. The train started up, they waved from their car—she waved, but he didn't see his friend, he had disappeared with his pistol, had dissolved, no longer existed. And the train carried her off in the same direction as the wind blew, that is—toward town.

He stood there a while longer and was happy. The thought that he would certainly see her in the city vaguely remained in him. Then with a sudden sharp tenderness he thought about his wife and son, about the house he was now returning to, and again about his wife, that he would see her now as if after a long séparation...

He slowly wandered back, against the wind, past the warehouse and the freight cars which were being unloaded, and rubbish flew into his face—"Such a mighty tem-pest"—he crossed the tracks, and in crossing the tracks there was such loneliness in all this emptiness, this windblown space all around—"Fell upon our is-land"—a feeling of isolation from the world seized him, and this was pleasant; an island...really an island!.. A smooth sandbar, a yellow turbid sea, and huts on slender legs, and roofs of broad stiff leaves—"And tore from homes the roof-tops"—the wind chased a large piece of cardboard: it stood up, stopped still for a moment, then slapped against the embankment and rolled on, raising dust; then it turned over again and for a short but seemingly very prolonged moment it stopped still and tremblingly opposed the wind...

And here was his quiet home, and the roof was whole. His home, his fortress,—the second floor... Alexei remembered how his study had flown in the hailstorm, and how the hailstorm had beaten down all the corn-shoots... "And it tore from homes the roof-tops, like foam from milk too fro-thy..." A chill passed thorugh him. He went up to the second floor—he was shivering...

In the evenings, when, quite drained, with a light, unreal ringing in his head he would come downstairs and drink tea with his wife, he thought that this was precisely what is called happiness. He turned on the radio, and a Frenchwoman sang her song, the tea was strong and hot, his wife, his eternal companion, sometimes sewed, sometimes drank tea with him—was nearby, and Alexei had no need to leave her for any place, and his son was not yet asleep and offered him a toy... And to Alexei it seemed that he would remember this peace and quiet all his life—after all, who knows what direction life might still take.

1963-1964

Translated by Carol G. Luplow and Richard Luplow
Edited by Priscilla Meyer

Fazil Iskander

BELSHAZZAR'S FEASTS

Life was good for Uncle Sandro after Nestor Apollonovich Lakoba brought him to the city, made him superintendent at the Central Executive Committee, and got him appointed to the celebrated Abkhaz Song and Dance Ensemble under the direction of Platon Pantsulaya. He quickly worked his way up to become one of the best dancers, able to compete with Pata Pataraya himself.

Thirty rubles a month as superintendent at the CEC, and as much again as a member of the ensemble—not bad money for those times, downright decent money, by God!

As superintendent at the CEC, Uncle Sandro kept after the maintenance staff, occasionally picked up hearing aids from Germany at the post office for Nestor Apollonovich, and also saw to the garage, including Lakoba's personal Buick, which he called the "Bik," to simplify the foreign pronunciation.

Of course Lakoba's personal Buick was at his disposal when Lakoba was away in Moscow or off some place at a conference.

At such times the people's commissars and other powerful officials used to ask Uncle Sandro for the Buick so that they could go to their village for some relative's funeral, celebrate a birth or a wedding or—if nothing else—their own arrival.

Barreling into one's native village in Lakoba's personal motor car, which everyone knew by sight, was doubly pleasant, that is, politically pleasant and just plain pleasant. Everyone understood that if a man arrived in Nestor Apollonovich's car it meant he was on his way up; maybe Nestor Apollonovich had let him into the inner circle and was always slapping him on the back, maybe he had even given him a bear hug and personally seated him in the car: Go on now, you son of a bitch, wherever you have to go, just don't throw up on the seat on your way back.

Of course, there were also unpleasantnesses. Thus a certain not-so-powerful but nevertheless highly placed comrade once used the Buick to go home to his village. There, at table, to someone's question about the Buick, he gave a craftily evasive answer to the effect that though he had not yet been given Lakoba's job, the matter was being decided at the very top, and one thing he could say for sure was that the car had already been transferred to him.

He did not have time to get away from this festive table, or to be more precise, he sat there so long that a party of three, Lakoba's nephews or namesakes, I think, had time to ride over from the neighboring village. Circumspectly, so as not to alarm the other people there, they dragged him away from the table, and in the yard they pounded the stuffings out of him, as he deserved.

To top it all off, they strapped him across the trunk of the Buick, planning to drive him through the village. In point of fact, the plan did not succeed, because they did not know how to drive the car themselves, and the chauffeur had fled to the cornpatch.

The plain truth is that the comrade should have known better. By his stupid remarks he had insulted not only Nestor Lakoba, but his entire clan. In those days an insult to a clan was something that rarely went unpunished.

After this incident, decent people were long amazed at the way this comrade had so openly dared to indulge in blasphemy, and mendacious blasphemy at that!

He himself said that his head was befuddled from drink, and the owner of the house where the feast took place swore by all his forefathers that no one had left the table, so that he never did figure out who had gone to inform the neighboring village.

Fortunately, none of this story reached the ears of Nestor Apollonovich, or everyone would have really caught it—all the nephews or namesakes, and Uncle Sandro, and, for the second time around, the victimized blasphemer.

Of course, Uncle Sandro did get something in return for these minor liberties with the Buick. Not that there was anything flagrant, mind you, but favors like getting a relative into a good hospital, obtaining some needed document in a hurry, having a friend's case re-examined—a friend who thought the times of Czar Nicholas were not over and stole some horses, and then at the trial, instead of denying it, turned to the audience and proudly told them all about it.

During these golden times Uncle Sandro did a lot for his friends, but not all of them repaid kindness with kindness; many of them subsequently proved to be ingrates.

Sometimes Uncle Sandro would go out on the balcony of the CEC headquarters and look down along the street, and there at the very end he could see the sea; and if a ship was in port, it was nice to think that he could get on a boat and sail away to Batum or Odessa. Although Uncle Sandro had no intention of going anywhere, because a bird in the hand is worth two in the bush, still and all it was nice to think that he could get on a boat and sail away.

If he stood on the balcony and looked in the other direction, there was nothing to see but mountains and forests, so that one might have said there was no reason to look over there.

Only once in a while, when a yearning for home crept over him, would Uncle Sandro look at the mountains and heave a furtive sigh. He sighed furtively because he considered it improper to sigh loudly when he had such honorable work—in power. Because if a man sighs when he's in power, it looks as if he doesn't like being in power, which would be ungrateful and stupid. No; Uncle Sandro liked being in power, and naturally he wanted to remain there as long as possible.

What Uncle Sandro really enjoyed, however, was to stand on the CEC balcony on a nice day and just look down at the passing crowds, among which there were many people he knew and many beautiful women.

Those who had known Uncle Sandro before and still liked him would look up and say hello, their cordial gaze indicating that they were glad he had been moved up. Those who had known Uncle Sandro before, but now envied him, walked on by, pretending not to notice him. But this did not offend Uncle Sandro: Let them go about their business, you can't please everyone by being moved up.

Those who had not known him before, but saw him now on the CEC balcony, thought he was a powerful official who had come out on the balcony for a breath of air. Uncle Sandro replied to their greetings with a polite nod, not because he was playing along with the involuntary deception, but simply because he knew how to forgive people their small human weaknesses.

Sometimes people he knew would stop under the balcony and ask in gestures, How is Lakoba? Uncle Sandro would clench his fist and shake it slightly to show that Nestor Apollonovich was solidly in place. His acquaintances would nod gladly in reply and stride onward with a certain extra briskness.

Sometimes, knowing that Lakoba was away somewhere, these acquaintances would ask in gestures, Where did he go? In reply, Uncle Sandro would point toward the east (which meant Tbilisi) or gesture more portentously to the north (which meant Moscow).

Sometimes they would ask—again, mostly through gestures—Well, has Lakoba gotten back yet? In these cases Uncle Sandro would nod affirmatively or shake his head negatively. Either way, the acquaintances would nod with satisfaction and walk on, glad to have shared, however transiently, in the affairs of state.

The fashion plates of Mukhus would click by in their high heels, and meeting their eyes, Uncle Sandro would twirl his mustache, hinting at mischievous intentions. Many an ingenious love affair was begun from this balcony, although he also struck up many new acquaintances from the stage of theaters and clubs where the troupe performed.

There were a few women who snickered at his flirtatious posing on the balcony. Uncle Sandro did not take offense, he just gave them a quick cold shoulder: Oh, you don't like me, well, I don't like you either.

The ones he liked best were the women who blushed when their eyes met his, only to lower their heads and walk quickly on. Uncle Sandro believed that shame was the finest ornament a woman could wear. (Sometimes he said that shame was the most irritating ornament, but basically this meant the same thing.)

Occasionally, as he stood on the CEC balcony, Uncle Sandro would see his old buddy Kolya Zarkhidi. He always greeted him heartily to show that he was not getting too big for his britches, that he still recognized and loved his old friends. From Kolya's eyes he could tell that Kolya felt neither spite nor envy over the fact that Uncle Sandro was playing host in his confiscated mansion, or that he was standing around on the balcony as he had in peaceful times.

Kolya would nod to him. "Try and get up there on a horse, why don't you?" he would say, reminding him of the feat he had performed so long ago.

"Not any more, Kolya," Uncle Sandro would reply with a smile. "Times are quite different now."

"Mmm," Kolya would say. As if he had received sad confirmation of the correctness of his own way of life, he would walk on toward the coffeehouse.

Uncle Sandro would look after him, somewhat sorry for him and somewhat envious, because sitting in a coffeehouse with a shot of cognac and Turkish coffee was pleasant even under Soviet rule, maybe even pleasanter than before.

The Abkhaz Song and Dance Ensemble was already making a splash all over Transcaucasia, and later made a splash in Moscow. I'm told they even performed in London, although I don't know that they made a splash there.

In the era I am describing now, their fame was already on the upswing, fame created mainly by Platon Pantsulaya, Pata Pataraya, and Uncle Sandro. On the anniversary of the Revolution, after the formal parts of the celebration, the ensemble would perform on the stage of the district theater. Moreover, they performed at Party conferences, at rallies for High Achievers in industry and agriculture, they were not too busy to go to the outlying districts of the republic, and they also put on shows for the larger sanatoria and vacation hotels on the Transcaucasian coast.

After a performance for any of the more or less important organizations, the members of the ensemble would be invited to a banquet, where they did more singing and dancing in close proximity to the banquet table and the higher-ranking comrades.

Uncle Sandro, as I have already said, was virtually an equal of the best dancer in the troupe, Pata Pataraya. At any rate, he was the only person in the troupe who mastered Pata Pataraya's most celebrated trick: getting a running start backstage, falling to his knees, and sliding, sliding, all the way across the stage, his arms thrown back like the wings of a soaring bird.

Well, Uncle Sandro became so good at this celebrated *pas* that many people said they could not tell the one dancer from the other.

One member of the ensemble, a dancer and lead singer by the name of Makhaz, said one day that if the dancer performing this number were to pull his turban down over his face, there was no way you could tell who it was sliding across the stage—the celebrated Pata Pataraya or the new star, Sandro Chegemsky.

Maybe Makhaz wanted to flatter him a bit, since he was from Uncle Sandro's home district, because after all you really could tell them apart, especially if you had a dancer's experienced eye. But that is beside the point. The point is that Makhaz's chance remark gave Uncle Sandro the idea for a great improvement on an already rather elaborate number.

The very next day Uncle Sandro started training in secret. Taking advantage of his official position, he trained in the CEC conference hall, behind closed doors so that the cleaning lady could not spy.

Incidentally, this was the very hall where Uncle Sandro had once galloped around on his unforgettable piebald charger, thereby saving his friend Kolya and bankrupting the Endursk cattle dealer.

Uncle Sandro practiced for about three months, and the day finally came that he determined to exhibit his new number. He did not feel it was sufficiently polished, but circumstances forced him to take the risk and play his secret trump on stage.

The previous day, the better part of the ensemble, twenty of the members, had left for Gagra. The ensemble was to perform at one of the largest sanatoria, where a conference of the Secretaries of the District Committees of Western Georgia was currently taking place. Rumor had it that the meeting was being conducted by Stalin himself, who was vacationing in Gagra.

Apparently the idea of convening the district committee secretaries had come to him while he was here on vacation. But why he had called a conference of the Secretaries of the District Committees of only Western Georgia, Uncle Sandro simply could not understand.

Apparently the district committee secretaries of eastern Georgia had committed some offence, or maybe he wanted to make them feel that they were not yet worthy of such a high-level conference, so that they would do better work in the future, competing with the district committee secretaries of western Georgia.

Or so thought Uncle Sandro, exerting his inquisitive mind—although strictly speaking this was not within his purview as superintendent at the CEC, or still less as a member of the ensemble.

So the better part of the ensemble had left, while Uncle Sandro stayed behind. The problem was that Uncle Sandro's daughter was very ill at the time. Everyone knew about it. Just before the group departed, Uncle Sandro had asked Pantsulaya to leave him behind, in view of his daughter's illness. He was sure that Pantsulaya would fly to pieces, would beg him to go with the group, and then, after being obstinate for a while, Uncle Sandro would sadly accede.

This would have preserved the proprieties in relation to his family: he could say he wasn't all that eager to dance himself, but he was forced to. Besides, the other dancers would have been made aware that while it was possible to go on without Sandro, the dance would not have been the same.

Quite unexpectedly, the director of the ensemble agreed right away, and there was nothing for Uncle Sandro to do but turn around and leave. That same day the manager of the CEC gave him an insulting reprimand.

"In my opinion, someone is stealing firewood from us," he said, pointing to the huge pile of logs that had been cut and stacked in the CEC yard back at the start of summer.

"It's just settling," Uncle Sandro replied carelessly, aching with the dullness of his artistic isolation.

"I never heard of a woodpile settling," the manager said, with intentional innuendo, or so it seemed to Uncle Sandro.

"I'll bet you never heard about the forest fire around Chegem, either?" Uncle Sandro asked insinuatingly.

This was the notorious Chegem sarcasm, which not everyone can handle.

"What's the Chegem forest got to do with it?" the manager asked.

"Why, I've been taking the CEC wood home to the hills," Uncle Sandro said, and he walked away from the manager. The manager just threw up his hands.

They've already gone through Eshery, Uncle Sandro thought as he went up the stairs of the mansion; they're probably getting close to Afon now. A cool draft touching his face seemed to him a breath of disgrace. The manager must know something, Lakoba must be cutting me loose, Uncle Sandro thought, correlating the manager's insulting tone and the even more insulting ease with which Platon Pantsulaya had acceded to his request.

It was particularly regrettable because everyone presumed that Comrade Stalin himself would be at the banquet. True, no one knew for sure. But one wasn't supposed to know for sure, somehow it was even sweeter that no one knew anything for sure.

The next day Uncle Sandro sat by his daughter's bed, dully watching his wife change the wet towel on her head from time to time.

The little girl had pneumonia. She was being treated by one of the best doctors in town. He had some doubt as to a favorable outcome, though he was relying, as he said, on her strong Chegem constitution.

Four Chegemians, distant relatives of Uncle Sandro's, were also sitting in the room, their hands warily on the table. In recent years they had started coming to town more and more often, and it must be admitted that Uncle Sandro found them a bit tiresome.

The historical development of the people of Chegem had been unnaturally accelerated. They managed this with a certain patriarchal clumsiness. On the one hand, at home, in complete accord with the march of history and the decisions of higher organs of government (in point of fact, the march of history was also determined by the decisions of these higher organs), they were building socialism, that is, engaging in collective farm agriculture. On the other hand, they came to town to sell things, engaging for the first time in capitalistic trade relations.

A double load like that could not pass without leaving its trace. Some of them, amazed that one could get money for such simple things as cheese, corn, and beans, went to the opposite extreme, piling on incredible prices, and they would stand in silence for days at a time beside their unbought produce. Sometimes, stung by the contempt of the customers, the Chegemians would cart their produce back: All right then, we'll eat it ourselves. However, as time went on there were fewer and fewer people so arrogant; the despotism of the marketplace did its work.

One thing the Chegemians could never get used to, that there was no fireplace fire in city houses. Without a real fire on the hearth, a house seemed unlived-in to the Chegemians, more like an office. It was hard to have a conversation in such a house, because they did not know what to look at. A Chegemian was used to staring into the fire while he talked, or at least, if he had to look at his companion, he could spread his hands to the fire and feel the heat.

This is why the four Chegemians were silent and kept their hands warily on the table, which added to Uncle Sandro's irritation.

Today, Uncle Sandro thought, our troupe may be going to dance for Stalin himself—and I have to sit here and listen to the silence of Chegemians. At the bazaar they had been offered a chance to stay in the Collective Farmers' Club, but they had indignantly rejected the offer on the grounds that their Uncle Sandro lived here in town, and as a relative he might take offence. It cannot be said that such loyalty to family ties particularly moved Uncle Sandro. Conceivably, he would not have been the least offended.

"Thank God our Sandro has gotten in with the watchers-over," said one of the Chegemians, making an effort to overcome his discomfiture at the lack of a real fire in the house.

There was a long, thoughtful pause. "Iron knees are valued more than ever by the powers-that-be," the second Chegemian said, explaining the reason for Uncle Sandro's success.

"I recall as how Prince Tatyr Khan valued good dancers too," the third

Chegemian said, drawing an historical parallel.

"Still, not so much," the fourth Chegemian added after a long silence. He had thought for a long time because he wanted to say something of his own, but, unable to find anything of his own, he had decided he would make a small correction in what had been said by someone else.

The Chegemians went on with their meager discussion. The wife, sitting beside the sick little girl, slowly waved a fan over her. A fly buzzed and beat against the windowpane. Uncle Sandro tried to be patient.

Suddenly the door burst open, and in came the manager. Uncle Sandro jumped up, feeling that the stalled motor of time had started up again. Something had happened, otherwise the manager would not be here.

The manager greeted everyone, went over to the sick girl's bed, and said a few sympathetic words before getting down to business. Uncle Sandro listened distractedly, waiting impatiently for him to say why he had come.

"Easy come, easy go," Uncle Sandro replied to his sympathetic words—using the Turkish proverb not altogether felicitously.

"I didn't want to bother you," the manager said, sighing, as he pulled a piece of paper from his pocket, "but there's a telegram for you."

"From whom?" Uncle Sandro said, snatching the folded blank.

"From Lakoba," the manager said with respectful wonder.

COME IF YOU CAN NESTOR, Uncle Sandro read, so happy that the words swam before his eyes.

" 'If you can'?" Uncle Sandro cried, and kissed the telegram with a smack. "Why, is there anything I wouldn't do for Nestor? Where's the Bik?" he added, turning imperiously to the manager.

"Waiting outside," the manager replied. "Don't forget to take your passport. They're really strict about that now."

"I know," Uncle Sandro nodded, and he snapped to his wife, "Get my cherkaska¹ ready."

Twenty minutes later, standing at the door with his professional case in his hand, Uncle Sandro turned to those who were staying behind and said with prophetic certainty, "I swear by Nestor, the girl will get better."

"How do you know?" the Chegemians said, brightening. His wife said nothing; she just watched her husband contemptuously as she continued to fan the child.

"I can feel it," Uncle Sandro said, and he closed the door behind him.

"Not everyone is allowed to swear by the name of Nestor," Uncle Sandro heard from behind the door.

"Not more than one or two people in Abkhazia," another loyal Chegemian said, making it more specific, but Uncle Sandro, was heading for his car and did not hear.

Incidentally, to jump ahead of my story, I can say that Uncle Sandro's prophecy—although based on nothing but shame for his hurried departure—did come true. The next morning, for the first time since she had been sick, the little girl asked for something to eat.

...After three hours of wild driving, the Buick stopped in Old Gagra at the gates of a sanatorium on one of the quiet green streets.

It was getting on toward evening. Uncle Sandro was nervous, suspecting he might be late. He ran into the gatehouse and went to a little lighted window, behind which a woman was sitting.

"A pass," he said, shoving his passport through the long tunnel of the bay window.

The woman looked at his passport, checked it against some sort of list, then glanced critically at Uncle Sandro several times, trying to detect alien features in his face.

Every time she looked at him Uncle Sandro froze, trying not to let any alien features materialize, setting his face in an expression of nonchalant likeness to himself.

The woman wrote out his pass. Uncle Sandro grew more and more agitated, sensing that this strict check-in process implied the nerve-wracking exhilaration of an encounter with the Leader.

With the pass and his passport in one hand and his suitcase in the other, he quickly crossed the deserted courtyard of the sanatorium and halted at the entrance, where he was met by the policeman on duty. For some reason the latter stared long and hard at his pass, checking it against his passport.

"The Abkhazian ensemble," Uncle Sandro said, by implication stressing the peaceful nature of his visit. The policeman made no reply. Keeping the passport in his hand, he shifted his gaze to the suitcase.

Uncle Sandro nodded joyfully in response, to indicate that he fully understood how crucial the moment was. He briskly opened the suitcase and took out his cherkeska, his Asiatic boots, his riding breeches, his Caucasian belt and dagger, laying them all at his feet. As he took out each article Uncle Sandro honorably shook it, thus providing an opportunity for any ill-meant object that might be there to fall out.

When he got down to the belt and dagger, Uncle Sandro smiled and slid it out of the scabbard a little way, as if distantly suggesting its utter uselessness for regicide, even if such an insane idea were to arise in some insane mind.

The policeman followed his movements attentively and nodded curtly, as if acknowledging the fact of the dagger's uselessness and cutting off all possibility of discussion on this point.

Uncle Sandro put all the things back in the suitcase, closed it, and was on the point of reaching for his passport and pass—but the policeman stopped him again.

"Are you Sandro of Chegem?" he asked.

"Yes," Uncle Sandro said. With a flash of insight he added, "But on the posters I'm Sandro Chegemsky!"

"Posters don't interest me," the policeman said. Without inviting Uncle Sandro to pass, he took a shiny new telephone from the wall and started calling someone.

Uncle Sandro felt desperate. He remembered the telegram—the document was his last salvation—and started rummaging through his pockets.

"Bik, CEC, Lakoba..." In his nervousness he muttered the words like a magic spell, rummaging through his pockets with no success.

Suddenly Uncle Sandro spotted Makhaz, his fellow ensemble member, coming down the broad carpeted staircase. Uncle Sandro felt that fate itself had sent him this countryman and neighbor. He gesticulated desperately, beckoning him over, even though Makhaz was coming down toward them anyway, slightly outdistancing the flaring hems of his cherkeska.

"Ask him," Uncle Sandro said when Makhaz came to a stop beside them, puffing out his chest and swelling with involuntary pride. Paying no attention to Makhaz, the policeman went on listening to the receiver. Makhaz's neck started to turn red.

If Uncle Sandro had been listening to the telephone conversation, however, he would not have had to worry so much, and Makhaz would not have had to tire his chest muscles, which were essential for the singing to come.

The problem was that the woman at the gatehouse had first mistakenly written "Chegen" instead of "Chegem" and then corrected the letter. This correction of the letter, apparently outside the rules for such a place, was what aroused the policeman's suspicion. Now, straightening out the misunderstanding over the phone, he convinced himself that she and she alone had corrected it.

Although the telephone was new, perhaps installed that day, it did not work very well, and the policeman had to keep repeating his questions.

When he finally hung up, Makhaz thrust his puffed-up chest forward and announced, "Member of the ensemble, the well-known Sandro Chegemsky."

"I know," the policeman said simply. "You may pass."

Uncle Sandro and Makhaz went up the red-carpeted stairs. It turned out that the director of the ensemble had already sent Makhaz out to meet him several times.

Uncle Sandro felt no enmity toward the policeman now. On the contrary, he felt that the strict precautions surrounding his passage into the sanatorium were a guarantee of the grandeur of the encounter that lay ahead. Uncle Sandro would probably have agreed to face even more obstacles, so long as he knew he would overcome them in the end.

"Will he be here?" Uncle Sandro asked quietly when they reached the third floor and started down the corridor.

"Why 'will be,' when he already is?" Makhaz said confidently. He already felt at home here. Makhaz opened one of the doors off the corridor and stopped to let Uncle Sandro go ahead of him. Uncle Sandro heard the familiar backstage hubbub, and with his excitement at fever pitch, he entered a large, brightly lit room.

The members of the troupe, already dressed in their costumes, were walking around the room limbering up. A few sprawled limply in soft chairs, their long legs stretched in front of them.

"Sandro is here!" cried several joyful voices.

Uncle Sandro embraced and kissed his comrades and showed them the telegram from Lakoba, which he had finally found.

"The manager brought it," he said, waving the telegram.

"Get changed quickly!" Pantsulaya shouted.

Uncle Sandro went to a corner where the troupe's clothes were hanging over chairs, and started to change, listening to the director's final instructions.

"The main thing is," Pantsulaya said, "when you're invited, don't jump at the food and wine. Behave modestly, but you don't have to play hard-to-get either. If one of the leaders invites you to have a drink, drink it, and then go back to your comrades. Do *not*—especially if you're chewing—stand beside the Leader as if you'd stormed the Winter Palace with him."

As they listened to Pantsulaya, the dancers kept walking around the room, limbering up, bending at the waist. From time to time one of them would rise up on his toes, lift one leg buttoned into a glove-soft Asiatic boot, and suddenly—hop, hop, hop!—take several giant leaps, all the while listening to the even, soothing voice of the director.

Pata Pataraya took several trial runs, practicing for his famous number. He did not fall to his knees, merely slid, in order to get a good feel for the floor. After each slide he would stop, turn around carefully, and measure how far he had gone by putting the heel of one foot to the toe of the other.

Uncle Sandro did the same thing. By now he could regulate the force of his running start and the distance of his slide with an accuracy of the length of his foot. True, Pata Pataraya did it with an accuracy of the width of his hand, but Uncle Sandro had his secret number in reserve, and now his soul was seared with nervous exultation: Would it work?

"Remember, there isn't going to be any stage," Pantsulaya was saying, pacing back and forth among his charges in his white cherkeska. "You'll be dancing right on the floor, the floor in there is the same as here. The main thing is, don't get nervous! The leaders are people just like us, only much better—"

Just then the door opened and a middle-aged man wearing a high-collared tussah jacket appeared. It was the manager of the sanatorium. Ominously, and at the same time fearfully, as if anticipating some failure, he nodded to Pantsulaya.

"Follow me, one at a time," Pantsulaya said quietly. He slipped softly to the door behind the tussah jacket.

Pata Pataraya went next; after Pata, Uncle Sandro; and then the others, who automatically made way for the best.

With the noiseless steps of court conspirators they went through the corridor and started into a room where a man in plain clothes stood at the door.

The sanatorium manager nodded to him. He nodded in reply and began letting them through, looking carefully at each one and counting with his eyes. The room turned out to be absolutely empty except for two men sitting at the far end by the window, wearing plain clothes like the one at the door. They were smoking, talking comfortably back and forth. On noticing the troupe members, one of them, without getting up, nodded to let them know they could pass.

The manager opened the next door and there was a roar of voices at table. Without going inside, he stopped at the doorway and silently, with a desperate gesture of his arm—Come on! come on! come on!—swept everyone into the banquet hall.

Within a few seconds the troupe members had flitted into the hall and lined up in two rows, blinded by the bright lights, the plenteous table, and the vastness of the crowd.

The banquet was at its height. Everything had happened so fast that not everyone noticed they were in the hall. At first isolated claps, then a joyous squall of applause greeted the twenty cypress-like knights who had sprung up from nowhere, led by Platon Pantsulaya.

One could sense that those who were applauding had eaten and drunk well and were now pleased to have their merriment prolonged by dint of art, in order, perhaps, later to return to fresh merriment at the table.

Regaining their wits, the troupe members tried to spot Comrade Stalin, but did not immediately locate him, because they were looking into the depths of the hall, whereas Comrade Stalin was sitting quite close to them, right at the end of the table. He was facing slightly away, toward his neighbor, who turned out to be the All-Union head man, Kalinin.

The applause continued, and Pantsulaya, his head bowed, stood before the cypress line like a marble image of gratitude. Then, sensing that the applause was not waning and that further silence from the troupe would therefore be immodest, he lifted his head, glanced sideways at the troupe members, and clapped his hands. In the same way, a horseman, after raising his quirt, looks back at his charger's croup before giving it a crack.

The troupe members began to applaud, the roar of their love forcing its way through to the very source of love, through the countering roar of governmental affection. Stalin suddenly got to his feet, and the whole hall rumblingly followed suit, everyone trying to catch up with him before he

. could straighten up.

It lasted for about a minute, this bloodless battle of mutual affection, like the friendly uproar of chums slapping each other on the back, a silly lovers' skirmish where the conquered thanked the conqueror and then lovingly conquered him, toppling his wave of roars with a new wave of roars.

The dancers continued to applaud while talking back and forth, as they were accustomed to do, without turning to each other.

"There's Comrade Stalin!"

"Where, where?"

"Talking to Kalinin!"

"Look, Voroshilov's short too!"

"And who's that?"

"Beria's wife!"

"The leaders are all short—Stalin, Voroshilov, Beria, Lakoba..."

"I wonder why?"

"Lenin was short—that's how it got started..."

"Sandro, you should be the tamada[2] at a table like that..."

"Our Nestor's the tamada!"

"Or maybe Beria?"

"No, see, Nestor's sitting at the head of the table."

"Stalin always picks him... He's his favorite..."

Gradually the mutual applause melted together and evened out, finding a common epicenter of love, its reason for being. And the fulcrum on which its being turned was Comrade Stalin. Now even the secretaries of the district committees, as if unable to resist the fascination exerted by the epicenter of love, turned their applause to Stalin. Gazing at him and raising their arms, they all clapped as if trying to throw their own personal sound wave to him. And he, understanding this, smiled a fatherly smile and applauded as if faintly apologetic for the treachery of his cohorts, who were applauding not with him but for him, which was why he was powerless by himself to answer their wave of applause with equal might.

He was gladdened by the sight of these well-built dancers, tightly buttoned into their black cherkeskas. At moments like this, he loved anything whose value was both obvious and irrelevant to politics, which sometimes wearied him. *Seemingly* irrelevant, that is, because subliminally he associated this obvious value and perfection with the cumbersome, crawly thing that metamorphosed from his every political act, and he interpreted it as a material, if small, proof of the thing's innocence.

Thus the twenty well-built dancers metamorphosed into flourishing delegates for his ethnic policy, just as the children who ran to the Mausoleum where he stood on holidays metamorphosed into heralds of the future, its rosy kisses. And he could appreciate these things as no one else could, stunning those who surrounded him by his unparalleled range—

from demonic mercilessness down to tenderness over what were, in point of
fact, very small joys. Noticing that he stunned those who surrounded him
by this unparalleled range, he more keenly appreciated his own ability to
appreciate the small joys of life that lay outside history.

As it happened, one of the rejoicing delegates for his ethnic policy—
Uncle Sandro, to be precise—had finished feasting his eyes on the leaders
and, still applauding, shifted his gaze to the table.

The table, or rather tables, traversed the banquet hall and at the end
forked into two fruit-laden branches. The platters of food stood out in
pleasant contrast to the cool whiteness of white tablecloths.

Gibbous turkeys lay in rich brown nut sauce, fried chickens presented
their bare rumps with a certain appetizing indecency. Vases bloomed with
fruit, candy, cookies, pastries. Split pomegranates, as if cracked by inner
fire, opened a glimpse of their sinful caverns crammed with precious stones.

Beds of salad greens glistened as if they had just been rained on. Young
lambs, cooked in milk in the ancient Abkhazian manner, mildly evoked a
lost innocence, while the roast suckling pigs, by contrast, clenched the
crimson radishes in their bared teeth with a sort of devilish glee.

Alongside every bottle of wine, like vigilant hospital orderlies, stood
bottles of Borzhom mineral water. The wine bottles were without labels,
obviously from local cellars. By the smell Uncle Sandro determined that
the wine was an Isabella from the village of Lykhny.

Most of the food was still untouched. Some had long since gone
cold—the roast quails had hardened in their own fat. Stalin did not like to
have waiters and other superfluous people flitting around at the table.
Everything was served at once, in a heap, although the kitchen was kept
ready in case of any sudden desires.

At the table everyone ate what he pleased and as he pleased, but God
forbid he should cheat and omit the required glass. This the Leader did not
like. At the table, the democracy of food was balanced by the despotism of
drink.

At the head of the table sat Nestor Lakoba. A large, dark horn with a
slight scorch mark lay beside him—the scepter of power at table.

To his right sat Stalin, then Kalinin. To Lakoba's left sat his wife, the
dusky Sarya; beside her the beautiful Nina, Beria's wife; and then Nina's
husband, with his pince-nez flashing energetically. Beyond Beria sat Voroshilov, who stood out because of his snow-white service jacket, his sword
belt, and the revolver at his waist. Beyond Voroshilov and Kalinin, on
either side of the table, sat secondary leaders, ones who were not known to
Uncle Sandro by their portraits.

The rest of the room was taken up by the secretaries of the district
committees of western Georgia, with their eyebrows raised as if frozen in
surprise. Scattered among them here and there were comrades from the
local secret service. Uncle Sandro recognized them immediately, because

unlike district committee secretaries they were not surprised by anything and did not have their eyebrows raised.

Nestor Lakoba, sitting at the head of the table, now turned abruptly to look at the ensemble. As the host, observing the proprieties, he applauded with much more reserve than the others.

When Stalin lowered his hands and sat down, the applause dropped and silence fell. But not all at once, because the people sitting farthest off could not see him. The silence fell like the wind dropping, rustling in the foliage of a large tree.

"Our beloved leader and dear guests!" Pantsulaya began. "Our humble Abkhazian ensemble, organized at the personal initiative of Nestor Apollonovich Lakoba,..."

Uncle Sandro observed that at this moment Stalin looked at Lakoba and smiled roguishly in his mustache, to which Lakoba replied with a bashful shrug.

"...will perform for you several Abkhazian songs and dances, as well as songs and dances of the friendly family of Caucasian peoples."

Pantsulaya bowed his head low, as if apologizing in advance that he must now turn his back on his lofty guests. Without raising his head—in one swift movement, striving to at least avoid offensive suddenness in the upcoming pose (since the pose itself was now inevitable), simultaneously wearing an expression of grief at having to turn his back—he completed his polysemantic turn, raised his head, waved his arms in the winged sleeves of the white cherkeska, and froze in mid-wave.

"O-rayda, siua-rayda, hey," Makhaz intoned, as if from deep in a narrow ravine.

And then, at the wave of the winged sleeves, the chorus took up the ancient song. Not everyone will return from the raid, the song says in sparing words... Not everyone is fated to see again the flame on his family hearth... And when the youth lying dead across his saddle rides into the yard of his father's house, the steed shudders, and the corpse moves, at the mother's scream.

But the father does not cry out and the brother does not weep, because only when he has taken revenge does a man gain the right to tears.

> Such is the will of fate and the fate of man.
> Woman ripens to give birth to a man.
> Man ripens to give birth to courage.
> The grape ripens to give birth to wine.
> Wine ripens to summon up courage.
> And the song ripens into dance to summon up the raid.

Gradually the energy shifts from the melody into the rhythm. The song tightens up, throws off excess clothes, as a warrior throws off his before entering the fray.

Uncle Sandro feels the approaching intoxication, feels the song pouring into his blood, and now he wants to become the dance, a fulfillment of the oath embedded in it.

The members of the ensemble are already clapping their hands, though all are still humming the tune, which is compressed to a minimum. Now all of the energy is in the rhythm of the clapping hands, but the dance must ripen, build to the right point, and therefore they go on warming it at the tiny fire of melody.

"O-rayda, siua-rayda!" the chorus repeats.

Tash-tush! Tash-tush!—clap the hands, continuing the process of drawing the dance out of the song.

Some of the spectators cannot resist, and they too start clapping their hands, trying to hasten the onset of the dance. Everyone in the hall, along with Comrade Stalin, is clapping his hands.

Tash-tush! Tash-tush! And at this point Pata Pataraya breaks forward. The mad dash of the steed breaking loose from its tether, and suddenly—he stops dead!... He stretches, up on his toes, arched taut, illustrating his readiness to fly like an arrow, to slice into enemy ranks, but at the last moment he changes his decision, and in a mad spin he quenches the insatiable thirst of the warrior to break through somewhere and slice into something.

Sandro Chegemsky throws himself into the circle! And now all the dancers soar in the black whirlwinds of their cherkeskas, illustrating man's ancient readiness to become a warrior, and the warrior's to slice, to fly, to break through... But at the last second it turns out that the order to slice, to fly, to break through has not yet been given.

"Oh, so it's like that?" the dancers seem to say, and ominously stamping their feet, they begin to whirl around. A moment later they stop spinning, only to learn that the order is again late in coming.

"Oh, so it's like that?" And again, stamping their feet, they whirl around.

"Like that? Oh, not yet?" And again.

"Like that? Like that? Like that?"

Circling and whirling they become thin, stratified, and finally semitransparent, like a propellor. It seems that by spinning around they can quench the insatiable thirst for battle.

"O-rayda-siua-rayda!" Tash-tush! Tash-tush!

Skillfully, and with perfect timing, the dancers replace one another, flying into the circle, and by now it seems that the carousel of the dance is moving of its own accord, by some ancient plan whose essence is the desire to stupefy the invisible enemy (in olden days, when the princes invited one another to feasts, the enemy was visible), stupefy him with the inexhaustibility of their fierce energy.

With brief intervals for songs, the ensemble dances Abkhazian, Georgian, Mingrelian, and Adzharian dances.

And now, the climax—a wedding dance. The long-awaited moment has come. With an abrupt shout, Pata Pataraya takes a flying start, tucks up his legs in mid-leap, thuds to his knees, and with arms outflung slides to a halt near the feet of Comrade Stalin.

This was so unexpected that some of the guests, especially those sitting farthest away, jumped to their feet, not understanding what had happened. Beria was the first one up. The lenses of his pince-nez flashing, he froze in a warlike posture over the table.

But there was no malicious intent, and Comrade Stalin smiled. A storm of applause broke, and Pata Pataraya, as if blown away by the storm, straightened up and flew back into the moving circle of dancers.

Now it was Uncle Sandro's turn. Catching just the right point in the music, he leaped whooping out from behind the backs of the clapping dancers and repeated Pata Pataraya's celebrated number, but stopped much closer, right at Comrade Stalin's feet. Uncle Sandro slid his eyes up from the Leader's well-cleaned and polished boots to his face, and was struck by the similarity between the oily glitter of his boots and the resplendent, oily glitter of his dark eyes.

Again applause.

"They're competing!" Lakoba shouted to Stalin, trying to shout over the roar and his own deafness. Stalin nodded and smiled his approval.

Again Pata Pataraya, crying out as if he had been stung, plopped to his knees, slid, and froze with arms outflung in a posture of audacious devotion, at Comrade Stalin's very toes.

Beria shook his head. "Out of bounds."

"Well, I think it's great!" Kalinin exclaimed, peering over Comrade Stalin's shoulder.

A storm of applause, and Pata Pataraya fell back into the whirlwind of dancers. The fact that he had succeeded in stopping a mere handsbreadth away from the Leader's feet had virtually assured his victory.

But a man from Chegem is not one to surrender without a fight! Now the fate of the best dancer was to be decided, and Uncle Sandro had something saved up for this occasion. Keeping a sharp eye on the distance from Comrade Stalin's feet to the spot where he was standing, he tried to intuit a moment when Stalin and Lakoba would not change their position. With the gesture of a knight covering his face with his visor, he jammed his turban down over his eyes, whooped a Chegem whoop, and charged straight for Comrade Stalin.

Even the other dancers did not expect anything like this. The chorus suddenly stopped clapping and all the dancers halted, with the exception of one who had been dancing at the opposite end of the room. A few more futile stomps and the dancer's feet fell quiet in terror.

In the silence, his face concealed by the turban, his arms thrown wide, Uncle Sandro flew crackling across the dance floor on his knees and came to a halt at Comrade Stalin's feet.

Stalin frowned in surprise. The pipe he gripped in one hand jerked slightly. But Uncle Sandro's pose, which expressed an audacious devotion—the poignant defenselessness of the outflung arms, the blindness of the proudly thrown-back head, and, paradoxically, a mysterious urgent stubbornness about the whole figure, as if to tell the Leader, "I won't get up until you give me your blessing"—made him smile.

Still smiling, indeed, he laid his pipe on the table, and with the expression of curiosity that one has at a masquerade, he started to untie the turban on Uncle Sandro's head.

When the tie-end of the turban slipped from Uncle Sandro's face and everyone saw it illumined with the blessing of the Leader, a hurricane of unprecedented applause broke out, and the secretaries of the district committees of western Georgia raised their eyebrows even higher in surprise, although it had seemed that their eyebrows were already raised as high as they could go.

Still holding Uncle Sandro's turban in one hand, Stalin displayed it to everyone with a smile, as if to let them see for themselves that the number had been done honestly, without any tricks. With a gesture he invited Uncle Sandro to stand up. Uncle Sandro stood up, and Kalinin took the turban from Stalin's hands and started examining it. All of a sudden Voroshilov leaned across the table and deftly snatched the turban out of Kalinin's hands. To the laughter of those around him, he held the turban to his eyes, showing that he really could not see through it.

Stalin looked at Uncle Sandro with his radiant eyes and asked, "Who are you, abrek?"[3]

"I am Sandro of Chegem," Uncle Sandro replied, lowering his eyes. The Leader's gaze was too resplendent. But that was not the only reason. An uneasy shadow had flitted through those eyes, and an alarm echoed in Uncle Sandro's soul.

"Chegem...," the Leader repeated pensively. His mind seemed to be elsewhere.

"Come here," Lakoba said in Abkhazian. He thrust Uncle Sandro's turban into his hands. Uncle Sandro walked away.

"What precision," he heard Kalinin say. Stroking his beard, Kalinin looked affectionately in Uncle Sandro's direction.

"You can see the sun even through a turban," Voroshilov observed pompously as he cut off the ear of a suckling pig. While he was working on the ear, the pig released the radish that had been stuffed in its mouth, and it rolled across the table, much to Voroshilov's surprise. He was so startled that he left his fork in the half-severed ear of the pig and started hunting down the radish in among the dishes and bottles.

Only now did Uncle Sandro turn his attention to the fact that those sitting at the table had had a great deal to drink. Now he trained his experienced eye on them and determined that they had already consumed twelve to thirteen glasses apiece.

Uncle Sandro used to say that from the appearance of men at table he could determine to within one glass how much they had drunk. He explained that the more people there were at the table, and the more they had drunk, the more precisely he could determine their consumption. But that was not all. It seemed that the precision of the estimate did not increase indefinitely with the amount of wine drunk. After three liters, Uncle Sandro said, the precision of the estimate decreased again.

...Platon Pantsulaya stood before the doubled cypress ranks of his charges. Now they were to sing *"Keraz,"* a song about the Red Partisan guerrillas. Everything was going as well as possible, and so Pantsulaya took his time, giving the dancers a chance to catch their breath.

"Good going," said Makhaz, the one from Uncle Sandro's home district. "Now you're set for life..."

"Oh, come on, Makhaz..." Uncle Sandro tried to be modest.

"And why not?" Makhaz said hotly, without looking at him. "Sliding right up to Stalin himself, and with your turban over your face, too! Even the Germans couldn't think up anything like that!"

Yes, Uncle Sandro understood perfectly well that this brilliant trick not only made him number one in the ensemble, but permanently established his authority at headquarters. Now, of course, the manager wouldn't dare bother him with stupid questions about the firewood.

When they started singing the Partisan song *"Keraz,"* Uncle Sandro just pretended to sing, opening and closing his mouth slightly in time with the melody. This was a first small reward for his feat.

While they were singing, Lakoba leaned over to tell Stalin something, and from the fact that he and Stalin glanced in his direction several times, Uncle Sandro sensed, with sweetly fluttering stomach, that they were talking about him.

When Nestor Apollonovich clenched his fist and swung his arm to illustrate something, Uncle Sandro surmised that he was telling Stalin about the Prayer Tree: his gesture meant that one had to strike the tree with something to make it sing *"Kum-khoz..."*[4] In any case Stalin leaned back and burst out laughing at this point in the story, and Kalinin nudged him to indicate that he was interfering with the singers. Stalin stopped laughing, leaned over to Kalinin, and, as Uncle Sandro surmised, began retelling the same story. When he reached the point where he had to illustrate how the tree was struck, he made several energetic gestures with the hand that clutched his pipe. At this, Kalinin could not restrain himself, and his little beard bounced as he went off in a fit of laughter, whereupon Stalin shook a finger at him, indicating that his laughter was interfering with the singers.

Taking the horn in one hand and a bottle of wine in the other, Stalin stood up and walked over to the dancers.

Nestor Apollonovich whispered something to his wife, and she seized a chicken platter from the table and hurried after Stalin. Before Stalin could reach the dancers, the sanatorium manager appeared and tried to assist him. Stalin shouldered him aside and himself poured a full horn of wine and served it to Makhaz.

Makhaz put one hand on his heart, accepted the horn with the other, and carefully raised it to his lips. As he applied himself to the horn and drank, Stalin watched him with satisfaction.

"Drink, drink, drink...," he said methodically, chopping the air with his small puffy hand.

It was a one-liter horn. Taking the empty bottle from Stalin, the manager put it on the table and ran for a fresh one. He took the platter from Sarya and held it for her to cut up the chicken. Either from embarrassment or because the platter shook in the manager's hands, Sarya managed the knife and fork clumsily. A blush appeared on her dark cheeks, and the manager began to gasp for breath.

Meanwhile Makhaz drained the horn, turned it upside down to show his honesty, and handed it to Uncle Sandro. Stalin, noticing that the food was late in coming, gave up on Sarya. Decisively, using both hands, he took the chicken by the legs and—with enjoyment, Uncle Sandro noted—ripped it in half. Then he ripped each half again. The fat dripped down his fingers, but he paid no attention to it.

It struck Uncle Sandro that the Leader's left hand was not entirely dextrous in its movements. Wonder if he has a withered arm, Uncle Sandro thought. Discreetly examining it, he decided yes, a little bit... I should get him together with Bad Hand, he thought for no apparent reason. Uncle Sandro felt that on the whole this slight impairment somehow diminished the Leader's image. Just a bit, but still...

Taking a chicken leg with his wet hand, Stalin gave it to Makhaz. The latter bowed again, accepted the leg, and took a decorous bite.

The manager was about to try and fill the horn, but Stalin again took the bottle away from him. Grasping it in fingers slippery with chicken fat, he filled the horn and gave the empty bottle to the manager. The latter ran for another.

"Drink, drink, drink," Uncle Sandro heard, as soon as he raised the horn. Uncle Sandro drank, smoothly tilting the horn with the nonchalant artistry of the true tamada—not drinking, but pouring the precious liquid from one vessel into another.

"You drink the way you dance," Stalin said. Proffering him a chicken leg, he looked into his eyes with his resplendent feminine gaze. "Have I seen you somewhere before, abrek?"

Stalin's hand, proffering the chicken leg, suddenly stopped motionless, and an expression of menacing alertness appeared in his eyes. Uncle Sandro had a sensation of mortal danger, although he could not imagine why. He knew that Stalin was wrong, that he, Sandro, would remember it if he had ever seen Stalin anywhere.

The ensemble, which was silent anyway, turned to stone. Uncle Sandro heard Makhaz's jaws stop chewing the chicken. He had to answer. He could not deny that Stalin had seen him, and at the same time it was still more terrifying to agree that he had, not only because Uncle Sandro did not remember it, but mainly because Stalin was inviting him to be part of some disagreeable memory. He sensed this immediately.

A mighty engine of self-preservation, developed through many dangers, turned over all the possible answers in a second or two and cast up to the surface the least dangerous one.

"They made a movie about us," Uncle Sandro said, to his own surprise. "You might have seen me in it, Comrade Stalin."

"Ah-h, a movie," the Leader said slowly, and the light in his eyes went out. He handed him the chicken leg. "Here, you deserve it."

Again came the gurgle of wine being poured into the horn.

"Drink, drink, drink," echoed beside him.

Uncle Sandro took a bite of the chicken leg and made a slight movement with his neck, feeling that it had gone numb, recognizing by the numbness that a weight had fallen from him. Well, well, Uncle Sandro thought, how did I remember that we had been in a movie? Hi-ho, Sandro, thought Uncle Sandro, intoxicated with joy and pride. No sir, it's not so easy to nip a Chegemian! Can we really have met somewhere? He must have confused me with someone else. I wouldn't want to be in the shoes of the man he confused me with, Uncle Sandro thought, glad that he was Sandro of Chegem and not the man the Leader had confused him with.

Stalin was already giving the horn to the last dancer in the front row when Nestor Apollonovich came over to him.

"Maybe we should invite them to the table?" he asked.

"Whatever you say, my dear Nestor; I'm only a guest," Stalin replied. Accepting a napkin from Sarya, he began wiping his hands, slowly and significantly, like a mechanic who has finished a job. Throwing the napkin on the ravaged platter, he walked to the table beside Lakoba, at a springy gait that carried his strength easily.

The members of the ensemble were seated around the banquet table, the best performers among the leaders, the more ordinary ones among the secretaries of the district committees of western Georgia. A rather considerable amount of noise now rose over the banquet table. Heterogeneous islets of conversation began to take on independent life.

Suddenly Comrade Stalin stood up with his wineglass raised. A thundering silence fell, and in an instant the air was cleansed of the rubbish of noise.

"I raise this glass," he began in a quietly impressive voice, "to this medal-bearing republic and its permanent leader..."

He stood motionless for a long moment, as if for the last time attempting to weigh this leader's lofty qualities, for which he himself had rewarded him by making his position permanent. Although everyone understood that he could now name no one but Lakoba, still, the lengthy pause engendered a fever of anxious curiosity: What if—?

"...my best friend, Nestor Lakoba," Stalin concluded, and his hand made an affirmative gesture, somewhat abbreviated by the weight of the wineglass.

" 'Best,' he said the 'best,'" buzzed the district committee secretaries, pondering how this remark would hit Party leadership in Tbilisi, and whether from there it might ricochet to hit each and every one of them. The eyebrows of every one of them were still fixedly raised in surprise.

"...In this republic you know how to work and how to make merry..."

"Long live Comrade Stalin!" one of the district committee secretaries shouted suddenly, jumping to his feet. Stalin swiftly turned toward him with an expression of menacing contempt, whereupon the secretary, a tall and mountainous man, slowly started to sag. As though satisfied of the certainty that the man would complete his slump, Stalin looked away from him.

"Some comrades...," he continued slowly, and in his voice one could hear distant rumbles of irritation. Everyone realized that he was angry at the district committee secretary for his inappropriate glorification of Stalin.

Beria fidgeted in his seat. Removing his pince-nez for a moment, he threw the man one of his notorious murky green glances. The district committee secretary recoiled as from a blow.

The district committee secretaries sitting beside him imperceptibly moved away, forming between themselves and him a gap that had an ideological nuance. All the district committee secretaries looked at him with their eyebrows raised in surprise, as if trying to see who he was and where the devil he'd come from.

Bracing his hands on the table, staring at Beria, he continued to sag slowly, trying to ease his way into the company at the table unnoticed, and at the same time holding himself back in case he should be ordered to leave.

"...some scholars, there in Moscow...," Stalin continued, after an even longer pause, and the note of menace and irritation sounded still more distinctly in his voice. It was immediately clear to everyone that he was deciding something very important in his mind and had long since forgotten the clumsy district committee secretary.

Beria removed his gaze from the man, and he seemed to collapse beneath his own broken backbone, tumble joyously down—it had passed!

"...Bukharin..." Uncle Sandro heard the whisper from one of the secondary leaders not known to him by their portraits.

"... Bukharin, Bukharin, Bukharin..." The whispers buzzed through the ranks of the district committee secretaries.

It was known in Party circles that Stalin did in fact call Bukharin that. In the days of their friendship, "our scholar." Now, "that scholar."

"...think that governing by Lenin's way," Stalin continued, "means holding endless discussions, timorously avoiding decisive measures..."

Stalin again lapsed into a reverie. He seemed to be listening to the buzz with the estranged interest of an outsider, and enjoying it. He loved this kind of vague innuendo. His listeners' imaginations inevitably widened the meaning of it, owing to the ill-defined margins of the contaminated area. They would all retreat farther than necessary, and later he could make political hay by accusing those who had retreated too far of vacillation.

"...but governing by Lenin's way means, first, not fearing decisive measures, and second, finding specialized personnel and adeptly placing them where they belong... A little example."

Suddenly Stalin looked at Uncle Sandro, and the latter felt his heart plunge straight down while he returned the Leader's gaze unblinkingly.

"...Nestor found this abrek in a distant mountain village, and made his talent universally accessible," Stalin continued. "Before, he danced for a narrow circle of friends, but now he dances for the enjoyment of the whole republic and for your enjoyment and mine, comrades.

"...So let us drink to my dear friend, the host of this table, Nestor Lakoba," Comrade Stalin concluded. Still standing, he drained his glass and added, "*Allaverdi*, Lavrenty..."

He knew perfectly well that Beria and Lakoba did not like each other, and he was amusing himself by making Beria be the first to drink to Lakoba.

With the tip of his knife, Stalin took a dollop of *adzhika* from the relish dish and transferred it to his plate. Slathering a chunk of lamb with the purple condiment, he put it in his mouth and crunched the milky gristle.

"Not too hot?" Kalinin asked warily, watching Stalin smear the meat with *adzhika*.

"No," Stalin said, shaking his head, "I think this Abkhazian *adzhika* has a great future."

Many of those who heard Stalin's remark reached for the *adzhika*. Subsequently this prediction of the Leader's, unlike many of his others, did in fact come true—*adzhika* spread far beyond the borders of Abkhazia.

Meanwhile, in no way betraying his feelings, Beria offered a toast and drank to Lakoba. Lakoba, who had listened to the Leader's toast on his hearing aid, now took it off and listened to Beria with his hand cupped to his ear. In no way did he betray his feelings, either; from time to time he nodded to show his gratitude and that he had heard the words.

After Beria, Kalinin took the floor and drank to Lakoba, saying a few words about scholars who had long been out of touch with the common people. Stalin liked his toast and reached over to kiss him. Kalinin unexpectedly ducked the kiss.

Stalin frowned. Uncle Sandro was again amazed at how quickly his mood changed. His eyes had just been shining resplendently at Kalinin, and suddenly they were opaque, withdrawn. Beria's pince-nez flashed animatedly, and the district committee secretaries stared at Kalinin, eyebrows raised in surprise.

That means he's with them, not with me, Stalin thought in fright, how could I have missed it? He was frightened not by Kalinin's betrayal itself—it would take nothing to crush him—but by the fact that his own sensitivity to danger, a sensitivity he trusted, had betrayed him. This was terrifying.

"Who wants to kiss a pockmarked fellow like you?" Kalinin said, looking at Stalin with an impertinent grin. "Now if you were a sixteen-year-old girl (he carefully cupped his right hand and gave it a slight shake, as if hearkening to the sweet bell of youth), that would be another matter..."

Stalin's face lit up, and a sigh of relief whispered through the hall. No, my sensitivity didn't betray me, Stalin thought.

"Oh, you—my All-Union goat," he said, hugging and kissing Kalinin, in reality hugging and kissing his own sensitivity.

"Ha, ha, ha, ha!" laughed the district committee secretaries, rejoicing in the leaders' mutual joke. Lakoba joined in a little belatedly after Uncle Sandro, who was now sitting beside him, explained the joke, which he had not quite heard. Lakoba's belated laughter sounded rather strange, and Beria, unable to restrain himself, guffawed ambiguously, although his guffaw might have been taken for an echo of Lakoba's laugh.

But Stalin perceived the mockery in Beria's laughter. Just now he found it disagreeable. He looked over at Beria and said, "Lavrenty, ask your wife to dance for us..."

"Of course, Comrade Stalin," Beria said, looking at his wife.

"But I can't, Comrade Stalin," she said, flushing.

Stalin knew she could not dance.

"The Leader wants you," Beria whispered threateningly.

"Why 'the Leader'—we all do," Stalin said. Encompassing the members of the ensemble in his gaze, he added, "Come on, fellows."

Clapping and humming as they went, the members of the ensemble formed a semicircle, the open side toward the head of the table.

"I'm not being coy, I really don't know how," Beria's wife said, trying to make herself heard over the clapping. But now everyone was calling for her. Urged on by her husband, balking timidly, she walked into the circle. At a moment when Beria turned his back to the table, Uncle Sandro noticed his distorted lips were whispering obscenities to his wife. Spreading her arms, she took a couple of awkward turns and stopped, not knowing what to do next. It was clear that she really did not know how to dance.

"Good girl," Stalin said, smiling and applauding her. Everyone applauded Beria's wife.

"Sarya, we want Sarya," called some voices. Sarya was sitting between Uncle Sandro and Lakoba. Her dark eyes flashed and she looked at her husband.

"Go on," Lakoba said in Abkhazian. She glanced at Stalin. He smiled back affectionately. Everything was going the way he wanted.

Sarya entered the circle. Her head somewhat tilted back by her heavy knot of hair, the dusky beauty took a few smooth turns and suddenly stopped beside Pata Pataraya, inviting him to dance. Smiling modestly, Pata glided alongside her.

Beria sat at the table without looking at the dancers, his head resting heavily in his hand. His wife, distraught, stood beside the ensemble, apparently unable to decide whether to resume her place.

"Lavrenty," Stalin said softly. Beria straightened up and looked at the Leader. "It looks like specialized personnel aren't the only thing the Deaf One knows best..."

Beria shrugged his shoulders as if to say, There's nothing to be done about it—it's fate. This made Uncle Sandro uncomfortable, he sensed danger lurking here for Lakoba. Oh no—the Leader shouldn't provoke him that way, Uncle Sandro thought.

At this point Sarya ran out of the circle, embraced Beria's wife, and kissed her on the eyes. Everyone felt a secret nobility in this impulse of hers, a desire to soften Nina's failure, to turn it all into a joke. Everyone clapped joyfully, and the women, their arms around each other, returned to the table.

"Tell me later what they said," Lakoba whispered to Uncle Sandro during the final burst of applause, while everyone was watching Sarya embrace Beria's wife. Lakoba had noticed Stalin saying something to Beria, and the latter shrugging his shoulders. He must have sensed that they were talking about him.

Almost simultaneously with Lakoba's words, three pistol shots rang out. Uncle Sandro leaped to his feet. Voroshilov returned a smoking pistol to his holster. Moved by Sarya's dance, and especially by her noble impulse, he could not restrain himself from making this little salute. Everyone buzzed gleefully and started looking at the ceiling, where beside the chandelier there were three little black holes joined by a jagged crack.

The plaster that rained down after the shots had covered a cooling turkey with a white deposit. Stalin looked at the powdered turkey, looked up at the black holes in the ceiling, and then shifted his gaze to Voroshilov and said, "You missed."

Voroshilov flushed darkly and hung his head.

"We have among us," Stalin said, "a genuine first-class sniper. Let's get him up here."

He looked at Lakoba, laid his pipe on the table, and began to applaud. Everyone amiably took up the applause, joining the Leader, although almost nobody actually knew what was going on.

Lakoba understood what was being asked of him. He ducked his head and shrugged in embarrassment.

"Maybe it's not worth it?" he said, glancing at Stalin. The latter held a match to his pipe.

"No, it is, it is!" the voices cried all around. Stalin stopped in the middle of lighting up and nodded at the cries as if to say, the voice of the people—what can you do.

Embarrassed at the pleasure that lay ahead, Nestor Apollonovich gestured helplessly. He started looking around for the sanatorium manager, but the man was already trotting toward him.

"Call him...," Lakoba said as the manager bent down to him.

"Should he change his clothes?" the manager asked, still bending down.

"Why?" Lakoba frowned. "Let's keep it simple..."

Nestor Apollonovich poured himself a glass of wine and gestured to indicate that everyone should follow suit. Everyone filled his glass.

"I want to raise this glass," he began in his splintery voice, "not to the Leader, but to the Leader's modesty."

Apropos, Nestor Apollonovich told the following anecdote. It seemed that last year he had received a note from Comrade Stalin in which the latter had asked him to send him some mandarin oranges, giving strict orders for the parcel to be accompanied by a bill, which the Leader would pay out of his very next paycheck.

Stalin pensively puffed on his pipe as he listened to Nestor's story. This is all true, he was thinking, the Deaf One is not flattering me. And I did send the money out of my next paycheck... A good lesson to all these secretaries, who don't know how to do anything but crane their eyebrows all evening long.

It pleased him that everything Nestor was saying was true, but, looking deeper within himself, he found another source of a more secret but also a more subtle joy. The source of this joy, he remembered, was that even as he was writing that note, he knew that sooner or later it would crop up and play its little historical role, just this way... So, who knew how to look into the future—he or those "scholars"?

"...One might wonder, would it really impoverish our republic to send this miserable bunch of mandarins to Comrade Stalin?" Nestor Lakoba continued.

"It wasn't you and I who put the mandarins in, my dear Nestor." Stalin jabbed his pipe in his direction. "The people put them in."

"The people put them in," buzzed through the ranks.

The people put them in, Stalin repeated to himself, still dimly groping after the explosive play on words imprisoned in this innocent expression. Later on, when his magnificent formula "Enemy of the People" was worked out and issued, there were those who tried to attribute its origin to the French Revolution. Maybe the French did have something of the sort, but *he* knew that he had nursed it to life himself, right here in Russia.

(Like a poet, for whom a sudden combination of words is a flare illuminating the contours of a future poem, he found in these chance words the embryo of a future formula.

It is terrifying to think that the mechanism for crystallizing an idea is the same for a hangman and a poet, just as the stomachs of a cannibal and a normal man accept food with the same good conscience. But if we think about it, what seems to be the indifference of human nature may be a result of the highest wisdom of man's moral nature.

Man is given the choice of becoming a hangman, just as he is given the choice of not becoming one. In the final analysis, the choice is ours.

And if the cannibal's stomach simply would not accept human flesh, this would be an oversimplified and dangerous way of humanizing the cannibal. No one knows where his proclivity might lead him next.

There is no humanity without triumph over baseness and there is no baseness without triumph over humanity. Every time, the choice is ours, and the responsibility for that choice as well. If we say that we have no choice, it means the choice has already been made. We talk about having no choice only because we are burdened by guilt for the choice we have made. If there were in fact no choice, we would feel no burden of guilt...)

...To the thunder of applause, Lakoba drained his glass. Before this thundering glorification of the Leader's modesty had stopped, the cook came through the door in his white apron, and behind him the sanatorium manager carrying a plate.

On hearing the applause, the cook tried to back out, but the manager gave him a little shove and drew him away from the door.

He was a plumpish, middle-aged man of average height, with the pasty complexion that cooks often have and a head of thick curly hair.

Gesturing for him to wait there, the manager, trying to hold the plate motionless, went over to Lakoba.

"Nestor Apollonovich, the cook is here," he said, bending down to show him what was on the plate. On the plate, rolling around a little, lay a half-dozen eggs.

"Good," Lakoba said. He looked frowningly at the plate.

Only at this point did Uncle Sandro guess that Nestor Apollonovich was going to shoot at the eggs. He had never seen this.

"Turkey eggs?" Beria asked suddenly. He reached over and took an egg from the plate.

"Chicken, Lavrenty Pavlovich," the manager supplied, holding the plate closer to him.

"Then why so big?" Beria asked, examining an egg curiously. The eggs really were quite large.

"I chose them myself," the manager giggled, nodding in the direction of the cook, trying to direct Beria's attention to the secret humor of the situation. But, paying no attention to the secret humor of the situation, Beria continued to examine the egg. The manager grew anxious.

"Maybe I should change them, Lavrenty Pavlovich?" he asked.

Beria collected himself and hastily put the egg back on the plate. "No, it was just a comment."

"He's jealous of the Deaf One," Stalin whispered to Kalinin, and laughed soundlessly into his mustache. Kalinin's little beard bounced in reply.

"I think that corner would be better," Lakoba said, examining the chandelier and nodding toward the corner opposite to where the cook stood. In the same way, a photographer tries to choose the best lighting effect before he starts shooting.

"Quite right," the manager agreed.

"Is he nervous?" Lakoba asked, indicating the cook.

"A little," the manager said, bending low over Lakoba's ear.

"Calm him down," Nestor Apollonovich said, pulling away from the manager, whose posture somewhat too insistently called attention to his deafness.

The cook was still standing in the doorway with the apathetic expression of a test subject. Only now did Uncle Sandro notice that he was gripping his tall white cap in one hand. The fingers of that hand were in constant motion.

The manager went over and whispered something to the cook, and they started for the opposite corner. The manager solemnly carried the plate of eggs in front of him.

It grew quiet. By now everyone clearly saw the meaning of all this. His starched apron creaking, the cook stopped in the corner and turned to face the hall.

"If you only knew how I hate this," Sarya whispered, turning to Nina. Nina did not respond: she was staring wide-eyed at the corner. From then on Sarya did not once look in the direction that everyone else was looking.

The cook stood tightly pressed against the wall. The manager was talking to him non-stop, and he was nodding. His face had turned the color of flour. The manager selected an egg from the plate and the cook watched his gesture—no longer moving his head, just his white eyes, which seemed to be floating detached from his face. The manager started trying to set the egg on his head, but either he was nervous himself or the egg was not a steady one, because it simply did not want to stay put.

Nestor Apollonovich frowned. Suddenly, still standing motionless, the cook raised his hand, felt for the egg, squinted his white, floating, detached eyes, found the balance point, and smoothly lowered his arm.

The egg perched on his head. Now he stood erect and immobile in the corner, and had it not been for the expression in his eyes, he would have looked like a draftee having his height measured.

The manager quickly glanced around, without finding anywhere to put the plate of eggs. Suddenly, as if afraid that the shooting would start before he could get away, he shoved the plate into the cook's hands and rapidly moved away toward the door.

Lakoba pulled his revolver from its holster and cocked it, taking care to point the barrel down. He looked back at Stalin and Kalinin, trying to stand in such a way that they could see everything. Uncle Sandro had to leave his place. He stood behind Sarya's chair, gripping the back with his hands. Uncle Sandro was very agitated.

Lakoba extended his arm with the pistol raised and started slowly lowering his hand. The arm remained steady, and suddenly Uncle Sandro saw Lakoba's pale face turn to a slab of stone.

All of a sudden the cook went white, and in the dead silence one could clearly hear the eggs rattling on the plate he held in one hand. Suddenly Uncle Sandro saw something yellow splatter on the cook's face, and only afterward did he hear the shot.

"Bravo, Nestor!" Stalin cried. He began to clap. Applause thundered like an electric discharge of relief. The manager ran to the cook, grabbed the cap from his hand, wiped off his yolk-covered cheek, and stuck the cap in his apron pocket.

He looked back at Lakoba, the way a firing-range attendant looks back to tell the marksman where his shot hit or to inquire whether the target is to be readied for the next shot.

"Go ahead," Lakoba nodded. This time the manager quickly stood the egg on the cook's head and went back to the doorway, crunching the shell of the broken egg underfoot. Again Lakoba's face went rigid, and only the wrist moved, slowly and mechanically lowering the gun barrel like a blunt clock hand.

And again this time Uncle Sandro saw the yellow fountain of egg splash up first, and only afterward heard the shot.

"Bravo!" Explosions of applause shook the banquet hall. Smiling a pale happy smile, Lakoba put away the pistol. The cook still stood in the corner, slowly coming back to life.

"Seat him at the table," Lakoba snapped to his wife in Abkhazian.

Sarya picked up a napkin and ran over to the cook. The manager followed her, and the cook angrily pushed the plate of eggs at him. Sarya stood in front of him, wiping off his face with the napkin, and said something to him. The cook nodded with dignity. The manager squatted down, set the plate of eggs on the floor, and picked up the shells of the broken ones.

Sarya started to lead the cook away, but he suddenly stopped to take off his apron and fling it to the manager. Evidently, what had happened gave him such rights for a little while, and he was showing the audience that he was not one to risk his life just for nothing, but had quite a bit to gain by it.

While the manager was hastily walking to the door with the apron slung over his shoulder and the plate in his hand, Uncle Sandro thought with amazement that the cook and the manager might well have traded places, because much in this life is decided by chance.

Sarya seated the cook between the last of the secondary leaders whom Uncle Sandro did not know from portraits and the first of the district committee secretaries.

Sarya poured the cook a glass of cognac, pulled over a plate for him, and put a splash of nut sauce and a piece of turkey on it. The cook immediately drank off the cognac. Now, looking around the table, he was nodding importantly to whatever it was Sarya was saying to him.

Poor Sarya, Uncle Sandro thought, she's trying to atone for the sin of this shooting, which she so disliked and which, incidentally, had once ended in trouble.

It happened in an Abkhazian village. After a long session at table, the guests had turned to target practice. Perhaps precisely because they were shooting at targets and Lakoba was not very careful, or for some other reason, he wounded a villager who had been running back and forth looking at the targets. The wound was not serious, and the man was immediately shipped off to the district hospital in Lakoba's Buick.

Lakoba rode back with the other members of the government in a second car. And on the way, one of the members of the government had a real quarrel with Lakoba and even made him get out of the car in the middle of the road.

"I'm sick of your guerrilla games," he is said to have told him. It is difficult now to determine why Lakoba agreed to get out of the car. He himself may have been so crushed by what had happened that he found it impossible to resist this insulting measure. I think the man who cussed him out was most likely older than he was. If the man said something like, "Either you're getting out or I am," then Lakoba, as a true Abkhazian, could not allow it and probably decided to get out of the car himself.

...When Nestor Apollonovich put away his pistol and turned toward the table, Stalin was on his feet with open arms. Smiling shyly, Nestor Apollonovich went over to him. Stalin embraced him and kissed his forehead.

"My William Tell," he said. Suddenly remembering, he turned to Voroshilov: "And who are you?"

"I am Voroshilov," Voroshilov said, quite firmly.

"I ask you, which of you is a Voroshilov Medalist in marksmanship?"

Stalin asked, and Uncle Sandro again felt uncomfortable. Oh no, he thought, he shouldn't provoke Voroshilov against our Lakoba.

"He's the better shot, of course," Voroshilov said in a conciliatory manner.

"Then why do you go showing off like a Voroshilov Marksman?" Stalin asked. He sat down, anticipating the pleasure of a long string of casuistical taunts.

The district committee secretaries, with difficulty raising their now-heavy eyebrows, began listening in surprise. Lakoba stole away and sat down at his place.

"Now, that's enough, Iosif," Voroshilov said, breaking out in crimson blotches and looking pleadingly at Stalin.

"That's enough, Iosif," Stalin said, gazing reproachfully at Voroshilov. "Opportunists all over the world say that. Are you going to start in too?"

Voroshilov, hanging his head, flushed red and began to sulk.

"Tell them to start his favorite song," Nestor whispered to his wife. Sarya quietly got up and went to the middle of the table, where Makhaz was sitting. Lakoba knew that this was one way to abort the Leader's sudden gloomy caprices.

Makhaz struck up the ancient Georgian drinking song, *"Gaprindi shavo mertskhalo"*—"Fly, Black Swallow." Voroshilov looked up and tried to say something to Stalin. But the latter suddenly raised his hand in an imploring gesture, as if to say, Leave me alone, let me listen to the song.

Stalin sat with his head resting heavily on one hand. In the other hand he clutched his extinguished pipe.

Nothing else—neither power, nor the blood of an enemy, nor wine—gave him such enjoyment. With an all-dissolving tenderness, with an all-submissive courage that he had never in his life experienced, this song, as always, liberated his soul from the burden of being eternally on his guard. It did not liberate him in the same way that the excitement of passion or struggle did, because as soon as the excitement of passion ended in the death of his enemy, a hangover set in, and victory started a putrid toxin flowing from the corpse of the vanquished.

No, the song liberated his soul in a different way. It colored his whole life with the fantastical light of Fate, in which his personal concerns became the concern of Fate, and where there were neither hangmen nor victims, but there was the movement of Fate, History, and the funereal necessity for him to take his place in this procession. And what of the fact that he was destined to occupy in this procession the most terrible and therefore the most magnificent place?

Fly, black swallow, fly...

But Fate's funereal procession gradually moves on, becomes the distant backdrop for a fairytale scene...

He sees a warm fall day, the day of the grape harvest. He is driving out of the vineyard on a cart laden with baskets of grapes. He is taking the grapes home, to the winepress. The cart creaks, the sun is bright. From back in the vineyard he can hear the voices of his family, the shouts and laughter of children.

On the village street a horseman has stopped by a wattle fence. He has never seen the man before but for some reason recognizes him as a visitor from Kakhetia. The horseman is drinking water from a mug that a local peasant has offered him over the fence. The well is right by the fence, which is why the horseman has stopped here.

As he passes the horseman and his fellow villager, he nods cordially to them, smiles fleetingly at the horseman, who peers at him and, though he looks like a modest winegrower, correctly guesses his essential greatness. His fleeting smile is a response to the horseman's guess, to show the horseman that he himself does not attach much significance to his own essential greatness.

He rides by and senses that the horseman from Kakhetia is still looking after him. He even hears the conversation between his neighbor and the visitor from Kakhetia.

"Listen, who's that man?" the horseman says, splashing the last of the water out of the mug and handing it back to its owner.

"That's Dzhugashvili himself," the owner says happily.

"Not *the* Dzhugashvili?" the visitor from Kakhetia says in amazement. "I thought it looked like him, but it can't be..."

"One and the same," the owner confirms. "The very Dzhugashvili who did not want to become the sovereign of Russia under the name of Stalin."

"I wonder why not?" the visitor from Kakhetia says in amazement.

"Too much trouble, he says," the owner explains, "and he says he'd have to spill a lot of blood."

"Tch, tch," clucks the visitor from Kakhetia. "I can't pass up a single grapevine root, but he passed up Russia."

"Why does he need Russia?" the owner comments. "He has a fine farm, a fine family, fine children..."

The visitor from Kakhetia continues to cluck. "What a man!" he says, looking after the cart, which is now turning off toward a house. "He passed up a whole country..."

"Yes, passed it up," the owner confirms, "because he's sorry for the peasants, he says. He'd have had to unite them all. Let them all live for themselves, he says, let each one have his bit of bread and his glass of wine..."

"God grant him health!" the horseman exclaims. "But how does he know what would happen to the peasants?"

"He's that kind of man, foresees everything," the owner says.

"God grant him health!" the visitor from Kakhetia clucks... "God grant..."

Iosif Dzhugashvili, who did not want to become Stalin, just sits on his cart, hums a little song about a black swallow. The sun warms his face, the cart creaks, he listens with a quiet smile to his neighbor's naive but essentially true story.

And now he drives through the open gate of his yard, where a peasant has been waiting for him in the shade of the apple tree. The peasant, who has evidently come to him for advice, stands up and bows to him respectfully. Well, he'll have to take the time to chat with him, give him some sensible advice. A lot of them come to him... Maybe it would have been better after all, to take power into his own hands, so as to help all of them at once with his advice?

Chickens drunk on grape-pressings wander around the yards hearkening to their odd condition, the peasant bows respectfully as he waits for him, his mother, on hearing the creak of the cart, glances out of the kitchen and smiles at her son. His kind old mother with her wrinkled face. Only in old age have respect and plenty come to her at last... His kind old... Damn her to hell!

Here, as always, the vision broke off. He could never carry it further, always got stuck at this point, because the blood of an old insult rushed to his head. There was no forgiving her, none. How stricken he had been once, how stricken, when, playing with the other boys on a green meadow, he had suddenly heard (tear up the meadow!) two grown men, chortling obscenely, start to talk about her.

They sat within ten paces of him in the shade of a cherry-plum tree (ax the cherry-plum, may it wither!) and talked about her. And then one of them suddenly stopped and nodded in his direction, told the other to lower his voice, because they thought it was her boy playing over there.

They lowered their voices and went on talking. Crushed with humiliation, he had to carry on with his game, so that his comrades would notice nothing and guess nothing. How he had hated them, how he dreamed of taking revenge on them, especially, for some reason, the second one, who had told the first to lower his voice. There was no forgiving her for her extreme shameful poverty, or for anything else...

Fly, black swallow, fly...

He raised his head, and as he looked around now at the singing district committee secretaries, he gradually regained his calm. With every wave of melody, the song was washing from their faces those pathetic raised-eyebrow masks of surprise, and under the masks, ever more distinctly, more independently, were revealed (never mind, it's all right so long as they're singing) the faces of winegrowers, hunters, shepherds.

Fly, black swallow, fly...

They think power is honey, Stalin reflected. No; power is the impossibility of loving anyone, that's what power is. A man can live his whole life without loving anyone, but he becomes an unhappy prisoner if he knows that he must not love.

Here I've grown fond of the Deaf One, and I know Beria's going to gobble him up, but there's no way I can help him, because I like him. Power is when you must not love anyone. Because the minute you love a man you begin to trust him, but once you begin to trust, sooner or later you get a knife in the back. Yes; yes, he knew this. And they loved him, and they got the knife for it, sooner or later. Damn life, damn human nature! If only you could love and not trust at the same time. But that is impossible.

But if you have to kill the ones you love, fairness demands that you make short work of the ones you don't love, the enemies of the cause.

Yes, the Cause, he thought. Of course, the Cause. Everything is done for the sake of the Cause, he thought, listening with attentive surprise to the hollow, empty sound of the idea. That's because of the song, he thought. I ought to prohibit that song altogether, it's dangerous, because I love it too much. Nonsense, he thought, it would be dangerous if others could feel it as deeply as I... But no one can feel it so deeply...

Continuing to listen to the song, he poured himself a glass of wine and silently drank it off without looking at anyone. After setting down the glass, he took his long-since extinguished pipe from the table and made several unsuccessful attempts to pull on it. Noticing that the pipe had gone out, he now pulled on it purposely, as if he were still deep in his reverie. The matches lay beside him on the table but he waited: Would someone think to give him a light, or not?

So there—you could be dying and they wouldn't give you a drink of water, he thought, pitying himself, but at this point Kalinin lit a match and held it to the pipe. Deep in his reverie, he waited until the match flame burned down to Kalinin's fingers, and only then bent for a light. As he lit up, he watched the bright flame touch Kalinin's trembling fingers. Never mind, he thought, I don't have to suffer alone.

He inhaled with pleasure and leaned back in his chair. His glance fell on Voroshilov. He was still sitting at the table hanging his head and knitting his brows, with the hurt expression of a child. Stalin was suddenly stabbed with pity for him. He too has a burden on his conscience, Stalin thought.

"Klim," he said, his voice thick with emotion, "where's Tsaritsyn, where are we, Klim?"

Voroshilov raised his head and gazed at Stalin with bitter, devoted eyes. "Why did you hurt me, Iosif?"

"Forgive me, Klim, if I hurt you," Stalin said, repenting and admiring his own repentance, "but they're hurting you and me even worse..."

"Never mind, Iosif!" Voroshilov exclaimed, electrified by the fact that the Leader not only understood his hurt feelings but placed them on a level with his own. "You'll show them a thing or two..."

"I think I will," Stalin said modestly. He puffed on his pipe. The song ended, and the swarm of dim, unsteady thoughts cleared from his sobered mind.

How could I be angry at him, Voroshilov thought, cheering up and looking discreetly around at the leaders to be sure they had heard Stalin elevate him just now. And how precisely he understood, Voroshilov thought triumphantly, that my enemies among the top brass of the army are a continuation of the anti-Stalinist line within the top echelons of the government.

"Comrade Stalin, what should we do with this Tsulukidze?" asked Beria, who had been listening attentively to Stalin's remarks. He had been wanting to ask about this for a long time and had decided that this was an opportune moment.

The problem was that this old Bolshevik, still respected as one of Lenin's cohorts although he had long since been relieved of any practical responsibility, continued to heckle and grumble at every opportunity. In his time he had dropped a remark, since picked up by the Georgian Communists, that Beria was trying to break into the Party leadership in Transcaucasia with a Mauser in his hand. ("You swine—how was I supposed to break into the leadership, with the Erfurt Program? Wouldn't you have ended up in the shitpile along with it?")

Any other man he would long since have strung up by the tongue for such a remark (now that he had broken into the leadership), but this one he was afraid to touch. The issue was not clear-cut. Stalin himself had annihilated many old Bolsheviks, but certain ones, for some reason, he supported and honored with decorations.

"What has he done?" Stalin asked. He looked pointblank at Beria.

"He blabs too much, he's gotten senile," Beria said, trying to guess what Stalin thought of this before he could express an opinion.

"Lavrenty," Stalin said, growing gloomy because he could not hit on the right answer, "I came here to take my rightful vacation. Why must you hand me a question like that?"

"No, Comrade Stalin, I merely wanted some advice," Beria replied hastily, fleeing ahead of Stalin's gathering gloom. His tone indicated that he was apologizing and did not himself attach any great importance to the question. Good thing I didn't liquidate him, he thought with a flash of joy and fright.

"...Lenin hated blabbermouths, too," Stalin said pensively.

"Maybe we should throw him out of the Party?" Beria asked, reviving. Maybe Stalin was not averse to punishing the son of a bitch somehow after all.

"Can't oust him from the Party," Stalin said, and added impressively, "We didn't admit him, Lenin did."

"What should we do?" Beria asked, utterly bewildered.

"He had a brother, I believe," Stalin said. "I wonder where he is now?"

"He's alive, Comrade Stalin," Beria said, breaking out in a cold sweat. "He manages a lemonade factory in Batum."

Stalin lapsed into reverie. Beria was in a cold sweat because he had not known of the existence of Tsulukidze's brother until just this past year, when he was gathering evidence against the formerly prominent Bolshevik and happened to learn about the brother. The dossier on the brother, requisitioned from Batum, contained nothing useful; he hadn't even been caught embezzling at his lemonade factory. But the fact that Beria knew of the man's existence, knew what he was doing and how he was getting along, now worked to his advantage. Stalin liked it.

"How is his work?" Stalin asked severely.

"Good," Beria said firmly, showing that his enmity for the blabbermouth in no way extended to his relatives, and that his knowledge of the lemonade-factory manager's business qualifications was the simple consequence of his being a Party-minded leader who knew his specialized personnel.

"Let this blabbermouth"—Stalin jabbed his pipe at the unseen blabbermouth—"regret all his life that he destroyed his brother."

"Brilliant!" Beria exclaimed.

"You people in the Caucasus are too strong on family ties," Stalin said, to explain his train of thought. "Let this be a lesson to other blabbermouths on the dialectics of punishment."

Realizing that by this remark Stalin had set himself apart from the Caucasus, several district committee secretaries began looking at him with melancholy reproach, as if to ask, Why have you abandoned us?

"Live and learn," Beria said, spreading his hands.

"But not at the expense of my vacation, Lavrenty," Stalin admonished severely, a joke that gladdened Lakoba. He considered it tactless of Beria, here at a festive table in Abkhazia, to get Stalin to sanction reprisals against his own enemies. This Beria's always trying to worm his way up, and I have only myself to blame for introducing him to Stalin, thought Lakoba. This was the right time to raise a toast to elder brother, to the great Russian People. Not without reason had Stalin said, "You people in the Caucasus..." It meant he already thought of himself as a Russian...

He signaled to the other end of the table for everyone to pour another drink.

"I want to raise this toast," he said, getting up from his seat, pale, stubbornly fighting off an early-morning drunkenness, "to our elder brother..."

The festive night caught second wind. Again they drank, ate, danced, and by now even Uncle Sandro, the greatest tamada of all times and nations, found his head spinning. It was a little too much even for him, to see in one night so many ominous and wonderful things.

Lakoba, as tamada, relaxed the reins a little, sensing that the strict ritual of the Caucasian table was beginning to weary the Leader.

"We want Sarya, beautiful Sarya!" Kalinin shouted, clapping his hands and tilting his bearded chin affectionately.

"'Mravaldzhamie,' we want 'Mravaldzhamie'!" called some people at the other end of the table. They struck up the song.

"'Many Summers'!" shouted others. They struck up the Abkhazian drinking song.

"Now you're off and away," Makhaz shouted from the other end of the table, his eyes meeting Uncle Sandro's. "Bliss has descended on you— bliss!"

"My hair is curly, like a fern," the cook was telling one of the district committee secretaries, letting him feel his hair. "The egg lies there like it's in a little nest."

"All the same it's a risk," the secretary said, dourly feeling the cook's hair.

"Some men's wives," Beria muttered, resting his head heavily on his hands.

"But Lavrik, try to understand... I was ashamed to, and he didn't even get angry."

"We'll talk when we get home—"

"But Lavrik—"

"I'm not Lavrik to you any more—"

"But Lavrik—"

"Some men's wives..."

"Where's the risk, my dear fellow? My hair is three fingers deep," the cook said enthusiastically, trying to out-argue the district committee secretary, who was touching his head mistrustfully.

"He didn't hit your head?"

"Of course not," the cook said, gleeful at his naivete. "There's a lot of fear, but little risk."

The district committee secretary dourly held to his own interpretation. "All the same, it's a risk, the man is drunk."

"'You people in the Caucasus,' he says," another secretary was saying, shaking his head. "What have we done to him?"

"Shota, I ask you as a brother, don't take offense at the Leader—"

"I'd lay down my life for him, but my heart aches," Shota replied, casting a bereaved glance at the far end of the table.

"Shota, I ask you as a brother, don't take offense at the Leader..."

"Lucky stiff! Lucky stiff!" Makhaz shouted drunkenly, meeting Uncle Sandro's eyes. "Now you've got all Abkhazia in your pocket!"

Uncle Sandro shook his head reproachfully, intimating that such shouts were indecent, especially when aimed into the thick of the government. But Makhaz did not understand his signal.

"Don't pretend it's not in your pocket!" he shouted. "Don't pretend, you lucky stiff!"

"What's he shouting?" Even Lakoba had noticed Makhaz.

"Just nonsense," Uncle Sandro said, and he thought to himself, "It's a good thing he's shouting in Abkhazian, not Russian."

"Now here's something!" The cook was trying to amuse the dour secretary. "I started out as an apprentice cook here in Gagra back in Prince Oldenburgsky's time. The prince used to carry a cane, like Peter. He sampled the workers' dinner himself. Sometimes he used to beat the cooks with his cane, but always for cause."

"All the same, it's a risk." The secretary shook his head dourly. He felt overwhelmed and could not get the egg-shooting out of his mind.

"Here's something!" the cook went on, trying to distract him with his remarkable memories. "His Majesty the Emperor came here—"

"Why make things up," the secretary said, distracted against his will.

"I swear by the cross—on a cruiser! The cruiser dropped anchor out at the roadstead... His Majesty came in on a motor launch; but Her Majesty didn't want to come ashore, which offended the prince," the cook said.

"Court intrigues," the secretary interrupted dourly.

...Early in the morning, when at Lakoba's order the sanatorium manager opened the heavy curtains and a soft pink August dawn peeped into the banquet hall, it (the soft pink dawn) saw many district committee secretaries asleep at the tables—some sprawled back in their chairs, and some with their faces right on the table.

One of the ones sprawled back in his chair held a radish in his mouth, stuck there by his friends. This could only have perplexed the soft pink dawn, because the suckling pigs, each holding a radish in its bared teeth, were no longer on the table, and the humorous analogy was intelligible only to the initiated.

The troupe members approached Stalin one by one. Stalin shoveled up candy, cookies, chunks of meat, fried chickens, cheese bread, and other eatables from the table. Holding up the hem of their cherkeskas or holding out their turbans, they accepted the gifts, said thank-you, and walked away from the Leader.

"Off you go!" Stalin said as he threw a batch of presents to each dancer in turn. He tried to give everyone equal shares, looked closely at the chunks of meat, at the fried chickens, and if he gave less of one thing he tried to pile on more of another. In the same way, a village patriarch, the Eldest in the

House, hands out shares for his neighbors and for guests who will be traveling home after a great feast.

"All the same they'll chalk it up to Stalin," the Leader joked, piling eatables into the wide-spread skirt of a cherkeska. "All the same they'll say Stalin ate it all..."

That being the case, several troupe members exchanged winks and grabbed bottles of wine to take with them.

* * *

The ensemble returned to Mukhus in three overcrowded motor cars. When they were getting into the cars, a curious mix-up occurred. Platon Pantsulaya, the director of the ensemble, got in next to the chauffeur of the first car, of course. Pata Pataraya, as usual, was supposed to sit next to the chauffeur of the second car. He was about to stick his head in the open door but then pulled it out and offered his place to Uncle Sandro, who happened (let us suppose) to be right beside him.

Uncle Sandro tried to refuse, but after some polite wrangling he was forced to yield to Pata Pataraya's urging and sit next to the chauffeur in the second car.

It had been decided to drive as far as the Gumista River and find a picturesque spot to have a picnic. They sang boisterously as they rode. Frequently they encountered children on the road and threw candy and cookies to them out of the car. The children rushed to gather this manna from heaven.

The dancers smiled wearily. "If they knew where it came from!"

Beyond Eshery, at a point where the road passed among thickets of ferns, blackberries, and wild nuts, their way was suddenly blocked by a small flock of goats. The cars braked, and the goats proceeded across the road, tossing their beards and snorting. The goatherd was nowhere to be seen, but his voice carried from the thicket; he was in there driving out a goat that had lagged behind.

"*Kheyt! Kheyt!*" the boyish voice shouted, awakening a strange alarm in Uncle Sandro. From time to time the boy threw stones, and they crashed through the tightly woven branches to land dully, at intervals, on the ground. When one stone hit the unseen goat, Uncle Sandro had a sudden feeling that he had known, the moment before, that this was the one that would hit her. And when the goat ran grunting out of the bushes, and after her the youth, who halted shyly when he saw the cars, Uncle Sandro went cold from agitation and remembered everything.

Yes; it had happened almost the same way back then. The boy had been herding the goats into Sabid's Hollow. And one goat had gotten stuck this same way in the bushes, and the boy had thrown rocks the same way and shouted. Just this same way, the goat grunted and jumped out of the bushes when the rock hit her, and the boy jumped out after her and halted in surprise.

A few steps away, a man was walking along the path, driving ahead of him some heavily-laden pack horses. Hearing the branches snap, the man started and looked at the blue-eyed youth. Never in his life had anyone looked at him with such malice.

At the first instant the boy thought the man's fury was due to the unexpectedness of the encounter, but after he perceived that it was only a boy and a goat, the man threw him another look, as if he were considering for a fraction of a second what to do with him: kill him or leave him. He went on without bothering to decide, merely jerked an elbow to hitch up the carbine that had slipped off his sloping shoulder.

The man walked unusually fast, and it was plain to the boy that he had left him alive only to save time. There was neither a stick nor a whip in the man's hands, and it struck the boy as strange that the horses moved so fast without any kind of goading.

After several seconds the path led into a grove and the man and his horses disappeared. But at the very last moment—one more step and he would be hidden behind a bush—he hitched up the carbine that had slipped off his sloping shoulder again, turned around, and caught the boy's eye. The boy thought he heard a distinct whisper, right in his ear: "You tell and I'll come back and kill you..."

His flock was already far below, and the boy ran down the green mountainside, urging on the goat. He knew that the grove the man had entered with his horses would soon end, and the path would lead them out to an open slope on the far side of Sabid's Hollow.

When he caught up with the flock and looked up, he saw the pack horses begin to appear, one after another, there on the green slope. Eight horses and the man, distinct against the green background of the grassy slope, quickly crossed the open expanse and disappeared into the woods. Even from here, at a distance of about a kilometer, it was noticeable that the horses and the man were walking very fast. And now the boy surmised that this man needed no stick or whip, he was one of those whom horses feared even without any kind of goading.

Before disappearing into the woods, the man again glanced back and jerked his sloping shoulder to adjust the slipping carbine. Although his expression was now impossible to make out, the boy was sure that he had looked back very angrily.

A day later rumors reached Chegem that some men had robbed a steamboat going from Poti to Odessa. The robbers had operated precisely and ruthlessly. Not only did they have a man waiting for them near Kengursk with horses bought beforehand, they had also been able to win over four of the sailors to participate in the robbery. By night, they bound the captain, the helmsman, and several sailors and locked them in the captain's cabin. They lowered the lifeboats, into which they had loaded their loot, and rowed to shore.

Late the next day the bodies of the four sailors were found in a marsh near the hamlet of Tamysh. A day later two more bodies were found, eaten away by jackals, beyond recognition. It was decided that the robbers had quarreled among themselves, and the two that survived had taken their cargo to some unknown place or maybe even perished in the marshes. After another few days, this time quite close to Chegem, they found the body of still another man. He had been killed by a shot in the back and thrown off the steep Atary road, almost on to the heads of the residents of the village of Naa, who had stubbornly settled below these precipitous slopes. The body was well preserved, and it was recognized as that of a man who had bought horses a month ago in the village of Dzhgerdy.

The Chegemians took the whole incident rather calmly, because it was a lowland affair—someone else's, especially since it had to do with steamboats. And only the boy, with terror, guessed that he had seen the other man, in Sabid's Hollow.

About ten days after that encounter, a horseman rode up to their house wearing an Abkhazian cloak but an official peak-cap, which indicated from afar that he was an important man, paid by the authorities.

The horseman, without dismounting, stopped by the wattle fence and waited for the boy's father to approach him. Then, after pulling his foot from the stirrup and resting it on the fence, he conversed with the boy's father. Shooing away the dogs, the boy hovered near the fence to hear what the grown-ups said.

"Have any of your folks," the horseman asked his father, "seen anyone go by with pack horses on the Upper Chegem road?"

"I heard about that," his father replied, "but I haven't seen the man."

"Not the Upper—the Lower!" the boy almost blurted, but he bit his tongue in time.

The man, still talking, found the stirrup with his foot and then rode on.

"Who's that, Pa?" the boy asked his father.

"The sergeant-major," the father replied. He went into the house without saying anything more.

Only in late fall, when he and his father, after packing a donkey with sacks of chestnuts and climbing up from Sabid's Hollow, sat down to rest on that same Lower Chegem path, almost at that same spot—only then could he no longer restrain himself, and he told his father everything.

"So that's why you stopped bringing the goats here?" his father grinned.

"That's not true!" the boy flared: his father had struck home.

"Why didn't you say anything before now?" the father asked.

"You should have seen the way he looked at me," the boy confessed. "I keep thinking he might come back..."

"By now you couldn't drag him back on a rope," his father said, standing up and urging on the donkey with a switch. "But if you'd told right away, they still could have caught him."

"How do you know, Pa?" the boy asked, trying not to lag behind his father. Since meeting that man he did not like this place, did not trust it.

"A man with pack horses can't get farther than one day's journey," his father said. He flicked the switch; the donkey kept wanting to stop, the grade was steep.

"But you know how fast he was walking!" the boy said.

"But no faster than his horses," his father objected. After a moment's thought he added, "And he killed that last man because he knew he had one day's march left."

"Why, Pa?" the boy asked, still trying not to lag behind his father.

"He probably left him alive," his father said, still thinking aloud, "so that the man could help him pack the horses for the last day's march. And then he got rid of him."

"How do you know all this?" the boy asked, no longer trying to keep up with his father, because they had come out on a slope from which their house was visible.

"I know their infidel ways," his father said. "They'd just as soon not work. I don't even want to think about them."

"I don't either," the boy said, "but for some reason I keep remembering about this all the time."

"It will pass," his father said.

It did indeed pass, and with the years receded so far that Uncle Sandro, remembering it once in a while, questioned whether it had all really happened or whether he, the little boy, had imagined it after people started talking about the steamboat robbery near Kengursk.

But then, after the never-to-be-forgotten banquet that took place on an August night in 1935 or the year before, but certainly no later, it all came back to him with uncommon clarity. Superstitiously marveling at the Leader's menacing memory, he thanked God for his own quick-wittedness.

Uncle Sandro often told his friends—and even, after the Twentieth Congress,[5] people who were merely acquaintances—about this festive night, appending to the story his own youthful imaginings or recollections.

"I can still see it now," Uncle Sandro would say. "His carbine kept slipping off his shoulder, and he kept jerking it up as he went, hitching at it without looking. A very sloping shoulder, That One had..."

So saying, Uncle Sandro would gaze at his companion, his big eyes tinged with mysticism. His gaze made it plain that had he told his father soon enough about the man who passed on the Lower Chegem road, the whole of world history would have taken a different path, in any case not the Lower Chegem path.

All the same, it was not exactly clear whether he regretted his long-ago silence or expected a reward from the none-too-grateful younger generation. Most likely his gaze meant that while he regretted he had not told, he was not averse to receiving a reward.

Then again, this ambiguity in his gaze implied a dose of demonic irony, which seemed to reflect the confusion and vacillation of earthly judges in appraising him.

The very fact that he died a natural death—if, of course, he did die a natural death—prompts me personally to the religious thought that God requisitioned the dossier on his deeds in order that He Himself might judge him in the highest court and Himself punish him with the highest punishment.

Translated by Susan Brownsberger
and Carl R. Proffer

Notes

1. Cherkeska: The traditional long, open-necked coat of the Caucasian highlander. Across each side of the chest is a row of polished cartridge cases.

2. Tamada: The head of the table, master of ceremonies (Georgian). He must be a skillful speaker, a master of ritual, an indefatigable drinker, and an expert in human nature.

3. Abrek: A member of the guerrilla bands formed by Caucasian highlanders to resist the rule of Czarist Russia in the nineteenth century.

4. Kumkhoz: Abkhazian pronunciation of the Russian word *kolkhoz*, "collective farm."

5. Twentieth Congress: The Congress of the Communist Party at which Krushchev delivered his famous "secret speech" about the crimes committed by Stalin.

Valentin Rasputin

DOWNSTREAM

Thank God, everything had ended. An end had come to that confused and exhausting darting from store to store, when you yourself don't even know what you're looking for, only that you must buy something, must not forget a gift for anyone, must not leave anyone out. That hurried casting off of all concerns, large and small, which had piled up, as always, till the last day had come to an end: the urgent running here and there, talking with this person and that, taking one thing and returning another, these frenzied preparations when you're constantly checking to be sure that you haven't forgotten anything. Everything ended at once, as if it had been cut out of his life as soon as Viktor walked into his cabin and put down his suitcase. And now an easy and pleasant period of idleness stretched before him, exciting him in advance with its promise of time off and freedom.

The weather for May had turned out to be surprisingly hot. It was baking all day, and now, just before evening, the heat grew even more intense and oppressive. In addition to all this the cabin smelled of paint and the air was musty and acrid. As soon as he entered, Viktor opened the window as far as it would go and thrust his head out. Although what he felt was warm and weak, it was nonetheless a light breeze; from the water came a barely noticeable hint of freshness. Until five, when the ship left, there were still fifteen minutes and passengers were still coming on board. You could hear people coming up the gangplank, but in everything you could feel impending liberation; the massive white hulk of the ship had already begun to tremble in impatience; a half-sleepy female voice on a record, teasing and exciting people, had already begun a standard farewell song about how "people say farewell completely differently when ships are leaving than when trains do."

The cabin was small, but cozy and comfortable enough: a sofa with a high soft back, a small table by the window with a lamp permanently clamped to it, a closet by the door for clothes and other belongings, and behind a heavy green curtain a sink. Viktor was taking a single cabin for the first time and was now impatiently waiting for the ship's departure in order to fully enjoy his solitude. Here he was his own master; here he would lie around and read as much as he wanted, without being in anyone's way or dependent on anyone. In the evening he would put up the window screen and light the table lamp; in the morning he'd sleep as late as he wanted, to the point where he would get up groggy and tired; he'd go out on deck, in the wind...

As a student he had travelled third class, then located below, in the hold, and every time those trips were a holiday for him about which he would already begin to dream during the winter and for which he got ready with all possible painstaking: he saved money, squeezing rubles from his meager stipend; he intentionally saved unread what was rumored by his fellow students to be the best book, improving as best he could his supplies for the trip. Here with every right, earned through months of grinding study, he would finally allow himself a small extravagance; he would go to the restaurant, take a table by one of the wide windows which took up half the wall and order a beer. This was in fact the main part, the most exciting part of the holiday—sitting carelessly slouched in a chair, sipping cold beer and pretending that you see the sense in it, unceasingly looking, looking out the window at the smooth, slow current through which the ship was cutting, at the shore, at everything which stood and lived upon it. At that time the song "water, water, water everywhere" didn't exist yet, which now the same half-sleepy voice continued to drag out with an expressive lack of passion; but even then the water had cast no less a spell than it did now—it now cast a spell, intoxicated and pulled you somewhere, evoking a vague, deep sense of anxiety. This was some kind of an unusual, inexplicable and unearthly condition when unexpected desires were suddenly kindled which aroused your soul and you seemed to envision unusual feats or experienced, out of the blue, a sentimental feeling for your own life, where your greatest happiness seemed to be seeing, thinking, and engraving everything upon your memory.

Here on the ship he had once been in love with a medical student, a girl who was pretty but so thin that you couldn't help wondering how there was any room in her for everything that a human being was supposed to have. She wasn't alone, but was travelling with her mother. Viktor no longer remembered now, how and when this acquaintance had begun, but he remembered well how later they hid the whole night from her mother, now hiding on the upper deck, now in the stern among barrels and huge spools of rope, now in the hold on his bench; how he covered her from the wind with his jacket, how happy he was listening to her hurried and in fact nonsensical whispering. That's what "water, water, water everywhere" does to people. The whole summer after that they dashed off impatient, tender letters to each other, but when they did meet in the city that fall, away from water, they parted quietly and without any regrets whatsoever.

At last there burst forth a march they play when a ship leaves shore, and at that moment the ship lightly pushed off, moving away from its berth. From the shore and on board, people began to shout and wave to each other; here and there were heard words of the command crew directed at the engine room; somewhere a child began to cry loudly and apprehensively. The ship first took a position perpendicular to the shore and then let the current swing it around facing downstream. From the shore it probably looked very beautiful now...white, light and long, gleaming with all its rigging. Today's sailing was its first, maiden voyage since an overhaul and the whole ship was clean, touched up with paint and brought to tiptop condition. The sailors looked smart in their new uniforms and the young stewardesses gave intriguing respectful smiles. Later all this would grow worn and dull or would seem simply unnecessary and superfluous, but for the time being, if you weren't too picky, everything was in reasonably good shape. If only it didn't smell so much of paint in the cabin.

Now they began to move on their own power. Alongside, the stirred-up water began to splash noisily, the shore receded more and more quickly, and the wind rushed through the window. It became easier to breathe. Viktor got off the couch, and adjusting himself without hurrying to the lazy, do-nothing life of the trip, he began to settle in. He got out of his suitcase what he would need here, and went and got bed linen from the stewardess. He was overcome with a tranquil, pleasant sense of self-satisfaction: here he is en route, despite everything, no matter what, he's on his way. Now he can go to the restaurant and, taking a seat by a window as he used to, order a beer. True, he's already lost his taste for beer, but in order to prove both to himself as well as to anyone else that he's the same man, it's worth downing a bottle.

For five years he hadn't been home in his village—five long years which had both changed and complicated his life greatly. During these years he had seen many other places, he had even gone abroad. All this was fine, useful and necessary because he would return filled with some kind of a special, inner direction. It was as if he were being transfused with new blood, bringing keenness and newness to the daily, regular existence of his feelings. But nevertheless how tired he would become on those trips! From beginning to end he had to live in a state of constant tension, something lying ahead always made him anxious, forced him to push himself or, on the other hand, to hold himself back; afraid of making a mistake, he had to make choices constantly: this or that, one or the other, here or there. On trips even the rare moments of physical weakness seemed like the peace of a man strung up by his feet. Only at home (he should no longer say "at home," but somehow something different, because he has his own family in the city which he had just now left), and only in his native village, with his father and mother, did he know that his rest would be complete, absolute and yet unnoticeable: he'd go where he felt like, he'd do whatever came into his head, he would immerse himself in that life as if it were a second childhood; and he would remain there for a long time in happy oblivion, not remembering anything about himself or about others, and giving in only to the simplest and most accessible desires. Even now he felt calmer and more comfortable than he had for a long, long time, as if each cell in his body, freeing itself from a tense mass, finally found its place.

He decided in any case to look in the restaurant, although he didn't know if he would stay there or not. A table by the window turned out to be free, as if especially for him, and so he didn't dare leave. Viktor had sailed on steamships before this; however, this was a motor vessel, and what is more, a motor vessel for ocean travel, unafraid of large waves; but its restaurant, it looked like, hadn't changed, as if it had been moved form a steamship complete and inviolable—the same moderately-sized semicircular room in the hold, which extended to the sides of the ship and had narrow doors on either side, the same picture windows, hung with yellow venetian blinds, and the same low, soft chairs with white slipcovers. Viktor would have bet that even the menu here had not changed in any way, except perhaps in some trifling detail. He opened the menu and smiled. Of course, everything was the same: cabbage soup, whose unpromising sour smell he remembered even now, fried eggs, steak, hot rice cereal, but the river catch had been replaced by sea catch, which he should have foreseen. In every other way the menu resembled a sign chiselled in rock once and for all.

To sit slumped in a chair with a glass of beer held in his hand was both comfortable and pleasant. Somewhere above him a fan was working silently and powerfully, circulating the air, and a breeze, moving in circles about the room, made the light high window blinds flutter and touched your face with a timid fading movement. On one side at a neighboring table a group of villagers were talking noisily over their beer; on the other side a family was having supper in silent, playful concentration like in a game: he and she with identically broad clean faces which were young and kind and for some reason (couldn't it be from their life together?) resembled each other, and a boy and girl of about the same age, around six or seven. The children, who couldn't reach the table sitting in a chair, ate standing up. Apparently this is what evoked the slyly attentive and happy mood of the parents: now and then they would glance at each other and smile. Watching them, Viktor, God only knows why, felt an incomprehensible envy toward this small yet complete family. Something other than the love and accord in this family touched and moved him—perhaps their resemblance to each other and their physical equality, which immediately struck you, as if he and she were created especially for each other, like the left hand for the right; or perhaps it was the careful, balanced moderation: mother, father, son, daughter—one of everything possible in a family, and it was all beautiful, strong, for the glory of mankind; or perhaps it was even something else, something hidden more deeply and firmly. And because he couldn't find an explanation for this feeling, his uneasiness did not go away but kept bothering him. Even after they had finished eating at the neighboring table and had left, it faded away slowly.

But outside the window, beyond the narrow strip of water, the shore kept gliding and gliding by; behind the stern the water churned about unwillingly as if taken by surprise, and splashing up, hurled waves to both sides. The river extending behind the ship seemed to rock gently to the left and then to the right; on its surface far and wide, as far as the eye could see, ripples left by breaking waves glistened in the sunlight. They both hurt and attracted the eye. The current seemed to grow weaker there, and even to cease flowing altogether. The shore changed frequently: in one place, low-lying and bright green, with cows grazing on fresh green pasture, in another, around the bend, a steep bank with buildings on top of it; steps led down to the water and boats, and by the boats children were jumping, shouting and waving their hands; near the houses, screening their faces with their hands from the sun, stood the adults.

Viktor had grown up on this river. He used to spend every Godgiven day on it from morning till night, and a large number of his childhood joys and those which followed childhood were connected with it. He would never forget how each year he feared missing the ice floe; with what fear and emotion, completely forgetting himself, he had looked at the wild, uncontrollable force pushing the ice downstream, forcing upward sluggish blocks of ice of a deep blue hue, and crumbling them—what a many-toned and drawn-out rumbling there had been all around, with sounds of groaning and despair.

One recollection, almost his earliest, was sharper than the rest. Then he had turned six, not just turned six, but turned six on that day precisely— on May 1. Usually the ice floe also started toward the end of April or the beginning of May. It wasn't enough for him, the little tyke that he was, that his birthday coincided so nicely with a holiday; he also wanted for the ice to start moving without fail on that very day; otherwise, he wouldn't be happy. From where, from what depths and dreams this superstitious connection between one and the other had arisen in him, he, of course, didn't know; but he only knew that even now—of course without the old undisguised frankness and personal interest—he continued to follow, as if in jest, when the ice on the river would break, before or after the holiday; whether success would smile on him today or not (here was yet another difference: happiness had been replaced by good fortune, which was easier and safer to deal with—even if you let it slip through your fingers, it was no great loss. As he grew older, it seemed, he had taught himself to risk only that which in the long run wasn't worth that much).

From early morning on May first he had sat on the shore, staring intently at the ice that had turned blue and had buckled. Never before had he had the chance to see the first, decisive push which ripped the ice from its place, and now he waited with impatience and grave concentration, fearing more than anything else in the world that the day would end before this happened. Somewhere in the village people were singing; the sun shone brightly; there wasn't even any wind from down the river, but there was a gentle, even breeze lightly moving above the river, bringing from somewhere the fresh, cool scent of pussy willows and water which had just broken free. The river moved restlessly, rocked, sighed; at times you could hear a hollow noise from within its womb, then a quick powerful sound of cracking would resound like a shot, and cracks would break out in the ice. Any moment now all of this was supposed to break loose and begin churning about, roaring, flowing, but there it stood. It was held in place by some kind of force, it was clutching at something, holding its ground, and would not move anywhere. He waited in vain all day; in the evening they took him home completely exhausted. Now all was lost: the war would never end, father would never come home from the front, the little girl Ninka next door would never fall in love with him. There was no point in living any longer.

In the middle of the night he woke to a vague, far-off hum, which now fell silent, now poignantly and uneasily rose again. At any other time the six-year-old boy would most certainly have hid from it with his head under the covers and would have tried to fall asleep as quickly as possible, but now a last bit of hope compelled him to overcome fear and get out of bed. Following some external powerful force, he groped his way to the door, opened it without a sound and slipped out into the street. Both heaven and earth were covered by complete pitch darkness, through which nothing penetrated anywhere, but he knew the road to the river even with his eyes closed. Ludicrously and clumsily jumping about, afraid of flying into a fence, but yet even more afraid of walking at a normal pace, he rushed to the shore.

It was brighter here. The ice gave off a faint gray shimmer and in it he easily discerned that the river remained just the same as before. Nothing in it had changed since evening. It was as if the river had settled down and grown quiet after the long labor pains it had expended in vain; indifference had taken over. Little Vitka grew numb from terror, not understanding what was happening to him, why he was here and not at home in bed. Having gotten here, he was now in no condition to run back. His legs were paralyzed with fear.

Somewhere far off in the taiga there began a rumbling which gathered strength and rolled, rolled straight up to the village, threatening to crush and overrun it; having almost reached the village, it subsided. A storm was approaching. What he had taken for noise from the river was thunder in the sky, the first of spring, born unexpectedly and producing at first a low rumbling. A brief flash of lightning flared up and immediately went out, again the thunder moved on, drawing its movement up over the river, again halting not far from the village.

The sky was now powerful and frightening. Its edges, merging with the earth, receding into endless darkness, and it hung above the earth like a huge restless weight. In the conglomeration of clouds some sort of stripes and spots glowed with an ominous blue as they advanced and charged. Between thunderclaps, when it grew quiet, an indistinct, barely audible noise was heard from above, either the rustling of clouds or the muffled whistle of the wind. Below, the air was alarmingly motionless and empty, without spring's sharp smells or night's usual freshness; the storm had managed to suck everything from it.

The thunder was now rolling over the village. It began reluctantly, lazily, as if it did not know if it were worth thundering at all; but aggravated by its own growling, it suddenly made an instantaneous and fierce leap to one side and with effort burst apart, exploded, strewing about lots of thundering fragments. Barely had one peal of thunder ended before another arose. In the bright, deathly luster of the lightning the huts seemed transparent; and if you couldn't see anything beyond their walls it was only because there really wasn't anything behind them except the forest, which was awesomely white and lifeless, with narrow long lifeless tree trunks.

Hunching his shoulders, the little boy sobbed forlornly, helplessly and what is even more, without realizing it. He stood on his feet, but had lost long before any sensation of the earth beneath him, as if he had been seized and borne away somewhere like a bit of fluff so that no one would ever find even a trace of this small, unfortunate little human being.

When it was just about to rain, the storm grew more and more threatening. From a solid impenetrable black the sky turned dark purple and could be distinguished more clearly. The thunder pounded steadily and maliciously, without the restraint and playfulness that had existed at first; it exploded immediately and pursued this explosion without weakening, until a new explosion began somewhere on the other side. Everything around was filled with this roar alone, which was whipped up by frequent flashes of lightning bolts. Everything shrank and trembled before him, and now there wasn't enough open space for him; he began to gasp from all the fury; any second now something was about to happen and without a doubt it had to be something terrible.

And it did happen. A lightning bolt flashed out in thin long strokes as usual, but it didn't go out; suddenly, as if confused, it began to swirl around and dance, and disintegrated with a broad finish, revealing an eerie light blue fire. With insane, fantastic power a roar immediately seized the whole sky, tearing it to pieces—the latter cracked and caved in.

The little boy cried out and fell down because he couldn't bear all this, but he jumped to his feet again immediately. He heard, although he was in no condition either to hear or to see—in some wondrous way he did hear—the sound of the sky being torn apart, a sound which grew weaker and lighter but nevertheless the same sound repeating somewhere not far from him. With frightening and unexpectedly joyous foreboding he threw his head back and saw the ice breaking and exposing the water in the middle of the river. The river had only just begun to break loose; the strip of exposed water was still quite narrow.

And then it immediately began to rain. The storm began to move off quickly; lightning flashed on one side, on the very edge of the horizon; thunder which had shifted in that direction subsided completely as well. The sky grew dark and quiet and rain poured down from it.

But the little boy kept on crying without wiping his tears and kept looking and looking at the river, at its noisy festive deliverance which had begun during the night, in the middle of a storm, far from people's eyes. ...My God, had it really happened? And had it happened the way he remembered or had he dreamed this in his pure, vivid childhood dreams? ...Ice blocks kept floating by; ice lay even on the river banks. But they, the little children, were already casting seines into the murky greenish water. The exposed swollen river flowed with a speed marked by impatience because it moved so openly and freely; there was immediately a feeling of more space all around; through the light clear air overhead with a whistling sound sand-martins were flying, descending, and striking the water with their little white chests; the sound of water dripping from heavy ice peaks formed above the layers of rock could be heard; the sun glistened everywhere merrily and brightly. There was a unique, keen and mysterious feeling of happiness in the fact that if you wanted to hear fish biting the bait while you held the top edge of the net over the water, your whole heart had to stand still in anticipation. And the whole wide world would be concentrated in that one thin thread which registered the tugging motion of the fish.

Soon the river began to take on a better appearance, having freed itself of everything superfluous and alien which had been brought down from the mountains by rushing spring rivers and brooks. Its water became a deep azure blue and it was so clear that you could see the bottom even at a distance. The current stretched out along its course, settling into a slow, peacefully quick pace which only a long period of bad weather could throw off.

Summers they would go with the whole family way down the river to the hayfields; they would pick berries, then mushrooms. Viktor would manage to beg from the buoy keeper two buoys nearest to the hayfields. In the evening he would light them and in the morning put them out. He learned to maneuver a boat with a pole as well as the villagers and to handle a paddle. He received untiring, endless pleasure from his stay on the river, from contemplating its frightening, alluring depths and its powerful swells as he sensed his own happiness; from pushing off and rowing from shore, further and further, riding the waves and dipping into them; and afterward, having made it back unharmed, from considering himself a victor and thinking that after this the river had immediately grown calmer.

On dark autumn nights his grandfather, now deceased, would take him spearfishing. In the boat's prow the tar resin burned bright and happy; his grandfather, with feet spread wide and peering patiently into the water, would stand by the fire with his spear ready, while he, sitting in the boat's stern, would noiselessly handle the oar. The river wearily and silently carried them downstream. In the heavy metallic color of the water a fallen leaf weakly glimmered, bubbles burst and disappeared, and somewhere in the middle of the river, in good weather, God knows why, a long band of ripples remained for a long time, sparkling with an incomprehensible shimmer that disappeared afterwards just as unexpectedly as it had appeared. It was damp and chilly; the flame only teased you with its insufficient warmth. But in your heart and soul there was also exciting sweetness and strangeness from the bushes which leaned away from shore and floated by in strict silence; from the mysterious splashing which appeared here and there; from the distant cry of a night bird; and from the fairy-tale-like treacherous dance of the flame, towards which a large fish, driven mad by the flame's glow, was rushing and could not stop.

Memories linked to the river lived within him distinct from other memories; they lived like a warm, heartfelt sorrow beside which he would often rest and warm himself before moving on. He understood: childhood had preserved them—everything relating to first impressions is preserved for a long time, perhaps forever, but the crux of the matter was that out of many other things childhood had set precisely these apart. The taiga neither moved nor tormented Viktor the way the river did; the taiga remained and had to remain in the same place, while the river could disappear, slip away, come to an end, exposing as a keepsake of itself a bare rocky river bed along which dogs would run. Each morning, afraid to admit it even to himself, he carefully went to check if anything had happened to the river and he couldn't understand why this no longer perturbed anyone, why everyone calmly felt that the river would flow tomorrow just as it has flowed yesterday and the day before.

He paid for the beer and went on deck. The large setting sun was extremely low and so near that it seemed as if it would not go down behind the mountains but would sit down upon the shore; and the shore, in expectation of this first wondrous and dangerous touch, fell silent. The mountain's shadow had already covered the shore, but the colors were bright, clear and distinct; in the utter green of leaves, aspen and birch trees could easily be discerned; the clay of the steep river bank looked a lush red. The opposite shore, flooded with sunlight, lay mournfully in the distance sloping gently and bare. Perhaps there was a swamp there because the tall dark grass grew unevenly, in clumps; nowhere did a living soul appear in the vicinity. Shortly thereafter the mountain on the left, western side also disappeared somewhere deep down, and the sun immediately moved off from the river, rose higher and grew smaller. Smoke began to stretch across the sky.

About fifteen minutes later the first stop was announced. The ship approached a town of which not so long ago (Viktor on his first cruises had still known that time) there hadn't even been a trace here. It had been built quickly, and while it was being built, much was written and spoken about it: in the remote taiga, in a bare place and so forth, although to Siberian understanding anything lying near a road, and a railroad at that, is certainly not any kind of taiga. Afterward other, more high-flown appellations appeared, and then the town quieted down for a while; but shortly after, it became famous again, this time for its demographic indices: it turned out that here, if you added the ages of the oldest and youngest and then divided by the total number of inhabitants, the youngest people in the country had settled here, who, calculated per 1,000 persons, had more weddings than any other group, and afterwards, naturally, had more children than any other group. But since then the town seemed to be lagging behind even in that respect.

It wasn't visible from the river; it stood off to the side, only its high, different colored chimneys jutted out. But in any case it did have its own moorage. Passengers usually take advantage of it on the return trip. The current is stronger here and the ship, going upstream, inches along from here to the last stop for a good eight hours, while the same route by electric train takes an hour in all. As a result the more impatient people disembark here and go to the train station. That's how it was before and, apparently, is to this day. The ship grows half-empty: only on the benches, surrounded by bundles, sit little old women, with unending patience on their faces; and on the upper deck, not finding places for themselves before the ship's arrival, stroll families with children. It grows quiet and forlorn: the crew is occupied with cleaning up and the remaining passengers are for some reason speaking in lowered tones, looking around pensively and sadly. Sometimes they isolate themselves completely, leaning for a long time against the ship railings and withdrawing into themselves. The two shores, it seems, do not draw together, do not recede downstream, but only barely seem to pull apart; they stir when the ship, in search of the easiest course, moves first toward one, then toward the other of them, but here and there the powerful counter current equally fiercely and noisily beats against the ship's prow, lifting high large, biting sprays of water. All this Viktor was to see and experience again on the return route; but earlier, he seemed to recall, he loved these last long and exhausting hours because he was leaving home and wasn't hurrying anywhere; the impatience and empty bustling of others who ran off now and then to see how much longer they had to sail, gave him some sort of unkind, malicious joy: could it be, he thought, that they don't understand that in this anticipation you should proceed not on the basis of distance or speed, but on the basis of the times given in the schedules which come out precisely as listed, no matter how quickly the ship moves. You should know that you will arrive at exactly 9 o'clock in the evening, not a minute earlier, and until then you should sleep quietly or read a short book and not wear yourself out or worry yourself for nothing—they won't let you miss your stop.

As if to remind you of what the town had been known for quite recently, a wedding party was waiting on shore for the ship. They lingered near a little bus in which they had apparently come here directly from dinner. The concertina wailed wearily and nervously, but now no one sang or danced to it; they only made a lot of noise to it while watching the ship being moored. As soon as it pressed up to the landing and came to a halt, the wedding party went up to the gangplank and gathered around its wooden railing. The fellows were trying to convince somebody not to leave, to stay and celebrate another day or two, but whom they were trying to convince could not be made out in the crowd. For some reason Viktor wanted the bride and groom to come away, for them to decide to arrange a small honeymoon trip for themselves, but he soon realized that they too were only seeing someone off. A pity, he thought, a great pity. A pure unconcealed secret, around which everything would take on a beautiful mysterious meaning, would settle with them on the ship. Recollections and dreams of love and happiness would come, as would come the sadness of what could have been achieved and could have turned out well, but was not achieved and did not turn out. Your heart would flinch bitterly and painfully, stung with the admission that at one time, in the best days of your youth, it had beat unhappily, and your soul would awaken in the faint and humble promise of something unknown. Could it be that it really didn't dawn on them to take a cabin and go where fancy led them, up and downstream along the river, as far as possible from the noisy drunk dinner guests, from friends and relatives, from shouts and the ring of dishes? Here no one would bother them, no one would disturb their solitude and people would look at them with envy and hope; people would envy their inexperience and naiveté, envy the fact that they didn't know and didn't want to know what would happen to them tomorrow, how much time they had to love each other, what children they would have, when they would part and meet again; they would envy the fact that they were bewitched and entranced with this initial closeness, which for them was more important than anything. They would have been the main passengers on board, and the ship would have sailed for their sake alone, and only because there were still empty places left would pick up anyone else along the route as well.

Viktor carefully studied the faces of the bride and groom, trying to find in them something special, some sort of unintentional surprised declaration, a bashful openness, but he saw only fatigue and, in the squinting, tenacious eyes of the bride, a cold challenge: "Why are you staring at me?" Judging by everything, the wedding had been going on for more than one day, but the young people had still not shed their wedding finery: he was in a black, by that time fairly wrinkled suit; she was in a white wedding dress, but it was short and narrow, much higher than her heavy strong knees; from her head a patterned veil hung lightly and broadly to her shoulders. The bride held the groom's hand and on her lips a smile struggled weak and forgotten. Around them people were again pouring wine, clinking glasses, and then offering some to them as well; the bride, not waiting for the groom, threw back her head, revealing a long red neck, and with one gulp drank it down like a man.

Next to Viktor someone whistled in surprise. He turned around; almost the entire deck was filled with people watching the wedding party with attention and curiosity. To Viktor's right, hanging over the side, stood a fellow with a happy round face that was hot and rosy from teh restaurant. His frank, trembling mouth betrayed a desire to interfere which he controlled with effort. When the bride drank her wine with such determination, the fellow couldn't restrain himself: "Boy, you surprise me!"

The bride put her arms around the groom's neck and drew towards him to whisper something. But this gesture was misinterpreted and so fooled and disappointed the ship's passengers.

"Bitter!"[1] cried out someone not too loudly from the back.

"Bitter-r-r!" the fellow next to Viktor bent down and bellowed as loudly as he could, deafening Viktor in the process. Some kind of chords rang out mournfully and delicately in Viktor's ears. "And what about you?" the fellow turned to the crowd and threw up his hands demandingly. "Come on! Three, four! Bit-ter!"

This time several voices joined in. The rest laughed, enjoying this incident. In response to the shouts people came running from the stern and bow of the ship. Excited faces, filled with curiosity, peered out of cabins. Up above, over Viktor's head, quick steps were heard and at that very moment the short deep whistle of the ship resounded.

"Three, four!" commanded the fellow. "Three, four!"

"Bitter-r!" the deck responded in a friendly strong voice. "Bit-ter!"

The young pair became embarrassed. The groom took his bride by the hand in order to lead her away but suddenly she quickly and decisively pulled the groom's head towards her with unexpected strength and passion and planted a long hard kiss on his lips.

Up on top people fell silent. The chuckle which escaped from someone's throat and had seemed almost mournful died away that very moment. The fellow who had been giving orders smacked his lips loudly and thoughtfully and said in a drawn-out way:

"You sure don't tire easily, honey."

The bride raised her eyes, which were screwed up even more than before, and now teasing the people on board, she again drew her lips to the groom's.

"I say, you haven't tired her out," with joyful malice the fellow shouted to the groom. "What kind of a man are you?"

"Get on your way!" said the latter, dismissing the matter with a wave of his hand.

"Don't worry, I'll go, but you watch out that one of your buddies doesn't put the make on her. There they are, all alike, like peas in a pod.[2] Watch out!"

A heated argument ensued. The groom, hurrying to get away from it all, shook the hand of someone about to leave and dragged the bride behind him. From the deck, above the landing dock, you could see them making their way up the bank and heading for the bus without turning around. The fellows in the wedding party tried to force the one who was about to leave on the boat to go with them too, but he broke away and jumped on board.

The fellow next to Viktor did not quiet down for a long time.

"My, what a rogue he is! Took her away. They would have devoured her here. She might still surprise him. She'll show him!" he threatened. "That girl—heh, heh, heh! Look over there, they've gone, he's taken her away. Go on, take her, take her, don't stop or else she might run away. I told him the truth, he'll mark my words more than once. Bridegroo-oom."

When they again lifted anchor, it was already beginning to grow dark. The sun had disappeared long ago, a solid thick blanket of shadows covered the shore, and only at the very water's edge there was a narrow broken band of yellow rock. The mountains in the distance, silent and hunched-over low, were being shrouded in a gray, barely perceptible layer of smoke. Here and there you could make out lights that glittered a while and then disappeared, dissolving into the uncertain, shifting light of dusk. The sky seemed to resemble thawing snow, to have faded; the stars had not yet pecked through, and the sky blended softly and imperceptibly with the earth along the horizon. From the water came a smell of dampness and rotting matter, but the weak pleasant smells of the hot day grown cool reached from the shore even through these smells. The river seemed to glow as if from within, from its very depths; and glistening, it shone from end to end like a clearly outlined deep blue ribbon, mysterious and coldly wondrous, with a pale illusory halo rising in the air above it. The water lapped the side of the ship rhythmically and quietly, and a guarded lazy murmur of waves rolling over rocks reached the ship.

Viktor stood, listened, looked. And these sad and touching scenes of a late summer evening by the river, with their somber warm colors that had not yet become fixed, the clear, quiet sounds breaking the silence descending over the earth, the sensitivity, responsiveness and unreliability of all this evoked a sweet and wearisome feeling of gratitude and love within him. "How can it be?" distressed and reproaching himself, he pondered. "Why do we, to our own detriment, not want to notice what we absolutely should know and see in the first place? Why do we spend so much time just worrying about our daily bread and so rarely raise our eyes and stop to look with surprise and alarm: why didn't I understand earlier that this privilege is mine and that you can't live without it? And why do we forget that precisely in such moments a man's soul is born and filled with beauty and goodness?"

He asked and could find no answer.

Later he no longer looked, no longer listened and no longer reflected. He floated in the air, all alone, now turning towards the distant silent mountains or black plough-lands, now turning toward the river; and everything that remained behind him faded into dreams. He floated, blessing the native places that had in their secret hour revealed themselves to him for his rest and health, and he heard them respond with a grateful whisper.

An island, high and rounded like a barge, drifted noisily by, and Viktor came to himself. Yes, they had passed an island.... How good life is now on the islands, where grasses grow soft and gentle like fur; where flowers bloom especially bright and bountiful; where the smells from water, earth and wild greenery blend into a delicate, sharp, intoxicating essence which, in spite of the evening breezes, is never lost, but only grows sharper and drier as fall approaches. The trees bend in one direction from the wind, but stand firm, revealing their thick stumps, their tenacious, taut roots spread wide. The water's edge is overgrown with alders and small willows, and among them there are berry patches, currants mostly. And on the island there is always a wondrous—deceptive and at the same time real—feeling of motion, as if you're on a boat, on a ship, moving slowly and with an air of importance; and this feeling arises not so much from the water all around as from the exciting feeling of being somehow raised above the earth, a feeling that you're sailing cautiously to a mysterious place. Suddenly Viktor remembered with a start: there really aren't any islands left near his village. There is no more Khlebnik[3] Island nor any Beryozovik Island, where once he used to pick currants and pull up wild onions and garlic, where he used to graze horses, plow fields and cut hay. They had been flooded. The water had risen higher than it had during any of the worst floods which the islands had seen in their long existence; it had swept over and crushed them when they tried to shrink away and stand still, to hold out until sunrise: it kept coming and coming, engulfing the trees and then rising even higher. A long time has passed since the river water washed away and redistributed the soil on which grains and grasses used to grow, and a long time has passed since it levelled the islands so that they formed its bottom. There are no more islands, and their names, forlorn and empty since they've lost their true meaning, are heard less and less and are receding into the distance from whence they are not fated to return.

Viktor grew a bit chilly from the wind and rather uncomfortable, and he felt pangs of guilt in his heart from these recollections; he went to his cabin.

Yes, it's true, he hadn't been to his native village for a long time. But he had a vivid memory of his last arrival there. It was precisely on the day before the flooding of the reservoir for the hydroelectric station that was being built further downstream, and the village was being moved to a new place. More precisely, the village was being torn to bits. The collective farm was moving somewhere to strange steppe lands 200 kilometers away; the forest industry complex, which maintained the reservoir, was being left behind, but all the equipment was being moved from the water site up the hill. The office located on a boat was being shifted to another village. The village itself was being taken down on three sides. No one was being forced to go anywhere he didn't want to, but even without this, it was no simple matter for a man to choose his fate if he didn't know any work other than tilling the soil, if he couldn't imagine life somewhere else where there was no river or taiga.

Just as he was doing now, Viktor had arrived by boat at the beginning of July, also in the evening around dusk. Even from the boat he had noticed how sparse and bare the village had become, its usual order and appearance gone. No one except a few children had come to the dock, which meant that people weren't up to it. Viktor headed for his house, keeping to the shore and avoiding the road; before turning onto the footpath between the vegetable gardens, he stood a while by the water, warming himself in the low warm sun which was striking his face from across the river. Only then did he move on. He was not surprised that, upon raising his eyes, he didn't see the familiar slope of the bathhouse roof: he was too late.

They had managed to take down the hut. One part of the high closely set fence, on which little Vitka had caught more than one pair of shorts, had been torn down as well; the second part, which adjoined the barn and ended in a heavy decorated gate painted long ago, stood looking mournfully out of place. The tightly closed gate with a portion of the attached fence gone looked particularly funny: right next to it a path leading into the yard had already been made. Viktor intentionally did not take this path but turned the large iron ring on the gate and raised the bolt. His mother came running from the barn toward him, but before reaching him she stopped and began to cry, pointing with her hand at the large darkening hut. His father came out, shook his hand and, averting his eyes, said: "It's really good that you've come. At least you'll help us now. We just didn't know what to do."

Viktor walked up to what was left of the hut and stood a long time over it, as if he were standing over a grave, gazing with sad bewilderment at the scattered ashes, at the pieces of stone-like clay from the Russian stove,[4] at the two small metal buttons which perhaps he himself had at one time let roll under the floor boards; he stood there, breathing in the warm sourish smell of daily human life which had not yet faded entirely. The cellar walls had crumbled, but on one remaining wall he could see green potato sprouts turning upwards. Little green beetles quickly darted along an old rotten piece of wood; a large gray spider, now crouching down, now raising itself on its long thin legs, stirred in a corner. And this little piece of land, on which the hut had stood and which now lay exposed before him, worn to dust by the wooden structure which had stood upon it, suddenly seemed so small and insignificant to Viktor and everything which had formed the hut and which now lay together in two neat piles seemed so coarse and hopeless—that he no longer knew if he should believe that all this had really been here and that it had made a sturdy, comfortable and roomy home. A feeling of some kind of bitter, old unreality which had receded into the past, of some kind of a mistake which he had known earlier and had again forgotten, seized Viktor and would not leave him for a long time.

That same evening he covered the whole village from end to end. There was little of it now. Only a few huts still stood peacefully; the rest were either torn down or were being taken down; the exposed rafters stuck out awkwardly and looked bare; the spaces left by the windows which had been taken out peered into the street lifelessly and yet with authority; behind the windows dust continued to swirl without ever settling, and Russian stoves "molded" from clay and not suited for moving stood out in the open, left to the mercy of fate. Pieces of broken glass, chunks of brick, wet, rotten, lichen-covered pieces of wood, light prickly balls of blackened fur resembling tumbleweed used to caulk walls—everything that usually appears during something's destruction—were strewn about the street; and a wet bad smell given off by decaying matter was also keenly perceptible. Only the kitchen gardens had not been touched, suddenly becoming, to their joy and despair, the center of attention. Left untouched also was the cemetery, located in the middle of the village, in a spot above the small bridge across the stream; it kept some kind of a particularly mysterious, terrible silence in the midst of this general commotion. For quite a few centuries since people had settled here it sanctified and filled this earth with those who had passed away, while disturbing the living with its mystery and pain. And now the time of parting was approaching.

People greeted Viktor, began conversations, and the first thing they asked was: "Have you seen what's going on, have you? The end of the world!"

He noticed that people were in some kind of an unnatural state of excitement and fear. Either they laughed in the wrong place or fell silent at a question and looked past him pensively and sadly, giving in to their own alarming thoughts. With difficulty forcing themselves to pull out the first nail and to remove the first board from the roof, they then rushed as if they were in the power of unbridled, fierce frenzy to tear things down, a frenzy which did not wane while anything was left to tear down. In the evening, afraid of being alone, they would meet at someone's house and sit on a piece of wood from a torn-down hut, smoking and talking about one thing—the move.

It was a hot, stifling and confusing summer. The forests were on fire and people did not have enough time to clear them of wood for their own use. Buildings were being moved on ferries (three more neighboring villages were being collected here, all in one heap); some sort of strange people kept darting about; cars and tractors, transporting the disassembled houses to the new location, crawled up the hill with great strain and effort; axes chopped away; cattle, sensing changes, mooed more than usual. As always happens during days of confusion and disorder, people argued a lot and quarrelled for no good reason; and at night, when all this noise and hubbub had died down for a while, dogs would begin to howl in a dreadful, frightening way in the silence that ensued.

And of course there were endless discussions about money: who had gained and who had lost in the resettlement; why the evaluation committee had set a high depreciation for one hut and a lower one for another; who had already managed to spend his money on drink and who had put the money away for a rainy day. They discussed how Nikolai Tochilov would extricate himself; a well-known crafty fellow in the village, he was at first going to move with the collective farm and had received money for the long journey, but he had then changed his mind and having made some more calculations, had refused to return the money, pleading that he didn't have it.

How many stories Viktor heard that summer and what only he didn't see!

It was then, while he was still there, that the kolkhoz workers were leaving. The convoy had been ready since evening; their homes were loaded on log transporters and tractor carts; belongings were piled into pickup trucks. They had agreed to set out at dawn in order to reach their destination in a day, but they barely got off by lunch. Not since the war had the village seen anything like this. The men drank vodka in farewell; the women wept, giving through their tears final orders on the cattle and gardens; the little children, gathering into flocks, scurried about with frightened quick motions. Two old women, Viktor's grandmother and their neighbor, the old woman Lukeya, embracing in the middle of the street, wailed bitterly and loudly. They had spent their whole lives living side by side; every day one would drop by the other's home for tea. They had decided a long time ago between themselves that they would come from the next world to visit people as a pair of two little identical, inseparable birds. But now they were taking old Lukeya away. In the head vehicle, sternly and solemnly, ready for any and all trials, sat deaf old Stepan in a police cap gotten somewhere and with two St. George crosses[5] on his military tunic, which had faded completely white. For a long time the tractor driver Ivan Zuev had been chasing after a male dog that he wanted to take home with him, but the dog could in no way be caught and Ivan shot it out of spite. Fifteen minutes later he got drunk and began to throw his bundles out of the vehicle. Someone sat in stonelike immobility in the cemetery, someone at the last moment suddenly remembered something and ran off for a dish at the neighbor's. The small kolkhoz stables, set on fire the evening before, were burning and the bitter smoke never lifted but hung in sheets over the street. A drunken song, in the course of which the command to get into the vehicles was heard more than once, kept bursting out and breaking off. At last they did set out, burst into tears, broke into shouts, began to sing louder; they headed out.

The day was quiet and not very bright, and the river flowed just as quietly and evenly as before, not recognizing in itself any blame or misfortune.

After the kolkhoz workers had left, those who remained began to hurry even more. Now only during the short hours of darkness did the pounding of axes fall silent. One end of the new village extended to the fields, the other was to cut into the forest. The plot of land Viktor's father received for his hut was fairly clear and fell within the boundaries of the old village, but he looked with melancholy and despair at the cool shady corner of the pine forest which was no longer young and which he would have to clear for the garden. Viktor helped his father set up the hut and left. It was time for him to go back to work.

He often got letters from home, telling him mostly who had died, who had gotten married and who had been born, but as to how the village was doing, how it was faring and prospering, they didn't know how to write. But now he only had to wait until tomorrow. Tomorrow he would see everything with his own eyes.

He sat on the couch of his half-dark cabin for a long time, without getting down to anything, senselessly and blindly staring at the wall. A cool breeze that made him tremble blew through the open window, but he didn't shut it. Gradually the memory faded and went away. Now he knew that he had deceived himself while preparing to come to the village; the whole time he had had in mind the old village and for some reason he had not wanted to remember that it hadn't existed for a long time. But it wasn't this that disturbed him now. When you get down to it, he was going to visit his father and mother, whom he needed to see, no matter where they lived.

Outside his window quiet, careful steps rose and then faded into the distance. Somewhere music was playing and a familiar voice, that seemed terribly sad now, again and again sang, "water, water, water everywhere."

He was waiting for something, for some remarkable and wondrous end to this long, restless day, for some kind of rare and happy emotions. Something had to happen. What exactly he didn't know and didn't try to guess, but he waited and feared letting something slip by which could happen today only and could never be repeated. The vague, undefined feeling that tormented him with its secret promise gave him no peace.

Later he went out on deck again. The sky was studded with stars; but the stars, which had not yet attained their full brightness, were distant and tiny, as they usually are in spring, while the moon, round and full, hung low and festive under the sky's canopy. In its silent, solemn, silvery light, everything lay in lazy, blessed stillness, and the river, in whose depths the night sky was reflected in all its fairytale splendor, shone with its own glassy-green, haughty radiance. The ship moved almost noiselessly, barely cutting through the water; and in the clean, cold air he imagined that he heard coming from the moon a happy aching sound which was plucked on a single string and which now fell to earth, now slowly ascended. It summoned him somewhere, brought to mind something marvelous and from long ago; and his heart, which was trembling with anxiety and didn't understand, began to pound in a despairing prayer: "What? Where?" Having resounded again, the sound returned and again and again troubled him with its sought-after sweet ache, beckoning again and again to pure, sacred far-off reaches.

At the stern people were dancing, and Viktor went there and began to watch them. Here were the husband and wife he had observed in the restaurant when they had been dining with their whole family. It seemed that only they were enjoying the dance; the rest were shuffling about with nervous obstinacy in their movements, with painful submissiveness on their faces. Delight shone on the faces of the man and wife. She placed her hands on his shoulders, leaned back her head and smiled, while he, slightly bowing, danced round and round with her in complete happy self-oblivion. But Viktor did not have the opportunity to admire them long. The husband said something in her ear; in response she began to laugh and shook her head, but she shook her head with such fascinating slowness and with such amazingly joyous responsiveness in her eyes, that it was impossible to interpret this refusal as anything else but consent. Soon, turning circles all the while, they tore themselves away from all the rest and floated along the deck to one side further and further away, until they disappeared completely. And they appeared no more. And again, just like the first time, Viktor caught himself feeling uncomfortably envious. He was glad that they had left; it was easier for him to observe lonely people like himself— tired people, exhausted by the unsuccessful hope of attaining their own happy moment.

No, something nevertheless should have happened and wasn't happening.

A star fell from the sky and drawing a burning line, went out. And right then, God only knows why, the whistle of the ship whimpered briefly and plaintively, as if half-awake. The sky rang out more closely and powerfully, and the earth became even more quiet and pale. Stars, lengthening into candles, danced in the wave that was moving away from the ship toward shore. The oncoming wind, tossing about the ship's flag that was lit by a searchlight, blew overhead and did not disturb the river's smoothness; but ripples did remain astern following the wave. From time to time yellow or red lights of buoys rose from the side; water lapped near them.

The bright May night, which was already summer-like, bold, reigned wide and brilliant; but there, to the right, in the east, where dawn was to break, the sky's edge was already beginning to grow lighter.

But his heart continued to be tormented and to ache in the same way as before, responding to some kind of beautiful promise that rang out in the night with violent, passionate force.

A long time ago, about two years ago, Viktor had a dream which stuck in his memory. Strictly speaking, it wasn't even a dream, but something in the middle between dream and fevered self-oblivion, the delirium of a mind worn out by doubts. At that time Viktor's book of short stories had come out which included one story about an old man dying, with all the ensuing sighs, moans, thoughts and sensations—not feelings, but precisely sensations, inasmuch as the latter assumes a more delicate cross-sectioning of the human soul. Moreover, like every inexperienced and therefore bold writer, Viktor went even farther: he tried to move beyond the line separating one state from the other. Later he had the sense to realize that he shouldn't have done this, but of course, he came to his senses too late.

And so it seemed as if a man with an old and almost transparent look stood on the threshold; he looked very much like Viktor's grandfather, but had a more delicate, intelligent, attractively elongated face. (Viktor's grandfather was an ordinary hunter, of bears in particular.) This man rose from his state of nonexistence and said:

"I read your book."

"And how was it?" asked Viktor, with hope, of course, that he liked the book.

"Well, it's like this," the other sighed and answered. "I don't understand...," he shook his head slowly and thoughtfully, with sad astuteness. "I don't understand why you have to write about what you can't know. You just can't know, no way. This story isn't like anything at all that you've ever run across. It's so much more, more meaningful, so much more un- believable than your poor imagination could think up.... And then," the half-grandfather, half-professor smiled sadly, "your words aren't suited for it. They're too insignificant. You," he sighed again, "can't speak properly about what you already know, about the human experience, but look at what you were striving to write about, about such a mystery. It seems so simple to say what you want to, but no, you can't. You see something, hear something, feel something, but what exactly, you don't say or say vaguely, inexactly, out of place. My, how you love to talk inexactly, to beat around the bush. Oh, good lord,... And you ask, how do I like it. When you are in my place and know what I know, only then will you really understand how weak and powerless you are right now. That's just the way it is. If you plan to write anymore, it's your own affair, only don't ever go beyond your own strength."

Viktor was awakened by a strange, long scraping sound, as if the ship were rubbing its side against something. He listened attentively: no, the ship was moving, its measured, frequent jolts, which followed one upon the other, could be felt distinctly. At an angle, through the bent wooden strips of the raised window screen, sunlight played on the floor with the same finely ruled design. The cabin was fresh and cool; in other words, the morning coolness had not yet given way to heat. It was just after 6 o'clock.

Again the same undefined sound dragged on from end to end of the ship, but now weaker and higher with a hollow tapping. Yawning and squinting from sleep, Viktor got out of bed, lowered the loose screen and bolted it with difficulty. Suddenly he gave a start: right in front of him a dirty sharp branch which almost hit him in the face snapped back and disappeared. The only thing to do was cross himself. The ship was going through a forest. Two birch trees, standing side by side, flowed past, scratching the ship's side and leaving twigs on deck; later the top of a pine tree appeared, and then again a birch.

Viktor got dressed in a hurry and went outside. The ship was making its way into some sort of unknown, wide cove from the banks of which trees extended far into the water itself. They jutted out both in front and in back of the ship. This first impression split into two and changed; it was unclear what was more amazing or improbable: whether to consider the ship, carefully crawling between the trees, a huge prehistoric monster, or to look at the trees growing out of the water as if they were part of some fantastic picture.

But then again, was it fantastic? The trees were bare and pitiful, without leaves, the pines with sparse curled up needles, and the birches, whose slimy branches were swollen with water,with black catkins that looked like caterpillars. Some still stood straight, others were already bent, being washed away little by little. A wave would splash up and roll over them and then they would sway with a squelching moan, tugging at their weakened roots even without the wave's pull. The trees rocked like water beetles, long and weakly, lacking that pliability and playfulness with which a forest usually moves in the wind. One birch tree stood on the shore's edge, its small leaves completely yellow; its branches hung down; for it, spring had not come after all. But further on, as if nothing were wrong, a forest of young sturdy pine trees crowding each other extended up the hill. A tall aspen burned bright, its May foliage filled with sap....

After the whistle blew unexpectedly, seemingly muffled, as if on purpose, the ship made its way toward the bare uninhabited shore where on a piece of board the name of some unfamiliar pier was scribbled, one which hadn't existed on the river before. Two women got off and headed uphill along the road. Here the ship turned around and slowly headed back, all the while stealing its way as before between the flooded trees where bubbles and ripples from fish could be seen. The sun had already risen high, the air became warmer and drier; and the land in the distance could be seen separating into two sides. On shore, flying from fir tree to fir tree, one after the other, and cawing loudly, two crows followed the ship; but in their harsh resounding cry there was nothing but curiosity. From the opposite direction a motor boat passed roaring like a tractor; a bearded villager, wearing a hat and padded jacket, sat in the back of the boat; in the front tangled nets lay strewn about.

As the gulf pushed apart the two shores, it kept getting wider and wider. Now they were already moving in clear water, unafraid of getting caught on anything and, picking up a favorable wind, they began to move more quickly. People on board were beginning to wake up, children were beginning to run around. Sailors in blue and white striped T-shirts were calling to each other from time to time and bustling over something in the bow. A young woman in an unbuttoned smock shuffled around the deck, wielding a broom; from the kitchen came the smell of cabbage soup being reheated.

Finally, after another half hour had passed, the ship made its way out of the gulf and without turning around headed for the opposite shore which loomed dark and barely visible far ahead. Viktor couldn't even imagine how far the water could stretch, and he looked around dumbstruck, not knowing what he should be surprised at more: the lazy might of the huge body of water, which was now referred to as the sea, having flooded thousands and thousands of hectares[6] of land, or at the fact that all this had been planned in advance and carried out with that precision and confidence which are not within the realm of comprehension of a man ignorant of such things. There was nothing left here of the river, of course, and you couldn't even vaguely tell where the river bed used to be. While it was still night and Viktor slept, the river choked and drowned in the indifferent gulf of water that lay before it. It was ten kilometers from shore to shore, if not more, because water usually conceals distance; and even in the north, where before this the current used to flow, the land didn't meet the far low horizon for a long time.

The water seemed motionless and gray. A log floating behind the ship did not move to the side but only kept drifting further and further away; and the sun, high and almost directly above, could not penetrate the water but only illuminate its dim, faint rocking. In it there was now no whimsical play of blue and green, no lively, exciting tirelessness in the beauty and joy of the motion being made; there was no dark bottle-green glow in the still depths, and no crystal sounding music in the rumbling; no wavy criss-crossing rivulets formed by mountain streams rushing down with force, and no majestic view of islands beckoning to you—there was nothing left of that which only yesterday the river had carried with it. From end to end the water lay quiet and solitary like one unencompassible expanse, overpowering with its weight the forlorn low-lying shore. The sky above was empty; no sandmartins flew about making shrill broken sounds, no swallows warbled, gathering in united, noisy (you might as well cover your ears!) flocks in order to drive off hawks. On the other hand, as Viktor knew would happen, seagulls appeared; large eagles never before seen in these parts, began to come from somewhere—a sea, no matter what kind, gradually develops its own life.

In the meantime, the ship was drawing closer to a large village that stood apparently in a clearing; below the streets round circles of tree stumps loomed yellow and thick. Among the old blackened huts were a lot of new ones, put up quite recently; their reddish walls, with streaks of baked-on sulphur, glowed with an even, intense heat under the sun; their steep plank roofs hung lightly and happily in the air, ready, it seemed, to break off and fly away. A few houses were even quite rich-looking, with slate roofs, an unheard-of luxury before. In the gardens in front there already grew mountain-ash, birch and fir trees. Here and there along the streets there were even pine trees left over from the forests, but as always happens when they live side by side with man, they rushed as hard as they could to push upward and so stuck out bare and sparse, with branches on top that weren't much to look at.

From all sides of this village people came running to the dock. Motorcycles crackled, dodging from side to side in unsuccessful attempts to avoid the treestumps, but all the same bouncing over them; dogs began an awful racket and ran along the shore; two cows raised their heads from grazing and gazed at the approaching ship with a fixed, startled look; from the ship's whistle a calf made a dash for the vegetable gardens and there began to moo pitifully, looking askance at the unfamiliar, noisy monster; behind the wattle fence near which the calf was trembling, a rooster flew up and settled on the head of a scarecrow, adding his contribution to the general uproar. And then there were children and more children, who were pouring out like peas from every crack. A chubby little fellow, his red little head shining in the sun, was not keeping up with the long stream of children older than he and was wailing from his hurt feelings as he ran, but no one paid any attention to him; all the people were running as if they were madmen. At last, stopping short, the chubby little fellow fell and let out a wail, calling someone—and that someone came. A little girl of seven or eight, who was red-headed like he, and had been running ahead, turned around, ran up to the little boy, spanked him angrily and quickly ran on. That instant he jumped up and ran after her; it was surprising and incomprehensible how he could run and at the same time scream so loudly and in such demanding tones without ever stopping, drowning out all other sounds with his wailing.

Once just like this, just like these little children, little Vitka too had rushed with all his might to his first ship, beside himself with joy, ready to jump into the water and submerge. After this, barely would the real summer come when the Lieutenant Schmidt—a passenger steamboat famous in those years, which constantly leaned to one side—would appear from beyond Verkhny Island[7] and give out a prolonged welcoming whistle. Oh, what didn't go on here! What bustling set in! Doors, wicket gates, larger gates, kept slamming in one polyphonic stream of sound; children rushed down the street, scattering various kinds of barnyard animals, for example, hens and pigs, to all sides Someone kept shooting his rifle, carts rattled along, overheated horses neighed. Anything that could walk splashed up to the shore. Although it wasn't marked on the calendar in red, or sweetened with a good dose of drinking, this was a holiday which was looked forward to no less than any other. And then afterwards, later on, each time the ship was due, a crowd would gather at the dock, they would light bonfires and wait until midnight or even later, if it were delayed, but they would not leave. Mothers who caught sound of the whistle would prod their children and say: "Run quickly, see who's come to see whom, but watch out, don't mix the names up."

What more can you say, in summer the village would come to life. Guests came in droves; they brought gifts, and even the villagers themselves occasionally allowed themselves to board the ship and go somewhere on business or other matters. There also came here with expeditions completely foreign, strange people from large cities with beautiful sounding names, which as it turns out really do exist in the world and are not invented in books (only the name of his own village seemed eternal and comprehensible to him, as if the earth had its source here; the rest for some reason sounded funny, comic, something you could believe or not). In addition to all this, it was always interesting to simply look at the passengers on deck in their amusing, strange clothes, and to imagine that you too at some point would pick up and take off somewhere no less than they, wherever your little heart desired.

But summer would pass and winter begin. And—my goodness, how melancholy and bitter (you could cry!) your heart would become when the last ship disappeared beyond that same Verkhny Island and right on its heels a cold low wind from the lower reaches of the river, mixed with rain and snow, would begin to blow. The sad, forlorn village was left by itself all alone in the whole wide world with its dull fate; for long months it remained waiting with patience and hope for the next summer. And again they lit a bonfire, but in farewell; and stood around it silent and depressed, warming their hands and backs; again someone was firing his rifle but your heart was no longer wrung by these shots.

But even winter passed. Believe it or not the Lieutenant Schmidt would again appear from beyond Verkhny Island....

To the noise, din, cracking, barking and howling of everything and everyone that had gathered on shore, the ship poked its prow against the river bottom at a fairly respectable distance from land and came to a halt. It became clear that docking here would be no simple matter; the shore was low, the bottom shallow because the water just barely covered it. Pushing off, the ship went in reverse and then tried to get through in another place; the same thing happened. After four unsuccessful tries at getting closer in which almost a half hour was spent—at the same time the crowd on shore did not stop giving advice, one comment better than the last—the captain, losing patience, finally shouted "stop" and the ship froze, after it had moved its stern toward the sea just in case. The mechanical ladder opened and hung beautifully in the air, not even reaching halfway to the ground. A young sailor, dragging behind him a stepladder, began to climb the ladder which was hanging in midair. But even the stepladder turned out not to be enough. Some people on shore shoved a board into the sailor's hand, then they ran and got another one; with great difficulty a way off the ship was nevertheless found, although it was unstable and full of holes, because water was splashing about at the point where the board and stepladder met.

And at that point the villagers made a dash for the ship. The sailor tried to stop them, shouting with a thin, breaking voice that they had to let arriving passengers off first; but finding himself in the water, he immediately quieted down and with concentrated, painstaking attention began to turn up his wet trousers. And the villagers kept shoving and shoving happily and desperately, and all without luggage, without things. With a wave of the hand, they refused the boarding passes which the crew tried to hand them at the gangplank. With their shoes clumping, they hurled themselves on board.

"Vaska-a! Don't forget about me! Vaska-a-a," someone yelled from shore, straining.

In front of the crowd on shore Victor caught sight of the familiar red-haired little fellow who before this had been trying to reach the dock so noisily and with such adventures. His face was freckled; his tears had dried long ago. Splashing through the water in sandals worn without socks, water he probably didn't even remember getting into, he observed the ship and all the hubbub connected with it with attentive and serious wonder. Behind him, without warning, the same little girl who looked like him and who was so quick to mete out punishment, ran up and hit him without explanation, and then returned to her girlfriends as if nothing had happened. The little fellow flinched but took it in silence. More than that, he understood the slap's intent: without rushing he undid his sandals and threw them on shore. He felt even better without them and now began to stroll boldly back and forth in front of the ship until he climbed on top of a stump lying beneath the water. He stamped his feet on it for a while and then decided to sit down. But the minute he dipped the place on which people usually sit in the water, the little girl again briskly threw herself at him and with an automatic, mechanical swinging motion found the usual, appropriate application for this place—with an alluring and resounding sound. But once again the little fellow figured out what's what and immediately began to pull off his shorts.

"Grinka, you parasite!" she warned him, chewing on her words. "If you take off your shirt too, I'll drown you! I warn you!"

This time Grinka didn't dare disobey her. He gave a sigh and sat down on the stump just as he had planned, sinking up to his chest in the water, and wetting, of course, the last thing that remained on him, his shirt.

The ship blew its whistle—one long blast followed immediately by three short ones. And back to the shore poured the villagers, who by now had grown bigger and rounder: as they ran, they were clinking bottles which were shoved into net bags, purses, pockets, shirts—anywhere they could find a place for them. Now there was an explanation of what it was that had led them to the ship with such a mighty burst of passion. As if trying to justify them, Viktor remembered that today was Sunday. The fellow in the blue sports T-shirt with a long numeral "1" on the back, displaying his strong muscular hairy hands, brought out a case of beer, carefully put it on the ground to one side of the crowd and, without paying any attention to his friends who had run up to him and were joyfully slapping him on the back, began to uncork[8] the first bottle. A tall, healthy woman, still young and beautiful in an easygoing sort of country way, was silently chasing an agile but miserable-looking fellow from the village. Dodging her in the crowd, he was managing to imperceptibly put clear bottles bearing a simple, expressive label into pockets extended and open in readiness. In a word, by the time the captain had given the command to weigh anchor, life in that settlement already held promise of continuing in an interesting way.

The ship, not without some difficulty, tore itself loose from the ground and began to move at a crawling pace; the gangplank, folding in two in the middle, swung upward; but right then two more villagers jumped out from somewhere, ran madly for the gangplank, grabbing hold of the rope, and began to climb up so that the gangplank had to be straightened out; then, just as if they were standing on a diving board and bouncing at its springiest end, they threw themselves into the water to the sound of laughter and shouting from all sides. A third villager, who was exhaling with a wheezing sound, kept quickly and nervously throwing bottles to shore. People kept at a distance from the bottles, ran in all directions, then gathered round again to pick them up; but two bottles which hit tree stumps broke. Freeing himself from his load, the villager threw himself overboard as well, but now he had to paddle a short distance before he was on his feet again. As if that weren't enough, there was still another person, a fourth whom Viktor could not see from up where he stood, but people on shore shouted and clapped their hands:

"Jump! Jump! Petro, jump!"

"But I can't swim," Petro answered in a soft Ukrainian accent.

"Then throw a bottle! A bottle!"

"But you'll drink it."

"Boy, Petro," loudly teased some woman's voice, "you'll get it from Anka when you come home. She'll give it to you...boy, oh boy, what did she tell you? What did you promise her?"

"Tell Anka to watch out for herself. Tell her that I'll be there soon."

"She'll take care of you. Just how are you taking care of yourself? And what is it that you promised her?"

"Petro-o!" someone suddenly sang out louder than anyone else through cupped hands. "Hold your ground, Petro, I'll save you. I'll come get you.... Hear me, Petro?"

"I hear you! Save me, Semyon." Semyon, standing on shore, jogged to the boats which were moored in a long row to the right of the dock. The initial rattling of the chain could be heard, then the motor sputtered and began to hum evenly. And in no time at all Semyon in the red-striped shirt reached the ship in his own boat and stopped alongside.

"Petro, do you have any money on you?" he asked.

"Well, yes, a bit."

"Why don't you pick up two or three for me? Will you have enough? As soon as I get home, I'll give it back to you."

"Oh, I have enough."

"And I, for my part, will save you. We'll be like a bayonet charge today. Your Anka won't even have time to get fired up because we'll get there before she knows it."

Viktor walked down to where the schedule was. It was more than forty kilometers to the next landing area, two hours by ship. When he went up to the deck area again, Semyon's boat was moving away from the ship, to one side, its nose tipped up, apparently following a shorter course; and as for Semyon, he covered himself from the rain and splashing water with what appeared to be a piece of canvas, and huddling low in the stern, he resembled a big bird with arched wings. But in about an hour Viktor heard in his cabin a voice, hoarse with cold, calling:

"Petro! Petro-o!"

Viktor peered out: Semyon's boat was again moving alongside, in front of a wave, and Semyon was sitting in his soaked, ripped raincoat; craning his neck, he carefully enunciated his words in a bass voice which betrayed how chilled to the bone he was.

"Petro-o! Where are you? Petro-o!"

Then the boat fell behind and disappeared, and a voice was heard indistinctly from the other side:

"Petro-o!"

Petro did not answer.

Semyon made it to the dock before the ship did. The gangplank was lowered, and he immediately took a position beside it with an uncertain frozen smile on his face which hadn't had a chance to thaw yet. The passengers began to leave: two old women, one of whom was being helped by a sailor, a woman with a child, and a soldier. The last one to get off, holding on to the top railings with both hands, but nevertheless staggering badly, was a rather short, well-formed villager, his head clean shaven, with only one narrow, ribbon-like, light forelock bouncing on his forehead. Semyon's face fell for a minute, but then broke into an especially big smile. He grabbed the villager under both arms, and saying something quickly and cheerfully to him, led him off to the boat. After he sat him down on the prow with some difficulty, Semyon asked him something. The villager nodded. Semyon said something more, after which the villager put his hand in his pocket, rummaged around for a long time and finally pulled out a bottle. Viktor, watching them, realized right away that this was not the bottle they were waiting for, that it contained, more probably than not, fruit-flavored soda pop. Semyon took it in his hands with a squeamish, guarded gesture and again asked something. The villager nodded his head and checked his pockets for effect and to convince Semyon. Semyon looked at him for a long time with what one must assume was an infinitely grateful look, and having reeled off one of those short and powerful words, for which there are and cannot be any substitutes in Russian, he forcefully swung the bottle against the boat's edge!

Oh Semyon, Semyon, what a strange fellow you are....

After dinner Viktor saw the seagulls for the first time. Two birds were following the ship in a beautiful, grand, leisurely way, keeping together all the while, moving their long wings smoothly and solemnly. The sun was out, but the sky had grown pale, and a hard wind began to blow which, it seemed, bent and brought down the sun's rays. They fell not where they should, and so you got the feeling that you were keeping warm with someone else's warmth. Waves rolled on the sea, churning up foam, and seagulls, settling on the water, immediately got lost in it. They often settled on the water as soon as they reached some particular boundary which they did not want to cross, so as not to find themselves closer to people than they should be. Then each time a guttural cry was heard from afar, and the seagulls, as if on command, would soar up at the same time.

The banks on both sides continued as before, depressing and monotonous. The sun brought them little joy. The forest, which had not been flooded but had by some miracle been saved from death, was on the brink of happiness, as if it did not quite believe in this miracle and was waiting for some kind of a new misfortune to befall it. It looked unkempt and overgrown, with trees jutting up in one place, trees which had been hidden earlier in the taiga and weren't prepared to stand out in full view. As for the river bank as such, a line between river and land, there wasn't much of one; one began immediately after the other, and even more than that—one had hardly finished when the other began. Nowhere, where they had sailed today, had Viktor seen either rocks or sand marking this boundary; nowhere was there to be seen a sharp bank with wonderfully colored clay and rocks in its wall and neatly arranged red layers of stone at its foot. When will all this take hold, settle down, come to order and attain its true beauty?

But sometimes a field would suddenly appear, and immediately your heart felt better. This small clearing in the mournful blue expanse in the heart of the forest was like much needed rest in the middle of a long and wearisome journey. Somewhere on the edge of a field a birch grove gleamed clean and white; farther on, where (he knew by heart) even shadows shone with reflected brightness, circles of fields swirled by with transparent greenness. And you had such a desire to rush there, to bury your head in the grass on which the sun was playing through the leaves of trees in intricate lace patterns, and to fall asleep, deafened by the chirping of grasshoppers and the grand, majestic sound of the high wind.

But after the boat would turn, the fields would disappear, and a damp gloomy forest would again swim into view, repaying you with endless melancholy for having been brought to the forefront without being asked or prepared.

The river got even wider since more water flowed here; its blind powerful flood evoked some kind of unsteady, mirage-like feeling of surprise and confusion. The waves stirred restlessly with a muffled hum, barely hinting at the power locked within them; bright sharp bits of the setting sun bobbed on the waves, different scattered sections of the river banks came into view in the cold windy haze. Far off to the right a self-propelled barge loaded with timber came towards the ship and then passed; music could be heard coming from it, and clothes could be seen fluttering on a clothesline. The wind, looking for an obstacle to amuse itself with, whistled with a long weary sound in the empty air. And the low stretched-out sky hung above like the mirror image of the longish hollow in which the sea lay.

A harsh scene and in its way, beautiful. Only everything in it was somehow simple and clear, like in a trunk made with your own hands, one you could be proud of and in which you knew every knot. The pure spirit of mystery didn't hover on high above these waters, forcing you to stand in childlike wonder before its beauty and question every day and every hour: how, why, since when, from where did this come and continues to come? Your heart stopped beating anxiously and ardently, paralyzed with fear at the depth as it stood over the abyss of time; and the feeling of eternity left, closed shut with a tight lid. Everything was clear here—how, and why, and since when, and with what purpose.

The wind intensified, got bolder; it really rocked now, not just playfully. But the seagulls continued to fly behind the ship as before, now settling on the water, now soaring away. Only their wings seemed to have gotten shorter, and they flapped them more often, overcoming the wind with apparent effort. But something, some purpose, some goal forced them to keep on flying and flying....

Viktor tried to read, but couldn't. Ever since he himself began to write, reading didn't give him the same pleasure as it does when you follow the author quietly and trustingly wherever the spirit leads him, when the events taking place in the book and the characters taking part in them are accepted as true reality, no matter whether you like these characters or not. His attitude to literature too had previously fit easily into three rather categorical responses: good, bad, so-so. Now there arose a purely professional interest. Oh, God, this professional interest!.... It seems to have no bottom, no top. How much simpler it was earlier and how much more difficult it is now—as if you are constantly on guard and don't want to but still see how an incorrectly inserted word fidgets and sometimes even struggles in tormenting convulsions; how empty, unnecessary phrases shamelessly hiccup or shout "hel-lo!" in the middle of a serious discussion because they have nothing to do there; how some positive hero, swimming in loud and respectful words as if they were soap bubbles, mouths beautiful sounding lies when, according to the author's intention, he should be speaking the truth, only the truth and nothing but the truth; how the whole book is having a tantrum, demanding that people read it and wailing about equal rights for books, although there isn't and cannot be any benefit from such reading. You see, you understand, but can't interfere—you can neither help nor check nor put to shame. It would be better not to see and to understand. The whole joke is that a good book, as well as a bad one, is created from one and the same material, from the very same words, arranged, of course, in a different word order, ringing with a different intonation and blessed with a different hand. But the fact that the primary raw material comes from one pile gives many people an excuse to think that the end product too must be evaluated with the same criteria.

But even if you have a good book before you, it isn't easy, thanks to all this professional discrimination. When you see the common phrase "she groaned" you shudder in pain from that groan; when you see the name of a color and clearly distinguish its particular shade and can smell its scent, when you hear with your own ears the sound of an apple falling off a tree and weep at the meeting of two people invented by the author's fantasy, you try to understand how all this was achieved, with what life-giving water it was sprinkled; you sort through the words again and again, following them like steps of an endless staircase, trying to penetrate into their wondrous mystery, which forces them to sound, to smell, to glow and to excite. And you see everything, because it's difficult to hide anything in a book—the whole network of words, their musicality, appearing note after note, the seams between phrases and the pauses between thoughts—you see everything and nevertheless understand nothing. Despairing, you put aside the book and weakly close your eyes, hating yourself for your helplessness, for your lack of talent and for everything else that is connected with this.

But you can't be without books. And you do, of course, keep reading, but, Lord, what difficult, nerve-wracking and endless work it is!

The last hours before their arrival were particularly hard. The wind had died down toward evening, the waves slept; the sea was still rocking, but somehow lazily and pointlessly, proudly boasting of being a sea. The sky had ripened and turned dark blue; the sun was setting on the horizon in a clear, evenly blazing circle. The seagulls were no longer flying behind the ship but were floating in the air, their wings flapping from time to time. What made them follow the ship? The water around it made a sticky, particularly drawn-out sound; the flag melancholically fluttered above; the children who had been running around the dock with intentionally loud steps had quieted down in their corners—everything all around had levelled off in the general great anticipation of all kinds of things: darkness, rest, the dock, newness.

In earlier times Viktor had known by heart the places they were passing by now. Since the fifth grade he had gone to school at the district center, fifty kilometers from home: there was no intermediate school any closer. Many times for winter and spring vacations, he had had to make his way home on foot—no one, of course, sent a car for him, and rides going that way rarely turned up, and even if they did, they weren't going far. Now he found it difficult himself to believe: as a twelve-year-old boy he would cover the whole fifty kilometers in a day. He would walk and keep a tally: a tenth of the way was behind him, a sixth, a fourth, a third...trying to deceive himself by leaving before him a few more kilometers than there really were so that they would melt away by themselves when he was totally spent and moving at a slow pace.

But now he didn't recognize anything. Even in the coves along the streams, in the crumbling stone, it was impossible to distinguish where they were or what anything was. Everything had either melted together or had washed away into a single and alien picture of the taiga. What was amazing was that he used to walk then not through the heart of the forest, but along a road, which the water by now had washed away. He was forced to orient himself only by the time listed in the schedule.

An hour remained, half an hour, then even less.

It was time to get his things together. Viktor packed his suitcase and for the last time glanced out the open porthole. The ship was clearly approaching the shore which was, as before, locked in by the thick forest wall. Even here, at the threshold of his native village, nothing beckoned to his heart beating with sweet and anxious excitement, nothing responded to his call, as if Viktor had come here for the first time.

"How could you? How could you? Aren't you ashamed of yourself?" He suddenly heard a quick, cutting voice and turning toward it, he shuddered involuntarily. He would have expected to see anyone and everyone, only not them, not those people who were so infinitely happy with each other, whom Viktor had first observed in the restaurant, then in the evening at the dance, whose love, accord and open tenderness he had regarded with sad melancholy and envy. Something had happened to them. The wife stepped up to her husband, her sharply outlined face burning with wrath; the latter, frowning, kept brushing her away.

"Stop it. I'm sick of it. Go to the cabin, don't scream here."

Right beside them, in calm expectation, as if such scenes didn't strike them as extraordinary, stood the little boy and girl who looked like twins.

"Mmm-yes," smiled Viktor, "here's still another unnecessary proof of the fact that any joy is short-lived." But he was nevertheless upset. Idiots. Really, couldn't they be patient for fifteen minutes—or even less, five or ten—so that he would have had time to leave and know nothing about it, so that in his memory they would have remained eternally beautiful and constant, because he himself had been witness to it, to the legend of undying love in one human nest. Idiots, idiots twice over. They can't deceive people and have their trust too—that's just what they deserve.

He said goodbye to the shop attendant who had come to return his ticket and went below. Passengers with their things were already crowded in the passageway on the right side of the deck. Viktor took a position to the side, by the railing, where he could see the shore. Far ahead neat rows of trees appeared and in front of them a cove stretched into the taiga like a wide sleeve. And right then, as soon as the crest of the hunchbacked cape had drawn back, a small square appeared, toward which people were running, and beyond the trees the roofs of houses began to glisten. The ship blew its whistle and turned sharply toward shore.

Strangely enough, Viktor still didn't leave the ship although it had already ceased to exist for him: it was as if it had moved on, faded away. In his heart there was a ringing, burning emptiness: he had already rejected one state of existence, the other had not yet come to pass. In the crowd which had gathered on shore he began to recognize familiar faces; among the little children he made out his nephews, two light-haired, stocky little boys in whose faces, as in his own, their Tungus[9] origins showed clearly— faint, yet unconquered from generation to generation. To one side, like always, with his cap pulled over his eyes and his hands in his pockets, stood his father. His nephews ran up to him and began vying with each other to say something and pointing at the ship—his father roused himself and came closer to where the gangplank was being lowered.

"Why didn't you write?" he said quickly and happily, when Viktor had disembarked and they were greeting each other. "We didn't expect you. And your mother, your mother's been wishing and dreaming for nothing else. Well, now she'll begin to bustle about."

Viktor slapped his nephews on the back and just before leaving looked back at the ship. On deck, right across from his cabin, stood the same woman from the deceptively happy family, but now alone, without husband or children. Her estranged, bitterly solemn face was directed somewhere into the emptiness; her eyes stared blankly, without seeing. Viktor searched within himself and found neither pity nor sympathy for her: for both happiness and unhappiness alike you have to have doors, and not parade these feelings before each person you meet.

"Well, shall we go?" his father pressed.

"Let's go."

Beyond the wide road, which had been beaten down by tractors, they turned to the left and went through the section of forest which remained by the shore. Viktor recognized it by the bare, trampled bushes of columbine and honeysuckle: earlier the path to the berry-patch had begun near the cemetery and had merged not far from there with the road to the fir grove.

That's how far the water had risen: it couldn't be less than two kilometers to the old shore line from here, and uphill at that. Somewhere around here, he remembered, a waste ground[10] of young spruce trees had stood, unusually thick, through which you almost had to crawl to get through and in which the very first saffron cup mushrooms would appear in profusion. Viktor looked around, but of course didn't find it. Calves strolled among the trees, hogs rooted about, the latter all spotted for some reason and resembling each other; hens strutted about, raising their legs high.

Up ahead, jumping between piles of cow manure and stirring big green flies from them, ran his nephews. The oldest was named Sanka; Viktor had forgotten the name of the younger one: when he had come the last time, the latter had been about a year-and-a-half old—he barely waddled on his short, incredibly crooked legs which were constantly scheming to become entangled beneath him. Now it seemed that the legs had straightened, at least to a reasonably acceptable degree. His father was walking a little to the side of him; Viktor noticed that his step had become completely that of an old man, heavy; he moved, hunching over more than usual, as if he were concealing someone and bowing forward much too much. Last year he had closed the door on six decades—no joke.

"Have you come for a long time? his father asked carefully.

"I don't know yet. I'll see."

The truth was he couldn't say anything definite. It wasn't worth guessing now as to how things would turn out. He was free all summer, and he secretly hoped that if everything went well, he would spend it here completely, working a bit and resting. In another month his wife would go on vacation and then she and their son would naturally come here—to fresh air, fresh milk, to fresh green vegetation and berries. Viktor would help his mother and father cut the hay and look forward to August, when mushrooms would begin to appear; he knew no greater spiritual pleasure, no greater joy than going out into the forest with a basket right after the morning dew had fallen to those special, sacred places which he knew so well and which saffron milkcaps or peppery milk caps favored, and having reached his goal and pricked up his ears, taking with rising, eager excitement a first sweeping look back from the forest's edge. But it was still a long time before that would happen; before that he'd be able to work some— quietly, enjoying every moment, without pushing himself; he'd be satisfied if he managed to write only two or three short stories.

They came out on a street and began to walk along it uphill. Viktor looked about with interest. What sort of village was this—before him stood a large workers' settlement. To this side and that houses stretched out in several long rows; a chimney of some definitely industrial significance was pouring out smoke to the utmost; beneath it you could see a low-lying building of brick construction.

"How many streets do you have here now?" he asked his father.

"Streets?" his father began to count on his fingers. "Down below—Naberezhnaya[11] by the fields—Nagornaya, where the school is—Shkolnaya. Ours is Krivolutskaya; more people from the village of Krivolutskaya live there. And then there's still Pochtovaya—named after the post office. Five or six. At first each village grew up around its own main street, but now everything's all mixed up."

"And are there a lot of people in all?"

"Who in the hell knows? I probably don't know half of them. I know the ones who have their own houses, but now this place is full of newly recruited workers. They come here and hurry back where they came from; you can't remember them all."

On the sidewalk dogs were lying everywhere. They raised their heads lazily, met your glance with a pensive, evaluating look, but didn't budge from their places, and you had to walk around them. Cows occupied shallow, overgrown ditches along the sidewalks. Standing by the gates were people who had come out to see who was coming from the ship. Viktor greeted everyone in turn, both those he did and didn't know. They answered him and said to his father:

"Well, Stepanych, you've gotten what you've been waiting for; your son's come."

"Yes, he's here," said his father.

From one street they turned into another and crossed onto the other side. His father paused:

"Recognize it?"

No, he hadn't recognized his own hut and, had he been alone, he probably would have walked right by. Now it looked very small and old to him, with little windows half peering out like in winter, with darkened, cracked beams in the walls and uneven corners jutting out awkwardly. But this was it, and both a warm and a bitter feeling of gratitude and blame suddenly overcame Viktor and wrenched his heart.

"Why aren't you coming out to meet your guests?" shouted his father.

"What guests?" Viktor heard his mother's frightened voice from the hallway and ran toward it.

In only an hour they were sitting around the table. All his kin had come together: father, mother, uncle, or more precisely, Nikolai, his father's brother, whom Viktor never honored with the name of uncle because the latter was only about five years older than Viktor himself was and a casual, friendly relationship had developed between them long ago; Nikolai's wife, Nastya, a surprisingly quiet and good woman with a face which looked a little strained with an excess of goodness; their children, Sanka and Genka, who had met Viktor at the dock and had turned out to be not his nephews but cousins; Galina, Viktor's aunt, in terms of family ties, whom he also didn't call aunt, although she was older than Nikolai. The whole district had known Galina in earlier days; she had received a medal for her kolkhoz vegetable garden, but now, it turns out, was working as a cleaning woman in the school. His grandmother didn't come to the table; she remained sitting on the bed where she was served tea. She drank it with a cube of sugar in her mouth, sugar brought for her by Viktor from the city; she listened attentively to the conversation, joining in from time to time and again falling silent to continue her tea.

His father poured vodka all around, telling how Sanka and Genka were the first to see Viktor on the ship and turn to him; but how he himself couldn't understand for the longest time what they were squealing about because no one was expecting Viktor then.

"But I knew he would come this year," his mother declared. "Perhaps I didn't expect him to be on the first ship, but still, all in all, I knew."

"How did you know?"

"What do you mean, 'how'? I just knew."

She had aged a great deal, her shoulders were bowed, and Viktor looked at her in bewilderment, with tender and sad disbelief: can this really be her, his mother? What had happened to her? And his father too.... Deep hollows had appeared behind his father's ears, emphasizing his skull; his head looked as small as a child's, and his thin face was completely lined with wrinkles. Only his grandmother, it seemed, hadn't changed, as if she couldn't get any older, as if she had come up against some final invisible barrier beyond which there was no continuation in this world. Viktor caught himself experiencing toward this whole family, the people closest to him, a strange feeling of love and alienation, a feeling of resisting them, their old age, their movement toward that perennial feature of man's life toward which they were involuntarily pulling him too, with an invisible, silent, unweakening chain. And it already seemed to him, he already seemed to believe, that he had come here only so that he could understand how far he had come along in their footsteps, at what a distance he now found himself, and to beg, to convince them, not to hurry.

The conversation was mostly about the old village, about who had left for where, about what form their lives had taken. They remembered the kolkhoz in which they had lived poor but happy, warm lives, where they all shared the zeal for work as harvest approached, and where they all con- spired together: they would conceal extra plots of land from taxation if someone came to inspect the gardens, and they would cite various illnesses, when they weren't supposed to work any longer on their own hay fields.[12] Exasperated and embittered by these memories, Galina gave a sob, com- plaining: "At the kolkhoz I was a person at least, but now...."

"And you should have left with the kolkhoz," said Nikolai.

She snapped back with unexpected malice: "And why didn't you go?"

"I didn't have to. I'm fine here."

"Well, I didn't have to either. Where would I go away from my own? Although my destiny in life was to till the soil and not to wipe up dirt left by kids every day."

"Ah-hah," suddenly his grandmother began to speak loudly and joyfully from her bed—joyfully because she had remembered, hadn't forgotten, to make her point at the right time. "There was Lukeya who left and she didn't last a year. How did that happen? And what if they had let her be?" And now in a more rational, sober voice, with a painful moan she said, addressing Viktor alone: "She died, you know, Lukeya did, may the heavenly kingdom be hers, she died. She couldn't last even a year in the new place. People say she kept longing for the old place, kept begging to go back. Here at least, the fir trees look like home, but over there everything to the last drop is foreign. And so she couldn't bear it. They say she wept bitterly before she died."

"And how did the water rise?" Viktor began to ask. "All at once, or did it increase gradually as it usually does after a rain?"

They were silent a while, collecting their memories and slowly sinking into that recent but important, critical time for all of them, when this had happened.

"Do you think it came in one big wave?" his father said and shook his head. "No. But it came swiftly." He was silent again briefly. "But I used to go down just before that. I'd sit awhile on the shore, walk down the street, where the huts stood; I'd take a walk...."

"It pulled you," affirmed Nikolai. "I'd go too. She'd scold me," he nodded toward Nastya. "This or that needed to be done around the house, but I was drawn down there. We knew that any moment now they were going to flood it. It was too bad. It was as if we'd go to say goodbye. I'd come from work, have something to eat or not, but I just would have to go down the hill. I'd run away quickly and hide somewhere. You'd see in one place one of our people roaming around, in another place.... Every day Mishka would swear and drive Uncle Yegor Plotnikov away from there. He'd sit down and stay whether it was night or day, as if he were glued to the place."

"Aha," his grandmother piped in, having listened with impatiently tormenting concentration on her face. "And the dead they made into drowned men. How could they do that? They'd already died, but nonethless, they didn't get their proper respect. How could they do that?"

"Why must you speak of the dead now?..."

"And why not? Your grandmother lay there. All our people lay there. And now where do we look for them, near which shore?"

'Well, there you are," continued his father. "And the last time this is what happened. Just as I am about to go down the hill, I take a look: the river is already agitated, boiling wildly. I hurry there more quickly. I'm afraid I might drown, but my legs still carry me, I can't stop them. I reached the road, and the water had come up from the other side, right up to our yard. And it's creeping and creeping up; you can see with your eyes how it's creeping up. I slowly edge away from it, but keep looking. I don't run away. It had lifted up whatever sort of litter there was, chunks of coal, nettles; it pulled at goose-foot weeds. The water rolled up to the huts, where our own hut stood, and began to swirl like a funnel, which meant it was rushing into the cellar. While I was watching, I looked around, and the water had snuck up on me from one side; I had to wade through it. I crawled to the first hill beyond Yegor's garden and saw people running from the village. But at first I was alone, there was no one else; I was the first to meet it, the plague on us."

"But we had gone to the haymaking that day," recalled Nastya. "You went then too, didn't you?" she said and turned to Nikolai.

"Who else, it would be interesting to know, could have been with you if not me? Or do you think Styopka the Cossack was cutting hay for our cow?"

"That's right, you were there. We went there in the morning—everything was fine, but when we ran back to the river—saints preserve us—what in the world is going on! The bridge across the stream has been ripped away; my dear, it is floating in the middle of the stream and the water rushing over the grass—shsh—kept making this noise over and over. How do we get home? We again crawled up the hill. We had to walk the long way around to the old high road. There was no other place to pick your way through. I keep running and worry: what if everything in the world has been flooded by this water, both the old village and the new one? He," she nodded toward Nikolai, "yells at me: 'what a fool you are!' Why a fool? If there has never been anything like it, you get scared against your will. How do you know anything? It doesn't take much for the one who let this water loose to make a mistake. Is there any way you could stop it then? And the children are there—of course your heart is in your throat. In the dark we darted out into the fields—thank God, our little huts are intact, are still standing. But there, where the old village had been, water is glistening."

"The first year it rose only to the lower hill and stopped. It kept rising, but bit by bit. The next summer it had crept farther."

"But you have to give them their due. They did predict exactly how far it would go. They knew how to figure it out. Grisha Suslov extended his garden below the markers, and half his garden was flooded."

"Now it's full of fish, though," said Nikolai.

"A lot of fish?" Viktor happily asked, interrupting.

"A lot. Only what fish: perch, Siberian roach, pike. The pike are immense, as big as logs. But the meat isn't the same anymore; it's true that it's like wood and smells of slime. We even feed it to the pigs."

"And what about grayling, lenok?"

"Where would we get them? They're clean fish and need clean, flowing water. To get grayling you now have to go to the upper reaches of the Zuy. There are people who go there. If you're going to stay a long time, we can arrange something with someone. With old Yegor Plotnikov, for example—he won't touch either perch or roach. Give him the kind of fish we used to have, clean water fish. But we've already begun to forget what it even tastes like. We have the fish we have today, and that will have to do."

"How long will you stay with us?" his mother asked.

And again Viktor answered vaguely: "I don't know. Until I get tired of it."

"Why don't you at least tell me how things are going. Are you still writing your books?"

"I am."

"And even now you're still writing?"

"And even now."

"And the fact that they criticized you, you didn't get in any trouble for this?"

Viktor noticed that upon hearing his mother's last words everyone fell silent and pricked up his ears. Galina quietly put the spoon down on the table so as not to make any noise, and bending over the table, leaned forward. His father grew deathly quiet in eager anticipation. Nastya didn't even say "tut-tut" when Genka began to fidget in his chair; she merely tugged at his sleeve. Even in his mother's voice tension could be felt as she posed her question.

"When I was criticized for what?" Viktor didn't understand.

"Oh, for that bit of writing, for that. In the newspaper. The teacher showed us the paper just so that we'd know. Got it still, father?"

His father without a word looked into the night table and handed Viktor the newspaper.

"Here it is," he said, noticeably agitated. "There, at the end."

"Everyone keeps asking us whether they've dismissed you from those writers,"[13] his mother said, "but even we ourselves don't know a thing. Many times I've imagined all kinds of things. What's more, your grandmother gives us no peace: what, oh what will happen to you because of it?"

Viktor unrolled the newspaper and found a small article in column four about his last book of short stories. He remembered this review which had appeared a month and a half ago in a regional newspaper; he had read it, but at that time he had not given it any thought. Can you really take seriously being reproached for some kind of superfluous psychologizing, for digging into people's souls too much, for the fact that there are no clearly expressed positive and negative heroes in your stories, but rather characters with an ill-defined philosophy of life, whom you don't know whether you should have as friends. As if people search for friends in books, and search according to the principle of who talks louder. The review was shallow and uninteresting, one of those composed of helpful rubber phrases which eternally stand in readiness and have the unusual talent of being suitable for any occasion—that's why Viktor had immediately forgotten about it.

"Oh, that," he smiled and gave the newspaper back to his father. "That's nonsense."

The people at the table were silent for a while. Then his mother said distrustfully: "It was printed in the newspaper."

"So what, so it was in the newspaper. People work there too—it means that like all of us, they too can make mistakes. Of course, there are things to criticize me for, but what he's listed here is nonsense." Viktor didn't know any better way to explain all this to them and so he began to offer a long confusing explanation. It was doubtful that they understood him.

"All the same, be more careful there," his mother said, "All kinds of things happen."

There was nothing left for him to do but agree with a smile. "All right mama, I'll be very careful."

That night he slept in a small extension to the hallway which was made of planks and used as a storeroom. It was cool here; there was a sharp smell of sheepskin and of something bitter and musty; mice scampered somewhere in the corner, but all the same his sleep, like in childhood, was full and deep. And he awoke only because morning came—with the cackling of chickens in the yard, with the satisfied, patient mooing of the cow, with the sparrows' cheerful and thin-voiced chirping being carried separately, as if on a special channel, with the sun's rays breaking through cracks into the storeroom; he awoke and, realizing that he was in the village, he happily roused himself.

He walked out on the porch and stood there awhile, letting his eyes get used to the bright sunlight. The morning seemed wonderful—bright and fresh; everything in it was there in full view and everything evoked in him an exhilarating feeling of space and the first creation, as if just now, an hour or two ago, fresh, completely new colors had appeared in place of the old. Filmy white clouds, transparent and bent like wings, were slowly melting in the sky now that night had gone; the sun filling with warmth and passion was gently rising on high; the air, glowing warmer, became lighter, shifted and turned steamy; beyond the vegetable gardens, nearby, rose a forest set in a wide semicircle, and from the other side, behind the roofs of houses, water rested quietly in an abyss that glistened in the sunlight.

From the yard came his mother carrying a milk pail whose weight dragged her down. She was surprised to see Viktor.

"Why did you get up so early? Go back to sleep, sleep a bit more. Only the women of the house get up at this hour here."

Viktor, squinting from the sun as he had before, gave a smile and didn't answer. He couldn't sleep now anyway. The morning, early by the clock, but clearly in full swing, evoked in him a rare, intoxicating feeling of participation in it, in its swift and well-done beginning; and from this feeling, as from any good work, his heart grew joyful and sensitive; he wanted new work just as big and unusual, and the new pleasure which would be derived from it.

Not knowing himself what to tackle and what to start, he went into the vegetable garden, took off his slippers at the gate and began to walk around barefoot on the black, cold, recently upturned soil. The earth had been turned over with a plough; on the transverse boundary lines hoofprints, and circles made by the plough when it was shifted from furrow to furrow, had not yet become covered with vegetation. In the middle of the garden stood two larch trees, which his father apparently could not bring himself to touch; one was still green, the other stood jutting out dry and bare. Strong, rough-textured seedlings bristled in hollows in the long cucumber patch. The potatoes hadn't been planted yet, and Viktor thought with pleasure that he wouldn't escape this simple, artless work today anymore than he would escape the many other tasks of village life which were half-forgotten and therefore seemed even more enticing.

Afterwards he enjoyed sitting on the porch, throwing grain to chickens and watching their hungry bustling, which turned into a scratching noisy game depending on how full they were. Among the chickens, sparrows were hopping about; looking around, they seized the individual grains of seed, again turned their heads from side to side, watching out for danger, and then they again plucked the grain quickly and tenaciously, while taking wing just to be on the safe side, and then came down immediately. A big pig lumbered out of a corner behind the barn, chased off both the chickens and the sparrows and began to run its snout back and forth along the ground, sucking dirt together with the remains of the birds' food like a magnet.

Viktor decided to go to the woods.

He drank a glass of fresh milk, but didn't eat anything; his mother had heated up the tile stove and was now preparing pirozhki. At breakfast he would have to try to eat a lot in order to please her, and so it wasn't worth spoiling his appetite right now.

Following a path with cows stretched out all over it, he unexpectedly came on an airfield behind the vegetable garden. To one side, by the road out of the village, stood a large new building with a white identifying cross on the roof and with the antennae of its radio station meeting at the top of the high tower. The landing field, a converted grain field, was beautifully and evenly outlined with whitewashed posts. But even here cows were lying about. Viktor, who had stopped for a moment because he didn't know whether he could walk on it or not, picked up his courage and took the short cut. But all the same he walked through the field with some kind of strangely distrustful, strangely confusing feeling of surprise and insult, as if he had been deceived in some way; but the insult and surprise didn't come from being deceived, but from the fact that this deception could in no way be defined.

Along the upper section of the airfield a ditch had been dug, which directed water from spring thaws away from the field; but its walls were already crumbling and the ditch had long ago shifted its course trying to cut its own comfortable path for the water. Immediately behind it lay a waste ground, where pines grew and where once there were lots and lots of butter mushrooms. But butter mushrooms at that time were not considered real mushrooms, except that perhaps you could pick some nice little fresh ones to fry once or twice, but after that no one even gave them a second glance: saffron milk caps and pepper milk caps would begin to appear. And in general either from lack of knowledge or from the great abundance of these mushrooms, except that perhaps once or twice you could pick some nice little fresh ones to fry up but after that no one even gave them a second glance: them for the winter in large tubs, and this particular type of mushroom stayed firm and pungently fragrant all the way until spring.

Viktor wanted to walk through this waste ground. He knew every corner here and remembered many trees individually. But it turned out that he was not able to walk through it; it retained the appearance of a forest only on one side, on the lower edge; in the interior it had been almost completely cleared of trees. It stood too close to the new village, where people had built fences around their vegetable gardens, put up pens for their flocks, and this was its downfall; the pine trees were used for poles and beams. Wood chips lay on the ground in blackening piles that were impossible to climb over; pine needles had turned brown and had been packed solidly into the ground by people's footsteps; tall, sharp stumps jutted out. Here and there you could even see fresh work under way; that which was growing and had become suitable for something quickly fell to the axe for that purpose. Viktor took consolation in the fact that at least there, where the villages had been taken down, no one was left to touch the forest—even for brooms, cemetery crosses and New Year's trees. As for the forest here, apparently such was its fate—you couldn't escape from it anywhere now.

For a long time he climbed up the hill along the edge of the forest, often glancing back, expecting the village to disappear from view. But its edge was visible all the time; on the lower end it merged with the water which stretched out from there so vast and wide that involuntarily you wanted to pinch yourself to make sure that you weren't off somewhere dreaming this in the dead of a bad night because of a melancholic longing for native places. Then the edge of the forest came to an end; he turned right and walked out onto a small path, but gave up after going a little way: a tractor road pressed right next to the path—heaven only knows where it came from—on both sides of which, like fences, lay trees stacked up in piles, their uncut branches sharply sticking out. And he went on simply where his eyes directed him and where it was easier to walk, coming upon familiar, memorable spots everywhere. Right here, under these bird-cherry bushes, so many pepper milk cap mushrooms were showing their heads that you could pick them every day; it was here that, finding enough courage for the first time, he grabbed a snake below its head and brought it into the village; vengeance had aroused this courage in him: he was going to leave the snake near Ninka, who didn't return—die, you wretched girl!—his love; and right here as little kids they had put up a shelter of branches—the darkened wooden wedge even now stuck out of the pine tree. He stopped now and then, stood still for long periods of time, peering into the grass and trees keenly, with some sort of overly close attention and curiosity, as if he were trying to establish for himself an important link with his own self, with what he was like in those years—and he kept coming away with nothing.

Later he wandered unexpectedly into a meadow which for some reason he did not remember, about whose existence he did not know; it was as if it had appeared here after he had left. He was already far from the village. He walked on with no road ahead of him, hoping to come upon a path and begin gently coming down the hill. His mother was probably worried now; and the pirozhki cold. Lost in these thoughts he didn't notice right away that from the gloomy forest packed with ravines he had stumbled into a completely different world.

It was spacious, light and festive here. Growing some distance apart in order not to block out the light from each other and not to draw each other's moisture from the earth, full magnificent birches stood importantly and stylishly, like grand ladies, their heavy branches spread wide and bent downward. Their leaves were still sticky like fish scales, and they were fragile, with delicate faint veins; each leaf by itself seemed timid, to be feverishly hiding itself, but all together they produced a long and happy song of peace. Circling before his eyes, the spotted birch tree trunks, which had been cleansed by spring, evoked a sad distant, blissful yet mournful weariness, which now struck with sudden power—when you seemed to think that any moment now it would reveal itself and expose its secret—now became enveloped in fog. In the gnarled patterns and scratches of the trunks drops of sap accumulated, broke off and fell downward. Down below, shadows from the birches streamed down and melted, and snowdrops bloomed; from the grass which was short and even as if it had been trimmed and above which bumblebees hummed and butterflies fluttered, there came a thick, pungent smell of honey, and there was a quiet prayer-like rustling in the air which rose in waves. And far, far away, teasing and frightening you, the resounding, indifferent sound of a cuckoo surrounded you with its fortune-telling.[14]

And it was so good, so sweetly frightening because of the life here and the sun; life was so wondrous and happy here that you wanted to cry from this inexpressible, unworldly happiness.

After dinner his mother made some clattering noises with the buckets and got ready to go for water. Viktor called to her:

"Where are you going? There is a full container of water over there. What do you need more water for?"

"Oh, Vitya," she said as she waved her hand at the small container. "I want to put on the samovar, but that water isn't good for tea. It's from a pump and somehow really hard. You can't wash your hair in it, for example, because if you do you won't be able to comb it out with any comb. For cooking we still make do with it, but for tea we bring water from the river, even though it's far away."

Viktor managed to note one peculiarity here: when it was a question of water which you could fill your buckets with and bring home, in which you could swim and fish, the people here said "river"; however, when the discussion touched upon movement on this water, distances of which now had increased many times over in comparison with old distances, they said "sea," although it was in reality neither one nor the other; for this there was a precise word—"water reservoir"—but it was just too unwieldy and cumbersome; the tongue, pronouncing it, seemed to be grinding boulders.

"What about me—can't I bring the water?" Viktor asked, offended. "You should have said something."

"All right, go, if you feel like it. I thought you were tired, that you had had your fill of wandering around today."

"How should I go, what's the shortest way?"

"Right down that little road. Keep straight until you come to the end of the road."

He hooked the buckets to the yoke and clanging them, walked out into the street. There was a light wind outside, but it was still hot; the summer nowadays began red-hot; it was time already for the rains to come, to show themselves and give support to that bit of moisture which still remained in the ground. Here people didn't till or sow grain, and the forest could be cut in any weather; but even here they thought about grain out of habit, about those who did till and sow, and after all, here they did keep vegetable gardens and cut hay.

Getting water turned out to be not such a simple matter. Waves lapped the shore, and the water was red and clayey, the kind which usually comes from fields in spring. Viktor shuffled his feet and lingered awhile near the boats cluttering the whole shore; he got into one, then another, and while standing at the stern he would scoop up some water and then throw it back—not only could you not drink this water but a good housewife would worry about pouring it on her cucumbers. What was he to do? He certainly couldn't return with empty buckets! Viktor began to undress without noticing a small kid approaching from behind.

"Are you going to swim, uncle?"[15] he asked.

Viktor, displeased, turned around: so here was the first witness already, someone who had seen with his own eyes that he didn't know how to get plain water from the river, from the sea, from the water reservoir—from all of them combined. They all couldn't be stripping naked to do this; they probably managed some other way.

"Yes, I'm going to swim," he answered. "You'll take up swimming here whether you want to or not."

He grabbed a bucket and waded into the water. Slime, resembling gruel, passed under his feet and he slipped and almost fell. This made him even angrier, the devil only knew what was really going on. Then, with effort, he pulled his feet out of this gruel that was swallowing them and stubbornly pushed forward.

"No," the boy shouted to him from shore, "You have to go by boat."

Viktor had scooped up what was before him anyway and nudging the bucket ahead of him, somehow made his way out of the water.

"You have to go by boat," repeated the boy. "You can choke on this water."

"What boat do you have in mind?" Viktor shook off the specks which clung to him and with fear and repulsion watched his whole body become covered with fine specks of dirt resembling pinpricks.

"You've come to visit Uncle Pyotr Stenovich?" asked the boy.

"Yes."

"Your boat is locked up. It's over there. You can use ours."

"And where do I go?"

"There," the boy pointed toward the sea.

"What is this—you now go for water in boats?"

"And how else?"

"And you always do this?"

"No-o, why always? If it's clean water, we take it from here. It was yesterday's wind that made it all muddy. At this point it may settle by tomorrow, or it may not."

"Made it all muddy," Viktor mimicked him. "Well, let's be off, where's your boat? Boat-water tote."

The boy was around ten or twelve. His shoulders and neck were already burnt black but a completely white stomach showed from beneath his T-shirt. On an expressive pug-nosed face his eyes darted quickly and businesslike, grasping immediately what they needed. But the boy's most important feature was the red rash on his hands, which Viktor got a good look at while the boy was putting the oars into the holders of the rowlock. He hadn't seen children with a rash for a long time—now it was a meticulous nation—and he rejoiced at the rash as he would at seeing old acquaintances from whom at one time he had rarely been apart. O rashes, rashes, offspring of dirt and water, aching at night with an unending hungry insistence, even with goose fat on them, so that you can neither open your hands nor move a foot without pain, but in the morning, as if nothing had happened, ready again for any adventure. What would life be without rashes? If there are rashes, it means there are boys in the world— not just any boys. Good lads.

They rowed about a hundred meters away from shore and Viktor finally got his water, which in terms of the effort expended should have been fresh water. It's true, something was also swimming in it, looking dark and circling around, but this no longer had any significance.

"Are we going to swim?" asked the boy.

"Swim?" Viktor grew pensive. "But isn't it early?"

"No, the water's warm. I've gone swimming three times this year already."

"Well, if you're not afraid, let's go. And for me it would even be good to wash off."

Viktor jumped in the water first; the boy dove in after him. The water burned, but Viktor soon understood that it was really bearable, much warmer at least than the water used to be in the river. There was no current and it warmed up quickly. The children now had vast expanses of water, while earlier they used to run from the river to a bonfire on shore.

"Over there," shouted the boy, pointing with his hand in the direction of some treetops sticking out of the water.

They swam on together. The boy moved quickly and easily; he turned on his back, then on his side, and again did the crawl, demonstrating for Viktor all his skill; and it was obvious that he could swim this way for a long time. Viktor was already falling behind. There, if you please, is the advantage of the sea: in warm water you can really learn how to swim. In the river it had been difficult to endure more than five minutes.

They were already drawing near the trees. The boy climbed a pine tree; Viktor, not far from him, a birch. It bent under his weight, but it didn't break. And here's a second advantage: who before dreamed of such places for resting in the middle of the water?

"Just don't dive there," warned the boy. "There's a fir tree somewhere under the water. Mishka Zhukov dove in last year and cut his whole side open. There sure was a lot of blood! Somehow we managed to get him to shore—and a red trail stretched behind us all the way back."

"And what happened? Is this Mishka alive?"

"I guess you could say he's alive. But his side became like a fir tree too.

He had an operation."

"What's your name?" Viktor asked.

"Filipp."

"It's Filka, then."

"Well, maybe it's Filka, only I don't like it when people call me that. It's too much of a nickname. Filipp is better."

Viktor began to laugh: "You sure are a serious fellow."

"Why?" The boy didn't understand.

"You have a good name, that's why. Now don't you go decide to change it when you grow up."

He truly felt that the boy with the rash really ought to have a name like that—Filipp.

"I was just on my way to look for you," said his mother, who was walking away from the gate. "I think to myself, maybe he's drowned somewhere. All this time and no sight of Vitya. Give me at least one bucket, your father asked for some tea a long time ago."

Viktor was talking with his childhood friend, the cheerful and fearless Slavka Kapustin[16] who loved to pick fights and who had now turned into a large, awkward looking fellow over six feet tall with huge arms and straight broad shoulders. Slavka had called out to him when Viktor was approaching his house with the precious water. It turned out that he lived directly across from them.

"I did hear people say that some important bigwig[17] had come to visit Uncle Petya," Slavka explained, squinting one eye. "Couldn't understand: what bigwig, who was it?"

"All right, all right, don't play dumb," cheerfully, in the same tone, answered Viktor. "Bigwig. You're the bigwig."

"Yeah, O.K., I am a bigwig too. Do you know how much good I bring the government? Oh, well! In the first place, I've produced four children and all of them boys. How many do you have?"

"One."

"It's time to castrate you. What kind of peasant are you if you can't even put in the right amount of work for you and your woman? Someone else later on will have to trample the ground for you. This is nothing to joke about."

Even in childhood, Slavka had one wonderful quality: you didn't have to question him, he himself gave out all the information there was about his life.

"I work on a tractor, in the forest. May the Lord give everyone that kind of work. Three hundred—four hundred little rubles free and clear per month. Do you make that much?"

"No."

"There, you see! Move here. Life's better here. We're different from the rest, here we're your own. And even if someone cusses you out—so what, it won't go beyond that person. You, on the other hand, were just barely criticized in the newspaper and the whole world knows about it. Now everyone subscribes to these newspapers. I get five different ones every day, have wrapped up everything I can in them; now I might as well wrap up wood for throwing in the stove. Now you come and see how I live. I live well. I'm not going to brag, you'll see for yourself."

"I'll come without fail."

"And if something really does happen, why don't you move here?" Slavka began to roar loudly with laughter. "But I won't take you into my brigade. Whether you're insulted or not, I won't take you. Do you know how quickly you have to move in my group? Oh, boy! But you with your cushy little job are not the same man you were. I'll slip you to Styopka Shelkovnik.[18] He'll take you. So think about it."

It was impossible to get angry at Slavka. There are some lucky people who, no matter what drivel they might utter, always come out sounding smooth, fine, and uninsulting.

And so there came a stretch of days—bright, sunny, and long.

Viktor could in no way get used to the idea that he had already arrived; it seemed to him as if he were still on his way and had stopped somewhere near his native village, so near in fact that he could at times come upon familiar places by accident, places which he remembered from childhood and from earlier visits; and he could immerse himself in their mysterious, cherished aura and feel within himself a pure and quivering excitement rising in response to their nearness. He was right next to these places and yet at a distance, and there, where he now found himself, a different kind of sky hung above him, lopsided and uneven, sharply shifted to one side above the water; a different land lay before him, reminding him in rare, cherished moments of the land where he had grown up but nonetheless foreign and obscure; the horizon in all directions curved beneath the sky differently and in the center of all of this stood a different village—large, colorful and noisy. He was ready to believe that he had arrived here at the wrong moment—either too late or too early, but not at the appropriate time, because he had gotten lost, who knows where on one side or the other of those days.

He wandered a lot around the forest; he found it pleasant to walk, plunging his feet into the grass, moving heavy stiff branches away from his face, and greedily, with some sort of heightened awareness listening attentively to the multitoned chirping of birds, to the pecking and hammering of woodpeckers, to the rustling of leaves; a gentle blessed peace came over his soul, lulling all his anxieties to sleep; but this feeling, he knew, could arise wherever you like, in any forest you like, not just here; he didn't have in him that one single unrepeatable, passionate and stupidly touching response which your native places evoke. Deprived of something important, basic, of some focal point that gathers these places into a single body, into a single circle, they wandered off in all directions, every which way; they turned into faintly familiar corners, which had grown old with time and seemed only memories which too can appear wherever you like.

On the third day after his arrival he went on a fishing trip with Nikolai. They brought the boat to a stop among water-covered trees, baited the hooks with worms and right then and there, from on board, from both sides of the boat lowered into the water the nylon fishing line, which was weighted down with a sinker, while they held one end in their hands. The whole trick consisted in tugging at the line from time to time, dangling the worm and snaring the fish as soon as it took the lure, which is why such a device is called "the tugger." Not even five minutes had passed before Nikolai pulled out the first perch. Then Viktor too felt the fishing line move in his hand and quickly began to pull it in. In two hours the two of them together tossed into the boat more than a bucketful of perch. The work was almost mechanical: lower the fishing line, give a tug, wait awhile, give another short tug, feel the despair of the deceived fish and pull it out into the air. The excitement which had first seized Viktor passed quickly, and the expectation, the impatience, the tormenting and sweet despair without which fishing is not fishing, burst and disappeared without reaching full force and without giving him the pleasure usual for such occasions.

He helped his mother plant potatoes, and with pleasure watered the cucumbers in the evening. But nonetheless more often than not he didn't know how to cope with his time, and so again and again went into the forest. He tried to write and once had taken pencil in hand, but his mother, upon seeing him, said with such decisiveness: "Why don't you just rest, you'll still have time, you'll still be able to wear yourself out with your scribbling," that he dropped his hands and gave into her. Most probably she never believed his explanations about the newspaper review, which he had been shown his first evening home, because more than once he caught her unsettlingly attentive, suffering glance upon him, and felt directed at himself her excessive, obsessive worry, the kind you have for someone ill. But Viktor did not want to try to prove anything beyond what he had already said, and in fact he probably couldn't have. He guessed that for many in the village he had apparently become a social outcast who had not found a place anywhere else, a failure who had come here to lick his wounds, or someone of that type; people looked at him with that intent gaze and interest which involuntarily betray an unhealthy yet sympathetic curiosity. He was needlessly convinced of this one more time by a meeting with his grammar schoolteacher, Vasily Petrovich, a man already well along in years, an inquisitive person, who loved more than anything else in the world to discuss the presidential elections in America and military upheavals in small countries. Seeing Viktor on the street, Vasily Petrovich rushed towards him as fast as his feet would carry him and before Viktor could even open his mouth, he began to soothe him in a cheerful, excited fashion, saying that everyone can have failures and make mistakes, even politicians, but that in any case one must not despair; saying that he understood how difficult it was for Viktor now.... Viktor listened to him and smiled, but this smile, not finding any encouragement, grew smaller and smaller and finally changed into a patient, painful grimace.

Two or three times, lost in thought about something, he had stopped in the middle of the village, bewildered and surprised: Where was he? Where had his wandering brought him? Around him stood unfamiliar houses and walked unfamiliar people who didn't have any connection with him—he had to force himself to remember why he was here, but even when he finally remembered, figured things out and found himself, he nonetheless felt vaguely bewildered: oh, yes, now it was clear why he had come, what he needed. And hurriedly he would turn back. He tried to convince himself that he had to wait a few more days to get used to things, to be at one with everything which surrounded him, with complete understanding and a feeling of closeness to combine in himself that notion of a village which had lived in him all these years with the reality which he had found here; but days passed by and nothing changed.

And so he gave up. Once, left alone with his mother, he said resolutely: "I'll leave on the next ship."

She raised her frightened eyes, looked for a long time at him and not knowing what to do, said: "You still don't find a place for yourself."

He agreed: "No, I don't."

Two days after this he got ready to leave. His mother and father quietly and sadly waited to walk him over to the pier; Viktor for the last time walked into the house to say goodbye to his grandmother. She got up from the bed with difficulty, started to cry, and while crying made the sign of the cross over him.

"Don't write there what they don't want you to," she said through her tears.

Viktor couldn't control himself and broke out laughing. "My dear grandma! What are you talking about?"

Oh, sweet innocence—how can we exist without you, how?!

And once again the ship. This time he hadn't managed to get a cabin: the whole ship was packed with tourists. (Oh, those tourists traveling on trains and ships, those women growing fat and men growing bald, who don't want to languish on their feet and who see the whole purpose of such trips as contact among themselves—who will build a monument to your bitter and comic indefatigability?) The rest of the passengers were packed into corners and looked out from them with fear and curiosity, while all around people laughed, sang, strummed on guitars and chased each other like children—the ship reminded you of a gypsy camp more than anything else. It was a good thing too that Viktor's mother had sent some kind of little baked things along with him for the trip, otherwise he would have had to go hungry: the restaurant had been given over to the tourists, and they'd already emptied the snack bar by that time.

Viktor left his suitcase below deck with some old women, all four of whom had squeezed together on one bench, and then took a walk on deck. The distant shore was motionless, the water still, and the ship pushing forward gave the impression that the oncoming current was slow and grand. The summer was at its height; it had become even more intense, it had risen even higher; on both sides of the water everything was enveloped in its even and light-green fire.

The days spent by Viktor in the village rolled into one hazy, indistinguishable ball of yarn which had managed to roll off somewhere, and Viktor just could not believe that he was already going back. He tried to understand what had forced him to leave, you could say, even run away from the village, but these attempts were weak. It seemed he wasn't sorry that he had left. Apparently, he had to leave. Apparently, he had to leave in order to repeat everything from the beginning: to get on the ship in the city, to admire the river along the way, its shores and current, to be awakened at dawn by a strange scratchy sound and to see the flooded trees, the new shores and new villages, to be amazed and frightened at the flood of water—to see and experience once again all that he had already seen and experienced during this trip, but now as a different person himself, more experienced and calmer, imagining clearly and well where he was going and what he was going to find there.

And he already knew that that's the way it would turn out—today, soon.

Translated by Valentina G. Brougher and Helen C. Poot

The translators would like to thank Georgetown University for providing typing funds.

Notes

1. "It's bitter," a call to the bride and groom to kiss and make the wine or vodka the guests are drinking "sweeter."
2. Literally, "all alike, like Komsomol volunteers."
3. "Khlebnik Island" is derived from the word for "bread" or "grain"; Beryozovik

Island, from the word for "birch tree."

4. A Russian stove is one made of brick or rammed clay, occupying a large room which in peasant homes constitutes the living room, bedroom and kitchen. The stove itself often provides a heated sleeping platform, usually reserved for the children or the old.

5. Cross of St. George: established in 1769 by Catherine the Great as the Order of the Great Martyr and Bearer of Victory Saint George, which was awarded to generals and officers for achievement in battle and for years of service (after 1855, only for achievement in battle). In 1809 a special decoration of the Order of St. George was established for soldiers in the lower ranks. In 1913 the Order of St. George became known as the Cross of St. George.

6. A hectare equals 10,000 square meters or 2.471 acres.

7. "Verkhny Island" means, literally, the "upper island."

8. If no openers are available, Russians know how to uncorck bottles by slapping the bottom of the bottle repeatedly until the pressure pushes out the cork.

9. Tungus: a tribe of Mongolian descent which lives in Siberia east of the Yenisei in the Amur Basin.

10. A waste ground is a stretch of uncultivatable land, often thickly covered with trees and underbrush.

11. Naberezhnaya Street means "Embankment Street"; Nagornaya Street, "street on the hill"; Shkolnaya Street, "school street," and Pochtovaya Street, "post office street."

12. I.e., so that they could continue cutting their own hay on the sly.

13. "Those writers" refers to the "Union of Soviet Writers," an organization to which a writer must belong in order to publish his works in the Soviet Union.

14. People of many cultures consider the call of the cuckoo to be an omen; for example, some Russians believe that if a person counts the number of times the cuckoo sounds its call, that number equals the number of years he has left to live.

15. Children address strangers as "uncle," where an American child would say "mister."

16. "Kapustin" comes from the word for "cabbage."

17. Literally, "rank."

18. "Shelkovnik" comes from the word for "silk."